ROOSEVELT
and
MARSHALL

ALSO BY THOMAS PARRISH

Simon and Schuster Encyclopedia of World War II

The Ultra Americans

ROOSEVELT and MARSHALL

Partners in Politics and War

THOMAS PARRISH

William Morrow and Company, Inc.
New York

Library of Congress Cataloging-in-Publication Data

Parrish, Thomas (Thomas D.)
Roosevelt and Marshall: Partners in politics and war
Thomas Parrish.
p. cm.
Bibliography: p.
ISBN 0-688-09099-0
1. Roosevelt, Franklin D. (Franklin Delano), 1882–1945—Friends and associates. 2. Marshall, George C. (George Catlett), 1880–1959—Friends and associates. 3. Civil-military relations—United States—History—20th century. I. Title.
E807.P27 1989
973.917′0922—dc20 89-30489
CIP

Printed in the United States of America

First Printing

1 2 3 4 5 6 7 8 9 10

Only keep up your position and character and let *no one* make you feel small.

—Sara Delano Roosevelt to her son, April 1900

He is bright, full of life, and I believe will get along well.

—George C. Marshall, Sr., to the superintendent of the Virginia Military Institute, September 1897

Remember well the great trust you have undertaken: You are as a continual sentinel, always to stand upon your watch to give [the King] true intelligence. If you flatter him, you betray him.

—Francis Bacon to Sir George Villiers

Everything is very simple in war, but the simplest thing is difficult.

—Karl von Clausewitz

. . . a teamwork which has succeeded and will succeed.

—Roosevelt to Marshall, January 31, 1944

CONTENTS

ROOSEVELT
and
MARSHALL

PREFACE

The idea of writing about the relationship of Franklin D. Roosevelt and George C. Marshall came to me unexpectedly one afternoon, when I had stopped at Warm Springs, Georgia, for a visit to FDR's Little White House. I had not been there for a number of years, but as I slowly walked back to the car after my brief tour, I found myself still struck by the simple tastes this powerful man displayed in his private life. With its plain chairs and tables, its uninviting beds, this Spartan cottage is wonderfully evocative; it seems to offer a message about the essential Roosevelt—though, certainly, only one of many possible messages about this complicated man.

Reflecting on FDR's personality, I then thought of the other great figure from the era of World War II, a man in whose life I have long had a special interest—the general who was renowned for his own kind of simplicity, but whose personality otherwise seemed to differ strongly from FDR's glittering style. Suddenly I found it strange that nobody had ever written about the partnership of these two giants, one of them unquestionably the preeminent American twentieth-century political leader, the other holding equivalent rank among soldiers.

In such a book I would obviously need to describe the evolution of the relationship—its clashes and compromises, its successes and failures, its clearly profound consequences for the United States and the world. I was proposing to myself not an exercise in hagiography—which, in any case, is no doubt a lost art nowadays—but a realistic account with light and shadow. I would have to try to get close to the two men, each of whom now lives on in a kind of legend, partly fact, partly fiction. These were not only strong and complex personalities, they were men who by upbringing and personal psychology hid much of themselves from the public and even from friends. I would have to look behind these commanding masks. (As I quickly began to see, when looked at in juxtaposition the two men revealed personal qualities more sharply than when regarded individually.) I also wanted to have room for irony and humor, because a picture of life cannot be truly painted if these qualities are left out.

An important feature—one, I believe, that distinguishes the finished book from any written about Roosevelt or Marshall individually—is the placing of them together, as president and chief of staff, in the context of American civil-military relations. (In what tradition, for example, did the chief of staff function? Were his powers automatic? Constitutional, perhaps? What did it mean to call the president the commander in chief? How much of the part he played in relation to the army and the navy was created by him?) By dramatizing these political and military roles and relationships and showing how they collide and overlap, I have sought to provide a full and three-dimensional account of these leaders during the prewar crises and the war itself. Beyond that, I have looked at the precedents they set that influence our lives today.

In telling the story, I have tried to keep a lively awareness of three golden principles (well put by Robert K. Massie): *importance, immediacy,* and *suspense.* The importance of the story speaks for itself, both in its own time and in the legacies it has given our present generation. To tell such an important story, an author must strive for the other two golden qualities through a variety of ways, but one point may be worth mentioning here. Immediacy and suspense come when we see and feel what the characters saw and felt at the time of the story, or what others knew and our principals could have known; hindsight is the deadly enemy of suspense. (The storyteller benefits from the mind's remarkable capacity to involve itself in the unfolding story even of such a universally known event as the Pearl Harbor attack on December 7, 1941; the outcome holds no mystery for us, but still, as we watch all the maneuvering and negotiating, we can hope that some person or event will somehow arise to stop the slide of the nations toward catastrophe.) And it is only through immediacy that we can come to know the characters as persons. Our present-day knowledge gives us the power of selection and arrangement, but that is a very different thing from interference in the story by means of hindsight and condescension. We have to dwell within the range of experience of our characters if we wish to share a compelling story. We are concerned with individual human character, not simply for the sake of drama, but because it illuminates history if it does not determine it.

THOMAS PARRISH

PROLOGUE: "I'M SORRY, MR. PRESIDENT"

The pilgrims who still come to Hyde Park, New York, to capture a touch of the president they revere find a fitting framework—the old house (spacious, but with nothing ostentatious about it), the fieldstone library and museum nearby, the broad hayfields left untouched as FDR wished, the wooded bluffs falling away to one of America's most magnificent rivers. The visitor to Hyde Park readily understands the president's love of his boyhood surroundings, an environment he never left for long.

The visitor who travels from Hyde Park to Uniontown in southwestern Pennsylvania meets a sharply contrasting scene. Here, in a parking lot next to a squat concrete building housing the local VFW post, the visitor can find a small plaque declaring this site to be the birthplace of George C. Marshall. Thriving farming country during Marshall's childhood in the 1880s, the area would lose its innocence when miners moved in to take the coal that underlay it. When Marshall was a boy, a good-sized, fresh-running creek curled around the property, and behind the house stretched a large yard; on an island in the creek stood an orchard, as the family called it, consisting of four apple trees. Now the black-topped home site is bounded by a stream little more than a filthy trickle. They "buried my youthful associations," Marshall once said, "under a twenty-foot fill."

These contrasting settings cradled two men who were to preside together over a period of extraordinary change in American life and power. But one day, in the autumn of 1938, the two seemed destined to have only a brief association. In the early afternoon of November 14, President Roosevelt held a special meeting in his office. A month and a half earlier had come the Munich conference, at which the frightened leaders of the British and French governments had placed the fate of Czechoslovakia in the hands of Adolf Hitler. For some time now, Roosevelt had been digesting various pieces of disturbing information. In a letter written well before the proceedings at Munich, the U.S. ambassador in Berlin had warned of Nazi Germany's developing might in the air. Two weeks after Munich, a memorandum drawn up in the War Department pointed to a five-thousand-plane gap between the existing—and truly meager—American air strength and the force said to be needed if war should come.

Most shocking to Roosevelt was the news brought to Washington on October 13 by William C. Bullitt, the U.S. ambassador to France. The president sat up late that night to talk with Bullitt, a man never noted for calmness and detachment. Now, under the impetus of Munich, the high-strung ambassador told a frightening tale of German air power as seen from the French point of view. Hitler had been so cocky with the British and the French, Bullitt said, because he not only possessed a huge bomber fleet ready to do his bidding but had a great array of aircraft factories that could rapidly expand this force. The terrified French air leaders believed that their only chance of safety lay in a rapid buildup of their own air strength, both in fighters for defense and in bombers for counterattack. These planes, the ambassador told the president, could come only from American factories.

The next day Roosevelt informed his press conference that new international conditions demanded a fresh look at the state of American preparedness. As always, FDR's developing conclusions flowed not so much from rational analysis as from his own special way of learning. He belonged to the order of politicians whose style often baffled more conventional observers, an order well described as one in which each member "possesses antennae of the greatest possible delicacy, which convey to him, in ways difficult or impossible to analyse, the perpetually changing contours of events and feelings and human activities round them . . ."

The November 14 meeting in the president's office drew a high-level mix of such civilian and military officials as the secretary of the treasury, Henry Morgenthau; the administrator of the Works Progress Administration, Harry Hopkins; and the chief of staff of the army, General Malin Craig. As was often the case, the president did most of the talking. He seemed not so much to be seeking advice as to be laying before this group the conclusions to which his recent appraisals of the defense picture had already led him; he focused almost entirely on the air. After pointing to the obvious weaknesses in American defenses, he declared that the first task was to build up a bomber force. France, he said, had only 600 front-line planes and could produce only 3,600 a year; Britain had about 2,000 planes, with an annual production capacity of 4,800. The figures for the Axis countries, though not precise, stood in sharp contrast. Germany, the president believed, had between five thousand and ten thousand planes and could produce twelve thousand a year. To this impressive strength Italy added 3,000 planes and an annual capacity of 2,400. This Axis air potency meant, FDR said, that the United States would have to be ready to fight off attacks on the Western Hemisphere "from the North to the South Pole."

As the president proceeded with his discourse, his reasoning appeared, at least to some of his hearers, to suffer from odd limitations. What he really wanted, FDR said, was a U.S. Army air force with a strength of 20,000 planes and an annual production capacity of 24,000. He had no hope, however, of winning congressional support for any such goals. Probably, he said, Congress would grant about half his request. Accordingly, he instructed the War Department representatives to draw up a program for 10,000 aircraft—2,500 trainers, 3,750 first-line, and 3,750 reserve—to be produced over a two-year period. New plants as well as existing ones would be needed to meet these goals; in fact, the president implied that the production capacity should be created for a program even larger than the one he was outlining.

What concerned the military professionals in the room was the president's single-minded concentration on the aircraft themselves. An air force, the officers well knew, consisted not merely of planes but also of pilots and crews, maintenance teams and equipment, and supply and other services, all properly organized and fitted into the overall structure of national defense. Besides, the air was not the only realm in which American military strength was meager. What about the ground forces? The national-defense structure must be carefully balanced, yet the president ignored this basic principle; it was as though an athlete were concentrating on developing the muscles of a single arm or leg while letting his other limbs atrophy.

But the president fully understood this point. Behind the curious pose of dilettante and dabbler he often chose to assume—he seemed, in fact, to relish playing the paradoxical part of a professional amateur—he was fully capable of absorbing and analyzing information, and remarkably capable of seeing its political implications. His real purpose in calling for planes, planes, and more planes seems to have been twofold—in the first place, the aircraft would be a deterrent ("he could not influence Hitler with barracks, runways, and schools for mechanics"); beyond that, as one of those present in the room concluded, these new planes "were, in his mind, principally destined not for the U.S. Army Air Corps but for direct purchase by the air forces of

Great Britain and France." But if the president said so publicly, he would defeat his own purpose, since the U.S. Treasury could hardly pay for factories devoted to producing matériel for foreign countries; he would be handing a banner to those who opposed American involvement in foreign quarrels, after Munich as well as before it. Thus, with at least a part of FDR's purpose veiled, the issue at this meeting seemed to be orthodoxy versus a new approach, or professionalism versus amateurism. The discussion ran around the room, and finally the president turned to an officer sitting on the end of a sofa "way off to the side." This officer, the newly appointed deputy chief of staff of the army (he had been on the job not quite a month), was a tall, sandy-haired, fifty-seven-year-old brigadier general, George C. Marshall.

The president and the new deputy chief of staff were barely acquainted. In the past they had met briefly—in 1928, when Roosevelt had come over from Warm Springs to pay a brief visit to Fort Benning, where Marshall served as assistant commandant of the Infantry School, and in 1937, when the two men had talked for a few minutes during a presidential visit to Oregon, where Marshall supervised Civilian Conservation Corps camps in the area in addition to his duties as commander of a brigade headquartered at Vancouver Barracks, Washington. And now, as the new deputy chief of staff, Marshall was participating in a full-dress conference at the White House.

As the president spoke, most of those present "agreed with him entirely, had very little to say, and were very soothing in their comments"—regardless, presumably, of what they actually thought about some of his plans. Turning to Marshall at "the end of this general outlining," Roosevelt said, "Don't you think so, George?"

Marshall was perturbed at the president's exclusion of men and equipment from his concerns, and the general wanted aircraft for the U.S. Army, not for countries overseas. As for being called "George," he felt a flash of irritation over "such a misrepresentation of our intimacy." After all, he hardly knew the man, president or not! "Mr. President," he replied, "I'm sorry, but I don't agree with that at all."

Roosevelt shot him a surprised look—"very startled"—and "that ended the conference."

Afterward, Marshall's associates told him good-bye. His bluntness toward the president, they said, had surely brought his tour of duty in Washington to an early end. Certainly his behavior had not displayed the political awareness that was expected in the capital. But, as forecasters, these associates proved to be quite wrong.

CHAPTER ONE

THEMES

Behind the presence of George Marshall at the White House in November 1938 lay, ultimately, a case of sibling rivalry—a condition common enough in families, but in this instance unusual not only for its marked power but for the fact that it drew its main inspiration from a single hot moment of reaction to sibling contempt.

Born in Uniontown, Pennsylvania, on December 31, 1880, Marshall enjoyed what glowed in his memory as a classic small-town childhood. In the horse-and-buggy 1880s and 1890s, the town resembled Mark Twain's Hannibal—the sort of place where a pranksterish child could find full scope for his talents, not simply in overturning outhouses and pulling similar standard capers on Halloween but in playing all sorts of practical jokes throughout the year. George Marshall, nicknamed "Flicker" because of his sandy hair and perhaps because of his general liveliness, took full advantage of all the local opportunities. No one, parent or child, could consider himself out of harm's way when young George had a prank in mind or when one naturally evolved in the course of the boy's ordinary activities.

One morning he managed to turn his regular chore of hosing down the brick walk in front of the house into a watery assault on his sister as she came through the front door—only to realize, belatedly and after administering a thorough soaking, that the victim was not his sister but his mother. After his mother recovered her glasses, he recalled, she laughed "because she knew the terrible plight I was in"; the "plight," in the form of an angry father, arrived very shortly to administer the last whipping of Marshall's childhood. On another occasion, barred from the house during a party given by his sister "because she regarded me as a rather turbulent member of the household," he and a chum decided for amusement to stir up a beehive, an activity that predictably led to a battle between the boys and the bees and then a chase, in which one determined bee pursued George straight into the forbidden house and then abandoned him as its quarry in order to seek out and sting his sister's guest of honor. It was an accident, George insisted, but "they wouldn't believe me," because "my reputation wasn't very good."

Always, however, regardless of the nature of the prank, Marshall's mother showed notable understanding. "Sometimes she may have been worried; sometimes she may have been ashamed; sometimes she may have been shocked; but she heard . . . what the affair was, and whenever there was any humor in it, it amused her very much."

As for his education, Marshall had "a very painful time" when, apparently as the result of the failure of his father's business, he was switched from the small private school he attended to the local grammar school. Except for the subject of history, in which he could "star," he had been poorly prepared by the genteel lady who had first taught him, and he was embarrassed to show the other children how little he knew about such subjects as arithmetic. Unremarkably, he hated to be laughed at; perhaps more remarkably, this distaste ran very deep, to his core.

When George was still in elementary school, his brother Stuart, almost six years older, enrolled in the Virginia Military Institute. Visiting his brother, young George was taken on a tour of the battlefield at New Market in the Shenandoah Valley, a hallowed spot in the annals of VMI. At New Market, on May 15, 1864, a mixed Confederate force, including 241 mustered-in cadets from VMI, had attacked and driven back an invading Union force; ten of the VMI boys were killed in the battle, and forty-seven wounded, and every spring their sacrifice was commemorated at VMI in a solemn review when each fallen cadet was said to have "died on the field of honor." The school had "a very famous record of fighting," and Marshall was "intensely interested" in the lore of New Market. One of the doomed cadets had been a distant cousin, Martin Marshall. Out of this experience and perhaps others—a Marshall relative had served as Robert E. Lee's aide during the Civil War—young George began to develop the idea of becoming a soldier.

Stuart Marshall did well as a student at VMI, emerging in 1894 as a chemist. Apparently he took great pride in his achievements. One day, at a time when George was "begging to go to the VMI," he happened to overhear a conversation between his mother and Stuart. To George's consternation, Stuart was pleading with Mrs. Marshall not to let his younger brother follow in his footsteps. If George got to VMI, Stuart said, he would disgrace the family name.

Immediately what had existed simply as a wish with George became an unshakable resolution. Stuart's contemptuous words hit his younger brother with far greater impact "than all the instructors, parental pressures, or anything else." Stuart simply was not going to get away with this; George decided "right then" that he would show his brother—he would "wipe his eye." He would go to VMI and he would succeed. It was no longer simply a desire, it had become an "urging."

In going to Virginia, this young small-town Pennsylvanian was actually moving closer to his family's roots. The Marshalls were of Tidewater origin—Chief Justice John Marshall was a collateral ancestor. They had come to Pennsylvania by way of Kentucky, to which George's great-great-grandfather had moved in 1780. Wherever they went, they took with them pride in their distinguished forebears. This kind of talk, particularly when it involved boasts about the great Chief Justice, produced a negative reaction in George; in a bit of resolution perhaps unperceived by his status-conscious older brother, the younger boy decided that "it was about time for somebody to swim for the family again." But the Chief Justice, though much the most eminent of the Marshalls, had not been the only successful one. In the two northeastern Kentucky towns in which the family lived, Washington and Augusta, the Marshalls owned the best residences, handsome three- or four-story brick houses with fine views of countryside or river. In his grandfather's house in Augusta, George's parents grew up "accustomed to a very bountiful living and continual hospitality," a sort of life they found lacking in Pennsylvania, where his father went to work a few years after the Civil War. Missing their Kentucky ways, when "there were always people for meals," the Marshalls established a continual open house after they moved to Uniontown in 1877. Young George thus grew up in a lively social atmosphere; it all made for a "pleasant little life."

In September 1897 Marshall, a tall and not overly coordinated sixteen-year-old, fun-loving but shy, left the pleasant little life of Uniontown for an austere, disciplined world in which he would learn much about what was inside him and would make one of the most important discoveries anybody can make. He would find what he wanted to do in life, and he would find that he could do it well. And for the first time he would "finally get ahead" of his older brother. In his third year at VMI he was to become first captain, the top cadet command post.

Sibling rivalry posed no problems for Franklin Roosevelt. Although he had a half brother, "Rosy," from his father's first marriage, this sibling was twenty-six years older than the "splendid large boy" to whom James Roosevelt's young second wife gave birth on January 30, 1882, and throughout Franklin's childhood Rosy played the part of an amiable uncle. "Doting" must be considered a weakly inadequate term to describe Sara Delano Roosevelt's view of her new son. So delighted was she, and so fulfilled, that she never contemplated having another child. Franklin thus grew up with no rivals for his mother's love. His father too played an active part in rearing his son, particularly on the sporting side, until he fell ill in 1890, when he was sixty-two. Loving the land and everything that grew on it, especially the pine trees, James Roosevelt passed this affection on to Franklin, and, along with it, a more subtle and general legacy; everywhere father and son went, James Roosevelt received deferential treatment, whether in the village of Hyde Park or in Mr. James's private railroad car traveling to Canada or through the Middle West. In every context, he would appear as the chairman or the supervisor or the owner, the dominant person in the room.

The subculture in which the eagerly greeted boy had arrived possessed qualities both tribal and cosmopolitan on a level unimaginable in a provincial Pennsylvania town. Marshall's father, a nineteenth-century entrepreneurial type, had aimed at amassing business wealth but missed his target and instead became a victim of the long depression of the 1890s. In contrast, the Roosevelts lived as landed American gentry, possessors not of riches in what they saw as the questionable Rockefeller or Vanderbilt manner, but of status and financial serenity (although Franklin's father made his own ineffective post-Civil War attempt to emulate the Vanderbilts). The world into which Franklin Roosevelt was born was socially the loftiest world America afforded; "nice people," its inhabitants called themselves. His father was a country squire and a like destiny awaited the son; the grandfather, curiously and perhaps significantly, had graduated in medicine but never practiced because, it was said, he could not abide the sight of blood.

The boy and his friends roamed the fields around Springwood, the comfortable but not showy house at Hyde Park, sitting on its bluff from which tree-covered slopes fell away to the broad Hudson River. It was a life of sledding and bird-watching, of carefully supervised shooting, of warmth and family fun, remote from any world of small-town pranks, of bee-fighting and upended outhouses on Halloween. It was a life complete with tutors and frequent sojourns in Europe, with knowledge of French and German automatically acquired by its favored young members. Young Franklin's parents encouraged him to be self-controlled and self-reliant, to wear an unvarying mask of good manners—a tendency furthered during his prep-school years at Groton under the awesome eye of the headmaster, the Reverend Endicott Peabody. It was not a world of crybabies. Out of it came a young man who grew up with an extraordinary assurance and inner security and a belief that "the wellborn must never compromise with evil."

One story from Franklin's mother caught the tone of the boy's self-confidence. An avid and skillful collector of birds, he came into the house one day, looking for his collecting gun but seeming in no great hurry to go back outside and get the winter wren he sought.

His mother laughed. "And do you think that wren is going to oblige you by staying there while you come in and get your gun to go back and shoot him?"

Franklin seemed surprised but hardly perturbed. "Oh, yes," he said, "he'll wait."

This upbringing had another side to it. His mother's love was limitless, but like all such loves it exacted its price. Reluctant to see Franklin leave for school, she kept him at Hyde Park until he was fourteen, two years later than the usual age for entering Groton. Finally she released him to "a world whose boundaries were not limited by the barriers the very intensity of [her] devotion imposed." During the years inside these loving barriers, Franklin had managed to develop the independence his family prized, but he had been forced to do it in his own way. One could not be independent and yet agree with every thought and yield to every whim of one's doting mother. One had to create an inner life that was one's alone. To the mask of class and culture, Franklin Roosevelt added a layer imposed by familial circumstance. He did not confront his mother's intrusive concern, he evaded it, he slipped past it.

Described as "dictatorial, Spartan, and immaculate," the Reverend Dr. Peabody had built Groton in his own image, thereby producing for the sons of old families a school devoted chiefly to "Christianity, character, and muscle." Awesomely impressive to his students, who called him "the Rector," Peabody took it as his mission to mold from the social elite a new class of national leaders with social responsibility; the privileged, he preached incessantly, must fight for the less fortunate. Neither Roosevelt nor any other boy of the time could escape intimate acquaintance with this insistent lesson in *noblesse oblige.* Not driven by any internal imperatives demanding scholarly achievement, Franklin nevertheless managed to stay in the upper fourth of his class at Groton; but, despite the fact that he arrived there as a skinny boy of five feet three inches, he fought his main struggle for distinction in athletics, where his success was limited. In another sphere, in a debate in which he spoke against American annexation of the Hawaiian Islands, he noted that "a little inexpensive dredging" could transform Pearl Harbor into a valuable naval base, but he went on to make the interesting strategic point that by acquiring Hawaii the United States would for the first time have taken on territory vulnerable to naval attack. At Groton he also learned something about living as a member of a minority: He held an unchallenged distinction as the only Democrat in the student body.

At Harvard, to which he went in 1900, Roosevelt entered a world far wider than Groton, and more relaxed. Although he concentrated in the social sciences, he still did not devote his main effort to scholarship but enjoyed considerable social success and worked hard for what he really wanted, a high place on the Harvard *Crimson.* In his junior year these efforts won full success, bringing him the compound post of president and editor in chief of the newspaper. He managed the *Crimson* effectively, in a style recalled by a colleague as featuring "geniality" that held "a kind of frictionless command." But certainly the most exciting happening during these years was the accession to the presidency of the United States of his distant cousin, Theodore

Roosevelt, and the consequent flamboyant and inspiriting use the new president made of his office.

Thus far in his life, Franklin Roosevelt had experienced only one important disappointment. Taught sailing by his father and reared to admire the maritime exploits of his mother's family, the seafaring Delanos, he had announced one day that he wished to go to Annapolis and become a naval officer. That was hardly suitable, his parents said; as a man, he would own land and have other responsibilities that precluded the choice of such a career. He must give up his dream; he was to go to Harvard and on to law school. Thus the way ahead seemed assured, if not so exciting as he would have wished.

Franklin Roosevelt and George Marshall—two young men who would have appeared quite different to anybody who happened to meet them both. But, curiously, each in his own way had succeeded at college in achieving an ambition, and neither ambition had academic qualities.

Two young men who had carefully fashioned masks for themselves—Roosevelt, in his charming fashion, hiding a part of his inner self that insisted on true independence, Marshall, in a drive for the kind of success he valued, suppressing under the weight of discipline the mischievous small-town lad called Flicker.

Two different young men, but perhaps not so different as an observer would have believed them to be.

Once, in conversation with a fellow law clerk, Franklin Roosevelt remarked that he thought he might be president some day. Although he was engaged at the time in humdrum legal work on Wall Street, the idea could not be dismissed as utterly far-fetched, because Cousin Theodore had done it—and not only did the famous cousin hold sway in the White House, but, preaching the same gospel as that of Groton's rector, he urged well-born young men to follow him into politics. Franklin even had in mind a detailed plan. As he explained to his friend, he would have to begin by serving in the state legislature, next acquire national experience in Washington, then become governor of New York. Finally from Albany he could take the one remaining step to the White House. The early Washington experience, he thought with noteworthy precision, should see him serving as assistant secretary of the navy. The program could hardly claim originality, because it drew its details from the career of the man then occupying the White House, but its application to somebody else was startling. Surely one could not expect a beginning career to follow an established one so closely, even to the assistant secretaryship of the navy. But even though the plan copied TR's progression, it also fitted Franklin's own interests. If he could not become an admiral, he would find another way to preside over the fleet.

All in all, the friend found himself astonished at what he had heard. And, as anyone could have noted, the plan took no account of the unpredictable—of changes of mind, of historical developments, of accident and illness. Yet, finding the practice of law somewhat less than enthralling, Roosevelt in 1910 succeeded in beginning his climb. Delighted at being asked, he accepted the Democratic nomination for state senator from his solidly Republican district, ran a zestful and innovative campaign—featuring the use of a bright red Maxwell touring car instead of the standard horse and buggy—and succeeded in becoming only the second Democrat to carry the district in more than fifty years.

In Albany he quickly proved himself a lively and reformist state senator, attracting even national attention by his role as a ringleader in a revolt against the bosses. In neighboring New Jersey a similar fight was being waged by a rather more highly placed Democrat, Governor Woodrow Wilson, and long before the opening of the Democratic party convention of 1912, Roosevelt declared himself for Wilson for president. A successful presidential candidate tends to reserve a special high place in his esteem for supporters who climb aboard his bandwagon while it is still a modest vehicle whose destination is in doubt. Proving himself no exception to this principle—which old politicians called "first on the bandwagon, first at the pie-counter"—Wilson, after his victory over Teddy Roosevelt and William Howard Taft, delighted the thirty-one-year-old Franklin Roosevelt by approving him for a Cabinet post. The position for which he was chosen? Assistant secretary of the navy! Although he had entered politics only three years earlier, Franklin had already reached the second rung of his four-level ladder. His name, his good looks, his charm, his connections—everything seemed to conspire in his advancement.

During the first three years of the great war in Europe that began in 1914, Roosevelt took a strong interventionist position, frequently expressing impatience with the caution and neutralism of President Wilson. After the United States entered the war in 1917, Roosevelt as the number two man in the Navy Department became an important figure in Washington. Responsible for the navy's personnel and physical plant, he now had to procure men, ships, and matériel on a great scale. In pursuit of his tasks he showed himself vigorous, unorthodox, a strong foe of red tape. "I get my fingers into everything," he said, "and there's no law against it." He liked to move quickly, and, if necessary, he could make it plain that he was not "just another rich man's son with nothing more to do than to dabble in politics," as he was regarded by a disgruntled Massachusetts shipyard executive, a twenty-eight-year-old apprentice tycoon named Joseph P. Kennedy.

Roosevelt wanted more from the war than contracts and production; he yearned to be overseas, playing a part in the great adventure of his generation. Finally managing to arrange an inspection trip in 1918, he showed his delight when on the western front he came under German artillery fire, recording with zest the "long whining whistle" of a shell that exploded at a spot he had left a few moments earlier.

His performance as assistant secretary during the war had been impressive. Yet many thought his ideas and his enthusiasms ill-considered, ill-organized, and essentially superficial. His lack of ideology, or rather his ability to move between ways of thinking, made him appear to some a lightweight, with no fixed point of view. Only a few observers seemed to divine any bedrock beneath the dash and the smiles.

Secretary of the Navy Josephus Daniels called Roosevelt "a twentieth-century Apollo" and "as handsome a figure of an attractive young man as he had ever seen." This personal attractiveness together with FDR's other great continuing asset, the Roosevelt name, helped win him the Democratic vice-presidential nomination in 1920. But the Democrats could not turn back the tide of national reaction against Wilson's League of Nations. So strongly did this tide run against Roosevelt's party that the Republicans were able to take the presidency with a candidate who had no qualifications, mental or moral, for the post. The winner, Warren G. Harding, became the first of three "heirs of fatigue" who would occupy the White House during the 1920s. It was an instructive lesson in the power of historical currents.

Never after making his first race, in 1910, did Roosevelt show consistent interest in any field of activity besides politics. But as an out-of-office Democrat in a world at least temporarily Republican, he turned after the election of 1920 to the law and to business. A bonding company presented him with a lucrative job—and even here he was actually involved with politicians if not with electoral politics, because the company did much of its business with officeholders who controlled city and state bonding. He even managed to discern a ray of light in the dark Democratic sky, telling a friend that such a moment of sweeping defeat was "the best time to lay plans for Democratic victories in the future."

In the summer of 1921 Roosevelt became the target of a congressional investigation having almost uniquely unsavory aspects. As acting secretary of the navy in 1919, he had presided over the creation of a vice squad to investigate homosexual activity at the Newport, Rhode Island, training center, but, with details *The New York Times* did not regard as "fit to print," the Republican majority on the committee accused FDR of condoning acts of sodomy by some of the young investigators. After the inquiry had dragged on for many months, the committee rushed out its printed report without allowing Roosevelt's defense to appear. LAY NAVY SCANDAL TO F. D. ROOSEVELT declared the headline over the July 20 story in the *Times,* which quoted heavily from the report. The assistant secretary's action was called not only "most reprehensible" but "unnatural," and Roosevelt, the committee said, was too intelligent a man to be allowed to get away with a plea of ignorance. Although FDR desperately fought back by deploring the committee's use of the navy as a "vehicle for cheap ward politics," the Republicans had unquestionably landed him a blow painful both politically and personally.

But within a month the bright young Democratic star would suffer an infinitely greater blow. Following the stressful events of July came a holiday on Campobello Island, off Maine, the family vacation spot where, as always, FDR swam, sailed, and played baseball and tennis with his children. Physically he presented a paradoxical picture: Although vigorous and active, hardly ever sitting still, he nevertheless "caught every bug that came along," as Josephus Daniels said; his immune system sometimes seemed unable to put up any resistance to attack. One day at Campobello, by spending an exhausting afternoon fighting a forest fire and then cooling off, first by a swim in one of the frosty ponds and then by a dip in the frigid waters of the Bay of Fundy, Roosevelt gave his body's defenses a challenge they could not fend off; he was stricken by poliomyelitis. Suddenly an absolutely unforeseeable change had taken place: The twentieth-century Apollo could no longer walk. If the congressional report had not finished his career before it reached the third of its planned four rungs, then surely the disease had toppled him from the ladder. In 1921 a cripple lived set apart from the mass of mankind, often shut away, whispered about like an idiot or a syphilitic. To some extent, society even seemed to blame such a person for his condition. And treatment sometimes possessed a perhaps unconscious punitive quality, with doctors advocating, for efficiency's sake, the amputation of useless legs. Gear like wheelchairs and braces was cumbersome, not designed to enhance the mobility of the handicapped individual. Certainly no country known to history had ever freely chosen a paralytic as its leader, nor did such persons dream of seeking high office.

Perhaps Roosevelt had not taken his four-stage plan with complete seriousness. Behind the mask worked a complex mind, with the activities of one compartment sometimes seeming unrelated or even contradictory to those of another. Still, he had followed precisely the path he had laid out as a young law clerk; he had even embellished it with a vice-presidential candidacy that had made him well known throughout the country. And now, when he was just thirty-nine, it all seemed over.

One autumn day in 1920, a major on the U.S. General Staff sat down at his desk to compose a letter to a friend. He had promised, the major said, to write the friend his observations about "what had constituted the success of the outstanding figures in the American Expeditionary Forces" in 1917 and 1918, and now he was making good on the promise.

The major had occupied an excellent position for viewing the "outstanding figures" in the U.S. forces in France. He had been a thirty-six-year-old captain when the United States declared war on Germany. During his fifteen years in the army up to that time, he had served in the usual variety of duty stations, in the continental United States and twice in the Philippines. In the first of these Philippine tours, 1902–1903, he had learned under hard circumstances, including a devastating cholera epidemic, to relate effectively to troops.

He developed the ability to command in the field, and he

quickly showed himself a resourceful and imaginative leader of men. He had a flair for inducing troops to take part in projects like recreational activities that were deemed good for them but were unenthusiastically received. As a leader he developed his own style. One day, while he was taking a patrol across a swampy stream in an area known to have crocodiles, the men heard a splashing noise ahead of them and one yelled, "Crocodile!" The whole patrol panicked, the men plunging ahead, flattening Lieutenant Marshall and running over him: "I was ground right down to the bottom." As he dragged himself up and followed the men onto the bank, he did "some very fast thinking." Panic could not be tolerated, but he felt that cursing the men, a traditional technique of command, would hardly suffice. Instead, he fell them in formally, "gave them right shoulder arms," as if on parade, marched them back across the crocodile-infested stream, and then back again. No further words were necessary.

Overall, the young officer developed a way of following his own path with an unusual mixture of quietness and audacity, so that frequently those who questioned his daring concluded by admiring his effectiveness. Later, after a year at the staff college at Leavenworth, he had been judged "an exceptionally capable man." In 1916 he had won from his commanding officer, Colonel Johnson Hagood, a remarkable tribute. In making out the captain's efficiency report, Hagood had to answer a standard question. Would he "desire to have him under your immediate command in peace and in war"? Yes, said the colonel, "but I would prefer to serve *under his command* [underscoring in original]. . . . He should be made a brigadier general in the Regular Army, and every day this is postponed is a loss to the Army and the Nation. . . . He is a military genius . . ."

Despite this unprecedented praise, George Marshall still held captain's rank when war came. In the middle of June 1917, he found himself aboard a troopship en route to France. One of his roommates was a young officer named Lesley McNair; the two had been assigned as assistant chiefs of staff of the hastily assembled and totally untrained U.S. 1st Division. Like most professional soldiers, Marshall wished to command troops, but his all-around skill as a planner decreed that he would spend the war as a staff officer with the 1st Division, the First Army, and General John J. Pershing's General Headquarters. He had a great deal of contact with troops and often came under fire, but he never got the kind of line command he hoped for.

One day when Marshall was still at 1st Division headquarters, he staged an unlikely and remarkable scene with Pershing. Marshall had just recently reached the rank of major, and Pershing—stern-faced, ramrod straight, immaculately turned out—strode into division headquarters with all the authority borne by the American commanding general in France. But for a few minutes Major Marshall seemed to forget this great gulf in rank. After watching a 1st Division exercise, General Pershing tore into the division commander, Major General William L. Sibert, and his staff, asking questions of officers who could not possibly have known the answers; "he just gave everybody hell." In such a circumstance, the normal reaction is to swallow the rebuke and lose one's temper later, cursing the high officer after he has moved out of earshot. But Marshall, furious, felt that he must make a "sacrifice play." As Pershing turned away, the major went up to him and attempted to explain matters; the general merely shrugged and continued on his way. Marshall then grasped Pershing by the arm, "practically forced him to talk," and proceeded to point out deficiencies in Pershing's own headquarters that were responsible for some of the First Army's problems. When Marshall became angry, an assistant said, "his eyes flashed and he talked so rapidly and vehemently no one else could get in a word. He overwhelmed his opponent by a torrent of facts." In view of the illustriousness of this particular opponent, Marshall's fellow officers were horrified at the scene, but Pershing took the major's tirade calmly, saying only, "You must appreciate the troubles we have." Marshall shot back, "*We* have them every day and we have to solve every one of them by night."

That was the end of the conversation. When Marshall's friends remarked that he had made a bad enemy and no doubt would be fired forthwith, he answered that such an outcome would not necessarily be bad news. "All I can see," he said, "is that I may get troop duty instead of staff duty, and that would be a great success." Had it not been such an extraordinary scene, one could have suspected Marshall of planning the outburst in order to disgrace himself with Pershing. If that had been his intention, it proved thoroughly misguided. Instead of ordering Marshall into the trenches, Pershing on his subsequent visits to the division would take the firebrand major "off away from the others" and query him about the situation. This served as a highly instructive lesson in leadership for Marshall. He had never before seen anybody like Pershing, a man "who could listen to severe criticisms, just as though it was about a man in another country. He never held it against you personally. He might not agree with you in any degree. But he listened to very, very frank criticisms in regard to his actions." Yet this forbearance came from a man in no degree unsure of himself. "General Pershing as a leader always dominated any gathering. . . . He was a tremendous driver, if necessary; a very kindly, likable man on off-duty status, but very stern on a duty basis."

Loyalty and temper, two of Marshall's most pronounced qualities, soon combined to keep him from being named chief of staff of the 1st Division. In December 1917 Pershing fired Sibert, replacing him with Brigadier General Robert L. Bullard. Here again, Marshall saw injustice; he was "vitriolic" and "bitter" and "het up"—not qualities the new division commander would seek in a chief of staff; the job went to somebody else. Enough, Marshall decided: He must face himself and his temper. "I learnt my lesson," he said; "I never forgot it." He realized that if he had been appointed divisional chief of staff, he "would very quickly have been made brigadier general." Although he was subsequently promoted to colonel, the transition to brigadier would have carried special weight because ranks in the army make up a pyramid divided into three layers—company grade, through captain; field grade, through colonel; and general officers. Promotion to brigadier would have seen Marshall moving up from the relatively wide middle layer to the loftier and narrower world of generals. It was a transition made by Marshall's contemporary, Douglas MacArthur, who commanded troops and who, as the son of a former senior general, benefited from his widowed mother's promotional efforts.

But, rank apart, Marshall acquired in France a very large part of what was becoming in the army the Marshall legend; earlier, in the Philippines, his conduct of maneuvers had impressed officers high and low, and had led at least one, a lieutenant named Henry "Hap" Arnold, to write that he had seen a future chief of staff in action. In September 1918 Marshall drew the assignment of planning the concentration for the Meuse-Argonne battle, "which was being prepared for at that time in the midst of the action of St.-Mihiel. It presented very complicated conditions," because the U.S. command "had to take troops out of a going battle, cross them over the rear zone, tremendously active," and move them into the sector of the new battle; it was "a terrific problem of logistics," involving some 600,000 men and the needed transport and supplies. Despite the difficulties, unprecedented in history, Marshall's plans worked as close to flawlessly as was possible for so complex a military operation; their creator was honored at headquarters with the nickname "Wizard." Pointing out that the matériel included 3,980 guns, 40,000 tons of ammunition, 34 evacuation hospitals, and 93,032 horses, all of which was moved without arousing German suspicions, General Pershing himself declared that "it seldom happens in war that plans can be so precisely carried out as was possible in this instance."

So far was Pershing from having given Marshall a black mark after their fiery encounter that in October 1918, following the colonel's Meuse-Argonne wizardry, the general recommended the younger man for promotion into the top layer of the pyramid of rank. But the nomination ran afoul of a delay imposed by the U.S. Congress, which had decided to postpone promotions until the Meuse-Argonne operation ended. Within a few weeks, however, the end came not only of the operation but of the war itself, and the armistice brought with it the end of all temporary promotions. Again, Marshall had missed his star.

In 1919 Pershing further showed his liking for Marshall by asking the colonel to become his aide. Although the war had been over for several months, Pershing as a major public figure had a variety of duties. Here again, Marshall felt himself pulled onto a path leading away from command of troops rather than toward this duty he most desired and in which he believed he would be most likely to progress to higher posts. But such a flattering offer, coming from the army's most eminent soldier, would not be easy to turn down—and Marshall decided he could not reject it.

The job immediately offered new kinds of experiences. As he accompanied Pershing to victory parades and celebrations first in Paris and then in London, Marshall encountered some of the great figures of the time. On arriving in the British capital, the party was greeted by the secretary of state for war, Winston Churchill, and later Marshall escorted Mrs. Churchill at a troop review. (At one point, acknowledging the coming of Prohibition in the United States, Churchill turned to Marshall and said of the American troops on parade: "What a magnificent body of men never to take another drink.") Socially, Marshall hobnobbed with such personages as the crown prince of Sweden and Lady Curzon, wife of the former viceroy of India; at a country-house party he refereed a tennis match between, he noted casually, "the Duchess of Sutherland with Lord Hope playing against Lady Drogheda and some other chap"; at a dance the blasé American colonel observed that "the usual crowd was present, including the Prince of Wales and his brothers."

Marshall's growth in worldliness had been remarkable in the two years since he had arrived in France. A zealous self-improver, bent on familiarizing himself with the language of the host country by speaking it "on every suitable occasion," on his first day he had turned to an escorting French officer and observed, *"Je suis très beau aujourd'hui."* After analyzing the "odd look" given him by the startled officer, Marshall resolved never to speak French again "except when forced to"; any comments intended to describe the weather or anything else would be made in English. Even so, he later succeeded in delivering an entire impromptu speech in French, although his fellow American officers claimed that it was utterly verbless.

After returning with Pershing to the United States, Marshall helped the general prepare testimony for a joint congressional committee that was considering the size and makeup of the postwar American Army; the Democrats had lost their Senate majority in the November 1918 elections, and "normalcy" in the form of Republican conservatism already spoke with a loud voice in Congress, even in advance of the 1920 presidential sweep. On Capitol Hill Marshall encountered still another new world, this one in its own way as exotic and ritualistic as that of Lady Drogheda and Buckingham Palace. Pershing attacked the Wilson administration's proposal for a large standing army, but strongly supported universal military training (UMT) for all young Americans. The senators and congressmen on the joint committee lapped up the first testimony, but no one displayed much enthusiasm for the second idea, a favorite of Marshall's. The principle of the "citizen army" stood at the core of his beliefs; with UMT "you can create a respectable military force . . . without having the fellows constantly in uniform." But in 1919 the war was just over, a great victory had been won, and who cared about any future dangers? In fact, what future dangers were there? As always between crises, the American public and its legislators willed the army into insignificance.

Not long after Marshall took up his duties as Pershing's aide, the 1920 presidential season dawned. As he toured the country on what was supposed to be an inspection of army camps and war plants, moving from city to city, the great American hero found the enterprise coming more and more to resemble a triumphal progress. Parades, receptions, dinners, balls—everywhere Pershing was feted in a thoroughly head-turning way, and in his speeches he seemed to respond by becoming increasingly political. A fine-looking man, a victorious general, a leader admired across the country—might not such a person dream of the presidency?

The general's aide frowned on these developments. The presidential bug had unquestionably bitten Pershing, but Marshall resolved not to allow any consequent infection to develop. The general must not "cut down his prestige by being involved in that sort of thing unless it was almost by acclamation." A soldier was a soldier and a politician was a politician, and, as Marshall shrewdly saw, the public might admire Pershing, but the politicians were hardly ready to hand him the nomination, nor did popular adulation necessarily equal political support. Some of Pershing's friends had "deluded" him, Marshall believed, and when one such group came calling from Tennessee only to find the general away, his aide unhesitatingly took it on himself to send them back home. Pershing, Marshall said, "was furious with me. I didn't even consult him." By now such an operating style had become a pronounced characteristic of Marshall's; when he knew what ought to be done, he simply went ahead with it, and he never doubted his capacity to make the right decisions. Not a patient man by nature, Marshall in army matters became particularly vexed at obfuscatory regulations and individual buck-passing, and he encouraged such an antibureaucratic attitude in others.

For all his on-duty sternness, Pershing out of the office was delightful, "almost boyish in his reactions," and Marshall found him a wonderful traveling companion. On duty, in addition, the general "had no hesitation at all" about taking advice from his aides; "it was one of his great strengths." The general handled most matters by picking up whatever document or other paper had been sent to him for action, writing "Colonel M" on it, and turning it over to Marshall, who was "to take a look at it and tell him what I thought." This arrangement, under which the aide freely expressed himself about various superiors, was kept between the two men as their little working secret. One day Pershing, in collaboration with another general, proposed an action counter to a decision taken by General Peyton C. March, a onetime subordinate of Pershing's who in 1918 had become chief of staff, an appointment that had led to continuing friction and disputes about authority between the field commander in France and the chief in Washington. Marshall told Pershing in a memo that this counterproposal was "entirely wrong," whereupon the general summoned his aide to his office to express his objections to the memo.

"Let me have it again," Marshall said. "I didn't express myself well."

The same thing happened again. Pershing rejected the rewritten memo, and Marshall took it back to his own office and "rewrote the whole thing to give it a brand-new flavor." But when Pershing read this latest effort, "he slapped his hand on the desk," an unusually strong reaction for him, and exclaimed, "No! By God, we will do it this way."

Marshall did not budge. "Now, General," he said, "just because you hate the guts of General March, you're setting yourself up . . . to do something you know damn well is wrong."

Pershing stared back at his aide, handed him the paper, and said, "Well, have it your own way."

The exchange said a great deal about both men. Marshall particularly admired the fact that, as far as Pershing was concerned, it "was the end of the affair." The general "held no griefs at all. He might be very firm at the time, but if you convinced him, that was the end of that." It was admirable, Marshall thought, that Pershing not only could separate—completely—personal feelings from considerations of fact but could seemingly will the inappropriate feelings not to exist. This detachment and objectivity, with the lamentable exception of Pershing's continuing feud with General March, constituted a lesson in leadership that appears to have impressed Marshall deeply. Marshall's own conduct as the general's aide won a sweeping tribute from Pershing's former chief of operations: "I know nobody in whom endowments of intellect, character, courage and rare tact are more abundantly provided and more perfectly balanced."

By the summer of 1920 Marshall had become a sophisticated

officer, an experienced military planner—considered by many the best in the entire army—an executive, and a diplomat, and he had begun learning something about politics as practiced in Washington, D.C. It was in the autumn of that year that he sat down to write to General John S. Mallory at VMI, making good on his promise to tell the general what advice he would give a young officer going to war, on the basis of his "observation of what had constituted the success of the outstanding figures" in the American Army in France.

"Assuming that you possess good common sense, have studied your profession and are physically strong," Marshall said, he found four qualities essential, and he was certain that "the average man who scrupulously follows this course of action is bound to win great success," although "few seemed equal to it in this war."

In the first place, Marshall wrote, "when conditions are difficult, the command is depressed and everyone seems critical and pessimistic, you must be especially cheerful and optimistic."

Second, "when evening comes and all are exhausted, hungry and possibly dispirited, particularly in unfavorable weather at the end of a march or in battle, you must put aside any thought of personal fatigue and display marked energy in looking after the comfort of your organization, inspecting your lines and preparing for tomorrow."

Third, Marshall said that the officer aiming at "great success" should "make a point of extreme loyalty, in thought and deed, to your chiefs personally; and in your efforts to carry out their plans or policies, the less you approve the more energy you must direct to their accomplishment."

Fourth, "the more alarming and disquieting the reports received or the conditions viewed in battle, the more determined must be your attitude. Never ask for the relief of your unit and never hesitate to attack."

Optimism, energy (with emphasis on the well-being of the men for whom one is responsible), loyalty, detemination—these were not only qualities that ought to be possessed by an officer determined to rise in his profession, they were also traits a wise high commander should look for in picking officers for responsible posts. They were solid qualities on which a commander could depend, qualities that would make a large organization function effectively. And among them Marshall inserted an explicit reproof to the individual ego: The less you agree with the policies of your superiors, "the more energy you must direct to their accomplishment." France had taught stern but thorough lessons, and Pershing seen close up had offered an inspiring example for at least one officer determined to "win great success." But where and how was he going to win it?

CHAPTER TWO

ON THE HORIZON

The new act of Franklin Roosevelt's political drama opened with a standard stage situation, a triangle made up of a man and two women—one of the women, classically, the wife; the other, however, not the mistress but the mother of the leading man.

To Sara Roosevelt, it appeared that her hour had struck. The polio attack that had taken away the legs of her beloved son surely meant that now, as before he went off to Groton, she could have him at Hyde Park, free of all his grubby and demeaning political associations, where he could live full time as a country squire, working over the books of the estate, reading and writing, playing with his stamp collection, spending the evenings in genteel conversation in the great south room of the big house. Certainly she wished for his recovery and supported him in his drive to make his way back, but she could hardly profess to being disappointed that he could no longer aspire to political office.

In sharp and imaginative contrast came the view of Roosevelt's wife, Eleanor, who with great insight into her husband's character believed that as much as possible he ought to continue to involve himself in politics and in the varied life of New York City. He did not possess a nature that could content itself in sitting by the fire up in Dutchess County, a scenic and charming area whose proximity to the city was purely geographic; psychologically and socially it could have been eight hundred miles away instead of eighty. Perhaps few marriages are typical, but this opinion came from a wife in the midst of a particularly unusual family constellation. Having been forced to battle her formidable mother-in-law for regard (and sometimes even consideration) in the eyes of her husband, she had then discovered his emotional involvement with her own social secretary, a beautiful young woman named Lucy Mercer; perhaps the relationship had involved sexual intercourse, perhaps not, but Franklin had clearly been in love and he and Eleanor had spoken of divorce. He obviously had not thought the matter out to its conclusion, because as a Catholic Miss Mercer could hardly have married him once he had become free; like many another affair, the relationship saw its end decreed in its beginning. A complicating factor in the unhappy situation was the fact that the Roosevelts, after having produced six children (one of whom died in infancy), practiced contraception only by means of abstinence, a device less appealing to Franklin than to Eleanor. She also offered her husband an alternative—they could stay together for the sake of the children. After intensive discussion, including the powerful intervention of FDR's mother, Franklin agreed to this solution. The elder Mrs. Roosevelt was said to have told her son that if he left "a wife and five children for another woman," she "would not give him another dollar." Franklin was her cherished son, but right conduct did not constitute a matter for debate. Aside from respecting the potency of his mother's threat, Franklin had to consider the lethal effect divorce would have on his political career—his only real life work. The Roosevelts resolved the problem through reconciliation, though apparently the sexual relationship that had lain dormant continued so.

Now, suddenly, Franklin needed his wife, as companion and nurse, and Eleanor responded with marked devotion. The two joined in transforming what had become essentially an official marriage into a new entity, a partnership.

But what did Roosevelt wish to do? After the first shock and depression, he reacted to the polio attack in his own individual way—a way utterly in opposition to standard medical belief. A person afflicted with such a disease is supposed, after absorbing the initial impact, to come to terms with the facts, to accept the nature of the condition and rearrange his life accordingly. Roosevelt approached the problem differently. All his instincts told him to hope for the best and ignore the possibility of the worst, to deny the obvious implications of his condition. He would work and struggle, he would strain and sweat, he would progress, and some day, by one means or another, he would walk again. He could conquer his affliction. After all, why should he not? If he set his mind and his will to anything, he could bring it about. And—a very important point—he would do it cheerfully. The stoicism he had absorbed as a child would support his cause.

In addition to his wife, FDR found another prime helper in his double fight to walk and to remain a force in politics. This was an ugly, gnomelike, minor-league newspaperman named Louis Howe, who had affixed himself to Roosevelt during the Albany days in the conviction that this handsome and dynamic young politician had limitless possibilities; Howe became the tactical adviser, the operator, and the in-house cynic. Together, he believed, the two might well one day reach the White House; even in 1912 the little man had addressed Roosevelt as "Beloved and Revered Future President." The jocularity conveyed by the capital letters could not disguise Howe's belief in the inspiring vision he saw. Now, in 1921, despite the evidence of his eyes, Howe kept his remarkable faith.

Running for office was out of the question, and would remain so for some years, but neither the Roosevelts nor Howe regarded this as any reason to avoid political activities. The early 1920s became for Roosevelt essentially the years of research, of contact-making and maintenance. He became a scholar and a specialist, with politics his profession as surely as theoretical physics was Einstein's. He and Howe built up files of contacts with key persons across the country, and streams of letters went out to them, all purporting to be written by Roosevelt himself. The seriousness of his condition was kept carefully hidden. He could never be seen as disabled, and certainly no photographs could be allowed to reveal his handicap. From the first days, Howe took care of that. The little man was shrewd, unrelenting, and effective. He had only two concerns: to advance Roosevelt's career by any and all means, and to maintain himself as the man closest to his hero.

Roosevelt entered the struggle for his future as a man able and talented but, at least in some eyes, superficial—a self-proclaimed liberal and progressive, but with no apparent strong views on economics or on society generally. Inevitably the polio and its victim's extraordinary fight for recovery brought about changes. The struggle could not create traits FDR did not already possess, but it reached deep into his personality and lifted to the surface characteristics previously unseen. He demonstrated a new kind of maturity and, as his sometime arrogance waned, of humility. He did not become a saint but he grew through his suffering.

The struggle produced simple and obvious practical effects as well. Before his polio attack, for instance, Roosevelt, like anybody else, could find all sorts of easy ways to end an unsatisfactory conversation; he could simply make an excuse and leave the room. Now he had to take people differently, to listen to them in a new way, to develop patience. He became closer to all sorts of people he might earlier have dismissed as unimportant or boring. He also developed his own recreational and self-defensive conversational style—he could not move away, but he could outtalk his visitor.

In consonance with his psychological and spiritual growth, Roosevelt developed physically in a way that seemed symbolic. Formerly slim and lithe, seemingly built for speed rather than for staying power, through persistent exercises he offset his wasted legs with a massively muscular upper body that made him literally a figure of strength and solidity. Through it all, he kept his Hyde Park–Groton mask firmly in place. Thus others found it easy to deal with him. They did not have to show pity, because they saw a man who obviously had no thought of needing it. Life after the initial period of adjustment was spirited and positive, whatever depression may have hidden behind the mask.

The 1924 Democratic national convention marked Roosevelt's surprisingly rapid return to the public stage. Favoring the presidential candidacy of Alfred E. Smith, the liberal governor of New York, Roosevelt agreed after some argument to deliver an already written nominating speech in which the brassy, derby-hatted, cigar-chomping Al was lyrically likened to Wordsworth's Happy Warrior "that every man in arms should wish to be." It was Roosevelt, however, who emerged from the speech as the true happy warrior. The conventioneers had eyed him curiously as he made his slow way on crutches to the lectern, and then his smile, his confidence, and his style swept everything before him. Though his man did not win the nomination, FDR proved the star of an otherwise pointless Democratic convention in a Republican year. After the Democratic defeat in November, Roosevelt made the prescient observation that he "did not think the nation would elect a Democrat again until the Republicans had led us into a serious period of depression and unemployment."

In 1928 Al Smith, who had compiled an excellent record as governor of New York, succeeded this time in winning the Democratic presidential nomination, which in realistic terms had little value—the "period of depression and unemployment" had not yet been delivered by the Republicans, and as an insular, raucous-voiced New Yorker, a Catholic and a foe of Prohibition, Smith despite his good gubernatorial record was not for export. But his nomination nevertheless had fateful consequences. It left the gubernatorial spot vacant on the party ticket in New York State. This was not the moment Roosevelt would have chosen—he still had some faith that continued intensive work at Warm Springs would at least enable him to manage walking with canes, and in any case it was very obviously not a Democratic year. Louis Howe's timetable called for a Roosevelt bid for the governorship in 1932 and a run for the presidency in 1936, after Herbert Hoover completed the second of his two expected presidential terms. But, pressed by Smith, Roosevelt yielded; he had, after all, held no governmental office of any kind for eight years, a very long time in politics, and he might bring on himself resentment by Democratic regulars if he refused the party's call. And he also had to explode the view held of him in many quarters that he was in some respects a sick man. Smith spoke bluntly to that point in assuring reporters at a press conference that the governor of New York had no duties that required him to be an acrobat, capable of performing "a double back flip or a handspring." The genuineness of the call for Roosevelt was attested to by Walter Lippmann: "The demand for Mr. Roosevelt came from every part of the state. It could not be quelled. It could not be denied. The office has sought the man." The curtain was rising on Roosevelt's Act III.

As he had done when he could walk, FDR campaigned strenuously, crossing New York State first by train and then by car, making numerous appearances in a day, drawing attention to his vigor by telling his audiences: "Too bad about this unfortunate sick man, isn't it?" To serve as a traveling aide and helper with speeches, Democratic party headquarters had supplied a young lawyer of thirty-two named Sam Rosenman. A devout Al Smith Democrat, Rosenman entertained a number of doubts about this Hudson Valley aristocrat who was supposed to be a liberal but, with his Groton and Harvard background, could hardly know anything substantial about the polyglot sidewalks of New York. But soon the helper was receiving lessons in speech-writing from the candidate himself. After producing an earnest effort on labor problems in the state, Rosenman learned that although his material was adequate, the draft itself was "a little on the dull side." That was Roosevelt's way, Rosenman found: "There was no effort to salve my feelings, but there was a ready acceptance of the parts that he considered good." FDR proceeded to dictate a series of inserts and changes, giving his assistant his "first lesson in how to pull a speech together and pep it up," particularly with the addition of graphic details and points aimed at the voter as an individual person. And that night, after delivering the speech to an enthusiastic audience, Roosevelt said, "It went over fine, Sam—good work," and then sent Rosenman off to begin drafting the next night's effort.

Although he had arrived with skepticism, Rosenman soon began to change his mind. He marveled at the courage and stamina of this disabled man for whom simply getting up and sitting down several times required as much energy as an ordinary person would expend in an entire day. Since of course FDR could not climb steps, members of his party often had to carry him, helpless as a baby, up and down the backstairs of the halls in which he spoke. "He always went through the harrowing experience smiling. He never got ruffled."

As the exhausting statewide campaign caravan continued, Rosenman viewed Roosevelt with increasing respect for his ability as well as with admiration for his courage. He had never met anybody "who could grasp the facts of a complicated problem as quickly and as thoroughly as he. He could listen attentively to a brief statement of the facts, and then dictate them into a speech"—on labor, water power, or any other subject; and then and there he could "walk onto a platform or rise at a banquet table and talk about them before an audience as though he had had a lifelong familiarity with them." And he always demonstrated his distinct touch; to an earnest and fact-packed Rosenman dissertation on efforts made through the years by Republican state leaders to turn the water power of New York over to private interests, FDR added opening lines describing the speech as "a history and a sermon on the subject of water power" with its text from the Old Testament: *"Thou shalt not steal."* He spoke of cheap electricity in terms not of kilowatts but of the farm wife's stove and sewing machine and the hired hand's milking. In addition to his editorial and rewriting skills, Roosevelt was such a fine natural orator that he could endow the most commonplace written words with "force, emphasis and charm."

Beyond all that, Rosenman found, the candidate was easy to work with. He had been told that this country squire was "aloof, reserved, lacking in humor, hard to get to know." Instead, Rosenman encountered a friendly man with an infectious sense of humor, who "knew how to stop work, even when hardest pressed, for a joke or an anecdote or a minute of light conversation or gossip"—a person "who really loved human beings." At the same time, as Rosenman had seen right away, FDR's bearing carried "an unspoken dignity which held off any undue familiarity." Beneath the labile surface always stood the solid core, of which Hyde Park and Groton formed the basic elements.

Although Al Smith at the head of the Democratic ticket took a bad beating, the party's candidate for governor of New York squeaked through to victory by about 25,000 votes out of almost four and a quarter million. Even many Democrats expressed surprise at this outcome; one story had it that some of the rustic folks upstate thought that one more time they were voting for good old Teddy. And on the morrow of the election, Louis Howe was exultant. He and his hero had come through the long night since 1921; right timing or not, Franklin now held the governorship of the nation's largest state, the state that produced presidents. Barring a loss in 1930 (New York governors then served two-year terms), he would be the automatic front-runner for the presidential nomination in 1932—all because of a winning margin in 1928 of a mere six tenths of one percent.

Then came the 1929 crash and the onset of the Great Depression, and as this unprecedented disaster progressively gripped the American economy, Herbert Hoover's luster as the "Great Engineer" dimmed and then winked out. The Democratic nomination in 1932 thus became a prize eagerly sought by a variety of aspirants, but after a series of back-room discussions and dealings, FDR emerged from the convention as the winner and likely next president; the deals became necessary even though Roosevelt ran up a large majority on the first ballot, because the party was still encumbered by the rule requiring the nominee to have two thirds of the delegate votes—a rule that in the past had repeatedly led to exhausting fights resolved by compromise on weak candidates.

Dramatically, in a precedent-breaking move, Roosevelt flew

to Chicago to deliver an acceptance speech to the weary delegates. During this address he made use of a phrase to which no one in his speech-writing team had attached any particular significance. It merely made a point the writers thought ought to be made, but it quickly became one of those expressions, casually uttered, that sum up a point of view or an approach so well that they become symbolic. In 1914, referring to the treaty guaranteeing the security of Belgium, the German chancellor had expressed amazement that the British would fight "just for a scrap of paper"; he made this comment in an interview with the British ambassador, hardly expecting it to ring around the world and damn his country in neutral eyes. In a parallel way, at the Democratic convention, when Roosevelt uttered a promise to the party and the country, he made a more momentous observation than he or anyone else realized: "I pledge you, I pledge myself, to a new deal for the American people." Whatever his point of view or his actions would prove to be, they had now acquired a label. And, in fact, this symbol exactly fitted Roosevelt's nature and purposes. He did not intend to create a new game, or to change the cards; he proposed instead to give the deck a good shuffling and to deal new hands, so that the poor, "the forgotten man at the bottom of the economic pyramid," would have a chance to win an occasional pot. As a Democrat and a progressive, he saw himself in a line going back to Jefferson, pitted against the Hamiltonians, the greedy plutocrats who would go to any lengths to keep all the face cards for themselves. In his own eyes, he stood very much in a sound, honorable, and much-needed American tradition.

During the 1920s, FDR had sought income from a variety of investments, most of them unprofitable. He had hoped to win quick riches from such schemes as a Zeppelin service between New York and Chicago and a power-generating system that would harness the Passamaquoddy Bay tides in Maine. But while doing his best to become a tycoon, he had also had occasion, in the only book review he ever wrote, to give voice to his basic political faith. On December 3, 1925, in the liberal New York *World,* he described the excitement with which he had read *Jefferson and Hamilton,* by Claude Bowers, a journalist, historian, and Democratic activist. "I felt like saying 'At last,'" Roosevelt declared in his review, not because of the historical interest of the book, but because the country must apply Jefferson's ideals "to the often similar problems that lie still unsolved before us." Jefferson, he observed, began "the mobilization of the masses against the autocracy of the few"—and, FDR said, "it was a colossal task." In Jefferson, the reviewer commented in a remarkable bit of analysis, "we see not only the savior of the deeper ideals of the Revolution, but also the man with human failings, the consummate politician." He concluded with a question bearing fascinating implications: "Hamiltons we have today. Is a Jefferson on the horizon?"

And now, in 1932, the book reviewer carried the banner of Jefferson's party. In November Herbert Hoover went down to the kind of overwhelming defeat that Smith had suffered four years earlier (the vote totals were similar, but with the party labels reversed), and on March 4, 1933, in the midst of the worst economic hour in the country's history, the paralyzed squire from Dutchess County took the oath of office as thirty-second president of the United States.

Immediately, what was perhaps the new president's greatest personal asset made itself felt not merely in Washington but in individual homes across the land. The people of the United States were frightened; times had been bad before, but no seemingly endless catastrophe like the Great Depression had ever fixed itself on the country. Withdrawn, weighed down by disaster, Hoover and his associates had sunk themselves in gloom. In dazzling contrast, making use of radio as if he had specialized in the still-new medium, the new president spoke directly to a troubled public, his lustrous voice carrying a message of confidence and courage.

Even in newspaper photographs Roosevelt seemed to sparkle with vitality. The great smile with the rows of strong if irregular teeth clenching the uptilted cigarette holder simply could not be produced by a worried man. Unlike his unhappy predecessor, he gave no sign of being "afraid of the big bad wolf," as the Depression had been symbolized in a popular song. Not only did Roosevelt appear unafraid, he actually seemed to be enjoying himself; he obviously liked his job and seemed to be sure he would do well at it.

He also kept a lively sense of humor. When a very proper lady cousin, Mary Roosevelt, wrote him from Paris to berate him for his "silly attitude about that 'forgotten man' and all the rest," and assure him that she did not support him, she addressed him as "My dear Franklyn." FDR responded with a light flick of the foil, calling her "Dear Marye" and telling her that "it really never occurred to me that you would vote for me."

FDR waved no wand and worked no miracles, but his reaching out to touch the people directly had an immediate effect on the national mood. Even without magic, his presence reached people's lives, as his mail showed. In an extraordinary letter for a citizen to write to the White House, a correspondent told how his home had been saved from foreclosure. And, he said, "you remember I wrote you about losing the furniture too. Well, your man got it back for me. I never heard of a President like you."

Roosevelt might be patrician—and he certainly made no attempt to tone down his elegant accent for the benefit of the average American—but as a cab driver put it to a reporter: "That guy has a slant in my direction." That confidence and that slant came almost palpably through the radio speakers. The nation swallowed the new president's tone and his words—not as a sedative but as a tonic.

In July 1924, after having served with ever-widening duties as General Pershing's aide for five years, Lieutenant Colonel George C. Marshall and his wife sailed for China, where he would take up a long-coveted assignment—troop duty with the 15th Infantry Regiment at Tientsin. Although eager for a field assignment, Marshall would miss the general; the two men had been genuinely fond of each other. Pershing's good-bye cable to the ship carrying the Marshalls to China concluded AFFECTIONATELY. And in each of the two preceding years the general had inserted in Marshall's personnel file this handwritten description of his aide: "A most efficient officer in every respect. Has superior knowledge of tactics and handling large bodies of troops. Able as a general staff officer. Should be made a brigadier general as soon as eligible. This officer should reach high rank and is capable of filling any position with ability and good judgment—a very exceptional man."

During his three-year tour in China, where the United States and other Western countries maintained small contingents of troops as a kind of police force to protect their own citizens and their interests, Marshall officially served as the executive officer of the 15th Infantry, but spent important periods as acting commander. "It was not long before it became clear to everyone that he was running the show," recalled a younger American officer, Captain Frank Hayne. This was not because of "any undue assumption of authority but because his ideas were sound and when put into effect at once began to improve the command in appearance, discipline, and particularly in training." The colonel's efforts soon produced striking visual results. When he arrived in Tientsin, the summer uniform of the regiment was "left-over wartime khaki of every shade from a dark olive to light beige, comparing very unfavorably with the smart uniforms of the British," but before long "the morale of the regiment had been raised to such an extent that every man in it bought with his own money a smart, tailor-made uniform of Hong Kong khaki." It was all, Hayne said, entirely voluntary, with pressure coming not from higher up but from the men themselves; Marshall had not said a word. His attitude toward the men in his command was strikingly revealed when he overheard the younger officer administering "a rather severe dressing down" to a surly enlisted man. Out of hearing of the men, Marshall said, "Hayne, you were perfectly right in reprimanding that man, but you weakened your point by losing your temper"—an authority on hot tempers and the importance of controlling them, the colonel knew what he was talking about. Then, after a pause, he made an observation that stayed with Hayne throughout his career. "You must remember," Marshall said, "that the man is an American citizen just the same as you are."

The years in China formed an interesting and instructive time; the Marshalls, like many other American military families, were captivated by the country. They returned to the United States in the summer of 1927, Marshall's service record now including still another of the accolades that were becoming almost repetitious. This one, from the officer who was U.S. commanding general in China during most of Marshall's tour, said simply that Marshall was "one of the best officers in the Army." The same general had earlier called Marshall "one of the most capable officers" who had ever served under his command.

The Marshalls had barely arrived in Washington, where George was to lecture at the Army War College, when Mrs. Marshall was forced to go to Walter Reed Hospital, first for an examination and then for a very serious thyroid operation. Never strong, she had suffered from heart problems even in the days when, as Elizabeth Coles, she had been courted in Lexington by Cadet George Marshall. A "very lovely-looking woman," she was some years—six or eight—older than he and, interestingly, had earlier been pursued by another Cadet

Marshall, Stuart. Although a reigning belle of the town, Lily, as she was called, had reached her late twenties with no marriage, not even an engagement, almost as though she were waiting for someone as single-minded and determined as George Marshall to appear and claim her. She was Marshall's first love and, characteristically, he gave her absolute devotion—so much so that, contrary to all regulations, he regularly slipped out of the barracks at night to see her. If caught, he would have been reduced from the lofty post of first captain to mere private in the ranks—or even worse. Despite his exceptional ambition and his drive to succeed in a military career, he was "very much in love," Marshall said. "I was willing to take the chance. It was a dismissal offense if they had discovered what I was doing." That had already become the personal strategy of the onetime Flicker Marshall, even at this early stage of his life. If you chose an objective, you should go straight for it and allow nothing to turn you aside. Acting in accordance with this principle, Marshall conducted Operation Lily with drive and unwavering consistency, and he saw his efforts crowned with victory.

He and Lily were married early in 1902, as soon as he received his commission as a second lieutenant in the U.S. Army. For George, the marriage had been more than happy: "To an extraordinary degree, his wife had satisfied every need of his mind and spirit, had absorbed every interest he had outside his profession and shared his burden in that." Lover, confidante, and adviser, she had also a lively spirit that lightened her husband's basic seriousness. And now, one morning in September 1927, while believed to be recovering satisfactorily from the operation, she was found dead in her hospital room. When Marshall was telephoned the news, he folded his arms on the desk and cradled his head in them. He did not disguise his grief at the sudden collapse of his world.

After a while he telephoned Frank Hayne, his friend from China, and another officer and asked them to meet him at his quarters. The two were sitting in his living room when he walked in "obviously under great emotional strain and white as a sheet." Marshall sat down at a desk, wrote a few lines, and handed the paper to the other officers. His note read simply: "Make all arrangements for the funeral. Don't ask me any questions." Then he went upstairs.

"Twenty-six years of most intimate companionship" had suddenly ended. It was "something I have known ever since I was a mere boy," he wrote Pershing a month later, and it "leaves me lost in my best efforts to adjust myself to future prospects in life. If I had been given to club life or other intimacies with men outside of athletic diversions, or if there was a campaign on or other pressing duty demanding a concentrated effort, then I think I could do better. However, I will find a way."

The secretary of the Infantry School at Fort Benning, Georgia, quickly discerned an interesting characteristic of the new assistant commandant. "I discovered," said the secretary, that "he was intensely interested in meeting and getting to know prominent people." Why such an interest? For one thing, to be sure, visits from such persons "stimulated pride and spirit in all personnel of the school." But, the secretary felt in retrospect, a different and far more sweeping purpose played a greater part: "It is now very clear that he was preparing himself for the great roles he was to fill . . ." The officer, the secretary believed, had a sense of destiny.

One of the prominent persons whose visits the secretary helped arrange was Governor-elect Franklin D. Roosevelt of New York, who came over to Fort Benning from his beloved polio-treatment center at Warm Springs; it was the first meeting of the two men. The secretary could see Colonel Marshall's genuine enjoyment of such visits, with "the opportunity they afforded to engage in lively discussion on national and international issues, and the human relations involved, outside the sphere of party politics." This particular sphere the colonel resolutely avoided, just as some years earlier he had managed to keep General Pershing out of it.

The secretary of the Infantry School was not alone in feeling a special impact from Marshall's presence and personality. In many ways, Fort Benning was China all over again, except that now Marshall found himself in an arena in which his ideas and methods could have much wider and deeper influence. The assignment to Benning had not only been desirable in the autumn of 1927, it had been necessary; Marshall could not have endured living in the house he had decorated and furnished in Washington while Lily was in the hospital, nor could he bear the thought of spending the daytime hours seated passively behind a desk at the War College. The Infantry School offered him the chance to engage in varied activities, to spend time outdoors, and to have an influence on the thinking of large numbers of younger officers. It was also a desirable assignment professionally, and Marshall had sought it in earlier years. One of its charms was the fact that he truly enjoyed teaching.

Marshall was eagerly awaited by the commandant, Brigadier General Edgar T. "Windy" Collins, who declared to one of Marshall's old friends that the new assistant commandant had "the soundest sense, the finest military background, and that rare thing, imagination—above any man I know." He would be expected "to come down here and take that academic training out of a rut"; this "rut" had developed with unusual speed, since the school was only nine years old. Although the post commander was formally the commandant of the school, in practice the assistant commandant held the executive direction; he served in effect as a dean with three hundred to five hundred students. The primary purposes of the school were to train leaders for infantry units and to develop infantry tactics and technique. In practice, these reasonable-sounding aims had become bogged down in a mess of rules, regulations, and "correct" solutions to tactical problems, all based on what U.S. officers thought they had learned from trench warfare in France. Marshall saw it as his mission to move the school's staff members from "the even tenor of their theoretical ways." But, as had become his habit, he would move carefully. In an age of "normalcy" and meager military budgets, army officers, members of a commonly derided social group, already possessed an ample supply of resentments. Besides, the doctrines taught and the practices encouraged at Benning reflected views held on high, at the Command and General Staff School at Leavenworth. Too much noise about changes at Benning, and the higher brass might squelch progress.

Just as he had done in China, Marshall won his way not by commanding obedience but by radiating influence. An officer who had attended the Infantry School before Marshall's arrival returned to Benning at the end of the new assistant commandant's first year. Immediately he felt "a noticeable change in the discipline at the school." For one thing, in his own student year, 1926–1927, officers had the habit of visiting a bootlegger and bringing back a supply of his product. But now, in the summer of 1928, officers appeared more serious and displayed a greater interest in other activities. Yet Marshall never issued an order concerning discipline: "The change was brought about by his force of example, character, and devotion to duty."

Marshall also promoted physical fitness, in particular encouraging mounted sports—which not only kept officers in condition but fostered comradeship and teamwork. Hunting, polo, paper chases, flag races, and horse shows occupied so much time and became so popular that the Infantry School officers were called a horsier crowd, with more enthusiasm for riding, than could be found at the Cavalry School. Marshall, who threw himself into all the activities, partly to ease the ache of Lily's loss, did not limit them to mounted sports. Golf, tennis, swimming, and even gardening all found favor with him, as did mental games—brainteasers and quizzes—and amateur theatricals. It all created a totally new climate.

As director of the school, Marshall grasped his great opportunity to exert influence over a variety of officers and hence, in the long run, over the whole army. He did away with demonstration maneuvers leading undeviatingly to a prearranged solution. Observing that students profited more from having the chance to make mistakes than from watching a flawless demonstration, he forced his charges to deal with unexpected problems presented on unfamiliar terrain. In a war they could not be sure of having convenient, well-paved roads and equally convenient communications, nor were they likely to have time either to draw up lengthy and densely written orders or to read and digest them—nor were such orders apt to fit the situation even if someone managed to produce them.

What Marshall wanted the students to do was to "think on their feet." He was concerned over the fact that American officers with World War service were "almost entirely without practical experience in warfare of movement"; it was perfectly natural that they would build up their experiences into doctrine, yet "the great military problem of the United States is the rapid mobilization and concentration of field armies and their early employment in warfare of movement." *Movement!* Marshall was not a technical or tactical pioneer, but he had his magic word, and along with it his belief in command responsibility for junior officers. In France, he pointed out, often a month would go by between the taking of a decision to attack a particular front and the beginning of the actual operation; "detailed orders were prepared long in advance, special maps were lithographed, ammunition and supplies were accumulated." But future tactics would "demand a knowledge of how to operate by means of brief, concise oral orders . . . ; they require a knowledge of how to maintain control and direction of units necessarily much dispersed. They compel action when very, very little is yet known of the enemy's dispositions." Summing up his gospel, Marshall said that "speed of thought, speed of action and direction and speed of operation is essential to success."

Behind this doctrine and this sense almost of urgency lay not only Marshall's understanding of the lessons of the World War, but also a particular experience in China when during a training exercise he had observed with some puzzlement that a perfectly capable officer had allowed a simple operation to collapse. This officer, it turned out, had graduated as a star from the Infantry School, but had become stuck trying to draft a written order "for seventy men" from a sketchy map. "I then and there," Marshall wrote a friend, "formed an intense desire to get my hands on Benning"—a school that could produce as a number one student a man who exemplified so absurd a system. In a war of movement no one was likely to have the time to sit on a riverbank composing paragraphs of English prose.

To spread his message and his methods, Marshall as dean of this specialized college recruited a highly able faculty—"the most brilliant, interesting, and thoroughly competent collection of men" he had ever been associated with. Among these professors were J. Lawton Collins, James A. Van Fleet, Joseph W. Stilwell, Harold R. Bull, Walter Bedell Smith, and Omar N. Bradley. It was from Marshall, Bradley said, that he learned the rudiments of command. Once he had assigned an officer to a job, Marshall did not hang over the man, watching every move he made. "During the two years I served him as chief of the weapons section in the Infantry School," Bradley observed, "he sent for me only once to discuss the work of my section. And during that same two-year period he visited me in my office but twice." Marshall's method inspired his subordinate "to do my absolute utmost." And Bradley divined Marshall's underlying purpose at Fort Benning—to develop techniques so short and simple they could readily be grasped and applied by a citizen officer of ordinary intelligence. The assistant commandant was looking far ahead—to a citizen army of the future.

One evening early in 1929, Marshall went to dinner at the home of friends in Columbus, the town nearest Fort Benning. He was not the only guest. As he stood chatting by the fireplace, a tall and elegant lady entered the room; Marshall's hosts had arranged a blind date for the lieutenant colonel and the new arrival, a widow who was visiting Columbus. Marshall made little attempt to hide the fact that he was staring at her; she remembered the moment as an example of his "way of looking right straight through you." After a little conversation, she decided that "this certainly was someone different." He even declined the proffered cocktails, behavior she thought odd for an army officer.

The striking lady, Katherine Tupper Brown, came from an unusual family. A native of Kentucky, like Marshall's parents, she was the daughter of a well-known Baptist preacher and author; her brother and sister were both writers. Mrs. Brown herself had toured in England as a Shakespearean actress, but after retiring from the stage because of physical problems had married a Baltimore lawyer. Her bereavement was more recent than Marshall's, and had certainly been traumatic; in 1928 her husband had been murdered by a client disturbed over the size of the bill he had received.

Mrs. Brown was accompanied by her sixteen-year-old daughter Molly, who recalled that she was "interested in her own date, not in this older man" who had been produced as escort for her mother. At the end of the evening the young people set off for the house where the Browns were visiting, and Marshall took the mother in tow. Suddenly this man who had seemed so capable appeared surprisingly inept. After they had driven around the town of Columbus for perhaps an hour, Mrs. Brown asked the colonel how long he had been at Fort Benning.

"Two years," he said.

"Well, after two years haven't you learned your way around Columbus?"

You had to know Columbus extremely well, he assured her, in order to avoid for an hour the block where she was staying as a house guest.

The next day Marshall invited Mrs. Brown to a reception at Fort Benning. Although she declined, he nevertheless sent a car for her; she changed her mind and came. Marshall had launched his campaign, and it moved straight to its inevitable conclusion. The objective was won in October 1930, when the two were married in Baltimore. By marrying again, Marshall was acting to restore his personal situation to its normal condition. He had grown up in the presence of women who were concerned with him, not only his mother but his sister Marie, who was four years older than he. In a time in which men took nurturing by women for granted, Marshall had enjoyed his full share of it.

Following the wedding the couple moved on to Fort Benning, where on their very first evening the commandant honored them with a reception, a splendid affair remembered by Mrs. Marshall as having the quality of a stage setting, with a full moon shining through the great oak and magnolia trees while bandsmen in smart uniforms played for officers in full dress and ladies in filmy evening gowns. To prepare his bride for greeting several hundred complete strangers, Marshall introduced her to the briefing system he had developed with General Pershing. As each person came down the receiving line, he would whisper a key word, such as "China" or "flowers," and she would respond with a comment about the officer's having served with Marshall in China or with thanks for the "lovely flowers" he and his wife had sent to welcome the newlyweds. All went well for "the first five hundred or so," but finally, to the tired bride, her husband's voice seemed to come from a great distance as it intoned the code words, and she felt "a whirling jumble" in her brain. Then, on hearing someone say "triplets," Mrs. Marshall graciously thanked the lady before her for her "lovely triplets." Marshall looked astounded, and later when his wife asked him how well she had done during the evening, he observed that she wasn't as quick on the pickup as General Pershing had been. She pointed out to the colonel that she was not competing with Pershing.

Although Marshall's tour at the Infantry School was scheduled to end in 1931, the army at the urging of the commandant devised a paper transfer to enable him to stay another year. By 1932, Mrs. Marshall felt, she had become a fair army wife; she had learned many things, her knowledge and insights including such detailed points as "lieutenants do not dance with colonels' wives for pleasure," and she had come to know a great many officers and their wives. During her two years at Fort Benning, she was often told how her husband was revolutionizing the Infantry School. He was a very brilliant man, her friends said, and some day he would be chief of staff. That lofty position seemed to her a long way from the world of a lieutenant colonel, but so frequently did she hear the forecast that she began to believe it.

The individual person versus the Industrial Revolution has been described as the greatest American domestic question of the twentieth century. As soon as Franklin Roosevelt took the oath of office as president on March 4, 1933, he had to begin producing answers to the great question—modern Jeffersonian answers devised for a world the Democratic patron saint had not imagined. Caught in a profound crisis—economic and financial and psychological—the American people needed work and income and reassurance. FDR made one thing clear at the outset: He did not look on the plight of twelve to thirteen million unemployed as a problem to be resolved, in its own good time, by the bloodless turning of the business cycle. He saw these workless legions not as figures in reports but in personal terms, as individuals and families, cold and hungry, dispossessed and dispirited.

One particular program, which represented the realization of a personal dream, received a presidential push during his first week in office. It always pleased FDR to think of himself as a farmer, with trees as one of his principal crops. "He loved trees," his secretary of labor, Frances Perkins, said, "and he hated to see them cut and not replaced." As governor of New York, he had pulled ten thousand men from the relief rolls and put them to work planting trees. Now he proposed to do the same thing on a national scale, with efforts directed to fighting soil erosion and engaging in flood control as well as reforestation. The program would benefit the land, but more important than the material results would be "the moral and spiritual value of such work." The president saw it as taking "a vast army of these unemployed out into healthful surroundings," away from the cities and the corroding effects of enforced long-term idleness.

There would be problems, of course. Some unemployed men might be physically unfit for work in the forests; others might be too antisocial to fit into group life. "You couldn't just open the forest and say to the unemployed, 'Go on in and we will pay you a dollar a day.'" To meet such objections, to ensure that the men were controlled and protected in the remote places to which they would be sent, Miss Perkins proposed that the army be put in charge of the camps; indeed, no other agency of government had facilities for taking care of hundreds of thousands of men. Who else had "tents, trucks, cots, blankets, shoes, underwear, sweaters, wash basins, soap, kitchen equipment, and officers trained in the organization of sanitary, orderly camps"? The Forestry Service could supervise the work itself, but the president readily agreed that the army would have to take on the responsibility of maintaining the operation. The moribund

U.S. Employment Service would be revivified and put in charge of recruiting the men. FDR carefully baptized the project the Civilian Conservation Corps (CCC).

Only one of the many proposals drawn up in the beginning weeks of the New Deal, the CCC bill did not at first attract undue public comment. But when a labor leader suggested that the CCC camps would represent "relief through the creation of a form of compulsory military service" and Norman Thomas, the head of the Socialist party, said that they smacked of fascism, Roosevelt immediately moved to blow these opponents out of the water. As the scene of his counterattack, he made use of one of his innovations, a press conference at which reporters asked questions and the president answered or parried or evaded them, as he chose. For some years previously, when the president of the United States met with reporters he had answered only questions that had been submitted in advance. Now FDR quickly made the press conference one of his most effective ways of reaching the public—and of winning over the men and women who wrote the news. It also seemed to serve for him as a kind of recreation, a game of wits. The "talk about military control and militarization," Roosevelt told the reporters, was "just utter rubbish." Some form of policing of the CCC camps was of course necessary. "In other words, you cannot allow a man in a dormitory to get up in the middle of the night and blow a bugle." The reporters laughed; the somber Herbert Hoover had never made cracks like that. You had to have normal order, Roosevelt said, "the same as you would have in any kind of a big job," and thus "so much for the military end."

On March 25 the new secretary of war, George H. Dern, informed the army corps area commanders that they must be ready to receive 100,000 men, though no one yet knew what would be done with them; the CCC bill had not yet even been passed. But it quickly became obvious that the army would have to operate the camps in all respects except those pertaining to the actual forestry work. Although some officers objected to duty of this kind, the program numbered among its immediate beneficiaries not only the young men who were to go to the camps but several thousand officers, including some on active duty who might otherwise have been dropped as part of an economy move, and also many reservists who had found themselves unemployed in civilian life and welcomed the summons to help with the CCC.

Secretary Dern's instructions filtered down through the army hierarchy to individual posts, including Fort Screven, South Carolina, an installation whose mission it had once been to protect Savannah harbor, but which now served only as home to one battalion of the 8th Infantry Regiment. Since the previous June, the commander of the four hundred men had been Lieutenant Colonel George C. Marshall, back with troops at last. It was hardly a major position—in contrast, Douglas MacArthur, only eleven months older, reigned as chief of staff of the army, and Franklin Roosevelt, a little more than a year younger than Marshall, sat in the White House as commander in chief and president of the United States. For Marshall, advancement up the ladder of seniority continued to prove painfully slow, in spite of the praise he invariably received. But, without fanfare, he always made the best of any assignment—and, serving with troops, he was happy at Fort Screven.

Miss Perkins's reconstituted Employment Service moved with thoroughly unbureaucratic speed to enroll CCC trainees; Marshall received his first group at Fort Screven late in April, barely a month after the legislation had been sent from the White House to Capitol Hill. But he was receptive and ready; with few exceptions, he said, he could make all of his officers available for this new kind of work. In June, having been named commander of the entire 8th Infantry Regiment, he also became commanding officer of a CCC district, an assignment that entailed the establishment of nineteen camps in Georgia and Florida. After getting them set up, he moved to the headquarters of the 8th Infantry, at Fort Moultrie, off Charleston. This move put him into a new CCC district, with the result that he now had all fifteen new camps in South Carolina to look after.

From the very first, the CCC held a special place with Marshall. Rather than finding objections to this dilution of his military duties, he showed himself, his wife said, "fascinated by the opportunity he felt it afforded to build up the minds and bodies of the youth of this country." Partly, perhaps, the colonel liked the CCC because even though it was not military it represented at least a suggestion of universal peacetime training and what it might accomplish. As a relative newlywed of two and a half years, Mrs. Marshall still found herself learning the intricacies of her job as an army wife. New challenges arose constantly. That summer she and her husband stood for hours "under the burning South Carolina sun on little pinewood platforms, hastily erected, so that he might be present at the raising of the flag over a new CCC camp." The recruits were pitiful, "rather frail, anemic-looking youths, half-fed, with poor carriage, and nearly always with poor teeth."

Marshall "ate, breathed, and digested the many CCC problems," said one of his assistants, and he felt pride and pleasure at the quick results his CCC camps were able to achieve. Also fully involved in the work, Mrs. Marshall delighted in the improvement in the young men "after six weeks of medical attention, regular hours and good food." Part of the success of the camps sprang from a typical bit of direct action undertaken by Marshall. In the early days, offsetting to some extent the benefits of good food and regular hours, bootleggers would appear as soon as a camp was opened. Local officials professed their inability to stem the flow of raw moonshine into the camps. Marshall went directly to the bankers and businessmen in the nearby towns. If the bootleggers were not put out of business in two weeks, the colonel said, the local camp would simply be closed and moved elsewhere. He hardly found it necessary to point out the financial losses a town would suffer if the CCC boys spent their monthly paychecks somewhere else (even though the pay was only thirty dollars a month, this was an era when army privates received just eighteen dollars). The small-town bankers and businessmen quickly proved to have remarkable powers of persuasion in relation to local law officials and thus, indirectly, with the bootleggers. And Mrs. Marshall was delighted to see that "without moonshine the boys began to look and act like different human beings." When CCC national headquarters offered an award for the best camp in the country, the honor was won by the camp at Sumter, South Carolina.

With the idea that he would hold his new post as commander of the 8th Infantry for at least two years, Marshall, now a full colonel, agreed that his wife should have a truckload of her antiques brought down from Baltimore to furnish the commander's quarters at Fort Moultrie, a great rambling building with forty-two French doors leading onto downstairs and upstairs verandas. "Colonel Marshall had his regiment," she said, "he was back with troops—all was well with the world." Marshall succeeded in acquiring WPA funds for refurbishing the entire fort, and his wife set to work with a seamstress to make up 325 yards of curtains for the array of French doors. But in September, as the last curtains were being hung, unwelcome news came from Washington. On orders of the chief of staff, General Douglas MacArthur, Colonel Marshall was being transferred to Chicago as senior instructor with the Illinois National Guard. He was being removed from command of troops and shunted onto what, in terms of advancement in the army, loomed as a possible dead end. Another staff job! Officers his age had passed him up, *were* passing him up. He had not entered the army and devoted himself with such thoroughness to his profession in order to occupy positions that would not make full use of his talents and his attainments. If he was ever to become chief of staff, he must get ahead, because the post by tradition would go only to a man who, first, was a general officer and, second, had at least four years to serve before retirement; thus it was inescapable that if Marshall did not become chief of staff by 1940, he never would.

Accordingly, for the first time in his career, he asked for special consideration, writing directly to General MacArthur to point out that after four years at the Infantry School, he feared that it would be fatal to his career to be taken away from his regiment and placed on this detached service. MacArthur, who had chosen Marshall from a list of "outstanding and suitable" officers drawn up by a subordinate, remained unmoved, though he was said to have called the colonel one of the best officers in the army. In a sympathetic letter, he urged the colonel to look on the Chicago post as his duty. Marshall gathered that the War Department considered the job of very great importance—not because of any sudden interest in making the National Guard more effective generally, but because, as Marshall wrote to Senator James Byrnes of South Carolina, "of threatened civic disorders out here, strikes and unemployment." The Depression still gripped Chicago, and winter was coming on; "an anticipated critical situation this winter with the hungry, and the striking coal miners caused my selection," he wrote to General Pershing. Unlike some of his friends and supporters, Marshall left no record that he held army factionalism responsible for his being shunted to Chicago; however, since the World War MacArthur had nourished an almost phobic distaste for Pershing and had supported General March, whose autobiography was designed to contradict and counteract Pershing's memoirs, which contained attacks on the War Department—and Marshall was a prime "Pershing man." (Had Marshall harbored such thoughts, he might have derived some ironic amusement from the fact that he had done his best to induce Pershing to soften his observations, expressing himself so strongly that he had actually irritated his old chief, who had brushed off his comments.) In any case, when news of MacArthur's action reached General Charles G. Dawes, a leading Chicago banker and a former vice-president of the United States, the reaction was explosive: "What? He can't do that. Hell, no! Not George Marshall. He's too big a man for this job. In fact, he's the best goddamned officer in the United States Army!" But the transfer stood.

During their first months in Chicago, Mrs. Marshall watched her husband uneasily: "He had a grey, drawn look which I had never seen before." The possible death of his ambition seemed to drag him behind it. But, mastering self-pity, Marshall by December was devoting himself to improving the Illinois National Guard in all the ways he had employed in China, at the Infantry School, and at Fort Screven—with the complication that the shaping-up of these weekend soldiers demanded almost endless ingenuity in the use of his meager budget. Marshall even found himself the editor, art director, and staff writer of the division's monthly magazine. He was, his wife said, "as enthusiastic and energetic an editor as if he had been responsible for *Time* magazine." But in action far more significant than his contributions as an editor, he convinced the division's politically influential civilian-officers that inspections and parades, though certainly necessary, must yield time to tactical exercises and war games; it was the purpose of training to prepare a unit for combat—a concept that had not always been followed in the National Guard. As Marshall said in a speech, the Guard must constitute almost the entire first line of American defense, since all the Regular Army combat troops in the country could fit into just one big-league ball park. Striking his favorite chord, he declared that warfare of movement demanded skilled officers, trained noncommissioned officers, and a very high standard of discipline. Any week—even the very week during which he spoke—Guard members should be prepared to undertake foreign service within seven days. They must make themselves ready for modern war.

CHAPTER THREE

RUMORS AND WARS

While George Marshall did his best, with limited means, to turn a group of Illinois Guardsmen into a fighting division ready to take part in modern war, across the ocean real war came. In October 1935 Italian aircraft bombed and strafed villages in Ethiopia, and tribesmen learned that spears could do little against rifles and machine guns. At Geneva the Ethiopian delegate to the League of Nations produced a copy of the organization's constitution, called in Wilsonian language the "Covenant"; he intended to remind the assembled powers that Article 15 called for the League to support hapless victims of aggression. The secretary general and the British delegate seized his document and threw it into the wastebasket. The League, it was clear, would do nothing but talk.

What did this international turmoil have to do with the United States? Were such quarrels America's quarrels, or could they become so? The president's naval aide, Captain Wilson Brown, felt that the Ethiopian tragedy played an important part in Roosevelt's international education. FDR spent several of the closing weeks of 1935 in travel, including a leisurely cruise from San Diego through the Panama Canal to Charleston, South Carolina. "Had he been in the treadmill of his office routine," the naval aide observed, "he could not have given developments his undivided attention; but in the quiet of shipboard life he had time to consider the significance of all that happened . . ." A great many Americans took a different view of the Old World's troubles—they were none of our business. As they saw it, we had sent millions of young men across the Atlantic in 1917 and 1918 to free France from the grip of the Kaiser's armies and win the World War for the Allies, and what good had it done? We must beware of making the same mistake again.

During his first years in office, the president did not disagree with this isolationist point of view. Preoccupied with the struggle for economic recovery, he and his New Deal associates pursued an essentially nationalist path, concentrating on trying to heal the ills of America. Even when FDR did make a mildly internationalist move, such as an attempt to join the World Court, the isolationist forces on Capitol Hill rejected the proposal; the president's glamour in domestic affairs in the early years simply did not transfer itself to the foreign arena. The ineffectiveness of the Democratic leadership in the Senate formed a significant part of the problem. Through the workings of seniority, as inexorable in Congress as in the army, control of the Senate Foreign Relations Committee rested in the hands of Key Pittman of Nevada, who devoted himself to keeping the price of silver as high as possible. A man not without perception, Pittman, coming to Washington in 1913, had written his wife that the Senate was "like a club rather than a legislative body," thus neatly if perhaps inadvertently drawing an absolute distinction between the two kinds of organization. Since 1913 the senator had concerned himself not with foreign affairs but with the welfare of mining companies, to the exclusion of almost all other considerations.

Having seen close up the disaster Woodrow Wilson had brought on himself by turning questions of foreign affairs into partisan issues and occasions for battles between the executive and the legislature, Roosevelt had no thought of alienating the Senate; nor could Pittman be outflanked. But in foreign affairs the senator proved a weak reed. Carefully included by FDR in the United States delegation to a monetary conference in London, Pittman seemed to revert to his youthful days in the Klondike gold rush. A newspaperman observing the conference remarked to one of the American technical experts that the senator appeared to be drunk nine tenths of the time. No, said the expert, "he was drunk all the time." Pittman had brought his silver Nevada shooting iron along and proceeded to empty it at London streetlights. This was the caliber of the chief Democratic spokesman on foreign affairs in the Senate. Nowhere in the international realm did FDR have a Herbert Asquith—whom the British used to call the "Sledgehammer"—a man who could enunciate the government's policy with crushing effect on the opposition. Pittman, an increasingly foggy practicing alcoholic, barely reached flyswatter status; however, as a member the Capitol Hill club he had joined in 1913, he stood in no danger of being replaced as head of the Foreign Relations Committee by any one more effective.

Yet at times it was not easy to know what Roosevelt would have wished a Sledgehammer to say, even had one been available. During the new turbulence in Europe, newspaper stories recounted the work of a special Senate committee chaired by Gerald P. Nye of North Dakota. Described by Secretary of State Cordell Hull as "an isolationist of the deepest dye," the slim, youthful-looking Nye crusaded eloquently against the "merchants of death" who were alleged to have fomented the World War for their own selfish ends—munitions makers and financiers, men like Pierre du Pont and J. P. Morgan. Looking across the ocean to Europe, hearing the rumble of fascist drums, American women organized peace societies, and college students created the Veterans of Future Wars with the bitterly ironic aim of collecting their bonuses now, before they had been killed in battle. "It was evident," said Hull, "that no one could withstand the isolationist cyclone."

Nor did Roosevelt try to withstand it. In political matters, including foreign affairs, the president often proceeded like the sailor he was, not trying to slam through the seas toward his objective but tacking, putting his helm over and shifting his sails and thus coming about in ways that sometimes puzzled even his confidants. When Congress produced the first of the neutrality acts, which would require the president to embargo the export of arms to all belligerents in any conflict, Roosevelt hoped to gain the power to discriminate between aggressor and victim. But the isolationists saw his request as a wish for an international loophole; Roosevelt was rebuffed, the original bill was passed, and the president signed it, even though privately he was writing scornfully of the senators and congressmen who were "suggesting wild-eyed measures to keep us out of war."

During the presidential campaign of 1936, Roosevelt dramatized his own feelings about war in an address that became famous both in its own right and because presidential mimics seized on one of its key lines. In his only speech dealing with foreign affairs, FDR declared dramatically: "I have seen war. I have seen war on land and sea. I have seen blood running from the wounded. I have seen men coughing out their gassed lungs. I have seen the dead in the mud . . ." and on and on, concluding n the line "I hate war"—three words that were to be cherished and repeated by legions of Roosevelt impressionists: *"I hate wa-ah!"*

Although the more paranoid isolationists concluded that if FDR said he hated war no one should believe him, the depth of his feeling lay behind his own isolationist utterances and actions in the middle 1930s. Yet his dread of war did not at all affect his staunch and unwavering love of the United States Navy, in which he had taken an active interest since the beginning of his term. One Sunday morning during this same summer of 1936, Captain Brown came to FDR's bedroom to tell the boss that, in accordance with regulations requiring alternation between sea and shore duty, he was now due to go to sea; professionally, the captain said, this was the step he ought to take, but he hated to leave the president and to put him to the inconvenience of training a new aide.

"His response was immediate," Brown noted. "He would miss me very much, but of course I must go." Then the president asked him what duty he would get. Brown told him that the secretary of the navy had said he would be given command of the training squadron—which at the time was in effect the U.S. Atlantic Fleet—and would "fly my flag as an admiral on board the battleship *Arkansas.*"

"You are the luckiest man on earth," Roosevelt said, looking up at the captain. "I would give anything in the world to change places with you."

In May 1935 Franklin Roosevelt had tried to take a purposeful hand in the career of George Marshall. Although he had adjusted with his characteristic dedication to life with the Illinois National Guard, Colonel Marshall had not wavered in his desire for promotion or in his ultimate high ambition.

Since he would soon be fifty-four, Marshall glumly observed to General Pershing in late 1934, "I must get started if I am going to get anywhere in this Army." He had no wish to use political influence, he said; he was perfectly content to be judged on his record, but he wanted Pershing to ask the secretary of war to read that record—his efficiency reports since 1915. "I am prepared to gamble on my written record . . . for I have been told no one else in the list of colonels can match mine." He concluded: "I have had the discouraging experience of seeing the man I relieved in France as G-3 of the army, promoted years ago, and my assistant as G-3 of the army similarly advanced six years ago. I think I am entitled to some consideration now. But I will confine myself to you."

A few months later Pershing raised the question with the president, who promptly cooperated; in a note to the secretary of war, FDR wrote: "General Pershing asks very strongly that Colonel George C. Marshall (Infantry) be promoted to general. Can we put him on the list of next promotions?" Although this presidential intervention constituted support on the highest level indeed, Roosevelt might as well have dropped his letter into the wastebasket; nothing happened. Undaunted, Pershing continued his efforts, including talks with General MacArthur, still chief of staff; MacArthur suggested that Marshall wait until the post of chief of infantry became vacant. But no one knew when that might happen. Unsatisfied with this notion, Pershing pressed MacArthur for more immediate action, and the chief of staff yielded, but his term had come to an end; on October 2, 1935, Roosevelt replaced him with General Malin Craig. Since the new chief was, like Marshall, a Pershing man, his arrival did not represent bad news; in 1934, in fact, Craig himself had recommended Marshall for advancement to brigadier. But soon the outlook darkened again. Colonels senior to Marshall might be deadwood, but Craig nevertheless found a number of them in Marshall's path, and the next promotion list, published on Christmas Day, appeared with no gift for Marshall on it. Craig "is strong for you," Pershing had written, but apparently that had not been enough.

Marshall's response to Pershing, written two days after Christmas, struck a bleak minor note: "I have possessed myself in patience, but now I'm fast getting too old to have any future of importance in the army." In four days he would be fifty-five; his career seemed to have reached its end.

In the election of 1936, Roosevelt won a record-breaking landslide victory. But this triumph led, curiously—so it then seemed—to a decline in his political strength, owing to the failure of his highly controversial plan to enlarge the United States Supreme Court—to "pack" the Court, said opponents—and to the coming, in the late summer of 1937, of the "Roosevelt recession," when stocks slumped and unemployment soared—after the administration abandoned the deficit-spending measures that had been working for four years. In September, concerned about the developing recession, FDR undertook an "intake" trip across the country in order to make his own first-hand assessment of the country's economic health (this was an era when even in good times money circulated slowly, and most people had little of it; "recession" described a slide into economic deprivation almost unimaginable by later standards). Even though domestic problems occupied most of his attention, the president received a steady flow of foreign news reports from the State Department.

He had much to be worried about. On July 7 fighting had broken out between Japanese and Chinese troops outside Peking, and an undeclared war followed. For some time Roosevelt had feared that Japanese expansionism would produce war in the Pacific, but Americans, although showing more concern for the Chinese than they had for the hapless Ethiopians, had no thought of intervening in this new conflict. For the president, who felt an emotional attachment to the Chinese going back to his grandfather Delano's exploits as a Yankee merchant, the situation was painful. He could not accept Japan's China venture, but he had no wish to try to put an end to it by force. The feelings that American and British trading families like the Delanos had toward the Chinese could not fail to be complex, because much of the wealth won by Western merchants in China came from the trade in opium. Colorful and adventurous, Grandfather Delano himself was not inclined to let his right hand know what his left hand was doing; opium apparently never received any mention in the family. Certainly Delano's grandson Franklin Roosevelt never spoke of it, but he inherited not only an interest in the Chinese but a fondness for his grandfather's practice of keeping one hand ignorant of the doings of the other.

One day on the train, when the president read a newspaper account of the first meeting in three years between Hitler and Mussolini—a scene of swastika banners, glittering Fascist medals, and bombastic declarations—he "rather glowered at the pictures of the two little men." In both Europe and Asia, it seemed, arrogant militaristic powers were stamping their feet. A few days later, Roosevelt came forth with a response. On October 5, speaking to an enormous crowd jammed around the new Centennial Bridge on the Outer Drive in Chicago, he declared that "the peace, the freedom and the security of ninety per cent of the world is being jeopardized by the remaining ten per cent who are threatening a breakdown of all international order and law." What ought to be done about it? FDR offered his answer in a familiar, homely, and brilliantly chosen figure of speech: "When an epidemic of physical disease starts to spread, the community approves and joins in a quarantine of the patients in order to protect the health of the community against the spread of the disease." And, he said, "war is a contagion, whether it be declared or undeclared" (an example of the latter clearly being the Japanese push in China).

This "quarantine speech" received mixed reviews in the press. Even the staunchly Republican *Philadelphia Inquirer* praised the president's denunciation of "terrorism and international lawlessness." Many other responses, however, were less favorable. Although guided solely by the whims of its rigidly conservative and isolationist owner, Colonel Robert R. McCormick, the *Chicago Tribune* offered comments that proved in fact sharply analytical. Seeing the president's strictures as aimed primarily at Japan, the *Tribune* expressed its doubt whether the threat of a boycott would be effective; instead, it might "only serve to inflame the ardor of the Japanese." (To make sure that the president, his traveling party, and the multitudes on the Outer Drive were left in no doubt as to the *Tribune*'s general view of the New Deal, the marvelously idiosyncratic Colonel McCormick had decreed, for Roosevelt's visit, that a huge sign be mounted on the paper's nearby lakefront warehouse: CHICAGO TRIBUNE UNDOMINATED.) When reporters asked FDR whether he had any definite action in mind, he danced away from their queries, saying nothing more concrete than "there are a lot of methods in the world that have never been tried yet."

Whatever its practical effects, the quarantine speech assumed importance because it constituted a landmark in the president's own thinking and speaking. He had been accused of being an internationalist disguising himself in isolationist clothing—Roosevelt haters thought him diabolically deceitful—but his dread of overseas involvement had been profoundly real. No longer the intemperate interventionist of World War days, he truly hated war. But he was alive now to the possibility that in the future the security of the United States herself might be threatened by international aggression.

After the flare-up and then dissipation of fresh excitement over the Japanese bombing in December of the U.S. gunboat

Panay twenty miles up the Yangtze River, the president made a new kind of move for peace, secret but potentially spectacular and by far his most important attempt thus far to create an American role in the affairs of Europe. It came from the side of his nature that looked on nations somewhat as individual persons and believed that national leaders, gathered around a table and talking in a frank and friendly fashion, might open the way to a lasting peace. The fact that little evidence existed to support such an idea did not deter him at all, perhaps because previous attempts to accomplish such aims had not enjoyed the benefit of his supervision. His self-confidence was unrivaled. "As far as I could ever see," his son James said, "Father always felt he could handle any office better than the man in the job"—and in early 1938 the "office" of peacemaker sat vacant.

Since Neville Chamberlain, the British prime minister, was engaged in attempts to reach some kind of understanding with Hitler, Roosevelt's plan called for the United States to summon an international conference to lend "impetus to the efforts of Great Britain and France" to reach the bases for a practical understanding with Germany both on European questions and on colonies. On January 11, 1938, the president sent Chamberlain a confidential cable describing his plan and its aims.

Whatever results it might have had in amending the status quo and thus settling the grievances of the Axis powers—the likelihood here was surely almost nonexistent—the effects of the plan on world public opinion could have been great. It would have dramatized the dangerous approach of general war. It might have extended a hand of encouragement to the smaller European countries, which, seeing no leadership emanating from the great democracies, nervously eyed alignment with Germany and Italy. If the Axis powers refused the president's proposals, they would thereby make it plain who sought peace and who did not. Vastly more important than these considerations, however, the simple dramatic fact of the president's willingness to use American influence in the search for a European settlement would represent a new and potentially decisive American involvement in the affairs of Europe.

But Chamberlain said no. He thought he could handle matters himself.

In February 1938 Hitler assumed supreme military power in Germany. In March came the annexation of Austria to the Reich, with Czechoslovakia, now squeezed in German geographical jaws, as the obvious next target. The time for conferences to offer any hope had now passed; in Central Europe the jackboots were on the march. As the shouting, stamping Nazi Germans moved into Austria and tension grew in Czechoslovakia, while British and French leaders looked on helplessly—leaders who seemed to many Americans to be tired men of few convictions and little democratic feeling—Roosevelt, in spite of the deep 1937–1938 recession and his other domestic difficulties, could make a cheery point in a letter to his ambassador in Ireland: "We in the United States are still better off than the people or the governments of any other great country."

On July 6, 1938, George C. Marshall reported for duty at the Winder Building, Seventeenth and F streets, across from the State, War, and Navy Building in Washington. He had been appointed assistant chief of staff in charge of the War Plans Division of the War Department.

Marshall came to the capital from Vancouver Barracks, Washington, where for almost two years he had been back with troops, serving as commander of the 5th Brigade of the 3rd Division; he had also been back with the CCC, since he had the happy duty of supervising the camps in Oregon and part of Washington. The posting to Vancouver Barracks had been the consequence of a notable and eagerly awaited event. One day in the late summer of 1936, Mrs. Marshall, returning from a vacation in Canada, had just entered the house when the telephone rang. Greeting her, the woman caller said, "I just called to congratulate *General* Marshall." Mrs. Marshall dropped the telephone receiver and sank into a chair, and she and her husband sat looking at each other. The phone call had deprived him of the chance to surprise her on her return home with the great news—Marshall was a husband who delighted in springing pleasant surprises on his wife, and what news could be greater than winning the coveted star? He was General Marshall at last. "I am sure," General Pershing had written him, "that you are destined to hold a very high place on the list of general officers before you reach the age of sixty-four."

Spiffily turned out in a double-breasted suit, polka-dot bow tie, and homburg, Brigadier General George C. Marshall, with his wife and his stepdaughter Molly, had driven up to the entrance of Vancouver Barracks on October 27, 1936, at the end of a three-week cross-country trip from Chicago; Pontiac, the family's Irish setter, had been sent out by train. Although Marshall had wired the acting commander that he wanted no welcoming ceremony, few colonels could resist the chance to put on a show for a new commanding general, and Colonel Hossfeld of the 7th Infantry was not one of that small group. The regiment stood in formation, and even Pontiac was present, held on a leash by an orderly. As the bank struck up the standard ruffles, Marshall got out of the car. Seeing his master, Pontiac gave a mighty leap, snapping the leash and landing on Marshall's chest, almost knocking him down. Then the dog ran in and out through the lines of soldiers, here and there jumping up on one of them and absolutely demolishing the ceremony. Colonel Hossfeld's look was murderous; he did not realize, Mrs. Marshall said, that "such a welcome from his dog meant more to George Marshall than any formal reception that could have been given him."

So began what Katherine described as "two of the happiest years of our life" and Marshall himself later called "one of our most delightful periods of Army service . . . a pleasant dream," in one of the most beautiful regions of the United States. Pontiac likewise enjoyed the assignment, since he had good pheasant hunting almost every afternoon. Marshall particularly delighted in the historic associations of the post, which had been established in 1849 on the site of a Hudson's Bay Company station and early in their careers had been home to Generals Grant, Sheridan, Pickett, and other Civil War figures.

In late 1936, however, Marshall suffered the recurrence of an old problem that finally demanded treatment; like his first wife, Lily, he suffered from a malfunctioning thyroid gland. Pershing wrote that he could not believe that George had a goiter, but it was nevertheless so, and it was terrible news, not only for obvious physical reasons but because as a society the army resembled a small town, with gossip flowing freely. Any talk about health problems—particularly talk with some basis in fact—could be damaging and even fatal to one's career. So much did Marshall believe this to be the case that, instead of dictating to a secretary, he often wrote his own letters when he wanted to discuss his health with doctors or friends. Marshall, in fact, was accustomed to having physical problems. As a youngster he had suffered from typhoid fever, measles, and scarlet fever—"all the common diseases of that day"—but, as he recalled, "neither my brother or sister did." The typhoid was serious, a "very long siege," which put him out of action for several months. In his teens he acquired a dislocated arm, which was never treated and for some years remained acutely sensitive; he had to use great care in riding—which was a passion with him and was of course *de rigueur* in the army—because he could not hold the reins with his left hand.

Marshall had first noticed a slight swelling of the thyroid about 1923, but metabolism tests indicated that the condition was quiescent. During his time at Fort Benning, his pulse developed irregularities, caused by the thyroid problem, and the condition recurred while he was in Illinois; his pulse started to miss beats and then began to accelerate from 72 to 90, then to 95 and up to 105—although, Marshall wrote to a doctor and fellow officer, "strange to say, I never felt better in my life." After thorough testing in Portland, Marshall was sent to San Francisco in February 1937 for surgery; the malfunctioning parts of both lobes of the gland were removed and within ten days his heartbeat was back to normal. But he remained so close-mouthed about his illness that even Pershing had to learn of it from others. There really wasn't much to it, Marshall assured his old mentor. "Usually patients for thyroid operations are much underweight, highly nervous, short of breath, and generally unstrung," he observed, but "I was fortunate to be in fine shape, and was told that I was farther along the fifth day than most patients were after several months." He wanted to reassure Pershing, of course—but he also wanted to do his best to guarantee that no negative stories about his health would issue from the revered and influential old hero-commander.

Some months later Marshall strove to leave absolutely no room for interpretation when he replied to a letter of friendly concern from an officer he had known for thirty years. In the letter the officer had affably pointed out that "you know as soon as we get along about 50 if we have a bad cold every one has us dying." He had not even had a bad cold, Marshall answered in effect: "I went to the hospital feeling better than I ever had but due for a corrective operation for a minor goiter of about fifteen years standing." He was back to normal in every way in less than ten days, he said, and in fact blood-pressure and metabolism tests had even shown him normal *before* the surgery. Since the operation he had been extremely active—"two big maneuvers, innumerable fishing and hunting trips, and am riding and playing golf daily." Hence he did not require sympathy, he said, but he appreciated his friend's interest. If words could rout any rumors, Marshall was ready to expend them. His heightened awareness of his physical state also led to concern for other officers whose careers were jeopardized by army bureaucrats. Of one second lieutenant "of unusual promise" who was found to be partially color-blind, Marshall wrote to the area adjutant general that the young officer had "successfully reacted to thousands of red and green stop lights in the every-day business of driving a car"; he urged the adjutant general to "see if you can't maneuver this business so that we do not throw out a superior type over a technicality, and carry along the dead wood, as is usually the case."

Marshall did not comment on the psychological benefits he reaped from the removal of a hyperactive thyroid. Ever since his explosive days in France, he had worked successfully to impose calmness on himself; now his body through its altered chemistry would render it easier to maintain a serene persona, although his choler would by no means be succeeded by excessive phlegm.

From the public point of view, Marshall's most notable venture at Vancouver Barracks was the hospitality he extended to three Russian airmen who were attempting to fly from Moscow over the North Pole to Oakland, California, but landed instead at the airfield close to the parade ground at Vancouver. Marshall's handling of the situation revealed an interesting and promising resourcefulness. He invited the men to his quarters, where his wife had been instructed to have breakfast ready. "Three polar bears walked, or more exactly, staggered into the house. They wore huge parkas of fur, only their faces showing, and these were so streaked with oil and dirt, so haggard and covered with beards, that the men hardly looked human." Mrs. Marshall sent them up bacon and eggs as they were taking their much-needed baths. The first aviators to attempt such a flight, the Russians attracted a mass of reporters, photographers, and generally curious humanity onto the post. With some irritation the newsmen learned that the general would not allow them to see the fliers until they had caught some sleep. Although it was a Sunday morning, Marshall induced a Portland department-store proprietor to allow an army truck to pick up complete outfits for the men. Then, rested and properly clad, the Russians were allowed to meet the public in contacts stage-managed by the general. The men became heroes across the country, and the army had scored a public relations coup.

In the style that had become habitual, Marshall proceeded at Vancouver Barracks less by thunder than by enlightenment. He had started with a detailed inspection of the post, poking into corners that for years had not come under the eye of a general officer. He dealt cordially with local civilian officials, accepting a wide range of speaking engagements. He arranged for the lieutenant in charge of WPA projects on the post (the military as well as the civilian world reaped important physical benefits from Harry Hopkins's organization) to convert an old theater into a basketball court and skating rink and the old gymnasium into a club for noncommissioned officers. When Molly Brown came back from a year and a half of world traveling, younger officers and their wives began to appear frequently at the general's quarters.

One incident suggested that he had evolved a method of personal command worthy of an adroit civilian politician. In arranging to distribute Christmas presents to the families of enlisted men, the post chaplain wished to include those of men who had married without the permission of their commanding officers; however, the chaplain told Marshall, far from approving the plan, the colonel commanding the regiment had instead ordered the chaplain to turn over his list of intended recipients. The chaplain wanted Marshall's help. No commanding general would welcome such a situation, but Marshall handled it by casually saying at a regimental party, within earshot of the colonel, that he had heard of the chaplain's plan to distribute Christmas baskets even to the men who were married without permission and that he and Mrs. Marshall enthusiastically approved. No confrontation with the colonel was required, and the chaplain's relationship with his superior was preserved. And, as always, Marshall had found a way to come to the aid of enlisted men in need. Besides, children were involved, and Marshall was one of those adults who, childless themselves, take special interest in children and special pleasure in their company. When with them, he did not pretend to be anything other than a grown-up, but he seemed almost to reserve a special kind of relaxation for such times.

On September 28, 1937, Marshall turned out the troops to greet a distinguished visitor—President Roosevelt, swinging through the West on the long "intake" tour that included, some days later, Chicago, where he delivered the quarantine speech. Marshall's men were paraded for a ceremony at the Bonneville Dam on the Columbia River between Washington and Oregon, where FDR pressed the button that started the first of the great generators. The new dam represented the fruition of a promise Roosevelt had made on a campaign trip in the Northwest in 1932, and it would be capable of producing more power than the Tennessee Valley Authority and Boulder Dam combined; it was a true New Deal project, the kind of undertaking close to the heart of FDR the conservationist. After the ceremony Marshall, who viewed the great dam rather mundanely as "the political football of the Northwest" because of all the disputes over public versus private power, boarded the president's train, he wrote a friend, and "saw him off here in Vancouver after a very strenuous day." Marshall did not seem unusually impressed by the high-level spectacle, noting to his friend that far from being a backwater, as he had expected, Vancouver seemed to be visited by everybody "from the Russian fliers and the President, on down through a succession of important lesser notables," and he had had just about enough. "I would like a long rest, and more time for fishing and hunting."

But, as he told General Pershing, he had a few words with Roosevelt and "was much amused to watch the maneuvers of the various shades of New Dealers who were trying to appear before the public eye in his company." One phenomenon, however, was definitely striking—"the tumultuous welcome accorded Mr. Roosevelt by the crowds in Portland and along other portions of his route"; in fact, the streets were lined almost solidly with cheering people, and so great, if benign, was the crowd in the center of the city that the police were overwhelmed. Whatever the politicians might be saying in Washington, FDR clearly still held his great popularity with the electorate.

Marshall appeared to make no particular effort to impress this visitor who, when it came to the highest service commands, held all the plums in his hand. Yet, since the general's own timetable required him to become chief of staff by 1940 or not at all, the appointment would have to come from FDR. Although from the vantage point of Vancouver, the national capital and the chief of staff's office looked a very long way off, the mild-looking, bespectacled Malin Craig was a probable supporter, and there was always General Pershing. Yet Marshall's tone in commenting on his prospects almost suggested that whether out of assessment of the odds against him (his age, and the fact that he still had only one star) or out of genuinely changed desires, he had developed a new outlook. In February 1938 Craig spoke to him about the possibility of his coming to Washington as head of the War Plans Division of the General Staff, but Marshall remarked to an old friend that he was "a country boy who rides every day before breakfast, walks in the woods every evening, or runs about the mountains or down the sea coast inspecting and playing"—activities that were hardly available to staff officers serving in Washington.

When the War Plans appointment became official in May 1938, Marshall fatalistically observed to Pershing: "I am fond of Craig personally, but I loathe a desk. I would not mind much, except that I have so few years left for active service that I hate to lose them to desk instead of command work." Marshall said this even though he had been told that within a few months he would move up from assistant chief of staff for War Plans to deputy chief of staff. Part of his reluctance to take the job no doubt stemmed from his knowledge of army history. When a president went looking for a new chief of staff, he rarely searched among deputies and advisers and planners, but chose his man from the generals exercising field commands. Craig, for instance, had served as a corps commander as well as commandant of the Army War College. Why should anyone expect Roosevelt to abandon the established pattern?

CHAPTER FOUR

"ALL I HAVE DREAMED OF"

Shortly after Mrs. Marshall arrived to join her husband in Washington, she underwent a chilling experience. Accompanying him to Fort Myer for a formal call on General Craig and his wife, Mrs. Marshall was struck by the chief of staff's greeting: "Thank God, George, you have come to hold up my trembling hands." And then, after the two men had withdrawn to Craig's study, Mrs. Craig turned to her guest and said with great bitterness: "I shall never forgive Washington. They have crucified my husband."

No one could have accused Mrs. Craig of exaggerating. The War Department in 1938 roared with sounds of confusion and conflict, as high-level combatants fought savagely for authority and power. Marshall quickly found that he had not only reported for work in an office, he had stepped onto a battlefield. The conflict arose from two main causes, one historical—having to do with the organization of the department and the General Staff—and the other purely individual, directly traceable to the personality and working methods of Franklin D. Roosevelt.

Although the General Staff had been in existence for thirty-five years, it had never won a high place in the affections of the American public, of Congress, or even of other components of the army. Created in the aftermath of the Spanish-American War to correct the army's appalling deficiencies in command, organization, planning, and supply, the General Staff had experienced a difficult birth and owed its existence chiefly to the hard work and political skill of its founder, a New York lawyer named Elihu Root who had reluctantly agreed to come to Washington as secretary of war. Almost everybody at the time seemed to find something objectionable about the idea of a general staff. The public and many members of Congress looked on it as an undesirable import from across the Atlantic, a device reeking of elitism and spiked-helmet Prussianism. Other senators and congressmen, and a number of army officers, objected to the creation of the General Staff because it threatened to disrupt long-established and mutually rewarding ties between army agencies and Capitol Hill.

For years, from the time of Andrew Jackson's administration, the War Department had existed as a house divided, with one side occupied by the secretary and the other by an officer called the commanding general of the United States Army. The important point is that this system set up a wall between command, on the one hand, and administration and fiscal affairs, on the other. The secretary of war and the commanding general both reported directly to the president; one man did not hold a higher position than the other, they simply operated in different fields. This "coordinate" organization, as it has been called, held particular importance for the army's administrative bureaus—ordnance, engineers, medical, quartermaster—which were staffed by officers who managed to acquire permanent tenure in Washington and to operate almost independently of any control; these were the men who had built up the cozy relationships with members of Congress. As for the commanding general, the system gave him little to do.

Ever since the Root reforms, the War Department had existed as a "vertical" structure, with authority descending in a straight line from the president to the secretary of war to the chief of staff, the last-named being the senior post created by Root to replace the commanding general. Even Root had not been completely clear about the chief's duties, but it was understood that this officer would be subordinated to civilian authority in the department. Along with the chief of staff had come the new planning and coordinating agency, the General Staff.

As General Craig and other chiefs of staff discovered, the Root reforms, though enormously valuable in many ways, had not solved all of the army's problems. Under the vertical organization devised by Root, the top officer of the army occupied exactly the same areas of responsibility as his civilian superior, the secretary of war: Both concerned themselves with the whole of the army. The chief of staff thus found himself forced out of his military sphere into realms concerned with purely political questions. "Under this system," as a commentator observed, "the Chief of Staff became a part of the administration in power." (Along with his organizational reforms, Root made another move with long-range implications. In 1901, because of the new colonialism that followed the war with Spain, the secretary succeeded in persuading Congress to increase the authorized strength of the army; 1,135 new lieutenants would be needed. Thus it was that in February 1902 a vacancy was waiting for a recent graduate of the Virginia Military Institute, George C. Marshall.)

In the late 1930s the General Staff still found its powers and duties shadowed by Elihu Root's own choice of a word to describe the organization's main function: "supervision." The great reformer had favored this word, not "command"; the General Staff was to be the "directing brain" of the army. The role of the chief of staff was to advise and assist his civilian superior, in whose name he would act. Twenty years earlier, during the World War, the feud had erupted between General Pershing, commander of the American Expeditionary Force (AEF) in France, and Major General Peyton C. March, who had been summoned from the fighting front to become chief of staff and stir up the sluggish War Department. The austere, hard-working March—who struck a younger officer, Colonel George C. Marshall, as "a master administrator" but "a very arbitrary, tactless man"—declared himself the country's chief soldier, taking "rank and precedence over all officers of the Army." Pershing, who acted independently in every sphere, thought otherwise. It was the chief of staff's job, he felt, to keep the AEF supplied with what it needed, not to nurture illusions of command; the position of chief of staff, he observed later, should not be confused with commanding general of the army. The feud between Pershing and March and their respective groups of supporters had never ended; in fact, in the early 1930s the flames had burned higher after the publication of the memoirs of the two generals. But March had nevertheless demonstrated a key point about the office of chief of staff: Like the presidency, its scope came not only from written mandates but from what the occupant could make of it.

Beyond any problems posed by the structure of the War Department came the difficulties directly due to President Roosevelt himself. In early 1937 FDR had filled the vacant secretaryship of the department by promoting the assistant secretary, Harry Woodring, a snappily dressed small-town banker who had earlier served as governor of Kansas. Still thinking as an isolationist himself, the president seemed unperturbed by the fact that Woodring was not only widely regarded as a lightweight but was an isolationist too. And Woodring had friends among high officers; Craig found him easy to work with, and Pershing, whose word always counted, said of the new secretary (presumably in support) that "he would be better than some man who thought he knew it all."

Then Roosevelt had proceeded to appoint as the new assistant secretary of war a prominent West Virginia corporation lawyer, Louis A. Johnson, who in 1932 had glad-handed his way to the post of national commander of the American Legion and ever since had given FDR valuable political support. Talkative and energetic, Johnson soon made it clear to everybody in Washington that his ambitions would not be satisfied until he had forced Woodring out of the secretary's chair and claimed it for himself. As the skies grew darker in Europe and Asia in late 1937 and 1938, history seemed to be coming to Johnson's aid. Moving steadily away from his isolationist position, Roosevelt found the assistant secretary, whose leanings were internationalist, a more congenial associate than the head of the department.

What kept General Craig and the General Staff squarely in the crossfire between Woodring and Johnson, with no place to hide, was the fact that the president, not content with having made these discordant appointments, allowed the fight to rage on when he could easily have stopped it, either by dismissing one man or the other or simply by muzzling Johnson. But since isolationism held strong appeal in many parts of the country, and notably on Capitol Hill, the presence of Woodring at the War Department served as a useful signal that the administration had no thought of building up an army capable of intervening in foreign wars.

Beyond that, Roosevelt had created in the War Department one of his favorite situations—an agency or function run by two persons of opposing views and antagonistic temperaments. He had acted that way at the State Department, where he had set the urbane and activist Sumner Welles, a fellow Groton alumnus, against the cautious congressional politician Cordell Hull. And in an absolutely spectacular fashion he had thrown the New

Deal's great relief effort open to a continuing fight for projects and power between Secretary of the Interior Harold Ickes, who on his own loved a good scrap and always had several in progress, and Harry Hopkins, a former social worker from New York. Even the initials of the Ickes and Hopkins agencies confused the public: PWA versus WPA.

Why should a president pursue such aims, complicating his administrative life rather than simplifying it? "He loved peace and harmony in his surroundings," observed Robert Sherwood, a leading Broadway playwright who served FDR as a speechwriter, "and yet most of his major appointments . . . were peculiarly violent, quarrelsome, recalcitrant men"—men, Sherwood might have added, who were yoked together but often tried to pull in opposite directions. "Being a writer by trade," Sherwood said, "I tried continually to study him, to try to look beyond his charming and amusing and warmly affectionate surface into his heavily forested interior. But I could never really understand what was going on in there. His character was not only multiplex, it was contradictory to a bewildering degree." Henry Morgenthau, Jr., FDR's old Dutchess County friend and neighbor and his secretary of the treasury, said that Roosevelt was "a man of bewildering complexity of moods and motives." His secretary of labor, Frances Perkins, called him "the most complicated human being I ever knew"; he was "not clear, not simple, with drives and compulsions in a dozen different directions."

Yet, behind his unruffled surface, in the "heavily forested interior," the president like anyone else had his reasons, good and not so good, conscious and unconscious, for his words and actions. Ideologically he followed the polestar provided by his simple Jeffersonian view of American—and essentially human—history, but his course left him ample room for all the tacking he thought necessary. As the pioneer in transforming the presidency from the limited office it had been even under Teddy Roosevelt and Wilson into the modern office concerned with every aspect of American national life, he inevitably engaged in many presidential activities for the first time. One of his most powerful weapons of control was the dependence of other officials—subordinate decision makers—on his favor and support. This dependence was partly material, since an official's tools for doing his job were ultimately provided by the president, but also psychological: The official wanted the president to give approval to his efforts, to stand behind him in his pioneering work. Subordinates like Woodring and Johnson craved FDR's blessing.

By establishing competition rather than unity at the head of an agency, Roosevelt achieved another desired practical result as well as satisfying his inner dislike of orthodox hierarchies. The quarreling, feuding officials would of course be unable to settle their disputes on their own and would therefore be forced to lay them before the one superior authority; the president could thus become the great referee and decide which of the feudists "would enjoy the prestige to be derived from laying the sewer pipes." He could play papa, which he enjoyed (he often spoke of himself this way), and he could also keep himself up to date on the activities and problems of his subordinates.

By making all the lines radiate directly from himself, Roosevelt could sit at the center of the administrative web and feel tugs slight enough to go unnoticed by a more orthodox executive; he could keep at least one hand on the bureaucracy and check its tendencies to swell in size and self-importance.

This style of management did not come free, one of its costs being the tremendous demands it placed on the chief executive himself. Roosevelt took great delight at being in the midst of the action, and for years he thrived on it, but the demands could hardly fail to take their toll. Further, his unconventional managerial approach caused him to spread his attention wide and thin, to busy himself more with responses to immediate specific problems than with longer-range reflection—although his methods offered him many delightful opportunities to make use of his great store of minute facts and figures from all realms of subject matter. A greater cost in some ways came from the energies FDR's subordinates spent in waging feuds instead of getting on with their jobs. Certainly from the middle of 1937 the squabbles between Harry Woodring and Louis Johnson hampered the effectiveness of War Department principals and of subordinates as well.

"General Craig was sitting on the fence between these two gentlemen," noted Mrs. Marshall. "If he followed the Secretary's instructions he would be in bad odor with the Assistant Secretary, who was quite powerful. If he followed the lead of Mr. Johnson, Mr. Woodring would have called him to account. It was an impossible and tragic situation." Thus was the general, as Mrs. Craig said, "crucified." Into this scene walked George

Marshall to take up his duties as assistant chief of staff, War Plans Division, U.S. General Staff.

His crucifixion began early. "Rumor is destroying me, I fear," Marshall wrote to General Pershing on September 26, 1938. "I am announced by Tom, Dick and Harry as Deputy Chief of Staff and Chief of Staff to be, the Asst. Secretary makes similar announcements. Probably antagonizing Woodring & Craig." With the tactless Johnson trumpeting his cause, Marshall feared, the Woodring faction in the department would feel compelled to oppose him.

It was also true that a plan that seemed to have evolved to move Marshall from War Plans to the post of deputy chief of staff and thence to chief grew out of no hallowed tradition. No precedent decreed that the deputy chief should succeed the chief; as Marshall well knew, such a transition had taken place only once since the World War. Marshall was also well aware that he possessed only one star, and his chances of acquiring a second one while serving in the "brain of the Army" did not appear great. Throughout his career, events seemed to have conspired to keep him from being in the right place at the right time.

In any case, it was all up to the president, of course. FDR looked on the chief of staff as his personal military adviser, and he could pick any eligible officer he chose; the man could have greater seniority than Marshall, or less. Roosevelt had selected General Craig without letting his predecessor, General MacArthur, know who was going to get the prize or when it would be awarded. The president could make the same kind of move again.

Once on the job at War Plans, Marshall, as always, attracted no attention by flashily wielding a new broom but instead settled in quietly, taking his measure of his men and their work. He was soon introduced to the great variety of "color plans" the staff had created. The planners designated each foreign country against which the United States might conceivably find herself fighting by a color (orange, for instance, signified Japan); the plan involved the activities the United States would undertake, or seek to undertake, against that country. In reality, these plans amounted to little more than paper exercises, not because of any deficiency in the staff, but because the army ever since the World War, and particularly since the onset of the Depression, had lacked the men and the means to conduct hostilities against any but the tiniest country. The operations described in these plans called for forces of a strength and power that could not come into being until long after a war began.

During the long, lean years since the triumphant days of 1918 in France, the army had developed the habit of approaching budget makers and legislators in the manner of a poor relation who knows that his kinfolk will keep him alive but will allow him few comforts and certainly no luxuries at all. Thrift-preaching congressmen made a special point of declaring that the great mass of weapons and equipment created for the never-fought campaign of 1919 must be used up, whether or not it had become obsolete, before the army went shopping for replacements. Accordingly, twenty-year-old tanks, as out of date as Model T Fords, rattled across training fields, and, democratically enough, the antitank weapons used against them dated back twenty years, too. Successive secretaries of war and chiefs of staff asked not for what the army needed but for what they believed they could get.

Early in September 1938, Louis Johnson drew a measure of public attention to the new division chief by having the general deliver an address to the West Virginia state convention of the American Legion. Since by law the assistant secretary held special responsibility for keeping the army supplied, Marshall diplomatically devoted considerable attention to "the necessity for adequate and modern matériel"; their fellow West Virginian, he told the legionnaires, was "at the forefront of the drive to modernize the equipment of the Army and to prepare American industry for the rapid conversion of its production machinery from peace to war purposes." These were "possibly uninteresting particulars," he conceded, but national defense must be looked at in a practical and sensible way. The speech, utterly free of rhetoric, contained not a word glamorizing war, nor did the speaker wrap himself in the flag while proclaiming special doctrines of his own. If the legionnaires wanted a stemwinder, a reminder of the great old days in the trenches of France, they did not get it. They heard instead about "the many factors that enter into the matériel problem" as the War Department sought a "symmetrical modernization and development of our military National Defense system."

Johnson apparently approved of the speech, even without fireworks, and of Marshall's conduct generally, because in the second week of October the assistant secretary made a bold move. Although the office of the deputy chief of staff had sat vacant for some days, Craig, and to some degree Woodring, had doubts about moving Marshall into the job, because as deputy chief he would be in a position to give orders to generals who outranked him. According to office rumor, Craig intended to postpone the decision until after the first of the year, although Marshall's degree of seniority was not a factor that would change during the ensuing three months. At this point one of Woodring's special talents caused him to be away from Washington. Well aware that he needed all the help he could get during the 1938 congressional campaign, President Roosevelt had dispatched the secretary, an effective speaker, on a speechmaking tour, which left Johnson presiding as acting secretary at the War Department. One day, before the beginning of a meeting of the war council, Johnson raised with Craig the question of a deputy chief of staff.

"We'll get that worked out, Mr. Secretary," Craig answered.

Johnson pressed the chief of staff. "What about George Marshall for deputy?"

"We'll work that out, Mr. Secretary," Craig said.

There would be no war council meeting, Johnson declared, until the matter *was* worked out. Craig left the room, and when he came back a few minutes later he said simply, "The orders have been issued." He saw no need to tell Johnson that Woodring was really a Marshall man, too, aside from his worries about seniority. (Woodring, though campaigning energetically during this period, did suffer a strange sort of setback. So lacking in charisma was he, at least in eastern eyes, that he arrived in Jersey City to make a speech only to learn that an unknown man in the crowd had been taken for the speaker and had been given the official welcome.) The secretary could not claim to be delighted that the appointment of Marshall had been made behind his back, but otherwise he was not displeased. As for going all the way and supporting Marshall for chief of staff, Woodring could not make up his mind.

The conversation resulting in Marshall's appointment as deputy chief of staff took place only a few days after the signing of the Munich agreement. No suggestion of any post-Munich initiative by the White House had yet come down to the War Department, but during this same week William C. Bullitt, the ambassador to France, paid his dramatic visit to President Roosevelt with vivid tales of German air might and French helplessness. Marshall's appointment became effective on October 15, and just a month later, on Monday, November 14, came the conference at the White House at which FDR advanced his startling proposal to build ten thousand airplanes, the proposal about which Marshall said, "I don't agree with that at all."

In the days following this meeting, Marshall, receiving no word that he was to be banished from Washington, went to work with Assistant Secretary Johnson to draw up budgets that over a two-year period would provide for a ten-thousand-plane air force and for procuring other needed equipment, supplies, and raw materials. Mindful of the fact that all the figures needed to be ready for processing by the Bureau of the Budget in time for the president's State of the Union address in January, Marshall pressed his associates. To the new chief of the air corps, Major General Henry H. Arnold, he said, "This is no time for normal General Staff procedure. Speed is essential and your efforts should be informal."

Not content to leave the president to his own devices, Marshall brought out the army's number one siege gun, ghostwriting a letter on defense policy for General Pershing to sign and send to FDR. In the letter Marshall, after duly acknowledging the need for more airplanes, caused his old chief to express careful concern about the pathetic deficiencies in "features of the defense mechanism that are vital necessities to air operations, though not organically of the air service" and, further, about the needs of the ground forces that must be met "at the earliest possible moment." The creation and dispatch of this letter present a vintage example of Marshall's relentless thoroughness at work. During a White House call, Pershing had spoken with Roosevelt about defense requirements, but when the general, in describing the conversation to Marshall, "made the familiar remark that Mr. Roosevelt had done practically all the talking," Marshall "began to be very fearful" that Pershing had not been heard and, obtaining some sheets of Pershing's stationery, dictated the letter and had it properly typed. Then it was flown to San Antonio, where Pershing merely had to sign it and send it on to the president, who was then at Warm Springs.

Toward the end of November, FDR began to pick up various details of the army's planning and budget-making efforts, and on December 1, when presented with Johnson's program as put together by Craig, Marshall, and their colleagues, the president reacted with anger to such items as $1,289,000,000 for an overall air program, $421 million for equipment for the army's Protective Mobilization Force, and $122 million for preparing industry for war. His military advisers had simply not divined his purpose. Summoning these men to a new meeting, FDR read them a blistering lecture. Whatever hopes they might nourish, it was most unlikely that he could ask Congress for more than $500 million, and he had already told his listeners what he wanted to buy with that money. He wanted airplanes, and here were his military advisers offering him everything else!

After some discussion, the two sides began to move toward common ground. Of the hoped-for $500 million, Roosevelt agreed to allot $200 million for matériel for the ground forces, and to allow another $120 million to be spent on what Marshall and Pershing had called "vital necessities to air operations," leaving $180 million that must be spent on combat planes—three thousand, FDR said—for the explicit purpose of impressing Germany. During the next months, before the defense program was presented to Congress and afterward as well, these figures underwent numerous changes, partly as the result of fiery attacks on them by isolationist senators. The program took final form in April 1939 as legislation that authorized an army air corps of six thousand planes, combat and noncombat, which was far less than Roosevelt had originally sought. Even so, it offered a great stimulus to the factories—which had been one of the president's aims—and it mandated a considerable increase over the existing strength of about 1,700 aircraft. The fact that Roosevelt began to listen to the views of his advisers with respect to the need for balanced forces, Marshall felt, owed a great deal to the Pershing letter, which "had a tremendous effect." It was all a "rather intricate procedure that we followed in order to get this going."

So, in this not only intricate but halting fashion, after twenty years of neglect, began the rearming of the United States, and the new deputy chief of staff took his stand in the thick of the fight alongside the president.

Sitting at his desk with its fantastic clutter of souvenirs, little ships, lighters, figurines, animals—everything suggesting a person who enjoyed a myriad of associations, who liked for things to remind him of people and happenings—President Roosevelt, for all his post-Munich concerns, did not strike observers as a troubled man. One interviewer talked with him not in his office in the executive wing of the White House, but in the oval study on the second floor of the mansion—a thoroughly Rooseveltian room with its marine prints, pictures of his mother and his wife and John Paul Jones, with books piled high on plump, chintz-covered chairs, stamp albums, ship models, all reflecting a bygone gentlemanly world, a time when sail rather than steam ruled the seas, when Delanos roamed across the Pacific to China. "After nearly six years in the White House, the center of deeper domestic controversies than have shaken this country for generations, the focal point of whirling social change, his personality is still oddly intact and unclassifiable"; the interviewer also discerned the "heavily forested" Roosevelt interior. Covering a wide range of matters, "he discoursed on all the large subjects with equal zest and fluency"; actually, this perceptive observer was struck as much by the style as by the substance. "The more an interviewer sees of the leaders of other nations the more he is impressed by the unique quality of interest and energy, and particularly of ease in energy, which Mr. Roosevelt possesses." The European democracies, Britain and France, might be led by tired old men, whom Munich would have made even wearier; but in FDR the United States possessed quite a different phenomenon. "Because of his interest in everything under the sun he can talk all day and refresh himself in the evening with more talk."

Wary of becoming involved in international power politics—and wary, too, of the isolationists and the turbulence they could stir up—the president nevertheless engaged in a highly secret game. So strongly did he hold the conviction that only through the possession of formidable air power would the Western democracies stand any chance of stopping Hitler that he pursued this end by any means, likely or unlikely. Long before the Munich conference he had assured a French emissary, Jean Monnet, that if war came while the arms embargo still stood (thus making it illegal to fly airplanes out of the United States to a belligerent), he would have aircraft on French order flown to a field on the northern border of New York State and then pushed across the boundary into Canada. He even drew a map showing possible places where this maneuver could be accomplished, and when his visitor asked for the sketch as a memento, the president with a grin handed it to him.

After declaring his wish to build up U.S. air strength and

aircraft-production facilities, FDR had to use all his authority to compel Secretary Woodring and General Arnold to allow the French to study an air corps light bomber, a new design from the Douglas Company. In great secrecy, French representatives went to California. When Captain Paul Chemedlin, a French test pilot, delivered some less-than-tactful comments about the new bomber, his annoyed American counterpart decided, as General Arnold said, "to make the Frenchman eat his words" and invited him to come aboard for a ride. The plane was put through some unusual maneuvers; finally, given too great a challenge, it stalled, then crashed in a Los Angeles parking lot. The American pilot was killed but, incredibly, the French passenger survived. An excited Frenchman in the group watching rushed up to him, speaking volubly in a language that no one could mistake for English. Although Douglas spokesmen tried to keep the secret by telling the press that the survivor was one "Smithins," a company mechanic, the truth quickly came to light.

Seizing the moment, isolationists demanded to know what business a Frenchman had on an American experimental plane. The members of the Senate Military Affairs Committee paid a call en masse on FDR, who used the occasion to paint a picture of the world as he saw it, a world in which Hitler loomed as a deadly menace to all and America's first line of defense lay in the continued existence of nations threatened by the Axis. War was imminent, said the president, and it would directly affect "the peace and safety of the United States," because "so soon as one nation dominates Europe, that nation will be able to turn to the world sphere." He therefore would see to it that the United States sent Britain and France everything they could pay for. In answer to a question, he said that yes, such a policy might not be neutral, but it was nevertheless necessary: "Self-protection is part of the American policy." Then, at his most earnest, he declared, "I hope to God they get the planes and get them fast and get them over there in France. It may mean the saving of our civilization."

The president's callers did not agree. Although they had pledged themselves to secrecy about the meeting, some of the isolationists among them broke the agreement immediately. The very next morning newspaper readers were told that the president had urged the members of the Military Affairs Committee "to regard France as the actual frontier of America in an apparently inevitable showdown between democracies and dictatorships." The secrecy deemed vital by the president had vanished. Instead of announcing an advance to the Rhine, FDR was forced to sound a hurried retreat. So loud became the national outcry that within three days he was denying the whole story: Anyone who claimed that in the meeting he had spoken of the Rhine as the American frontier, he told reporters, was telling a "deliberate lie"—indeed, had he chosen, he could have produced the twenty-seven-page stenographic transcript, in which no mention of the Rhine appears. But his meaning was perfectly clear, and now the wariness with which he normally approached the isolationists seemed freshly justified; he had been candid in the meeting and he had been stung. (As a result of the loose talk about the Rhine, FDR and a secretary experimented unsuccessfully with a device to make secret recordings of sensitive meetings—an idea that bore brief fruit some months later when for a few weeks a recording machine that worked on the principle of a movie sound track captured some press conferences and parts of several conversations. Not particularly happy with the device, Roosevelt let it fall into disuse.) In spite of the uproar, however, the French were allowed to sign contracts for one hundred new bombers and for as many other planes as the American aircraft industry was capable of turning out for them. The number was discouragingly small.

"Drum, Drum!" cried President Roosevelt one day. "I wish he'd stop beating his own drum!"

Fact or reportorial fiction, this outburst seemed a plausible presidential response to the loud self-advertisement of Major General Hugh Aloysius Drum, who in 1938 and 1939 believed that destiny intended to crown his career by making him chief of staff of the United States Army. Not only was Drum the Army's senior major general, but he had been a protégé of Pershing's since serving as chief of staff of the First Army in France, and he enjoyed important political and social connections. He also had many friends in the press who seemed to take it for granted that he would receive the top job.

Besides Drum, more than thirty major generals and brigadiers ranked ahead of George Marshall. Hence, in the competition to become chief of staff, he seemed to observers who looked only at the numbers to be hopelessly lost in the pack. But the rule requiring a nominee for chief of staff to have four years to serve before retirement swung a sharp scythe, cutting down all but three other senior generals besides Marshall and Drum, and none of these men had either sought support or acquired it; for one reason or another, none was seriously regarded as a possible successor to General Craig. One, an able leader of troops, suffered from the serious handicap of having been born in Germany; another had spent much of his career, unfittingly, in the supply services; the third simply had no following. Only Drum, of the officers who outranked Marshall, counted as a serious rival, but he was formidable indeed (although at least one junior officer thought of him as the "biggest stuffed shirt" in the army), and in the eyes of Craig and other Marshall supporters, he possessed one particular advantage. As commander of the First Army, based at Governors Island, New York, Drum did not belong to the decision-making apparatus in Washington, whereas Marshall, by his frank talk against a great air buildup at the expense of other branches of the army, might well have alienated the president, as some of his friends suggested. Besides, even if FDR did not choose Drum, he was fully entitled to reach below Marshall on the brigadier generals' list and pluck someone like Dan Sultan, an engineer officer with an administrative flair, or Adna Chaffee, a devoted and hardworking pioneer of armored force.

While Drum pressed into service every contact who might advance his cause, Marshall was making important friends of his own. His acquaintance with one governmental figure took on special significance. Marshall met Harry Hopkins for the first time at the fateful November 14 White House conference. No sudden friendship sprang up, but late in December Hopkins, who was coming to be widely regarded as the man closest to the president and had just been appointed secretary of commerce, informed Marshall's office that he wished to have a conversation with the deputy chief of staff. A man on whom FDR could rely to carry out a mission without argument or reservations, Hopkins during the fall had made for the president an eyes-and-ears tour of aircraft factories, and in his typical style he had told one of his companions, the General Staff liaison officer with the WPA, that "the Army and the Navy are sitting pretty to get a lot of money in the next relief bill for the national defense if they can sell the idea to the President." The liaison officer, Colonel Arthur Wilson, wrote urgently to the War Department that "Mr. Hopkins has the ear of the President as no other man, probably," and "the Chief of Staff or the Deputy [should] get an appointment with him." Knowing the normal pace of the General Staff's work, resulting both from the standard bureaucratic mentality and from understaffing, Wilson said bluntly: "This question is not a matter of weeks and general staff studies but a matter of fast action and days." Privately, Wilson thought the War Department was "sleepy."

As if to prove his point, neither Craig nor Marshall leaped into action, and in the last week of December Hopkins made the first move, asking for the meeting with Marshall. Here Marshall employed a technique he was to find increasingly useful. Instead of inviting Hopkins to the State, War, and Navy Building—to which he had moved on becoming deputy chief of staff, with an office close to General Craig's—Marshall paid a call on Hopkins, thus giving up the advantage of operating on home territory but preserving his freedom of movement. It was characteristic: When he had finished his business, he could simply stand up, express his thanks, and leave.

Marshall spent more than an hour in the splendid paneled office to which Hopkins, as the secretary of commerce-designate, had moved from his shabby WPA headquarters on New York Avenue. Sallow and skinny, Hopkins at the end of 1937 had lost two thirds of his stomach in a cancer operation, and after the surgery had suffered various bouts of illness, some of them severe, caused by complex nutritional problems. Though far from robust, the blunt and often sarcastic Hopkins was extraordinarily useful to Roosevelt; in telling General Marshall that "the entry to the President is through Mr. Hopkins," Colonel Wilson was on absolutely solid ground.

The discussion between Hopkins and Marshall covered the whole realm of defense, with the general drawing for the civilian a picture of overall American inadequacy and weakness. Much of this came as news to Hopkins, who though an extremely quick learner had no military background. His response was typical of him: Marshall must see the president at once, wherever it could be arranged, at Warm Springs or Hyde Park. Marshall declined, his expressed reason having to do with protocol: He was not the chief of staff. But Hyde Park, Warm Springs? These were places where the friendly, charming Roosevelt treated you as a guest, and over drinks or dinner turned what seemed to be a social conversation into a discussion that might end in an undesired agreement of some kind. Getting onto a "basis of intimate relationship with the President," it seemed to Marshall, might have its dangers; FDR's conversational wizardry was famous. The deputy chief of staff's attitude suggested the fears of a virgin who believes that the preservation of virtue comes most surely from avoidance of the first date.

Even without a meeting between Marshall and Roosevelt, the general's conversation with Harry Hopkins produced quick, tangible results. Colonel Wilson noted the secret switch of several million dollars in WPA money into the defense stream, to be spent in creating machine tools for the manufacture of small-arms ammunition. This unspectacular move would give the United States vital lead time in an important area of military production.

The meeting had another result as well, one not tangible but highly important in a different way: George Marshall and Harry Hopkins had begun to know each other.

On February 21, 1939, sitting at the witness table in a hearing of the Senate Military Affairs Committee, General Marshall delivered one pithy sentence that summed up the state of American preparedness. After telling the senators that the ordnance department had developed a new 37mm gun to replace .50-caliber machine guns in the mobile antiaircraft regiments, the general said simply: "We consider [it] very fine, but at present we have only one gun." Marshall had come up to Capitol Hill to argue the army's case for acquiring new matériel—equipment not designed and manufactured during the World War or even earlier. He wanted a semiautomatic rifle to replace the veteran Springfield (M1903); new artillery; enough antitank and antiaircraft cannon to supply the troops, not numerous, that would use them; and ammunition to replace the old and decomposing stocks built up twenty years earlier. As for field artillery, the army was like a prudent housewife turning shirt collars, altering some of the 75s to permit a higher angle of fire and making these guns and also the old 155mm howitzers more mobile but not daring to ask for replacements—while European armies were being outfitted with new artillery such as 105mm howitzers.

Presenting testimony to Congress counted as a prime part of the job of a high military or naval officer, and Marshall found this legislative session hectic; "the pressure," he told Major General Stanley Embick, his predecessor as deputy chief of staff, "seems to continue without interruption." The day following his testimony he came back to Capitol Hill to be available "in connection with the final vote by the Senate committee on the Army bill." During the past three months, he told Colonel Edwin Cole, under whom he had served at Leavenworth thirty years earlier, he had been busier "than at any time since the World War and with just about as many conflicting interests and problems to deal with." Military life had become so complicated, with its demands for scientific, mechanical, technical, and political knowledge, that he looked back with envy "on the peaceful days of the old Army when we debated the relative merits of a chuck wagon attachment for the escort wagon." Sadly, "all the glamour, if there ever was any, has gone out of the business of war."

Marshall also thanked his old superior for "all the kind things" Colonel Cole had said about him in a recent letter. One of the observations Cole had offered was a categorical forecast: "I have for years predicted that if we again went to war when you were not too young or too old to be considered that you would undoubtedly be the Commander in Chief."

Marshall could not be so sure. Increasingly, he found himself caught between Secretaries Woodring and Johnson. Although each man now supported him (Johnson had never wavered), the absurd factor was that neither knew what the other thought. The situation demanded that Marshall walk on eggs. As he summed it up: "Johnson wanted me for Chief of Staff, but I didn't want Woodring to know he was for me. Craig was for me, but I wanted it kept from the President. Woodring was for me, but I didn't want the others to know."

Caught in this bizarre situation, which was extreme even for wide-open New Deal Washington, Marshall uttered words of caution to well-wishing friends. To one supporter who suggested a public relations campaign, Marshall replied that he had enough trouble already. "Reference any publicity regarding me, or 'build up' as it is called," he said, "I am now, in my particular position with low rank, on the spot in army circles. The fact of my appointment as Deputy while a brigadier general, junior to other generals of the general staff, makes me conspicuous in the army." And he added, "Too conspicuous, as a matter of fact."

But in any case, Marshall thought, the path of his own advancement did not lead through publicity and promotional campaigns. "My strength with the army," he said, "has rested on the well known fact that I attended strictly to business and enlisted no influence of any sort at anytime. That, in army circles, has been my greatest strength in this matter of future appointment, especially"—and it was not necessary actually to mention the name "Drum" in the following clause—"as it is in strong contrast with other most energetic activities in organizing a campaign and in securing voluminous publicity." Marshall had not heard Roosevelt cry "Drum, Drum!" but he was coming to know FDR; the president liked to make up his own mind. "Therefore, it seems to me that at this time the complete absence of any publicity about me would be my greatest asset, particularly with the President." Besides, "the army would resent it, even some of those now ardently for me. In other words, it would tar me with the same brush to which they now object."

A concern that had not left Marshall since his medical examinations and surgery on the West Coast tugged at him. He had made an informal arrangement with his old friend from China and Fort Benning, Colonel Morrison C. Stayer, who was both an able soldier and a doctor, to visit Washington from time to time to check up on his heart condition; he still occasionally experienced an irregular pulse, for which Stayer prescribed medication. Entire letters to Stayer, or sometimes simply the portions relating to his physical problems, were written in longhand; Marshall's well-founded fear of rumors circulated by secretaries remained as great as ever.

The pressure and the sedentary life of Washington, he felt, did him no good. To ensure a favorable report on his annual medical examination, he had carefully "resumed" regular dosage of Stayer's prescription a week before he expected to have the checkup, and he planned a quiet morning in the office on the day itself. But General Craig upset the schedule, suddenly suggesting one "hectic" day, as the two were having a quick sandwich lunch, that Marshall go straight out to Fort Myer and take care of the matter quickly and quietly; Craig even picked up the telephone and made the appointment. Marshall could hardly demur. In the checkup the doctor found a slight irregularity in his pulse before exercise and none after, and his blood pressure was a satisfactory 132 over 78; the examiner recommended exercise to fight "desk belly" and benefit the pulse. All in all, Marshall thought the checkup went well. If Craig happened to hear of the irregularity, he decided, it "would be credited . . . as a more or less natural reaction to the really terrific strain of the past three weeks, during which I have had to work like lightning, compromise endless disagreements, sit in on most difficult scenes, etc." On the whole, indeed, he felt "fine and in high spirits."

At the end of March, getting ready for a trip to Warm Springs for some hoped-for days of relaxation, President Roosevelt asked the secretary of war to send him the service records of generals eligible for appointment as chief of staff. General Craig, who carried out the request, took it on himself to leave out two of the top five who met the requirement as to remaining length of service; he included along with Marshall and Drum, only the German-born Walter Krueger, and he dutifully added four generals junior to Marshall. The chief of staff thought that the president might well prefer one of the younger men.

While in Georgia, FDR wrote his daughter Anna about his delight at the birth of her third child, Johnny Boettiger (Anna's second marriage had taken her to the West Coast, and her father, to whom she was very close, missed her greatly); he responded to a telegram from Eleanor, in which she asked: ARE YOU AND STATE DEPARTMENT DOING ANYTHING? about Loyalist Spanish leaders trapped in Madrid, which had just fallen to the forces of General Francisco Franco; he discussed the "current picture" in a memorandum to Sumner Welles (it was an ominous picture indeed, since on March 15 the Germans had trampled on the Munich agreement by marching into Prague and taking over the truncated Czech state); he corresponded about arrangements for the forthcoming visit to the United States of the king and queen of England. But he kept his own counsel with respect to the choice of a new chief of staff. In the middle of April, General Craig still told confidants that he saw a good chance of the president's choosing one of the junior generals; in particular, he had picked up a rumor that FDR's jovial appointments secretary, Brigadier General "Pa" Watson, favored Dan Sultan, five years younger than Marshall.

On Sunday, April 23, Marshall was summoned to the White House. No one else—Woodring, Johnson, Craig—knew of the appointment. Marshall arrived at 3:35 in the afternoon and was shown into the president's oval study. "It was an interesting interview," Marshall said later, with impressive understatement. After being informed that he was to be the next chief of staff, Marshall told the president that he wanted the right to say what he thought and that it would often be unpleasant.

"Is that all right?"

"Yes," said Roosevelt.

"You said yes pleasantly," Marshall said, pursuing his point, "but it may be unpleasant."

One fact was clear: FDR held no resentment about Marshall's outspoken opposition to the unbalanced big-air program. "I want to say in compliment to the President," the general observed later, "that that didn't antagonize him at all. Maybe he thought I would tell him the truth so far as I personally was concerned." His appointment, Marshall felt, came "on the recommendations of other people," and since the president did not really know him he could not yet have FDR's entire confidence. But at the outset of their relationship as commander in chief and chief of staff, the two men had staked out an area of understanding marked by candor. Marshall had wished for the appointment, indeed coveted it, but he had not connived in order to get it, he had neither covered up any of his views nor professed opinions that were not genuine; nor had the president even by implication invited any such behavior. The job of chief of staff came to Marshall without strings; once again, Roosevelt had chosen for a high-level post one of the strong men (if no longer so choleric) described by Robert Sherwood.

This fact escaped some journalists, particularly those with an animus against the New Deal. Some members of this group habitually saw Roosevelt's every act as coming from either hypocrisy or deviousness, and thereby charged (or credited) him with a Machiavellianism beyond anything preached by the master. What had happened to the appointment of General Drum? For what sinister reasons had the president passed over the strong and able senior major general of the army in favor of a relatively unknown brigadier? "Tremendous pressure was exerted upon Mr. Roosevelt to appoint General Drum," wrote Boake Carter, a broadcaster and syndicated columnist who unwaveringly opposed the New Deal. "But perhaps Hugh Drum's friends should have read the history of the past seven years and known better. The greater the pressure exerted on Mr. Roosevelt for an appointment to an office, the greater the determination of the President not to yield, regardless of the merits of the candidate involved." But there was more to the shabby business than this, Carter thought. Speaking of Marshall, he observed that, although "it would be unkind to say that he is expected to be simply a willing 'order-taker,'" what "is expected of him by the

White House is that he will not 'talk out of turn.'" Neither Carter nor any other member of the press had been present to hear Marshall's dissent in the November 14 conference in the president's executive office, nor had reporters been privileged to take part in any subsequent discussions of American rearmament. So, believing that they saw the issue clearly, makeup men at William Randolph Hearst's New York *Daily Mirror* headed the story of the appointment FDR WANTED A "YES-MAN."

Drum was "vigorous, keen, ambitious to go to the top," said *Time,* and "until last week, most Army men would have bet that 'Drummie' was about to go on to Malin Craig's job." But, unlike Boake Carter, the news magazine saw nothing sinister in the appointment of George Marshall, the first non-West Pointer to hold the job since Leonard Wood in 1914 (by coincidence, Drum also was not a graduate of the academy). Marshall was given credit for "his brilliance at staff direction" during the World War, and when the magazine characterized him, in its standard style, with an attributive adjective, the word employed was "able" (a year earlier, in an article on defense, the same magazine had granted Marshall two adjectives: "brilliant, taciturn"). In commenting that the president had "dipped down past Hugh Drum and the 33 next-ranking officers of the Army" to find his man, however, *Time,* by ignoring the four-years-to-retirement rule, made FDR's choice of Marshall seem far more idiosyncratic than it actually was, and helped launch something of a myth.

Among the "other people" to whose recommendations Marshall's appointment was due, Pershing, his constant supporter, ranked high. But he owed his primary debt, Marshall believed, to his influential new friend, Harry Hopkins, who had respected and admired him from their first dealings.

General Pershing was ecstatic. "George's appointment has met with universal approval," he wrote to Katherine Marshall. "Of course all this pleases me very much and I do not have to tell you how I feel toward him. He is in a position where he will make a great name for himself and prove a great credit to the American Army and the American people."

Mrs. Marshall agreed. Thanking President Roosevelt for choosing her husband, she said, "For years I have feared that his brilliant mind, and unusual opinion, were hopelessly caught in more or less of a tread-mill. That you should recognize his ability and place in him your confidence gives me all I have dreamed of and hoped for."

Only an incorrigibly myopic and thoroughly prejudiced observer could have looked on the subject of her letter as a "yes-man."

CHAPTER FIVE

"TRAGIC MESSAGES IN THE NIGHT"

On March 15, 1939, eight days after seizing Czechoslovakia, Adolf Hitler sent his troops into the Baltic port of Memel, an East Prussian area given to the new state of Lithuania after the World War (and guaranteed in this status by Britain and France). On March 28 Madrid fell to the army of Francisco Franco, thus bringing victory in the Spanish civil war to the side supported by Hitler. And three days later, having tried to brush off criticism of his failure to oppose Hitler's move into Czechoslovakia, Prime Minister Neville Chamberlain took the extraordinary step of announcing to the House of Commons, and thus to the world, that Britain "in the event of any action which clearly threatened Polish independence and which the Polish Government accordingly considered it vital to resist with their national forces" would come to the aid of Poland.

In view of all these events, it was hardly surprising that three fourths of Americans responding to a *Fortune* magazine poll expected war in Europe in the near future. Could the United States keep out of such a war? Opinions were not only divided but passionately held.

"Certain types of propaganda are today fertilizing our soil for our entry into war," said former President Herbert Hoover in an eloquent plea for Americans to stay out of the European game of power politics. Drawing on his experiences in the World War, Hoover painted a vivid picture of the horrors of trench warfare as he had witnessed it at the Battle of the Somme, where a million and a half men "here and there, like ants . . . advanced under the thunder from 10,000 guns—until half a million had died." If we must go to war again, he said, let it be "on this hemisphere alone and in defense of our firesides or our honor. For that alone should we pay the price." In general, those of isolationist persuasion mistrusted anything on the order of a new crusade to make the world safe for democracy, since the "last effort to enforce civilization on the world resulted in at least 15 dictatorships replacing prewar constitutional governments." The isolationists foresaw the loss of civil rights and individual liberties; already the stress of rearming merely under the threat of war was forcing "even England and France into disguised dictatorship."

But the other great camp of opinion in 1939, the interventionists, actually believed not in intervening in a war but in playing a strong enough part in international affairs to prevent war. The widely syndicated columnist Dorothy Thompson argued that "we are already engaged in a struggle which will certainly result in war or in the defeat of this whole American way of life without war, unless we are willing to use right now the political and economic weapons which are in our hands." Whatever happened in Europe, wrote Heywood Broun from a more moral viewpoint than that of most commentators, Americans should not imagine that "we can remain untouched by the brutal spectacle," because "there are no caves in which men can hide when their fellows cry out in agony."

Amid these swirling currents of passionately held opinion, President Roosevelt had to find his course.

One morning in early May 1939, a young Washington matron, answering her telephone, heard a familiar voice on the line. Could she meet him at three o'clock sharp that afternoon? asked the newly appointed chief of staff of the United States Army; he had a project for which he needed her help.

When the two met, General Marshall declared that he had to go shopping for summer clothes because he was leaving immediately for Brazil. He needed help in picking out the suits. "I have to look real snazzy," he said, "because I'm supposed to outdo the charming Madame Ciano."

"Brazil?" the young woman cried. "Madame Ciano—old stinko Mussolini's daughter? What are you talking about?"

What Marshall was talking about was a great diplomatic game. Increasingly, President Roosevelt and his military advisers were expressing concern about German and Italian activities in Latin America and their possible effect on the control of the great and strategically important Brazilian bulge into the South Atlantic; in response to a question from Marshall, the Joint Planning Committee in March proposed the creation of a 100,000-man expeditionary force that would be prepared to take emergency action to forestall any Axis move in the area. In an attempt to impress the Brazilians with their country's military might, the Germans had invited the Brazilian chief of staff, who had spoken admiringly of the German Army, to pay a visit to Berlin. To sweeten the invitation, the Germans' Italian friends were sending Countess Ciano to Rio; besides being Mussolini's daughter, she was the wife of the Italian foreign minister. Upset at these maneuvers, the Brazilian foreign minister had proposed that the United States forestall the Germans by sending General Craig to Brazil as part of an exchange of visits that would also include a trip to Washington by his Brazilian counterpart. President Roosevelt had heartily approved of the plan. But after Marshall's appointment was announced on April 27, Craig handed on the assignment to his designated successor.

It was "in order to suppress these intimacies" between Brazil and the Axis powers, General Marshall said later, that he was being dispatched on this quick trip. As he summed it up for his young woman friend: "Latin America is a vitally strategic area and I'm supposed to spread good will in Brazil for the United States. That's the story, so let's get on down to the Young Men's Shop. I don't have much time; I've an appointment later this afternoon."

Aghast at the general's plan to buy clothes for this ceremonial trip at the bargain store he had mentioned, the young woman persuaded him to go to the best haberdashery in town. After choosing two suits, half a dozen shirts, and several ties, Marshall remembered that he had forgotten to pick up his new eyeglasses. But that presented no problem, since he did not require professional service but merely bought his glasses at the five-and-ten; at the nearest Woolworth's he chose four pairs in five minutes. He was now outfitted for his mission.

The young matron was Rose Page Wilson, whom the general had known since coming to Washington with Pershing in 1919, when Rose was eight years old; Marshall had taken an apartment in the building in which the Page family lived. Rose, an exceptionally lively child, had heard inviting reports from a friend about "that wonderful Colonel Marshall" who was said to be a whiz with children and, not willing to wait for a formal introduction, proceeded, as she said later, to pick him up in the elevator.

Their first outing, a walk in Rock Creek Park, began unpromisingly. Five minutes late for their meeting in the lobby of the apartment building, and loaded with guilt for having lied to her mother about the way she had met Colonel Marshall, Rose was downcast to hear him call, "Come along, hurry! It's two thirty-five. You're late!"

Fighting back tears, she replied with as much dignity as she could summon up, "Thank you for waiting."

Looking into her unhappy face, the colonel then surprised her by giving her a gallant salute, making a jaunty bow, and saying with no trace of mockery, "Not at all. It's a pleasure to wait for a charming young lady."

"Oh, my goodness!" she cried. "You really are nice!"

Four years later Marshall became Rose's godfather. In spite of lengthy separations in the succeeding years, the two had always remained close, Rose in many ways filling the role of the child the general could never have. In a bit of humorous verse written when Rose was about ten, the colonel, making fun of her appetite for toast and honey, called her "a little girl I strive to please," but predicted that her clothes would finally split, leaving her "with nothing whole except her hat."

With Rose, Marshall saw himself not only as an entertaining companion but as teacher and mentor, just as he always regarded himself in relation to men under his command. Beginning with a demonstration of the best way to dry socks, he then moved into intangible realms, refusing for instance to listen to lobby gossip reported by Rose and pointing out to her the harm careless talk could do to a person's reputation. He displayed particular anger when the child relayed rumors that an exotic young Cuban woman was General MacArthur's "sweetheart." His response was a command: "Don't you ever repeat talk like that again!" Several years later he not only encouraged but ordered the girl to write a note to a senator who had befriended her when her family had come to Washington and who had been featured in a story in *Collier's* magazine. The senator had been nice to her when she was a child, Marshall said, and she could "damn well" take the time to congratulate him. A few days after she had complied with the colonel's order, Rose to her surprise received a reply from the old senator, who was touched that she had "bothered" to write him. She had bothered, Rose recalled, because Colonel Marshall had insisted—"but then, few people are as thoughtful as he was and fewer still trouble to act on a kind impulse."

As a diplomatic mission, the Brazilian trip represented a new experience for Marshall, since it served a mixture of political and military purposes. In telling Rose that he was "supposed to spread good will for the United States," however, the general had caught its essence. He undertook "a very strenuous program everywhere and a devilish number of speeches a day"; the Brazilians greeted him "with a steadily increasing enthusiasm," he reported to General Craig (whom he had earlier told that he would send only a brief report because airmail cost twenty-five cents a sheet). In one town, opposing the glamour of Countess Ciano with a spontaneous countercoup, Marshall won over the children of the area and then, when word spread, of all Brazil and hence of their elders as well. Reviewing a parade of schoolchildren, he was struck by a group of two hundred little boys dressed in blue overalls with pink piping and carrying or pushing hand cultivators and other farm tools. When he discovered that the boys came from an agricultural school for foundlings, he induced the governor of the province to give him a tour, and the next day, wishing to repay some of the bounteous hospitality he had received, he decided that instead of feeding the dignitaries at a banquet, he would give each of the children a pound of candy, a decision that meant a busy morning in the local shops for one of his aides. From then on, the tour swelled into a triumph ("a regular Lindbergh reception," Marshall said of his welcome in the heavily Germanic town of Rio Grande do Sul), with children and their parents turning out in enormous numbers. "General Marshall received all honors everywhere he went," his orderly wrote Mrs. Marshall; an American officer in Brazil declared that he "had never seen its equal."

When Marshall sailed for home on the cruiser *Nashville* on June 7, he brought along as his guests a distinguished group—the Brazilian chief of staff and a party of five—who were to make a reciprocal tour of the United States. Not only had Marshall's goodwill efforts borne abundant fruit, but the American and Brazilian officers had reached practical agreement on such concrete points as the use by American forces of airfields in the great Natal bulge. The Brazilian chief never got to Berlin.

A week after returning from his Brazilian mission, Brigadier General George C. Marshall, General Staff Corps, was detailed by War Department Special Orders No. 149 as acting chief of staff, effective July 1, when General Craig would begin his longed-for two-month terminal leave. The permanent title would not be Marshall's until September 1, 1939, but he would take on the duties and responsibilities the very next Saturday. On his last day in office, General Craig wrote a farewell letter to his successor. After observing that it was not his nature to say the many things in his heart that should be said, the retiring chief of staff gave Marshall his warm good wishes "for a future career even more brilliant than the past."

Keenly aware of the power of the isolationists in Congress—proportionately greater than among the people as a whole—Franklin Roosevelt found the spring of 1939 a trying time. As diplomatic and military temperatures rose in Europe, FDR, with a matching sense of urgency, sought to induce the Senate and the House to repeal the 1935 neutrality legislation forbidding the sale of weapons to any nations at war. If Europe should erupt while this arms embargo stood unchanged, the United States would be prohibited from extending any material help to the British and French even for cash on the barrelhead. Spurred on by Harold Ickes and other administration officials who declared that Congress did not have the right to interfere with the president's conduct of foreign affairs, FDR called on his attorney general for an opinion as to the constitutionality of the arms embargo. If he failed to obtain a new law that would untie his hands, the president asked, "How far do you think I can go in ignoring the existing act—even though I did sign it!?" FDR raised the question out of some desperation; he could hardly hope that the attorney general would advise him to evade the law. The only real solution would have to come from Congress.

During these months, the president found himself caught in a trap both frustrating and unflattering. Since the onset of the 1937 recession, and particularly since the anti-New Deal gains in the 1938 congressional elections, Roosevelt had viewed his influence on Capitol Hill as a fragile asset, one so delicate that sometimes it ought not even to be used at all. The best way to get rid of the arms embargo, he believed, was to play no part in the whole business, neither to lead nor to negotiate. With respect to the members of the Senate Foreign Relations Committee, his view could not be considered unrealistic; the committee room housed a pride of isolationist lions—renowned senators like William E. Borah (actually dubbed the "mountain lion" from Idaho), Arthur Vandenberg, Hiram Johnson, and the Progressive Robert M. La Follette, Jr., of Wisconsin. Nowhere did FDR have a Sledgehammer, since the chairmanship was still held by the tippling Key Pittman who, as the price of his support on the neutrality legislation, extorted from Roosevelt the promise of a higher government subsidy for silver.

Promising action ("Two weeks more and we'll be getting somewhere," he would report to FDR every fortnight), Pittman nevertheless produced none, and the president's hopes, such as they were, switched to the House Committee on Foreign Affairs. In the late afternoons, the president emerged from the legislative shadows and, to House leaders who had been invited to his office, presented his deterrent thesis, which held that repeal of the arms embargo would likely prevent war from starting in Europe; further, if war should come, repealing the embargo would help make the victory of the dictators less probable than it would be as matters stood. The committee reported out a favorable neutrality bill, but during the evening of June 30 the whole House, in a narrow-shave vote (159 to 157), cut out the vital clauses that removed the arms embargo. The bill, shepherded unwatchfully by Representative Sol Bloom of New York, who was called "one of the Congressional seniority system's broadest jokes," faded away in amendments passed late at night after many administration supporters had gone to bed. Such was the congressional raw material with which FDR, an increasingly frustrated political craftsman, found himself forced to work.

Thus, despite his intentions, Roosevelt had ventured into open conflict with the legislative branch over a question of foreign policy—the kind of Wilsonian mistake whose potential disastrous consequences he had seen close up in 1919. Making little progress in the House, he turned to the Senate, whose members were motivated at this time of the year primarily by a desire to go back home and work on the mending of their political fences. Even those in the Foreign Relations Committee who favored repeal of the arms embargo saw nothing to get excited about because there surely was not going to be any immediate war in Europe; the men of Munich would no doubt go on yielding to Hitler's threats. On June 11 the committee voted 12 to 11 not to report out a bill to the full Senate. He could not swallow this without a fight, FDR decided, and on a hot summer evening the members of the committee gathered at his invitation in the upstairs oval study of the White House. The president contrived a clubby, even jovial atmosphere for the occasion, providing a drinks tray in one corner of the room. As he relaxed in shirt-sleeved ease on an overstuffed couch, he joked with Vice-President John Nance Garner about the best way to make an old-fashioned.

But then, calling the meeting to order, Roosevelt sought to change the mood, as a conductor's downbeat stills a chatty theater audience. It would probably be proper, he told the senators, to open with a prayer, since the decision to be made might well affect the peoples of the entire world. The idealism quotient of these congressional veterans was surely no higher than the average for the Senate, but FDR perhaps hoped that the suggestion of a prayer might at least startle them enough to claim their attention. He then recounted the familiar story of the danger of war, presenting it factually and not dramatically, with an array of supporting evidence. He spoke for a full hour, and at the end, in response to a question, he told the senators that even if there was not a probability of war before the next session of Congress, there was "a strong possibility."

It was more than a possibility, said Cordell Hull, who definitely forecast war by the end of the summer. Unlike the president, Hull spoke with visible emotion, pleading with the members of the committee to listen to his evidence. But Senator Borah, the seventy-four-year-old mountain lion from Idaho, dissented. There was not going to be a war, he said: "Germany isn't ready for it."

Sadly, Hull replied, "I wish the Senator would come down to my office and read the cables. I'm sure he would come to the conclusion that there's far more danger of war than he thinks."

No, no, Borah said. He had his own sources of information (in fact, his news came from a ragtag international newsletter produced in London), "and on several occasions I've found them far more reliable than the State Department."

At this shocker, even the other senators remained silent for a moment. Tears sprang to Hull's eyes, and he told the members of the committee that he had nothing further to say. Vice-President Garner went around the room, polling the senators, and then he turned to the president. "Well, Cap'n," he said, "we may as well face the facts. You haven't got the votes, and that's all there is to it."

Unlike Hull, who was not a Hudson Valley patrician and had

not had the advantage of Groton training, Roosevelt took the result quietly, leaning back in his seat, puffing on his cigarette, keeping his mask firmly in place. What thoughts and passions flitted from tree to tree in the thickets of his mind, no observer could know. Whatever his inner feelings, the man who did not reveal them to his wife and children would certainly not display them to this crowd. Nor, in truth, did the outcome surprise him. Having long accepted the separation of powers cherished by the Founding Fathers, he had grown accustomed to living with its often less-than-happy consequences. Experience had shown him the truth of the principle that effective leaders, unlike dictators, are "painfully aware that they are not in control of the universe." He also knew—perhaps intuitively—that a president "must never cease to press for action" and yet that "he cannot seem to dominate for fear of injuring Congressional pride." The job was designed for "a man who delights in the political process," and Roosevelt was that man. Calmly he told the group that he had done his best; the Senate must now take the responsibility for the results. Still buoyed up by his own arrogance, Borah assured him that there would be "no difficulty about that."

Congress adjourned early in August, leaving the arms embargo firmly in place. In a matter calling for the Senate's advice and consent, its advice to Roosevelt had been negative, and its consent to his policy had been withheld. He had lost his last chance to influence the march of events in Europe. Less than a month after the legislators left Washington, the Germans unleashed the world's first blitzkrieg, with Poland as its victim.

One of the greatest problems Franklin Roosevelt encountered on taking office as president of the United States had been not economic or social or political, but simply organizational. The structure of the executive branch, created in an era of limited government, had almost immediately revealed its inadequacy. The president turned for help to management experts, who began to develop plans for reorganization, including providing an adequate staff for the chief executive himself. When Louis Brownlow, a Chicago management specialist, sought the advice of a veteran British public servant, he was told that presidential aides should be "possessed of high competence, great physical vigor, and a passion for anonymity."

Reorganization took several years to flower, partly because

of congressional fears (whether genuine or expressed simply for tactical purposes) that FDR was seeking to create a framework for a dictatorship. But on April 3, 1939, Roosevelt signed the much-needed Reorganization Act, which created the Executive Office of the President, to be staffed by aides with the requisite passion for anonymity. Thus, as pressure was building up in Europe, the U.S. government took a big and vitally needed step out of the administrative dark ages. While Congress was tying FDR's hands overseas—or refusing to untie them—it at least granted him ammunition for his administrative wars.

Actually, Congress did considerably more than that. Unperturbed at seeming to contradict themselves, the legislative chambers that discouraged American involvement in Europe and professed to see little likelihood of imminent war readily produced their checkbook to underwrite activities devoted to defense in the Western Hemisphere. On July 1, 1939, the day after the House had voted to preserve the arms embargo, Congress provided the president with a $525 million defense budget—a relatively large sum at the time.

Despite his disappointment over the arms embargo, the president now had an organization of his own and he had money. Immediately, on July 5, he took an interesting and important step with respect to the army and navy by issuing a Military Order—a presidential device rarely used—transferring a whole array of military bodies from their places in the hierarchies of the War and Navy departments to direct supervision by the president as commander in chief. Of particular importance here were the Joint Army and Navy Board (usually called just the Joint Board) and the Army and Navy Munitions Board, the former the instrument of the chiefs of staff, the latter the organization in which Louis Johnson, the assistant secretary of war, represented the War Department.

Since Elihu Root's day, the Joint Board had been charged with coordinating army and navy planning and with creating agreement on military policy. In 1939 the members were: from the army, the chief of staff, the deputy chief of staff, and the head of the War Plans Division; for the navy, the chief of naval operations, the assistant chief, and the director of the navy's War Plans Division. The continuing work of the board was handled by a subordinate group, the Joint Planning Committee, which had earlier produced the series of "color plans" studied by General Marshall in 1938. President Roosevelt's order of July

5 bore a great deal of significance. Until this time the chiefs of staff had possessed no legal right of direct access to the president. The Joint Board had come into being as the result of an agreement reached in 1903 between the two service secretaries, to whom the board reported. Now the president's move took the secretaries out of the flow of strategic discussion and decision; the civilian president would deal directly with the official organ of military control. Nothing could have made it plainer that Roosevelt as commander in chief had no intention of limiting himself to predigested information passed on by the service departments. As for the secretaries, it was clear that their positions would become whatever they could make them out of what was left.

No one could say how everything would work out. For the new chief of staff, holder of an office whose own authority in wartime did not possess clear boundaries and had not done so even prior to Roosevelt's July 5 order, the reorganization would constitute a new kind of challenge.

On Friday morning, September 1, at ten minutes of three, President Roosevelt was awakened by a telephone call from Ambassador William C. Bullitt in Paris, passing on fateful news he had received from Ambassador Anthony Biddle in Warsaw. Bombs were falling on Polish cities; the European war had begun in earnest. Propping himself up on his pillow and lighting a cigarette, the president telephoned his men at State, War, and Navy—Hull and Welles, Woodring, and acting Navy Secretary Charles Edison. Woodring conveyed the news to George Marshall.

Having issued his alerts, the president did something that would have been remarkable for many men in the face of such momentous news but was wholly in character for him. Aware that he could do nothing more at the moment, he went back to sleep. At 6:30 he was awakened again by another call from Bullitt, who reported further momentous news—a talk with the French premier had convinced him that France would fight. Again, displaying remarkable serenity, FDR returned to sleep, only to be roused forty-five minutes later by a call from Ambassador Joseph P. Kennedy, who reported from London that Neville Chamberlain declared himself ready to honor Britain's pledge to Poland. This time there would be no appeasement of Hitler. The frightful prospect of a general European war had left

Kennedy deeply depressed, and after spending a few minutes cheering up his ambassador, the president decided that he had had all the sleep he was going to get, and he rang for his valet.

He had a feeling he had been through it all before, Roosevelt told his Cabinet later in the day. "During the long years of the World War the telephone at my bedside with a direct wire to the Navy Department had time and again brought me other tragic messages in the night—the same rush messages were sent around—the same lights snapped on in the nerve centers of government. I had *in fact* been through it all before. It was *not* strange to me but more like picking up again an interrupted routine." But this time he held the presidency of the United States, and he told the Cabinet that the parallel with 1914–1918 must go no further. "No warlike events" should be allowed "to disturb the peaceful and orderly pursuits of the American people." Americans must refuse to be lured into wartime profiteering and speculation "and thus neglect the task that lies before us—to defend our country and our people."

On this same morning, with dramatically appropriate timing, George Marshall took the oath as chief of staff of the United States Army. Smartly attired in a white Palm Beach suit and flanked by Secretary Woodring, he was sworn in by the adjutant general of the Army. A week later the chief of staff and his wife went up to Uniontown, which he had not visited for many years, for a welcome, as he termed it—a congratulatory homecoming, with a round of visiting topped off by a banquet.

Everything seemed to have changed in the old hometown. The hotel in which the dinner was held occupied what had once been the big cobblestoned courtyard of an old inn Marshall had known as a boy; in the past the inn had been an important stopping point on the old National Turnpike for "all the great of those days who went to the West." Not wishing to make any comments about the war that had broken out in Europe, and having spent a richly retrospective afternoon, Marshall decided that in his remarks to the crowd of four hundred people in the dining room he would offer comparisons between the present-day building and the features of the site as he had known them in boyhood. Picking out a lady in a red evening dress he observed that she was sitting where the old blacksmith's shop had been. Another elegantly dressed lady, seated somewhat farther away, was singled out for special prominence. She, the general told his audience, was sitting where in the old days hogs had been butchered in the fall and where the boys of the town assembled to get the hogs' bladders to use as footballs. Mrs. Marshall, the general recalled, did not seem thrilled at this discussion of bladders; in fact, "she sort of shrank into insignificance." But, undeterred, Marshall went on with his identification of the present in terms of the past.

Aside from the general's regrettable lapse in taste, his wife found the homecoming "memorable and touching." In particular, an editorial in the local newspaper offered what she long thought of as her favorite tribute to her husband. Now he had become chief of staff of the United States Army, the paper said, but "our special welcome is for 'Flicker,' the snub-nosed, freckle-faced red-head who was a natural leader of boydom in the 90's, who coasted on Gilmore's Hill, staged shows in Thompson's stable, and kept things generally astir."

At the dinner Marshall relaxed his self-censorship enough to offer some thoughts more serious than those relating to the blacksmith's shop and the hogs' bladders. Again, as in his address to the West Virginia legionnaires a year earlier, he sounded no trumpets and clothed himself in no glamour. Difficult times lay ahead for the United States, he told his audience, but "I will not trouble you with the perplexities, the problems and requirements for the defense of this country, except to say that the importance of this matter is so great and the cost, unfortunately, is bound to be so high, that all that we do should be planned and executed in a businesslike manner, without emotional hysteria, demagogic speeches, or other unfortunate methods which will befog the issue and might mislead our efforts." Giving no call to battle, he offered something more important—a clear declaration of the way in which he intended to carry out the duties of his new office. The homecoming, although intended as recognition of Marshall's accomplishments—"for almost 40 years," the local paper said, "you have been preparing for the position you now hold"—also marked a beginning. Having refreshed himself with memories, the chief of staff could now pursue his difficult goal of preparing the United States Army—but preparing it for what? Would the army have to fight and, if so, against whom and where? In September 1939 President Roosevelt could offer no answers. No one could.

CHAPTER SIX

SOLDIERS AND CIVILIANS

When George Marshall moved into the chief of staff's office, the United States Army, by most reckonings, ranked seventeenth in the world, numbering some 174,000 men, with an authorized strength of 210,000. "Ineffective," as Marshall said, it was virtually the army of a third-rate power, and its problems were not limited to lack of size. Not organized in units of effective strength but scattered here and there on 130 posts across the country and in American overseas dependencies, the army in its dispositions had changed little from the old Indian-fighting force that had suddenly found itself called on in 1898 to go to war with Spain. "We had no field army," Marshall said simply. Nine infantry divisions existed on paper, but only three were actually organized as such and none could claim even half strength. The one cavalry division likewise fell far short of its authorized size. The armored force consisted merely of one half-strength "mechanized cavalry" brigade, numbering 2,300 men, and a few tank companies assigned to the nonexistent infantry divisions. No larger formations, even corps, existed except on paper. No divisions were actually fit for combat, aside, perhaps, from two in Texas—one infantry, one cavalry—that stood in some degree of readiness, not to fight a European-class army but to repel raids across the Rio Grande by Mexican bandits. The great American Expeditionary Force of 1918 was only a collective dream, so completely had it vanished—except for its unwelcome legacy of twenty-year-old tanks and field guns.

With respect to weapons, the army had inherited various difficulties and limitations. In the first place, as Marshall had explained to legislators in his testimony of February 1939, the

World War matériel had outlived its usefulness, either being literally worn out or having been bypassed by technological developments. Second—particularly during the 1930s—army leaders, seeking to make the most effective use of their very limited funds, had skimped on research and development in favor of buying actual hardware they could put into the hands of troops. Certainly some advances had been made. For one thing, an inventor and designer named John C. Garand had produced a superb semiautomatic rifle, designated by the army the M-1 and destined to replace the veteran bolt-action Springfield. But even in cases in which European armies had served as the testing laboratories, as with the replacement of the famous 75mm field gun by the new and more potent 105mm howitzer, United States leaders had favored only a slow changeover. Marshall himself thriftily opposed quick replacement, since the army had on hand six million rounds of ammunition for the 75s. How could he justify such a waste to the congressmen who wrote the army's checks?

But the U. S. Army suffered from theoretical as well as practical problems. One of its leading strands of thought ran back to the old days on the western frontier, where it had performed as a constabulary force devoted to pushing the Indians ever westward and establishing civic order. In that era, mobility had constituted the army's ideal characteristic and the cavalryman had thus been its ideal type. But the Civil War had come along to contribute an entirely different set of ideas. In this first great modern war, in which industrial production, railroads, and other advances made it possible for combatants to face each other with large and powerfully equipped forces, General U. S. Grant led his army to unconditional victory by applying what one scholar characterized as "relentless, continuous pressure" to the weaker Confederates, taking away their ability to maneuver. Thus the idea of victory through the employment of mass force entered army thinking, to dwell there incompatibly with the constabulary tradition of mobility. In practical terms, this schizoid legacy meant that if the United States should find herself in a land war, the heirs of the lightly armed and fast-moving cavalrymen must contrive a way to win by crushing the enemy with irresistible power.

In most army minds, the experience in France during the World War strengthened the belief in mass force. General Pershing even hoped to use American power to smash a great hole in the German line and achieve a genuine breakthrough, thereby demonstrating the traditional American desire for short and decisive wars (although Pershing, a true product of the constabulary tradition, held the remarkable belief that this breakthrough, if it came, would be led by rifle-toting sharpshooters who were accurate at six hundred yards. "Spirit and aggressiveness," preached the general).

After a great war dominated by defensive firepower, some military philosophers looked for offensive inspiration to such enticing infant factors as aircraft and armor. In the United States the possibility that armor would bring back war of movement was clearly envisioned by Major Adna R. Chaffee, a lean-faced driver of a man who in 1928 commanded a short-lived experimental mechanized force. Another exponent of movement, in lectures and speeches both at Fort Benning and later, was George C. Marshall. But unlike Chaffee and such European thinkers as Heinz Guderian and Charles de Gaulle, Marshall viewed mechanization as affecting war but not revolutionizing it—a view he shared with the chief of staff in the early 1930s, General Douglas MacArthur, who believed that an independent mechanized force would have no value. Army regulations adopted in 1923 had declared that "the mission of the infantry is the general mission of the entire force," with the other arms performing supporting roles. Although these regulations breathed the spirit of Grant, Chaffee conducted his tank experiments in the cavalry tradition, on the light-footed, free-ranging model of Jeb Stuart. In speed and armor, the tanks that would be created for the U.S. Army would reflect this origin.

As Marshall took office in 1939, the infantry, the traditional "queen of battles," was experiencing streamlining of its own. The big American division with its four regiments—a powerful formation created during the World War on Pershing's urging and thoroughly in the Grant tradition—was succumbing to criticism that it was fit for nothing but static warfare; it would not be mobile enough to be effective in the initial wartime period of movement and maneuver. (Where U.S. forces would find themselves involved in a war in its first stages remained an unanswered question.) One of the most influential of the critics was Brigadier General Lesley J. McNair, Marshall's old roommate on the transatlantic trip in 1917. McNair favored abolishing the brigade level of command and dropping one of the regiments, thereby converting the "square" division into the "triangular" division. Could these new formations succeed in blending the mobility they sought with the power they must have in order to apply irresistible pressure to the enemy? The question would have to be answered by McNair—a small, wiry man with a personality of "extreme firmness," as Marshall put it—to whom the chief of staff soon entrusted the design of the army ground forces.

In late September the Marshalls moved into the chief of staff's official residence, Quarters One at Fort Myer—a roomy red-brick house utterly lacking in architectural distinction but comfortable nevertheless. The general and his wife were shown through the house by the post commander at Fort Myer, Colonel George S. Patton, Jr. The Marshalls found their new home much to their liking, particularly an upstairs sun porch that overlooked the garden and, in the distance, presented a view of the Capitol. This quiet spot immediately became the couple's refuge.

The versatile and brilliant Patton, whom Mrs. Marshall had not known before, soon became a great favorite. Marshall thought him an extraordinary character. "He would say outrageous things and then look at you to see how it registered." He would "curse and then write a hymn." Stepdaughter Molly, who still lived at home, took to the post commander, finding him very amusing—not only his conversation but some actions not intended to be funny; in many ways, Patton "was like a little boy." Molly, who was Marshall's favorite riding companion, would be especially amused when she and the general would arrive at the stables to see, most mornings, Patton waiting there, mounted and ready to ride. But, ignoring the colonel, Marshall would turn to Molly, saying, "Come on, let's get out," and away the two would go, leaving Patton sitting at the stable. "He was always trying to be with General Marshall, but he never once was invited to join in the morning ride."

In handling Patton this way, Marshall was not merely poking a bit of fun at his subordinate for his "little boy" demeanor. The chief's refusal to invite Patton along bore a relationship to his conscious overall plan for the day. When not in the office or otherwise performing some official function, General Marshall wished as much as possible to spend time with his wife, who "satisfied a whole area of need"; she was his constant companion and certainly his principal and almost exclusive confidante.

Although, like everyone else, he had married for a variety of reasons, he seemed, far more than most men, to place supreme value on companionship. He did not join men's groups, as he had said to Pershing after Lily's death, and he seemed to feel a need to balance his essentially masculine daytime company with that of women before and after hours. Since Mrs. Marshall did not favor early-morning rides, Molly served as a welcome surrogate.

Always "very good with young people" and always fond of them, Marshall had quickly established close ties with Mrs. Marshall's children, particularly Molly and Allen, the younger son; Clifton, the older boy, remained more reserved. Initially Allen, as a twelve-year-old, had felt some doubts about his mother's involvement with this new man. On hearing that she had invited Colonel Marshall to pay a visit to the family summer place at Fire Island, New York, Allen had suggested that "we're happy enough as we are." But, on thinking it over, he had come forward with the sort of half-funny, half-touching gesture with which youngsters will often surprise adults. After Marshall arrived for his visit, he told Katherine the boy had written him a letter saying, "I hope you will come to Fire Island. Don't be nervous, it is OK with me." As his complimentary close, Allen added, unforgettably, "A friend in need is a friend indeed." General Marshall "was crazy about Allen," Molly said, "and Allen was crazy about him too."

When it became clear that Marshall would soon become a member of the family, the children held a council to discuss an important subject: What should they call their stepfather? After some debate one of them suggested "Colonel," and the motion carried unanimously; when Marshall was informed of the decision, he approved it immediately. With children, as in the early days of his friendship with Rose Page, Marshall would often tend to be indulgent but with a sort of grave gaiety; now, however, at home with his new family, he could simply relax and thoroughly enjoy them. For him, the need to relax provided one of the prime reasons for having such a home. It was where one took one's ease and recharged one's batteries and from which one returned refreshed to the military world.

Marshall shared with Franklin Roosevelt a liking for anecdotes, both men preferring to be on the giving end of them; for each, storytelling constituted a favorite form of relaxation. The doings of Maine lobstermen and old Hyde Park retainers provided FDR's favorite material; Marshall liked to talk about his early life in the army, particularly his days in the Philippines. In fact, like Roosevelt he was a great talker, and at the dinner table, as Molly put it, "he controlled the conversation." Normally, whether in the office or at home, he spoke in a quiet voice with a pleasant, rather gentle tone.

Essentially a perfectionist, Marshall did not interfere with the children's activities but proceeded on the presumption that their undertakings would "come out right"; whatever they did, they would do well—he did not hang over anybody's shoulder to make sure—and he showed pleasure when they succeeded. "When you had done something dreadful, he would look at you, and you knew you were wrong. But if you were in trouble and you came to him, he would help you solve the problem, whatever it was."

With just a few minor adjustments, Marshall's way at home reflected his leadership style as he had perfected it through the years. Letting his expectations be known, quietly and without fuss, lay at the heart of it. Once, in a situation that arose when he was commander at Vancouver Barracks, he had made a remarkable use of this technique. At a time when the troops at Vancouver were preparing to go to Fort Lewis, Washington, for training, the guardhouse held about seventy prisoners, not members of Marshall's command but deserters who had been picked up in the Portland area. The post adjutant submitted to Marshall a list of the names of twenty soldiers who he thought should remain behind as guards for the troublesome men in the stockade. "The general deleted the whole twenty and left me only two old sergeants to care for these seventy prisoners," the adjutant recalled. Assuring the skeptical officer that the men would cause no trouble, Marshall went to the guardhouse and spoke to the prisoners, not at great length, simply telling them what was to happen and making it plain that he trusted them. "During that summer," the adjutant said in admiration, "not one man ran away and all did their jobs under the planning and supervision of the two sergeants. They caused no trouble at all."

As one of Marshall's officers said, "he listened and had all the essential facts before him before he drew any conclusion or announced any decision. He was a gentleman of the old school." Because of this, "people were at ease in his company. He did not talk down to anyone. He never tried to impress his listener. His subordinates were made to feel that they had a fair hearing of their case and that proper action would be taken. This inspired confidence." Leadership is hard to define. One could speak of it at length, as Socrates did of justice, and likewise never offer a concise definition. But it can make itself felt unmistakably.

On November 29, 1939, the American Export liner *Excalibur,* bringing a number of Americans home from warring Europe, docked at Jersey City. Among the disembarking passengers was a well-turned-out figure with a neat military mustache, Major Percy Black, the acting military attaché at the American embassy in Berlin, who had returned to the United States to make a confidential report to the State Department on conditions in Germany. Major Black chatted with the press on his arrival. He had a great many interesting matters to talk about, since he had accompanied the German Army during part of the blitzkrieg in Poland and had seen its operations on the outskirts of Warsaw. The Poles, he said, had been demoralized, and German soldiers had rounded up women and children and fed them in soup kitchens, and, he added, "I do not believe any of the atrocity stories." His own treatment by the Germans and that of other Americans he knew, he declared, had been uniformly friendly.

Speaking more generally, Major Black said that in his opinion reports of internal dissension in Germany were largely exaggerated. "Remember, any people who go to war feel their cause is just and that they are being attacked. The German people from the top to the bottom are more afraid of another Treaty of Versailles than of anything else, and they feel that if they let themselves be beaten it will be the end of Germany." The morale of the German people was "as good as could be expected."

Hearing of Major Black's arrival, Adna Chaffee, now a brigadier general, showed immediate interest. Since the major had accompanied the German Army in Poland, said Chaffee, he obviously had enjoyed "an exceptional opportunity to view the usage of the German mobile mechanization." Here was somebody surely worth hearing, a man who had seen at first hand armies using tank power to win victories Chaffee had foreseen in the 1920s, when he had been dismissed by many of his fellow officers as an impractical dreamer. Now serving as commander of the 7th Cavalry Brigade, Mechanized, at Fort Knox, Chaffee wanted General Marshall to send Major Black out to talk to the officers of this small armored force, and "let us draw from him as much professional information as we can."

Appreciating Chaffee's keen specialist interest in the use of armor in battle, Marshall not only gave the idea his immediate approval but expanded it into a proposed tour of seven army installations on which Major Black could share with infantry, cavalry, and other officers his impressions of the German Army in action. Impressive in its power, the blitzkrieg had smashed Poland in just three weeks, although Warsaw had held out several days longer and one pocket of fighters had resisted some days more. Certainly Major Black would have a great deal of "professional information" to pass on to his listeners. But a little more than a week later, the chief of staff informed the eager general at Fort Knox that "it is not advisable to initiate these discussions at the present moment."

What had happened was that a nonmilitary factor—a political consideration—had upset Marshall's plans. As the chief of staff explained to Chaffee in a postscript, some of Major Black's remarks to the press had "produced a violent Jewish reaction" (apparently having been taken as expressing sympathy for Germany) and therefore for the present the army was not "advertising" the major. A regimental or divisional commander could function simply as a soldier and enjoy great success, but a chief of staff had to develop a good measure of political adroitness. Earlier, as a post commander, Marshall had demonstrated a real flair for public relations, as in his management of the Russian fliers at Vancouver. Now, however, he belonged to a team, with all the responsibilities and the limitations such membership carried with it, and this team performed not at army bases tucked away in South Carolina or the Pacific Northwest, but in the eye of the nation, with the press constantly at hand. Like the president, Marshall would have to deal with interest groups of all sorts—ethnic, economic, sectional, ideological. Some of these dealings would of course concern relatively minor matters, such as Major Black's proposed tour, but many would obviously have the greatest significance. And inescapably the most important and demanding of all the interest groups would be the Congress of the United States.

The relationship between the chief of staff and Congress was especially significant in 1939 because of the continuing "holy show," as Harold Ickes called it, between Secretary of War Woodring and Undersecretary Johnson. Whatever the War Department's organizational chart said, Marshall in fact would often have no choice but to act as the independent spokesman to Congress for the War Department. One day Johnson even went so far as to call the new chief of staff down for his refusal to abandon the secretary of war. "You clouded up on me," Johnson charged. "I thought you were for me."

Marshall was having none of this. "Listen, Mr. Secretary," he said. "I was appointed chief of staff and I think you had something to do with it. But Mr. Woodring was secretary of war, and I owed loyalty to him." Marshall sharpened his thrust. "I can't expect loyalty from the Army if I do not give it."

Revealingly, Johnson could not see the point.

Although far from ideal, this situation existed in a context of civil-military relations in the United States that had never reached a plane close to the ideal. The pattern was not of the army's making. In the period before the Civil War, in the time in the life of the army that is justly called preprofessional, civil-military relationships had been fluid; people believed that any competent executive could succeed as a leader of troops. After the great mid–nineteenth-century war, with a general rise of professionalism in the armies of the world, the U.S. Army had increasingly developed its own professional outlook. Like European officers, American officers did their best to stay aloof from political and social fads and trends, and, thanks largely to the relative insignificance of the army in American life, they had an easier time of it than their transatlantic counterparts, who faced such shocks as the Dreyfus affair in France and the post-1918 upheaval in Germany. And where the Germans in the 1920s depended on old Field Marshal von Hindenburg to hold the state together, the American people in the postwar decade acquired no ersatz kaiser but only Calvin Coolidge. Coming late to the World War, the Americans also spared their national psyche the deep wounds inflicted on the British and the French by four agonized years in the blood and slime of the trenches—although the United States went on to experience the same postwar pacifism and disillusionment and even added a distinctive American touch, the rejection not only of war but of the European countries that seemed addicted to it.

As they began to work for greater American preparedness, President Roosevelt and General Marshall had to face homegrown problems woven by the Founding Fathers into the U.S. Constitution. Genuine military professionalism and civilian control of the military—a control generally desired in the United States and generally assumed to exist—both rest on a clear delineation of the two spheres and, as the Prussian military educator and reformer Karl von Clausewitz declares, of the responsibilities that fall to each. But the Constitution, written before the civil-military distinction came into being, divides control of the militia between the federal and the state governments, thus setting up a political role for militia (National Guard) officers and a military role for state governors. It also divides control of the armed forces between the president and Cabinet-level officials, the instrument here being the clause declaring the president "commander-in-chief of the army and navy of the United States." This was the provision on which FDR based his July 7, 1939, Military Order calling for the Joint Board to report directly to him, the effect being to mingle the military in the highest level of government while removing it from departmental direction.

By basing their work on the structure of British government at the time, the framers of the Constitution created a system differing greatly from the cabinet form of government, which combined the executive and the legislature, that took shape in England a generation later. In the guise of "separation of powers" and "checks and balances," the Founding Fathers willed their political and military successors a system characterized by overlapping authority, with the functions relating to foreign policy and war being the exclusive concern of no one part of the government. The House of Representatives was given the power of the purse; the Senate was to confirm appointments and participate in the making of treaties (or at least approve them); the House and the Senate jointly were empowered to declare war and "to raise and support armies"; and the president was to make appointments, to be commander in chief of the armed forces, and make treaties.

Thus the Constitution not only failed to provide for any clear-cut civilian control of the military but also guaranteed that the U.S. government would experience continual internal confrontation, in a tug of war between the Congress and the president with the legislature attempting to expand its own territory and curb the executive, while the president strove for room to maneuver. The chronic tension between Roosevelt and the Senate Foreign Relations Committee offers a perfect example. By setting the branches of government against each other, the

Founding Fathers did a great deal to accomplish one of their prime purposes, the checking of the growth of any arbitrary and abusive power in the state. One retired general has praised them for this achievement by asserting that it enabled them "to create a 'standing army,' the hobgoblin of a century of Anglo-American rhetoric, by taking pains to establish much tighter control over the armed forces than existed in any contemporary European country." In any case, the Founding Fathers created a large, lumbering, inefficient machine, designed not for speed but for safety, and in Congress they established a body whose power far exceeded its responsibility and whose seriousness of purpose would therefore constantly be tempted to yield to the blandishments of frivolity.

Now, in 1939 and 1940, Roosevelt and Marshall would increasingly find themselves forced to deal with the practical effects of these constitutional provisions. How did they influence the work of military preparedness? If the army was supposed to be controlled by civilians, exactly which civilians were they?

One day, as General Marshall sat in a congressional committee hearing, a member remarked to him that he had probably had no dealings of any kind with Congress until he became chief of staff. No, said the general, that was not correct. His relationship with Congress actually went all the way back to his early boyhood, and he therefore could not legitimately be accused of having the sort of purely military mind often deplored by the legislators. On being asked just what his connection with Congress had been, Marshall explained that as a very small boy he, together with a partner, had set up a greenhouse business in an old stable (which they had painted green because they thought the name referred to the color of the house). They had enjoyed a considerable success, producing a tomato praised by seed company executives as the largest they had ever seen. When they learned that congressmen would send their constituents free seeds, the boys decided to branch out, and on their toy typewriter they wrote such a request for their district's representative. Back came a packet of seeds, but "the only trouble," Marshall said, "was they were cotton seeds, which was sort of out of place in Pennsylvania." Never after that, the general told his listeners, had he had any other relationship with his congressman: "The cottonseed experience was enough for me." The listening congressmen were much amused.

General Marshall's rapid development of an effective touch with Congress perhaps did not come as a complete surprise to President Roosevelt. At least, FDR could hope for better results than had sometimes been yielded by the efforts on Capitol Hill of General Craig or Secretary Woodring, both of whom, in one notable session, had seemed to encourage Senate hostility toward Roosevelt's dealings on aircraft with the French. In meetings with Marshall from the autumn of 1938 until his appointment as chief of staff, the president had learned to appreciate the authority with which the general spoke and the conviction his words carried. "The spectacle of General Craig 'protecting' the national security by attacking the Commander-in-Chief," one observer believed, "spurred Roosevelt to form a clear mental picture of the man to take over as Army Chief of Staff"; whatever the new man's other qualities might be, "the role for which Roosevelt had to cast him was that of star witness for the Commander-in-Chief at Congressional investigations."

Marshall himself made a striking point in relation to the public side of his job. He quickly realized that even though war had broken out in Europe, the president still intended to move carefully on preparedness, as his scaling-down of the new authorized size of the army suggested. It was even the case, Marshall said, that "it was very difficult to get action on important military requirements of that day." Some members of the Senate, impatient at FDR's caution, "were very intent on going ahead more rapidly than the administration was willing to do," and they put heavy and continuing pressure on the chief of staff to support them. But Marshall had made a key decision early in the game. So far as possible, he "was going to operate as a member of the team, political and otherwise." He knew he would often be pressed to appeal to the public, but, he said, "I thought it was far more important in the long run that I be well established as a member of the team, and try to do my convincing within that team, rather than to take action publicly contrary to the desires of the president and certain members of Congress." He wanted to make it plain to the president that he would not "run off to a public appeal." Marshall also was aware that he must try to understand the president and his motivations—to read his mind—and he could readily see and sympathize with Roosevelt's feeling that the Middle West was so solidly opposed to him on defense questions that sudden and dramatic moves would only defeat both his immediate military purposes and, with a presidential campaign due in 1940, his longer-range political purposes.

Marshall also studied the president's mind for direct practical reasons. The differences in the styles of the two men could be symbolized by their desks—Roosevelt's with its letters and documents bordered by the clutter of trinkets, Marshall's presenting a polished surface holding only a bare blotter, a nearly empty IN box, a pen holder, and sometimes a pair of steel-rimmed glasses. In dealing with the complexities of the commander in chief, Marshall decided he must make use of imaginative attention-getting devices. A staff officer came away amused and impressed from witnessing the method by which Marshall "explained and sold to the President the various types of army organizations which were being established and trained." Since FDR always declared himself a sailor, Marshall ordered the creation of a visual aid consisting of a large cardboard diagram representing a ship. "Comprising the forward section, or bow, of the ship was the newly designated regular army triangular division. Back of that were two or three square National Guard divisions and at the stern were the service elements to support the forward divisions." By encasing these organizational facts in a nautical container, however unrelated the two subjects may have been, Marshall succeeded in catching FDR's eye.

In November 1939 the chief of staff made sure that the commandant of the Infantry School would take full advantage of a forthcoming presidential visit to awaken FDR's interest in the army's training methods. He made the following "suggestion," Marshall said mildly, proceeding to give thorough orders that no one press Roosevelt "to see this or that or understand this or that; that whatever is furnished him in the way of data be on one sheet of paper, with all high-sounding language eliminated, and with very pertinent paragraphed underlined headings." He observed that "a little sketch of ordinary page size is probably the most effective method, as he is quickly bored by papers, by lengthy discussions, and by anything short of a few pungent sentences of description. You have to intrigue his interest, and then it knows no limit." To Marshall, FDR was a bird of passage who, if not caught at the right moment, would simply soar away. He had not been trained in an army in which careers rose on piles of reports, orders, and endorsements.

For years now Roosevelt had been accustomed to dealing with questions of national and global scope, to acting on a wide range of matters having to do with the life of everyone in the country, to working with persons of great individual influence, and so too, to a large extent, had the secretaries of war and the navy, and men like Harry Hopkins and Henry Morgenthau. Veterans of high-level political life, all were men whom experience had shown the ways through the mazes of Washington. But Marshall, for all his days as General Pershing's aide in the early 1920s, was a newcomer to the highest levels. During the international political and economic storms of the 1930s, his concerns had been focused on the camp and state levels; as a military commander he had put his hand on nothing greater than a brigade; his public speeches had been delivered to local Rotary clubs. In 1937 he had hoped briefly to be given command of the 1st Division—one single division—but actually had felt that, much as he desired the assignment, he lacked sufficient seniority to receive it. And now his selection by the president and the outbreak of a major war had propelled him to the national summit, where he would meet and cope with unlimited new challenges. Now he would have ample opportunity to demonstrate how great a part he would play on the team.

As its first order of business with Congress after the British and French declarations of war on Germany, the administration sought repeal of the president's old bugaboo, the arms embargo. For this purpose Roosevelt called Congress into special session for September 21. Some of the president's advisers, Hull among them, argued for the repeal of the entire Neutrality Act, but one senator countered this notion with the remark that "people would think, if we repealed the whole Neutrality Act, that we were repealing our neutrality." Having no desire to create any such impression, Congress, while voting to allow the sale of arms to belligerents, imposed the "cash and carry" principle, under which purchasers of American war materials would have to carry these goods away in their own ships and would have to pay for them before being allowed to leave. The act became law on November 4, 1939. The vote in the Senate was an impressive 63 to 30, but the new law was full of compromises. Yet "we have definitely taken sides with England and France," wrote the isolationist Senator Arthur Vandenberg in his diary. "There is no longer any camouflage about it." Sadly he added, "What 'suckers' our emotions make of us!" Isolationism was far from dead, but at last FDR had been freed from the clutch of the embargo.

It had not been easy. "I am almost literally walking on eggs," he had said at one point; "having good prospects of the bill going through, I am at the moment saying nothing, seeing nothing and hearing nothing."

Although Marshall took no part in the cash-and-carry debate, he spent a great deal of time on Capitol Hill. Modest as it was, the increase in the size of the army meant that the chief of staff had to go to Congress with a revised budget; if he was to get more men and more munitions right away, he must have more money. Marshall wished to transform the "pathetically incomplete square divisions" into real, functioning triangular divisions, complete with $12 million dollars' worth of new motor transportation. He also wanted to acquire "heavy artillery, engineers, medical regiments, signal battalions, quartermaster truck trains" with the aim of holding genuine, large-scale maneuvers in 1940—the first true corps and army maneuvers in the nation's history.

But events in Europe quickly let Marshall—and Roosevelt—down. After the German destruction of Poland, a great calm seemed to fall on the Continent; "the situation in western Europe was to all intents stabilized. There was a feeling by many that the field fortifications established in France and Belgium furnished ample security to those nations." If that was so, did not requests for building up the armed forces of the United States constitute acts of warmongering? Anyway, asked a congressman from West Virginia, why should the army be enlarged when the European countries were busy fighting each other and had no time to worry about the United States? Marshall brushed the warmongering question aside, assuring the congressmen who held the pursestrings that the War Department and the chief of staff had "an earnest desire, a desperate desire, to keep out of trouble." Besides, the army was not being expanded but was merely being brought up to the authorized strength adopted by Congress in 1920.

As winter unfolded and the "phony war" continued in Europe, any sense of urgency in Washington seemed to ebb. The proposed $853 million budget for the army looked large at the time, but Marshall knew that it did not really meet the army's needs. He made a shrewd point with his staff: "It will react to our advantage if our bill is acted on at the latest possible date. It is probable that events in Europe will develop in such a way as to affect Congressional action." With spring would come the season for military campaigns.

In his determination to build up the army, Marshall made forays into public relations. He spoke to the American Historical Association in December on the topic of military history and why the schools should teach it. But he made the headlines by telling the historians that the army was less than 25 percent ready to fight. Some weeks later, in a radio address urging preparedness, he warned that time was running out for America. Americans nevertheless continued to assume that the Allies would probably win on their own, or that the stalemate might go on indefinitely. Foreseeing a third possibility, some thought the Germans might begin to look like the winners. In that case America would have to bestir herself to give the Allies greatly increased help. But nowhere did one find any sense of urgency. Across the Atlantic, Prime Minister Neville Chamberlain could tell his supporters that he felt ten times as confident of victory as he had at the beginning of the war. By not attempting to overwhelm the unready British and French at the outset, he said, Hitler had certainly "missed the bus."

General Marshall took a more realistic view. On February 23, 1940, he made a striking appearance before the House Appropriations Committee. The touch he had shown with Congress was now developing into an effectiveness that veteran Washington correspondents called unprecedented. Even his accent was helpful, with its basic Uniontown quality softened by the influence of his Kentucky-born parents and by his years at VMI. Although pleasant, it was, as one correspondent observed, "not so mellifluous that it would put up the hackles on a New England senator's neck." Under questioning, the general showed patience and good humor, although he was not given to jokes, and he stuck to his point. When he was warmed up, he spoke so fluently and rapidly that the stenotypists had to struggle to keep up with him. Unlike some of his predecessors, it was said, he "neither barks at congressmen as if they were rookies" nor "condescends to them too obviously." And, as had been the General Staff's peacetime custom for some years, he normally wore civilian clothes, thus helping to allay grass-roots prejudices against brass buttons. (During this same February, Marshall won favorable mention by living up to a prejudice of his own. He refused to appear at a White House reception in the rather baroque uniform designed by General Craig, which featured a wide, gold-fringed sash. Instead, he wore a plain blue army dress uniform that had the effect of making him appear a straightforward military personage amid all the stripes, aiguillettes, and epaulets surrounding him in the East Room.)

The problem was that the United States could not merely wait in the old Minute Man style for some emergency, and then plunge into "a sudden expansion of personnel in such a manner that our small nucleus of trained troops would be fatally diluted." What Marshall sought were definite measures to be taken "step by step to prepare the nation against the possibility of chaotic world conditions." One can almost see the general's forefinger raised as he declared to the listening legislators: "If Europe blazes in the late spring or summer we must put our house in order before the sparks reach the Western Hemisphere."

But, much as they had come to like and respect Marshall as a witness, the congressmen did not approve his requests. Some weeks later, in fact, the appropriation bill became bogged down in both the House and the Senate. Since nobody seemed to be shooting at anybody in Western Europe, the legislators were as complacent as Neville Chamberlain, with the added justification of holding their deliberations three thousand miles from the scene of Marshall's anticipated blaze. On April 3 the House Appropriations Committee chopped 10 percent from the proposed army budget. On April 8 Marshall wrote a friend that he was "involved in infinite possibilities with the Senate in connection with the Army Appropriation bill."

Hardly twenty-four hours later, Adolf Hitler showed that he, too, was involved with infinite possibilities. On April 9 the Germans occupied Denmark and, in a series of lightning moves, seized key ports and airfields in Norway, right under the nose of the Royal Navy, which traditionally regarded the North Sea as its own exclusive domain. Within two weeks the invaders had taken control of southern Norway, and in two weeks more the Allies had been pushed out of the central part of the country. The phony war had ended, but what happened in Scandinavia was merely a light overture. On May 10 the Germans struck in the west, quickly smashing Belgian frontier defenses and setting the stage for a great armored thrust through the Ardennes. Only three days after the campaign opened, Heinz Guderian showed that he was not only a prophet of armored warfare but a driving leader in the field. After his assault troops paddled their way across the Meuse River and put out of action the French pillboxes on the west bank, engineers followed with pontoon bridges, and behind them came columns of panzers which, lashed on by Guderian, reached the English Channel only a week later. The Allied armies were split in two, the British began an evacuation by sea at Dunkirk on May 26, the Belgians surrendered on May 27, and the French First Army capitulated to the invaders on June 1. Scarcely stopping for breath, the Germans then turned south, piercing the French front and taking Paris on June 14. On June 22 the French and the Germans signed an armistice, the meeting being held at Hitler's insistence in the old railroad car in which Marshal Foch had received the envoys of a defeated Germany in 1918. France had vanished overnight as a world power, the British Army had lost almost all of its heavy equipment, and many observers expected the British Isles to be invaded within days or weeks. From his retreat in the Netherlands, the aged ex-kaiser telegraphed Hitler: WHAT A TURN OF EVENTS BROUGHT ABOUT BY DIVINE DISPENSATION.

To the Western world, the turn of events that thrilled the old kaiser was horrible and incredible. The army of the French *poilu*—the man *Life* magazine called the world's best soldier—had been destroyed in a campaign lasting less than six weeks. Few American observers had realized that the French Army represented an illusion, like a fortress in Hollywood with nothing behind the façade, or that if Germany and Russia continued their "friendship," the democratic countries had no chance of defeating them. A fourth alternative outcome of the war suddenly loomed up, frightening and previously unimagined—that, as two reporters wrote, "German victory, sweeping and decisive enough to change the whole face of the world we live in, may be at hand *before this country is ready* to increase its aid to the Allies."

Europe had blazed, sending out far greater showers of sparks than anyone had dreamed possible.

CHAPTER SEVEN

"FORCES OF DESTRUCTION"

Fed by dramatic and frightening reports of German victories, a fire was racing across the United States. How deep the new attitudes went had yet to be seen, but evidence for a profound change could be found everywhere. A man in Clarksville, Tennessee, observed that "for the first time in many years people in this little town are no longer finding arguments for Germany's aggressions"; no longer were they saying, "Well, Britain and France brought it on themselves. That Treaty of Versailles . . ." Arguing that the United States ought to supply the Allied air forces with thousands of planes, a woman in Lincoln, Massachusetts, said, "Whether we like Allied policies or not, it is necessary for the U.S. to recognize its stake in an Allied victory." If "we do not help stop the drive now, we shall be fighting Hitler for 20 years." Similar sentiments came from a man in Saco, Maine: "The U.S. should do something besides 'holler' for peace." With a touching faith in the eighteenth-century way of war, three hundred sharpshooters of the Illinois Skeet Association and kindred clubs formed the Sportsmen's Defense Reserve. The California legislature rushed through a plan to set up Citizen Guards, modeled after the famous Swiss Home Guards. As shooting clubs began popping up all over the map, the National League of Mothers of America joined in by organizing in New York the Molly Pitcher Rifle Legion, pledged to target practice once a week.

Congress shared the excitement. The legislators were ready to provide all the money needed for national defense, a senator assured Hap Arnold: "All you have to do is ask for it." But confronted by this proffered bounty, the army reacted like a starving castaway sailor suddenly surrounded by a bevy of eager native beauties; its machinery proved unequal to the challenge. The changes in the public and congressional moods had outpaced the General Staff's administrative capacities. And no one seemed slower to realize the intensity of the change than the old master of public opinion in the White House. On May 13, three days after the German cataract of fire and steel had roared into the Low Countries, Marshall and a new ally, Secretary of the Treasury Morgenthau, met with FDR with the aim of obtaining his support for still more money for the army than had been sought in April. Others present at that session were Harold Smith, the keen-minded director of the budget, and the two-headed civilian leadership of the War Department, Secretary Woodring and Assistant Secretary Johnson. Marshall, to his displeasure, realized that the president, "it was quite evident, was not desirous of seeing us." Something else that could hardly have been pleasing was the disarray in the War Department's presentation, with Woodring sitting on his hands while Marshall and Johnson contradicted each other on various points.

Since FDR did not wish to talk about anyone's returning to Congress hat in hand, he put into play a favorite Roosevelt tactic of dominating the conversation; "all of it for a long time was between the President and Mr. Morgenthau, and he was getting very little chance to state his case." The talk, in fact, turned a bit rough, with FDR riding his Dutchess County friend and neighbor; Marshall assumed that "the President was staging this rather drastic handling of Mr. Morgenthau for my benefit." In effect, Roosevelt belittled Morgenthau, suggesting that in supporting Marshall's requests the secretary was out of his depth.

Finally Morgenthau said, "Mr. President, will you hear General Marshall?"

"Well, I know exactly what he would say," FDR replied. "There is no necessity for me to hear him at all."

Roosevelt may have been making a sort of joke of it, but Marshall felt in no mood for games. "It was a desperate situation," one that was "catastrophic in its possibilities." Thus, reminding himself that "a man has a great advantage, psychologically, when he stands looking down on a fellow," Marshall, as he admitted, "took advantage, in a sense, of the President's condition." Advancing to the desk, he said earnestly, "Mr. President, may I have three minutes?"

Immediately FDR dropped his contentious manner, saying in his most gracious way, "Of course, General Marshall."

Twenty-three years magically fell away, and the fiery Major Marshall who had torn into General Pershing long ago in France now stood before this even more illustrious chief, venting in a passionate flood of words his needs and worries, his fears about the organization of the American defense effort, his requirements in weapons and equipment. "You've got to do something," he said, "and you've got to do it today!"

Morgenthau had earlier told Marshall to speak his piece to FDR when he got the chance, because the president actually liked frank talk, and the secretary was pleased that his advice had been taken so literally; the general "stood right up to the President," the result being that FDR asked him to come back the next day with a list of specific requirements. When he returned the following day, Marshall brought not only information but the draft of a presidential message to Congress, and after some presidential whittling had been applied to the estimates, FDR appeared before a joint session on May 16 to ask for 896 million additional dollars and, as if casting his budgetary caution aside, to declare that "this nation should plan at this time a program that would provide us with 50,000 military and naval planes" and the ability to turn out fifty thousand a year. Fifty thousand planes a year! The president's words drew cheers from his audience.

On May 26, in his first fireside chat in many months, FDR spoke of the existing strength of the army and the navy and of his resolve to build up national defense "at this moment of sadness throughout most of the world," when "those who would not admit the possibility of the approaching storm" could no longer cling to the illusion that "we are remote and isolated and, therefore, secure against the dangers from which no other land is free." But despite these dangers, he assured his listeners, he was not abandoning the kinds of goals for which the New Deal stood: "There is nothing in our present emergency to justify a retreat from any of our social objectives—from conservation of natural resources, assistance to agriculture, housing, and help to the underprivileged."

After delivering this speech, the president was driven to the Washington Navy Yard, where he boarded the yacht *Potomac* for a cruise down the river. As always, he was sleeping well even during this time when the world was "threatened by forces of destruction"—six or seven hours a night—but being aboard any boat had an especially soothing effect. He slept until eleven o'clock the next morning and at noon returned refreshed to the White House. He had been looking tired, observers had noted, with dark shadows under his eyes and two deep seams cutting into his face from his nose down past his mouth. Yet, as he sat at his cluttered desk, he impressed visitors with his air of total confidence. He averaged fifteen callers a day, dictated fifteen or twenty letters, scanned endless memos, reports, and documents. He studied his beloved maps, in this grim spring discussing minute details of battlefield topography with his military advisers; as the Germans slashed through Flanders, FDR discoursed on towns, bridges, and even minor creeks.

His day began around 8:30 with breakfast in bed, a session with a variety of newspapers, and a chat with Steve Early, his press secretary, about the day's expected events. To this standard program he now added a look at overseas cables that had come in during the night and, frequently, held talks with State Department officials. The party was often joined by Harry Hopkins, still secretary of commerce but also receiving presidential training in international affairs. Around ten o'clock FDR's valet would help him into his little armless wooden wheelchair and push him to the elevator for the beginning of his official day. Bells would ring to alert the staff to his approach. Once in his office, after making a deft transition from the wheelchair to the seat behind his desk, he would look up to see Grace Tully popping in for a quick good morning and a chat, often enlivened by such Rooseveltian remarks as "Have you seen so-and-so lately? She's as big as a house" or "Eleanor had a lot of do-gooders for dinner and you know what that means." And during his appointments, crisis or no, persons in the outer office would often hear bursts of lusty Rooseveltian laughter. His innate cheerfulness stayed with him. He still enjoyed his work, doing the job that even in easier days had worn down many of his predecessors; and to one observer he seemed to wear his crushing responsibilities in this apocalyptic time "as familiarly, as easily as his speckly seersucker suit, buttoned into thick wrinkles over his paunch."

At the end of May, the chief of staff foresaw an army of 500,000 men by July 1, 1941, of 1 million by January 1942, and of 1.5 million by July 1942. For the present, Marshall thought the most the army could handle would be 335,000, but the new appropriation, which had sailed through both houses of Congress almost like the New Deal emergency legislation in 1933, provided for fewer men. Marshall sought Roosevelt's support in once more going back to Capitol Hill; FDR, who like many army officers seemed to have problems in accepting congressional bounty, declined.

"I just sent a message to Congress three weeks ago," he said to Marshall. "What will they think of me?"

"Well, Mr. President," the chief of staff answered, "the world has changed since three weeks ago."

Despite his refusal to seek more money for the army, FDR cheerfully allowed Marshall to conduct Capitol Hill operations on his own. In doing so, Roosevelt acted in harmony with a suggestion from Henry Morgenthau, who told him: "Let General Marshall, and only General Marshall, do all the testifying" on army appropriations.

Unfortunately, "some fool," as Marshall called him, made in public the same point as Morgenthau's: The bill would go through if FDR would leave it in Marshall's hands. This was true, the general agreed, and for three reasons: "In the first place, they were certain I had no ulterior motives. In the next place, they had begun to trust my judgment. But most important of all, if Republicans could assure their constituency that they were doing it on my suggestion and not on Mr. Roosevelt's suggestion, they could go ahead and back the thing. He had such enemies that otherwise the members of Congress didn't dare seem to line up with him. And that was true of certain Democrats who were getting pretty bitter."

Although Roosevelt was hardly pleased at the observation made by "some fool," he did not allow any resentment to affect his use of Marshall. His chief Senate spokesman on foreign affairs, Key Pittman, remained only a flyswatter, but now, clearly, in the swelling realm of defense and defense-related policy, Roosevelt at last had acquired a Sledgehammer that could deliver the needed blows. And, a most unusual instrument, it was capable of swinging itself. It also had quickly revealed another important quality.

One day Marshall brought home to Fort Myer for lunch a civilian lawyer, a prominent citizen who had long been active in military affairs. Midway through the meal the guest, a worldly and sophisticated man, dropped his fork, and as Marshall rang for the steward the guest said, "General, you must excuse my awkwardness. I'm all too well aware that I am lunching today with the man who has more influence in the federal city than any man except the President of the United States. That's why I am ill at ease."

General Marshall, with his dread of seeming to seek or enjoy prominence, was not at all pleased. He said stiffly, "I don't know what you are talking about."

The guest hurried to explain that at a recent dinner party the Speaker of the House, Sam Rayburn, had told him that he ought to make a point of getting to know the chief of staff. "Of all the men who ever testified before any committee on which I served," Rayburn said, "there is no one of them who has the influence with a committee of the House that General Marshall has." On being asked why, the Speaker said, "It is because when he takes the witness stand, we forget whether we are Republicans or Democrats. We just remember that we are in the presence of a man who is telling the truth, as he sees it, about the problems he is discussing."

There was more. One day, lunching at the White House, Speaker Rayburn had made the same point to the president, and FDR had answered, "Sam, you don't admire General Marshall any more than I do. I'm not always able to approve his recommendations; history may prove me wrong. But when I disapprove his recommendations, I don't have to look over my shoulder to see which way he's going, whether he's going to the Capitol, to lobby against me, or whether he's going back to the War Department. I *know* he's going back to the War Department, to give me the most loyal support as chief of staff that any President could wish."

The guest concluded, "General, you're the only man in the federal city of whom these things could be said by two such witnesses."

Marshall seemed "less offended" then, saying, "The President and Mr. Rayburn are much too generous, and so are you."

The chief of staff had already given Washingtonians ample demonstration that for him, as a management specialist would later say with high approval, leadership offered "responsibility rather than rank and privilege." Marshall's refusal in 1938 to hunt for headlines had come from deeper causes than simply the fear of hurting his chances to become chief of staff. The look he took one day into the career of an obscure Lieutenant Jones makes clear his basic feeling. In requesting the adjutant general to check on Jones, Marshall said of the lieutenant that "he has asked for nothing, as a matter of fact, he is conspicuous in my mind because he does not want anything. But he came to my attention from his outstandingly efficient work in another camp, and I am always on the lookout for the real performers who are self-effacing."

In a small but important incident with Major Walter Bedell Smith, the secretary of the General Staff, Marshall showed two other aspects of the kind of leadership he sought to exemplify. One day Smith interrupted a conference in the chief of staff's office ("which was his privilege") to say that a visitor had just shown him drawings of what looked to be a most promising small vehicle. In his attempts to induce the army to test it, the caller, who represented the Bantam Motor Car Company, had been bounced from one office to another—"from the Quartermaster Corps, from the Field Artillery, regarding which he had been very hopeful, and from the Air Corps." Finally the secretary's office had sent the desperate man to Smith's office.

"Well," Marshall said, after making sure that Smith had checked the plans thoroughly, "what did you think of it?"

"I think he has a find," Smith said.

"That's enough for me," Marshall said. "Order one."

Smith answered that for a test the army would need at least fifteen of the cars. Could he find the money? Marshall asked. Smith said he thought so.

"Do it!"

Smith left but returned in a few minutes.

"What's the trouble now, Smith?" Marshall asked.

One of Marshall's old boys from Fort Benning, Smith was brusque and outspoken with the mighty and the powerless alike. "Well," he said, "that's the first damn time we've been able to get anything for this fellow in the whole War Department, and I think it's worthy of special comment."

Marshall's decisive response to Smith's request did not immediately translate itself into action, since the first proposals to test the vehicles encountered a not-unprecedented military resistance to technical change. Certainly these little cars—eleven feet long, fifty-six inches wide, forty inches high, with a four-cylinder, sixty-horsepower motor—resembled none of the existing army vehicles. To those who raised objections, Smith pointed out that the test was mandatory because the order had come from the chief of staff. So began the career of the highly mobile, multipurpose combat vehicle that soon became known as the jeep.

During the summer of 1940, Marshall did not believe that he had yet won the president's full confidence, although he felt at perfect liberty one day to counter FDR's chronic preference for the navy by making a mild joke: He wished the president "would not speak of the Navy as 'us' and the Army as 'they.'" Actually, Marshall saw no problem in their relationship, but believed that Roosevelt had chosen him on the recommendations of other persons and after a single year could hardly have had time to understand him and his methods. The Sam Rayburn anecdotes offered strong evidence that Marshall stood on firmer ground than he thought. Essentially Marshall, like Roosevelt, possessed a high degree of self-confidence. Natural enough in Roosevelt, the trait was remarkable in Marshall. FDR had grown up on the Hyde Park estate as the son of elite and devoted parents (his much older half brother playing in every way the role of an uncle). As a student of family patterns has observed, such a child is used to being the pride and joy of two adults. "He is used to winning acclaim, arousing sympathy, concern, sorrow, and the like, and getting all possible support on a moment's notice"—an upbringing that, in his career, tends to make him believe that he should be "the center of his peers' and his superiors' attention." He may even nourish somewhere inside himself the idea that "his entire work situation has been arranged so that he may display his talents." Supplementing young Franklin's family picture was the fact that his playmates frequently were not his social equals but the children of persons employed on the estate; although he may not have known why, he found it necessary to direct their play. "If I didn't give the orders," he explained to his mother, "nothing would happen!" A further factor relating to the influence of FDR's mother on his career is indicated by a psychological (though hardly literary) study showing that the best predictor of "achievement behavior" in men is "the mother's almost excessive concern with the boy's achievement, and her constant encouragement of his mastery behavior."

As a youngest child reared amid some economic uncertainties, Marshall met an enormous challenge in building himself into a leader—literally making himself respond more like a firstborn or an only child. And the personality he constructed, beginning when he overheard his brother Stuart's contemptuous remark to their mother, proved sturdy and durable. George Marshall quickly became as authoritative a figure in Washington as he had ever been at an army post in Georgia or a CCC camp in Oregon. In this respect the very different superficial styles of Roosevelt and Marshall cloaked two identical men. But during the difficult time with Congress in the early spring, Marshall had felt doubts about his effectiveness. For help in dealing with the problem, he had turned to Bernard Baruch, the eminent Wall Street speculator who had served as Woodrow Wilson's economic chief in the World War when Marshall was merely a young officer in the AEF. Marshall "sent for Baruch and said if he wanted to do something, here was a job."

For his part, Baruch, eager to be involved again in great affairs, had been courting the chief of staff. Marshall had already made adroit use of the older man's proffered services, having sent him in April the plan of a much-desired Alaskan air base with the suggestion that "if the opportunity presents itself I believe it would be very helpful if you could say a word to the President in support of this proposition. His active interest is of far more importance to us in getting results than that of men on the Hill." Then Marshall had told Baruch that he "wanted money in large amounts, a change in the attitude of Senate committees toward the war effort." Working through Senator James F. Byrnes, whom Marshall liked, Baruch "the next night" held a session with a group of senators. He began by outlining the weaknesses of the U.S. defense program, but then the "usually contained" Marshall interrupted him. "Let me take over, Baruch," he said, and with fervor and eloquence he spoke for several hours, concluding at two or three o'clock in the morning by saying that he felt culpable. "My job as chief of staff is to convince you of our needs and I have utterly failed." He told the group, "I don't know what to do."

"Yes, you do," answered the chairman of the Appropriations Committee, Senator Alva Adams of Colorado, previously a critic of preparedness. "You come before the committee without even a piece of paper and you'll get every goddamned thing you want."

Baruch regarded the meeting as a turning point, and on April 22 he wrote with satisfaction to Marshall: "I presume everything is all set now. I received word which leads me to believe that you got everything you asked for." The old speculator added a shrewd if commaless suggestion: "If there is anything more you need you had better get it now because the going is awful good and if you have not got a well-rounded program you are going to get badly blamed."

Marshall hardly needed the advice, but he did fall in with Senator Adams's suggestion. Discovering that it was "a good idea," he had returned to the Appropriations Committee "without a piece of paper" and "got what I wanted." Baruch he viewed with a touch of condescension—"He wanted to get in with me," the general said—but he continued to make careful use of the influential older man and his connections, handling him much as a senator or congressman deals with a well-connected constituent, replying fully to his letters, passing on information "for your eyes alone," arranging entertaining visits to army posts, patiently enduring such obvious suggestions from Baruch as that production of airplanes and production of armaments for those planes ought to be coordinated. Baruch's well-known tender ego received deft massaging from Marshall. Replying to one series of suggestions, the chief of staff reported that not only had he gone over them himself, very carefully, but he had "had them studied by a particularly able officer of the Staff." If a man like Baruch had influence, Marshall would make full political use of it.

One day in late June FDR put on a dazzling political demonstration of his own. For some time he had been playing with the idea of creating a sort of coalition cabinet, although such a device would possess more symbolic value than real meaning under the American system of government, in which no such concept as Cabinet responsibility exists. FDR had fixed his eye on two eminent Republicans—Henry L. Stimson, a veteran statesman who had served as Herbert Hoover's secretary of state and two decades earlier as William Howard Taft's secretary of war, and Frank Knox, publisher of the *Chicago Daily News* and vice-presidential candidate in 1936.

The president must not overlook one important consideration, said one of his aides: Stimson would no doubt want the freedom to choose his own assistant secretary. Thus, as Harry Woodring departed from the scene, along with him would go his fierce antagonist, FDR's faithful Louis Johnson, who had awakened every morning for the past three years in the hope that this would be the day he would become secretary of war. Agreeing with his aide, FDR promptly telephoned Stimson, who was astonished by the invitation, partly because he was almost seventy-three years old. But the two men reached a quick understanding, and thus, for the second time in his life, the chief civilian post in the War Department came to a man who had begun his professional career as a clerk in Elihu Root's law firm as long ago as 1891, who had always tried to model himself on Root's example of "rectitude, wisdom, and constructive sagacity," and whose friendship with the great reformer had first aroused his own interest in the army and the War Department. Had Root's long life been extended by only three years, he himself could have witnessed this act of almost dynastic succession.

In his conversation with Stimson, Roosevelt—not surprisingly—brought up no political aspects of the appointment, and Stimson presumed that politics was not a relevant consideration. But politically Roosevelt had managed to deliver a thrust to the heart of the Republican corpus. Knox also having agreed to serve, the two appointments were announced on June 20, only four days before the opening of the Republican national convention. Now, it seemed to some GOP leaders, two of the most outstanding Republicans had deserted the party by agreeing to serve under the archenemy of Republicanism; the GOP chairman took it on himself to expel Stimson and Knox from the party. This irate and self-defeating reaction could hardly have surprised the subtle Roosevelt, who had pulled off a coup highly satisfactory from every point of view; in both content and timing it was perfect.

Winston Churchill had never doubted where Britain's salvation lay. On May 15, five days after succeeding Neville Chamberlain as prime minister, he had sent off to Washington a message in which, after warning Roosevelt that "the voice and force of the United States may count for nothing if they are withheld too long," he presented the president with requests for "several hundred of the latest types of aircraft," for antiaircraft equipment, for steel and other raw materials, and, notably, for "the loan of forty or fifty of your older destroyers." Aside from the destroyers, the requested supplies fell, from the American point of view, into two groups—those that could reasonably be regarded as surplus and thus readily available for sale, and those that were essential to the defense of the United States.

On May 21 General Marshall ordered the chief of ordnance,

Major General Charles M. Wesson, to draw up a list of the matériel that could be sold. (This same General Wesson had recently startled observers who already doubted the army's state of mental preparedness for modern war by declaring of the country's great defense needs that the figures ought to be "emblazoned on the sides of the Flatiron Building," a twenty-one-story structure in New York that as a symbol of bigness had been out of date for several decades.) The list came back from Wesson the next day and was checked by the president, who ordered the chief of staff to stretch the definition of surplus as much as possible and also to seek other legal means of releasing equipment to the Allies. Marshall assented, as far as such items as .30-caliber ammunition were concerned, but he regarded aircraft as a very different matter: Airplanes could in no sense be called surplus. As he told Sumner Welles and Henry Morgenthau, the army had to be sure of keeping enough planes to train its new pilots, 220 of whom were now being turned out every month, and to fill out its operating units. The loss of just a hundred planes, Marshall said, would create a six-month delay in the pilot-training program.

The crux of the matter was that while preparedness was, all in all, a cause being lifted by a rising tide in Congress, the other side of Roosevelt's military policy—aid to Britain—had to struggle to stay afloat in quite different waters; in fact, the more desperate Britain's situation appeared, the less many legislators, and military professionals as well, wished to send her any of the scanty stock of American aircraft and other weapons. On June 17, after the Battle of France had been lost, Major General George V. Strong, the brusque cavalryman who was serving as head of War Plans, recommended to the chief of staff that the United States make no further commitments about matériel, in "recognition of the early defeat of the Allies." If a healthy person did not have enough food to support himself, would it not be criminal folly to weaken himself further by sharing his limited rations with somebody clearly moribund? What really constituted the best American defense?

For Marshall, such concerns represented a long step into a new dimension. Like other American officers, he had spent his professional life in an institution that, except during the World War, had held little interest for the public at large. When people thought of the army, they had done so at best with indifference and often with scorn. Since the army had few supporters, aside from suppliers who did business with the posts scattered across the United States, Congress had always found military appropriations to be defenseless against budgetary attack. Marshall and his fellow officers had endured their often marginal existence, knowing that if real trouble came—as many expected—their service during the long lean years would find its reward; the army would no longer have to live as the national stepchild. Now, in these late spring days of 1940, that foreseen trouble had arisen. Suddenly the desperately needed funds were becoming available. Here at last, it seemed, the professionals had the opportunity to build up the modern balanced force they had dreamed of—a new army with tanks and aircraft, well supplied with equipment and logistically sound. But now, with real progress at hand, Marshall felt himself being pressed to give away his new assets before he could even get them to the bank. Actually, these assets still amounted to little more than promissory notes; as Marshall said in a speech on May 27, "the public indifference of the past to our national defense requirements is a matter of fact which we are powerless to alter, and we must accept the resultant situation as our base of departure to remedy our deficiencies."

The national cupboard still sat almost bare and the British cried for sustenance. How should the chief of staff respond? His duty was to the United States, not to Great Britain. Since military men are "by tradition and training xenophobic, patriots rather than internationalists," Marshall found himself in a difficult spot; if not literally xenophobic, he as a professional soldier was sworn to think in nationalistic terms. No one could know Britain's fate, but everyone knew for whose army the Congress of the United States had made its appropriations. Secretary Woodring thought that the army could not legally sell *any* military property, and many of Marshall's subordinates felt that in any case they had none to spare.

But Marshall had another side, one that had been noted years earlier by Major General Fox Conner, an urbane Mississippian who had always been considered "one of the smartest men in the Army," and who except for the accident of age might well have become chief of staff. In the early 1920s Conner had already decided that the deficiencies of the Treaty of Versailles would inevitably lead to another great war in twenty years or less. The Americans would find themselves caught up in it, he told a young subordinate, Major Dwight D. Eisenhower, whom he advised to prepare himself to take part in a war fought with allies. The best way to do that, Conner said, would be to serve under George C. Marshall, who "knows more about the techniques of arranging allied commands than any man I know. He is nothing short of a genius." Marshall would be a leader who could "overcome nationalistic considerations in the conduct of campaigns."

Now Marshall was being powerfully asked, by the president and others, not necessarily to overcome nationalistic considerations but to take a broad view of them. The chief of staff saw the two sides clearly. "It is a military consideration to us that the Allies succeed in stopping this flood," he conceded to Morgenthau; on the other hand, "we have got to weigh the hazards in this hemisphere of one thing and another." Concerned about the British, Marshall, together with Roosevelt's civilian advisers, had to decide whether even old Enfield rifles and World War field pieces could lawfully be sent to a belligerent. Marshall's conscience was literally involved in the dilemma in two ways: Could the transfers be made legally? Could the army spare the matériel? In the case of the old World War guns, Welles, Morgenthau, and others worked out a formula whereby Marshall would certify them as surplus and they would then be sold to American companies that would hand them over to British purchasing agents, strictly "cash and carry."

Where he thought it justified, Marshall showed himself completely cooperative. He could also be imaginative, as Morgenthau assured Arthur Purvis, the able and versatile Scotsman who directed the British purchasing mission in Washington; if there was a way to get something done, the chief of staff would find it. In China, Morgenthau said, Marshall had once wanted to hire instructors to teach his men Chinese, but had no money to pay them; the only item of any value his outfit possessed was manure from the stables. He therefore advertised the manure for sale, but stipulated that the purchaser must provide "services"—the services being the teaching of Chinese. The plan to swap manure for language instruction, Morgenthau said, had proved quite successful.

"You are very reassuring," murmured Purvis—drily, no doubt.

But when Roosevelt and Morgenthau agreed to give the British twelve of the earlier-model B-17s, Marshall pointed out in a memo that the air force possessed just fifty-two B-17s, with only *two* scheduled for delivery during the summer, and that if the twelve B-17s were transferred to Britain, they could not be replaced before December. Adducing supporting reasons for his objection, the chief of staff declared that "it would be seriously prejudicial to our own defensive situation to release any of these ships." The president bowed to Marshall's wishes.

Then there was the matter of the destroyers. One reason FDR had decided to "lay off on the four-engine bombers" was his fear that a debate over the airplanes would increase the opposition to sending destroyers to Britain. Originally the president had told Churchill that such a transfer would require the approval of Congress and that, as Churchill put it, the moment was not opportune. But on June 11 the prime minister renewed his request. As their rhetorical technique, Churchill and his ambassador in Washington, Lord Lothian, fanned the fear in American minds that "they were in danger of losing the British Fleet altogether if the war went against us and if they remained neutral." FDR needed no convincing of the desirability of the transfer, but on June 28 Congress put up a huge roadblock, when the anti-British senator David I. Walsh of Massachusetts succeeded in attaching to an authorization bill an amendment whereby no matériel belonging to the army or the navy could be disposed of—in any manner—unless the chief of staff or the chief of naval operations certified that it was not essential to the national defense. Chronically distrusting the president, Congress grasped this opportunity to hamper him in his conduct of foreign affairs. As Roosevelt philosophically said in a note to Frank Knox, the new secretary of the navy, the move was "intended to be a complete prohibition of sale"—and, he added, "I fear Congress is in no mood at the present time to allow any form of sale."

Congress was, however, in a mood to pose problems for FDR's nominee to take over the War Department. In Henry Stimson's long public career four earlier presidents had submitted his name to the Senate, and never once had his fitness for office met anything more than the most routine questions. Although a believer in collective security, Stimson, as secretary of state in the early 1930s, had generally practiced the traditional American diplomacy by exhortation, with its laudable faith in the "sanctity of treaties," its more questionable belief that such moralizing unrelated to action constituted a policy, and its consequent production of irritation among both friends and potential foes. This behavior was well understood on Capitol Hill, where respect for the distinction between word and deed required no justification. The greatest personal weakness Stimson had ever displayed was probably a fondness for tennis so pronounced that he had placed on the State Department payroll a special messenger charged with bringing his white flannels to the office in the afternoon. But now, Harold Ickes said, "the pacifists and the anti-third-termers in the Senate proceeded to have a Roman holiday," as was shown by the fact that Stimson had to undergo hearings; his earlier confirmations had been pro forma affairs. Nevertheless, after baiting by Senator Robert A. Taft and Senator Arthur Vandenberg, the nominee was confirmed on July 9 by the full Senate by a vote of 56 to 28.

Sure of winning approval despite the attacks, Stimson had already wound up his personal affairs in New York, and on July 8, he returned to Woodley, his Washington estate overlooking Rock Creek Park. Not waiting for confirmation before renewing his acquaintance with General Marshall, whom he had heard lecture in 1918 at the U.S. Army staff college in France, Stimson invited the chief of staff for an overnight visit at Highhold, his farm in what was then a rural area near Huntington, Long Island. Before flying up on June 27, Marshall asked one of his old mentors, Major General Frank McCoy, for "a tip on Mr. Stimson, what you may happen to know of his special ideas and what advice you would give me in my approach to him." Such a precaution, although perfectly sensible, hardly proved necessary. The two men talked until almost midnight, Marshall wrote his wife; Mr. and Mrs. Stimson "are both delightful people," he said, "and their farm is charming." The next morning, after a 6:30 breakfast, the chief of staff flew back to Washington. What appears to have been the only discordant note was struck by telephone calls during the evening for Stimson from friends associated with the Plattsburgh movement, a 1915 plan for enlisting army officers directly from civilian life and training them in special camps—an idea that had been fine in its day, Marshall thought, but that did not fit the needs of the new army he was beginning to build. But a battle over this issue was not joined during this particular evening. And, as individuals, the two men could hardly fail to get along. Although they were somewhat different in age and notably so in background (Marshall could in no way be described as a member of the American eastern establishment), if history had ever brought into close association two men with more similar ideas of duty and responsibility, no record of that relationship has survived.

On the day Stimson returned to Washington, he had a further long talk with Marshall, and he "began to know and appreciate still better the quality of the Chief of Staff. He soon understood that the greatest problem a Secretary of War can have would never face him while Marshall was alive and well. He would not have to search the Army for a good top soldier. The right man was already there." The thought suggests that Stimson came into office with an expansive view of the secretary of war's power of appointment, but his satisfaction with the chief of staff meant that this view would not have to undergo testing.

As Stimson readily saw, the War Department had huge tasks before it. Rearmament had barely begun; the needed great expansion of the army's manpower had been "but sketchily charted"; new capable and trusted civilian assistants must be recruited to replace those who had staffed the department during the vexed Woodring-Johnson regime—and meanwhile "the last bastion of freedom in Europe was in deadly danger." Overall, two great issues challenged the new Stimson-Marshall team. One involved the "sketchily charted" expansion of the army's manpower; the other had to do with creating a response to urgent and repeated cries for help from Britain. Amid all the discord of an election year, President Roosevelt and his advisers thus had to deal with a draft for Americans and destroyers for the British. The advocacy of a draft would test the depth of congressional feeling for preparedness at home, while a push to provide destroyers (and other matériel) to Britain would give the isolationists and their allies as solid a fighting issue as they could wish for.

On June 22 General Marshall and the chief of naval operations, Admiral Harold R. Stark, put their stamp of agreement on a document called "Basis for Immediate Decisions Concerning the National Defense." Stark was an unusual naval officer in that he truly believed that the U.S. Army and Navy served the same country and therefore ought to cooperate freely and willingly. Marshall had carefully developed a working relationship with Stark that the chief of staff thought "without previous precedent"; Admiral Stark, he told a friend, "is a splendid fellow"; the general even went so far as to call the admiral not by his surname but by his rather lamentable nickname, "Betty."

At the White House the two chiefs went over the document item by item with FDR, whose comments were jotted down by Marshall. As one of their recommendations, the chiefs asked for the immediate enactment of selective service, to be followed "at once by complete military and naval mobilization." The president changed "complete" to "progressive," Marshall noted, and, disappointingly, he did not embrace the idea of a purely military draft, saying "at considerable length" that he favored a year of service for each young man that might put him in the armed forces but could see him in the CCC or in the arsenals or pursuing mechanical training. On June 27 the chiefs returned to the executive office with a new document, amending several proposals in light of FDR's comments but still calling for a draft act and "progressive mobilization." While they wrote and rewrote these proposals and plans, in the world outside the White House and the War Department mandarins of the eastern establishment were raising their authoritative voices.

The mandarin brotherhood included among its leading members Henry L. Stimson's longtime friend and fellow Wall Street lawyer, Grenville Clark, who shared with Elihu Root, Jr., Judge Robert P. Patterson, and other prominent conservative New Yorkers a view of international affairs that has been characterized as Hamiltonian, because it held that the first responsibility of the statesman is to develop a national policy that primarily reflects "not abstract ideals but a realistic understanding of the national interest." The original high priest of the sect was Theodore Roosevelt, who had welcomed the end of the nineteenth-century American isolationism and had rushed to embrace power politics. Many of the original "neo-Hamiltonians" had thought in ways very similar to those of the then new military professionals, and an interest in military affairs had been common among them, as it was with their latter-day successors in 1940.

Grenville Clark was old enough to have been prominent in the World War era, when he had been a leader in the Plattsburgh movement for businessmen's training camps. As it happened, the spring of 1940 marked the twenty-fifth anniversary of the establishment of the first such camp, and Clark determined to make good use of this symbolic fact by leading a campaign for preparedness in this new emergency. On May 22 a dinner in New York attended by a hundred mandarins produced a strong consensus in favor of draft legislation. A little over a week later Clark and Julius Ochs Adler of the *New York Times* family descended on Marshall's office; the chief of staff, they said, must recommend that the president support selective service legislation.

Moving only slowly toward the idea of a draft, Marshall turned his callers down flat, telling them that he did not wish to destroy the army's few effective units for the sake of providing cadres to train masses of recruits. Besides, he regarded selective service as simply too controversial a matter to bring up at a time when he was concentrating on prying loose large and essential appropriations from Congress. This was the message the disappointed Messrs. Clark and Adler carried away, but Marshall in fact had more than one string to his bow. The Clark-Adler appointment had been set for 9:00 A.M.; at 9:30 the chief of staff received another caller, the veteran Representative James Wadsworth of New York, who not only favored the draft but stood ready to introduce the legislation when the proper time should come.

At this point, perhaps without fully recognizing the similarity, Marshall was playing the sort of game typical of President Roosevelt, who would help to create a wave of public opinion on a particular issue that would then push him into doing what he had wished to do at the outset. After less than a year in office, Marshall showed himself as sensitive to public opinion as many an officeholder who owed his position directly to the voters; he, and all army planners, had never doubted that a draft would be necessary, but they expected it to come only after the United States was engaged in a war, and even then it must enjoy full public support. To guarantee such support, Marshall believed profoundly, he must make sure that any movement for selective service did not begin inside the army and that nobody could claim that it had. As a loyal chief of staff, Marshall also could not allow himself to advocate an act of high national policy, such as the enactment of the draft, until the president declared himself in favor of it.

As part of his strategy, Marshall had to keep his game secret. He characterized this time as "a very difficult period," when "it was very hard to keep my temper. I was being dictated to, and I mean dictated to. I was being sent for by a conference of this important New York fellow and this other important New York fellow." But, he said, "I tried to listen politely." What he wanted these "important fellows" to do was not to argue with him but to go ahead and marshal public and congressional opinion. After all, he said, "I understood what we needed far better than they did."

After being turned down by several cautious senators who normally supported the president, the persistent New York mandarins found a senator, Edward R. Burke of Nebraska, a Democrat though no strong New Dealer, who agreed to sponsor a selective service bill; on June 20 Burke introduced it in the Senate, Wadsworth doing the honors the next day in the House. The general reaction surprised those in Washington who had not gauged the force of the revolution in popular opinion. Even as Marshall and his colleagues promoted a recruitment program called the Civilian Volunteer Effort, since they had not been wildly optimistic about the immediate prospects for selective service, the Burke-Wadsworth bill rapidly won significant support on Capitol Hill and in the editorial pages of leading newspapers.

Now that civilians had created a movement for the draft, General Marshall felt able to change his strategy. He had spoken with perfect truth in telling the New Yorkers that the adoption of selective service would pose problems for the War Department, but a possible solution existed. If the whole National Guard could be summoned to active duty, it could absorb many thousands of raw recruits and provide them with at least beginning training, and the federalizing of the Guard would leave various units of the Regular Army intact for emergency duty. (Marshall worried about such "imminently probable" eventualities as "Nazi-inspired revolution in Brazil" and "widespread disorders with attacks on U.S. citizens in Mexico and raids along our southern border," as the dangers were put in a memo drafted by Major Matthew B. Ridgway of the War Plans Division.) Roosevelt now encouraged Marshall to testify on Capitol Hill in favor both of the draft and of calling the National Guard to active duty.

On July 12, appearing before the Senate Military Affairs Committee, Marshall spoke of the change that had come to the world with the fall of France (a change that had come to his own thinking, as well). Although enlistments had risen, no longer could the army take its time about reaching its authorized strength. He then linked together the draft and the mobilization of the National Guard. The army needed thousands of men now, but it could not train them without the help of the Guard. On July 24, the general told the House Military Affairs Committee that speed was vital. "My relief of mind," he said, "would be tremendous if we just had too much of something besides patriotism and spirit."

So busy had Marshall become that he wrote to a friend: "More occurs here in a day now than used to occur in a month, and it seems to grow a little worse each day." Almost his only time for relaxation came when he "read or slept on an airplane flying here and there." Yet, busy as he was, he could not resist answering, almost by return mail, a letter from a youngster in Dubuque, Iowa, who had joined the Junior R.O.T.C., but was disappointed to find that he was being taught nothing about military strategy. Commending the boy for his interest in learning, the chief of staff suggested that he read some books on military history and advised him to "remember that the eminent commanders usually rose to great heights only after they had mastered the fundamentals such as are now being taught to you." Marshall closed his letter "Faithfully yours," the style he used with presidents, generals, old friends, and schoolboys he had never met.

Despite the feeling of emergency in the air—the widespread belief that, with France crushed and Britain perhaps open to invasion, Western civilization itself stood on the brink—the men and women of the U.S. Congress could not bring themselves to hurry the draft legislation through the labyrinthine processes their predecessors had long ago set up. On August 5 Marshall, who seemed to have taken up residence on Capitol Hill, chastised the senators for the delay, pointing out that they were squandering the best weather for constructing camps and other facilities. Three weeks later, on August 27, Congress approved the calling of the National Guard into federal service, and on September 14, one month after German air attack opened the Battle of Britain, the Selective Service and Training Act was passed by a vote of 45 to 25 in the Senate and by 232 to 134 in the House; two days later the president signed the act into law. That same day sixty thousand members of the National Guard left their homes to begin a period of intensive military training, and that evening General Marshall appeared on the CBS radio network to declare that "for the first time in our history we are beginning in time of peace to prepare against the possibility of war. We are starting to train an army of citizen-soldiers which may save us from the tragedy of war." Then, in words carrying a resonance more political than military, more characteristic of a civilian leader than of a soldier, he concluded: "If we are strong enough, peace, democracy, and our American way of life should be the reward."

A month later, on October 16, which he had proclaimed draft registration day, President Roosevelt in a typical reference spoke of the sixteen million young registrants as "reviving the 300-year-old American custom of the muster"—the "first duty of free citizenship." The establishment of the first peacetime draft Americans had ever known signaled a triumph for the national-defense side of FDR's military policy. But this success bore one regrettable similarity to the old Colonial muster. The citizen three centuries ago would leave his fireside, join his fellows to take care of whatever trouble there was, and then come back home and return his musket to its place over the mantel. The draft act of 1940 likewise called for temporary service: Draftees, reservists, and National Guardsmen called to the colors were all supposed to be returned to civilian life after one year in uniform. Thus the cornerstone of the structure that Roosevelt, Marshall, and their associates had built held a political time bomb, one whose ticking would inevitably become louder as the months passed.

Meanwhile, there remained the elusive question of the destroyers Churchill had asked for. In early August Roosevelt's Cabinet, which like most U.S. Cabinets did not sit as a truly collegial body and rarely discussed important matters to any effect, spent some time trying to devise ways to get the old warships to Britain. "It was agreed that legislation to accomplish this is necessary," Roosevelt noted in a memo to himself, and "it was agreed that such legislation if asked for by me would meet with defeat or interminable delay in reaching a vote"—and yet Churchill had declared the need urgent. The president thought that the best quid pro quo the British could offer would be a pledge to send the fleet to America in case of disaster. The prime minister at no point really believed in the likelihood of this disaster, with the destroyers or without them. His faith in the quality of the Royal Air Force and its radar defenses, his knowledge of the complex difficulties involved in overseas invasion, and his awareness of some of the fresh successes of British signal intelligence with German ciphers all contributed to an unshakable belief that matters would not in fact come to this dark pass. Certainly the destroyers would be desirable, but, as Churchill later confessed, the fact of their transfer from the United

States to Britain—a "decidedly unneutral act"—would bring the United States closer to Britain and closer to involvement in the war. Unfortunately, from Churchill's point of view, he could see no hope that such a move would lead Hitler to declare war on the United States, justified though the führer would have been by the traditional standards of history. Nor did Roosevelt fear such an outcome.

Neither Marshall nor Admiral Stark appreciated the idea of the Walsh amendment, which required them to certify that matériel to be sold was not essential to national defense. The chief of staff actually considered it unconstitutional because it gave him the authority to veto decisions made by his commander in chief. Of course the law had not undergone any test in court, and the service chiefs took care to abide by it. "I tried not to crowd the issue at all," Marshall said, with his usual careful eye to congressional thought processes, because "it was imperative that Congress feel that they could trust me, and then I could get them to do things that otherwise they would oppose." (Marshall's conscience was troubled by this—he felt that his approach held "a certain amount of duplicity"—but at least once he proved to be ethically hyperactive. After a number of Flying Fortresses had been sent to England officially for "experimental" purposes—a subterfuge that left Marshall feeling "a little ashamed"—the British quickly discovered that the bombers were useless as delivered because of their inadequate defensive arrangements. Actually, Marshall then realized, this kind of opportunity for laboratory testing ought to have been seized much earlier.) But in completely good conscience he could take the position that any action to "prevent the complete collapse of Great Britain was of importance to the United States, because it would put war on a very different front, very threatening to us, and would permit its easy transfer to this side of the ocean and threaten the Panama Canal." Far from reacting to the new stresses of 1940 by sticking to a narrow nationalism, he allowed himself to see the soundness of the president's broad strategic view and to make it his own, even if at times he felt that he must object to certain particular proposed actions. (The obsession running through the entire War Department envisioned a Hitler victorious in Europe soon turning to feast on Latin America—a projection of "worst case" fears, perhaps, as much as an analysis of likely eventualities.)

The push to transfer the forty or fifty old destroyers to

Britain squeezed Admiral Stark into a tight corner. He was urgently appealing to Congress for the enormous sum of $4 billion over a just-approved naval appropriation to create a "two ocean" navy that would give the United States a strong presence in the Atlantic as well as in the Pacific. He could hardly declare the destroyers to be surplus in view of the fact that the navy was briskly reconditioning more than a hundred of them for American defense purposes; indeed, in current congressional hearings he had spoken of their value when he was asked, "Why should we go on, year after year, wasting the taxpayers' money keeping these old 'boats' in cold storage?"

But strong forces assailed the president. Pressures to solve the problem came from members of his own Cabinet, from concerned citizens, from the British. At the beginning of August, Secretary of the Navy Knox told Harold Ickes that he had seen the British ambassador, Lord Lothian, "almost tearful in his pleas for help and help quickly." Clearly, if the destroyers were to be transferred, a deal must be struck, a quid pro quo found. Knox, for one, suggested the answer—the transfer of some strategic British island territories in the Western Hemisphere in exchange for the warships. This idea opened the door. In an August 13 meeting with Morgenthau, Stimson, Knox, and Welles, Roosevelt himself drafted the basic principles of such an agreement; in return for fifty destroyers, the British would grant what amounted to leases, giving the United States the right to fortify and defend specified British bases deemed important for American security. With no reservations whatever, Admiral Stark could certify that this arrangement would have the net effect of strengthening the defense of the United States.

By this time President Roosevelt had become Candidate Roosevelt as well. For months, insiders in Washington had tried to fathom his intentions: Would he run? Wouldn't he? In the press he had been caricatured as a jaunty Sphinx complete with cigarette holder, knowing what he would do but keeping the decision to himself. He spoke of being tired and wanting to go back to his beloved Hudson, and he had signed a writing contract with *Collier's* magazine for $75,000 a year, a salary equal to his pay as president. Apparently he had not made up his mind until the fall of France created a clearly perilous world situation, and now here he was, running for a precedent-breaking third term. Reason and ego may have combined to define his duty, but the campaign also offered him the remarkable chance to exceed the achievement of his career model, Cousin Theodore Roosevelt. TR had won fame as a war hero—acclaim denied Franklin—but the first Roosevelt president, having in effect served two terms, had failed in his comeback try to win a third.

As a candidate, FDR took care to obtain for the destroyers-bases deal the private blessing of Wendell Willkie, the Wall Street holding-company executive who had captured the Republican nomination from the party regulars in an operation as startling as a commando raid. As it happened, Willkie was the only conceivable Republican nominee who would not have turned this extraordinary transaction into a campaign issue.

In public, the president led up to the consummation of the arrangement in a wholly characteristic fashion, telling a press conference on August 16 that the United States was "holding conversations" with Great Britain with regard to the acquisition of land and air bases for the defense of the Western Hemisphere. The United States would of course give Britain something in return, whatever it might be. Here Churchill proved something of a stumbling block, because for various reasons he wished the two transfers kept separate; but only through their being tied together could the Americans deliver the goods. In America the deal was displayed as being advantageous to the United States, which it clearly was, and in Britain Churchill described it in his own fashion, focusing on the British contribution to American security. In presenting the question to the House of Commons, the prime minister almost chortled; the process bringing the British Empire and the United States closer together, he declared, resembled the Mississippi: "It just keeps rolling along. Let it roll. Let it roll on—full flood, inexorable, irresistible, benignant, to broader lands and better days."

President Roosevelt during this fateful period had "a political calculating machine in his head," thought the Harvard historian Samuel Eliot Morison, "an intricate instrument in which Gallup polls, the strength of the armed forces and the probability of England's survival; the personalities of governors, senators, and congressmen, and of Mussolini, Hitler, Churchill, Chiang, and Tojo; the Irish, German, Italian, and Jewish votes in the approaching presidential election; the 'Help the Allies' people and the 'America Firsters,' were combined with fine points of political maneuvering." This political calculating machine, after due whirring and clicking and flashing of lights, produced the destroyers-bases deal as part of an overarching policy of extending all aid to Britain short of war. The president had outflanked Congress and done it legally and openly, but in the midst of a presidential campaign he had courageously taken an enormous political risk. One day at Hyde Park while dictating a memorandum on the agreement, he had said to Grace Tully, "Congress is going to raise hell about this, but even another day's delay may mean the end of civilization." It had taken him several months to see his way clear to making this unprecedented exchange, and even now he knew that "cries of warmonger and dictator" would be raised. But even the most virulent congressional critics could hardly complain that "the old Dutchman and Scotchman," as he described himself, had made a bad bargain.

CHAPTER EIGHT

"THE BEST IMMEDIATE DEFENSE"

Although he was a businessman with no experience in elective politics, Wendell Willkie proved to be an energetic campaigner, delivering so many stump speeches that his voice degenerated into a croak rivaling a whiskey baritone. Playing a different game, Candidate Roosevelt devoted himself to his high-level presidential duties and made sure the public saw him doing so. Finally he emerged from the White House for a few effective speeches, and in November, despite all the talk about his flouting of the two-term tradition, the voters gave him a 55 percent majority. Yet Willkie, whose nationwide campaigning revealed a likable personality, amassed almost six million more votes than Alf Landon had won in 1936, showing special strength in the isolationist heartland—the Middle West and the Great Plains states.

Out of all the mail coming to the White House to express the writers' devotion to FDR, one particular letter may have given him special inspiration. A lady told him: "I pray every night that you will get the chair." This endorsement, with its phrasing inadvertently suggestive of a Warner Brothers death-house movie, bore an eerie similarity to the sentiment once expressed by another female well-wisher: "I love you so mutch [*sic*] I want to see you die in the White House."

A month after winning the election, Roosevelt set off on what seemed to be another of the seagoing vacations he loved. Appearing relaxed and casual, he joked with reporters at Miami, where he left his train to transfer to the U.S.S. *Tuscaloosa*. At the start of a previous cruise, he said, he had deceived the press by "mentioning some phony islands." He wouldn't do that again. This time, "We're going to Christmas Island to buy Christmas cards and to Easter Island to buy Easter eggs." Earlier the White House had indicated some more likely stops—various pieces of the Caribbean real estate turned over by the British to the United States in fulfillment of the destroyers-bases deal. But when asked point-blank where he was going, FDR lightly replied, "I wish I knew."

The president's party included Pa Watson; Rear Admiral Ross McIntire, the White House physician; the naval aide, Captain Daniel Callaghan; and only one guest, Harry Hopkins. Also aboard the *Tuscaloosa* was a notable first-time participant in a presidential cruise, FDR's newly acquired Scottie dog, Fala, given him by a lady cousin. At Jamaica and other British possessions, the president received colonial officials; off Eleuthera Island the duke of Windsor, governor general of the Bahamas, came aboard the *Tuscaloosa* for a chat. But no one seriously believed that FDR intended to subject the sites of the new bases to detailed inspection; and fishing, loafing, and the cronyish horseplay he loved in fact constituted the main visible activities of the cruise. The party spent the evenings playing poker or watching movies, which included such Hollywood features as *Northwest Mounted Police* with Gary Cooper, *I Love You Again* with William Powell and Myrna Loy, and *Tin Pan Alley* with Alice Faye and Betty Grable. The fishing itself produced no results that could be the basis of future bragging. Hopkins made the biggest catch, a twenty-pound grouper, but he lacked the strength to reel it in and had to yield the rod to McIntire. In the 1,500-foot waters of Mona Passage between Puerto Rico and Hispaniola, FDR trolled for an hour or more without even a strike—despite a radioed recommendation from Ernest Hemingway of the locality as one in which "many big fish" had been caught with a feathered hook baited with pork rind.

The vacation party had left Washington on December 2. About a week before the president's departure, Lord Lothian, who had just come back from a visit home, paid a call. The ambassador had money on his mind, but the president told him that it was not yet time for the British to ask for American financial help; first they must liquidate their investments in the Western Hemisphere, a move Roosevelt thought should yield some $9 billion. To the surprise and concern of FDR and his advisers, Lothian had already told reporters that Great Britain was running short of ready cash. Henry Morgenthau chastised him for having made such a statement in public; now, Morgenthau said, a senator like Gerald Nye could question the placing of any future British orders (since the "cash and carry" law required the proffer of cash before any carrying could occur), but unlike FDR, Morgenthau did not credit the British with much ability to pay. Their available assets, he thought, amounted to no more than $2 billion. Thus he agreed with Lothian's point, although regretting the form in which it had been made. (Reportedly, Lothian had declared to the press: "Well, boys, Britain's broke; it's your money we want." At the time no one realized that the ambassador, a Christian Scientist, suffered from untreated uremic poisoning, a condition that can sometimes induce a mental fog. He died while the president was in the Caribbean.)

It seemed to many observers that the president had lightheartedly gone off on a holiday, leaving behind a huge financial problem to be chewed over by his advisers and associates. But even before Lothian's call, FDR had been perfectly aware that at some time—and that time not in the remote future—the British would run out of dollars. (The British Empire was not poor, but it could make purchases in the United States only with dollars earned by sales in America or by the conversion of gold or other assets into dollars.) In one particular area, cargo ships, Roosevelt had asked himself whether it might be possible for the U.S. government to build them and then lease them to Britain for the duration of the war. He told a Cabinet meeting that he thought it would be possible to lease ships or any other property "that was loanable, returnable, and insurable."

As the president loafed and fished, Stimson, Morgenthau, and the others back in Washington could see no solution to the money problem except submitting it to the dubious mercies of Congress. Before taking this step, Morgenthau said, the administration must be sure that it would be desirable from the American military point of view; otherwise, obviously, Congress would shoot down the administration advocates before they could make any case at all. General Marshall, who was attending this particular meeting, reassured the secretary. The General Staff had studied the matter, he said, and had concluded that British orders were "useful to us because they carry us beyond the two-million-man point in production of critical material"—that is, factories built to fill British orders would provide the country with a greatly increased capacity to meet U.S. military requirements. He was ready to prepare a study to prove the point to Congress, the general said, but his offer of course did not carry with it an answer to the financial question. Before leaving on his trip, the president had addressed the same point, saying that the government could build new factories and sell the war material they produced to the British. But where would the money for payment come from? Congress would hardly find overdrafts acceptable.

Although more than 1,500 miles away from Washington, the president had not put himself out of touch; navy planes regularly brought letters and documents to the *Tuscaloosa.* During the morning of December 9, as the cruiser lay off Antigua, a seaplane splashed down nearby and a pouch of White House mail was transferred aboard. Included in the correspondence was a long letter from Winston Churchill. Since the year 1940 was ending, the prime minister wrote, "I feel that you will expect me to lay before you the prospects for 1941." Although he did not give the reasons for this presumption, he seemed to imply that he was performing the kind of duty required of a corporation president *vis-à-vis* the stockholders. Actually, Lothian, on his recent visit home, had urged Churchill to write "a full statement of our position" to the president, as he believed that Roosevelt and his advisers were genuinely seeking the best way to help Britain (particularly since the election was now over); this statement would serve as a prod to the Americans, detailing British needs as well as the inability of Britain to meet those needs financially.

In the letter, which Churchill had been eager for Roosevelt to receive before he got back to "the bustle of Washington," the prime minister covered the entire strategic situation. Treating the British and the Americans as acknowledged partners, he discussed the duty of the former "in the common interest, as also for our own survival, to hold the front and grapple with the Nazi power until the preparations of the United States are complete." He dwelt on the heavy losses inflicted by German U-boats on British merchant shipping, and called for American warships, cargo ships, and aircraft, suggesting that ships could be transferred by "gift, loan, or supply." In the closing paragraphs Churchill confronted the question of finance. Reaffirming the points Lothian had made with the president, he then declared that while Britain would do her utmost "and shrink from no proper sacrifice to make payments across the exchange," the president would surely agree that it would not be to the "moral or economic interests of either of our countries" for the United

States to squeeze Britain dry. He did not suggest what Roosevelt might do to solve the problem, contenting himself with the trusting assertion that "the rest we leave to you . . ."

Harry Hopkins found the letter fascinating; it filled him "with a desire to get to know Churchill and to find out how much of him was mere grandiloquence and how much of him was hard fact." Discussing the letter with the president as the two sat quietly on the *Tuscaloosa*'s deck, Hopkins could see the great impression it had made on FDR; he read and reread it, Hopkins later told Churchill. When a radio message arrived from the Morgenthau working group in Washington, proposing various detailed short-run schemes for joint U.S.-British financing of war-plant construction, Roosevelt told Hopkins that the ideas were not satisfactory. Why not make outright gifts to Britain? Hopkins asked. No, said FDR, who knew his Capitol Hill, that would be too sweeping—and would also wound British pride. He ordered Morgenthau to hold off on any action until he had returned to Washington.

What was taking place in Roosevelt's mind—the "political calculating machine" that was also something more, an instrument with an artistic flair, capable at times of making imaginative leaps and unexpected syntheses? "I didn't know for quite a while what he was thinking about, if anything," Hopkins said later. "But then I began to get the idea that he was refueling, the way he so often does when he seems to be resting and carefree. So I didn't ask him any questions."

What the refueling and synthesizing process had produced was revealed to the world on Monday, December 17, the day after the president returned from his trip. Tanned and fit, jaunty as ever, he faced story-hungry reporters packed around his desk. No actor in modern memory ever possessed a greater sense of drama than Roosevelt's; in timing and in effective use of his voice he always proved himself an intuitive professional. And he also brought to the arena a sense of humor.

"I don't think there is any particular news," he began quietly, as he often did, but his bantering tone and fiercely uptilted cigarette holder suggested that the reporters would not leave his office without a story; his eyes danced. He established his ground immediately. "In the present world situation of course there is absolutely no doubt in the mind of a very overwhelming number of Americans that the best immediate defense of the United States is the success of Great Britain in defending itself" (FDR had not drawn this opinion from a hat; the polls had consistently shown such a belief, although they had often shown doubts about Britain's ability to survive her ordeal).

In the last few days, the president said, he had read "a great deal of nonsense" about finances—nonsense put out by people he dismissed as able to think only in traditional terms. But the point to remember was that no major war had ever been won or lost through a lack of money. What America really needed now was productive power, and here British orders were important because they created additional facilities. To further this process we did not have to repeal the neutrality legislation and lend Britain money to be spent in the United States, nor should we manufacture matériel and then give it to the British—both these approaches were "banal" (nor did many persons advocate either of them; FDR merely set them up as straw men). What he favored instead was for the United States to manufacture the materials and then divide them up as the "military events of the future would determine"; we would either lease the materials or sell them "subject to mortgage." The plan rested on the idea that such materials would make a greater contribution to the defense of the United States if they "were used in Great Britain than if they were kept in storage here."

Having sketched the background, FDR then told the reporters, "What I am trying to do is eliminate the dollar sign . . . get rid of the silly, foolish old dollar sign." It was the moment for an analogy, and one had been playing in Roosevelt's mind for months, since a conversation he had had the preceding summer with Harold Ickes. "Suppose my neighbor's home catches fire, and I have got a length of garden hose four or five hundred feet away; but, by heaven, if he can take my garden hose and connect it up with his hydrant, I may help him put out his fire." But in such a case you don't make the neighbor buy the hose from you; you lend it to him, and all you want is to get it back after the fire is out, and if it should be damaged, then he would of course replace it. Thus, "when the show was over," the president said, "we would get repaid in kind sometime." It would be "a gentleman's obligation."

Nobody at the press conference asked what sort of garden hose the British would return after winning a war with Germany, nor how they would be able to replace a hose that had been damaged—and so, with its homey and memorable image of a good Dutchess County squire rushing to the aid of an unfortunate neighbor, did this press conference launch the idea that was to be called "lend-lease."

"There were probably very few," Robert Sherwood felt, "who had any expectation that we would ever get the hose back," but at least no haggling over war debts would arise to foul international relations for another twenty years—no haggling would arise, that is, if the administration transformed lend-lease into a concrete program and Congress wrote it into law. FDR's declaration at the press conference, effective as it was, simply fired the opening salvo of the campaign. Then, during the week before Christmas and for a few days afterward, he seemed to be neglecting the follow-up; his subordinates could only shrug off queries about the plan, because they had no concrete details to pass on. The British made polite inquiries but could learn nothing. Allowing suspense to build among press and public—and refusing to be diverted from the old-time Christmas rituals he loved, celebrated in the White House with Roosevelts of all generations on hand—the president set his staff to work on what he intended as a major speech on the war and national security.

On the evening of Sunday, December 29, sitting before a battery of microphones in the oval diplomatic reception room on the ground floor of the White House and facing a group that included Cabinet members and Hollywood's reigning couple, Clark Gable and Carole Lombard, FDR declared that the United States "must be the great arsenal of democracy." Now that the election had become history, he felt that he could be blunt and name names: The Nazis must be defeated; "it is a matter of most vital concern to us that European and Asiatic warmakers should not gain control of the oceans which lead to this hemisphere." If Great Britain should go down and the Axis win the war, "all of us here in the Americas would be living at the point of a gun—a gun loaded with explosive bullets, economic as well as military." The United States must therefore "do all we can now to support the nations defending themselves against attack by the Axis." Of course such a policy entailed risks, but smaller ones than the country would run by allowing Britain to be defeated. The purpose was not to get the United States into war but "to keep war away from our country and our people." Without referring to his plan by any specific name, the president declared that "as planes and ships and guns and shells are produced, your government, with its defense experts, can then determine how best to use them to defend this hemisphere.

The decision as to how much shall be sent abroad and how much shall remain at home must be made on the basis of our overall military necessities."

In essence, the speech and the legislative strategy it foreshadowed turned on a simple idea. The United States could best avoid war by keeping Britain in the fight against the Axis, with lend-lease serving as the device by which this purpose would be carried out. No one could say whether Roosevelt really believed that Britain could somehow defeat Germany without active American intervention; but, as a supreme optimist, he normally shaped his actions in the belief that doing one's best today is likely to bring the kind of tomorrow one seeks. His psychological makeup, his rearing, his uncomplicated Christian faith, and his experiences as an adult all combined with a sense of special mission to render this belief unassailably strong (so strong that he could accept compromise and setback without feeling that he was deserting his purposes). Near the end of the speech he said: "I believe that the Axis powers are not going to win this war. I base that belief on the latest and best information." What information did he possess in December 1940? Just his belief, Hopkins told associates, that Congress would pass a lend-lease act and that the resulting program would make an Axis victory impossible.

"Arsenal of democracy": This ringing Rooseveltian phrase had been picked up by Hopkins in his newspaper reading and passed on to FDR, and whatever its origins it provided a memorable capsule identity for the president's December 29 fireside chat and for the ensuing campaign for support. The speech itself seemed to be a remarkable success. Steve Early, FDR's press secretary, reported telegrams and letters were running one hundred to one in support of the president's ideas, and a Gallup poll showed 61 percent favorable with only 24 percent opposed. More remarkably, perhaps, 59 percent of those polled had listened to the speech on the radio and another 16 percent had read it in the newspaper; this combined 75 percent audience was the greatest that had ever been recorded for any of FDR's speeches. The public, it was clear, shared the president's thoughts and hopes—victory over Hitler with American help but without an American army.

As always, Congress presented problems. On December 30, the day after the fireside chat, Roosevelt ordered the Treasury Department to prepare a bill along the lines he desired. What he really wanted, he told Morgenthau, was "authority to allocate as many of these combined orders as might seem necessary at the particular time." What he did *not* want was for Congress to stipulate "ten million, let's say, for the United States, five million for England." He wanted the bill drawn up, Morgenthau said, in "blank check form," an aim the secretary thought desirable but not very likely to be achieved.

On January 15, 1941, the House Foreign Affairs Committee opened hearings on the bill, which the ingenious parliamentarian of the House had tagged H.R. 1776 in order to give a patriotic boost to the majority leader, John W. McCormack, who represented a heavily Irish district of Boston; his constituents did not number aid to Britain among their favorite causes. The sessions of the committee proved the hottest ticket Washington had seen in many years, with five hundred people jamming the committee room almost every day and forty special policemen detailed to control the crowd. The *Washington Post* looked on the hearings not only as occasions for general coverage but as functions like receptions or dinners suitable for chronicling by the society editor, who could tell her readers when such notable capital ladies as Alice Roosevelt Longworth had attended. The country stood at a crossroads, the president was proposing an irrevocable step, and everyone sensed this historic fact. In addition, the committees of the House and the Senate offered as attractions a variety of notable guests, from such Cabinet stalwarts as the white-haired Cordell Hull and the dignified Henry Stimson to celebrities like Charles A. Lindbergh, representing the anti-interventionist America First Committee, and the demagogic Gerald L. K. Smith, who professed to be an admirer of Hitler.

But the leadership of the Foreign Affairs Committee hardly seemed fit even to preside over a town council trying to choose a new fire truck. The chairman was the same Sol Bloom who had been caught napping during the fight over the Neutrality Act in 1939 and who was considered by both Democrats and Republicans, as one historian has remarked, "pompous, arrogant, and an inveterate publicity hound"; the ranking Republican was FDR's own congressman, the Dutchess County isolationist Hamilton Fish, rangy and loud-voiced, who took it on himself to invite witnesses as though he were the head of the committee and antagonized Bloom by requesting persons to come and speak on "the President's dictator bill." (During the recent campaign, Fish had acquired a new reason to detest Roosevelt; in a speech at Madison Square Garden, FDR had given the congressman a sort of temporary immortality by linking him with Joseph Martin and Bruce Barton in a congressional isolationist triad: *Mah*tin, *Bah*ton, and Fish, so delightful a combination that the next time FDR used the phrase, the crowd chanted it along with him, the words sounding like an echo of Wynken, Blynken, and Nod.) In the realm of foreign affairs, Roosevelt had enjoyed no more luck in finding effective voices of leadership in the House than he had in the Senate (though he no longer had Pittman to deal with; the alcoholic senator had died in November).

The General Staff, which had not been consulted during the drafting of the bill, at first had some in-house doubts. But the deputy chief of staff in charge of supply quickly saw that whatever lend-lease might accomplish for Britain, it would produce long-desired benefits for the U.S. Army by forcing the coordination of military production. His recommendation bearing this specific point went to Secretary Stimson, who passed it on to the House Foreign Affairs Committee. As matters stood, Marshall had serious problems with the existing arrangements for dividing up the output of the factories.

During this crowded time, as Marshall wrote Rose Page Wilson, events had "developed too rapidly for me to turn to anything pleasant or personal." In this note he included what amounted to a direct order for her to write him about her recent move to New York, and he went on to say, with a touch of humorous archness, "So that you may not think I have neglected you, I will mention that I am due in ten minutes to leave here to appear before the Foreign Relations Committee on the famous 'lend-lease' bill, so I am sandwiching this in between some pretty important affairs of the world." His testimony, as he did not tell Rose, would be given in his unofficial role as FDR's Sledgehammer. Although Morgenthau acted more or less as the administration's official shepherd for the lend-lease bill, the Roosevelt-Marshall partnership, in which the president created and enunciated broad policies and the chief of staff carried them through the legislative committees, continued to evolve. In the football language Marshall often liked to use, the attack featured FDR as the veteran quarterback calling the plays, then nimbly stepping aside to allow his potent and still relatively fresh fullback to punch the ball through the enemy line.

To his VMI classmate Major Charles Roller, it appeared that Marshall might be fitted for more than the fullback role. Walking along a Washington street one January day, Roller heard his old friend's voice coming from a storefront radio. The buildup of the army, the chief of staff declared, not only promoted American defense but also could "develop a fine citizenship" among the men: "I believe the best medicine for the ailments of democracy flows from association in a common effort. Our self-imposed military program provides the opportunity." When Marshall finished, Roller remarked to persons in the crowd around him that here was "the kind of man we should have for the next President." His fellow listeners warmly agreed, which led Roller to propose that Marshall launch a drive for support among VMI alumni.

Marshall's answer presented a precise and revealing summary of his thoughts on such questions; it did not contain a single equivocal word. After thanking the major for his "flattering reactions," the chief of staff said "with complete sincerity" that Roller's idea possessed two qualities that would be "fatal to my future. In the first place, putting such an idea into a man's head is the first step toward destroying his usefulness, and in the second place the public suggestion of such an idea, even by mere rumor or gossip, would be almost fatal to my interests"—that is, the development and carrying out of the right military policy for the United States. "So long as the various servants of the Government in important positions concerned with national defense devote all their time and all their thoughts to the straight business of the job, all will go well with America, but just as soon as an ulterior purpose or motive creeps in, then the trouble starts and will gather momentum like a snowball." So much did Marshall dread the faintest appearance of such a possibility that he asked Major Roller not even to mention the idea to his wife.

It was a neat point: The presidential syndrome would destroy a man both internally and externally. Some two decades earlier, when a presidential bee had been released in the vicinity of General Pershing, Marshall, the faithful and self-confident aide, had moved immediately to kill it, but he had seen how its buzzing affected the general's behavior; fortunately, Pershing's war had already ended. Now, when the United States found herself on the edge of peril, Marshall as a general would allow no presidential bee even to begin making its tempting sounds. But Roller had not spoken idly, a point Marshall gave no sign of seeing. In extolling the benefits of a military training program, the chief of staff was making civilian-oriented points as a civilian would and he was taking on the attitude and tone of a politician. In his reply to Major Roller, however, he unmistakably killed the presidential bee with one convincing swat.

On the day after New Year, 1941, a forty-seven-year-old cavalry major named Paul Robinett took up his duties as an assistant secretary of the General Staff. A Missourian, Robinett was an expert horseman who as a member of the army equestrian team had taken part in the 1924 Olympic Games. He later went to Panama as aide to General Craig, and in 1932 he served as a staff officer in an interesting joint army-navy war game designed to test the defenses of Hawaii against sudden attack. In his most recent assignment Robinett had been detailed to the G-2 division of the General Staff, where he compiled and revised manuals relating to military intelligence.

On coming to work for the secretary of the General Staff, Colonel Orlando Ward, Robinett found himself at the control center "of a vast machine which is growing and not without the pains of growth." Colonel Ward seemed to do as much as anyone could to tie matters together and "prevent affairs going off at a tangent," but with the recently adopted arrangement involving three deputy chiefs of staff and with few problems fitting neatly into pigeonholes, the secretary of the General Staff had an extremely difficult job. Among Robinett's new associates were Major Walter Bedell Smith and Captain William T. Sexton; the duties of the latter, whose book on the U.S. occupation of the Philippines had first drawn Marshall's attention to him, included handling all the chief of staff's personal letters, and working with Sexton was Captain Frank McCarthy, "a bright young man from VMI."

The chief of staff occupied rooms in the old Munitions Building, "not only bare but uncomfortable and unsightly," except for the office of the chief himself and that of the secretary of war, which though not elaborate possessed a few niceties. Economy still reigned as the watchword, with little money spent on furnishings or any decorative features. Robinett's main complaint was the inadequate lighting, which led to a great deal of eyestrain as the staff "plugged away at our papers, finishing each day's batch regardless of hours."

The chief of staff himself, Robinett decided, "is the most

self-contained individual I have ever encountered." Although provided with an aide, the general made little use of this officer. In addition to the underused aide, General Marshall had the services of a personal secretary, Maude Young, who had served in the same post for every chief of staff since General March, and an appointments secretary, who was stationed across the hall. The general's immediate staff was rounded out by Mrs. Harry Chamberlin, who filled an interesting role in the office. A niece of the pre-World War chief of staff, General J. Franklin Bell (an early admirer of Marshall's), Mrs. Chamberlin with her vast list of acquaintances served as a sort of universal army contact person and a performer of special missions having a social flavor.

General Marshall, Robinett quickly saw, could digest a paper rapidly, pierce instantly to the heart of a problem, and express himself briefly in idiomatic English. Nothing irritated him more than receiving a long and involved presentation, either oral or written. The general read every letter addressed to him personally and, if an answer was drawn up for his signature, he would go over it carefully; he edited even the least important letters to fit his own style. In dealing with his staff, he seemed not to take kindly to yes-men. Along with these characteristics, which appeared designed to promote efficiency in decision making, Marshall displayed "a golden streak of imagination." He was also "smarter than any of his contemporaries known to me."

After a few days' further contact, Robinett singled out another important characteristic of the chief of staff; Marshall impressed the major as "a consummate Army politician." It was his way "not to cross swords with individuals" but "to let them down gracefully, if at all." He had "an uncanny eye for the political angle of every problem." Like many another traditionally nonpolitical professional soldier, Robinett seemed a bit uneasy in the presence of political maneuvering; although the chief of staff's skill at the game evoked the major's admiration, at the same time it seemed a blemish, a trait somehow unworthy of the top officer of the army.

Marshall's own feelings about his work came out in a personal letter he wrote to a field commander who felt misunderstood by the planners in Washington. Brushing aside the officer's complaint, the chief of staff said, "Frankly, while you have your difficulties with the Government of Panama, I do not think you have quite enough. You lack the flood of daily irritations and disturbances that we have every hour which eventually produces either prostration or a case-hardened front to the world." Sensing the great pressure exerted on Marshall from every conceivable angle, Colonel Ward observed to Robinett that he would not be chief of staff for anything on earth. Robinett readily saw why the general kept his life sharply divided into two parts—why, when he was through with his work at the office, he "jumped" into his car and "scurried" to Fort Myer, changed clothes, and went off for a canter on his favorite mount, either alone or with somebody who could not talk shop. This defense mechanism, Robinett thought, was surely what enabled Marshall to keep fit in spite of the burden of work and responsibility he carried.

During the previous year, the Marshalls had acquired another haven from the stresses of office. In the spring of 1940 they had bought a Revolutionary War–era house called Dodona Manor in the old red-brick town of Leesburg, Virginia, thirty-five miles northwest of Washington and Fort Myer, but this retreat could only be used on weekends and not even on all of those. Mrs. Marshall had taken care of the whole transaction, the general being so busy that the family had owned the large white brick house for several months before he found time to run up to Leesburg and take a look at it.

It was not clear how much would be demanded of Marshall's "uncanny eye for the political angle" as Congress took up the lend-lease issue. After six days of debate at the beginning of February, the bill with some amendments passed in the House by a vote of 260 to 165. (The discussions were enlivened at one point by a pamphleteer from New York, a woman calling herself "Andra," who appeared in the chamber outfitted in a black gown and death's head mask, a bit of theater that irritated some of the congressmen but apparently frightened few of these stalwarts.) While these deliberations took place, the Senate Foreign Relations Committee met under new and improved leadership; after Pittman's death the chairmanship had gone to Senator Walter F. George of Georgia. The committee heard its own parade of witnesses, including such heavyweight supporters of the bill as Wendell Willkie and a variety of opponents, ranging from Colonel McCormick of the *Chicago Tribune* to a Yale senior named Kingman Brewster.

Under Senator George's supportive guidance, the bill encountered little trouble in the committee, but when it reached the floor complications arose, the chief one being an amendment that would limit the president's freedom to make transfers of war goods. This change, Secretary Stimson declared, would "take the guts right out of the bill." If matériel obtained through military appropriations could not be sent to Britain without congressional approval, the unhappy result would be separate military and foreign-aid programs and the end of joint procurement. Seeing flexibility as the heart of lend-lease, Stimson, Morgenthau, and their allies determined to do battle, but the president, laid up with an attack of influenza, offered little inspiration—not only because he was sick in bed, it seemed, but also because of his constant and, in some minds, exaggerated desire to avoid open conflict with Senate leaders. FDR simply told the Cabinet members to get together with key senators and solve the problem. A meeting called by Secretary Hull on March 2 produced no progress at all. Then Morgenthau's chief counsel, Edward Foley, the principal drafter of the act, devised a technical compromise that, despite seeming restrictive, would actually leave the president with considerable discretion.

With this new ammunition in hand, the concerned Cabinet members met again on March 4 with Senate Democratic leaders. Here Stimson had devised a small plot of his own; during the discussion General Marshall appeared, and as the secretary had anticipated, the chief of staff made effective use of his earnestness and conviction to argue for the greatest possible flexibility in lend-lease, emphasizing the benefits the United States had reaped from the efforts to aid Britain. The general, Stimson noted, "gave a ripping good speech on it"; the secretary felt that Marshall "made a great impression on the Senators, who evidently don't know much about the whole situation."

After the bill's managers beat back a series of amendments, all of which attempted to impose one restriction or another on the administration's conduct of lend-lease, the Senate on March 8, nearly fifty-eight days after Congress had received it, passed the bill by a vote of 60 to 31. After the House agreed to accept the changes the Senate had made in the bill, the act was signed into law by the president at 3:50 in the afternoon on March 11. Finally, passing out the ceremonial pens with which he had signed the law, FDR could smile; Congress, even with its restrictions, had enabled him to make good on his promises to Britain. His view of the measure seemed in essence to be very much like that of a senator from California who, in a letter to his seventeen-year-old son explaining why he intended to vote for lend-lease, said that long before the bill was introduced, Americans were "morally committed" to aid "one party in the dispute" and that "to aid him stingily" would be "no more neutral than to aid him generously." As General Marshall saw it, the passage of the act declared the "intimate relationship" of the United States with Great Britain.

On March 12, the day after signing the Lend-Lease Act, the president asked Congress for $7 billion to finance the program. The very next day, his Sledgehammer appeared on Capitol Hill to urge favorable action from the House Appropriations Committee, and a week later the general performed the same mission on the Senate side, testifying again—perhaps now by rote—about the benefits lend-lease would bring to the defense of the United States. Having gone through something of a struggle to authorize the program, Congress quickly acted to make the necessary appropriations.

Although the fight for lend-lease had lasted almost two months, involving in the Senate the delaying tactic described by some as a "gentlemen's filibuster" with a time consuming series of petty amendments, the outcome had not been in serious doubt. But lend-lease was not to be the greatest congressional battle concerning defense in 1941. That drama, starring the president's Sledgehammer, was still to come.

As the summer of 1941 approached, no one could fail to hear the progressively louder ticking of the time bomb contained in the draft act adopted the previous September. In order to wring the legislation from Congress, Roosevelt and Marshall had accepted the one-year limitation on the draftees' length of service (which had given a songwriter the chance to turn out a tune called "Goodbye, Dear, I'll Be Back in a Year"). Now the day of reckoning was coming; the National Guard units first called up were due to go home on September 15, and in about two months the first draftees would follow them.

But the defense emergency had not yielded to any time limit, though the situation had undergone a dramatic change since the previous summer. Britain had survived without being forced to fight off German invasion, and on June 22 Hitler turned east, mounting the greatest land operation of all time against the Soviet Union, his forces driving into the Russian depths with the power of 180 divisions, 20 of them armored. General Marshall's intelligence specialists produced pessimistic forecasts, just as they had in relation to Britain during the previous summer. If these proved correct, the Nazi regime would emerge from the attack mightier than ever. Unlike his military advisers, President Roosevelt (as was true of Winston Churchill) did not expect a quick German victory over Russia. In any case the opening of this great new front proclaimed a cataclysmic change in the war, one that would profoundly affect the West. The likely American response, it appeared, would be the dissolution of the country's fledgling army.

At the time the draft act was passed, the *Chicago Tribune,* whose Colonel McCormick was always looking for a presidential weak spot, had declared that Roosevelt would find a way to break the one-year promise. Now FDR could see problems everywhere he looked. If he proposed legislation bearing out the *Tribune*'s prediction, he would encounter real trouble with Congress; Democratic leaders insisted that they could not round up enough votes to do away with the one-year limitation, and discontent seemed to reign among the soldiers themselves and among their families (who wanted their "boys" back on time, and no mistake about it). The army having no clear mission, in this twilight time of neither peace nor war, the morale of the troops sagged. Doubtful of the future, soldiers began to scrawl "OHIO" on walls in training camps; the term had nothing to do with the Buckeye State but was an acronym for "over the hill in October," telling the world that if the men were not released when their time was up, they would simply desert.

Writing to General Marshall, an angry mother even made a rhetorical issue out of the salutation of her letter. She was not sure she ought to address the chief of staff as "dear sir," she said, because of his intention to lift the twelve-month limit; "if you do that, you will have the hatred of every mother, wife and sweethearts *[sic]* and also the boys themselves." Replying on June 28, Marshall told the mother that "unless the military situation becomes very acute the bulk of the selectees will be sent home after they complete their year of service," but he added a characteristic thought: "Millions of European mothers would be offering grateful prayers of thanksgiving if the only sacrifice they were called upon to make for their country was to be separated from their sons by a few hundred peaceful miles." What Marshall told the angry mother about the "bulk of the selectees" was literally true at the moment, but that was not the way he wished the situation to stay.

The president decided that submitting the issue to Congress would lead to a bad strategic defeat. He was, Sherwood remarked, "afraid of fear itself," although it was true that the 1940 legislation provided for extending the twelve-month period of service "whenever the Congress has declared that the national interest is imperiled." This clause had nothing mysterious about it, but in 1940 the proponents of the draft had not gone out of their way to call it to anyone's attention. The realistic political fact now was that the army would disintegrate unless those who wished to preserve it took strong steps to extend the time in which draftees must remain in uniform. On June 19, concerned at Roosevelt's drifting, Stimson and Marshall took advantage of their presence at a meeting in the White House to make this point with the president. But Marshall quickly changed his approach. Increasingly accustomed to sniffing the winds of Capitol Hill, he now decided to outflank the Roosevelt haters by having the War Department take the lead.

When the chief of staff reached for the football, the presidential quarterback cheerfully pressed it into his hands. Then Marshall unveiled a remarkable secret play. Since protocol and practice forbade his issuing a formal appeal to Congress, he decided in the latter days of June to turn to print. At the end of the fiscal year in 1940, he had not bothered to make a written report to the secretary of war on the state of the army, as had long been customary for chiefs of staff; now he found the timing just right. If he and his staff worked at a breakneck pace, they could produce his first *biennial* report, and in it he could say what he pleased about the development of the army under his stewardship—and about the need to prevent the army's crumbling away as draftees with a year's training went home in dribs and drabs, to be replaced by raw recruits.

Putting aside his cherished private life, working day and night for the best part of a week, Marshall set down his view of the problems facing the army, and into his narrative wove material supplied by his assistants on the details of army activities. The document appeared in print on July 3, only three days following the end of the biennium to which it was devoted.

No one could charge the chief of staff with being evasive. After fourteen pages of texts and charts reviewing the progress of the army since July 1, 1939, Marshall presented a section boldly headed "Recommendations for the Elimination of Certain Legal Limitations and Restrictions," in which he flatly declared that the War Department should be given "authority to extend the period of the Selective Service men, the officers of the Reserve Corps and the units of the National Guard." Besides that, eager to make all his points, he introduced a discussion of "task forces" being trained for "possible special operations," and he declared that legal limitations acceptable when they were adopted "now hamstring the development of the Army into a force immediately available for whatever defensive measures may be necessary" (as the law now stood, draftees could not be sent to such possible outposts as Iceland or smaller islands in the Atlantic).

For all his authority, all the respect he had won in the past two years, all his skill in dealing with persons of different kinds, Marshall had not yet perfected his knowledge of the sensibilities of senators and congressmen. He had not thought to send informal word of his intentions to such congressional overlords as Speaker of the House Sam Rayburn, who read Marshall's declaration only after it was printed and bound. Dwelling in a subculture that viewed no action as innocent and every move as a calculated attempt to manipulate or coerce, the Speaker exploded: The army was not going to push him out on a slender political limb that would almost certainly break. Fortunately, the chief of staff managed with some effort to soothe Rayburn. With the president the report offered Marshall some immediate benefits, since its publication led to a meeting at which "he let me do all the talking for a change."

Although Marshall said that he had deliberately used the term "task force"—an expression not in general usage at the time—it quickly proved to be another land mine, arousing congressional suspicions that what he was really talking about was a new American Expeditionary Force, like Pershing's, to be sent off to fight overseas. That was not the case, he told the Senate Military Affairs Committee on July 9. He was merely speaking of the efficient creation of a "self-contained, self-supporting force" for carrying out specific missions; depending on the job, it might be five thousand men or thirty thousand. That was all. Nevertheless, in a White House meeting on July 14, attended by the president and the chief of staff and a constellation of sympathetic congressional leaders of both houses and both parties, agreement was reached, against Marshall's wishes, to disregard the proposal to remove the geographical restriction, in order to avoid a legislative storm that might destroy the chances of extending the time in service. Marshall and Stimson spoke sternly to Roosevelt, attempting to hold him in line on the geographical point, but FDR felt that the danger of losing the whole cause was too great.

On July 15, with the campaign in progress, FDR now "put the problem squarely up to Congress," as a reporter observed, telling his press conference that if the extension did not pass, the army would face serious disintegration. But he had not yet sent a formal message to Congress. As a believer in the pivotal importance of timing, he wished to make this move at the psychological moment. To take the temperatures on Capitol Hill and so determine when this moment had arrived, FDR deputized not a veteran legislative hand but the chief of staff, who then conferred with Senator Alben Barkley, the majority leader, and with others high and low, and reported on July 16 that the time had come; the message should be sent as soon as possible. "There is evidently," said the general, "a much better understanding of the situation than was the case a few days ago."

Much—probably most—of this improved understanding was due to Marshall himself and the trust he had built up over his two years in office. As the first result, after various weakening amendments had failed, the Senate on August 7 passed, by a vote of 45 to 30, a bill empowering the president to continue the active military duty of draftees, reservists, and National Guardsmen for eighteen months beyond their original one-year terms. Newspaper reports referred to this resolution as having been "urgently requested by General Marshall." Without him, there is little doubt, the bill would not even have been introduced, and if it had been it would have rapidly foundered.

But there remained the House of Representatives, much more divided on this issue than the Senate. Marshall spoke to the congressmen with his customary candor. Discussing newspaper stories about the plight of the unhappy draftees, the general said: "It is exceedingly difficult to develop military forces, because soldiers are only human; they read the papers. Like all of us humans, with a little encouragement they can feel very sorry for themselves." Marshall also commented on reports that "some source outside the Army" was circulating petitions for soldiers to sign and send to Congress in an attempt to defeat the extension bill. "We cannot continue to ignore such actions," the chief of staff said firmly. "We must treat them as soldiers; we cannot have a political club and call it an Army." To end the uncertainty, he said, the legislators must make up their minds and act rapidly—unless they chose to reverse American policy and create a large professional army (a development about as likely as an outbreak of brotherly love between Capitol Hill and the White House). He could get billions of dollars now, Marshall told the congressmen, but supplying money would be "futile unless you provide the highly trained personnel."

Still, the prognosis in the House was no better than doubtful. A Gallup poll published on August 5 showed a national split, with 50 percent in favor of extension and 45 percent opposed, the most favorable section being the South, with 63 percent supporting the bill. Congressmen, many of whom hated Roosevelt and all of whom would face election in 1942, wavered. At least seventeen members of Irish descent were said to be basing their votes on anti-British feeling; some Republicans who hated Wendell Willkie as a traitor to Republicanism opposed the legislation because Willkie supported it; other congressmen thought they would be breaking faith by holding draftees past their year of service. The America First Committee did an effective job of stirring up opposition to the bill. Another notable factor was the decision of Joseph Martin, the Republican leader in the House, to make the vote a strictly party-line affair—it seemed so tempting an issue for his minority party to exploit—in spite of his own personal if unspoken belief that for the good of the country the bill ought to pass.

So close did the issue seem as discussion raged that Marshall decided on an extraordinary step. He, more than the president or any other politician, had become identified with the bill; now, profoundly worried that his hard-won and still raw army might melt away before his eyes, he induced Representative James Wadsworth, the original sponsor of the 1940 draft bill in the House, to invite forty of his fellow Republicans to a meeting held in the private dining room of the Army and Navy Club. "I talked to them from seven o'clock at night until two in the morning," Marshall said, exaggerating the time by perhaps an hour or two, though it was certainly a long and exhausting session. "Struggling with them," the chief of staff drew on all his information and presented his case with all his earnestness.

Unmoved, one congressman counterattacked, saying with

absolute frankness, "You put the case very well, but I'll be damned if I'm going along with Mr. Roosevelt."

Marshall had only one response to such behavior. Twenty years earlier he had not allowed General Pershing to act unwisely out of personal hostility to General March, and now he was not going to allow this willful congressman to escape unscathed. With righteous anger he said, "You're going to let plain hatred of the personality dictate to you to do something that you realize is very harmful to the interests of the country."

So it seemed, not only for this congressman but for a number of others. Marshall felt that, at best, he was picking up only a handful of votes, not only because the congressmen hated Roosevelt but because many of them feared the reaction of their constituents if they supported the extension of service time. Going all the way politically, the chief of staff assured these men that if they would vote for extension he would campaign for them in 1942—"I would personally do everything I could."

Even this remarkable and potent promise left most of the group unmoved. Declining the offer, they told the chief of staff that even with his support they would be defeated in 1942 if they supported the legislation. But others agreed to vote for the bill, saying that they could see the need for it. Marshall actually wrote down their names, fully intending to make good on his campaign promise in 1942.

On August 12 Marshal Pétain, chief of the Vichy French state, turned over the effective control of his government to Admiral Jean Francois Darlan, considered one of the most pro-Nazi French leaders; now, said the aged marshal, all Frenchmen should collaborate willingly in the building of Adolf Hitler's New Order in Europe. On the same day Secretary of State Cordell Hull, in association with British diplomats, attempted to convince the Japanese that the United States and Britain would resist any move by Japan that threatened the independence of Thailand. And only seven weeks after the opening of the Russian front, the greatest of the war thus far, the German Army's southern drive had reached the Black Sea, cutting off Odessa and creating frightful visions in the minds of strategists who could see Hitler's legions soon assaulting the gates of Asia.

In the evening of this eventful day, the eyes of America and of much of the rest of the world were focused on Washington where, after wearying hours of debate, the galleries packed with spectators, the House began its roll call on the draft bill. The

Democratic leaders had made telephone calls to influential Democrats in states across the country, urging them to put pressure on doubtful members. Countering these moves, Representative Clare Hoffman, a Michigan Republican, had that morning sent a letter to his colleagues assuring them that "if you don't watch your step, your political hide, which is very near and dear to you, will be tanning on the barn door." Now all must watch the tally. The suspense deepened as for forty-five minutes the clerk growled out the names from his list of 432, listened for the answer, then repeated the member's vote. One Democrat from New York, now hoping to defeat the bill, changed his vote from aye to nay. The majority leader, Representative John McCormack of Massachusetts, scurried about the chamber, foraging for support, and succeeded by a personal appeal in inducing three Democrats who were abstaining to agree to switch their votes to aye if the need should arise.

Finally the clerk rumbled out the last name. Speaker Rayburn, after pounding the gavel block, declared in measured tones, "The yeas are 203 and the nays are 202 and the bill is passed." A one-vote margin! Then confusion. A Republican member claimed that his vote had not been recorded; another joined him. The Speaker dismissed the claim of the first congressman. Republicans sitting near the second member shouted arguments on his behalf, but the clerk, after consulting his roll call, reported to the Speaker that the member had indeed been counted against the bill. Democratic leaders were visibly relieved, and Rayburn announced: "The vote stands and the bill is passed." But the fight was not over until, after shouted parliamentary exchanges, the Speaker declared "in positive tones" that "the chair does not permit to have its word questioned."

Nor could the Senate question the House version. To avoid any further discussion in the House, the Senate leadership agreed to accept the House bill with no changes. On the day after the House vote, Hamilton Fish declared that the administration had won a "Pyrrhic victory through the use of power, patronage, and political bosses." And he seemed to feel that the isolationists were actually enjoying the last laugh. The one-vote margin, Fish said, proved that Congress could "be depended upon to vote three-to-one against involvement in wars in Europe, Africa and Asia"—with one proviso—"unless we are attacked." Senator Wheeler commented that the vote gave "notice to the administration that they should go slowly in trying to further commit this country to war."

The breathtakingly close vote and the political conclusions being drawn from it provided much for the veteran Congress-watcher in the White House to ponder. Without the powerful blows struck by General Marshall, always steady and decisive in his dealings with Congress, the U.S. Army would have been going to pieces as trained men were replaced by green recruits, with the autumn of 1941 approaching. For the chief of staff the whole affair offered one striking lesson: He could generate support and votes on Capitol Hill just by being himself in situations in which not only Roosevelt but Democratic congressional leaders would almost certainly fail. It represented a curious turn of events for a professional soldier who had not the slightest scrap of personal political ambition—but who had "an uncanny eye for the political angle of every problem."

One of the Republican congressmen at the meeting at the Army and Navy Club whom Marshall did succeed in winning over justified his vote to his district party chairman by the thought that General Marshall "is a fighting man and an able man, and if the politicians would leave him alone I think he would be much better off." Indeed, he declared, "I would stake my life that he is sound."

CHAPTER NINE

LORD BEAVERBROOK'S CRYSTAL BALL

Where was the president of the United States?

On the morning of August 3, 1941, seeming like anybody else who could escape the humid heat, he had left Washington by train. That evening, at New London, Connecticut, he had boarded the yacht *Potomac,* which had then moved down the Thames River channel and sailed eastward on Long Island Sound. For several days now the Navy Department had issued reports, based on word from the yacht, containing such dull and innocuous news as "all members of party showing effects of sunning. Fishing luck good," and "all on board well and weather excellent." But anyone reading these words could note a certain lack of explicitness; the dispatch did not say *the president* was showing the effects or enjoying the fishing or, indeed, was aboard at all. Reporters were annoyed that for the first time no representatives of the press had been permitted to cover a presidential vacation cruise; they had all been left behind in New London.

Roosevelt had hardly been out of the White House for the past four or five months. During much of this time, he had stayed shut up in his big bedroom on the second floor of the east wing, complaining of colds and sinus infections and the influenza he had pleaded as an excuse to stay out of the lend-lease quarrel with the Senate; he had rarely appeared in his executive office. But associates wondered how sick he had really been. FDR's confidential secretary and intimate friend and adviser, Missy LeHand, diagnosed her boss's ailment as mostly "a case of sheer exasperation"—both with the isolationists, who claimed that he was rushing the country into war, and with the interventionists, who claimed that he was doing far too little to hinder Hitler.

Noting that the trip had no sooner begun than the president seemed to be recovering "his usual gaiety of spirit," Dr. McIntire, as always a member of the party, felt much encouraged. Like others in the White House circle, the doctor, a Navy admiral, had been concerned that throughout the spring his eminent client had been "more reserved than usual, less inclined for company." But on the second day of the outing, FDR performed like his normal self. After he treated a group of royal Scandinavian exiles to a day's fishing in Buzzards Bay, he returned three of his guests—good-looking princesses—to the local yacht-club dock in a speedboat with himself at the wheel (the others had to go back in a launch). The next day, August 5, the *Potomac* appeared in public again, cruising slowly northward through the Cape Cod Canal while men in civilian holiday garb, one of them wearing glasses and flaunting an impressive cigarette holder, waved jovially to onlookers on shore.

But this latter group of holidayers was actually drawn from the *Potomac*'s crew. As for the president himself, at 6:17 in the morning on August 5, he and Dr. McIntire and the other members of the party had transferred from the yacht to the heavy cruiser *Augusta,* which lay waiting in Vineyard Sound. Nearby rode another of FDR's seagoing homes, the *Tuscaloosa,* and five destroyers, and when the transfer of the distinguished party was completed, the flotilla put out to sea, heading east past Nantucket Shoals lightship and then, well out in the Atlantic, bearing northeast at a brisk twenty-one knots. Roosevelt enjoyed the success of his own plot—the "delightful story" he created for the *Potomac*'s mission of deception. He expressed particular amusement at having deceived even the "good Colonel" Starling, the head of his Secret Service detail, who kept a careful eye on the *Potomac* as she moved through the Cape Cod Canal.

Greeting the president when he came aboard the *Augusta* were General Marshall, Admiral Stark, and the commander in chief of the Atlantic Fleet, Admiral Ernest J. King. The chief of staff's orderly had packed winter clothes, but that was the only clue Mrs. Marshall had picked up about her husband's destination (Marshall, on FDR's orders, had not even revealed it to Hap Arnold, who was aboard the *Tuscaloosa*). When a reporter from the *New York Herald Tribune* telephoned the Marshalls' house in Leesburg and asked, "Do you know where General Marshall is?" Mrs. Marshall's sister, who took the call, responded, "That's funny. I just bought a *Herald Tribune* to try to find out." "You win!" said the caller, and hung up. Now after three or four days, noting the consistent thinness of the news from the *Potomac* and the absence from Washington of the chiefs of the services—and, interestingly, seeing that their speculations met no official denials—the reporters began to suspect that somewhere in the North Atlantic a truly big story was taking shape.

The beginning went back to September 1939, when President Roosevelt had taken an unusual step for a head of state. In a letter congratulating Winston Churchill on his appointment as First Lord of the Admiralty, making the somewhat exaggerated observation that "you and I occupied similar positions in the World War," FDR offered Churchill the opportunity to "keep me in touch personally with anything you want me to know about." Unlike Neville Chamberlain, Churchill recognized an important hand of friendship when it was proffered, and he "responded with alacrity," signing himself "Naval Person." Thus began not only a correspondence unique in modern history but a study in long-distance friendship and mutually growing curiosity about the participant at the other end.

After returning to Washington from his Caribbean cruise in December 1940, while he was evolving the idea for lend-lease, Roosevelt remarked to Harry Hopkins one day that some of the questions of interest to the United States and Britain "could be settled if Churchill and I could just sit down for awhile." This was pure Roosevelt—person-to-person dealings at the highest level, unhampered by titled intermediaries or obfuscating bureaucrats: two men simply sitting by a fire and talking things out. He had hoped to use this kind of approach with Britain in 1937 or 1938, to stave off the advance of international menace, but Neville Chamberlain had dashed that plan. Now it seemed the perfect way to clarify a relationship and solidify a tie that was not quite an alliance.

"What's stopping you?" Hopkins asked.

Suggesting by his answer that he was not being completely serious, FDR said that such a meeting could not be arranged at the moment, because neither country had an ambassador in the other's capital.

Hopkins pounced on the possibility glittering before him. "How about me going over, Mr. President?"

Roosevelt rejected the idea out of hand, and in spite of Hopkins's subsequent lobbying refused to change his mind—or so it seemed until January 3, when, unknown to Hopkins, FDR told his press conference that Hopkins would be going to England as his "personal representative for a very short trip"; he was "just going over," the president observed lightly, in the manner he enjoyed employing with the press, "to say 'How do you do?' to a lot of my friends."

When he heard the news, Hopkins rushed from his bedroom to the president's office in the west wing, not only to make sure that the report was accurate, but to inform FDR that he would be leaving right away, before he was made to seek advice from "a lot of people" in the State Department.

On hearing that Roosevelt was sending Harry Hopkins over to England for a visit, Churchill exclaimed: "Who?" But it did not take him long to learn Hopkins's status in the Rooseveltian world. The prime minister had the visitor's aircraft met by a guard of honor and laid on a special train to take him to London. From this beginning the visit unfolded as an Anglo-American event of the first importance, for the understanding of Churchill it gave Hopkins (and hence Roosevelt), for the picture of a defiant Britain FDR's trusted emissary could take back home—a Britain whose situation was certainly serious but not at all as close to desperation as it had been painted by the recently departed American ambassador, Joseph P. Kennedy—and for the insights into Roosevelt that Hopkins offered Churchill. Hopkins thus became a switchboard connecting the two leaders in London and Washington. In a letter handwritten on hotel stationery—Claridge's—Hopkins reported to FDR that "*Churchill* is the gov't in every sense of the word—he controls the grand strategy and often the details," though he added an insightful qualifying point: "The politicians and upper crust pretend to like him." Essentially, however, Churchill "is the one and only person over here with whom you need to have a full meeting of minds." And Churchill was eager to see Roosevelt, "the sooner the better."

For various reasons—the length of congressional deliberations over lend-lease, successive British military disasters in the Mediterranean—the much-desired meeting had to be postponed several times. For many weeks Roosevelt's spring malaise, when lend-lease did not prove the hoped-for sweeping answer to interventionist-isolationist hostilities, took some of the edge off his anticipation of a rendezvous with the prime minister. During this gray period, Harold Ickes noted that the president "still has the country if he will take it and lead it. But he won't have it very much longer unless he does something." Then, for reasons he did not disclose, FDR revived his interest in a meeting at sea with Churchill, a "something" that could be shrouded in secrecy before the event and dramatically revealed to the world afterward. It would offer personal excitement and fulfillment, and it could constitute a dramatic affirmation of Anglo-American solidarity.

From the chief of staff's point of view, the meeting could hardly do more than that. He and Admiral Stark had received little advance notice from the president; they and their accompanying officers had hurried to New York and then transferred by destroyer to the *Augusta,* Admiral King's flagship, and the *Tuscaloosa.* During the trip north, the service chiefs, who were embarked in the *Augusta,* traveled separately from the planners and the other officers they had brought with them, who sailed in the *Tuscaloosa.* Since the whole mission came "as a complete surprise," Marshall said, "there was not much opportunity to plan for a specific meeting." Only matters "that were almost self-evident" could be discussed by the American military and naval officers. Marshall looked on the coming sessions as an opportunity to meet the British chiefs of staff and "to come to some understanding with them as to how they worked and what their principal problems were." He did not anticipate much more in the way of results; the president's overriding concern with secrecy, he felt, had decreed that the Americans could undertake no discussion of "heavy matters" with the British. So completely had FDR's mantle of mystery cloaked the operation that he had not even discussed the agenda for the meeting with the British or with his own aides; the planning for this conference presented an almost pure example of Roosevelt's propensity for holding all the threads in his own hands. It had been his project from the outset; Churchill, though the other essential participant, had been allowed to do little more than give his approval. In the circumstances, the prime minister was unlikely to play hard to get.

Early in the morning of Thursday, August 7, Admiral King's flotilla sighted the rocky southern coast of Newfoundland, and at

9:24 the *Augusta* anchored in Ship Harbor, Placentia Bay, a bleak inlet framed by low hills garnished with scattered pine trees. During the morning, FDR and members of his party fished from the forecastle of the *Augusta,* the most notable presidential catch being "a large and ugly fish" no one could identify; Roosevelt ordered it pickled for presentation to the Smithsonian Institution on his return to Washington. In the afternoon, after more fishing and an inspection of the U.S. naval air station under construction at Argentia, the president held a conference with the military and naval members of his party. To these American leaders it was not so much a time for drawing up war plans as it was the day when the army's struggle for survival approached its climax. That same evening, hundreds of miles away in Washington, the Senate would vote on the draft-extension bill, and action by the House would follow within a few days. Particularly poignant to Marshall was the fact that if the bill should fail to pass, the army would actually find itself less effective than it had been before the passing of the 1940 draft act, because regular units had been split up in order to provide leadership for the new formations that had been created. A military planner—particularly since the outcome of the House vote looked very much in doubt—could not help seeing that this was an awkward time to meet with British leaders. "We were," said Marshall, "in a very desperate plight."

Despite the various handicaps, one member of the American team had produced a short list of principles he believed ought to guide the Americans in the forthcoming discussions. Having seen British staffs in action on a visit to England, Hap Arnold knew that Churchill and his advisers would not come unprepared to Argentia; the Americans ought not to "come into this one cold" either. After being told en route the purpose of the voyage, Arnold, who a few weeks earlier had become the chief of the newly created United States Army Air Forces, therefore suggested that the president and the service chiefs agree: *a)* to develop a plan to build up the U.S. Army and Navy so that they could meet the present international situation; *b)* to give the British and other foreign governments only items that they could use effectively and that were not required by the army and navy; *c)* to make no commitments in the meetings in response to British requests until U.S. authorities had carefully studied them. This third principle, probably aimed at the president (no one, and certainly not one of Marshall's subordinates,

nates, could regard the chief of staff as impulsive and open-handed when it came to giving away army equipment), like the others seemed to find no objections from Roosevelt or the chiefs.

At the afternoon meeting aboard the *Augusta,* FDR outlined American policy, stressing the protection of shipping in the Atlantic—on a map he drew a line extending from *east* of the Azores to *east* of Iceland, thus enlarging the "Western Hemisphere" far beyond the definition offered in geography textbooks—and the ensuring of aircraft deliveries to Britain. In the Pacific, he said, U.S. forces in the Philippines ought to be strengthened and Japanese incursions into the Dutch East Indies must be resisted. He also approved a plan to send the Soviet Union a small number of planes—not many could be spared, his advisers told him. He informed these advisers, who knew it as well as he did, that they could expect the British to ask for ships, tanks, and aircraft.

At 7:30 in the morning, August 9, American destroyers made contact outside the anchorage with H.M.S. *Prince of Wales,* which unlike the shining U.S. ships wore wartime camouflage stripes and still bore scars from her battle in May with the formidable German battleship *Bismarck.* Then, after taking on an American pilot, the *Prince of Wales* surprised most of those aboard her by turning about and steaming out to sea. The great and novel occasion had been marred by the overlooking of a small detail: The U.S. and British ships were not keeping the same time, and as the guests at the party, (even if Newfoundland belonged to the British Commonwealth), Churchill and his associates had arrived an hour and a half early. But when the *Prince of Wales* returned later, steaming through a lane of ships that brought her abreast of the *Augusta,* with her band playing "The Star-Spangled Banner" and the Americans responding with "God Save the King," she dropped anchor on the stroke of nine. The mist that earlier shrouded the bay had disappeared to reveal a harbor crowded with ships flying the Stars and Stripes, their decks lined with sailors cheering and waving. On the bridge of the British battleship stood a plump figure in a blue uniform that looked to be possibly naval, possibly something more arcane. He and his companions stared across the intervening strip of water at the *Augusta,* on whose quarterdeck an awning had been erected. Beneath the awning clustered a group of officers and a tall man in a Palm Beach suit, who was as eager for his first glimpse of Churchill as the prime minister was to see him.

At eleven o'clock the admiral's barge from the *Prince of Wales* brought Churchill to the *Augusta* for his official call on the president, who received him standing, his back against the rail, on the arm of his son, Army Captain Elliott Roosevelt, who for the sake of a family reunion had found himself temporarily assigned as an aide to his father, along with his brother, Ensign Franklin D. Roosevelt, Jr. After presenting the president a letter from King George, Churchill introduced the accompanying members of his staff. "One look at the Prime Minister's company," said Admiral McIntire, "made us know that he had come prepared for full discussion of every possible topic." Churchill had brought his longtime friend and personal scientific adviser, the acid-tongued Professor F. A. Lindemann—known as "the Prof"—who had recently become Lord Cherwell; Sir Alexander Cadogan, from the Foreign Office; and an array of military, air, and naval officers, headed by the First Sea Lord, Admiral Sir Dudley Pound; Sir Wilfrid Freeman, vice-chief of the Air Staff; and the chief of the Imperial General Staff, General Sir John Dill, a tall, bald, bony-faced officer who displayed great charm and directness.

Another passenger aboard the *Prince of Wales* was Harry Hopkins, who as administrator of the lend-lease program had gone to London in July to discuss the new situation created by the German invasion of Russia, although he was so feeble from his chronic illness that he seemed to one British officer to be "dying on his feet." Realizing that at the forthcoming Atlantic meeting Roosevelt and Churchill would be limited in their global thinking without a clear idea of Soviet needs, Hopkins had accepted a Russian suggestion that he go to Moscow and had won quick approval for the trip from both the president and the prime minister. Anyone else in his physical state would have been propped up in a hospital room with a shawl over his shoulders, but the zealous Hopkins gave little thought to the hardships he would endure in a long, cold flight across the top of Europe (he spent most of the trip huddled in the tail blister of the Catalina flying boat, ready as the substitute tail gunner to squeeze off bursts from his weapon if enemy planes should appear). Hurrying back from the Soviet Union in order to catch the *Prince of Wales* for Placentia Bay, Hopkins found that the bag of medicines that kept him functioning had been left behind, and he arrived at Scapa Flow so sick that the admiral commanding feared that his visitor might die before morning. But after enjoying the benefits of two long nights of sleep in the admiral's quarters, Hopkins had improved enough so that Churchill could radio Roosevelt: "Harry returned dead-beat from Russia but is lively again now." Much moved, the British captain of the Catalina spoke in his report of his passenger's "unbelievable courage, determination and appreciation for the services of others. He was a noteworthy example of unparalleled devotion to duty."

Eager to smooth the way for the meeting of the two leaders, Hopkins had come over to the *Augusta* almost as soon as the *Prince of Wales* dropped anchor. He was not free of the jitters. For the good of the common cause, these men, one an old friend, one almost brand-new but nevertheless a person to whom he felt close, must take to each other. As a marriage broker on a grand scale, Hopkins had waited nervously for eleven o'clock to come. To his relief and pleasure, everything went well. After the ceremonial greetings, the scene on the quarterdeck easily turned into a friendly occasion, with little groups chatting as if they were attending a cocktail party, the American officers of each service talking with their British opposite numbers. Hopkins had encouraged Roosevelt to include the service chiefs and other officers in his party, in order for the Americans to become acquainted with the British chiefs' ways of thinking and operating. So it was that General Marshall first came to know the man who was then his British counterpart, General Dill. While Roosevelt and Churchill were making contact on their lofty level, the two chiefs of staff—who found that they had many traits in common—more quietly took their first steps into a friendship.

For the next three days, through lunches, dinners, a church service with U.S. and British sailors intermingled on the afterdeck of the *Prince of Wales,* and formal and informal conferences, with launches busily passing to and fro, the American and British leaders and their staffs discussed and debated political and military questions. The British, as Marshall said later, "would have liked to go ahead with fixed plans." From the military point of view, however, such goals lay beyond the American grasp, and politically they were not even deemed desirable. In spite of Churchill's hopes, Roosevelt proved as difficult a fish to net as American politicians had always found him. Some members of the British party had even dreamed that this great secret expedition across the Atlantic might end in a declaration of American belligerency. One evening the prime minister had remarked to a member of his party: "I have an idea that something really big may be happening—something really big." He did not seem to understand that not only would America proclaim no alliance with Britain, but that for Roosevelt the idea of providing "all aid short of war" meant exactly what it said; the president still clung to the hope of ensuring the defeat of the Axis powers without the participation of American troops. Through all the changing circumstances, FDR with perfect consistency had held this position since 1938, when he declared his desire for great fleets of airplanes to deter Hitler—a desire General Marshall and the other military leaders had found questionable then and with which, in its recurring forms, they had differed since. Roosevelt's wish to send all possible aid to Russia fitted perfectly into his overall outlook.

Now, at Argentia, realizing that the British had an illusory view of the United States as a vast warehouse stocked with military supplies, Marshall revealed again the tension between the president and the armed services on the question of matériel by putting forth Hap Arnold's point *a):* American requirements, not British needs, should determine what aid the United States could offer. Although Roosevelt did not formally differ with this idea, he still placed all his emphasis on pushing goods across the Atlantic. To him, it continued to be more important to keep Britain at fighting strength than to build up well-nourished American forces. His political opponents, incessantly accusing him of preparing the United States for war, never seemed to grasp this point.

At Argentia, Roosevelt, as Admiral McIntire said, "had no mind to go further than a statement of common purposes and principles in the peace that would follow war." Before leaving Washington, FDR had told Sumner Welles (bypassing Cordell Hull) that he wished to draw up a "general agreement" between the United States and Britain, and in the first meeting on the *Augusta* Churchill said to the president that he hoped that at the end of the conference they could issue a joint declaration of the "aims and desires of the two governments." The result, drafted by Churchill, Welles, and Cadogan, and then chewed over by all participants through successive versions—since both Roosevelt and Churchill were concerned about appeasing various sectors of opinion back home—was the declaration of principles known as the Atlantic Charter. The president and the prime minister declared that on these principles they based "their hopes for a better future for the world." In so doing they committed themselves to self-government for all people, with no "territorial changes that do not accord with the freely expressed wishes of the peoples concerned," and they proclaimed their belief that all peoples should be able to choose the form of government under which they would live. They also advocated economic cooperation and a Rooseveltian "freedom from fear and want." Although necessarily vague, because of differences in the American and the British points of view, these commitments had the ring of effective and not surprising propaganda. At the same time, as freely made undertakings, they held the possibility of future problems. A unique feature of the charter as a war document was its birth as the offspring of a belligerent power and a country officially neutral. Certainly it engaged in no euphemism but spoke bluntly of the "destruction of the Nazi tyranny."

The charter took final form on Tuesday, August 12, the very day of the narrow-squeak vote in the House of Representatives on the draft-extension bill. This final form was merely an approved typescript, with telegraphic versions sent off to the two capitals; FDR wanted no embossed and engraved document, embellished with seal and ribbon, that Senate isolationists could interpret as a treaty.

Shortly before five o'clock on this Tuesday afternoon, under drizzly gray skies, the *Prince of Wales* weighed anchor and began to move out of Placentia Bay. As she passed the *Augusta,* her band gave the Americans a farewell of "Auld Lang Syne." Then the American party began to disperse. Some of the officers were to fly back to Washington; Marshall and Stark, accompanied by Welles, would make the first leg of the return trip in the *Tuscaloosa,* leaving Roosevelt, Hopkins, and the rest of FDR's original party as a civilian group relaxing on the *Augusta.* The president intended to make a slow voyage home, in order not to attract attention while Churchill was moving through waters infested with U-boats. As a proud navy man, FDR pointed out in notes he dictated for a possible magazine article that "every night of the whole trip, either when we were at sea or in Argentia harbor, we 'darkened ship' after sundown, and although there were twenty-eight ships in Argentia harbor, this was carried out so effectively that not a single light could be seen on any ship." The United States might officially be at peace, but the commander in chief believed that his navy was on the alert.

At a port in Maine, Roosevelt and his party transferred to the *Potomac* for a little final pleasure cruising before boarding the train at Rockland for the return to Washington. The train paused at Portland while Roosevelt had a short conference with a forty-year-old assistant to Navy Secretary Knox, Adlai Stevenson, who remembered bumping into the door on his way out. Never one to waste any time in making use of first names, even strange ones, FDR called the younger man "Adlai" right away.

On the first day of the Atlantic Conference, a member of Churchill's party watching the prime minister and the president from the deck of the *Prince of Wales* had been moved to recall famous journeys and encounters from earlier times—Alexander the Great traveling to Siwa to meet the god Ammon, "one of history's remarkable encounters"; Cleopatra sailing to Tarsus to ally herself with Mark Antony; Napoleon and Czar Alexander meeting on the raft at Tilsit. Might it not be that this Council of Placentia would be inscribed in the pages of history, and that future schoolchildren would be required to learn August 9 along with the dates of Magna Carta and the Declaration of Independence? On the way home this observer and the rest of the ship's company learned of the Atlantic Charter not from those who had taken part in drawing it up but through an official broadcast from London, picked up on a radio in the wardroom. Eagerly the officers clustered around the speaker, waiting to hear what had happened behind the scenes at the show they had just witnessed. But as they heard Clement Attlee, the deputy prime minister, drily delivering one by one the clauses of the charter, the swollen balloon of excited expectation was deflated by anticlimax; faces grew long. There was no alliance, there were merely words. Yet the listener comforted himself with the thought that the charter at least amounted to a beginning and that the president had "set down his love of freedom." The Englishman did not seem to understand that the American system, with its separation-of-powers principle, did not permit the president to proclaim an alliance with a wave of his wand—or his cigarette holder. Nor could he appreciate the fact that by proclaiming his love of freedom jointly with Churchill, Roosevelt had given himself a political platform on which to base his actions in support of Britain.

One of the most striking aspects of the Atlantic meeting, thought this Englishman, was the evidence that the Americans still belonged to peacetime, with their magazines crammed "with almost eatable coloured illustrations of gigantic boiled hams, roast beef and other rationed food, to say nothing of rich, creamy puddings"; they dwelt in a world of "gleaming touring cars, new clothes, luxury." Between "ourselves and those charming and virile young Americans was the War, strange and impalpable as a curtain." The Englishman could hardly know that the American president, working in his own fashion day by day, hoped and intended to keep that curtain in place.

What Churchill and his generals and admirals sought at Placentia Bay was commitment: The United States must agree to definite military plans involving times and places. In trying to put their understandings with the Americans into the indicative mood, however, the British failed; the United States was not ready to regard its participation in the war as a fact. Viewed as a possibility, however, participation took on a different look. The president and his military and naval advisers had long been ready to engage in discussions held in the subjunctive mood: *If* the United States should become an active belligerent, *then . . .*

A year earlier, in the summer of 1940, General Marshall and Admiral Stark, in agreement with Roosevelt, had dispatched observers to London to see with their own eyes exactly how well Britain was standing up to the onslaught of the Luftwaffe (would sending more aid to the British really constitute a sound investment?) and to engage in informal discussions with representatives of the British chiefs of staff. (As an indication of the Americans' unreadiness for war in earnest, while the officers were aboard the liner *Britannic* on what was supposed to be their secret mission, the ship's radio picked up a news broadcast announcing the trip.) Making it clear that they were empowered to do no more than talk, the Americans in London had listened to British views on strategy, arms production, and other matters, and had agreed that exchanges of information between the two countries ought to be put on a regular basis. The Americans soon passed one highly important piece of news to the British: In an operation dubbed "Magic," American cryptanalysts had created a machine that enabled them to read Japanese diplomatic ciphers; and not long thereafter a group of young American intelligence representatives arrived in England bearing one of the actual decrypting machines (which were code-named "Purple").

Following the talks with the British chiefs of staff, who had not been content to send subordinates to the meetings but had themselves taken part, the Americans, on returning to Washington, gave long and hard study to questions of strategy and arms production. Marshall's planners readily accepted the principle that if the United States entered the war, the Atlantic would be the prime theater, but they saw probable trouble in the Pacific as well; U.S. policy, they said, should be based on keeping Pacific operations secondary to those in the Atlantic. Speaking as men who knew the relatively bare state of the American military cupboard, they urged caution in diplomatic dealings with Japan, because "we are not now prepared and will not be prepared for several years to come" for a major effort in the Far East. Thus in October, when Churchill asked the president to send a naval squadron to Singapore, Marshall called it "as unfavorable a moment as you could choose" for stirring up trouble with the Japanese.

Although the navy traditionally gave greater weight than the army to Far Eastern concerns, Admiral Stark agreed with Marshall's planners that if the United States became involved in war, Germany would be the principal enemy. In November the admiral produced a document succinctly outlining American strategic possibilities. He seems to have created this draft, a copy of which was sent to Marshall, partly out of the sense of grappling with thin air that often frustrated Marshall and his planners at the time. Designed to reach the president, Stark's reasoning was "presented for the purpose of arriving at a decision as to the National Objective in order to facilitate naval preparation." In its formal version, dated November 12, 1940, the memorandum discussed four possible plans for American action. The first one—Plan A—would be the limiting of U.S. activity to the defense of the Western Hemisphere and the fourth—Plan D—would call for a strong offensive in the Atlantic and a holding defensive in the Pacific. Although accepting for the present the need to adhere to Plan A, with the United States still officially a neutral, Stark spoke out for Plan D—"Plan

Dog," in army and navy argot—as the guide for future U.S. actions.

Since the army did not readily swallow all of the admiral's reasoning, back-and-forth discussions followed between the services and in the Joint Planning Committee. General Marshall expressed some fear that even under Plan Dog the navy contemplated a greater commitment in the Pacific than the United States should make: "It would be just what Germany would like to see us undertake." He suggested to Admiral Stark that the United States ought to reorder her war plans on the assumption that the national interest demanded the rejection of proposals "that do not have for their immediate goal the survival of the British Empire and the defeat of Germany." But Stark saw the Pacific situation in realistic terms. With fire smoldering behind the official, typewritten phrases, he denied that he in any sense sought war with Japan; if such a war arose, it would "not be through my doings, but because those in higher authority have decided that it is to our national interest to accept such a war." After all, he said, the navy had to plan for every possibility since it must "begin shooting the day that war eventuates."

Finally, knitting together recommendations from the two services and from the State Department, the Joint Planning Committee proposed that the United States abstain from any actions that could provoke attack by any other power, and that she make a decision "not willingly to engage in any war against Japan"; if forced into such a war, the United States should restrict operations in the Pacific "so as to permit use of forces for a major offensive in the Atlantic." The planners attached to this statement a proviso that no important Allied decision be accepted "save with clear understanding as to common objectives, as to contingents to be provided, as to operations planned, and as to command arrangement."

On January 16, as a climax to this series of requests and recommendations for a clarification of U.S. policy, the president summoned Marshall, Stark, and the secretaries of state, war, and the navy to a meeting in the White House. The group concluded, Marshall noted, that "we would stand on the defensive in the Pacific with the fleet based on Hawaii" and that "there would be no naval reinforcement of the Philippines." The navy was to become prepared to convoy shipping all the way to England. The army "should not be committed to any aggressive action until it was fully prepared to undertake it"; meanwhile, the government must pursue a conservative course. Finally the United States must make every effort to continue supplying Britain—primarily to upset what the president thought would be "Hitler's principal objective in involving us in a war at this particular time, and also to buck up England."

In his Plan Dog memorandum, Admiral Stark had recommended that the army and navy lose no time in entering into "secret staff talks on technical matters" with the British. In the midst of debating with Marshall, Stark had said he felt it essential for the Americans to "know a great deal more about British ideas than we have yet been able to glean." Did they have "realistic ideas as to what help they think they need from us to defeat Germany and Italy"? Marshall concurred. In London, Admiral Pound, the First Sea Lord, was making the same point from the other side of the table; the British, he believed, should send representatives to Washington for talks with U.S. Army and Navy representatives. The delegation "would consist of a small party which would easily pass unnoticed in the stream of missions, observers, and other officials." It was obvious to everybody on both sides of the Atlantic that in dress and activities the visiting Britons must exhibit a thorough passion for anonymity. If they attracted the attention of isolationists, in Congress or outside it, they might as well forget about any staff talks. All participants would wear civilian clothes and hope to pass as purchasing agents or members of trade delegations.

In the last week of January the new British battleship *King George V* arrived off Annapolis, bringing with her not only the new British ambassador, Lord Halifax, but a contingent of British staff officers accompanied by the able and highly literate U.S. military attaché in London, Brigadier General Raymond E. Lee. (President Roosevelt took the unprecedented step of sailing out to meet Halifax; whether he was motivated by a wish to honor the ambassador or a desire to see the new battleship remained a moot point.) The initiative launched by Admiral Stark in Washington and Admiral Pound in London was now to bear fruit in the form of fourteen U.S.-British staff conferences, spread over a period of exactly two months. Although the British representatives always appeared in mufti, their disguise could have been penetrated by any half-determined isolationist, since in ruddiness of complexion and sweep of mustache at least two of these officers carried the popular idea of a British general and admiral almost to the point of caricature.

Marshall, currently caught up in the midst of the fight for lend-lease and preoccupied with all the problems relating to the buildup of the army, seemed to regard the meetings mainly as Stark's show (perhaps because the navy more than the army felt the need for immediate information about British plans), but along with the admiral he was "rather disturbed that this might leak out" and cause an uproar, "particularly by those who were opposed to any preparations of any kind, particularly from the Middle West" (Marshall tended to use "Middle West" as a synonym for "isolationism," which was accurate in many respects but did not tell the whole story). To underscore the American refusal to make commitments, the talks were conducted "without regard to the President," in order "not to involve our government in any seemingly fixed understandings." Deniability, as it would be called in later years, was important here as well; as Marshall remembered, the president was not even supposed to know about the talks, at least not officially. At the same time, the Americans, by choosing to view the discussions in a nonpolitical light, deprived themselves of political guidance in an encounter with officers who spoke for a policy compounded of both political and military elements.

At the very first session, held in a conference room in the Navy Building, the British presented the three legs on which their strategic policy stood. Two of these, if somewhat redundant, agreed exactly with general American ideas; the European theater was the vital one, "where a decision must first be sought," and therefore Germany and Italy should be defeated first, after which would come Japan's turn. At this early point in Anglo-American collaboration, no one was spelling out just what operations U.S. forces ought to undertake in the European theater should the United States be "compelled to resort to war," as the president put it. But a statement delivered to FDR by Marshall and Stark spoke of the need to "contribute most directly to the defeat of Germany." Whatever strategy this might imply to the British, to men like Marshall—inheritors of the Grant and Pershing tradition of war—it could mean nothing less than directly assaulting the enemy, as soon as possible, with mass force.

On the third point the two sides disagreed entirely; Singapore, said the British representatives, represented the key to the defense of the British Far Eastern position, including Australia and New Zealand, and its security must accordingly be assured. Churchill pressed this same point on Roosevelt, when he asked more than once that an American squadron visit what he thought of as the Far Eastern Gibraltar. Since American naval forces might thus become involved in the defense of Singapore, the U.S. representatives objected to the introduction of political pressure, as they regarded it, into the staff decision-making process. As far as the Americans were concerned, the loss of Singapore and Malaya would no doubt mean a serious economic and moral setback to the Allies, but the first concern of the planners could not be the maintenance of British prestige in the Far East. British and American strategic interests coincided primarily in the defense of Great Britain, "and it was up to the British to do the best they could to take care of their interests elsewhere, even as it was up to the United States to defend American interests overseas." Whatever deterrent influence the Americans could exert on Japan must come from the basing of the Pacific Fleet at Pearl Harbor. (During this time, Marshall in fact expressed concern about the state of Oahu's defenses; he thought a Japanese attack was possible, and he asked for the army aircraft defending the island to be replaced by newer planes.)

At the conclusion of the American-British Conversations (ABC), as the discussions were termed, the combined staffs issued a report called ABC-1, which outlined the areas of general agreement—particularly the joint emphasis on the primacy of the European theater—and called for the immediate exchange between the two countries of "nucleus missions"—each consisting of a general, an admiral (and, in the case of the British, an air marshal), and a supporting staff. Thus would come the regular flow of information back and forth that had been foreseen during the previous summer, and if the United States should enter the war, the missions would then take on public and official character as fully empowered representatives of the respective chiefs of staff. But that would happen only *if* the United States should become a belligerent. The ABC sessions produced a great many understandings, but it all remained tentative. And as the summer of 1941 advanced, in spite of their escorting convoys far into the North Atlantic and their occupation of Iceland, the Americans' mood remained subjunctive. A despairing British officer stationed in Washington was even said to have suggested to his superiors that a Royal Navy submarine torpedo an

American ship with the aim of putting the blame on a U-boat and thus sticking Germany with the hoped-for consequences.

In the aftermath of the Atlantic Conference, the British could draw little encouragement from the president's comments. In his deeply ingrained fashion, having taken a step forward, Roosevelt then moved to one side and a little to the rear. Fending off isolationist attacks, he declared that the conference had not brought the United States closer to war and that, contrary to widespread speculation in the press, he had made no secret commitments to Churchill. Deeply depressed, the prime minister cabled Harry Hopkins, whom he genuinely admired: I DON'T KNOW WHAT WILL HAPPEN IF ENGLAND IS FIGHTING ALONE WHEN 1942 COMES. Reporting this message to the president, Hopkins observed that "all the British people I talked to believed that ultimately we will get into the war on some basis or another and if they ever reached the conclusion that this was not to be the case, that would be a very critical moment in the war and the British appeasers might have some influence on Churchill."

In an almost desperate tone, the prime minister concluded his cable to Hopkins with the wistful thought that he would be grateful IF YOU COULD GIVE ME ANY KIND OF HOPE. But Churchill's mercurial friend Lord Beaverbrook, the Canadian-born press tycoon, had no illusions. Following the Argentia conference, he had gone on to Washington and at the prime minister's request had conducted a sort of one-man opinion poll. There was not the slightest chance of the Americans' entering the war, Beaverbrook reported, until they were compelled to do so by being directly attacked. Seeing Germany as the potential attacker, he did not expect such an event to occur until both Britain and Russia had been defeated. A shrewd and accurate reader of opinion, Beaverbrook nevertheless possessed a crystal ball with an unsuspected flaw.

On February 7, 1941, Lieutenant General Walter C. Short, an officer of Marshall's age, became commanding general of the Hawaiian Department. On the same day, the chief of staff wrote the new commander a letter, not to greet him as he took up his new job but to pass along some insights into the personality of the commander of the U.S. Pacific Fleet, Admiral Husband E. Kimmel. Short's direct naval counterpart was actually Rear Admiral Claude C. Bloch, a former commander of the fleet who now, as commandant of the Fourteenth Naval District, held the responsibility of defending the navy yard. But, working in this structure of overlapping responsibilities, Short would necessarily do much business with Bloch's superior, the commander of the Pacific Fleet. Though brusque and "rather rough in his methods of doing business," the highly respected Admiral Kimmel was described to Marshall by Admiral Stark as "at heart a very kindly man" who was "entirely responsive to plain speaking on the part of the other fellow."

Kimmel, who himself had taken naval command in the Pacific only a week earlier, immediately informed Stark that he found the army arrangements for the defense of Pearl Harbor markedly inadequate. He expressed particular concern about the deficiencies in aircraft and antiaircraft guns. The admiral was right to be worried, Marshall acknowledged, but "what Kimmel does not realize is that we are tragically lacking in this matériel throughout the Army and that Hawaii is on a far better basis than any other command in the Army." Everybody lacked equipment and would continue to do so "until quantity production gets well under way." In any case, Short must always remember that the army's mission in Hawaii was to protect the Pearl Harbor base, and he should make sure that Kimmel and he understood each other without any hangover of the "old Army and Navy feuds" that still persisted "in confusing issues of national defense." Marshall suggested as a model his own relationship with the chief of naval operations: "Stark and I are on the most intimate personal basis, and that relationship has enabled us to avoid many serious difficulties."

In the scheme of American defense in the Pacific, Oahu had long been considered one of the keys. Together with Alaska and Panama, the island made up a strategic triangle giving the United States advance bases in the Pacific for offensive action against an enemy and also keeping that enemy many hundreds of miles away from the American mainland. But in May 1940 Oahu had become the most acute of the three angles because, on the order of President Roosevelt, the U.S. Fleet had transferred its base from the California coast to Pearl Harbor. FDR sought by this move to check Japanese expansionist activities, just as he had hoped to impress Hitler in 1938 by producing a flood of airplanes. But to Admiral James O. Richardson, commander of the fleet, the possible psychological effect on Japan's militarist leaders did not equal the cost of the move, which imposed on the navy the task of keeping its principal body of ships supplied over a two-thousand-mile lifeline from the mainland. The admiral saw another problem. As S. E. Morison put it, "The average young American of that era, conditioned by twenty-one years of antimilitarist doctrine by movies, books, preachers and teachers, could be induced to enlist in the armed forces . . . only by making things pleasant for him—not too much work and plenty of recreation." Thus, no matter what training the crews received during the week, the fleet customarily returned to port for weekends "to keep officers and men happy." California seemed a safer place for such indulgences than Hawaii. But the fleet existed to support national policy, not to suit the convenience of its commanders or the off-duty desires of its men. If the president's use of it "involved an element of danger," it was later observed, "such was the nature of the Navy's business. The Pacific Fleet did not exist to be safe; it existed to fight if war came." The president responded to Admiral Richardson's concern by replacing him with Admiral Kimmel.

Pearl Harbor cast a net of influence all the way across the Pacific. As the home of the fleet, the great base became the key to maintaining the American presence in the Philippines. More than twenty years earlier a Joint Board memorandum had pointed out that "without a naval superiority no military garrison, however large, will be able to defend the Philippines indefinitely as it could not be supplied with food and munitions." A revised Joint Board judgment of 1936 discussed the possibility of Japan's launching a surprise naval and air raid on Oahu or even attacking the islands with a landing force (a possibility developed in the 1932 war games in which Major Robinett had taken part). The army generally believed that Japan held her historic mission to be the attainment of preeminence in the Pacific, and a 1938 syllabus again discussed the possibility of a surprise attack. A curious piece of evidence in support of this possibility was offered by the veteran United States ambassador to Japan, Joseph C. Grew, in late January 1941, just a few days before General Short and Admiral Kimmel took up their respective posts in Hawaii. The Peruvian minister, Grew reported, had picked up rumors that the Japanese were planning a mass attack on Pearl Harbor. The idea seemed "fantastic," Grew said, but nevertheless he thought Washington ought to know about it. It seemed fantastic to the navy too; "no move against Pearl Harbor appears imminent or planned for in the foreseeable future," Kimmel was assured.

But American worries about possible Japanese actions were not groundless. Relations between the two countries, never good since the World War, had become increasingly hostile as the "China Incident"—the Japanese term for the war they had launched in 1937—continued year after year, with no resolution seeming possible. On July 26, 1940, in response to Japanese demands on Britain and France in Asia, Roosevelt issued an order restricting U.S. exports to Japan, and in September followed it with an embargo on iron and steel scrap. On July 27 Japan signed the Tripartite Pact with Germany and Italy, thereby branding herself with membership in the Axis. Although the embargo had struck Japan a truly damaging blow, it gave no evidence that it had changed the thinking of Japanese leaders.

American policy toward Japan seemed paradoxical. The United States dreaded the prospect of war in the Pacific, and yet the administration took steps that might well drive the Japanese into further adventures in Asia, against British and Dutch territory, and possibly even against the Philippines. As the president characterized it one day in October 1940, the Japanese wanted the United States to "demilitarize all of its naval and air and army bases in Wake, Midway, and Pearl Harbor." Chatting in his office, FDR then exclaimed: "God! That's the first time that any damn Jap has told us to get out of Hawaii!" But, he said, American public opinion would not "stand any nonsense."

During the ensuing year, while the two countries engaged in endless diplomatic talks and skirmishes, relations between them drifted toward disaster.

General Marshall had found the autumn of 1941 trying. In October he unburdened himself in a letter to Molly, now married to an army officer and living in Panama, where her husband was stationed. "Each day I think I have reached the peak of difficulties and pressures," wrote the general. The previous week had been the worst of all—"a combination of Russian affairs, the Japanese situation, supplies to England, the political pressures, developments in relation to National Guard and some Regular officers over relief from command, the development of the next period of training for the Army, the approaching hearings on the Lease-Loan, etc., etc., do not give me many peaceful hours." Unwisely, perhaps dangerously, the chief of staff seemed to be trying to do it all.

In dealing with FDR, Marshall, even after two years as chief of staff, had not yet perfected what each of the president's associates attempted in his own way to create—a method of handling this resourceful, charming, labile veteran of political encounters on all levels. "I didn't understand that I must find a way to do the talking," Marshall said. He did not feel that he had become "sufficiently adept in dealing with a man who was as clever as Mr. Roosevelt was about holding the boards and putting over his ideas." Persuading the president of a point could require "a great deal of wear and tear."

In a meeting on September 22, Marshall, despite his best dialectical efforts, lost what at the moment seemed an important battle with FDR. The president decided to act in accordance with a widespread opinion, which he shared, that the national defense would be well served by switching some manpower from the army to the industrial production lines. General McNair then came forward with a scheme to rotate National Guard divisions into the reserve and create new divisions in their place, and thus perhaps satisfy the president's desires while causing the least disruption to the army. Frustrated and unhappy, Marshall had no choice but to regard a version of this plan as the best he could make of a bad bargain. In his single-minded effort to build up the army, the chief of staff seemed to meet a succession of obstacles beyond imagining.

Yet he and the other American leaders held what seemed one indisputable advantage in dealing with the dangers that loomed around them. The army and navy code breakers with their remarkable Purple machine supplied the president and his advisers with a variety of Japanese diplomatic messages intercepted on their courses between the Foreign Ministry in Tokyo and Japanese representatives overseas. The handling of these intercepts, however, suffered from insufficient manpower, poor organization, and excessive secrecy. Besides, they were cast in the diplomatic cipher, used by the Japanese Foreign Office, and did not concern themselves with the movements of the armed forces. Still, by requiring extremely tight security procedures, General Marshall himself rendered the information in the messages less useful to analysts than it might otherwise have been. Thus, for all the wonderful work of the decrypters, a sort of intelligence haze swathed Japanese intentions. Despite her involvement with Britain since the summer of 1940, the United States was still a country at peace—which meant that when it came to war, the country was an amateur. Roosevelt and Marshall had both taken intimate parts in war a quarter of a century earlier, but since that strenuous time they had pursued their careers through many years of easygoing peace, when decisions did not have possibly deadly consequences. The two now resembled a small-town mayor and his police chief, ready enough to deal with shady land developers or pickpockets and purse-snatchers but lacking the grim experience required to grapple successfully with gangsters.

Even so, as November drew to its close, the diplomatic intercepts made it plain that the Japanese government planned a hostile move of some kind—although Japan's aggressive designs appeared so obvious that "an intelligence officer reading the *New York Times* could be almost as well informed on Japan's future policy as another officer scanning a number of random diplomatic messages coming off the decoding machines." On November 25, in a meeting in his office, the president told Marshall and other advisers that "we were likely to be attacked perhaps next Monday for the Japanese are notorious for making an attack without warning." Two days later the War Department informed all the commanders in the Pacific that "hostile action possible at any moment." Obsessed with the threat of sabotage, General Short assured the department that he had taken all the proper steps. So limited and creaky was the organization of the General Staff, even after two years of Marshall's leadership, that nobody in Washington had any clear idea of what the commander in Hawaii was doing or failing to do. It had never been army custom to hang over the shoulder of a commander in the field, but even the reports from this general did not receive the attention that would have made his views clear. In a separate message he called a "war warning"—not a standard term—Admiral Stark forecast aggressive Japanese action but directed the attention of his commanders in the Pacific toward the Kra Isthmus, the strategically important neck of the Malay Peninsula. This or some other point in Thailand, and Malaya and the Netherlands East Indies, were places where the planners foresaw Japanese moves—not American territory, not even the Philippines. But if the Japanese attacked any of them, what would the United States do?

On December 3 word went out from Washington to Admiral

Kimmel that the Japanese Foreign Office had instructed its diplomats at posts in British and American territory to destroy their codes and some of the cipher machines. Whatever the Japanese move would be, it would surely come soon; the destruction of coding equipment must be an immediate preliminary to war. The admiral, however, drew no conclusions from the news. Reflecting the bafflement at the top, Attorney General Francis Biddle noted after the Cabinet meeting on December 5 that the "Jap situation seems to have eased off."

During this same week, turning to a strikingly different realm, Marshall dealt with an inquiry from a congressman concerning the army's establishment of prophylactic stations near training camps. The editor of a religious magazine had termed them an "incentive to sin"; but in fact, Marshall said, the army was not encouraging prostitution. He even asserted that the rate of venereal disease was "considerably lower than that of civilian communities corresponding in size to our large camps." On the previous day, Marshall had taken time out from his pressing duties to dispatch a radio message to Sir John Dill, whose personal style and stamina had not proved equal to the almost continuous demands the prime minister made on a chief of the Imperial General Staff. Dill had resigned his post and was now to become governor of Bombay. Marshall, who had taken an unusually strong liking to the pleasant and thoughtful Englishman, invited him to proceed to India by way of the United States. The chief of staff offered to play host on a trip across the country for the visitor.

On the morning of Sunday, December 7, Marshall took his usual horseback ride. He rode alone. With Molly away now, and Katherine Marshall laid up with four broken ribs, he had no regular companion for a ride at any time of day. After returning from his constitutional, which normally took about fifty minutes "at a trot and a canter and at a full run," Marshall learned that he was wanted at the War Department; the excited caller, Colonel Rufus Bratton, did not explain why (no doubt an instance of more hypersecrecy). The chief of staff showered and then prepared to go to his office—the high command had no days off, although the general hoped to get away for a visit to Molly and her new baby in Panama, possibly in January.

Marshall arrived at the Munitions Building some time after eleven, to find a long diplomatic decrypt on his desk. Logically enough, he began reading it at the beginning. The watching army officers fidgeted with impatience, because the last portion of the message—Part 14—had burst on them like a flare, but after one or two attempts to direct the general to this final part, they waited for him to reach it himself, afraid perhaps of irritating him by pressing him. It had apparently not occurred to the officers, if they were so timorous, to put the significant part of the decrypt on top; nor had it occurred to anyone in the building to act without waiting for the chief of staff to appear in the office. The whole affair suggested more serious weaknesses in the structure and conduct of Marshall's office. Structure aside, Marshall himself as a younger officer would never have hesitated to annoy a chief of staff if it was necessary to accomplish his purpose. (Admiral Stark had read the fateful Part 14, but had thought it unwise to pass on the information to his commander in the Pacific, because he felt that Washington had rung too many alarms in recent weeks.)

The intercepted message presented overall a long and unstartling summary of Japanese-American relations, but Part 14 was different and unusual: It directed the envoys to deliver the message to the United States government, "if possible to the Secretary of State," at 1:00 P.M. that very day. It was certainly not customary for a precise time of day to be specified for the delivery of a diplomatic communication. As soon as he read this sentence, Marshall rushed into action, writing a message alerting yet one more time the overseas commands: "Just what significance the hour set may have we do not know, but be on alert accordingly." The chief of staff's handwritten instruction was then turned over to the army message center, whose head, in a remarkable series of bungles, finally sent it off to Hawaii by Western Union. The problems affecting the fate of the telegram were not explained to Marshall. Among the reasons for hurrying the message was the fact that 1:00 P.M. Washington time was 7:30 A.M. on Oahu, shortly after sunup, half an hour before morning colors, the official beginning of the day. In any case, the men at the War Department felt more concern for Manila; the telegram to Hawaii was marked third in priority, after both the Philippines and Panama.

Believing he had sent the message posthaste, Marshall drove back to Fort Myer for a quick lunch before returning for a conference the president had called for three o'clock. While at home he received a telephone call from an officer on the General Staff. A message had been received declaring that Pearl Harbor was under air attack.

During this same midday hour, Harry Hopkins was lunching with the president at his desk in the oval study. They "were talking about things far removed from war" when, at about 1:40, Secretary Knox called to say that the navy had picked up a radio message from Honolulu. Soon to become famous, the brief broadcast said simply: "Air raid Pearl Harbor. This is no drill."

Hopkins thought this could hardly be correct. Surely the Japanese would not attack Hawaii. The president disagreed. It was probably true, he said. As he had remarked in November, it was just the sort of unexpected thing the Japanese would do.

It was, indeed.

Asked later why, after receiving Admiral Stark's so-called war warning on November 17, he had left the battle fleet moored in Pearl Harbor, Admiral Kimmel replied with unvarnished candor: "I never thought those little yellow sons of bitches could pull off such an attack, so far from Japan."

As the first wave of Japanese planes from the aircraft carriers came in over Oahu, the pilots were amazed to see what a complete surprise they had achieved. How wise they were, said Major Robinett of the General Staff, to "American habits and customs of the Army and Navy." In one respect, however, the Americans had not been wrong. The Japanese had in fact launched the expected great push to the south. The raid on Pearl Harbor simply constituted an element of this advance, an operation to guard its flank. In a way Lord Beaverbrook had not anticipated, the Japanese had made him an accurate prophet, and at Pearl Harbor the enemy had handed President Roosevelt a more resounding symbol than the guns of South Carolina had given Abraham Lincoln eighty years earlier at Fort Sumter.

CHAPTER TEN

TWENTY-FOUR DAYS IN ARCADIA

On December 21—a clear, crisp Sunday—Paul Robinett broke off his work at the General Staff long enough to get in a welcome gallop on his horse Kansas Red. During the two weeks since the disaster at Pearl Harbor, rumors about high personnel changes had swirled and eddied through the capital. Some developments were obvious; Admiral Stark's stock was declining, while Admiral King was moving up, perhaps even "to top place as right-hand man of the President." Robinett, now a colonel, was surprised, however, when a friend stopped him on the bridle path to pose a question: Was General McNair going to succeed Marshall as chief of staff? Rumors had circulated about possible changes in the higher levels of the army, but nothing of this sort had come to Robinett's ears. Washington had always been filled with speculation about promotions and assignments; these rumors played a large part in the gossip of the legions of retired officers in the district. Many a great career in the armed forces had been nurtured by officers' kinsfolk living in Washington, some of them belonging to families going back to the early days of the Republic and operating effectively through a web of personal connections. But no one, Robinett thought, stood in line to succeed General Marshall. He told his friend he knew nothing about any such report.

The next day Robinett learned that, far from saying goodbye to the General Staff, Marshall was about to take part in a series of very important high-level conferences and, in connection with these meetings, had a special assignment for him. At Sunday's staff conference someone had asked where Winston Churchill could be found at the time. A superior, Brigadier

General Harry Malony, had scribbled on a pad and then slid it in front of Robinett; on it he had written "Washington, D.C." Now Malony told Robinett that the chief of staff had chosen him to be head of the American secretariat for staff conversations with the British chiefs, who were due to arrive in Washington that same evening. Although Robinett, like almost all officers, including the chief of staff, preferred troop duty—a sentiment that accounted for the low esteem in which his previous division, G-2, was generally held—he recognized the compliment implied in the assignment, and he felt that his background, particularly his service with the State, War, and Navy departments' standing liaison committee, had prepared him well for such high-level work.

These conferences would present a challenge of the first magnitude for all the Americans taking part. The United States had not chosen her moment to enter the war, but had seen hostilities suddenly explode overhead in a series of bomb bursts. Fighting off the inevitable sense of shock, the country was striving to develop a wartime outlook and ethos, but these characteristics did not come instantaneously after the long years of peace, as Pearl Harbor had dramatically demonstrated. (Just as shocking, if less publicized, was the fiasco in the Philippines, where some nine hours after the Pearl Harbor attack had signaled war, General Douglas MacArthur inexplicably allowed his air force to be annihilated on the ground.) Realizing the appalling deficiencies laid bare by the events of December 7, General Marshall and other U.S. military leaders felt the pressing need to put their house in considerably better order than that in which the Japanese had found it. A meeting with the British, though no doubt desirable at some early date, could be put off for a while.

At the outset of an alliance, joint planning, perhaps even joint control, might appear desirable, but it could not be considered inevitable. Coalitions in history had not been distinguished by the harmony with which they had operated. As a British general with a sense of humor would one day put it: "Allies are the most aggravating of people"; for one thing, "even when one agrees with them on common objectives their methods towards obtaining them are so queer, so very queer." And as their most annoying characteristic, "in the most astonishing way they seem quite incapable of recognizing how sound, how wise, how experienced are our views; how fair, indeed how generous, how big-hearted we are. They even at times credit us with the same petty jealousies, narrow nationalistic outlook, selfish maneuverings, that obviously sway them." In 1917 the United States had entered an alliance that after three years of hard war still made plans in a haphazard fashion; the participants related to each other more as acquaintances than as members of the same family facing a common fate, and not always as very friendly acquaintances. But when the Americans came into that war, they could at least prepare to fight on an already established front. Once the United States decided to build up an expeditionary force, there was no mystery about where it would go. But now, in 1941, Britain had no front except in Northeast Africa. The British Army had been driven from Europe, and in the Far East all Allied bastions were crumbling under the blows of the Japanese. Whether they liked it or not, the British and the Americans had little choice about planning together to create theaters of action against the Axis. The two countries could hardly launch independent and unrelated operations on the Atlantic coast of Europe or Africa or in the Mediterranean. Even so, the closer the British and the Americans should come to joint control of their forces, the further they would move from all historical precedent.

Churchill did not have joint control on his mind, but he was eager for meetings with the Americans as soon as possible. The prime minister had learned of the attack on Pearl Harbor in a way not complimentary to the intelligence services or other arms of either Britain or the United States. The news came while Churchill and his guests, including U.S. Ambassador John Winant and Averell Harriman, were dining at Chequers, the weekend residence of British prime ministers. The medium of transmission was a fifteen-dollar portable radio, the gift of Harry Hopkins; Churchill turned it on to hear the nine o'clock BBC news program, and so received the shocking intelligence of the Japanese attack some two hours later than it might have been made available. (A British embassy official in Washington, telephoning the Foreign Office in London to inform it of the Japanese attack, had asked that the news be given immediately to the prime minister. Not easily moved to action, the clerk on duty asked deliberately what the name of the place was and how it was spelled; he did not seem at all sure the prime minister would be interested.) Announcing with admirable faith in the reliability of the BBC that "we shall declare war on Japan,"

Churchill leaped up and strode out of the room. He and Winant immediately telephoned the president. Yes, it was all true, FDR said, and within a day the president had agreed to the prime minister's proposal that he and his chiefs of staff come to Washington as soon as the trip could be arranged.

Almost immediately the British had reason to question American intentions; the War Department placed a ban on all lend-lease deliveries, even of cargoes already loaded onto ships. Did this mean, as it very well might, that the Americans in their national fury intended to abandon all the subjunctive agreements arrived at during the past year and a half, now that real war had been forced on them? Would ABC-1 with its Germany-first principle be thrown overboard in order to clear the decks for vengeful action against Japan? The allocation of supplies was only one of many questions that Churchill felt must be thrashed out; his staff radioed the Americans from the battleship *Duke of York* en route to the United States that it was "hoped to reach agreement to following main points during conference," the first point being "fundamental basis of joint strategy."

Although they had not sought the meetings at this time, Marshall and his staff moved to prepare the way, and what had seemed to the British as a possibly overwhelming problem in reality amounted to no problem at all. The chief of staff and Admiral Stark (still chief of naval operations) reported to the president on December 21, the day before the British phalanx moved into Washington, that they continued to believe, despite the entry of Japan into the war, that "Germany is still the prime enemy and her defeat is the key to victory." Marshall and Stark held to this principle even though the Pearl Harbor attack, by destroying the great American strategic weapon in the Pacific, seemed to have left the United States naked to her aggressive enemy.

Besides making the point about the need to establish a fundamental basis of strategy, the message from the *Duke of York* listed, as other items to be decided on at the forthcoming conference, agreement on "immediate military measures, including redistribution of forces," the allocation of the forces of the two countries to carry out the agreed strategy, a "long-term programme," including "forces to be raised and equipped required for victory," and the creation of "joint machinery" for carrying out decisions. As soon as the message was received, Marshall's planners, headed by Brigadier General Leonard T. Gerow—and joined just that week by Brigadier General Dwight D. Eisenhower—began preparing statements of American policy in response to the points made by the British and to other questions raised by Secretary of War Stimson. Their efforts ended in a document fetchingly and cautiously titled "Tentative U.S. Views on Subjects of British Memorandum, Dec. 18."

What made planning particularly difficult, and in some cases gave it an unreal air, was that the Japanese had not flown back home from Pearl Harbor and Manila after their attacks, to wait and see what their opponents would do, but were pouring across the western Pacific at a ferocious rate not imagined in any prewar estimates. The British had shared in the force of the onslaught from the outset, the Japanese having invaded Malaya on the day of the Pearl Harbor attack; on December 10 the battleship *Prince of Wales,* which had carried Churchill to the Atlantic Conference, and the battle cruiser *Repulse,* unwisely committed to the Gulf of Siam without air cover, had perished under the blows of Japanese bombers and torpedo planes; and on December 16 the enemy had invaded Borneo. Within a few days Wake Island would fall and Hong Kong would surrender. All the Allies had quickly felt the power of the Japanese. But, on the other hand, planning was simplified by German and Italian declarations of war on the United States in the days following the Pearl Harbor attack. The British and the Americans now stood as complete allies in every part of the globe.

To ensure their safety, Churchill and his party were sealed below decks on the *Duke of York* as she crossed the stormy North Atlantic. But the prime minister found this confinement no problem. His personal physician, Sir Charles Wilson, saw him as "a different man since America came into the war," for now, "suddenly, the war is as good as won and England is safe." Churchill would sit for hours at table, enjoying himself in a flood of talk, and would spend the rest of the time in his cabin, "dictating for the President a long memorandum on the conduct of the war." With the experience of almost two and a half years of war behind them, the members of the British delegation shared a perhaps natural feeling that they must induce the unfledged Americans to follow their lead, even though Britain herself had thus far experienced little success against any enemy anywhere except the Italians in East Africa. Some of these officers perhaps deeply believed that the merit of an aristocratic society lay not in its performance but simply in its existence. Aboard the *Duke of York,* while the prime minister produced his papers on the future course of the war, his chiefs of staff were drawing up their own memoranda for the coming meetings with the American chiefs. Aside from their experience of war, the British brought into the conferences another advantage—the fact that, whether or not the method had always worked effectively and with foresight, they had grown up within an organized and well-understood committee system.

Having already seen the British mechanism at work at Argentia, the Americans felt a bit leery of this polish and professionalism. Shrewdly, Harry Hopkins had suggested to Churchill that he not appear in Washington with all the answers wrapped up in a complete program. Marshall saw that "our people were always ready to find Albion perfidious." In many cases this attitude had not arisen recently but reflected long-standing anti-British feeling among members of the officer corps, and it could only be enhanced if the British struck poses suggesting that they were "out here" visiting a branch office of the Allied war-making firm to bring it the latest wisdom from corporate headquarters.

American suspicions were not altogether ill-founded. Influential Britons peered down at their transatlantic partners from mountain peaks of condescension. "They strike me as very crude and semi-educated," Lord Halifax wrote privately in early 1941. "The Americans, more than any other people, are prone to emotionalism and exaggeration," observed the head of the North American department of the Foreign Office. A member of Parliament would shortly say, with cloudy grammar, that "the reason they dislike us is, because they realise their inferiority." These unflattering judgments no doubt rested on the fact that an American, as a speaker of English ("Cherokee," John Maynard Keynes called it) and frequently as the bearer of an Anglo-Saxon name, was looked upon not as a foreigner with his own national habits but as an even more deplorable creature, an Englishman *manqué.* Besides, Britons like Halifax dealt in their working lives at home with persons from their own social sphere; the more varied nature of American officialdom thus tended to confront them with unexpected instances of non-U behavior. The more the British indulged the tendency to see themselves in the great drama as the worldly Greeks guiding the raw American Romans, the greater the strain they would put on the alliance and the less they would face their own resentment at having become dependent on a country that had begun life as their colony. Happily, the chief of staff showed himself free of even a flicker of the nervous suspicion to which his subordinates were subject, and he consciously made it his policy "to be on a very warm and understanding basis with the British."

Churchill had been "panting to meet the President ever since Pearl Harbor," and Roosevelt for his part eagerly awaited the arrival of the prime minister. Having been assured by radio that "the house" was "large enough for him to have his secretary and his valet with him," Churchill moved into a bedroom in the White House across the hall from Harry Hopkins's room, an assignment that put the latter, who had already become the most effective Anglo-American working link, at the place where he was most needed. "We live here as a big family, in the greatest intimacy and informality," Churchill soon reported to the War Cabinet, with which he kept in what seemed almost continuous touch. Indeed, the Arcadia conference, as the meetings were cheerfully code-named, evolved on two interpenetrating but separate levels. In the White House the president, the prime minister, and sometimes other leaders engaged in conversations that went on from early in the morning till late at night, with Roosevelt staying up well past his bedtime to share the fun with Churchill and Hopkins; and the military staffs of the two countries held conferences in the new Federal Reserve Building on Constitution Avenue.

During this time, FDR also managed to keep up much of his normal life, seeing callers of various kinds, and Eleanor continued her self-created role as a kind of talent bank, bringing to the president's attention persons whose ideas she liked. It was a time when writers of all varieties produced articles telling how the United States ought to go about winning the war and managing the ensuing peace. Arriving for dinner on Eleanor's invitation one crisp January evening, one author and his wife found themselves part of a jolly little family group, with a gentleman cousin of Mrs. Roosevelt's and two English girls, one of them FDR's goddaughter. The president looked "extraordinarily fit, self-possessed, relaxed—on top of the world." The headlines in the evening papers had announced continuing Allied defeats, but the cocktail conversation in the president's oval study was light and amusing, much of it having to do with the famous Fala. "One of my Scots ancestors way, way back," said FDR, laughing, "was Murray the outlaw of Fala Hill." The visiting writer decided that such a social evening must serve as the president's way "of keeping sane while in the dead center of an overwhelming insanity."

Then came an unexpected treat for the writer and his wife. Mrs. Roosevelt suddenly rose from her chair and rushed to the door to greet another guest, who came waddling into the study, scowling, holding before him a long, fat cigar. Winston Churchill! During the evening, as the writer watched the two leaders joke about such points as their failure to include the exiled King Zog of Italian-occupied Albania among the signatories of the United Nations declaration they had drawn up, he saw them as "a couple of emperors" making light of deadly serious issues. Yet, he conceded, "I suppose it's the way momentous things get started. Maybe it's the only way." He visualized it as a little scene: "Says one emperor to the other across the dinner table: 'Oh say, we forgot Zog.' It's funny as hell." But was it *too* casual?

The first of the Anglo-American staff sessions got off to a poor start when it became apparent that the lieutenant colonel in charge of arrangements had selected a room too small to seat even the chiefs of staff and their assistants, not to mention others who would be present. "Apparently," Colonel Robinett noted, "he had not even found out how many would be involved" in the conference; it "must have been embarrassing to General Marshall when he saw what had been done." From the outset Robinett admired the cohesion of the British half of the secretariat, directed by Brigadier General L. C. Hollis, an aide to Churchill in the latter's role as minister of defense. Unlike the American group, this team had not been hastily formed but had been working together for some considerable time—a comparison that could accurately be made between any of the British groups and its American counterpart.

But Robinett decided that he was less impressed with the British chiefs of staff and other representatives. Among these was Sir John Dill, who though no longer chief of the Imperial General Staff (CIGS) had accompanied Churchill to Washington. He was a fine-looking man, but he seemed old and tired. Dill was indeed weary. His nerves strained by worry over the condition of his long-ill, paralyzed first wife, who had died just a year earlier, he not only had found himself unable to provide the round-the-clock attention Churchill required from his military chief, but could not stand up to the hectoring to which the prime minister subjected his closest associates when they disagreed with him. A longtime admirer and disciple of Dill's, General Sir Alan Brooke, felt that "for all his brilliant intelligence" Dill was "temperamentally unfitted to work with anyone so overwhelming and impulsive as Churchill." Their clashes angered the prime minister and exhausted Dill. Hence in late November Churchill had seen to it that Dill was promoted to field marshal and appointed to the governorship of Bombay, and Brooke, a man of very different personality, named CIGS. (The press was fed, and dutifully swallowed, the story that Dill was leaving because at sixty he had reached retirement age—a concept that in wartime applied neither in Britain nor in the United States.) But then came the explosive American entry into the war, and with it the vision of a new kind of service for Dill. Brooke, whose teacher Dill had once been, never wavered in his admiration of his predecessor, "his great friend and hero," and he felt that in view of the new situation the British could have no better chief military representative in Washington than Dill, who of course thoroughly understood British strategy and the staff machinery by which it was carried out. After "a good deal of discussion," the prime minister agreed. If Dill struck Colonel Robinett as a tired man, the impression was accurate; but as the meetings quickly showed, there was more to the field marshal than his appearance.

At the conferences of the chiefs of staff, in which the talks ranged around the globe and through long lists of projects large and small, Marshall and his associates quickly saw that in discussion, the British, like the prime minister in his shipboard memorandum, were reiterating the strategy with which the Americans by now were thoroughly familiar. Their aim was ultimately to capitalize on the anticipated Allied advantages—command of the sea and air and the help of the people of occupied Europe—to establish at various points in Europe armed forces which, aided by risings of underground armies, would liberate the occupied countries, roll back the German armies, and in the end defeat them. Under this doctrine the British chiefs saw limited offensives on the Continent as possible in 1942 but more likely in 1943, particularly in the Mediterranean; this was the picture the visitors drew of the ultimate Allied transition from the defensive to the offensive. This mobile, opportunist, open-ended view stood utterly at variance with the purposes for which General Marshall was laboring to create a great mass United States Army, an army that on the plains of northwestern Europe "must come to grips with the enemy ground forces." The U.S. planners sought to discourage action in "subsidiary" theaters, a category that included not only the western Pacific but Africa and the Middle East. Only in northwestern Europe, said the planners in the strategic review drawn up for the Arcadia conference, would it be "feasible from a logistics viewpoint to transport and maintain forces required for an operation of such magnitude."

Looking at the situation existing in December 1941 and January 1942, however, the Americans saw little point in getting into lengthy arguments about the strategy the Allies ultimately ought to adopt. The best the British could do in the near future, it seemed to Marshall's planners, would be to hold on in the home islands and in the Middle East, and to try to send reinforcements to the Far East (where, in January 1942, they still held Singapore). Any other kind of operation the British might undertake would have to be very small and would have only "very doubtful" chances of success. The planners saw the United States as similarly limited. The Americans must first try to defend their coasts against air raids and to hold Hawaii, the Panama Canal, and other bases; they could also complete the replacement of the British as the garrison in Iceland, reinforce the Philippines or the East Indies, and occupy Natal on the Brazilian hump or possibly some other undefended base; also, in the coming months some armored or infantry divisions might be sent to Britain, but even these operations faced limits owing to the shortage of shipping.

In accordance with Churchill's wish, however, the British representatives pushed for the adoption of what they called "closing and tightening the ring around Germany," because the prime minister envisioned one of the operations under this concept as an Anglo-American move into Northwest Africa, territory over which flew the Vichy French flag. Marshall's leading adviser on strategy, Lieutenant General Stanley Embick, no great Anglophile or admirer of British strategic thinking since his World War I days, opposed an Allied North African venture, considering it not "rational" and "motivated more largely by political than by sound strategic purposes." Although Marshall publicly neither accepted nor rejected this view, he was beginning to become acquainted with the notion that the Allies could not confine themselves to what he thought of as purely military projects. At a White House session with Roosevelt and Churchill, he had heard the president say that he considered it very important "to give this country a feeling that they are in the war, to give the Germans the reverse effect, to have American troops somewhere in active fighting across the Atlantic." Not only did Churchill's North African plan interest the president, but the area was one to which he himself had long given thought. Although finding the idea strategically incompatible with his own aims, the chief of staff therefore did not raise objections to it, and he assigned Major General Joseph W. Stilwell to study the operation that might be mounted.

Two days after this meeting Marshall experienced one of the nightmares of the kind he and other presidential associates and advisers dreaded when they saw FDR in a cozy situation with a persuasive figure like Churchill. At dinner or in a meeting with the prime minister without the chief of staff or another U.S. military adviser on hand, FDR might allow American views to be argued away and American plans to suffer. The "family" situation in the White House seemed particularly tailored to create such problems, and one of them arose on Christmas Eve when the president, in conversation with Churchill and members of the British party, told the prime minister that he would consider diverting to Singapore reinforcements intended for MacArthur's forces if the evolving situation made it impossible for them to reach the Philippines. When notified that discussion of such a proposal appeared on the joint staff agenda, Marshall, worried that the War Department would seem to be abandoning the battling U.S. forces on Luzon, protested to Stimson. The secretary, who admired Roosevelt in many ways but thoroughly disapproved of the president's unsystematic methods of making decisions, telephoned the indispensable Harry Hopkins with an ultimatum: There must be no more such decisions or there would be no more Henry Stimson at the War Department. Hopkins did not claim to be a maker of policy, but he had his own concerns about the ease with which Roosevelt seemed to accept many of Churchill's ideas, although he was well aware that FDR's affable receptivity as a good host did not necessarily signify that he agreed with what he heard.

When Hopkins bluntly presented Stimson's ultimatum while FDR sat talking with Churchill, he was rewarded by hearing a denial of the whole affair not only from the president but from the prime minister. Even though Churchill's proposal had nothing intrinsically sinister about it—if troop ships found themselves in the western Pacific with no place to land, Singapore at the time would offer a reasonable option—Marshall could hardly allow the matter to be discussed in depth without a General Staff representative participating. When a report of the agreement, or whatever it actually was, reached Colonel Robinett, he was disturbed not only because the U.S. chiefs had not had an opportunity to study it, but also because "the British had heard the discussions that led up to it." Like other Americans, the colonel stayed on the alert for British attempts to steal a march on the war-green Americans.

Aside from the reaffirmation of the Germany-first strategy, Arcadia stood as an Allied landmark in two different areas. During the first two days of the conference, Roosevelt and Churchill produced drafts of a declaration by what were then called the "Associated Powers"—a statement of the intended nature and aims of the coalition against the Axis. The two drafts were combined, and the resulting product was cabled to London for approval by the War Cabinet. In essence the powers signing the declaration would pledge themselves to honor the principles of the Atlantic Charter, to cooperate with each other, and to make no separate peace with the enemies. After some back-and-forth discussion, the Allied governments agreed that all the nations "rendering material assistance and contributions in the struggle for victory over Hitlerism" would have the opportunity to sign the declaration before it was made public, and as a final touch FDR rechristened the drably named Associated Powers as the "United Nations"—a move in which he took great pride. On New Year's Day, 1942, representatives of twenty-six countries gathered in the White House to sign the joint declaration, this wide participation being considered by Clement Attlee and the British War Cabinet as proof that the war was "being waged for the freedom of the small nations as well as the great powers." The Soviets, along with China, the Western Allies, and the smaller countries agreed to defend religious freedom and to "preserve human rights and justice in their own lands as well as in other lands" (this wording itself was actually a Russian revision of an equivalent draft passage).

The declaration of the United Nations, if not a great piece of prose, constituted the notable achievement of the Arcadia conference in the realm of politics and publicity; it contrasted effectively with the lack of any such sign of unity and purpose among the Axis powers. The other great landmark of the meetings, actually twofold, was established in the sphere of military command. Christmas Day had begun inauspiciously for General Marshall with the discovery of Roosevelt's agreement to discuss diverting the troops bound for the Philippines. Then, after his and Stimson's effective counterattack, the day had improved for the chief of staff as he played host at what his wife regarded as a "family Christmas dinner"—the family including such brand-new members as Lord and Lady Halifax, Lord Beaverbrook, the British chiefs of staff, and Admiral King and his wife. When Mrs. Marshall learned that Christmas Day was also Field Marshal Dill's birthday, she saw to it that a cake was provided. Pleased at giving his guests an opportunity for relaxation amid the cares of the conference, Marshall became the butt of some badinage when someone discovered that the little American and British flags decorating the cake were attached to staffs imprinted MADE IN JAPAN.

After this noontime dinner came Marshall's great moment of the day. Although his counterattack on the question of the Philippine reinforcements had resulted in a cease-fire with the president, the proposal was scheduled for discussion at a 4:00 meeting of the British and American staffs. With the picture in the Far East changing violently every day and with the forces of four Allied countries involved—American, British, Dutch, and Australian—the chief of staff had a perfect opportunity to make a point that had long been of cardinal importance to him. At the conference "he took the view that it was premature to make such a decision" as that involving the reinforcements. Questions like this "would come up again and again until unity of command" was achieved over all Allied forces in the whole wide area. Marshall believed absolutely that liaison and consultation would not do the job; as Pearl Harbor had bitterly shown, this way of doing business did not even work between two different services of the same country—and this was true even though, at the top, Marshall had with great care cultivated a close working relationship with Admiral Stark, who had been reciprocally cooperative. But that was only at the top.

The chief of staff explained to the group his idea concerning unity of command. He said, Robinett noted, "that no local commander could see the situation but a single commander, responsible for the whole theater, could decide the question of the allocation of defense forces." Speaking with fervor that broke through his controlled exterior, Marshall told the Anglo-American staffs that "with differences between groups and between services, the situation is impossible unless we operate on a frank and direct basis." Cooperation would not work because "human frailties are such that there would be emphatic unwillingness to place portions of troops under another service." The theater commander must have authority over all arms—"air, ground, and ships." This was a proposal to blend command not only of different services but of the forces of different countries. "We had to come to this in the First World War," Marshall said, "but it was not until 1918 that it was accomplished and much valuable time, blood, and treasure had been needlessly sacrificed."

Marshall had told the group that these were his "personal views and not those as a result of consultation with the Navy or with [his] own War Plans Division." Nor, obviously, had he talked the idea over with any of the British chiefs; the prime minister had certainly not heard of it. Taken by surprise, Air Chief Marshal Sir Charles Portal, the youngest of the British chiefs, temporized. The present discussion, he suggested, should be limited to dealing with the immediate problem. Disagreeing, Marshall reaffirmed the need for "a broader solution." After the meeting had adjorned to allow the American chiefs to go to a meeting at the White House, Admiral Pound told Colonel Robinett that he "was afraid of unity of command." It was abundantly clear that, in spite of his eloquence and conviction, Marshall had work ahead of him if he wished to win the point he believed would "solve nine-tenths of our troubles."

For all his hard-won experience as the administration's Sledgehammer on Capitol Hill, the chief of staff had forgotten for the moment that surprise, though valuable in war, can be counterproductive in politics—and the Arcadia conference was inevitably a political event. The next day he moved to mend his fences by bringing up the subject with Secretary Stimson, who on the following morning read a statement on unity of command drafted by Marshall, and then enthusiastically took the chief of staff with him to a White House meeting to win Roosevelt's assent. After receiving the president's full approval, Marshall moved along to Admiral Stark's office, where, Robinett felt, he presented his case for a unified command "in a most persuasive manner. His grasp and understanding of the entire situation is away in front of the others." Displeased by the overall American performance in the joint sessions, the colonel decided that "the one real contribution from the United States has been General Marshall's idea of unity of command." (Robinett was not impressed by the overall quality of the deliberations. To record the remarks, he would make brief notes, often in parallel columns according to subject. Major Sexton, who was also serving in the secretariat, took down comments consecutively in shorthand, but so erratic were the discussions that Sexton's notes "failed to make sense.")

Now, despite the chief of staff's persuasiveness, the U.S. admirals seemed to balk. If such an arrangement were adopted in the Far Eastern theater, who should be the commander in chief? Marshall had his own nominee ready—General Sir Archibald Wavell, the British Army commander in India, a distinguished and literarily inclined soldier who, like Dill, had encountered problems with the impetuous prime minister and as the result had been transferred away from the desert war in North Africa. Perhaps unaware of Churchill's less than admiring view of Wavell's aggressiveness, Marshall in making his choice employed some simple reasoning: "We had to do something. I picked the Britisher because he was there . . ." No doubt relieved to hear that at least in this theater they would not be compelled to suffer the indignity of being forced to serve under a U.S. Army officer, the American admirals began to shift ground. King declared for the plan, and "when he said this, all the other Navy people smiled and concurred in their own way."

That afternoon, having secured the support of his own countrymen, Marshall formally put forward in the joint staff meeting his proposal for unity of command. He brought with him a written directive to accompany his words. This document, which defined a supreme commander's mission and authority, had been drafted by the new man in War Plans, General Eisenhower, whom Robinett had already seen as the rising star of the division (in comparison with his chief, General Gerow, Eisenhower "moved quietly and without fuss and seemed to be more of General Marshall's type"). After hearing the proposal, the British chiefs offered various objections; the Royal Navy, predictably, was unhappy; Portal, whose alertness and intelligence particularly impressed the Americans, said gravely that the subject should be studied because the decision would be "momentous." Then, surprisingly, Dill declared for the idea, but said that the directive was too restrictive on any prospective supreme commander. Pleased, Marshall replied that he had "tried to be a realist in drawing up the paper."

Suddenly the mood in the room changed. The group agreed that a directive should be drafted for the approval of the political masters, the president and the prime minister. "The old" Admiral Pound rushed up to Marshall and put his arm around him, to the chief of staff's "complete astonishment"; Dill followed suit, embracing Marshall; and a third British officer "acted explosively." On the professional level the game was won, and the president had already approved the idea. But a formidable opponent remained; Churchill had told Roosevelt in a conference that unity of command had been a reasonable idea in France in the First World War, with a continuous front from Switzerland to the Channel, but that it could not very well be applied in the great distances over which Allied forces were scattered in the Far East. All the commanders of different nationalities and services should act independently under the general supervision of the Allied high command.

Hearing this strongly expressed opinion, Beaverbrook, the veteran political fixer, passed Hopkins a hastily jotted note telling him to "work on Churchill." Thus encouraged, Hopkins arranged for Marshall to confront the prime minister in his White House bedroom the morning after the Allied staffs had accepted the plan. In this meeting the chief of staff employed the tactic he had once used in a heated discussion with the president. He found Churchill in his standard morning working posture—lying in bed but propped up; "I didn't want to sit down and look up," said Marshall, "so I stood up and looked down," a stance that did not prevent the prime minister from giving vent to a fiery oration in which he indicated his belief that it was "inconceivable for an Army officer to have anything to do with the Navy"; he declared that "a ship was a special thing . . ."

Marshall fired back that he was "interested in having a united front against Japan, an enemy which was fighting furiously." If the Allies did not make a move right away, they were "finished in the war." Marshall had never hesitated to declare himself to Pershing or to Roosevelt, his two loftiest and in their differing ways most formidable superiors; now, moved by absolute conviction and a sense of urgency, he did not temper his bluntness for the benefit of the illustrious and formidable guest in the White House. Stalling because he wished to talk to his chiefs of staff, Churchill climbed out of bed and stalked into the bathroom, returning in a while "with only a towel around him." He then sent for the chiefs, and in an Anglo-American meeting that followed, although seeing grave problems in the specific case of Southeast Asia, he gave way—not altogether out of conviction but "to meet the urgent wishes of the President and General Marshall."

The Americans were not the only participants who approached the Arcadia discussions with suspicion. On hearing that General Wavell was the American nominee for the supreme command in Southeast Asia, some of the British officers, seeing the overwhelming likelihood of a disastrous outcome to the fighting in that theater, suspected an American design to fix the British with the responsibility for the defeat. Certainly, as Churchill said, the offer to Wavell was one that "only the highest sense of duty could induce him to accept." But the prime minister would have none of the staff's suspicions; to him, the American suggestion of Wavell represented an expression of confidence in him; the Marshall plan was therefore officially adopted. "If success should come out of the dark picture in the Pacific," Robinett wrote, "no little of the credit should go to him. His honest and frank presentation of the facts has persuaded the British to accept a unity of command which they have never been able to achieve with their own forces in any given area."

The odds for success, however, could not be called high. At the very moment the arrangements were being drawn up, the enemy "was rapidly knocking out the very concepts and assumptions on which they were built." But, against odds, Marshall had succeeded, at the outset of American involvement in the war, in winning both American and British acceptance of his principle of unified command; he saw the ABDA Theater, as the Southeast Asia area was called, only the beginning. As Fox Conner had long ago told young Major Eisenhower, Marshall knew "more about the techniques of arranging allied commands than any man" he knew. Marshall, observed Churchill's confidant Sir Charles Wilson, was "the key to the situation." The prime minister "has a feeling that in his quiet, unprovocative way he means business, and that if we are too obstinate he might take a strong line. And neither the PM nor the President can contemplate going forward without Marshall."

Operational theaters were not the only level at which Marshall saw the need for unity of command. In their December

18 message sent from the *Duke of York* while crossing the Atlantic, the British chiefs had listed as one of the points for agreement the need to "set up joint machinery" for implementing decisions on strategy. What shape should this Allied high command take? The British themselves functioned with a traditional and well-defined structure for providing command and strategic direction to the armed forces and military advice to the prime minister and the War Cabinet. The body holding this corporate responsibility was the Chiefs of Staff Committee, consisting of the First Sea Lord, the chief of the Imperial General Staff, and the chief of the Air Staff. The Americans had no counterpart organization with such responsibility; the lines of authority still ran directly between the president and the army and navy chiefs individually, and no independent U.S. air force existed at all. Somehow, out of British precision and American amorphousness, a new structure must be shaped. For one thing, an immediate practical question presented itself. If General Wavell was being appointed as an Allied-theater supreme commander, to what higher authority was he supposed to report?

Admiral King, whose star was indeed enjoying a rapid rise—he had, Robinett said, "caught the President's eye"—suggested in a conversation with FDR that a single-purpose group be set up in Washington to deal with strategy in the ABDA area, including representatives of the Netherlands and Australia as well as of the U.S. and British governments. Because of his constitutional distaste for devices that tended to remove his hand from the levers directly controlling action, Roosevelt took to this limited plan. Giving automatic power over the whole war effort to a layer of British and American officers, he thought, might make it harder for him to arrive at politically sound strategic decisions with the prime minister. But setting up a special group for Southeast Asia seemed a reasonable notion. The British Chiefs of Staff, however, thought otherwise; for them, such a body would add to the problem instead of to the solution. They declared themselves willing to participate in a single overall combined group, although this had not been their original intention. The chiefs had earlier envisioned two staffs, in London and in Washington, with decisions affirmed by telegraphic liaison. Now, in agreement with Marshall and the U.S. Navy chiefs, the British chiefs proposed to put the ABDA supreme commander under the direction of a combined U.S.-British committee. But when this proposal reached the president, he took out his pen and performed a heavy piece of editing, for example changing "*no* special body" to "*a* special body" for handling the Southwest Pacific and writing in the proviso that its headquarters should be Washington; he also added New Zealand to the list of participating governments. Although these drafts and discussions focused on the "higher direction" of the ABDA command, what was emerging was the machinery for the higher direction of the overall Anglo-American war effort.

On receiving the ball FDR had smashed back into their court, the chiefs of staff did not simply drop their rackets and walk away but kept the ball in play, modifying the proposal but not essentially changing it. None of the professionals thought it desirable to bring representatives of the British dominions or of the Netherlands government into the new combined Allied game; those groups were already being consulted through arrangements that had been made in London. Marshall proposed that the American and British chiefs of staff adopt the final British suggestion of a single body, the Combined Chiefs of Staff, which would consist of the U.S. chiefs and British representatives, and this plan won the approval of both the president and the prime minister. In accordance with the president's wish, the Combined Chiefs would sit in Washington, a position that could be justified on the grounds that the United States was situated geographically between the German and Japanese wars, and that it would contribute the great bulk of armaments and other matériel and, in the long run, of men.

This arrangement, thrusting the raw newcomer into the center of the action, inevitably did not please all the war-hardened British veterans. Roosevelt "got what he wanted," Sir Charles Wilson noted in his diary, but the doctor saw it as "an unequal contest." He missed Sir Alan Brooke, the new CIGS, who had been left in London to familiarize himself with his new duties and to mind the store. Had the tough, no-nonsense Brooke been on hand, Wilson thought, the outcome might have been different; the president and General Marshall might not have had their way. The "peace-loving Dill" was no substitute: "What he lacks is the he-man stuff." But the decision had been made—the war would be run from Washington. "Our people are very unhappy about the decision," Wilson said; but what he and they overlooked in their bitterness was that strategy could be formulated anywhere and debated everywhere. And Brooke would surely take part in future conferences.

In the official conference paper titled "Post-Arcadia Collaboration," the Combined Chiefs were described as the British chiefs of staff (although deputies would represent them in Washington) and their "United States opposite numbers." Since no U.S. counterpart existed to the British Chiefs of Staff Committee, the term "opposite numbers" had to be defined. No question arose concerning the army's representation on the Combined Chiefs; General Marshall stood in a position very similar to that of the chief of the Imperial General Staff. But with the U.S. Navy, the position was not clear-cut; by Roosevelt's order of December 18, the navy had acquired two professional heads of virtually equal standing. Admiral Stark remained as chief of naval operations, but the December 18 executive order created new powers for the commander in chief, United States Fleet, placing his office in the Navy Department in Washington and giving him supreme command of the operating fleets and the naval coastal commands. Two days after issuing the order, Roosevelt gave this post to the rising naval star Admiral King, another of the formidable and independent types FDR favored for high positions; like the chief of naval operations, King would have direct access to the president, a fact of which the participants in the Arcadia staff meetings were already well aware. (One day, Robinett observed, the admiral in reporting to the group on conversations with Hopkins and Roosevelt "was quite rude to Admiral Stark," which suggested to Robinett that the latter was "on his way out.") Since neither Stark nor King wielded authority comparable to that of the First Sea Lord, Admiral Pound, both had to be taken onto the Combined Chiefs to give the navy adequate representation.

The air posed another problem. Nowhere was there a U.S. "opposite number" to Portal, chief of the Air Staff and professional head of the Royal Air Force, which enjoyed autonomy equal to that of the U.S. Navy or Army. Whatever the hopes and aspirations of the fliers might be, the U.S. Army Air Forces in January 1942 were only one of several arms and services making up the United States Army. (Naval aviation did not enter the equation; as in Britain, it belonged integrally to the fleet.) But no one doubted who the air candidate for the Combined Chiefs would be. As chief of the U.S. Army Air Forces and deputy chief of staff for air, Hap Arnold, recently promoted to lieutenant general, had in response to Marshall's wish attended the Arcadia meetings as the air expert. But Arnold was not a chief of staff and Marshall had no intention of stirring up a legislative battle to make him one. Instead, Marshall took advantage of his friendship with Marvin McIntyre, one of Roosevelt's secretaries, to produce a change in a presidential statement praising the military leaders; to the names of Marshall and the navy representatives McIntyre agreed to add that of Arnold as air chief of staff. "I tried to give Arnold all the power I could," Marshall later commented. "I tried to make him as nearly as I could chief of staff of the air without any restraint, though he was my subordinate." The presidential statement, the only action taken with respect to Arnold's membership in the Combined Chiefs of Staff, established his position.

It also established Arnold as a member of a body that more or less automatically came into being as another result of Arcadia, the U.S. Joint Chiefs of Staff (by Allied agreement, the word "combined" was to be used for collaboration between two or more of the United Nations, with "joint" designating interservice collaboration within one country). This group, created to represent the United States on the Combined Chiefs, began to function as a corporate military directorate for the American war effort; it held its first meeting on February 9, 1942, but never by any law or executive order was it officially established—it simply grew, the closest approach to a documentary basis for its reality being nothing more than an "OK FDR" scribbled on a charter of the Combined Chiefs of Staff that referred to the "United States Chiefs of Staff," thus seeming to take for granted the existence of that body. As the coordinating agency for the army and navy, the Joint Chiefs of Staff (JCS) replaced the ineffectual old Joint Board. But the fact that Hap Arnold sat as a member of the JCS by presidential declaration did not overly impress Admiral King, who seemed to feel that if the chief of naval aviation could not be a member of the Joint Chiefs, then Arnold had little business as a member either. Probably as territorially minded an officer as the navy had ever produced, the crusty admiral would sometimes show his distaste for Arnold's comments by directing his responses to Marshall as if Hap were only a ventriloquist's dummy whose words had actually fallen from the unmoving lips of the chief of staff.

If General Brooke's arguments had not persuaded Churchill of Sir John Dill's potential value in Washington, the prime minister realized on seeing the field marshal with the Americans that "his prestige and influence with them was upon the highest level." Surely fortune had sent the perfect man to head the British mission in Washington and to serve as senior British officer on the Combined Chiefs of Staff, acting as the prime minister's personal representative. Dill, an Ulsterman like Brooke and many another British general, enjoyed a fine reputation as a strategic thinker and some of his fellow officers liked to call him "our best general since Marlborough"; the fact that the aggressive-minded prime minister did not share this opinion was not widely known—and in any case, no one would be surprised to hear that for Churchill his ancestor Marlborough stood on a pedestal shared with nobody. Twice already during the war, Dill had come close to death, though not in combat. Once, during the London blitz, the flats above and below his own were bombed, but he miraculously escaped; his other narrow shave came when an airplane carrying him and Anthony Eden on a mission to Cairo was almost forced down in the Mediterranean. As the prime minister's chief military representative in Washington, Dill would now, it seemed, face difficulties of a different sort.

He and Churchill confronted one problem right away, and the unlikely source of it was General Marshall. Much as he had come to like and admire Dill, at first in their contacts at Argentia and now in the Arcadia meetings, Marshall did not believe that anyone should set up shop on a level above that of the Combined Chiefs—that zone was already occupied by Roosevelt and Churchill—and also serve as a member of the group. Acting as the prime minister's personal representative would give Dill more authority than any other member of the chiefs; besides, Marshall, at this point thinking as an orthodox professional officer, saw such a role as an undesirable mixing of military and political authority.

Arcadia had ended on January 14, and after pondering the question on his homeward voyage, Churchill cabled Hopkins that he anticipated "great difficulties arising from Dill's vaguely defined outside influence and special relationship with me"; it would indeed be "far simpler and plainer" for him to sit in the combined staff simply as the chief British military representative. Having grasped early on not only Hopkins's unique position but his ability to perform without fuss a wide range of tasks, the prime minister asked his friend to point out the advantages of his proposal to Marshall and King, who he thought would like it because "they would not feel that between me and the President stood a senior allied officer in a somewhat undefined relationship." Since these were Marshall's own thoughts, he was unlikely to withhold his approval. Churchill even requested Hopkins's approval of the proposed message to Dill describing the arrangement. In his first move, as the prime minister no doubt expected, Hopkins presented the telegram to Roosevelt, who casually responded the following day in a memo: "I think this suggestion of Winston is all right."

Thus the arrangement was made. Although not the CIGS, Dill for practical purposes would function in Washington as Marshall's opposite number on the Combined Chiefs; nothing could have suited the U.S. chief of staff more. Of all the plans and decisions adopted in and around Arcadia, this little-heralded appointment was probably the most important and was certainly the happiest. Marshall found Dill "a most unusual man"; he not only "had a very remarkable character" but deserved great respect for his "even more remarkable courage in carrying out his duties." The U.S. chief had seen enough of Churchill in action to appreciate the courage it took to stand up to this torrent of a man and resist military schemes likely to bring disaster if carried out. Dill talked, Marshall said, "with extreme frankness"—a comment that constituted an unwittingly apt self-description. Besides, the field marshal did not look down on the Americans from a mountaintop, and gave no evidence of seeing himself as a Greek among barbarians.

Marshall took to Dill as a friend and seemed to regard him as a remarkably sensitive conduit for conveying his views to the British chiefs in London; the field marshal was just the instrument the chief of staff needed if his influence was to become effective in British councils. Such a thought would have nothing cynical about it—Churchill and Brooke envisioned for Dill exactly the same role with the influence flowing in the opposite direction.

Dill himself moved quickly to call attention to his usefulness, which he did not see as confined to his relationship with Marshall. On January 16, two days after the end of Arcadia, he wrote Hopkins: "I hope that you and the President will realize that I am entirely at your disposal, day and night, for consultation in my capacity as representative of the Minister of Defence"—i.e., Churchill. "I could, for example, have come last night, had I been wanted in that capacity, when the question of Wavell taking up his ABDA area command was under discussion." The later Churchill telegram, and Roosevelt's agreement with it, was supposed to have removed that "capacity," but on January 31, FDR could not resist muddying the administrative waters. He did not seem to have understood that Dill would replace Lieutenant General H.C.B. Wemyss, the army representative on the British mission. To Churchill, Roosevelt expressed the hope that Dill would sit on the Combined Chiefs in addition to Wemyss and the naval and air members; "but I particularly hope," said the president, "that I can regard him as the representative of you in your capacity as Minister of Defense"—exactly the role Marshall had opposed. "Perhaps," Roosevelt told the Former Naval Person, "this latter status could be put on an informal basis but one which would be understood between you and me." However, he assured the prime minister, "all of this is wholly agreeable to my people on the Joint Staff and also to Harry." Perhaps—and perhaps with his military seniority and his prestige such a role to some extent would have fallen to Dill whatever the formal arrangements; on the British side he certainly stood first among equals. But once again Roosevelt had shown that for him administrative lines of authority were first and foremost bonds to be wriggled free of, if not broken. By return cable, Churchill expressed his agreement.

Dill moved into a small house on Q Street and took up the life of an official in wartime Washington, working long hours at his desk in quarters provided in the Public Health Building and spending the evenings either entertaining at home or dining out with other officers on the Combined Chiefs. He got on well with Americans; he had an easy wit and a politician's ability to remember first names and nicknames. Dill had spent less than a year as a widower, and he was joined now in Washington by his new wife, who presumably had expected to become first lady of Bombay and now found herself in the teeming center of wartime activity. Something of a bird lover, the field marshal had little time to study the new American species or engage in much other recreation; apart from his regular office duties, Marshall kept him busy. Eager for Dill to grasp the nature and scope of the American military buildup to which he was devoting his thoughts and energies, the chief of staff began including the Briton on his flying inspection trips to training camps and air bases. As their friendship grew, Marshall began looking out for Dill's health; there were quiet weekends at the Marshall home in Leesburg and sometimes canoe trips on the Potomac. But strong as his liking for Dill became, there is no evidence that the chief of staff ever allowed himself to call the field marshal "Jack."

At the beginning of December 1941, Captain John McCrea, who served as aide to the chief of naval operations, had been all set to go to sea. He had in prospect a naval officer's dream, command of his own ship, this one to be a cruiser. Instead, one day the chief of personnel presented him with a memo addressed to the president and signed by the secretary of the navy, in which FDR was informed that Captain McCrea, who was "thoroughly conversant with the present state of naval affairs" and possessed the appropriate record and personality, was therewith nominated to be the president's naval aide. Upset at losing his command before he had received it—and concerned about the expenses that were supposed to come with the proposed job—McCrea rushed to Admiral Stark's office, where he encountered Admiral King as well as the chief of naval operations. After hearing the captain's protest, King broke in sternly to say, "This country is at war, and you can afford anything your assignment might require." It was not the moment for the captain to point out to the admirals that although he had never voted, he had been reared as a Republican and was certainly no New Dealer.

Accordingly, on January 16 McCrea, after working as a naval member of the secretariat for Arcadia, reported to the White House, where he was met by Pa Watson, who was not only the president's military aide but had served for several years as appointments secretary—as well as story-swapping friend and companion. McCrea received his job description directly from FDR himself as he sat behind his desk in the executive office. Observing that one of his earliest ambitions had been to attend Annapolis ("my mother vetoed that"), the president then described his enjoyment of his association with the navy as assistant secretary during the Wilson years and his acquaintanceship in those days with many young officers who now held high positions. "Briefly," Roosevelt said, "I would like you to be my eyes and ears in the Navy Department. I'm sure you won't burden me with nonessentials, but I must confess that little things about the Navy will be of more interest to me than the same sorts of things about the other services." Having put McCrea at his ease by making him a sort of jocular co-conspirator (although the navy did indeed come first with him, as Marshall for one had long since learned), the president went on to say that he expected to see the naval aide twice daily, in the morning and in the late afternoon, seven days a week "if I'm in town," and he was sure that McCrea would be available at other times if necessary.

With that, the briefing was concluded. Talking afterward with Pa Watson, the captain inquired about the management of the president's office—the "plan of the day." The backbone, said Pa, was provided by the president's appointment list drawn up by FDR and Pa jointly, while the president had his breakfast in bed; sometimes the list became "formidable"—as indeed it might, since FDR's relative immobility decreed that for him almost all action had to radiate from the chair behind the executive desk. Aside from these appointments, the important events were regularly scheduled meetings with congressional leaders and twice-a-week press conferences.

On returning to the Navy Department, McCrea answered a summons from Secretary Knox, who invited him to attend the departmental morning conferences at which the staff tried to put into focus all the happenings of the previous twenty-four hours; these summaries, Knox thought, might help the naval aide keep the president up to date. That was fine, McCrea answered, "but if there is anything you don't want the President to know, I trust it will remain unsaid." He felt it necessary to point out to Knox that the assignment to the White House was not particularly welcome, not only because it meant the loss of his cruiser command but because the job, he suspected, possessed political overtones—and his politics, such as they were, were not those of the executive office.

Well, said the thoroughly Republican Knox, "I've enjoyed knowing and working with the President," and he shared with McCrea the notable discovery that "New Dealers have the same love of their country that I have." In fact, "my bet is that you will enjoy the assignment."

In showing Captain McCrea through the White House offices, Watson made a special point of taking him into what he called the goldfish room, "where we park people who are waiting for appointments with the President." Since the attack on Pearl Harbor had brought about the immediate involvement of American forces in war, this onetime Cabinet room had acquired a few maps for the president to study from time to time.

But so casual were the arrangements and the thinking behind them that the maps were simply spread out on the old Cabinet table, being turned face down when the room held visitors. McCrea noted perhaps half a dozen charts covering the Atlantic and Pacific oceans; as accoutrements the table held *in toto* a pair of parallel rulers, a set of dividers, and a reading glass. Such, together with the globe in his office, were the visual aids available to the commander in chief of the army and navy of a nation engaged in a war around the world.

No one in the White House could know how clearly Field Marshal Dill was etching the Washington scene in communications to Brooke back home: "At present this country has not—repeat not—the slightest conception of what the war means, and their armed forces are more unready for war than it is possible to imagine." Eventually the Americans would do great things, but for now "the whole organisation belongs to the days of George Washington who was made Commander-in-Chief of all the Forces and just did it. To-day the President is Commander-in-Chief of all the forces, but it is not so easy to just do it."

In any case, it was obvious to some in the White House that, even without reference to the Father of His Country, improvements must quickly be made in many spheres. One of these changes came immediately after Churchill's visit. FDR had been exhilarated by the prime minister's presence as his guest, even if their late-night talk caused him to miss sleep. He had even called on Churchill in his bedroom, with its rumpled bedclothes, its cigar smoke, its floor strewn with newspapers. He had enjoyed taking the prime minister to church, telling others in the group that "it is good for Winston to sing hymns with the Methodists"; Churchill had agreed. Although it was perhaps not vitally important that the two men actually become friends, Hopkins certainly need not have worried about the relationship that might be struck up by his two prima donnas. Very different men—Churchill seemingly blunt and all of a piece, Roosevelt discursive and complex—each possessed thinking patterns that vexed his associates, and for the same reason. The sort of charge that was often leveled at FDR was made by Brooke against Churchill: He would not reason matters out but "just flits from one idea to another like a butterfly." Both men, to the bafflement of their logically trained chiefs of staff, approached the world as artists, finding in intuition an indispensable if not infallible guide. Churchill, brought up to have a hierarchical mind, paid careful deference to Roosevelt not simply as the object of a long transatlantic courtship and as a great potential benefactor but as a head of state equal to George VI. Altogether, the two men got on. And when, shortly after returning to England, Churchill cabled birthday greetings to the president, FDR responded with one of his characteristic graceful gestures: "It is fun to be in the same decade with you."

While in the White House, the prime minister turned the quiet upstairs hall into the headquarters of the British government, with a continuous bustle of officials and messengers coming and going with their "boxes"—the ancient red leather dispatch cases in which British official documents are circulated—all part of the ordered flow in which state business was conducted. What seems to have struck the president most vividly about Churchill's managerial world was a "traveling map room" supervised by Commander "Tommy" Thompson, the prime minister's flag commander, or naval aide. This condensed and visual version of Admiralty intelligence gave Churchill quick access to the overall strategic scene or any part of it. Captain McCrea soon felt pressure coming from the top down: FDR wanted a map room of his own and "something had to be done in that direction at once."

Not sure how to begin, McCrea had a stroke of luck. He happened to hear that a naval reserve lieutenant, currently on duty in the Office of Naval Intelligence, had in London spent several weeks as an observer in the Admiralty map room. McCrea sought him out at once and found him both an adventurous fellow—he had driven a Red Cross ambulance during the fighting in France—and an intelligent and modest person who was eager to be of help; the modesty was an important feature, because this man was well known around the world as Robert Montgomery the movie actor. With the help of the chief usher of the White House, McCrea found a possible location that Montgomery said looked large enough to serve the purpose. About the size of two ordinary living rooms, the area was situated on the ground floor of the White House between the oval diplomatic reception room and Dr. McIntire's office. It had a large lavatory, important in case the map room should acquire a large staff, and it was located just across the hall from the elevator the president used on his way from the White House living quarters to his office. FDR could easily stop in at the end of the day, since he usually came to McIntire's office about 5:30 to have his troublesome sinuses packed and to receive a massage.

Within a few hours of deciding on the office, McCrea had disposed of the room's odds and ends of furniture, acquired a desk, a file cabinet, and a few chairs, and seen to it that a stack of towels had been placed in the lavatory. He now had an office for himself and a secure room for the storage of secret dispatches like the increasing volume of messages between the president and the prime minister. As the next item of business, McCrea set about acquiring the charts that would enable the map room to live up to its name. Soon the walls were covered with large-scale charts of the Atlantic and the Pacific and smaller maps of such areas as Southeast Asia, the Mediterranean, and the Persian Gulf. The housecleaning called for a special approach. Mrs. Nesbitt, the housekeeper of the mansion, would knock on the door to announce that she was sending a member of the household staff to tidy up the room. Those on duty inside would reply: "Send us a dumb one."

When McCrea showed off his setup to Pa Watson, the general expressed his admiration but wanted to know what part the army would have in this promising operation. He was so busy as appointments secretary, he said, that he could not possibly keep the president adequately informed on military matters. The two aides struck a bargain whereby both "Army and Navy information"—seemingly an artificial distinction, but that was the way the services thought—would be centered in the map room, with the operation remaining under McCrea's direction and drawing its personnel from both services; this bit of interservice integration, easily arrived at and unbureaucratic, constituted no minor landmark.

Soon the map room was operating with a twenty-four-hour watch, each shift manned by two men from a team of three navy officers, two from the army, and one from the air force. Dispatches from the decrypting centers of the War and Navy departments came in at all hours. The president began making regular visits on the way to his executive office in the morning and after receiving his sinus treatment and massage in the afternoon. Usually an officer of the watch would describe the contents of significant messages; if FDR felt particular interest in a dispatch, he would read it himself and then hand it back to the officer. At other times, if the president expected particular news, he would appear during the day, and when necessary an officer would deliver a dispatch to the executive office. Captain McCrea began to enjoy the presidential afternoon visits, since FDR would scan the evening papers while chatting about the happenings of the day; "his asides about certain of his callers were always pointed and amusing."

Just two or three days after McCrea had come on board, FDR had taken from his desk and handed over for safekeeping a small bundle of papers clipped together—the file of messages to and from Churchill. Now the map room became the repository for all such traffic, not only with Churchill but with Stalin and Chiang Kai-shek; aside from the map room personnel, access to the file was limited to Roosevelt and Hopkins. The maps presented the location of U.S. forces of all services; changes were posted day by day in the positions of military and merchant convoys, capital ships, and naval task forces. Montgomery added a Hollywood touch by creating special pins to show the whereabouts of the Allied Big Three; Churchill's was shaped like a cigar, Stalin's like a brier pipe, and FDR's, inevitably, like a cigarette holder. Another distinctive pin, large and bright-colored, indicated the location of the only small vessel marked on the charts—the destroyer on which Franklin D. Roosevelt, Jr., served. His father always checked it first.

Concerned about conserving the president's time, McCrea developed the idea of briefing him, when it was suitable, while he was sitting in Dr. McIntire's office, but "we were always pleased when he visited us." Before McCrea took up his White House duties, a senior admiral had remarked to him that Roosevelt was genuinely fond of the navy and was greatly interested in everything it did. "You will like the President," said the admiral. He was turning out to be right.

With the establishment and efficient operation of the map room, Franklin D. Roosevelt had taken a giant step out of the world of George Washington. No longer was it true, as it had been even in the days following Pearl Harbor, that at night the sole military or naval person in the White House might be a young lieutenant serving as watch officer. And the president had acquired an indispensable tool for the work he intended to do. Before the war he had made it clear, time and again—as far back as the November 1938 meeting in which he had angered General Marshall and others by insisting on giving first place to aircraft production—that he had no intention of leaving military policy to the official experts. By his Military Order of 1939 bringing the service chiefs into a direct relationship with the president, he had demonstrated his interest in putting himself in touch with specific military concerns. Now, as the commander in chief of an army and a navy called on to fight a global war, he would not leave the making of the strategy of that war to others. Writing before the era of military professionalism, the framers of the Constitution had decreed that the commander in chief of the army and navy, should be, in effect, "an amateur strategist of high and unrivaled rank." Since the unusual—actually unique—feature of the clause making the president the commander in chief was that it did not assign a function but conferred an office, any president could tailor it to fit his own desires and capacities. Roosevelt intended to make it a very large garment, as loose-fitting and as suitable for all occasions as the navy cape he wore.

After putting his signature to the declaration of the United Nations, FDR had said that perhaps he ought to have signed it "Commander in Chief." Hopkins's dry wit proved equal to the challenge: "'President' ought to do," he said.

"He relished the title," said Secretary Hull. In talking with Captain McCrea, FDR characteristically had spoken of his service as assistant secretary of the navy as "when I was in the Navy"; earlier, in his famous "I hate war" speech, he had gone to vivid lengths to demonstrate his familiarity with the fighting in France. Much as he regretted it, however, he had not served in the navy and he had not seen combat; but now his big cape could become the uniform of all the U.S. armed services and he could be the permanent draftee. At a Cabinet dinner, where Hull was to propose the toast, FDR made a request: "Please try to address me as Commander-in-Chief, not as President." Aside from the enjoyment he derived from the use of the title, the practice certainly reminded everyone of the identity of the man at the head of the army and the navy, the chief strategist of the American war effort.

CHAPTER ELEVEN

"WE'VE GOT TO GO TO EUROPE"

One day in September 1941, General Marshall's plane, carrying no aides or any other passengers besides the chief of staff, had touched down at the airfield near Shreveport, Louisiana. The tourist attraction bringing the general to the South was large-scale army maneuvers featuring some 420,000 men of the Second and Third armies—the greatest U.S. military exercises ever held in peacetime. Whenever possible during the summer, Marshall had slipped out of Washington to take a personal look at these activities, which were spread out over Louisiana and east Texas, with their employment not only of infantry but of the new armored corps and parachute troops. Short as the forces were of equipment—trucks bearing identifying signs often had to serve as tanks—the exercises gave the troops experience they could have gained in no other way. To their higher officers, the maneuvers offered the novel opportunity to show how well they could lead large forces in action. Some members of Congress seemed to have difficulty grasping these obvious facts. One senator reproached Marshall for all the mistakes that were exposed in after-exercise critiques. Since so many errors were made, why was the chief of staff holding these maneuvers? "My God, Senator," said Marshall, "that's the reason I do it. I want the mistakes down in Louisiana, not over in Europe."

In typical style, the chief of staff insisted that he be greeted with no fuss at the airport. Accordingly, a single staff officer was always detailed to meet him with a car. On this particular visit, the chief of staff had more on his mind than observing the progress of the maneuvers. He asked the officer to take him to

Colonel Dwight D. Eisenhower, chief of staff to Lieutenant General Walter Krueger, commander of the Third Army.

After a two-hour drive, the car pulled up in front of a bank in downtown Lake Charles, and the staff officer led General Marshall upstairs to a small room with just enough space for a desk and two or three chairs, where they found Eisenhower alone. After presenting the colonel to the general, Marshall's escort stepped outside as Eisenhower, using a large wall map, proceeded to brief the chief of staff on the exercise in progress. Some conversation followed, but Marshall soon came out into the hall. He was ready to return to Shreveport, and on arrival there he left immediately for Washington.

For his planning of the Third Army's rout of the Second Army in the maneuvers, Eisenhower won wide publicity, and shortly thereafter Marshall approved his promotion to brigadier general. Despite the fact that he not only had met Eisenhower previously but had awarded him the honor of a listing in the little black book holding the names of approved Fort Benning alumni and other men deemed worthy of high responsibilities, Marshall clearly believed that, in a day when general officers were nominated one at a time, duty required him to make sure of Ike's quality by paying him a personal visit.

A week after the Pearl Harbor attack, having summoned Eisenhower to Washington, Marshall asked the younger officer a daunting question with respect to the Philippines: "What should be our general line of action?"

Jolted by the question but hoping he "was showing a poker face," Eisenhower answered, "Give me a few hours." Dusk had fallen when Ike returned to the chief of staff's office with a paper containing "bleak conclusions." The Philippines could not be saved if the enemy committed sizable forces there, Ike wrote, but the United States must do everything humanly possible for them; American prestige in the Far East was at stake; the first step should be to build up a base in Australia: "In this last, we dare not fail."

Marshall answered simply, "I agree with you"; Eisenhower divined from the chief's tone that he had been given the problem as a check on the conclusion Marshall had already reached. Then the chief of staff added, "Do your best to save them." With his eyes now looking "awfully cold," Marshall leaned forward and issued an unmistakable challenge: "Eisenhower, the department is filled with able men who analyze their problems well but feel compelled always to bring them to me for final solution. I must have assistants who will solve their own problems and tell me later what they have done." One of these unsatisfactory "able men" was General Gerow, and on February 16 Eisenhower was to succeed him as chief of the War Plans Division.

Ike's advocacy of support for the Philippines had certainly not sprung from any loyalty to the local commander, General MacArthur, under whom he had served during the 1930s. (After retiring as chief of staff, MacArthur had become field marshal of the Philippine Army; in 1941 he had successfully urged his own recall to duty in the U.S. Army and, after a day's delay, had received the less glamorous but more substantial rank of lieutenant general.) MacArthur was "as big a baby as ever," Ike noted one day, but "we've got to keep him fighting." And when MacArthur radioed his recommendation of Major General Richard K. Sutherland as his successor in case of "my death"—Ike himself supplied the quotation marks—the conclusion was that MacArthur "still likes his boot lickers." After MacArthur had left the islands for Australia, Ike wryly observed that "he's a hero! Yah."

Between MacArthur and Marshall, Eisenhower drew a contrast that approached the absolute. The chief of staff became a study to Ike, ten years his junior. "I knew about his reputation, of course," Eisenhower wrote, "but before long I had conceived for him unlimited admiration and respect for my own reasons"; and even though Marshall seemed austere, Ike developed an affection for him "because I realized the burden he was uncomplainingly carrying." Marshall's way of leading seemed ideal. Unlike MacArthur, the chief did not engage in tirades, he treated his subordinates as members of a team—with himself, quite properly, as unquestioned head—and he dealt with even frustrating matters calmly. It was not truly an Olympian calm, however, and here Eisenhower found Marshall a bit puzzling. "I've never seen a man who apparently develops a higher pressure of anger when he encounters some piece of stupidity than does he," Ike noted in his diary; yet "the outburst is so fleeting, he returns so quickly to complete 'normalcy,' that I'm certain he does it for effect." At least, Ike said, "he doesn't get angry in the sense I do—I blaze for an hour."

Eisenhower's insight was at least half right. Like anyone

else, Marshall could become angry, but "he had disciplined himself for the past forty years in the Army," Mrs. Marshall said, "far more rigidly than he had disciplined his men." During this winter of retreat and defeat, the Marshalls took long walks at twilight, when the chief of staff came home from the office. Listening to his quiet voice as they moved at a brisk pace, Mrs. Marshall heard a man "steeling himself to carry a burden so tremendous in magnitude and so diverse in its demands that it was difficult to comprehend how one man could carry it alone." She felt as he talked that he was viewing himself from the outside and that "George Marshall was someone he was constantly appraising, advising and training to meet a situation." He would enunciate a principle: "I cannot afford the luxury of sentiment; mine must be cold logic. Sentiment is for others." Then would come the particulars that had given rise to the thought—the subordinates he had been forced to criticize, the proposals he had been compelled to turn down. "It is not easy to tell men where they have failed."

As he had for some years now, Marshall paid close attention to his health, watching his body as if he were an athlete. Anger—the old choleric heat—lurked as the great evil. "I cannot allow myself to get angry," he said one day. "That would be fatal—it is too exhausting. My brain must be kept clear." And he could not appear in public seeming tired. One day General Pershing had leaned back in a car on a long trip, he said, and that trivial fact had given rise among the troops in France to the rumor that the general was discouraged and the war going badly.

The selection of officers for high positions demanded the chief of staff's greatest attention. Eisenhower, who saw Marshall every day and had already begun to look on him as a leader to emulate, paid close attention to the way the chief went about the task, noting the types of personalities that did not win favor. Marshall viewed with particular distaste the kind of officer who "seemed to be self-seeking in the matter of promotion" and who sought to bring pressure to bear on his own behalf. Another category that vexed him, as he had earlier told Ike, was that made up of officers who could do detailed work but would not take the responsibility for making decisions. Similarly, he objected to men who immersed themselves in minor details and so lost sight of general issues. The group in disfavor also included the fiery types who did not know the difference between strength and bad manners, those who loved the limelight, and those who had trouble getting along with others. Nor could the chief stand pessimists. He would never give a command to an officer who was less than enthusiastic about the post or operation in question. When, as inevitably happened, he had to choose from a pool of officers who did not meet all these criteria, the chief of staff, Ike observed, always maintained reservations about the candidate he had felt compelled to select.

One problem some officers had was unwittingly caused by Marshall himself. A legend grew up in the War Department that a young officer suddenly called to the chief of staff's office had responded to the summons by having a heart attack. This story, though apocryphal, suggested the reality exemplified by Brigadier General Robert W. Crawford, an able planner. Eisenhower, who worked with Crawford, found him a brilliant man, but General Marshall had no way of knowing his quality because Crawford, when appearing in the chief of staff's office, simply froze in terror.

Certainly the routine could have its unnerving side. Colonel John E. Hull, who came to the War Plans Division in the week before Pearl Harbor, saw how General Marshall's manner of conducting business with his staff led many persons to regard him as cold-blooded. The general did not try to do two things at once. When duty brought an officer to his presence, the man was supposed to walk into the office, not saluting, and quietly sit down in the chair directly opposite the general, facing him. Marshall would not look up until he had finished reading the paper in front of him; the officer would sit silently until the chief had completed his task. Marshall would then look at his caller and wait to hear a brief explanation of the purpose of the visit. In using this method, the chief of staff was faithfully applying the principle of keeping his brain clear by avoiding clutter; for him, a discussion in the office in no sense constituted a social occasion.

In listening to a presentation of this kind, Colonel Hull observed, most people will nod their heads from time to time if they are in general agreement with what is being said, or express partial approval or disapproval, or somehow suggest the nature of their own opinions. "But not General Marshall—not by the slightest change of expression or movement of his head would he indicate whether he was in agreement or disagreement with you. When you finished he might ask a few questions. He then gave his approval or disapproval to your proposal."

To Hull, who like Eisenhower did not find this procedure intimidating, it had the virture of offering no handholds to a sycophant or a bootlicker; "it was simply not possible for a 'yes man' to get by with General Marshall." But unfortunately, this style, although admirably conserving the chief's energies, made no provision for an officer, no matter how able, who, finding himself across the desk from the chief of staff with those blue eyes fixed on him, became tongue-tied. Or perhaps the chief simply viewed the attrition of the General Crawfords as an unavoidable cost of his deliberately chosen way of doing business.

Marshall's style with prominent civilians who came to see him differed in details but not really in kind. These callers would be seated on a sofa instead of in the inquisitional chair, and the chief of staff "would seem to have all the time in the world. The only times he was interrupted would be when the secretary of war would open the door which opened directly into his office, and then General Marshall would go right in to see him. He was always accessible to the secretary of war." Once on such an occasion Marshall told the caller to wait and then apologized for having had to leave him. This particular visitor produced the keen observation that "when you are in the presence of General Marshall you have his complete attention. But I never found myself believing that you could ever wish to remain in his presence one minute after he became bored. You would probably just feel it."

Even though General Marshall had insisted long before Pearl Harbor that the General Staff decentralize its work, he had failed to translate his wish into action. Instead, as the number of officers serving on the staff had grown from 122 to almost 700, he found himself trying to relate more or less directly to about 60 persons, clearly an unworkable number. This inadequate structure, and the consequent fragmenting of Marshall's attention, had contributed heavily to the fouling of communications with General Short on Oahu and to the creation of all the other misunderstandings that, from the army side, had helped ensure the success of the Japanese attack. Fortunately, as Colonel Robinett divined in December, these organizational inadequacies had not caused the president to lose faith in the chief of staff; nor did any land equivalent of the stern old sea dog Admiral King venture on the scene to challenge Marshall for military leadership. All the same, Marshall could perhaps consider himself lucky that the army on Oahu had not possessed cherished and costly assets like the battleships whose spectacular destruction provided inflammatory pictures for movie newsreel audiences.

Under the challenge of real war, Marshall now moved to bring about the most drastic reorganization of the War Department since Elihu Root established the General Staff almost forty years earlier. Against the resentful opposition of numerous officers entrenched in the status quo, a committee headed by a solemn-faced air force officer, Major General Joseph T. McNarney, quickly put together a plan for a tripartite army structure, consisting of the Army Ground Forces, the Army Air Forces, and the Services of Supply (later to be renamed the Army Service Forces). Under this genuinely modernizing plan, each of these components would have its own commanding general, who would have control over many officers who had previously reported directly to the chief of staff, and such posts as chief of infantry and chief of artillery would be abolished. Winning the president's prompt approval, the plan took effect on March 9. Within less than two months, this long-desired decentralization had shrunk the General Staff's roster by almost six hundred officers. Although McNarney, whom Marshall regarded as "a true hatchetman," had swung the ax, doing for Marshall what in the first war General March had done personally in his reorganization of the department, many of the officers who were now reduced in status or shunted aside were never to overcome their bitterness against the chief of staff.

Beyond such structural questions, Marshall faced a problem of personal definition. Two possible wartime role models existed—General March, the strong World War I chief of staff who had insisted on his preeminence in the army, and General Pershing, the field commander who had regarded himself as the army's number one soldier. According to the plans drawn up after the first war, the chief of staff was supposed to move to the theater of war as "commanding general of the field forces." But how and where could one assume such a post if these forces were engaged at the same time in operations on opposite sides of the world? And if the chief of staff remained in Washington, what authority would he have?

The planning committee had not failed to see the need, as McNarney tersely put it, "to fight the current war." In a global war the high command in Washington must have primacy, and at the top of this command stood the chief of staff. One planner said simply, "We have to centralize the direction of operations." By speaking of the chief of staff's "direction" of these operations, the new regulations also went further, than Elihu Root had been willing to go. To supply the chief with the personal command post he would need, the planners transformed the War Plans Division into the new Operations Division, which would have as its concern not merely plans but supervision and direction. (With Eisenhower remaining as director, this new headquarters quickly took on the no-nonsense character of its executive officer, Colonel Charles K. Gailey. Queries and plans coming from the chief of staff's office by the Operations Division were dubbed "green hornets," not merely because of their special green covers but because of the speed with which they were supposed to zoom through the office and the sting they would administer to anybody who held them too long. The intense atmosphere, suggestive of a command post somewhere in the field, proved very much to General Marshall's liking.)

Although Secretary Stimson felt that no officer should bear the title commanding general of the army, because such a position would seem to conflict with the powers of the commander in chief, everybody, including the president, now accepted General Marshall as the de facto commanding general. Marshall himself seemed to take it for granted. As a high officer he had come of age a Pershing man, but as chief of staff he totally shared the view of General March. With no fuss, he would have all the authority March had sought, without having to fight for it through orders and regulations, and theater commanders would be chosen by him or on his advice; none would have any reasonable warrant for viewing himself as either superior or equal to the chief of staff.

One field commander, however, had already been supplied by events. On March 11 General MacArthur left Corregidor by PT boat for Mindanao, and from there he flew to Australia. In spite of the fact that all MacArthur's predictions about the defensibility of the Philippines and the readiness of his forces for action had proved wrong, the public, Eisenhower observed, had "built itself a hero out of its own imagination." Roosevelt and Marshall had jointly played a large part in the process; for FDR, the celebration of MacArthur and his appointment to a high command could perhaps serve to placate still-unreconciled isolationists. The newly created hero was destined not for command of U.S. forces in Australia, as had first been intended, but for the supreme command of a brand-new entity, the Southwest Pacific Area, established under the Allied unity-of-command principle successfully urged by Marshall at Arcadia. The president wished the announcement to be made immediately, without waiting for the fine print, for a political reason—to forestall Japanese propaganda claiming that the United States was abandoning the Philippines—and the news won applause in the press. Did the president and the chief of staff weigh the fact that when one creates a hero, one becomes a captive of that hero? They did not say. Strictly speaking, MacArthur's new appointment made him an agent not of the War Department but of the Combined Chiefs of Staff, acting for the Allies. But in reality he had been chosen by Roosevelt and Marshall; whether or not they had much choice they had anointed not merely a field commander but a military viceroy with the outlook of a sovereign.

Even though he now had a Joint Chiefs of Staff organization and a slimmed-down and invigorated General Staff, George Marshall saw one more important organizational world to conquer. The Joint Chiefs existed but had not yet become what the chief of staff had in mind for it. It was hampered by its dependence on unanimity; an officer who wished to dig in his heels and insist on the point of view of his own service could not be overruled simply because he represented a minority opinion. As the chief of staff did his best to push for agreed decisions on important questions, he had to cope with the antagonism of Admiral King, to whom FDR in March had given the post of chief of naval operations along with command of the U.S. Fleet; unable to cleanse himself of the taint of Pearl Harbor, Admiral Stark was packed off to England to handle liaison between the U.S. and Royal navies.

If anyone from any other service could develop a relationship with King effectively free of turbulence, that person was surely Marshall. This harmony would grow not only from the chief of staff's general outlook on interservice cooperation but from his handling of one particular small but explosive situation. As everybody knew, Marshall said, King was "a very difficult individual, because he was very short of temper and very sensitive." One morning in early 1942 the admiral paid a singularly ill-timed call on Marshall, who at the moment faced verbal attack in his office from Herbert Evatt, the firebrand Australian foreign minister. (Evatt, who did not know General Marshall, came to the War Department with the extraordinary idea of giving the chief of staff a dressing down because of what he perceived as inadequate U.S. concern about the possible fate of Australia at the hands of the advancing Japanese. After hearing a few sentences of "what I would call a tirade," Marshall informed the foreign minister that if he intended to continue in that vein, he would have to take himself elsewhere: "I've heard how you conducted yourself in other offices. Now you are not going to conduct yourself like that here!" He then suggested that the two get down to a realistic discussion of the business at hand.) While the chief of staff tamed the Australian, Admiral King sat fuming with impatience in the reception room, and when Marshall finally "got rid" of Evatt, he found that King had angrily stalked off. Losing no time, Marshall trailed the admiral to his lair in the Navy Building, and after being shown with naval formality into King's office, he told the admiral why he had come right over. "I think this is very important," Marshall said, "because if you and I begin fighting at the very start of the war, what in the world will the public have to say about us? They won't accept it for a minute." They could not afford to fight, he told King—"so we ought to find a way to get along together."

The admiral sat for some moments, pondering this little speech, and then he said, "Well, you've been very magnanimous in coming over here the way you have. We will see if we can get along, and I think we can."

Even with King more or less tractable, Marshall believed that the Joint Chiefs could not function effectively until it acquired a head. Marshall hoped to weave an organizational net so finely meshed that even the wily FDR could not slip through it. The need for a chief became pressing when Stark's departure for Britain became imminent. Now the army would have two votes, Marshall's and Arnold's, to the navy's one. As the senior member, Marshall presided over the meetings, but even the finickiest impartiality would be unlikely to satisfy King.

After a chat with Marshall, Secretary Stimson carried away the impression that the general had in mind the creation of a unified command for the army and navy, with a single chief of staff over both. Marshall, however, could hardly have been so utopian; even if he were willing to see such a post created and filled by someone else, Roosevelt would certainly not have accepted a superchief over all the armed forces with the power to issue orders without reference to the president except for matters of broad policy. FDR had not drawn up his Military Order in 1939 only to be relegated to the sidelines now that war had actually come. But creating the position of chairman of the Joint Chiefs of Staff seemed to Marshall a reasonable aspiration. His thinking on this point was somewhat fluid; this chairman, he believed, could also fill the very useful role of chief of staff to the president, serving as the communicator of information, opinions, and decisions between the White House and the chiefs. The chairman would bring order to the JCS and also some much-needed regular procedures to the White House.

Seeking the aid of Harry Hopkins, who almost invariably supported him, the chief of staff sprang the idea on the president. FDR seemed surprised. Why was such a person necessary? "I'm the chief of staff," he said. "I'm the commander in chief."

But, said Marshall "with great frankness," it was "impossible to conceive of one man with all of his duties as President being also, in effect, the chief of staff" of all the military services: "You are not Superman."

Drawing on his increasingly maturing political skills, Marshall had carefully chosen a nominee for the proposed post. Not only must he be a person of broad experience and sound judgment, to have any chance of succeeding he must be acceptable to Admiral King and he must be someone liked by FDR. Remarkably, a man who seemed to meet all these stringent standards not only existed but was available. William D. Leahy, an admiral—no one but a naval officer could conceivably have been deemed acceptable by King—was in fact the senior U.S. officer, having been Stark's predecessor as chief of naval operations. He had also been a great favorite of FDR's since World War I days, when as commander of the secretary of the navy's personal dispatch boat he had become a good friend of Assistant Secretary Roosevelt; in the very traditional Rooseveltian world of personal relations, no friend counted like an old friend. After the end of Leahy's tenure as chief of naval operations, the president had made further use of him, first as governor of Puerto Rico and then, beginning in November 1940, in the highly sensitive post of ambassador to the Vichy French government of

Marshal Pétain. (Just before Leahy departed for France, he received a note from General Marshall praising his "integrity of purpose.") By early 1942 the admiral had become so disgusted with Vichy's collaboration with the Third Reich that he urged his own recall. Now sixty-seven years old, he had retired at the peak of his profession, he had always been considered in the navy an effective administrator and diplomat—even something of a "fixer"—and he had no advancement to seek and presumably no axes to grind. Although Marshall did not know him well, he said, "I was willing to trust Leahy to be a neutral chairman of the American chiefs of staff."

But Roosevelt did not eagerly grasp Marshall's suggestion. He did not seem especially pleased at the remark about Superman, and Marshall felt he did not seem to understand the role of the proposed chairman. More likely, FDR understood what it was but was not prepared to welcome it before thinking the matter over, chewing on it, and changing it to suit himself. In the following weeks Marshall persisted in bringing up the subject, always prominently mentioning Admiral Leahy as the nominee for the job, and Roosevelt persisted in fencing with the general, professing to see no need for this chief of staff to the commander in chief; he seemed to feel that Marshall himself should simply continue to preside at the meetings of the Joint Chiefs.

Then, on July 21, when Marshall was away on a mission to England, the president announced at his press conference the recall to service of Admiral Leahy as "chief of staff to the commander in chief of the United States Army and Navy." Defining the admiral's duties, FDR said that he would perform leg work for the commander in chief. When Marshall returned to Washington, he was sought out by Leahy, who asked what he was supposed to do; he did not even have an office. Explaining that the president did not "know what a chief of staff is," Marshall, who on his own had arranged for an office and a secretary for Leahy, led the admiral to his new quarters in the Public Health Building and then to the nearby room in which the Joint Chiefs met. Waving toward the chair at the head of the table—unused up till then because Marshall, though acting as chairman, always sat on one side—the chief of staff suggested that at the next meeting of the Joint Chiefs, Leahy simply walk in, sit down in that chair, and begin presiding. King might be furious, even though Leahy was a navy man, but he presumably would not be able to resist the *fait accompli.*

So began Admiral Leahy's tenure at the head of the Joint Chiefs' table. Marshall nevertheless remained disappointed that the admiral had not officially been named chairman of the group. His appointment represented great progress, but how well he would balance the role desired for him by Marshall and that prescribed by the president could not yet be known. Leg man? That had hardly been the aim. For all his careful efforts, the general had not woven a net fine enough to trap the endlessly resourceful FDR.

Day and night, in the early weeks of 1942, messages of all sorts—reports, calls for help, intelligence summaries—poured into the offices of the General Staff from points around the world. Every continent, it seemed, and a great many islands cried out for an infusion of American strength in the form of men or supplies or both. The United Nations found themselves on the defensive from the Russian front to the Pacific, and the resulting problems had to be dealt with as they came up rather than after leisurely strategic deliberations. Though Arcadia had reaffirmed the Germany-first principle, the Anglo-American staffs and their political chiefs had reached no other conclusions about strategy. As all the Allies—Britain, the Soviet Union, China—came calling with lend-lease shopping lists marked "urgent," Marshall's planners saw the specter of American strength dispersed everywhere, in each instance for seeming good reasons, with no strategic focus; "Germany first" might simply die of malnutrition.

To bring a measure of order to the strategic picture, Roosevelt and Churchill adopted a proposal of the president's to divide the world into zones of respective American and British military responsibility: the Pacific, to the Americans; the Middle and Far East, to the British; and Europe and the Atlantic, to be shared by the two powers. In the first two areas Britain and the United States would "supplement" each other as suitable.

The demands placed on U.S. shipping by the incredible Japanese victories, together with British reverses in Libya at the hands of General Rommel, led FDR to tell Churchill that the Allies must lay aside the proposed offensive in Northwest Africa. When they heard this news, Marshall's planners breathed more easily. Concerned about the danger of dispersing American strength, they also fretted about the deliberate adoption of offensive plans that would consume men and shipping without threatening either of the chief Axis powers in a vital area. "Decisive" sounded as the watchword in the War Plans Division—and to the planners, landings on the coast of French Northwest Africa seemed no more than hacking at Axis arms or legs while leaving the head and trunk untouched. These American officers breathed an air filled with the aroma not only of the offensive but of the mass offensive—the big squeeze and the great breakthrough, the achievement of Grant, the dream of Pershing.

When, in a message to Churchill, the president observed that he was "becoming more and more interested" in the establishment of a new front on the continent of Europe, he was moving in harmony with the thinking of his military advisers. All in all, FDR lost no time in showing himself the opposite of his own wartime leader, Woodrow Wilson; his finger, if not stuck into every pie, probed an impressive number of them. A variety of queries and suggestions flowed from the White House to Marshall's Munitions Building office, and the chief of staff, for his part, took pains to keep the president interested and informed on all sorts of matters, some of them quite specific. On January 19 Marshall reported on the tonnage of matériel being shipped to the U.S. supply missions in Egypt and Iran. On January 20 the president wanted to know what guns the War Department could make available to a group of South American countries for coast defense; the chief of staff sent him a "very impressive" list. Roosevelt's interest was not superficial; he instructed Marshall to make sure that Sumner Welles, the intermediary with those countries, received the "estimated time for dismantling and new installation." A few days later the chief of staff sent over a report detailing U.S. troop and supply movements since December 7. On another day he replied to a suggestion Roosevelt had made in talk that troops be sent directly to New Caledonia without detouring via Australia to pick up their equipment; it all came down to loading and reloading, said Marshall, and these arrangements would have to be continued until ample cargo space became available.

On February 26 the chief of staff sent Roosevelt an informative memo about arrangements for a new air-transport service from Sadiya, India, to Chungking, at the time the capital of China. A heroic sort of American pioneering endeavor, this service would call for airplanes, then barges, then trucks—all to try to assure a flow of supplies in support of General Stilwell, the new American commander in China. As a careful student of

Rooseveltian psychology Marshall made sure to enclose a visual aid—a sketch map—with his memo.

Demonstrating that even with its peculiar organization the White House could act effectively, the president's staff performed such feats as the production of a memorable send-off for a small signal company that had been given the mission of establishing radio and telephone communications along the Burma Road from Rangoon to Chungking (a mission soon aborted by the Japanese occupation of Rangoon). When, having finished training, the company sailed from Charleston for Burma, "a personal representative of President Roosevelt was at the dock to express the President's interest in helping General Stilwell and wishing us success in our mission." Such a gesture, the company commander recalled, "gave us a feeling that we were contributing something important at a critical early stage of the war."

Of course the number of questions with which FDR could or would deal was quite small in comparison with the possible total—inevitably, it was for General Marshall as well—but the president nevertheless presented an ear and a voice of which the chief of staff always had to take account. Roosevelt's reaction to the coming of the war had worked a change in Marshall's view of him. Previously the general had harbored his doubts about the caliber of the politician: "He wasn't always clear-cut in his decisions. He could be swayed." But in the aftermath of the Japanese attacks, when Roosevelt responded to disasters with courage and boldness, Marshall decided that the commander in chief was a great man. Their relationship changed, too. Marshall had been affirmed as de facto commanding general of an army whose men were committed across the world from Australia to Ireland, though he remained the president's personal military adviser; the establishment of the Joint Chiefs of Staff would not change that fact. In addition, Roosevelt persisted in the style dictated by his basic personality; he continued to favor the individual conversation, not the collegial way of reaching decisions. Nor, to Marshall's frustration, did he wish to have discussions recorded in any fashion. One day the chief of staff brought along to FDR's office a General Staff officer with "a big notebook," and "the President blew up." The next time, still thinking notes would be useful, Marshall had the officer in tow again—but this time with a book "so little he couldn't use it." Dedicated to his eternal campaign to impose some degree of administrative orthodoxy on Roosevelt, Marshall had to acknowledge failure, but somewhere, he seemed to feel, he would sooner or later discover a stronger, finer net that could contain his clever quarry.

Although General Eisenhower had begun his work for General Marshall as an apostle of aid to the Philippines and an opponent of the buildup of U.S. troops in Northern Ireland, by January 22 he had breathed in so much of the charged air of the General Staff that he vented quite different feelings in his diary: "We've got to go to Europe and fight . . . we've got to begin slugging with air at West Europe, to be followed by a land attack as soon as possible." A few days later he noted that "we must win in Europe." Eagerly, Ike, along with Hap Arnold, began pressing for action in 1942.

Although more cautious with respect to timing, the chief of staff continued to hold his own deep-seated Europe-first sentiments. Often misunderstood by many observers in both the United States and Britain, sometimes even by the president—could the chief of staff really produce a great army from scratch?—Marshall had consistently given the highest priority to the creation of a mass United States citizen army; much of its specific design and training he had entrusted to General Lesley McNair, but he held its purpose clearly before him. With due regard for the strategic situation existing at the time, that army must be hurled against the German forces defending northwestern Europe—the direct way to the enemy's heart.

On March 25 Marshall had the opportunity to state his views at a luncheon in the White House given by the president for the Joint Chiefs, the service secretaries Stimson and Knox, and Harry Hopkins. Although FDR had earlier written Churchill about his interest in action on the European continent, he began this day's discussion in a manner that disappointed and even "staggered" Stimson, a man of orderly and not overly flexible mind who disliked dealing with more than one proposition at a time. As the president with bold strokes sketched the world situation and the possibilities it offered, the secretary of war thought he was "going off on the wildest kind of dispersion debauch"; he "toyed a while with the Middle East and the Mediterranean," which, Stimson noted ominously, "he seemed to be quite charmed with."

Working jointly and carefully, the secretary and the chief of staff nudged the discussion toward the Atlantic. This intervention could hardly have surprised Roosevelt, who in the previous weeks had been made thoroughly familiar with the thinking in the War Department; the pleasure he drew from indulging in a *tour d'horizon* did not communicate itself to his advisers, who wished to move straight to the target, and if he wished them to keep the Mediterranean in mind, they wanted him to forget it. Drawing on the skill and force that enabled him to carry the day with such varied listeners as U.S. congressmen and British generals, Marshall in "a very fine presentation" persuaded FDR to give his support to a cross-Channel attack. As the lunch was winding down, the president suggested that the proposal now be turned over to the Combined Chiefs of Staff. Here Hopkins entered the discussion. Giving the plan to the Combined Chiefs, he said, would simply be asking for emasculation. The way to get action would be for someone—he meant Marshall—to take it directly to London, to Churchill and his chiefs of staff—Brooke, Pound, and Portal. This suggestion hardly amounted to an endorsement of the new Allied instrument of strategy and command, but FDR accepted it. He ordered Stimson and Marshall to put the plan "in shape if possible over this weekend."

On April 1 Marshall and Stimson came back to the White House with a memorandum and a plan for Allied invasion of Western Europe. The memo, one of several explaining the reasons for the plan, was well crafted to catch and hold FDR's interest. A series of simple and clear sentences explained the reasons for choosing this theater: "It is the only place in which a powerful offensive can be prepared and executed by the United Powers in the near future. . . . It is the only place where the vital air superiority over the hostile land areas preliminary to a major attack can be staged by the United Powers. . . . It is the only place in which the bulk of the British ground forces can be committed to a general offensive in cooperation with United States forces." If FDR had any intention of waffling, such hard-hitting points, backed up by more detailed reasons, should keep him on the track. "The United States can concentrate and use larger forces in Western Europe than in any other place, due to sea distances and the existence in England of base facilities. The bulk of the combat forces of the United States, United Kingdom, and Russia can be applied simultaneously only against Germany, and then only if we attack in time. We cannot concentrate against Japan. Successful attack in this area will afford the maximum of support to the Russian front." Strategic ideas, geography, logistics—all supported the plan.

The proposal also struck a note of urgency: "The element of time is of the greatest importance. We must begin an offensive on a major scale before Russia, now practically alone, can be defeated and before Vichy France, Spain, Portugal, and Turkey are drawn into the ranks of our enemies." The decision must be made now, "even if the actual attack cannot be launched during this year," because "a major attack must be preceded by a long period of intensive preparation."

Since the United States did not yet have Marshall's battle-ready citizen army, the target date—"the earliest possible moment that the necessary tactical forces can be accumulated"—was April 1, 1943, exactly a year in the future. The United States would supply 30 divisions (about 1 million men), with the aid of British shipping, and 3,250 aircraft; the British would be called on for 18 divisions and 2,550 airplanes. The memorandum also offered the possibility of an "emergency" offensive, which could be launched about September 15, 1942, "if the imminence of Russian collapse requires desperate action"; the planners frankly viewed this attack as a sacrifice effort. On the other hand, if the Germans should become almost completely absorbed on the Russian front, then the Allies ought to be ready to take advantage of this opening with a quick move across the Channel.

All in all, the army had produced a daring plan, a true offspring of the pioneering, damn-the-obstacles spirit that had impelled the Americans to supply Chiang Kai-shek with a U.S. chief of staff and undertake by road, barge, and aircraft to maintain the lumbering Chinese in the fighting line of the new United Nations. Less than three weeks after this White House meeting, the American refusal to keep within conventional bounds would show another side when the veteran flier Jimmy Doolittle and sixteen army B-25s took off from the deck of the carrier *Hornet* to bomb Tokyo and other Japanese cities in a surprise raid. The American war effort had barely begun, yet General Marshall and his planners were looking over the heads of their untried ground divisions and unfledged airmen toward decisive combat with the battle-hardened legions that controlled Europe from the North Cape to Sicily, from the Bay of Biscay to the Russian steppes.

Was it a wise plan? Seeming to harbor no doubts, President Roosevelt gave it his quick approval and ordered the chief of staff to take it to London, as Hopkins had suggested; Hopkins would go along, a decision to which he responded with delight. Having shivered through previous visits to England, Hopkins gleefully wired his friend Churchill: WILL BE SEEING YOU SOON SO PLEASE START THE FIRE. Although not intending to speak metaphorically, he was in fact defining the purpose of the Americans' forthcoming trip.

The president and the chief of staff had agreed on the theme of action in Europe as soon as possible. Marshall saw the key word as "Europe." He did not sense the weight Roosevelt gave to "action."

CHAPTER TWELVE

THE DOORS OF PERCEPTION

When Captain Albert C. Wedemeyer reported to the General Staff after returning to America in 1938 from two years' study at the Kriegsakademie in Berlin, he was disillusioned by the tenor of the questions put to him. In Germany this U.S. officer had studied tactics, technical principles, the command of large units, with such lecturers as Heinz Guderian on armor; he had seen grand strategy through the geopolitical perspective of the eminent Professor Karl Haushofer, mentor of Hitler's deputy, Rudolf Hess (although sometimes the professor had credited his insights with such importance that he required foreign students in the class to leave the room). Countries were analyzed from the German point of view with respect not only to their military strength but to their political, economic, and psychological qualities. At the time of the German *Anschluss* of Austria during the preceding March, the captain and his classmates had been engaged in ski training in an area near the Austrian border, and he had gone to Vienna to watch the arrival of the goosestepping Nazis.

All in all, Wedemeyer had received a kind of intellectual training few American officers had enjoyed, and he felt that he had come back to the United States very well informed about German ideas and capabilities. He had submitted a hundred-page report to his superiors, but when he personally appeared at the General Staff, his fellow officers barraged him with questions about such matters as Hitler's personal peculiarities and the love lives of Joseph Goebbels and Hermann Göring. Not many of his interlocutors seemed interested in the organization and training of the German Army or the strategy that could be expected to guide it.

One officer was a notable exception. When Wedemeyer entered the office of the chief of War Plans, General George Marshall, he saw a copy of his report on the desk, and it quickly became evident that the general had read it with care. The two men discussed Germany at some length, then Marshall took the captain to lunch, after which they returned and continued the conversation through the afternoon. The general showed more interest than Wedemeyer "could have imagined possible"; the two men "were very drawn to each other." (Actually, Wedemeyer, an imposingly tall—six feet six inches—gregarious man with a charming manner, could have told his fellow officers quite a bit about a number of German personalities; at a party he had chatted with Göring, Martin Bormann, and other leading Nazis, and his chief instructor during his first year at the Kriegsakademie had been Ferdinand Jodl, a specialist in tactics, whose brother Alfred was a rising star in operations and intelligence. A classmate who became a special friend, and at whose apartment Wedemeyer attended parties, was a tall, strikingly handsome young captain from southern Germany, Claus von Stauffenberg.)

Although Wedemeyer went off to Fort Benning to command troops, Marshall would certainly not forget him, not only because of their daylong discussion of the German Army but because the captain was the son-in-law of Marshall's friend and adviser on strategy, General Embick. When Wedemeyer reappeared in Washington assigned to War Plans, however, the move was said to have been suggested by General Gerow, who had succeeded Marshall as chief of that division. One day, frowning over the prose of a memo on the strategic importance of "some island group," Marshall handed it to an aide, saying, "Take this back to Gerow and tell him to get it to that long-legged major in War Plans and have him fix it up. He seems to know how to write." The general's failure to identify Wedemeyer by name had nothing odd about it; his memory, excellent and even remarkable in many respects, frequently failed to produce a name or sometimes produced the wrong one. Marshall's aide tactfully forbore to mention that the inadequate memo had been written by the "long-legged major," but took it straight to War Plans, where with some amusement he reported the chief's order to Wedemeyer. Since the memo represented his thoughts accurately, the major merely tinkered with it a bit, changed some short words to polysyllables, and sent it back. Later, Marshall said to the aide, "You see, that's the way it should be written." Wedemeyer was highly pleased, but he had also been lucky, because the chief of staff when editing letters and documents usually moved toward terseness and simplicity.

In mid-1941, at a time when conflicting demands for matériel and supplies were straining high-level nerves in the War Department, pressure from various sources—William S. Knudsen, the director of the Office of Production Management; the undersecretary of the army, who by law was responsible for procurement; and last, but hardly least, the White House—led General Marshall to order the creation of a new kind of estimate, one that would describe in detail what the army would need to win the war in which the United States was not at that point engaged. Then Roosevelt took a more direct hand, with an order to Stimson for the army, and to Knox for the navy; the secretary passed it on to Marshall, who delegated the task to Gerow; the directive reached the end of the army line when Gerow assigned the estimate to the relatively new Major Wedemeyer. "Although the procedure was normal," Wedemeyer observed with no overstatement, "the task was more than usually challenging." Who had ever tried to draw up such a war plan? How could one judge the "over-all production requirements required to defeat our potential enemies"? What, indeed, was the objective of U.S. national policy? These were particularly challenging questions for Wedemeyer to confront, since he did not in his own thinking support Roosevelt's policy toward Britain.

Despite the problems he faced, including presidential amplifications of his assignment, Wedemeyer completed his labors by early September, and on the twenty-fifth, the consolidated army-navy program was presented to the president. Along with it went a "Statement of Ultimate Requirements," which included a complete outline of the army's—hence, Marshall's—outlook on strategy; it immediately engaged FDR's interest. The document declared that the United States "must be prepared to fight Germany directly and defeat her"—which meant defeating the four hundred divisions the Germans were expected to have available in the European theater in 1943 (the planners gloomily presumed that Russia would have left the war). The United States would have to defend the Western Hemisphere, provide what would clearly be large forces for operations in Europe, and continue to furnish supplies to allies. Using a standard method of computation, Wedemeyer had calculated that the army and air force together would require close to nine million men; the navy had estimated its own manpower needs at 1,500,000. In an America not at war with anyone, with limited ideas of her productive capacity and of the possible maximum size of any army that could be raised, these came as colossal figures. The chief of operations and training in the General Staff found the timing and magnitude of the great task outlined by Wedemeyer "beyond his imagination or grasp."

This officer was not the only person impressed and even staggered by the scope of what quickly came to be called the "Victory Program"—as Major Wedemeyer discovered when he arrived for work at the Munitions Building at 7:30 in the morning on Friday, December 5, 1941. Office chatter suddenly stopped as Wedemeyer's secretary handed him the morning's *Washington Times-Herald,* which bore a Page One banner headline: FDR'S WAR PLANS. Subheads declared that the "goal is 10 million armed men; half to fight in AEF" and highlighted the "proposed land drive by July 1, 1943, to smash Nazis." The story was written by Chesly Manly of Colonel Robert McCormick's *Chicago Tribune,* with which the *Times-Herald* was associated. As Wedemeyer scanned the story he saw that it was perfectly authentic, containing "an exact reproduction of the most important parts of the Victory Program." The plan, marveled the disapproving Manly, "is a blueprint for total war on a scale unprecedented in at least two oceans and three continents, Europe, Africa and Asia." The most tightly guarded secret in Washington lay there, spread across the front page of a virulently anti-Roosevelt newspaper, bearing the by-line of the Washington correspondent of the leading America First publication in the country. Wedemeyer "could not have been more appalled and astounded if a bomb had been dropped on Washington." Later in the day, John J. McCloy, who had recently come to the War Department from Wall Street as assistant secretary and whom Wedemeyer viewed as something of a climber, kept the major standing at attention in his office as he portentously declared, "Wedemeyer, there's blood on the fingers of the man who leaked the information about our war plans."

Shortly after the major returned to his own office, he received a visit from two agents of the FBI. They made their suspicions quite clear. Wedemeyer did not sympathize with the administration's interventionist policy and he had friends among America First leaders; he had a German name and was friendly with German officers; and during the previous week he had been to see a Washington lawyer who happened to be the son of the isolationist Senator Burton K. Wheeler, who had once accused Franklin Roosevelt of wishing to "plow under every fourth American boy." Although purely circumstantial, the evidence even led some of Wedemeyer's associates to feel that he might indeed be the source of the appalling leak. A few days later some ill-wisher sought to bolster the case with an anonymous letter to Secretary Stimson declaring that "Wedemeyer thinks and says Hitler is a saviour."

In public, at least, the Germans reacted calmly to the sensational story. The idea that the United States planned to create an expeditionary force of five million troops, said a German official, was nothing but "fantastic." The whole world could not muster enough shipping to transport such an army to Europe, let alone keep it supplied. Very likely the Americans had produced the story simply to "bolster England's waning prestige," although it was singularly ill calculated to accomplish such a purpose, since the plans seemed to be "based on the theory that both Russia and the British Empire will be defeated by 1943." Perhaps the story was nothing more than a plan worked out on paper by "some crazy general."

The officer who had coordinated the development of the Victory Plan was neither crazy nor a general, but he had other troubles: He had no way to dispel the suspicion surrounding him except to declare his innocence. A secretary in the office had said, sobbing, "How did he get into my safe?" But who was the "he" in question? Whatever others might think, one man remained unperturbed by any circumstantial evidence or by any of Wedemeyer's personal political views; "General Marshall," said Wedemeyer, "never doubted me." In fact, within a few weeks the major was promoted to lieutenant colonel, and after the establishment of the Joint Staff Planners as an arm of the Joint Chiefs of Staff, Wedemeyer became one of the army members of this group.

On April 1, 1942, Wedemeyer received some interesting news. He would be leaving Washington shortly to accompany General Marshall on a highly secret mission.

* * *

In all the territories and outposts of the British Empire, by ancient custom, the senior civil official present was asked to read the first lesson at the Easter Sunday service and the senior military officer was called on to read the second lesson. Easter 1942 found General Marshall and his traveling party in Bermuda, and as the preeminent military personage present, the chief of staff was asked by the governor general to take part in the service.

This stopover on Sunday had not been planned. Enjoying the civilian comfort of a Boeing flying boat requisitioned from Pan American, the party had left Baltimore on Saturday morning, April 4, intending to spend the night at Bermuda and depart early the next morning for Britain. The officer in charge of assigning code names to this small group had brought very little flair to his task. The operation itself was accurately but unoptimistically called "Modicum"; the participants were likewise drably named. General Marshall was Mr. C. G. Mell, Hopkins was Mr. A. H. Hones, Commander James R. Fulton (a doctor sent along on Roosevelt's order to keep an eye on Hopkins) was Mr. A. L. Foss, Colonel Craig (the air force officer in charge of the arrangements) was Mr. J. H. Case, and Colonel Wedemeyer, who was to serve as Marshall's aide, was Mr. J. E. White—not a polysyllable in the lot; an enemy agent studying the list might well have found it suspect. As another feature of security, the officers had been told to wear civilian clothes, but, to Wedemeyer's surprise, the chief of staff had arrived at the pier on the Baltimore waterfront dressed in his regular uniform. When the lapse was pointed out to him, he conceded that Frank McCarthy, who was increasingly serving as his all-purpose aide, had no doubt cautioned him about the uniform but that he had forgotten his instructions. What had perhaps been forgotten too was the thoroughness of the staff work with which the British had approached previous Anglo-American meetings—ABC-1, Argentia, Arcadia. Although he might expect some help from the U.S. military headquarters in London, Marshall would be assaulting the British command citadel with the support of only one American officer, an air force colonel, besides Wedemeyer.

Halfway to Bermuda the Pan American Clipper had lost an engine; the stopover had to be extended while a replacement was flown in from New York. Saturday evening during dinner at the governor general's residence, the Americans discovered that the security supposedly cloaking their mission was so transparent that jokes were made about it; "apparently everyone on the island knew exactly who we all were, and precisely why we were going to England." Like the British before them in 1939 and 1940, the Americans continued to learn that a complete wartime mentality did not spontaneously appear with the beginning of hostilities.

Pleased to learn of the governor general's invitation to Marshall to take part in the Easter service, Wedemeyer conscientiously read over the assigned passage—Revelation 1:1–8—checking for verbal pitfalls. He saw none, and after a rehearsal at breakfast the chief of staff, his performance approved by Hopkins and Wedemeyer ("All of you be prepared to criticize," the general had said), seemed ready to play his part. But at the church, after the governor general read the first lesson, Marshall checked the slip of paper just handed to him: His assignment was not verses 1–8 but verses 1–18, and he soon discovered that the additional portion included the names of the seven churches of Asia Minor; names like Thyatira and Laodicea loomed as tongue twisters. Gallantly Marshall proceeded with what Wedemeyer called "undulating effect" until he came on such a welcome term that he intoned it with dramatic intensity: *Philadelphia*! Afterward, as the congregation was leaving the church, an elderly lady rushed up to Marshall, proudly exclaiming that she too was from Philadelphia.

Early Wednesday morning, after a twenty-hour flight over water (a venture that was still novel), the Clipper landed on Lough Erne, in Northern Ireland, and as soon as their luggage was transferred, the Americans took off from the adjacent airfield in an RAF transport for Hendon airport, outside of London. Arriving early that afternoon, they were greeted by a distinguished party, including the prime minister and the chiefs of staff. On the way into the city, and later in the evening, the Americans were struck by the signs of enemy attack, the heaps of rubble and the cleared areas like promiscuously scattered parking lots, and the thorough blackout, with its dim traffic lights and shadowy pedestrians. The next morning Wedemeyer discovered another fact of British wartime life, as he was served for breakfast two pieces of stringy bacon, several venerable mushrooms, toast, and "execrable coffee." On this first visit to London at war, the Americans had entered a world remote from their home cities safe from enemy bombs and free of even a suggestion of deprivation.

The first afternoon and evening, while Wedemeyer took a look at London and worked on staff papers, his chief and Harry Hopkins met with Churchill at 10 Downing Street for a two-hour discussion in which Marshall gave Churchill an overall description of the American proposals for offensive action against Germany. "It was perfectly clear that the Prime Minister was well aware" of the proposals, Hopkins noted, because the British had been studying such points for many weeks. Marshall and Hopkins came away with differing impressions of Churchill's reaction, Hopkins feeling that it was guarded, Marshall expressing the optimistic thought that the prime minister had gone "a long way" toward falling in with American ideas. The visitors in fact had found Churchill in none too sanguine a mood. He expressed concern over the crumbling of the British position in Asia and what he saw as the dilatoriness of his commander in the Middle East, General Auchinleck, in dealing with Rommel's Afrika Korps.

At dinner that evening Churchill played host to his two American friends and to Clement Attlee, the Labour party leader and deputy prime minister, and General Brooke, chief of the Imperial General Staff. The dinner proved to be primarily a social occasion in which the prime minister dominated the conversation with an extended monologue of the sort with which his associates had become more familiar than many of them would have liked. "Displaying his talents as a military historian," Hopkins said, Churchill "spent most of the evening discussing the Civil War and the World War and never really came to grips with our main business." But the evening possessed exceptional significance, nevertheless, because it saw the first meeting of Marshall and his British opposite number, the fifty-eight-year-old Alan Brooke, swarthy, eagle-faced, stoop-shouldered, immaculately turned out. For an encounter of which much good might have been hoped, the meeting produced disappointing results. Looking at Brooke, a man whose aquiline features struck many as fitting accompaniments to a quick and incisive mind, a complex man but one so methodical in his habits that he often appeared mechanical, Marshall saw in this successor to his great friend Sir John Dill someone who, he told Hopkins, "may be a good fighting man" but "hasn't got Dill's brains."

The next morning Marshall, Wedemeyer, and Major General James E. Chaney, the U.S. commander in England, met with the British Chiefs of Staff Committee in the Cabinet war room in Great George Street, Whitehall. The Americans confronted an imposing British array, with Brooke presiding, the others present including Pound for the navy, Portal for the RAF, and a newly appointed member, Vice Admiral Lord Louis Mountbatten, chief of combined operations; the other committee member, who played a part of great importance though it lacked clear definition, was Major General Sir Hastings Ismay, known to everyone as "Pug" for physiognomic reasons that were obvious at first sight; in essence, Ismay represented Churchill in the latter's self-styled function of minister of defense. Urbane and charming, Ismay struck Wedemeyer on first acquaintance as smooth but superficial. As the link between the fiery and impetuous prime minister and the chiefs of staff, Ismay needed an ample store of tact and deftness if the machinery of war was to be kept in running order, but in reality his smoothness carried with it nothing superficial. Ismay was a factotum with a mind of his own, even if he was not, as some in the British press alleged, Churchill's *éminence khaki.* Like the Americans who had taken part in the Arcadia meetings, Wedemeyer considered Portal the outstanding figure of the British group—thoughtful, clear, responsive, never smug.

After being formally welcomed by General Brooke, Marshall discussed the reasons for his visit and drew the strategic picture as the Americans saw it, emphasizing the "two main considerations" he believed ought to determine the principal British-American effort against Germany: continuance of Russian resistance and exposing the new U.S. Army to active operations that would give it war experience. What he aimed at was not a detailed discussion of logistics and matériel but the adoption of "a decision in principle as soon as possible," so that U.S. planners could settle questions of production, training, and troop movements. He also brought up the "emergency operation" described in his memorandum, doing his best to make it clear that he saw a landing in France in 1942 as only a contingency that would depend on events on the Russian front. His talk was well organized and straightforward.

Brooke, who had won no previous acclaim as a diplomat, responded tactfully with the observation that the British staffs had "been thinking much on the same lines as General Marshall had described." (In February, in fact, British planners had foreseen a possible quick return to the Continent, in the event of a German disaster in Russia, or a major effort in 1943. In addition,

Mountbatten's Combined Operations planners had produced a proposal for the seizure of a bridgehead on the Cotentin Peninsula [Cherbourg] or a large-scale raid on the Pas de Calais—all of these possibilities having features in common with American thinking. They were, however, staff plans, not policies that had won high-level support.) What Brooke said now was that the British had studied the possibilities of action in case of either heavy Russian or German reverses—although they thought that if events developed badly for the Russians, no good could come from attempting landings in France except where land forces might be used "as a bait to bring on air battles advantageous to ourselves." At best Britain could land on the Continent in 1942 only seven divisions and two armored divisions, a force too small to maintain a bridgehead. The British staffs were extremely worried, Brooke said, by their weakness in India and the Middle East; if the Germans should decide to switch their efforts from the Russian front to the Mediterranean, the British would not be strong enough to resist them.

This meeting, and others that followed, rested in good part on two important subtexts. Marshall and his associates did not agree with the British about the importance of India and the Middle East, because they could envision the Allies working to maintain the British position in those areas and at the same time failing to help keep the Russians in the war; as Wedemeyer noted, the Americans were sure that the Germans aimed at the destruction of the Russian armies in 1942. The other factor was that until an American buildup of forces should be achieved in the United Kingdom, any operation undertaken on the Continent would have to be primarily British in character, and therefore the British held an absolute veto power. Trained men, shipping, and time—these elements did not favor the American argument. Later Brooke noted in his diary, with questionable accuracy, that Marshall had given "a long talk on his views concerning desirability of starting a western front next September and that the U.S.A. forces would take part." Since this participation could consist of only two and a half divisions, it represented "no great contribution!" The Americans, Brooke felt, had simply not even begun to realize the implications of their proposed plan. As for his opinion of the U.S. chief of staff, Brooke returned Marshall's faint favor of the previous evening: "I liked what I saw of Marshall, a pleasant and easy man to get on with, rather over-filled with his own importance. But I should not put him down as a great man." The Allied war effort was primarily guided by four men—Roosevelt, Churchill, Marshall, Brooke. The two politicians had developed what was in many respects a uniquely close relationship for heads of two different governments. The two generals had not got off to a promising start at all.

During the next few days, amid a whirl of social activities that included a dine-and-sleep at Chequers with the Americans as fellow guests, Brooke and his colleagues worked to frame a reply to Marshall's proposals. An incident at Chequers seemed to suggest that a bird of ill omen, albeit one with a sense of humor, had decided to hover over the relationship between Marshall and Brooke. In Bermuda, Hopkins had asked Wedemeyer to arrange for two crates of fresh vegetables—great rarities in Britain, thanks to the U-boats—to be put aboard the Americans' plane, one to be a gift from Hopkins to Churchill and the other to be presented by Marshall to Brooke. The ensuing procedure exactly mimicked the method by which Wedemeyer had been assigned to coordinate the writing of the Victory Plan: Wedemeyer passed the request on to a major in the Quartermaster Corps who bucked it along in the familiar army way so that it ended in the hands of some anonymous enlisted man, who indeed saw to it that two crates arrived at the pier to be loaded onto the Clipper. At Chequers, where the gift for Churchill had been delivered, the prime minister, Marshall, Hopkins, and Wedemeyer watched as the yard man pried open the crate, Churchill no doubt feeling the greatest anticipation. Fortunately, the relationship between Hopkins and the prime minister rested solidly on mutual liking and respect and was not apt to be easily shattered, because as the contents of the crate were revealed, everybody could see that this precious bit of cargo consisted entirely of Brussels sprouts. Since wartime restrictions had made this drab vegetable an everyday feature of the British diet, it was magnanimous of Churchill to break into a laugh; Brooke's reaction to his separately delivered gift was not recorded.

Following the weekend the British chiefs succeeded in producing a draft statement, which Brooke read aloud to Marshall at a meeting on Tuesday, April 14. This document expressed in very careful wording the British chiefs' "general agreement" with Marshall's proposals. Indeed, they said, "it fits in with the way we had been thinking," and they went on to discuss in some detail the nature of their agreement. They wished, jointly with the Americans, to proceed with preparations to go on the Continent. The Americans must send whatever forces they could, particularly air strength, to help in any 1942 operation that might be undertaken, and in view of the importance of maintaining the British position in India, "we most urgently require American naval assistance." Marshall responded with a promise to point out on his return home the seriousness of the situation in the Indian Ocean, reverted to the theme of giving American troops battle experience, and then expressed what was at once a cardinal point and his personal great concern: He was "anxious that dispersion of forces should be reduced to a minimum" (his strategic adviser, General Embick, had long before warned him to beware of Churchill's fondness for diversions). The "main project"—operations on the Continent—"should not be reduced to the status of a 'residuary legatee' for whom nothing was left."

Brooke concluded with the clear observation that all were completely in agreement with respect to 1943, but "if we were forced this year to undertake an operation on the Continent it could only be on a small scale," and its military value, which "could not be great," must be weighed against the danger of Germany and Japan joining hands in the Indian Ocean area; this latter possibility, though unlikely, gave recurring nightmares to the British staffs, who could see Persian Gulf oil being cut off and the Middle East falling into the hands of the Axis.

That evening after dinner Marshall and Hopkins attended the capstone meeting of the Modicum mission at 10 Downing Street, at which the Defence Committee of the War Cabinet would in formal session discuss the American plan. This body included Churchill, Attlee, Foreign Secretary Anthony Eden, the service ministers, and the minister of production; the chiefs of staff were also present. Actually, the discussion was preempted at the outset by the prime minister, who after declaring that the committee had met to consider the "momentous proposal" proceeded to announce that he had "no hesitation in cordially accepting the plan." He praised its underlying idea, which, he said, "accorded with the classic principles of war—namely, concentration against the main enemy." Like the chiefs of staff, he professed only one reservation—India and the Middle East must be successfully defended, and likewise Australia.

Admiral Mountbatten, the young chief of the commandos and other unconventional forces, declared that the American commitment to send a million troops to the United Kingdom during the next year changed "the whole picture of combined operations against the Continent." Now great projects could be conceived; the Allies could plan "that real return to the Continent, without which we could not hope to bring the war to a successful conclusion."

Three projects or operations had been put on the table, and all of them had won some measure of agreement; at least, none had been rejected out of hand. They had all acquired code names: "Bolero," for the proposed U.S. buildup in England; "Roundup," for the full-scale invasion of the Continent in 1943; "Sledgehammer," for the emergency or opportunistic landing, as the case might be, in France in the autumn of 1942. As the group discussed the first two projects, the meeting became fired with a spirit not merely of optimism but of enthusiasm. The two nations, said Churchill, "would march ahead in a noble brotherhood of arms." Sledgehammer, which posed more immediate problems, came in for less attention; but Hopkins, scrawling notes and doodling as the others spoke, observed to the group that although the American people could hardly help considering Japan the enemy whose deeds must be avenged, the American leaders saw Europe as the place where the enemy could be fought earliest and most effectively—and the British must realize, despite their concern over Japanese successes in Asia, that if Americans crossed the Atlantic they would not be arriving "merely for purposes of sightseeing." The American people wanted to come to grips with the enemy and get the war over. As Hopkins had privately told Churchill, the United States could not indefinitely immobilize large numbers of troops.

Summing up the meeting, Churchill declared that a complete unanimity of opinion existed, and he later reported to Roosevelt: "We wholeheartedly agree with your conception of concentration against the main enemy"—with the one qualification that the Allies must prevent a junction of the Japanese and the Germans: ". . . We are starting joint plans and preparations at once."

Thus, it seemed, Marshall had won the prize he sought—concentration against Germany leading to a mass attack across the plains of northwestern Europe. But the spirit of Henry James hovered over the meetings between the American chief of staff and his Old World hosts—the formidable, impatient Brooke; the suave and engaging Ismay; and the redoubtable prime minister himself. To some British eyes, Marshall seemed, and commendably enough, a "simple, straightforward soldier," and in observing the Americans as a whole, Brooke and his fellows saw an energetic people accustomed to carrying out large projects, "to hustling and getting things done" and, as Hopkins said, wanting to get on with the war and get it over. Applying themselves to the new problem of war in Europe, the Americans therefore appeared hasty and naïve, blind to its Old World subtleties and complexities.

Lunching with Marshall the day after the Defence Committee meeting, Brooke decided that the American might be "a good general at raising armies" and at bridging the deeps between the military and political worlds, "but his strategical ability does not impress me at all"; Marshall "had not studied any of the strategic implications of a cross-Channel operation." In letters from Washington, Dill had praised Marshall to Brooke, though not as a strategist; indeed, Brooke concluded, the U.S. chief of staff was "a big man and a very great gentleman who inspired trust but did not impress me by the ability of his brain." Here, Brooke felt, fate had given him still another wearisome task: The Americans and their top general must be taken by the hand and led into the real world with all its contradictions and pitfalls.

The picture looked quite different to one of the Henry Jamesian Americans, Colonel Wedemeyer. Since the beginning of the war British strategy had been limited by the relatively slim military resources of the United Kingdom. The arrival on the scene of the United States, with her vast potential war-making power, administered a wrench to the British frame of reference, and the British chiefs of staff and the prime minister, set in their peripheral ways, could not appreciate the rightness of a strategy based on a mass force delivering the knockout blow. Nevertheless, it seemed to the American colonel that "with their ingrained habit of assuming authority," the British automatically expected the Americans to follow their strategic lead. This condescension struck Wedemeyer as particularly odd since, aside from the small force fighting to and fro in North Africa, the British Army had so far in this war acquired very little experience in offensive warfare.

Perhaps inevitably, the representatives of the two allies found themselves peering at each other through cloudy doors of perception, ready not so much to see their opposite numbers approaching with ideas of independent merit as to witness them performing according to the dictates of presumed national characteristics. These doors presented observers with those tired old figures, the hustling and simple Americans, the lofty and stodgy British. If the doors were cleansed, as an English poet had long ago told the world, "every thing would appear to man as it is, infinite." Instead, man "sees all things thro' narrow chinks of his cavern." Still, the limited view the doors reciprocally afforded the British and the Americans could not be considered wholly false.

In failing to strike any clearly audible discordant notes, General Ismay later remarked, the British acted unwisely. Perhaps they should have leavened their assent to Marshall's proposals with greater frankness by saying that on first reaction they agreed in principle with Roundup but were not at that point ready to commit themselves to a date as early as the summer of 1943. They could also have been direct about Sledgehammer, expressing their thought that it was "an extremely doubtful proposition" and asking whether the Americans had "given sufficient weight to its immense difficulties and embarrassing implications." Then they could have agreed, nevertheless, to study the plan and, if they saw a reasonable prospect of success, to do their part faithfully. "But nothing of the kind was said," Ismay observed, and the Defence Committee adopted Marshall's proposals in principle.

What had really happened in the Modicum meetings? Had the "straightforward" American chief of staff allowed himself to be taken in by what an American novelist has called, in a very different context, "the classic waffling manner of the British upper classes"? Would the United States have been better represented by the allusive, discursive, cosmopolitan Roosevelt, who could veil his thoughts and slide from one point to another as dexterously as any Briton? On April 13, the day before the last meeting, Marshall made some suggestive comments. Reporting to his deputy, General McNarney, back in Washington, he observed that everybody was agreeing with him "in principle" but held "reservations regarding this or that." Particularly with respect to keeping the Sledgehammer option alive, the Americans would have to exercise "great firmness" to prevent diversion of troops and resources to other operations. Yet the next evening, showing that even he could be carried along by a tide of masterly rhetoric, Marshall felt on hearing Churchill's praise of the plan that Roundup, at least, was assured for 1943. As for Brooke, Marshall realized that, like many American skeptics, the CIGS did not expect the United States to produce "workmanlike divisions" from conscripted civilians without a great deal of time being consumed; the British chief would therefore take lightly any American talk of operations on the Continent against the war-hardened Wehrmacht. Nor did Marshall fail to sense some of Brooke's reservations about him personally; Brooke had performed outstandingly as a corps commander before Dunkirk and after that famous evacuation he had been sent back to France on the short-lived mission of commanding a new British Expeditionary Force, whereas Marshall had never led troops in battle: "While I had been chief of operations in an army in the first war, I had done nothing like it." Not surprisingly, Marshall felt, Brooke and his colleagues credited him with little understanding of the problems of the battlefield.

Guided by his view of strategy itself, Marshall conducted the Modicum conversations the way he proceeded in any situation. He concentrated, and kept his British listeners concentrated, on his main strategic objective—confronting the Germans where it would hurt them most and where the Allies ought to be able to make the best use of their forces. Sledgehammer? Perhaps he had oversold it to the British, because it was not only a proposed operation, it was an insurance policy. As long as it sat on the boards, with plans going forward, the forces that would carry it out would not be scattered here and there—"diversion" continued to be one of the most negative words in the lexicon of the U.S. General Staff—and Roundup, the crux of the matter, would remain safe for 1943. But let men and resources be assigned to other tasks in other areas, Marshall was convinced, and the insurance policy for 1943 would lapse. The Americans had to put Sledgehammer forward, said Wedemeyer, "simply to restrain wild diversionary efforts proposed by the British Prime Minister." The operation could also serve a purpose at home, by providing a reason for the army to resist pressure from the navy to send more troops to the Pacific.

But Marshall's heel offered one clearly vulnerable spot; he had no experience of the most difficult and complex of all great military operations, an amphibious invasion. Churchill, who had presided as First Lord of the Admiralty over the Dardanelles landings in 1915—an imaginatively conceived operation thoroughly bungled in its execution—knew the dangers of a landing from the sea all too well, and he also, Marshall believed, shrank from re-creating an arena for the kinds of slaughter that had marked the First World War; he had the bloodletting of the Somme in his bones, and "a horror of bodies floating in the Channel."

Other factors, not emphasized to the Americans, almost surely played a large part in tempering any British enthusiasm for large-scale operations on the Continent. Churchill had openly criticized General Auchinleck, his commander in the Middle East against Rommel's Afrika Korps, and he had been aghast at the feeble conduct of the British defense of Singapore; in the spring of 1942, indeed, the prestige of British arms had sunk almost below the horizon.

But more than the British Army's leadership had come into question; in morale, organization, training, and equipment, the army showed no likelihood of fighting more than a few German divisions on anything like equal terms. The British had been driven out of Crete in May 1941, though outnumbering the attackers, and in North Africa Rommel had displayed a disconcerting habit, however much he might be outgunned, of turning defeat into victory. In February 1942, after the crumbling of the British front in Malaya, General Wavell, the luckless Allied supreme commander, concluded that "for the time being we have lost a good deal of our hardness and fighting spirit." Until the army acquired or trained soldiers "whose first idea is to push forward and get to grips with the enemy on any and every occasion and whatever the difficulties and odds," he said, "we shall not recover our morale or reputation." Accordingly, France, with Germans as the enemy, hardly seemed the place to begin regaining these vital qualities.

Unsure of their own army, dubious of whatever forces the Americans might offer, Churchill and Brooke and their colleagues could draw little cheer from the view across the Channel. To keep these men looking in that direction, General Marshall would indeed have to exercise all the "firmness" he could muster. And he must also see to it that the gaze of one other very important person remained fixed on France. The commander in chief of the army and navy of the United States had a seemingly casual way of tossing out new operations with what Marshall called his cigarette-holder gesture, but no such diversionary ideas from on high must be allowed to interfere with the Bolero buildup in England and the operations it could make possible.

One afternoon in late May, a White House valet, unpacking the bag of a guest who had been placed in the Rose Suite, was startled to discover that in addition to clothing and personal effects the visitor had arrived with a roll of sausage, a hunk of black bread, and a pistol. Apparently word about the shortcomings of the White House cuisine (as monotonous as the fare offered in a boardinghouse, said Robert Sherwood) had reached far beyond the boundaries of the United States; the bread and sausage had come all the way from Russia. The Secret Service men felt little concern about the snack food, but the pistol was another matter. Since the visitor was the foreign commissar of the Soviet Union, however, the guards did not impound the weapon. But the presence of the food and the gun together suggested that when it came to survival, Comrade Vyacheslav Molotov felt only limited faith in his bourgeois allies.

Molotov arrived directly from a stop in London, where he had negotiated a long-term treaty of alliance with Britain and had pressed his hosts to declare their intentions about the establishment of a "second front" against the Germans. The coming weeks and months on the Russian front were "fraught with serious consequence to the Soviet Union and their allies," he said, and it was to discuss this vital question that President Roosevelt had invited him to visit Washington. Making no promises, Churchill had pointed out all the problems involved in mounting such an undertaking, asking Molotov in particular to remember the difficulty of an amphibious invasion.

During the first afternoon and evening at the White House, Molotov engaged in long conversations with the president, Hopkins, and Hull. As the great exponent of personal diplomacy, FDR drew on all his conversational talents to establish a human connection with the solemn, slab-faced Bolshevik, who only a year and a half earlier had visited Berlin to discuss in his methodical way an alliance with Hitler exactly as he was now doing with the Western Allies. So unswerving and insistent did the Russian prove, so seemingly content to sit for hour after hour, sticking to his argument, that Roosevelt at some point bestowed on him the nickname "Stone Ass."

The next morning at eleven o'clock General Marshall and Admiral King came to the president's office to join the conversations. Molotov had been received politely on his visit to London, explained the president, but he had obtained no commitment about a second front from the British. What he wanted was an Allied agreement to mount an operation in Western Europe big enough to draw off forty German divisions from the Russian front. Indeed, said the Russian, the Allies must act in 1942, before Hitler tried to crush the Soviet Union with one mighty blow.

The president turned to Marshall. Were Allied plans sufficiently advanced so that the Americans could assure the Russians that a second front was being prepared?

To this comfortably general question, Marshall could readily answer yes.

Turning back to Molotov, Roosevelt authorized him not only to say that a second front was on the way but that it was expected "this year." Cautiously Marshall observed that the United States would do as much as shipping would allow. But in a meeting with the chiefs the next day FDR, feeling that the situation on the Russian front was so critical that Molotov needed more than vague answers, proposed to tell Churchill that the United States wished to make a commitment for an operation by August. Not long back from his extensive Modicum discussions, Marshall knew how quickly a promise tied to a definite date would put up British hackles; Hopkins supported his objection. The chief of staff wanted to keep the president's eyes fixed on France, but this new commitment went beyond the limits of prudence.

Roosevelt felt the Russian situation so keenly, however, that neither Molotov's gruffness in the final meeting on Monday morning, June 1, nor Marshall's opposition to mentioning any time limit deterred him from adopting the Russian draft of a statement summing up the agreement reached during the discussions. This document was a strange bit of prose, written by somebody whose English was fuzzy or who for some reason chose to be less than pellucidly clear: "In the course of the conversations full understanding was reached with regard to the urgent tasks of creating a Second Front in Europe in 1942." No White House editor took pencil in hand to tidy up those ambiguous "urgent tasks." When Hopkins telephoned from Hyde Park to check the statement with Marshall before it was released to the public, the chief of staff told him that the reference to 1942 should be dropped. But Roosevelt insisted that it stay in; thus this imprecise American commitment was published to the world. For the president it represented an attempt to assure the hard-pressed and always suspicious Soviets that the Allies, and certainly the United States, intended to play a full part in the land war. Roundup was of course out of the question for this year, but Sledgehammer was at least a possibility, and stepped-up air activity and coastal raids were more than that.

When the statement was released on June 11, after Molotov was safely back home, it met with great acclaim not only in the Soviet Union, as was hardly surprising, but across the United States, and it thereby triggered that great bugaboo of planners, the law of unintended consequences. Second front—immediately! That was what people eagerly awaited. The announcement enjoyed auspicious timing, because during the first week in June the U.S. Navy's great victory over the Japanese fleet in the Battle of Midway had transformed the strategic picture in the Pacific; a handful of American fliers in small planes had stopped the advance of the enemy toward Hawaii, and by sinking four of the Japanese Navy's six first-line aircraft carriers had guaranteed that the victory was decisive. In April pilots flying from U.S. carriers in the Coral Sea had checked the Japanese advance in the Southwest Pacific; now the enemy had been beaten and turned back in the Central Pacific. The strategic initiative was passing to the Allies, and far sooner than anyone had dreamed in the wake of the disaster at Pearl Harbor. In the Pacific the Americans had shown what they could do, and now the public was hearing official good news from the Atlantic side of the war. Ignoring the lack of adequately trained men, and unaware of all the problems of supply and equipment and the shortage of the landing craft that would be required for such an operation, the American public not only welcomed the news about the second front but clamored for such an attack. Then, as days and weeks passed and no second front appeared, public impatience grew. Soviet supporters found ample voices to join them in their often-repeated cry: "Second front now!"

Roosevelt indeed believed that the Allies could mount some kind of European ground operation in 1942—his advisers had proposed Sledgehammer and the British had not ruled out it or something like it—but the military staffs faced the daunting problem of transforming the idea into reality. Public enthusiasm, which if not gratified could turn into public disillusionment and anger, constituted a factor the politicians could not ignore.

Churchill had played his part in creating the second-front clamor by agreeing to the release in Britain of a communiqué containing that same murky sentence about "urgent tasks."

The prime minister had not only general strategic concerns but more immediate practical worries. During the night of May 26–27, the daring General Rommel had launched an attack in Libya, at Bir Hacheim southwest of Tobruk, the main British fortress and supply port for the Eighth Army. By the time the Molotov communiqué appeared on June 11, the British knew a major struggle was taking place in the desert, but no matter how the battle should go, Churchill and his chiefs in London believed that Tobruk must be "held at all costs." In any case, the British had to reach a clear understanding with the Americans about the strategy to be pursued against the European Axis in 1942. What exactly had the president meant by his promise to Molotov?

CHAPTER THIRTEEN

"TAKING UP YOUR DISHES"

The small plane hit the airstrip with a jolt, bumped and bounced high and came to a stop, and presently out climbed Winston Churchill. Waiting at the wheel of his little Ford, with its special hand controls, sat Franklin Roosevelt, and in a few minutes the illustrious pair drove off toward the Roosevelt home at Hyde Park. While the president showed the prime minister over the estate, including the fine views from the heights overlooking the Hudson, Churchill experienced some "thoughtful moments" as the car backed and turned near the edges of the bluffs. Reassuringly, Roosevelt invited his guest to feel his biceps, which he said a famous boxer had envied, but Churchill hoped that the special driving devices would prove equally reliable. "All the time we talked business," the prime minister observed later, "and though I was careful not to take his attention off the driving we made more progress than we might have done in formal conference."

Although he had other concerns, the chief business that had brought Churchill to America was the need to make the decision about Allied operations in 1942 and 1943. Always thorough and careful in his dealings with the president, the prime minister had prepared the way for his own visit and the views he would express by sending as advance man Admiral Mountbatten, who had suggested to Marshall and the other U.S. chiefs that the agreement made in London only six weeks earlier might not prove inviolate. The dashing admiral, a man of the sort admired by both Roosevelt and Churchill, then was a guest at a dinner that turned into a long evening with the president and Hopkins during which he made a clear case against Sledgehammer in

1942. The British felt that with so few landing craft available for the operation, Sledgehammer would be such a minor affair that the Germans would not move any ground forces from the Russian front to oppose it (the Germans, it was believed, had about twenty-five divisions in France, though Marshall thought they were of "poor quality"). Well, countered Roosevelt, what about putting off the operation until later in the autumn, perhaps even December, when more men and landing craft would presumably be available? Such a postponement would, however, leave the Allies little time to seize Cherbourg or some other port, which would be needed to keep the troops supplied during the winter. If they launched the operation, Mountbatten said, they must be sure to capture a port. (Since his planners had looked with some favor on a Cherbourg landing, Mountbatten understood the requirements clearly.) In a positive note about Sledgehammer, Lord Louis in reply to Roosevelt's question assured the president that the British were ready "to follow up a crack in German morale by landing in France this autumn."

Roosevelt found all this most unsatisfactory, telling Mountbatten that he "did not wish to send a million soldiers to England and find, possibly, that a complete collapse of Russia had made a frontal attack on France impossible": not only no Sledgehammer, in other words, but no Roundup in 1943 either. Here Gymnast, the landings in North Africa discussed at Arcadia during the winter, came back into the picture. To a telegram to FDR about the Molotov visit, Churchill had neatly tacked on a reminder that "we must never let Gymnast pass from our minds." Roosevelt told Mountbatten how struck he had been by this remark.

The conversation between Roosevelt and Mountbatten represented the side of the president that Marshall found perhaps most frustrating. Cordell Hull had long endured the same sort of information shortfall when FDR discussed foreign affairs with Hopkins or Sumner Welles while Hull, though secretary of state, was excluded; but Hull, as a political appointee, had through the years accepted the president's way of doing business and had carved out his own areas of concentration, notably Latin America. Now, in a matter of vital concern to both the army and the navy, Roosevelt had conducted business without inviting the service chiefs to take part, shutting one group up in its own separate compartment. Still dwelling inside FDR lived the boy who quietly insisted on hiding important areas of his inner life from the potent scrutiny of his mother; as chief executive, he divided his correspondence among various secretaries, to keep any single person from possessing a complete file; in the map room, outgoing and incoming messages were handled by cipher personnel of different services, so that neither the army nor the navy could know the whole story.

Besides excluding his military advisers from his talk with Mountbatten, FDR gave them no account of the meeting. They learned what had been said only when the admiral's report to the British chiefs filtered back to America through the machinery of the Combined Chiefs of Staff. The key element of this machinery was Sir John Dill. Early in the field marshal's stay in Washington, he and Marshall, as part of their increasing friendship, had begun having confidential lunches once a week, at which they discussed and often resolved problems before they arose in that week's session of the Combined Chiefs of Staff. Dill had once characterized his duties as chief of the Imperial General Staff as requiring him to spend his time "trying to prevent stupid things being done rather than in doing clever things"; he brought much the same attitude to his task of Anglo-American harmonizer and coordinator.

But for Marshall, Sir John also served an even more unusual purpose. Seeking a way to penetrate the "very sensitive" manner in which Roosevelt cloaked his conduct of affairs, Marshall turned to his friend Dill. Although Roosevelt "didn't give us the messages he was sending half the time," matters on the other side of the Atlantic were handled with great bureaucratic orthodoxy; as Marshall enviously said, when the president sent a message to Churchill "everybody that should know that immediately got a copy of it"—and in due course a copy would arrive in Dill's office in Washington. Dill then brought the news to Marshall.

The same method came into play when the traffic flowed in the other direction. If Dill's office received a copy of a message from Churchill to Roosevelt, Dill passed it on to Marshall. To the chief of staff this arrangement constituted one of the greatest secrets of the war: "I had to be very careful that nobody knew this—no one in the War Department and certainly not the [British] chiefs of staff." If the secret came to light, Marshall felt, "Dill would be destroyed in a minute." Since, in a familiar prophet-without-honor situation, Dill's stock stood much higher in the United States than at home, the chief of staff perhaps had good reason for his fear. But Dill was not the only person at risk. Because the whole procedure had been created to thwart "Mr. Roosevelt's desire for secrecy," Marshall's standing with the commander in chief would hardly have benefited from discovery. Yet he simply had to have the information; more than Roosevelt, he felt, he knew how important it was for the War Department to know not only what was happening but why it was. The risk of discovery had to be run. If the president would not conform to traditional lines of information and responsibility, then Marshall would devise his own unorthodox methods.

In the case of the president's meeting with Mountbatten, Dill drew on another source of intelligence: Harry Hopkins gave him a full account of the conversation. Here the two chief Allied coordinators were working together in what amounted almost to a professional capacity. In addition to his report to the British chiefs, Mountbatten wrote the president a letter summarizing the conversation as a check on his own understanding of it. When Marshall later learned about the letter, he credited (or charged) it with influencing FDR against Sledgehammer.

On June 17, the day before Churchill and his small traveling party arrived in the United States, the president in a meeting in his executive office upset Marshall and Stimson by declaring that since Sledgehammer seemed doubtful for 1942 and it was vital to "bring additional pressure to save Russia," he wished to discuss Gymnast again. Though concerned, the chief of staff was not taken by surprise; he had come prepared with a study drawn up by his planners in which the by-now ritual arguments against the North African landing were arrayed and forcefully stated. But the army representatives had to fight off a surprise flank attack delivered by Admiral King, who suddenly offered to supply the convoys for Gymnast by moving ships from the Pacific. Stimson, no doubt inaudibly, snorted with disgust. "King wobbled around in a way that made me rather sick with him," the forthright secretary noted in his diary. "He is firm and brave outside the White House but as soon as he gets in the presence of the President he crumbles up." Stimson added with a measure of self-satisfaction, "A few words of cross-examination on my part put him in a rather indefensible position," and the old advocate went on to counterattack two days later with a long letter to Roosevelt, approved by Marshall, in which he presented a powerful plea on behalf of operations in Europe. Marshall's plan, he said, ought not to be put in jeopardy by any "additional expeditionary proposal"; it was "an essentially American project, brought into this war as the vitalizing contribution of our fresh and unwearied leaders and forces." Here the secretary showed himself not above giving the president a little psychological armor for his meetings with Churchill and the British staff, whose forces, judging by the reports from the Libyan desert, were anything but fresh and unwearied; nor did their leaders seem capable and effective.

While the statesmen were talking and sightseeing at Hyde Park, the Combined Chiefs of Staff met in conference in Washington. The participants included not only the U.S. chiefs and the members of the British permanent mission, but Brooke and Ismay, who had accompanied the prime minister to America. Although Ismay had met Marshall during the Modicum sessions in London, it was the first time he had seen the U.S. chief of staff in action with his peers. He was "greatly impressed," Ismay wrote; Marshall "was a big man in every sense of the word, and utterly selfless. It was impossible to imagine his doing anything petty or mean, or shrinking from any duty, however distasteful. He carried himself with great dignity."

During the Combined Chiefs' discussions, an interesting phenomenon appeared. In the Modicum meetings in London, the divisions of opinion had generally run along national lines, American versus British. But side by side with the bond of national kinship existed the tie of professional brotherhood, of a common military way of regarding a problem. During the meetings, lunch, and casual chat of June 19, Brooke felt that the U.S. and British staffs were in general agreement on military policy for 1942 and 1943, but he was concerned about "what P.M. and President may be brewing up together." The next day—Saturday, June 20—his apprehension increased; the military men, he said, "fear the worst."

What had brought about this shifting of alliances? In the first place, because no one could predict what would happen in Russia, Marshall and Brooke and their staffs agreed on the importance of building up a strategic reserve in England; these forces might be needed for offensive purposes in the event of Soviet success or for defense in case the Soviets should collapse and the Germans return to the west—and for Marshall, still holding on to the possibility of Sledgehammer, the buildup had to come before the operation could be mounted. Brooke's nervousness about the schemes being hatched up at Hyde Park also sprang from his anxiety about the situation in Africa. The Eighth Army was now in full retreat, fleeing across the desert toward Egypt, leaving doubtful the security of that British bastion in the Middle East. Every effort must be made to save it, and that included shipping and matériel that otherwise might go for Gymnast; only after the Eighth Army was recast and revivified would landings in Northwest Africa make strategic sense. Thus, for somewhat differing reasons, Marshall and Brooke found themselves in welcome harmony. Pleased, the U.S. chief of staff even offered to send an armored division to the Middle East to give the British a hand.

Brooke had planned to spend a quiet Sunday morning with Dill, putting on old clothes with the intention of playing tourist on a sightseeing visit to Mount Vernon. But first he had to check at the office of the British mission in the Public Health Building, where bad news awaited him. Instead of spending Saturday night at Hyde Park, as had been expected, Roosevelt and Churchill had changed plans and were taking the president's special train to Washington; Brooke was expected for lunch at the White House.

Before leaving Hyde Park, the president had telegraphed an assignment to Marshall and King. A large scale Soviet attempt to recapture the city of Kharkov had failed, and now the great German summer offensive was opening. Anxious about the danger of a Russian collapse, Roosevelt and Hopkins produced a message (drafted by Hopkins, edited and supplemented by FDR) asking where American ground forces, "prior to September 15, 1942," could launch an attack on German forces or in German-controlled areas that could compel the Germans to withdraw from Russia. This message followed one of Churchill's most persuasive performances. In a slashing note on Sledgehammer, he had asked the president questions about details of the plan—where would the landing take place? what shipping was available? who would command the operation? what British help was required?—unfair questions, since the planning was supposed to be carried out in London, but effective. If these questions found no good answers, Churchill said, then the Allies should pay attention to Gymnast. Better this than, as the prime minister was given to declaring, the Channel should become a "river of blood." Since Roosevelt also abhorred the thought of casualties on the scale of the first war and had expressed interest in the occupation of Northwest Africa even before the United States entered the war, he found Churchill's reasoning persuasive. Gymnast, then, was what the statesmen had been "brewing up together" out of earshot of their military advisers. The true alley cat of operations, often given up for dead, explicitly executed on occasion, Gymnast always came twitching back to life.

On Sunday morning the president's naval aide, Captain McCrea, arrived at the map room at 7:30, checked the overnight cables, and then walked to the south entrance of the White House to greet the president, having left instructions that any important dispatches that might come in should be brought to him immediately. Just as FDR was being helped from his car, the assistant watch officer of the map room came up to McCrea with a message. Then, when the president was wheeled into the building, Roosevelt invited McCrea to join him and the prime minister for breakfast. After the captain, who had already breakfasted, declined, FDR asked, "Any news of interest?"

Since he had taken a quick look at the message that had just been handed to him, McCrea said yes, there was indeed news of interest.

"Very well, come on up," said Roosevelt, and the three men went to the study on the second floor next to the president's bedroom. After FDR had seated himself behind his desk, McCrea handed him the dispatch. The president read it carefully, then said quietly, "Show this to Winston."

Taking the paper from the president, the naval aide crossed the room to the couch on which Churchill had taken a seat. As he read the dispatch, Churchill's pink cheeks faded visibly. It was grim and shocking news: Tobruk with its garrison of 25,000 men (the actual number proved later to be 33,000) had surrendered to Rommel, who commanded half as many. This vitally important fortress, as Churchill thought of it, had fallen to the Germans in a battle that had effectively taken only a single day. The prime minister spoke his shock. "I can't understand it," he said. "I simply can't understand it!" First Singapore, now Tobruk—the outposts of empire were compiling a dismal record; Alexandria, the British fleet base in the eastern Mediterranean, and the Suez Canal lay in peril.

Roosevelt expressed his sympathy, observing that in time of war one must expect the unexpected—although he conceded that the speedy fall of Tobruk was an unexpected event of considerable magnitude. Later in the day, when the statesmen were meeting with the generals, Roosevelt spoke his thoughts in a way that left Brooke "impressed by the tact and real heartfelt sympathy which lay behind these words. There was not one word too much nor one word too little." The president also put his sympathy into a practical form, saying in one of his finest hours as an Allied leader, "What can we do to help?" Nothing, said Churchill, "could exceed the sympathy and chivalry" of Roosevelt and Marshall. "There were no reproaches; not an unkind word was spoken." The outcome was that three hundred of the new Sherman tanks, which had already been issued to the U.S. 1st Armored Division, were withdrawn from the troops, put on fast transports, and sent off to the Middle East; Marshall even improved on the arrangement by adding a hundred self-propelled guns. As Churchill, not knowing the part the adage had played in Marshall's life some years earlier, later said: "A friend in need is a friend indeed."

Although the political leaders made it plain that they did not accept the generals' idea of Bolero itself as a sufficient principal activity by the Western Allies against the European Axis in 1942, "everyone's thoughts," Ismay said, "were on the disaster in the Egyptian Desert, and the discussions centred round the steps which should be taken to restore the situation." One proposal called for sending large American ground forces to the Middle East; another even recommended that the Americans take control of operations in the area. When Roosevelt put forward such a suggestion in a late-night White House session with the British visitors, Marshall was horrified. Fearing what he might say if he began to vent his feelings, he told the president that he would not discuss the idea at that hour of the night. Then he turned and strode out of the room. After cooling off, he summarized his objections in a memo to FDR: "logistical, serious confusion of command (further complicated by strong racial and religious prejudices), and"—the sort of factor that was ever dominant with him—"the indecisive nature of the operation."

Churchill had come to the United States to settle the question of the second front, but this issue became lost in plans for shoring up the Middle East. On June 25 the prime minister and his entourage took off for England, to face the deteriorating military situation and the political storm that had blown up because of it. Thus the second Washington conference, as it was called, ended with no clear outcome. With utterly unexpected help from Erwin Rommel, General Marshall had managed to keep Sledgehammer alive, if only barely.

The chief of staff made another move in the same direction, this one psychological rather than strategic. The day before the British visitors left, he played host at a party at Fort Jackson, South Carolina, at which he and his co-host Stimson entertained Churchill, Brooke, Dill, and Ismay. Well aware that the British, and particularly Brooke, were skeptical of American plans to mass-produce divisions the way Detroit turned out cars, Marshall, like a military Cecil B. De Mille, had made meticulous arrangements to produce a spectacle on the plains of South Carolina. Three divisions took part in the exercises, with tanks and cars, while Churchill, looking in his zip-up siren suit and floppy hat like an aging baby, clutched his walkie-talkie, a new toy the Americans had given him. He recorded the impressiveness of the airborne demonstration—"I had never seen a thousand men leap into the air at once." But the men were still green. "To put these troops against continental troops would be murder," Ismay told the prime minister. Churchill disagreed: "You're wrong. They are wonderful material and will learn very quickly." But by no means did he mean that they would learn in time to make Sledgehammer a practicable operation in 1942. Marshall had scored some points but not nearly enough to make the lead in the game change hands.

On July 3 General Marshall turned for a few minutes from his strategic worries to a more pleasant concern. A telephone call that morning from Harry Hopkins had confirmed an item the general had seen in the newspaper—his friend had become engaged to Louise Macy, a New Yorker who in seeking war work had been introduced to Hopkins by mutual friends. In his note of well-wishing to Mrs. Macy, Marshall produced a vintage blend of diplomacy and bluntness. "To be very frank," he told the lady, "I am intensely interested in Harry's health and happiness, and therefore in your approaching marriage." Hopkins, he said, "has been gallant and self-sacrificing to an extreme, little of which is realized by any but his most intimate friends." Accordingly, the chief of staff had some instructions for the prospective bride. Her fiancé "is of great importance to our National interests at the present time, and he is one of the most imprudent people regarding his health that I have ever known. Therefore, and possibly inexcusable as it may seem to you, I express the hope that you will find it possible to curb his indiscretions and see that he takes the necessary rest."

Behind Marshall's words lay deep affection as well as admiration. On one trip Marshall had been moved by the fact that "Hopkins had ten blood transfusions in the previous twelve days. He had more nerve than anyone I had ever seen." Hopkins had indeed become a special friend, not only as one of Marshall's first supporters for the post of chief of staff, but as the never failing medium of communication with the president; Hopkins listened and Hopkins acted. Marshall had written "of great importance," but more likely he thought "indispensable."

The president would probably have used the same word. When Hopkins told him of the wedding plans, FDR invited the couple to live in the White House after their marriage, thus continuing the arrangement that had existed when Hopkins was single. Mrs. Roosevelt put forward some objections, saying that it would hardly be fair to the couple to require them to begin their married life in someone else's house, "even though that house happened to be the White House." Roosevelt rejected the argument, making it plain that his invitation was more in the nature of an executive command; "the most important thing in the world" was the conduct of the war, and for that Hopkins must be close at hand in the White House.

A few days later, on July 8, Marshall had to face less pleasant news. A message from Churchill to Roosevelt declared that, on recommendation of the Chiefs of Staff Committee, the War Cabinet had voted not to try to mount Sledgehammer in 1942; Marshall received the news directly from Dill. The British presented a lengthy list of objections; the odds against success were heavy and, for an operation that was contingent in nature, the costs would be too great. Even if one did not question the soundness of these observations, such points had been just as true three months earlier—although in April the British had not yet lost Tobruk and been driven out of Libya. The new message represented "a rather staggering crisis in our war strategy," Marshall told the sympathetic Stimson; the chief of staff was "very stirred up and emphatic over it" and weary of "these constant decisions which do not stay made." Accordingly Marshall proposed a showdown with the British, and Stimson agreed to support him.

At the meeting of the U.S. Joint Chiefs of Staff on the afternoon of July 10, Marshall, after announcing the British veto of

Sledgehammer, raised two vital questions: Should the Americans agree to landings in Northwest Africa? Did the British really intend to invade the continent of Europe in 1943? The framing of these questions displayed his main concern, which was not Sledgehammer itself but the preservation of Roundup, the major landing planned for 1943. Earlier than anyone else, politician or soldier, American or British, Marshall seemed to understand that the mounting of Gymnast in Northwest Africa would almost certainly make Roundup impossible for the following year. He therefore put forward his "showdown" strategy—if there was to be no decisive action against the Germans in Europe, then the United States should turn to the Pacific and undertake decisive action against Japan. This action would "tend to concentrate rather than to scatter U.S. forces"—*decisive action . . . concentration:* Here Marshall was proclaiming the essence of the War Department gospel, and in saying it to Admiral King he was certainly preaching to the choir. Promptly picking up the theme, the gruff admiral declared that as far as he was concerned "the British had never been in wholehearted accord with operations on the continent as proposed by the U.S.," and when Marshall produced a memorandum for the President summarizing his argument, Admiral King delightedly added his signature to that of the chief of staff; the navy in the Pacific would cheerfully welcome any morsels that fell from the army's European table.

Was the chief of staff serious in proposing such a reversal of the War Department's carefully conceived strategy? Actually, he was not expressing a wholly new thought. Four months earlier a subordinate committee of the Joint Chiefs had declared that if the British rejected the idea of a cross-Channel attack in 1942, the Americans should consider "the possibility of concentrating U.S. offensive effort in the Pacific area." This argument had been well timed to find favor with the navy, because it was advanced just after Admiral Stark, the chief naval proponent of a European strategy, had departed for England. In putting his proposition to the commander in chief, Marshall had challenged the one man who could and would immediately find out how serious it was. Receiving the message at Hyde Park, FDR telephoned on Sunday morning, July 12, to order the chiefs to rush a detailed plan of their "Pacific Ocean alternative" to him by airplane that very afternoon. FDR did not make the assignment easy—he wanted to know the time schedules and the numbers of ships, planes, and ground troops that would be involved, and what changes these moves would cause in Atlantic dispositions. Marshall of course had no such "detailed, comprehensive outline" as Roosevelt was calling for, but he came to the office from his Sunday in the country to assemble an answer.

Meanwhile, Field Marshal Dill was alerting his colleagues in London to the hornet's nest they were stirring up. If they pressed Gymnast on the Americans, Dill said, the result would be exactly what Marshall was advocating with the president. The British chiefs must convince Marshall and his colleagues that they were still completely in favor of Bolero and Roundup and did not support such diversionary ventures as Gymnast. Otherwise, they might soon see the U.S. Army joining the navy in putting the Pacific war in the first place on the American agenda. The telegram owed much of its persuasiveness to the contributions made by Dill's unacknowledged coauthor, General Marshall, who provided not only his own ideas but factual American information. Marshall-Dill collaboration in the drafting of messages from the field marshal to his masters in London had become frequent. When Churchill would ask Dill to sound Marshall out on some issue, the field marshal would simply read Marshall the request and then, said the chief of staff, "he and I would make up the reply." Although some of Dill's countrymen liked to accuse him of "going native" in the United States, there was never any genuine question as to where his first loyalty lay. Dill was a British officer, but he was also devoted to the idea of Allied victory. He did not believe that such a victory would be won by quarrels and recriminations. This clarity of purpose seems to have been one of the qualities that first drew Marshall and Dill together.

On July 15 the president returned to Washington from Hyde Park, and on that morning he met with Marshall. He had already let his feelings be known about the "Pacific Ocean alternative," having told the chief of staff the day before that he was rejecting it. He had also made it plain that he intended to move rapidly toward a strategic decision; Marshall, King, and Hopkins would be leaving for London immediately—the next day, if possible. Marshall superintended the preparation of his own instructions; the draft came back from the president with "Not approved" written boldly across the upper right-hand corner; under that rejection Roosevelt had written, "See my substitute." It was not that the president had become unsympathetic to

Sledgehammer or Roundup; in fact, he instructed the chiefs, in his substitute memo and in meetings on July 15, to urge with the British chiefs that Sledgehammer "be pushed with utmost vigor" and even that "it be executed whether or not Russian collapse becomes imminent." But if Sledgehammer proved to be finally and definitely impossible to carry out, the chiefs must determine "upon another place for U.S. troops to fight in 1942" (this phrase was handwritten into the draft of instructions by the president); the principle of action against the enemy by U.S. ground troops in 1942 had appeared earlier in the document as one of FDR's cardinal themes—a point "of the highest importance." Saying that he hoped for total agreement within a week, Roosevelt told the chiefs to proceed on three principles: "speed of decision on plans, unity of plans, attack combined with defense but not defense alone." To remove any doubt about the capacity in which he spoke, he signed the document as commander in chief.

Nerves were stretched taut in those White House discussions of July 15. Thoroughly disgusted with what he regarded as the shifting British views on the whole second-front issue, Marshall saw the president as "all ready to do any sideshow," particularly with Churchill prodding him. "My job," Marshall said, "was to hold the President down to what we were doing." FDR made it clear, however, that he objected in principle to issuing any ultimatum to the British, and he also declared that an attempt to defeat Japan before Germany would be misguided. Since this was the view General Marshall and his planners had consistently expounded from the time they had begun studying the question several years earlier, FDR was merely acting as their disciple—although in an excess of optimism or rhetoric he went so far as to say that "defeat of Germany means the defeat of Japan, probably without firing a shot or losing a life." In any case, said the president, there would be no American threats to the British. That would be like "taking up your dishes and going away." Humanely, Roosevelt as a political leader did not wish even to appear to be bullying his fellow practitioner Churchill while the latter faced the domestic political crisis resulting from the Eighth Army's fiasco in Libya. Marshall could make one last try in London for Sledgehammer, but if he lost—as it seemed obvious he would—then he must push for the adoption of another offensive scheme against Germany, to take place before the end of the year. That plan could only be Gymnast. In effect, the president had made the decision for the operation before his chiefs left Washington. As a student of government has remarked, "decision-making is a process, in which all but the most trivial decisions are developed over a series of stages extending from the first glimmer of an idea to the last time it is put into effect."

Marshall, who could not be accused of yielding even to the inevitable without first getting in as many solid counterpunches as possible, determined to make a good final try for Sledgehammer, and thus for Roundup in 1943. On the day after the discussions in the president's office, he, Hopkins, and King took off for London, flying in a Boeing Stratocruiser. Among the other members of the party were Brigadier General Walter Bedell Smith, Colonel Hoyt S. Vandenberg of the air force, and Frank McCarthy, the last-named serving as Marshall's aide. Apparently content to leave the technical aspects of negotiating to Marshall, King took no staff except a single aide. For this trip FDR had shown that he was a far more effective deviser of code names than the anonymous functionaries of the War Department. For use in their cables he and Hopkins drew up a list of names that included "Plog" for General Marshall (after William Plog, the longtime superintendent of the Hyde Park estate); "Moses Smith" for Churchill (Smith was a farmer who rented land from the Roosevelts); "Rev. Wilson" for Air Chief Marshal Portal (Wilson was the rector of St. James Church at Hyde Park); and "Mrs. Johansen" for Sir Stafford Cripps, the prominent Labour party politician and member of Churchill's coalition government (Mrs. Johansen ran a small restaurant near the Roosevelt property). This list of code names constituted by far the most lighthearted aspect of the mission.

The visit began undiplomatically. Immediately after the Americans landed at Prestwick, in southern Scotland, an invitation came from Churchill to spend the weekend at Chequers. It was the sort of summons that made no allowance for refusal, yet Marshall and King turned it down, leaving Hopkins to deal with the prime minister's anger, because they wished to spend the time conferring in London with the commanders of U.S. forces in the British Isles—a team now made up of Eisenhower, Major General Mark Clark, Major General Carl "Tooey" Spaatz of the air force, and Admiral Stark.

Before leaving Washington, Marshall had received a cable from Eisenhower telling him that the "British military authorities are most fearful that in making this decision"—the abandonment of Sledgehammer—"they may be giving you a feeling that they have partially let you down." Ike could hardly have put the case more mildly, but he went on to say that he did not believe the British lacked the desire to take the offensive; on the contrary, "the fixed purpose among the staffs to adhere to a decisive purpose grows daily more noticeable . . ." During the first three days of the ensuing week, Marshall tested this resolve by putting forward a plan the Americans cobbled together during the weekend meetings—with, paradoxically, important help from a group of British planners—younger members of Mountbatten's Combined Operations staff who favored the Cherbourg alternative and provided technical details of such an operation to a U.S. liaison officer. Under this scheme Sledgehammer would take on a new look, becoming not simply an emergency landing but a deliberate attempt to seize Cherbourg and the Cotentin Peninsula and establish a permanent lodgment. The insistence that the Allies not plan to land in France at all unless they intended to stay had been one of Churchill's prime political points, but in advancing it, Marshall and his associates proposed a move that the British chiefs of staff had unequivocally declared impossible.

On Monday afternoon, at 10 Downing Street, began three days of "long arguments," as Brooke called the talks. Even his compatriots found the CIGS difficult in discussion, because his high-strung nature expressed itself in fast and abrupt categorical statement of his views, his tongue "shooting out and round his lips," as one colleague observed, "with the speed of a chameleon." For the Americans, the CIGS posed a double problem: To his compatriots he was only an individual person, but to his allies, he was not only Brooke, he was British.

What Brooke seemed to regard as the mental sluggishness of his American listeners was often simply an auditory problem. "He talked so damn fast," said Admiral King, "that it was hard to understand what he was saying." Brought up in France, Brooke spoke not only rapidly but with an idiosyncratic accent that to one U.S. officer sounded almost Cockney, so that many Americans besides King found it difficult to understand his words.

During these July sessions, however, it made little substantial difference whether Brooke sounded like Alfred Doolittle or Professor Henry Higgins. If work in an ideal committee is regarded as "a matter of invention, rational discussion, compromise, and eventual agreement on the best practical solution," then this group of chiefs did not approach the ideal. At one point in the full-dress meeting in the afternoon of July 22, Hopkins scribbled on Churchill's memo stationery two little notes that told the story. One said: "Br. say no, we say yes." The other consisted of four glum words, apparently written for Marshall's eyes: "I feel damn depressed." At the end of the session, Marshall cabled Roosevelt that the discussions were deadlocked: Sledgehammer was dead. It was, said Eisenhower, still new to the European war, "the blackest day in history."

Roosevelt responded to the chief of staff's announcement by listing five possible alternative Allied operations, in the order in which he favored them. To no one's amazement, landing in Northwest Africa took first place. (Such an operation appeared to be a popular idea at the time. During July, persons outside the government, including a Dutch major general, sent FDR memos suggesting it.) The president also reminded his representatives in London that he still wanted a quick decision.

Could he even now find some way to save Roundup for 1943? This was the question Marshall asked himself, and the U.S. staff spent the day of July 23 in putting together a plan designed to accomplish the chief's desire. The proposal actually involved a postponement, or keeping the Allied options open. It called for carrying out preparations for both a cross-Channel operation and Gymnast simultaneously, with the final decision not to be taken until September 15. By that time, ran the argument, the Allies ought to have a clearer idea of the fate of the Soviet armies—whether or not Russia could maintain herself in the war.

The next day, Friday, July 24, Marshall laid this new American proposal on the table before the prime minister and the British and American chiefs. Delighted at a plan that seemed acceptable to everybody, the generals and the politicians quickly agreed to it—all except one. At this point Marshall's faithful ally, Harry Hopkins, who often saw the political and psychological issues more clearly than the generals and who understood the reasoning behind Roosevelt's insistence on putting American troops into combat against Germany somewhere during 1942, made a move that stopped the forward motion of the chief of staff's battle plan. A postponement, Hopkins saw, was no solution at all. The spectacle of the Allies standing and waiting to see what might happen on the eastern front was not going to stiffen Russian resistance to the Germans. "What I fear most," Hopkins cabled the president, "is that if we do not now make a firm decision on Gymnast and fix a reasonably early date, there may be procrastination and delay." Hopkins suggested that Roosevelt choose a date for Gymnast not later than October 30, 1942, on the assumption that mounting the operation would probably require three months' time after the decision was made. If matters were put off until the middle of September, the operation would face winter weather and thus might well have to be canceled.

The president replied promptly, and exactly as Hopkins had wished, employing the exuberant words "full speed ahead." As commander in chief, he had told Marshall what the limits of policy were, and he had allowed—even encouraged—the chief of staff to fight for Sledgehammer. But now that the battle was lost, it was time to move on. Although, back in Washington, Marshall, seeming obsessed, still made one more attempt to push his last plan, he found himself alone. On July 30 Roosevelt made the decision official and categorical: Sledgehammer was truly dead. What lay ahead now was the move into Northwest Africa, which henceforth had a new name along with a new charter. Optimistically the operation was rebaptized Torch.

It had been a head-on collision, a war *à outrance,* and Marshall had been completely defeated. He had pitted himself against the president as if strategy existed in isolation—even though before the war he had always been especially aware of the army's need for public support. FDR, the professional dramatist, knew that he could not allow a whole year to pass after Pearl Harbor without giving the public a direct sense of involvement in the war against Germany, the enemy that was most dangerous but was not the one that had attacked the United States. He had granted Marshall plenty of room for maneuver, and he had been willing to settle for any feasible operation that would bring American troops into action on German-controlled territory in 1942. Torch clearly shone as the only reasonable response to the president's conditions. The commander in chief had exercised his prerogative as chief strategist.

Marshall had learned a great lesson. He had not appreciated the calculus of military need, political pressure, and psychological understanding that guided the president in making the decisions of grand strategy. It was now clear that future strategic decisions must be reached in cooperation with Roosevelt;

Sledgehammer had proved too heavy a weight to be swung by the chief of staff alone. As Marshall later conceded in an oddly worded phrase that nevertheless left his meaning clear, "I did not realize how in a democracy the public has to be kept entertained."

Nor had he thought about one highly practical aspect of Torch—the benefit a successful landing might bestow on an administration hoping to hold its own in the 1942 off-year congressional elections. This would be the first opportunity for the voters to pass judgment on the shock of Pearl Harbor and the loss of the Philippines, on the organization of the United States for war, on the administration's response (or lack of response) to popular pressure for a second front—and, of course, on the great victory at Midway and the battle on Guadalcanal that had begun in August. One day, in a conversation about Torch in his office, FDR folded his hands, as if in prayer, and said, "Please make it before election day." Since the original date suggested by Hopkins was October 30, that would have left only a four-day margin for any delays—not a schedule that would have been proposed by a Machiavellian president intent on tying military operations to political events (especially since Marshall had first been given a thorough chance to fight for Sledgehammer). Not that Roosevelt would have objected to Torch on the eve of the elections—"but when he found we had to have more time," Marshall commented, "he never said a word. He was very courageous."

The general perhaps was able to enjoy a wry chuckle at a subsequent story in *Time* crediting him with a mind that worked "with an earthbound simplicity that is the precise opposite of Hitler's 'intuition,'" and declaring that his strategic design had as its first aim "to clean Hitler out of Africa" before moving into Europe. Readers of the magazine could not know that Marshall's fight against Gymnast-Torch was one of the fiercest battles of the war. And now the general himself had to deal with all the consequences of his defeat.

The Virginia Military Institute, about 1900: Cadet George C. Marshall is third from left in the front row. *(George C. Marshall Library)*

Warm Springs, Georgia, about 1930: Governor Franklin D. Roosevelt engages with friends in a favorite form of therapy for polio survivors. *(Franklin D. Roosevelt Library)*

FDR pays a visit to the CCC camp at Big Meadows, Virginia, in 1933. *(Franklin D. Roosevelt Library)*

Brazilians give GCM an enthusiastic welcome during his 1938 visit. *(George C. Marshall Library)*

FDR the sailor enjoys a winter cruise on the U.S.S. *Houston* (February 1939). Seated next to him is Admiral William D. Leahy, then chief of naval operations. In the rear, from left: Captain Daniel Callaghan, Major General Edwin M. "Pa" Watson, Dr. Ross McIntire, and Captain G. N. Barker. *(Franklin D. Roosevelt Library)*

The Marshalls dine at Fire Island, New York. With them are her children, Molly, Allen, and Clifton. *(George C. Marshall Library)*

Heading for retirement, General Malin Craig welcomes his successor in the chief of staff's office. *(George C. Marshall Library)*

FDR, famous as a cluttered-desk man, dictates to his secretary and confidante, Marguerite "Missy" LeHand (1940). *(Franklin D. Roosevelt Library)*

July 1940: GCM displays his deft touch with Congress at a critical time—during the debate over the draft. His companions are members of the Senate Military Affairs Committee. *(George C. Marshall Library)*

Above, September 16, 1940: FDR signs the country's first peacetime selective service act. Watching are (from left) Secretary of War Henry L. Stimson, Representative A. J. May of Kentucky, GCM, Senator Morris Sheppard of Texas. *(Franklin D. Roosevelt Library)*

Below, GCM and Katherine Marshall with Fleet, the general's beloved but famously stupid Dalmatian.
(George C. Marshall Library)

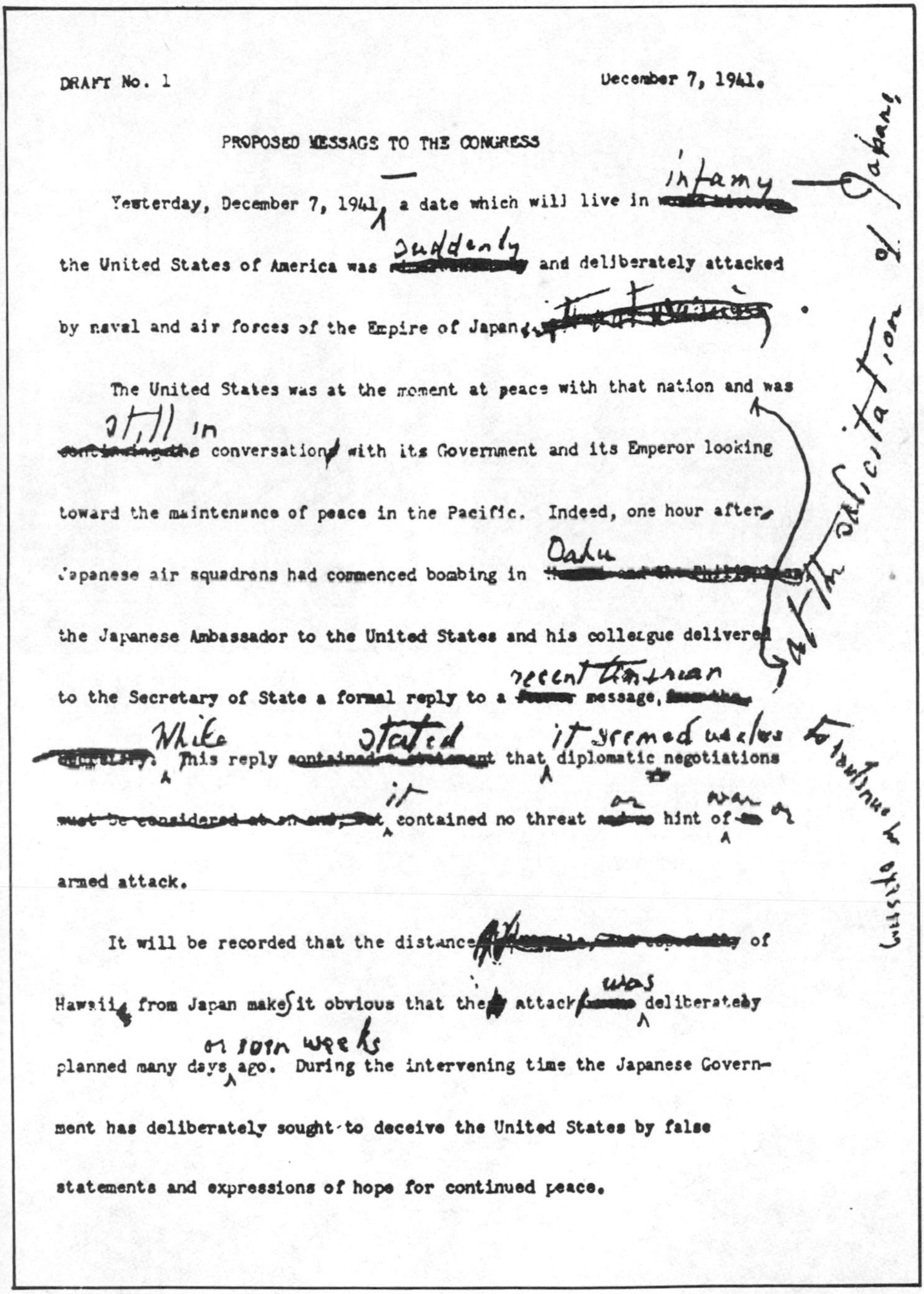

DRAFT No. 1 December 7, 1941.

PROPOSED MESSAGE TO THE CONGRESS

Yesterday, December 7, 1941 — a date which will live in infamy — the United States of America was suddenly and deliberately attacked by naval and air forces of the Empire of Japan.

The United States was at peace with that nation and was, at the solicitation of Japan, still in conversation with its Government and its Emperor looking toward the maintenance of peace in the Pacific. Indeed, one hour after Japanese air squadrons had commenced bombing in Oahu the Japanese Ambassador to the United States and his colleague delivered to the Secretary of State a formal reply to a recent American message. While this reply stated that it seemed useless to continue the existing diplomatic negotiations it contained no threat or hint of war or armed attack.

It will be recorded that the distance of Hawaii from Japan makes it obvious that the attack was deliberately planned many days or even weeks ago. During the intervening time the Japanese Government has deliberately sought to deceive the United States by false statements and expressions of hope for continued peace.

Typescript of the first page of the president's war speech shows FDR's talents as writer and, notably, as editor. *(Franklin D. Roosevelt Library)*

GCM takes two British colleagues—his close friend Field Marshal Sir John Dill (left) and Lord Louis Mountbatten—on a 1942 tour of U.S. military installations. *(George C. Marshall Library)*

A strong supporter of the Women's Army Auxiliary Corps, GCM looks on as Oveta Culp Hobby is sworn in (May 16, 1942) as the first director of the corps, which would soon lose "Auxiliary" from its name.
(Franklin D. Roosevelt Library)

ight, in a message drafted by Harry opkins, FDR gives GCM the order for s July 1942 trip to London to settle strat- gy with the British.
'ranklin D. Roosevelt Library)

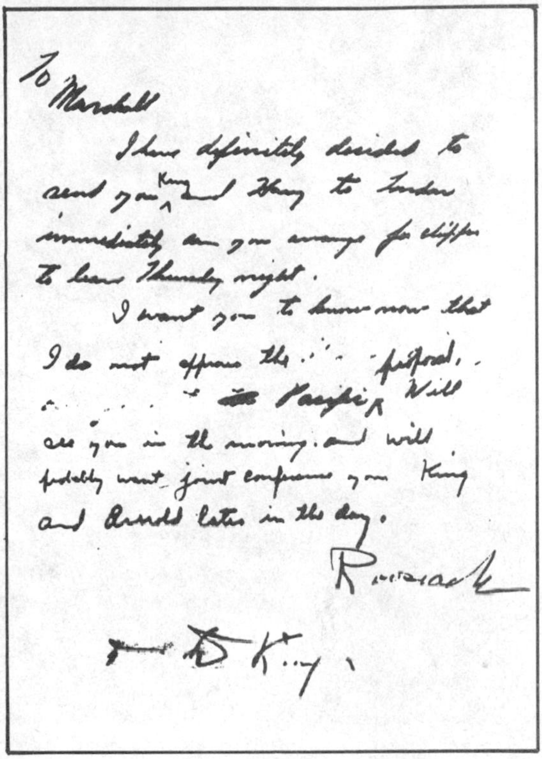
To
Marshall
I have definitely decided to send you, King and Harry to London immediately as you arrange for clipper to leave Thursday night.
I want you to know now that I do not approve the [illegible] proposal [illegible] the Pacific. Will see you in the morning and will probably want joint conference you King and Arnold later in the day.
Roosevelt
[illegible] King.

elow, at a luncheon of the Joint Chiefs f Staff in December 1942, Hopkins is anked by GCM and Admiral Leahy.
'ranklin D. Roosevelt Library)

December 1942: FDR contemplates his Christmas present from GCM. *(Franklin D. Roosevelt Library)*

In a Combined Chiefs of Staff session at Cairo, November 1943, the U.S. chiefs—General Henry "Hap" Arnold, GCM, Admiral Leahy, Admiral Ernest J. King—confront their British opposite numbers (the officer between Marshall and Leahy is unidentified). *(Franklin D. Roosevelt Library)*

Right, a beaming FDR presides over the reluctant handshake of French Generals Henri Giraud (left) and Charles de Gaulle—Casablanca, January 24, 1943. *(Franklin D. Roosevelt Library)*

Below, Allied leaders gather during the Trident conference—Washington, May 1943. Behind Winston Churchill and FDR stand (from left) Air Chief Marshal Sir Charles Portal, General Sir Alan Brooke, Admiral Sir Dudley Pound, Admiral Leahy, and GCM. *(George C. Marshall Library)*

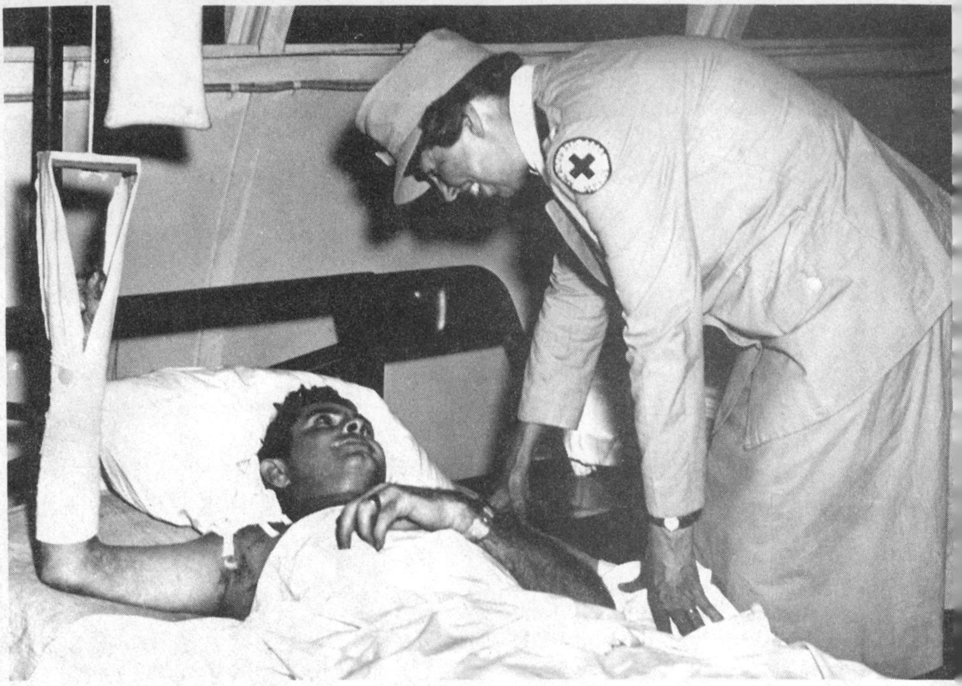

During her long Pacific tour in the summer of 1943, Eleanor Roosevelt spent much time visiting hospitals. *(Franklin D. Roosevelt Library)*

At the Tehran Conference (November 1943), the Big Three—Marshal Stalin, FDR, Winston Churchill—pose in their oddly assorted chairs. *(Franklin D. Roosevelt Library)*

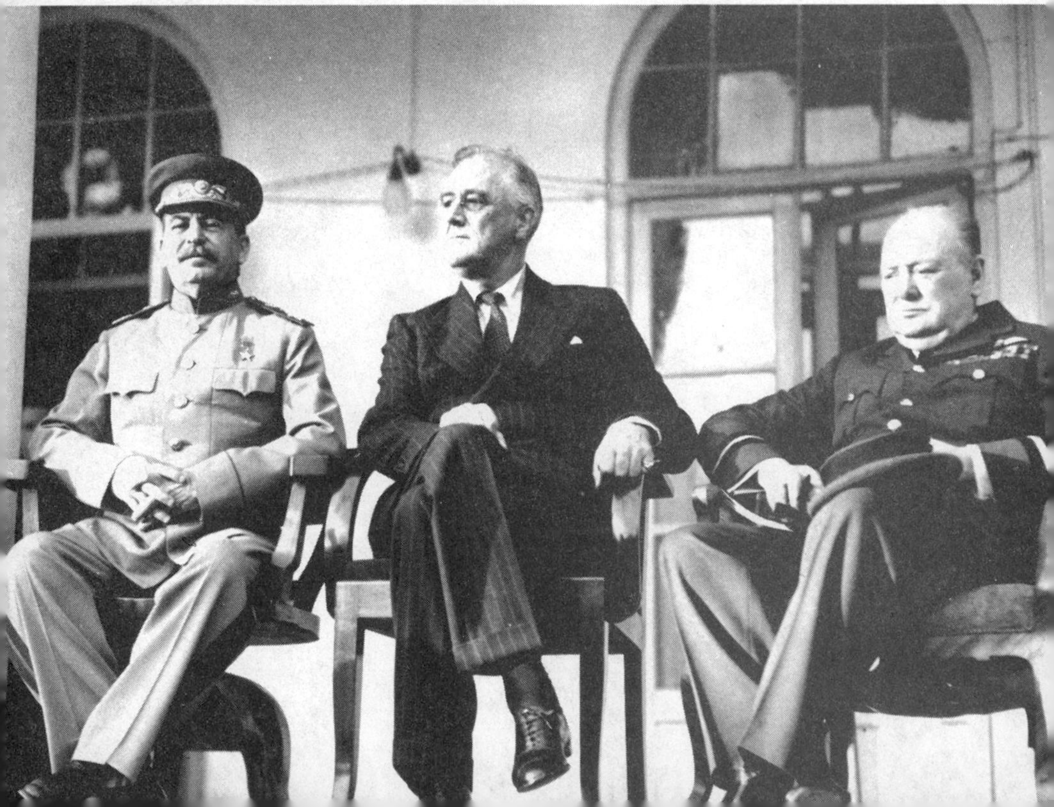

Flanked by Dr. Ross McIntire (right) and "Assistant President" James F. Byrnes, FDR arrives at Malta en route to the Yalta Conference. *(Franklin D. Roosevelt Library)*

FDR confers with Leahy, King, and GCM aboard the U.S.S. *Quincy* in Malta harbor. *(George C. Marshall Library)*

GCM with his indispensable aide, Colonel Frank McCarthy.
(George C. Marshall Library)

Young doctor Howard G. Bruenn, FDR's last physician.
(Courtesy of Howard G. Bruenn)

Having just arrived in the Crimea, GCM stands with Soviet Vice Admiral Kucherov, commandant of the Saki airfield, and a U.S. officer.
(John L. Bates)

Conversational group in the Crimea includes FDR's daughter Anna, Wilson Brown, Averell Harriman, and Edward R. Stettinius.
(Franklin D. Roosevelt Library)

Above, the Big Three and their military advisers during the Yalta Conference. Leahy stands behind FDR; behind the admiral is GCM.
(Franklin D. Roosevelt Library)

Left, almost forty years after the end of the war, Mona Nason, GCM's personal secretary when he was chief of staff, stands in a State Department reception room beneath a portrait of GCM.
(Courtesy of Mona Nason)

CHAPTER FOURTEEN

DECISION AT ANFA CAMP

One day in November 1942 President Roosevelt dictated an eloquent if brief note to General Marshall:

Dear George:
You win again.
F.D.R.

The note honored the chief of staff for the leading part he had played in persuading Congress to agree to the drafting of eighteen-year-olds. The legislative battle had been complex, because even some of the senators and representatives who agreed that the army needed the younger men had sought to escape the wrath of American mothers by insisting that eighteen-year-olds not be sent into combat outside the United States until they had received at least a year's training. "I am fully aware of the peril of employing partially trained troops in combat," Marshall had told Congress, urging the lawmakers not to "hamper us at this critical period." His powerful intervention had yielded its usual positive results.

Since Roosevelt had also worked for passage of the bill, the note was a graceful gesture for him to make. Certainly it constituted an acknowledgment of professional accomplishment from one effective politician to another. Marshall's political success possessed a remarkable feature: Regardless of the extent to which he involved himself in legislative questions, lawmakers and public approvingly looked on him as nonpolitical. His position *vis-à-vis* Congress resembled that of a person who has carefully and patiently invested in a stock that seems to have an uncertain future but suddenly becomes the hottest item on the market; the honesty and thoroughness with which he had spoken to congressional committees during the years before Pearl Harbor now paid enormous dividends.

At Christmastime General Marshall took a step toward simplifying the formulation of strategy by the commander in chief by sending him a four-foot globe. (A twin globe went to Churchill; now neither leader would have any excuse for failing to see the scope of global war.) FDR was delighted with his big toy. "I have set it up in my office directly behind my chair," he wrote back. "I can swing around and figure distances to my great satisfaction." As time went on, Marshall saw that he "became stronger" with the president, and at the same time his admiration for FDR as the cheerful bearer of enormous burdens steadily grew. But he rationed his visits to Roosevelt's office; every day a staff officer would go to the White House to take replies to queries and see what matters Pa Watson wished to bring up. When Marshall called on the president, he did so as a presence, thus marking the occasion as important, and he usually went alone. The relative infrequency of his visits disappointed Roosevelt's secretaries, Grace Tully and Dorothy Brady, who counted themselves among the general's leading admirers. "Harry Hopkins used to rib us occasionally about our favoritism," Miss Tully wrote, "and when we playfully stuck on our wall an envelope bearing the General's signature, Harry made a facetious complaint to the President that we were being unfaithful." Hopkins said this when Marshall was in the office, and Miss Tully thought the general was probably embarrassed by it. He did not say.

Miss Bessie Boggess, a small, prematurely gray Mississippi lady, rarely hesitated to say what was on her mind. The daughter of a onetime Confederate captain, she had been orphaned at an early age and through drive and hard work had acquired a college education. She abhorred double negatives and poor eating habits and spoke out firmly against both. One wartime day she was distressed to see an army stenographer who was so weak and gaunt that she resembled a refugee suffering from pellagra. Since the health of this young girl and that of thousands of other persons came within her professional purview, Miss Boggess felt entitled to ask some questions. The answers she received appalled her. The stenographer allowed herself only forty cents a day for food. She ate no breakfast, had only coffee and doughnuts for lunch (at a cost of ten cents), and spent the remaining thirty cents for supper. The money she saved through this austere regimen went home to her family in Minnesota. But after she received a stiff lecture from Miss Boggess on the evils of malnutrition, the girl promised to mend her ways.

Having studied nutrition at Columbia and spent some years on the staff of the University of Georgia before becoming director of the Department of Health Education at the U.S. Army's remarkable new headquarters, Miss Boggess held the responsibility of inducing civilian employees to eat well-balanced meals in the institution's cafeterias. She brought a kindly human touch to the extraordinary new environment in which employees not only might eat unwisely but tended to complain, paradoxically, of both claustrophobia and agoraphobia. Unique in the world, the building was so enormous and yet seemed so self-contained with its many windowless offices that a psychologist readily agreed that it might indeed upset those who feared isolation and also those who feared being smothered. But whatever these people dreaded, he suggested, if they worked in the building long enough they would get used to it.

One of the most remarkable features of the great building was that it had become a legend even before it was finished. Developed under the overall management of Brigadier General Brehon B. Somervell, a driving empire builder who commanded the supply services, and the direct supervision of an engineer colonel named Leslie R. Groves, the project caught the imagination of the public both by its scope and by the speed with which it was carried out; begun in the summer of 1941, the building began receiving some tenants within a year. On November 15, 1942, when great events had just begun unfolding across the Atlantic, General Marshall became one of those tenants, moving into a large third-floor office with a row of tall windows looking out across the river toward the monuments of Washington.

Well before Pearl Harbor, the army had been pressed to find space for its workers. At the time that the decision was taken to build the headquarters across the Potomac in Virginia, 24,000 army clerks were lodged in offices scattered throughout the capital. To create great space that would also provide efficiency, the designers shied away from using a rectangle (because offices in opposite ends would have been almost a mile apart) and came as close as seemed feasible to a circular plan, by constructing a concentric series of five-sided rings. Each side of this pentagon measured 921 feet in length, making a building so enormous that all of it could not be seen except from distant hills or from the air. So gigantic were all the dimensions, both fiscal and physical, that reporters could not keep them straight. Although originally expected to cost $35 million, the building consumed $64 million. Or was it $70 million? The structure covered thirty-five acres, or perhaps forty-two. The lengths of five ring corridors added together amounted to 16½ or seventeen miles. The building in full use would house hordes of workers, 30,000 or 40,000. In any case, the Great Pyramid could be set inside the walls with two hundred feet to spare. And unlike most wartime ugly-duckling buildings, the Pentagon, a solid reinforced-concrete fortress, was permanent.

The entire country quickly heard some of the stories the building inspired, the most famous of them concerning a Western Union boy who innocently wandered into the maze of endless corridors and emerged three days later a lieutenant colonel. Some officers of course denied the story, while others insisted that the boy had come out merely a major. Another story told of the woman visitor who entered the building a virgin and by the time she made her way out had become a mother. Behind these jokes seemed to lie a kind of national pride in the Pentagon as a home-front manifestation of the American can-do spirit that was producing prodigious logistical feats overseas.

Having the world's largest office building at his disposal, General Marshall decided in the interest of unity between the armed services to offer a large part of it to the navy, so that the top commanders could keep in close touch. Amused at the prospect, an anonymous navy wag produced a memorandum declaring that "all personnel being moved will provide themselves with a sleeping bag, clothing for one week, food and water for one week, three extra pairs of shoes, a compass, a scout knife, a pistol and roller skates or a scooter. All Section Chiefs will be suitably labeled and packed." Comfortingly, he added that "rumors concerning lost safaris in the Pentagon are hereby discounted."

Soon discounted also were the reports that the navy would accept Marshall's invitation; the section chiefs would not have to worry about finding themselves boxed and labeled. Claiming a need for more space than the chief of staff had offered, the navy brass could not bring themselves to share the army's quarters. It was bad enough to have to fight a war alongside the army; any moves toward unification definitely held danger.

Public speculation soon arose about the use that might be made of the great building after the war. The large number of windowless rooms seemed to rule out one suggested possibility, that of converting it into a hospital. In the better world of tomorrow, some thought, all that endless space might be turned into a last resting place for federal archives.

During the morning of January 8, 1943, two Boeing 314 flying boats, coming in from New York, landed at Dinner Key, the Pan American Airways base off Miami. The pilots had been told that they were to perform a special mission, but not what it would be; their departure was scheduled for six o'clock in the morning of January 11. One of the aircraft, the *Dixie Clipper,* was commanded by a handsome young Pan American flying officer, Howard M. Cone, who was also a lieutenant in the naval reserve; for this secret mission he had donned his service uniform. For some time Cone knew nothing about his passengers except that he would have nine—no names provided. Then, at 5:40 on the eleventh of January, only twenty minutes before flight time, he was handed a more detailed list. The mysterious bestower of Washington code names had for this occasion produced perhaps his most unusual performance; the list bore at the top "Mr. Jones," which was followed *en clair* by such names as Harry Hopkins, William D. Leahy, Ross T. McIntire, and John L. McCrea.

Cone turned to the dispatcher. "No! Not really!"

The dispatcher assured him that what he had concluded was indeed the case, and in a few minutes a navy launch glided alongside the flying boat. "Mr. Jones," who was physically handicapped, was lifted into the *Dixie Clipper,* where he received a proper salute from Lieutenant Cone and a historic greeting: "Mr. President! I'm glad to have you aboard, sir."

The Clipper taxied across the water and rose into the sky, bearing with it the first president of the United States to make a journey by air (FDR's previous flight had come when, as the Democratic nominee in 1932, he had flown to Chicago to address the party convention—a venture that also broke precedent); Roosevelt on this trip also became the first president to leave the country in wartime. The first leg had been accomplished by special train from Washington to Miami; so secret was the project that the Pullman porters and cooks were replaced by five Filipino messmen from the presidential yacht *Potomac,* who were quickly applauded by the passengers for providing tasty meals of steak, chicken chow mein, and the like at cost—fifty cents apiece.

After gaining altitude for forty minutes, the Clipper leveled off at nine thousand feet and headed for Trinidad, one of the stops made necessary by its cruising range, when fully loaded, of just 2,100 nautical miles. Arriving off Port of Spain at 4:45 in the afternoon, the travelers spent the night at a U.S. Navy base; on returning to the Clipper early the next morning, the president was delighted to be greeted by signal flags arranged by the crew, spelling out HAIL TO THE CHIEF. During this stop Dr. McIntire discovered that Admiral Leahy was running a fever, and, fearful of risking complications, he ordered the president's chief of staff to sit out the trip in Trinidad—a decree that did not appear to upset the admiral; Hopkins felt that Leahy would have been perfectly happy to have stayed behind in Washington.

The party made its next stop at Belem, Brazil, 1,075 miles away. From there the *Dixie Clipper* took off for a 2,100-mile leap across the South Atlantic to Bathurst, Gambia. All along the way from Miami, the president, who was always at home no matter where he found himself, was, Hopkins saw, "happy and interested" in what was happening. During the first hours, "he acted like a sixteen-year-old," making a point of directing Cone to fly over Henri Christophe's citadel in Haiti and otherwise studying the chart as if he were the navigator for the flight. He chatted, napped, ate, even played a little solitaire. Dr. McIntire had expressed some concern about the effects the altitude might have on FDR's heart, but no problems arose. One reason for Roosevelt's general exuberance, Hopkins felt, was that "he was tired of having other people—particularly myself—speak for him around the world." Besides, "he was sick of people telling him it was dangerous to ride in airplanes. He liked the drama of it." Above all, "he wanted to make a trip."

The impetus for this trip came from the need for Allied leaders to decide what moves to make after the Germans were driven out of Africa. This happy event had not yet occurred, although the Torch landings had begun on November 8, almost on Hopkins's originally proposed schedule (but five days after the congressional elections, in which the Democrats lost forty-five seats in the House). The Allied forces had been slow to reach Tunisia, winter rainstorms had arrived, and Hitler, instead of acknowledging defeat in Africa as he might have done in view of the convergence of the Anglo-American Torch forces from the west and the British Eighth Army from the east, had flung reinforcements across the Mediterranean. It was a curious if characteristic move for the Führer, because he had kept his resourceful Afrika Korps commander Rommel on thin rations when greater support would have won North Africa for the Germans, and only now did he direct attention to this front. But the support he sent could only delay the outcome, not change it.

Where were the Anglo-American forces to be employed after the inevitable collapse of German resistance in Tunisia? During back-and-forth correspondence, Roosevelt and Churchill had agreed that Stalin should be included in any forthcoming discussion of Allied strategy, but the Soviet premier rejected two invitations to join his high-level colleagues in a conference, insisting that operations at Stalingrad and elsewhere made it impossible for him to be absent "even for a day." The "next-best thing," Hopkins thought, would be a meeting between Churchill and Roosevelt and their staffs. Fearing that public opinion in the United States might object to his being absent from his presidential post on what was regarded as a hazardous trip, Roosevelt suggested that if the conference were held in Africa he could justify his presence by seeing U.S. military commanders in the area and inspecting some American troops. (The idea of the trip won no popularity in FDR's own circle. Captain McCrea thought the president was needlessly exposing himself to danger, and Pa Watson said, "There's only one son of a bitch around here who's crazy enough to promote such a thing and his name is Hopkins.")

Nestling quietly in the middle of one of FDR's messages to Churchill sat this revealing sentence: "In view of Stalin's absence, I think you and I need no foreign affairs people with us—for our work will be essentially military." This notion grew into insistence; to the first great Allied meeting to be held outside the United States, FDR did not wish to bring his secretary of state, Cordell Hull, and he made it plain that he would be pleased if the foreign secretary, Anthony Eden, were likewise not present—thus rendering Hull's absence less conspicuous. Although dominated by Churchill and his untiring pursuit of his objectives by any means—oratory, fits of temper, sulks—the

British government shone as a model of order compared with the Roosevelt administration, and in the normal course of events the foreign secretary might well have taken part in such an international meeting. Churchill, however, yielded to Roosevelt's insistence. He could hardly claim unfamiliarity with FDR's methods. For almost three years now he had adapted himself to the Rooseveltian system of communication, working directly with the unportfolioed Hopkins instead of through the Foreign Office and his ambassador in Washington.

Stung by being excluded from meetings concerned with military matters, and seeing clearly that "scarcely any large-scale military operations could be undertaken that would not have diplomatic aspects," Hull several times brought up the question with the president, even using Eden's role in the British government as an example to be followed. The president brushed aside this argument, saying casually that the American system was different from the British. It was not, Hull thought, *that* different, and in any case military and political issues often arose intertwined—a truth of which FDR was thoroughly aware, as he demonstrated by his decision on Torch. Hull, however, was arguing on the level of principles, while FDR was thinking personally—he did not want an institutional foreign-affairs voice at his ear, especially Hull's, nor did he wish for any civilian semblance of the British War Cabinet. Hull did not prove to be the only person left at home; neither Stimson nor Knox received an invitation to take part in this conference.

The *Dixie Clipper* landed off Bathurst, on the coast of British West Africa, late in the afternoon of January 13. After spending the night aboard the cruiser *Memphis,* which lay in harbor, the president entered on the last leg of his long journey, this time transferring to a Douglas C-54 four-engine transport for which a big wooden ramp had been built to accommodate his wheelchair. As the plane, which cruised at 180 miles an hour, covered the last 1,500 miles of the trip, the pilot admiringly noted the president's cheerfulness despite the fact that he had been in the air or otherwise shuttled from place to place for almost three days; he even refused the offer of an improvised bed because those traveling with him would have no such luxury. Finally, at 6:20 in the evening, local time, the C-54 touched down at Medouina airport, Casablanca—journey's end.

* * *

The military staffs had arrived at Casablanca several days earlier to "clear the ground," as the president put it, and "have plans in fairly good tentative shape." As a matter of course, the arrangements for Marshall's travel were made by Frank McCarthy, whose relationship with the chief of staff was developing into what Molly Winn regarded as the closest tie Marshall maintained with any officer in the war. An engaging man, liked by everybody, McCarthy was a Virginian from Richmond and a VMI graduate who had gone to work for Warner Brothers in the late 1930s; one of the films in which he was involved had been the 1938 production *Brother Rat,* in which the action took place at VMI. (Starring Eddie Albert and Priscilla Lane, the movie included in its cast what one reviewer called "a mettlesome group of juniors"—one of these a gangly young actor named Ronald Reagan who played the role of Cadet Dan Crawford, "who's always going along for the ride.") During the war McCarthy and other reserve officers increasingly rose to prominence in the General Staff as part of the legacy of Marshall's experience in World War I. Always ruefully aware of the problems a regular officer could encounter as the result of spending his time on staff duty, the chief of staff wanted those men who made the army their profession to have every chance for command experience—though he could perhaps have reflected that his own lack of such experience had not kept him from reaching the top of the ladder; in fact, since modern war at the highest levels was a vast enterprise involving figures in the millions—of men, of armaments, and of supplies—it demanded (as the War Department had discovered in World War I) that its leader be not a fiery, sword-waving figure on horseback but an experienced and skillful military manager.

In spite of his liking for McCarthy, Marshall found that the younger man's surname presented him with a formidable challenge. Katherine Marshall, who often had problems with names, called the major "McCartney"—a usage Marshall regarded as a great joke, although, either from repetition or from his own difficulty with names, he adopted the same version of his aide's surname before finally settling for "Frank" (a rare instance of his calling someone by his first name). The chief of staff had two other foibles in the area of names. He tended to call a General Staff secretary by the previous secretary's name; "he was one jump behind," a General Staff officer said, "which was a funny thing because he had such a retentive memory." Marshall also employed the device of describing a person physically (for example, by calling Wedemeyer "that long-legged major"). Sometimes he failed to be even as precise as that. One day McCarthy wrote a friend that he was beginning to know whom the chief had in mind whenever he would say: "Get me that fellow I want to see." Having problems with names was markedly Marshall's most unpolitical trait, contrasting sharply with Roosevelt's free and easy use of first names, initials, and nicknames. Marshall had flowered brilliantly in his dealings with congressmen and other Washington figures, but he had done so in his own quiet style; he lacked the zest with which born politicians like FDR made use of names and details of personal lives on all occasions.

In accordance with the arrangements McCarthy had made, Marshall, Sir John Dill, Hap Arnold, General Somervell (head of the U.S. Army Service Forces), Wedemeyer, and McCarthy himself left Washington National Airport at eight o'clock in the morning of January 8, flying in a C-54 which, like the president's plane, would make a number of stops en route to Africa. A believer in thorough preparation, McCarthy had loaded Marshall's plane with clothing and other items for any eventuality, including beads and similar trinkets in case a forced landing in the desert made it necessary for the party to negotiate for transportation with the local Arabs. At Bathurst, McCarthy revealed that he had outdone himself. Having been warned by supposedly knowledgeable persons that mosquitoes were prevalent in North Africa, he had requisitioned sets of special boots, gloves, and hats with veils. Accordingly, following his aide's instructions, Marshall on arriving at Bathurst led the way off the transport thoroughly booted, gloved, and veiled, only to see, to his evident disgust, that the members of the welcoming party were casually attired in shorts. For this performance McCarthy earned one stern look. But when Marshall was told about the trinkets for trading with the natives, he enjoyed "one of the best laughs he got during the war."

Gloveless and unveiled, the chief of staff and his associates arrived at Casablanca about four o'clock in the afternoon, Monday, January 11, while the president's party was still on the Caribbean leg of the trip. After considerable research in the area, the American and British scouting parties had chosen as the site of the conference the Anfa Hotel, a large, modern, oval-shaped building rising from its surrounding palm trees like a white ship riding a green sea. The hotel was located in the town of Anfa, which sat on a hill overlooking Casablanca six miles away. The sumptuous villas surrounding the hotel had been requisitioned and a ring of barbed-wire fence thrown about the area; a telephone network connected the villas with each other and with the offices established in the hotel itself. U.S. transportation officers set up a livery service, impressing a French officer by the fact that "a car had scarcely been ordered when it was at your door to take you wherever you wanted to go." This officer noted in general a great lavishness of personnel and equipment, "in the American style." The bright sun and the palm trees and orange groves, with the ocean only a mile away, gave a midwinter holiday cast to "Anfa Camp," as the site was called.

The British chiefs had planned to travel to North Africa by flying boat, but in view of heavy seas they were switched at the last minute to B-24s, in which they slept in unwilling intimacy in bomb bays and other narrow spaces, arriving hot and grubby at Casablanca, while the American chiefs emerged spruce and well fed from their C-54 transports. But in other respects, the British stood a good distance ahead of their transatlantic colleagues. Although FDR had hoped and expected that the conference would be conducted as a small affair of the political leaders and the "three top men" on either side, the British contingent arrived with a six-thousand-ton liner fitted out as a command and communications ship, manned by an abundant staff. Thus when technical problems arose, demanding detailed solutions, the British would have the means of producing "every quantitative calculation that might be called for"; the U.S. chiefs faced the unpleasant realization that, as one British staff member observed, "they had left most of their clubs behind," although Dill had warned Marshall that "the British would be ready."

On a higher level, the British marched onto the Anfa scene in intellectual unity. Clearly, the Allies must choose for 1943 between two main possibilities. They could conduct major operations in the Mediterranean and in the Pacific (in the latter theater, the first American offensive of the war anywhere had been launched on Guadalcanal Island the preceding August, and was now winding down), while continuing the Bolero buildup with forces not used in these theaters, or they could give priority to the buildup in Britain and to an Asian counterpart having as its aim the recovery of Burma from the Japanese. In the only meeting the president and his chiefs had held prior to Casablanca to discuss the matter—during the afternoon of January 7—Marshall, who made no secret of his feelings, had been forced to admit that the U.S. planners disagreed among themselves. But, he said, what would particularly threaten Roundup—the invasion of Western Europe—would be operations in the Mediterranean that would cause heavy Allied losses in shipping. Although FDR warned his advisers to be ready for the British who "will have a plan and stick to it," the White House meeting ended with no consensus. In making his point the president put his finger on one of the greatest British sources of strength in Allied conferences: Whatever the behind-the-scenes disagreements might have been (with both Brooke and Portal, Churchill engaged in some memorable bloodlettings), at the conference table the British side spoke in a harmonious chorus.

When the president arrived at Anfa Camp on January 14, he was installed in a splendid villa named Dar es-Saada. By this time Marshall and Brooke had become locked in the expected debate over strategy; the meetings, some of which provided heat unneeded even in the winter climate of Anfa, took place in a large, airy semicircular room off the main hall of the hotel. Operating without extensive staff help, Marshall thought of himself as "shooting off the hip" and "shooting off the cuff all the time." Whether or not he still nourished any real hope of Roundup for 1943, the U.S. chief of staff insisted that Bolero-Roundup must continue to be the main Allied aim in Europe; the buildup in Britain must come first. Brooke, though often testy in discussion, now viewed the battle loftily, rather in the manner of a kindergarten teacher or an animal trainer working with his charges. He found dealing with the Americans "a slow and tiring business which requires a lot of patience. They can't be pushed and hurried, and must be made gradually to assimilate our proposed policy." (Field Marshal Dill's aide said that Brooke "rather gave me the feeling that in his view children should be seen, not heard"—and, certainly, not all of the children were American.) As a negotiator, the highly capable Brooke added to the difficulties caused by his personal style a basic problem of attitude. Whether or not his ideas were sound, he was unable to see the possibility that any of them might conceivably not be, or that anyone else might have a better one.

For his part, Wedemeyer, now a brigadier general and

Marshall's chief planner, felt that the "peppery and terse" Brooke, whom he saw as "intelligent but not intellectual," was enunciating a policy guaranteed not to win the war in any reasonable period of time because it rested on the avoidance of a major cross-Channel operation. In Wedemeyer's view, Torch had already accomplished its purpose of ridding Northwest Africa of the Germans (except for the forces in Tunisia) and thus of providing the Allies with air and naval bases that would enable them to protect shipping through the Mediterranean.

But the conclusion was really foregone. Torch had opened up an offensive Allied theater and brought large forces into the Mediterranean, giving rise to the opportunistic approach to 1943 that became known as the Mediterranean strategy. At a point on January 18 when Marshall and Brooke seemed far apart, with the Mediterranean and Roundup and various Pacific projects all in competition, Dill entered the picture as mediator. This intervention constituted a tribute to Marshall's foresight, since the field marshal had come to Anfa because the U.S. chief of staff, not the British, had invited him; more and more, Marshall looked on Dill as an essential member of any Anglo-American party. (Taking notice of such a need and then fixing on someone to fill it was a characteristic operating procedure for Marshall—although his liking for Dill may well have preceded his insightful grasp of the field marshal's potential value in inter-Allied negotiations. Dill, indeed, beguiled the Americans like a temptress; he served as an efficacious antidote to Brooke. He was "one of the finest gentlemen I have ever known," said General Hull of Marshall's planning staff, "a courteous, kindly man." Another staff officer remarked that "like most truly great people, Sir John had the gift of being able to meet and talk with people of any station and make them comfortable in his presence.") Dill emphatically told Brooke that the British must reach an agreement with the Americans and that it must be accomplished by the generals; if the unresolved situation were to be put into the hands of the president and the prime minister, he declared, "you know as well as I do what a mess they would make of it." That same afternoon Marshall, conceding that Roundup was gone for 1943, after a talk with Dill assented to a draft statement that proposed no long-range Allied objectives but asserted that operations would continue in both the Pacific and the Mediterranean, the latter looking to an invasion of Sicily after the Germans should be beaten in Tunisia. The cross-Channel operation, Marshall's great aim, was left to simmer on the fire.

Both the British and the Americans tended to place great faith in air power, the British often seeming to believe that a great bombing offensive might by itself so shatter both the German economy and German nerves that the Third Reich would collapse under the blows. This belief meant that one American general, at least, left Casablanca a happy man. Major General Ira C. Eaker had come to the conference to defend the U.S. daylight-bombing strategy against Churchill's desire to switch the American effort to night operations alongside—and perhaps under the control of—the RAF. A fervent believer in precision bombing, Eaker, who commanded the Eighth Air Force, was also a hands-on leader who for example refused to receive ULTRA intelligence information produced by the code breakers because "it would keep me from flying missions" (since ULTRA recipients were not supposed to expose themselves to possible capture by the enemy). Told by Hap Arnold that Roosevelt had accepted Churchill's proposal, Eaker exploded: "If these people are going to be that stupid, count me out!" But then, although speaking quietly, Eaker, in a half hour's talk with the prime minister, argued his case with such conviction that Churchill gave his approval to what Eaker enticingly called "around the clock" bombing. Since the plan concentrated on bringing the attack to Germany as the main foe, Marshall naturally gave it his support.

Despite the fact that Marshall came away from the sessions of the Combined Chiefs of Staff with relatively empty hands—certainly he won no concrete assurances about Roundup—he impressed the British by his "friendliness and honesty of purpose." It came as a relief, said one officer, "to find that he was not obstinate or rigid in his strategic views"; the U.S. chief of staff was not going to sulk or "take up his dishes and go away." In any case, the decision to extend operations in the Mediterranean surprised nobody. If no Roundup would be mounted in the coming months, other work must be found for the Allied armies. The outcome of the Sledgehammer debate with Roosevelt had made that point abundantly clear.

The planning and execution of Operation Torch had led two politically unsophisticated American generals, Dwight Eisenhower and Mark Clark, into a maze of French politics in which even experienced statesmen and diplomats found themselves at dead ends. Since the spring of 1941, Robert Murphy, a State Department career officer based in Algiers as a consular official, had been involved in negotiations with Frenchmen opposed to the Vichy regime. (The performance of this mission by Murphy and his American colleagues actually marked the first U.S. use of diplomatic status as a cover for secret activities.) Murphy devoted his efforts to preparing the way for support by a resistance movement of Allied landings in French North Africa and, further, for cooperation between the Vichy armed forces in the area and the arriving Allied armies.

Some optimists in the Allied camp even imagined that Marshal Pétain, the aged Vichy leader, might fly to Algiers to cooperate with Allied forces when the day came, but this view rested on the idea that the marshal anticipated the reentry of France into the war on the Allied side; in fact, Pétain, who had established a state that was "fascist around the edges," believed that the armistice had settled matters between France and Germany and that any new French activities would only bring fresh trouble for *la patrie*.

Actually, even French Army and Navy officers who detested the Third Reich and hoped for an Allied victory found themselves caught in a net of "obedience and legality," as one scholarly French diplomat called it, which paralyzed them; Kenneth Pendar, one of Murphy's subordinates, observed that "legalism and hierarchy mean everything to the officers of the French Army and Navy"—even though this obsession with the letter of the regulations ignored the fact that Marshal Pétain was not a free agent acting in an independent country, but the leader of a nation half occupied by an enemy army and constantly under the threat of total occupation. The duty of obedience, the French diplomat observed, "does not extend to the absurd or the absolute"—or, as a French marshal once put it, "blind obedience is for second lieutenants, not for responsible leaders." Even officers who might concede these points felt bound to Marshal Pétain by a personal oath that had been exacted from them.

Aware of many of these considerations, the Americans knew that if they were to have any chance of winning the support of French military officialdom in North Africa, they must keep General de Gaulle and his Fighting French out of the secret and far away from the arena—a fact eminently agreeable to President Roosevelt, who from a distance looked on De Gaulle with deep distaste as a self-appointed spokesman for France and probably a would-be dictator. In casting about for a figure around whom French officers might rally, the Americans came across General Henri Honoré Giraud, a much higher-ranking officer than de Gaulle who had escaped in April from imprisonment in Germany and was eager for action against the enemy. Almost a caricature of the fighting leader, overflowing with *élan,* the general was a tall man with impressively branching mustaches, but, unfortunately, with little feel for politics.

After Torch was launched, the Allies made the disagreeable discovery that "Kingpin," as Giraud had been code-named in all the planning, evoked no obedience from the legalistic local commanders pledged to Marshal Pétain, nor were the Americans themselves welcomed. The marshal expected French officers to resist any invaders, whoever they might be, and that was what most of them did.

At this point an unpredictable event pushed Dwight Eisenhower, the overall commander of Torch, and his deputy on the spot, Mark Clark, into the depths of the French maze. During the middle of October, less than a month before the launching of Torch, a French naval officer named Alain Darlan, while on a trip to Tunisia, had contracted poliomyelitis and been taken to the military hospital in Algiers. Not just another officer, Darlan was the son of Admiral François Darlan, former head of the Vichy government under Pétain and still commander in chief of all French armed forces and the marshal's anointed successor. Having come to North Africa on official business, the "dauphin" saw his son on October 28 and 29, and he then returned to Vichy, comforted by the doctors' assurances that Alain was out of danger. But on November 3 heart and lung complications arose—"The assembled specialists agreed that I was lost," Alain later remarked—and the next day his coffin was ordered. On being informed of the bad news, Admiral Darlan flew back to Algiers, arriving at midday on November 5; next day his son rallied, but the admiral decided this time not to take the optimism of the doctors at face value but to keep watch for a few days and return to Vichy on November 10. In the early hours of November 8, Operation Torch intervened.

Of all the personalities involved in the political drama surrounding Torch, Admiral Darlan stood out as probably the most complex. Short and round-faced, he affected the bluff style of an old sea dog, and his bearing and manner gave few clues to his thoughts. The admiral had never rebelled against his father's meddling in his life, his son Alain later said, but—in a fashion much like that of a very different man, Franklin Roosevelt—Darlan "little by little acquired the habit of making his most important decisions in his innermost self, of carrying them out with a sometimes obstinate determination, while refusing to explain them." He was bitterly anti-British, especially after the Royal Navy attacks on the French fleet in 1940, though he professed respect for the "stubborn [*farouche*] egotism" of the British to which he credited their survival in earlier times of trouble.

During his tenure at the head of the Vichy government, Darlan, like Pétain and Laval, had worked with seeming eagerness with the Germans—"collaborated" was the opprobrious term—and was thus viewed as the enemy by the Anglo-Americans. When the Torch forces came ashore, the Americans took the admiral prisoner, but he refused to make any move to stop the fighting without an order from Marshal Pétain; as it became obvious that the French forces could not continue their resistance indefinitely, however, Darlan yielded to the extent of ordering a cease-fire. After byzantine negotiations with Mark Clark and others—the American general wanted Darlan to order the French fleet to North Africa—and exchanges of telegrams with Vichy, the admiral claimed that Pétain had empowered him to act as he saw fit. Darlan swung over to the American side (because of French hostility to the British, the Allies maintained the fiction that Torch was solely a U.S. operation), declaring that in the name of the marshal he was taking the leadership of the French Empire, in its return to the war against the Axis. This proclamation was an even greater piece of fiction than the Allied story about the makeup of Torch, but it produced many of the desired results—although the French fleet remained in Toulon and the French forces in Tunisia rejected the admiral's orders to turn their guns on the Germans.

By November 13 the harassed Mark Clark had worked out an arrangement whereby Giraud would serve as commander in chief of French forces in North Africa and Darlan "would head up the political and civil end of the government of North Africa." Alain Darlan's attack of polio had by an incredible fluke reversed his father's career, unexpectedly offering him what seemed a bright future. What feelings moved this strange little man? "It is impossible to say with certainty," wrote one colleague from earlier times, "any more than we can know in which of his opposed activities a double agent is acting in accord with his conscience."

Reporting to his official masters, the Combined Chiefs of Staff in Washington, that "the actual state of existing sentiment here does not repeat not agree even remotely with some of prior calculations," Eisenhower stoutly defended what immediately became labeled the "Darlan deal." He had been sickened at the reluctance of the French to work together: "All of these Frogs have a single thought—ME." To Marshall, Ike had hotly written that "I find myself getting absolutely furious with these stupid Frogs." To get on with his job, which he was empowered to manage as he chose, he had countenanced a deal with one of Hitler's leading French collaborationists. He was not prepared for the hurricane of criticism that blew through the British and American press and governmental circles; critics called Darlan "the first quisling employed by the United States" and "a rat used against his masters." The Allies must make no compromise with Vichy, it was said, and if they took up a man like Darlan, what would they stoop to next? Although describing himself as "idealistic as hell," Eisenhower as a traditional soldier placed his emphasis on winning the campaign that had been entrusted to him; he did not expect to be branded a fascist around the world. The storm grew so great that Ike's brother Milton, an experienced journalist serving in the Office of War Information, flew to Algiers to help save his brother's reputation.

Eisenhower also had an unwavering backer at home. General Marshall had picked Ike for the U.S. command in England and supported him for the command of Torch; the chief of staff did not desert his protégé now that a storm had broken. Drawing on all his political sophistication, Marshall went to work on Congress, the press, and administration officials—including the president. "I brought down a group of members of Congress," he said, "particularly of the Senate—very carefully selected men—and explained to them what the situation was and read them a message, a long message I just got from General Eisenhower that day, which explained his point of view at that moment." This move, Marshall commented, "gave us defenders on the floor of the Senate and the floor of the House." Convening a press conference, the chief of staff abandoned tact in favor of an all-out offensive, telling reporters that the deal with Darlan had saved 16,000 American casualties and that criticism of Eisenhower was "incredibly stupid" and might lead to his replacement by a British general; national prestige was thus at stake. Overawed by this onslaught, some (but not all) of the reporters and their newspapers abandoned their criticism of Ike.

With FDR, Marshall produced Eisenhower's long telegram of explanation and insisted that the president support the commander in the field. In response, Roosevelt wrote Ike on November 16 that he fully appreciated "the difficulties of your military situation: I am therefore not disposed in any way to question the action you have taken." But the president enjoined Eisenhower to keep three points in mind: "1. That we do not trust Darlan. 2. That it is impossible to keep a collaborator of Hitler and one whom we believe to be a fascist in civil power any longer than is absolutely necessary. 3. His movements should be watched carefully and his communications supervised." Clearly, the president was unhappy about the deal but did not feel he could take on Marshall and reprove Eisenhower. Here arose in reality a classic clash between the traditional military view of conflict, conservative and little concerned with ideological questions, and the liberal political view that saw war being waged between ideas as well as between nations. From a purely military standpoint, the enemy was the German Army; for the politicians it was Hitler and Nazism. Attempting to bridge the gap, the president, in a thoroughly worked-over statement drawn up for the press, said that he accepted Eisenhower's political arrangements "made for the time being," but declared "the present temporary arrangement in North and West Africa is only a temporary expedient, justified solely by the stress of battle." Americans, said the president, "are opposed to Frenchmen who support Hitler and the Axis." Wielding a heavy editing pencil, FDR revealed his discomfort by seeing that the statement contained the word "temporary" five times in addition to "for the time being."

The vociferous public reaction to the deal with Darlan and FDR's repeated use of the word "temporary" were hardly calculated to imbue the turncoat French admiral with a sense of security. "I am," Darlan wrote to Clark, "only a lemon that the Americans will drop after they have squeezed it dry." But a very different and more rapid end awaited the admiral. For some weeks, diners in Algiers had drunk toasts to his death, and handbills had called for "death to the traitor Darlan!" On Christmas Eve, 1942, the admiral was shot dead by a young man said to have been a member of a group that drew straws to determine which one would free Algiers from tyranny. Darlan's reign had proved temporary indeed. But during it he had received and accepted a characteristic offer from Roosevelt. Whatever Admiral Darlan was, his son had been attacked by polio, and the president had informed the admiral, through Robert Murphy, that Alain was welcome to come to Warm Springs for treatment. FDR always looked on a fellow polio survivor as somebody special.

Admiral Darlan had been dead exactly a month when, as the Casablanca conference was coming to its end, the president stage-managed what amounted to a theatrical production and then proceeded to make the most striking policy statement of the war. It was the time for tying up loose ends and for summarizing the discussions.

Two of the loosest ends flapping about were the separate French entities now associated with the Allies—Charles de Gaulle's London-based Fighting French organization and the Algiers administration, which, after Darlan's death, the Americans had put into the hands of General Giraud as high commissioner. In the aftermath of the Darlan deal, Roosevelt came under strong pressure from American liberals to straighten out U.S. policy toward France and rid it of any taint of grubby expediency (as if Darlan had not been trouble enough, the administration had been involved in the installation of a former Vichy minister of the interior as governor general of Algeria). The obvious answer, and one in which Churchill concurred, was to arrange a shotgun wedding between the reluctant bride and groom; accordingly, de Gaulle and Giraud were invited to Anfa. Giraud accepted the bid eagerly, but the deliberately haughty de Gaulle refused both British and American invitations several times until Churchill flourished the diplomatic counterpart of a shotgun by threatening the general with the loss of British support if he failed to come. Finally de Gaulle arrived on January 22, but he brought his intransigence along, refusing for a while to call on Giraud (who outranked him in the French Army five stars to two).

Meanwhile, Giraud had thrived in the atmosphere of Anfa. He was pleased to find in Marshall an officer who in 1917 had missed serving on his staff by only a few days, and with whom he shared many acquaintanceships and memories; it made a "favorable climate." As for the president, the general was impressed by his "keen eye" and by the fact that he spoke fluent French. (De Gaulle proved less complimentary: "The President's knowledge of French was not very good," reported a member of the general's entourage, and he had difficulty understanding de Gaulle's "classic and sophisticated" speech.) After several talks with the president, Giraud concluded that the American leader was indeed "a great statesman—very clever, very adroit, farseeing."

When de Gaulle appeared at Giraud's villa, he quickly made it plain to his host that he had little use not only for Roosevelt (to whom, indeed, he owed nothing) but for Churchill (to whom he owed everything, including such material support as he received from the United States). He had not wished to come to Casablanca, he said, because he and Giraud "did not need these gentlemen to act as intermediaries"; he would not discuss matters under their aegis. In separate meetings with the two Frenchmen, the president and the prime minister urged them to resolve their differences and in any case to keep in contact. When de Gaulle paid his obligatory call on Roosevelt, Hopkins was startled and amused to realize that concealed behind the living room curtains and prowling the gallery above were members of the president's Secret Service detail "with, perhaps, a dozen Tommy Guns among the group." It all struck Hopkins as something out of Gilbert and Sullivan, but it demonstrated a high-level American distrust of de Gaulle; no such attention and weaponry had been in evidence when Giraud came calling.

Nevertheless, at noon on January 24, Roosevelt, Churchill, and the two French generals appeared on the rear lawn of the president's villa; an unscheduled meeting of the four had produced an agreement that de Gaulle and Giraud would issue a joint statement proclaiming their good mutual intentions. Then FDR suggested a photograph—"American publicity never loses its privileges," Giraud observed—and the four men took seats in chairs on the lawn. Their surprised audience was a crowd of perhaps fifty reporters and photographers who without knowing what story they would be covering had been flown in from Algiers the previous day. There, in front of them in the bright sunshine, they saw the president and the prime minister, Roosevelt seated between Giraud and de Gaulle, Churchill at the end of the row on de Gaulle's left, while cameras whirled and clicked. Then FDR came forth with an inspiration. Would the two generals stand up and shake hands to show their friendship to the world? Obediently they rose, Giraud tall but de Gaulle towering over him, and extended their arms, their hands meeting. Obviously feeling that he was in the clutches of a relentless blackmailer, de Gaulle wore the expression of someone being forced to retrieve an object from an unflushed toilet. But Roosevelt had his photograph. So it is, Giraud observed philosophically, that opinion is made.

After the departure of the Frenchmen came the official business of the moment, the press conference for which the journalists had been brought to Anfa Camp. Following the president's suggestion, the newspapermen seated themselves in a large semicircle on the grass, most of them taking a cross-legged position, from which they stared up at the great men seated side by side before them. Leading off, FDR described the nature of the conference, why the chiefs of staff had been brought together and, in a general way, what they had accomplished. The participants in the meeting, Roosevelt said, had discussed, "I think for the first time in history, the whole global picture." They had made plans covering the "maintenance of the initiative during 1943." Then the president moved onto new ground. Peace could come to the world, he said, "only by the total elimination of German and Japanese war power." The Americans had once had a general named U. S. Grant, who in "my, and the Prime Minister's, early days" was called "Unconditional Surrender" Grant. "The elimination of German, Japanese, and Italian war power means the unconditional surrender by Germany, Italy, and Japan. That means a reasonable assurance of future world peace."

Unconditional surrender? Where had this new doctrine come from? Discussing the question subsequently, Roosevelt described it as having arisen in impromptu fashion. "We had so much trouble getting those two French generals together that I thought to myself that this was as difficult as arranging the meeting of Grant and Lee—and then suddenly the press conference was on, and Winston and I had had no time to prepare for it, and the thought popped into my mind that they had called Grant 'Old Unconditional Surrender' and the next thing I knew, I had said it." If this was indeed the way the president had arrived at the formulation of a war aim and doctrine of the first magnitude—to use U. S. Grant's battlefield ultimatum in western Tennessee (not his meeting with Lee) as an overall policy not just of a nation but of a great Allied coalition fighting a global war—then such casualness would surely represent an act of towering irresponsibility. But, remarkably, FDR's explanation held no truth at all. It seemed to come not from a desire for accuracy but from Roosevelt's continuing fondness for playing the part of the facile, opportunistic amateur; he was a gentleman farmer and he would be a gentleman politician and statesman. The fact that he was a professional politician and had been one all of his adult life he perhaps saw as being softened by this squirish behavior.

Actually the president, in meeting with his advisers during the afternoon of January 7, had used the very words "unconditional surrender." After discussing plans for the Americans' forthcoming trip to Africa, he turned to General Marshall and suggested that after the conference the chief of staff might go to Moscow.

Such an idea seemed not to have entered Marshall's thinking. "What would I be expected to accomplish there?" he asked.

The purpose would be to lift the morale of the Russians, the president explained; he thought that Stalin "probably felt out of the picture as far as Great Britain and the United States were concerned." He intended to speak to Churchill about the advisability of telling Stalin that the United Nations would continue on "until they reach Berlin"; their "only terms would be unconditional surrender." If Churchill agreed with this and other points he intended to raise, then the chief of staff could be the emissary to bear the news to Stalin. But even this was not the first enunciation in Washington of the unconditional-surrender principle; a State Department advisory group had included it among ideas that earlier had been passed on to the president as being worthy of consideration. The formulation of such ideas presented a striking validation of Thorstein Veblen's insight of twenty-five years earlier: Wars fought by democratic societies are seldom ended by negotiated peace.

At Casablanca Roosevelt mentioned the idea to Churchill at least five days before the news conference, because on January 19 the prime minister cabled the War Cabinet seeking a reaction to the inclusion of "unconditional surrender" in the final conference statement. In this message Churchill made the specific point that both he and Roosevelt thought that Italy should be omitted "to encourage a break-up there." In their answer, sent on January 21, Clement Attlee and Anthony Eden—the deputy prime minister and the foreign secretary—objected not to the unconditional-surrender formula but to the exclusion of Italy, whose people ought not to be spared "knowledge of all rough stuff coming to them."

During the two days preceding the press conference, the president had taken time to dictate and edit notes for his remarks; this material included statements about unconditional surrender that were almost identical to those he was to make to the reporters. As he spoke, he held in his lap a sheaf of papers that presumably included his dictated and edited "Notes for F.D.R." The only improvisation was the typical device by which Roosevelt gave personality to his theme—the reference to "Old Unconditional Surrender" Grant. He had discussed the principle with his military advisers (although he had not asked for their opinions of it) and with Churchill, and he had embodied it in written notes. As he sat in his chair in the midday sunshine, proclaiming to the reporters a new and potentially fateful doctrine, he was speaking not off the cuff but from a background of solid tactical preparation (but he had not sought advice from such potentially valuable consultants as students of German psychology). He had planned what he wanted to do, and the British government had agreed with him. He was making a statement to the world and, inferentially, to his own generals: They would arrange no more Darlan deals. No one need fear that as the Allies began to bring the land war home to Germany, they would consider making any arrangements with Hermann Göring or some other alleged moderate leader; nor would any equivalent deal be made with any Japanese. (The most doctrinaire antifascist in the Allied camp, however, took a contrasting view. On November 28 Stalin had cabled Churchill his thought that "the Americans used Darlan not badly in order to facilitate the occupation of Northern and Western Africa. The military diplomacy must be able to use for military purposes not only Darlan but 'Even the Devil himself and his grandma.'" Ivan Maisky, the Soviet ambassador in London, added a comment: "This is a strong Russian proverb." Stalin's statement amounted to a reasonable summary of the thinking behind the "military diplomacy" of Eisenhower and Clark and behind the support Marshall gave it. But even this encouragement from "Uncle Joe," who had no parliament or public opinion with which to concern himself, did not alter Roosevelt's thinking or that of Churchill and Eden.)

However the doctrine of unconditional surrender might be interpreted in practice, the President in proclaiming it, had taken a step having a deeper meaning than anyone was likely to see; he had brought General Marshall and his other military advisers to a crossroads. This was so because of the assumption on which FDR based his reasoning. In the preparatory notes for the press conference, he wrote that unconditional surrender by Germany, Italy, and Japan "means a reasonable assurance of world peace, for generations"; as given to the reporters, the thought stood almost unchanged: Unconditional surrender would mean "a reasonable assurance of future world peace." In the sphere of national rivalries and war, the president seemed to say, all the trouble at the time and into the indefinite future was caused, and would be caused, by the three Axis countries; the sovereign cure was therefore "elimination of German, Japanese and Italian war power."

This was not the way Marshall and the other military leaders had viewed the world when the War Plans Divisions of the army and navy were putting together a national policy to guide them in devising the Victory Program. In the Joint Board report submitted to the president in September 1941, they had, with respect to the military situation, put forward five national objectives: "1) preservation of integrity of the whole Western Hemisphere; 2) prevention of disruption of the British Commonwealth; 3) prevention of further extension of Japanese dominion; 4) eventual re-establishment in Europe and Asia of a balance of power furthering political stability in those regions and future security of the United States; 5) establishment, as far as practicable, of regimes favorable to economic freedom and individual liberty." Three of these points concerned military objectives; the last two set forth the purposes for which military power ought to be used, number 4 putting the point quite clearly, number 5 expressing a hope that ought to be realized "as far as practicable." Number 4, the sort of realistic statement that professional military planners might be expected to make, did not assume that the defeat of Germany and Japan would solve the problems presented by international relations in Europe and Asia, but saw the current conflict as part of the continuing drama of international life; today Germany or Japan might be the disrupter of international harmony, tomorrow other European or Asian powers could be the troublemakers. The United States should use her strength to restore order in

Europe and Asia by a classic means—the balance of power. This was the way to protect and further the American national interest. Marshall and his planners had indeed looked to the "total defeat" of Germany, but they contemplated a military victory that would be followed by the establishment of a balance-of-power situation.

Now, at Casablanca, the president was proclaiming an Allied policy that was exactly the opposite. He presented the elimination of Axis "war power" as a permanent condition—"for generations." Here was no balance of power, no assumption that trouble was a chronic concomitant of international dealings and could not be done away with simply by defeating one or two national states. Europeans had made such a mess with their balance-of-power thinking, FDR seemed to believe, that in the future peace must be maintained by other means—which at this point he did not bring forward. The only objective that would count now would be to win the war by the most expeditious means, because the defeat of the enemy would bring about lasting peace—however that defeat might be achieved. This kind of thinking held more persuasive force than it might have possessed at any other time in modern history because of the extraordinary barbarism of the Nazi regime (even so, the Soviet Union had to be redefined as a country that was, or wished to be, democratic in Western terms).

The proclaiming of unconditional surrender as a war aim did not necessarily surprise Europeans, to whom the United States resembled "a secular church, or perhaps a gigantic sect" more than a traditional nation-state. Like a sect, the United States could operate within the international system with a clear conscience "only if it could remake that system in its own image." Woodrow Wilson had tried and failed; his World War II successor would not repeat his mistakes. But such a view was not restricted to Americans: Clement Attlee's Labour party as a matter of doctrine opposed the balance-of-power principle and in 1943 favored complete disarmament and the long-term military occupation of Germany—hence Attlee's approval of FDR's design for unconditional surrender. The new doctrine also represented a generous response to the feelings of Europeans who could not take a detached view of the war—to a sentiment a British major in the Middle East called "the confident will of whole peoples, who have known the utmost humiliation and suffering and have triumphed over it, to build their own lives once and for all." Albert Camus declared that he and his comrades in the French Resistance never lost sight of "the idea and hope of Europe." In 1943 even Churchill agreed in his own fashion with Roosevelt; his often-stated preferred policy was to support "whoever is killing the most Germans."

The signal sent to Marshall and the other U.S. chiefs was clear, and it offered them a far greater challenge than the British chiefs faced because they constituted the only organized body of advisers the executive had or wished to have. On hearing the declaration of unconditional surrender, General Eaker recalled, everybody he knew said, "How stupid can you be?" But henceforth, the chiefs of staff would be required to look at the world from a political as well as military point of view (in truth, so pervasive was the belief that the Axis constituted the root of all international trouble, the chiefs had already begun the process) and would formulate strategy as subscribers to the civilian aim. In a great irony, by concentrating on destruction of the enemies rather than on victory over them, the U.S. chiefs would be accused, by Churchill and lesser figures, of engaging in purely "military" thinking at the expense of political considerations. Actually, Marshall observed later, nothing except the shortage of landing craft "came to our minds more frequently than the political factors"; the chiefs of staff "talked politics more than anything else." The conference at Anfa Camp represented the crossroads, and—no doubt inevitably—the chiefs followed the president onto the path he had chosen. Thus polio, which had played a leading part in the drama of Roosevelt's own life, had returned through the obscure medium of Alain Darlan to influence the future of the great Allied coalition.

Casablanca was the first Allied conference with the political leaders and all the chiefs of staff present. It was a landmark, because it not only fixed the aim of the Anglo-American war effort but declared the strategy by which it would be achieved—the Mediterranean in 1943, Roundup in 1944. On the latter point, it was up to Marshall now to hold the president in line, to make sure that the British did not seek to evade that commitment, and to see that if they did, FDR refused them aid and comfort.

Wedemeyer's reflections were somber. He felt that Marshall had done a "magnificent job but that he had been almost entirely on his own." To a friend Wedemeyer wrote: "We came, we saw, we were conquered." He later recalled that when he advanced an idea the British disliked, "they swarmed upon me like a bunch of locusts." But they had not converted him to the Mediterranean strategy.

Adherents of a cross-Channel operation had one small victory to carry away from Anfa: The Combined Chiefs of Staff agreed that an independent Anglo-American staff should be created immediately to plan and develop training for such an operation. The resolution referred to the possibility of an invasion in 1943, but this was merely rhetoric, a verbal sop to Marshall and other disappointed Americans. They knew better. They knew that not for at least a year would the world begin to see anything created in the spirit of Grant and Pershing.

After completing this pioneering trip with all its resounding realms of meaning, FDR received a curious acknowledgment of his efforts from the veteran Kansas Republican editor William Allen White. "Well, it is now 60 hours since the Old Smiler returned to the White House from his great adventure," White began. "Biting nails—good, hard, bitter, Republican nails—we are compelled to admit that Franklin Roosevelt is the most unaccountable and on the whole the most enemy-baffling president that this United States has ever seen. He has added a certain vast impudent courage to a vivid but constructive imagination and he has displayed his capacity for statesmanship in the large and simple billboard language that the common people can understand." The editor concluded: "We have got to hand it to him."

CHAPTER FIFTEEN

THE PRESIDENT'S PLUM

In early March 1943 General Marshall treated himself and his wife to a brief vacation in Florida. Having boarded the plane at Bolling Field as the chief of staff, Mrs. Marshall noted, he "stepped out of it at Miami as a rather tired-looking businessman wearing dark glasses." The general had good reason for weariness. Casablanca had not been a pleasure trip, and since coming back from Africa he had been heavily involved in attempting to induce Congress to increase the army's share of the national manpower pool (a task that naturally involved detailed testimony before committees on Capitol Hill); besides, he was suffering from a cold. He was also girding himself for personal intervention in two of the wars in which the United States was engaged—that against the Japanese in the Pacific, and the fierce but separate conflict between the U.S. Army and the U.S. Navy in the same great arena.

The war between the army and navy in the Pacific had special complexity, because in one prime respect the two were firm allies. Each believed that the commander in chief and the Joint and Combined Chiefs of Staff were devoting resources to the war against Germany that could be more profitably used against Japan. But beyond that, strong personal hostilities inflamed the relations of the two American commanders between whom the Pacific had been divided—Admiral Chester W. Nimitz and General Douglas MacArthur.

Although Nimitz possessed his full share of the keen territorial sense with which admirals seem natively endowed, he "was not a quarrelsome man," according to Marshall, and he was much easier to work with than his superior in Washington,

Admiral King. Nevertheless he took his orders from King. As for MacArthur, no one could say that he needed prompting from anybody before putting obstacles in the way of interservice cooperation. He "just took a decided stand" on anything that affected his command, Marshall commented; "there were no concessions on his part whatsoever"—but war, as Anglo-American dealings amply demonstrated, was a matter demanding continual concessions. Yet Nimitz's staff had developed such bitter feelings toward MacArthur, and MacArthur's staff toward Nimitz, "that it was almost impossible to get them together on anything." Although the chief of staff stood up for MacArthur, he regarded the general as the aggressor in the interservice war.

Both as a Pershing man and as a onetime colonel to whom MacArthur, as chief of staff, had denied advancement and the duty assignment of his choice, Marshall occupied a ticklish position in relation to the imperious ex-Philippine field marshal. He devised a twofold solution to the dilemma—to behave with perfect correctness toward MacArthur, and wherever possible to lean over backward to send him help. For the time being, Allied strategy had relegated the Pacific to the official status of a sideshow, and MacArthur resented it; Marshall sympathized with that feeling. This enabled him to turn the other cheek to such MacArthurisms as the fashion in which the general would often conclude a demand for aid: "To deny this request is contrary to the fundamental principles of the art of war." Seldom openly critical of a high officer, Marshall would occasionally allow himself to blurt out in the office, "That fellow MacArthur!" And he might add, "He's got the strongest case of localitis in the Army"—localitis being a field commander's fervent belief that his area is both crucially important and yet thoroughly neglected by the high command. MacArthur's curious inner insecurity also revealed itself in a particularly exasperating habit: When Marshall would send greetings to one of his old friends serving in the Southwest Pacific, MacArthur might hold the message at headquarters for as long as two months before forwarding it. Fully aware of the fact that MacArthur was always on the alert for slights, Marshall rarely allowed any letter for the general to leave the office until he had gone over it himself. Marshall's correspondence with Eisenhower, the other American overseas military proconsul, was cast in a friendly and sympathetic and easy style, almost in the tone that would be used by a father or a kindly uncle. With MacArthur, matters were handled with full regard for all the diplomatic niceties. (Once, when Marshall allowed himself to produce a "stiff reprimand" for MacArthur, a staff subordinate induced him to soften it.)

Roosevelt's support of MacArthur was also not a simple business. During his term as chief of staff in the 1930s, the general had once reviled the president for not offering the army adequate budgetary support. (In this confrontation with Roosevelt, the general had erupted into melodrama: "When we lose the next war and an American boy, lying in the mud with an enemy bayonet through his belly and an enemy foot on his dying throat, spits out his last curse, I want the name to be not MacArthur but Roosevelt!") On another occasion FDR observed that MacArthur was one of the two most dangerous men in America (the other being Huey Long). In addition to these negative points, MacArthur was not a truly professional officer in the nonpolitical sense. He liked the picture of himself as president of the United States, as he began demonstrating more or less openly in early 1943 both in conversations with his staff and in correspondence with Senator Arthur Vandenberg ("'Mac' is certainly not 'running away' from anything," Vandenberg noted in his diary in April). All in all, since chance had decreed that MacArthur be the commander on the spot in the Southwest Pacific when war erupted, it probably seemed a suitably remote arena in which to make use of the self-dramatizing general's talents and experience. Roosevelt and Marshall then had to face the result—MacArthur's continued charges that Washington favored other theaters and deliberately neglected the Southwest Pacific.

To deal with Pacific questions, Marshall convened a conference in Washington. It was partly to collect his personal forces for these sessions that he had gone to Miami Beach (social functions in Washington offered no surcease from care; once, keeping track of the correspondence generated by requests made to him at a single dinner party, the chief of staff calculated that he sent thirty-two letters and several radio messages).

On the first evening of their vacation, as the Marshalls reclined in beach chairs outside their cottage, the general, apparently forgetting that he was not in uniform, objected to a U.S. Coast Guardsman's order that they leave the beach because of a seven o'clock curfew. He said quietly, "I think it will be all right," closed his eyes, and lay back in his chair. In a few minutes a squad arrived, led by a notably overweight petty officer.

Before Marshall could say a word, the leader "let loose a tirade so violent that his whole body quivered like a bowl of clabber." Where did these people come from? Didn't they know there was a war on?

Without saying a word Marshall stood up and headed for the house, pursued by the squad leader who said over and over, "Don't you know there's a war on?"

Marshall turned around to face his unwanted escort. "That is enough," he said. "What is the reason for this ridiculous display? Does it take you and a patrol of six men to tell me we are at war?" Then he walked into the house. But on future days, even with his dark glasses, he would be readily recognized on the street. He had become too great a public figure to be incognito anywhere in the country.

For his part, MacArthur had asked for the Pacific Military Conference, as it came to be called, in response to requests from the Joint Chiefs to see his plans. The meetings were enlarged to include officers from Nimitz's headquarters and also from Admiral William F. Halsey's South Pacific Area, the naval command that operated, under Nimitz, adjacent to MacArthur's Southwest Pacific Area. What the conference quickly demonstrated, apart from the army-navy rivalry, was that the Allied chiefs at Casablanca had bitten off far more in the way of plans than their resources would enable them to chew. With U-boats netting an enormous catch of Atlantic shipping and with operations lagging in Tunisia—the latter thanks largely to the resourcefulness of Field Marshal Rommel—the Bolero buildup was languishing. In the Pacific the Americans had no possibility of assembling enough forces to carry out in 1943 the planned advance to the important Japanese base of Rabaul, at the eastern end of New Britain. After two weeks of meetings, the participants agreed on a more modest program; on March 28 a new, more realistic directive went out to MacArthur, Nimitz, and Halsey.

The drama featured familiar performers: George Marshall and Alan Brooke. This time the action took place in the boardroom of the Federal Reserve Building in Washington, with the British and American chiefs facing each other across a long, polished table. The issue they now debated was not simply operations in the Mediterranean versus Roundup in 1943, or even 1944, but versus Roundup at all—or at least at any definable future time. If, said Brooke, the Anglo-American forces did not continue their offensive in the Mediterranean after driving the Germans out of Sicily (an operation that had not yet been launched), then he saw no possibility of a landing in France. The available forces would be too small, the troops too inexperienced.

Marshall came onto the attack. Now they were "getting to the heart of the problem," he said. He feared that the landing of ground troops in Italy would suck the Allies into a vacuum that would rule out a successful cross-Channel operation. Aside from the bomber offensive adopted at Casablanca the Allies would restrict themselves for 1943 and even 1944 to a wholly Mediterranean policy, thus prolonging the war in Europe and, correspondingly, delaying the defeat of Japan—a state of affairs the American people would not tolerate.

Indeed, agreed Admiral Leahy, who as senior officer chaired the meeting. The Pacific could not be neglected; it was "too vital to the United States."

"The European war must be ended as fast as possible," Brooke conceded, but stopping operations in the Mediterranean after taking Sicily would lengthen the war; only by continuing in that theater could the Allies "achieve the maximum diversion of German forces from Russia."

But, said Marshall, if a maximum effort were made, the United States could have eleven divisions in England by April 1944. Even so, Brooke countered, these forces would be sufficient only to hold a bridgehead on the Cotentin Peninsula, not to move into France. In previous wars, his hearers must remember, "our side" had always had the participation of some eighty French divisions, which was now lacking; an advance toward the Ruhr would leave the Allied armies with dangerously long lines of communications, the RAF could not yet be considered ready to operate on a tactical basis with armies, and the British manpower situation was weak—all of which meant that "no major operation would be possible until 1945 or 1946."

Nineteen forty-five or 1946? Brooke's declaration struck Marshall like a blow. Roundup, he responded, still seemed to be regarded as a "vague conception." Did this mean that the British chiefs looked on operations in the Mediterranean as the key to winning the war in Europe? The whole battle for the landing in Western Europe, it appeared, would have to be fought again.

This discussion, held on the morning of May 13, 1943, formed part of the Anglo-American conference code-named

"Trident." On May 2 and again on May 9, the president had met with the Joint Chiefs to discuss the coming sessions with the British. After the May 9 meeting, Marshall told Secretary Stimson that FDR had accepted "in principle" the position the Joint Chiefs intended to maintain, but the chief of staff nevertheless expressed doubt: How firmly would the president hold to his approval? Stimson shared this fear. "The man from London will arrive with a program of further expansion in the eastern Mediterranean and will have his way with our Chief . . ." If the secretary had seen FDR's marginal notations on a Joint Chiefs memo, he would have felt even greater concern. Next to a discussion warning of the dangers of British action in the Aegean, Roosevelt had written simply: "Spinach."

In his remarks at the opening of the conference in the White House on the afternoon of May 12, Roosevelt did nothing to ease Marshall's mind. Favoring definite action in northwestern Europe in 1944, FDR nevertheless phrased his support in a disturbing way. "Sledgehammer or Roundup," he said, "should be decided upon definitely as an operation for the spring of 1944." Sledgehammer *or* Roundup? What Marshall wanted at this point was not Sledgehammer, the relatively small-scale landing, but a major cross-Channel offensive operation.

And now, the next morning, here was Brooke saying that continuing the operations in the Mediterranean would be "more valuable than building up for a 1944 Roundup which might not even then be possible." Meeting later with his American colleagues, Admiral King pounced on Brooke's comment. All the British wanted to do, it appeared, was drift, undertaking Roundup only when Germany had reached the point of collapse, and if they were not pinned down they would simply continue to "fiddle fuddle" and "limp along." If they would not agree to Roundup in the spring of 1944, the Americans should switch their effort to the Pacific. Marshall offered no disagreement. So often had these positions been taken now, and these rebuttals offered, that the participants almost could have achieved these results merely by reading the minutes of previous meetings.

But at the same time all the chiefs, British and American, realized that they were not members of a debating society, sequestered in their boardroom with unlimited time to play with ideas. They must reach conclusions that could be presented to their political masters. Where Marshall and Brooke really differed was not on the logistical feasibility of mounting

Roundup—although most of the discussion seemed to focus on it—but in their estimate of the resistance Allied attackers would meet from the enemy. "Whoever has not fought the Germans does not know war" runs an old axiom, and Brooke believed that he knew the Germans very well; landings in France would succeed only when the Germans had become much weaker—a state that would come about primarily after more fighting in Russia and also after more Anglo-American activity in the Mediterranean. Marshall expressed greater optimism. Long interested in the use of air power, he felt that, properly employed, it would make an effective Roundup possible with fewer divisions than Brooke regarded as essential. And he saw the operation as a help to the Red Army, not as a move to be made only after the Russians really required no help.

Six weeks before the Trident conference, Marshall had also pointed to another possible dimension of Roundup. He had spoken seemingly in political terms but actually as an orthodox military officer concerned with the shape of the world that would follow the end of the war. If the Allies moved into France only at the finale, he said, and were merely fighting on the fringe of the Continent while the Russian Army was approaching Germany, "there would be a most unfortunate diplomatic situation immediately involved with the possibility of a chaotic condition quickly following." Although neither Marshall nor anybody else advanced this opinion in any recorded discussion held by the Combined Chiefs of Staff, it took its place among the considerations in the argument for the vital importance of Roundup.

The relationship between the United States and Britain had changed since the earlier conferences, even since the meetings at Anfa. American forces had now confronted Germans in a campaign; they had been green and made many mistakes, but in Tunisia, where the fighting had ended just a few days before Trident began, commanders and men had made long strides forward. In manpower and material the might of the United States loomed like a growing mountain. And despite Marshall's worry about Roosevelt's steadfastness with respect to Roundup and ready ear for the flow of Churchill's dialectic, the president now showed interest in working for the earliest possible end to the European war by the classic American means urged by the chief of staff—the great push across the plain of northwestern Europe.

During a Combined Chiefs of Staff session on May 19, the

discussion grew hotter and hotter; Brooke tended to be "easily excited," Wedemeyer said. Finally, not wishing to put on a show of fireworks for the supporting staff members and secretaries, General Marshall suggested that everybody but the chiefs should leave the room; if the discussion was to be frank and forthright, then it should be limited to the principals. Certainly the problem must be solved. "It was the most difficult day of the conference," Brooke noted—which meant that it was rough indeed—but he and Marshall and the other chiefs had what Brooke delicately called a "heart to heart talk," and as the result "at last formed a bridge across which we could meet."

Two days later the chiefs had managed to draft declarations of policy for presentation to the president and the prime minister. As the two political leaders offered their own thoughts on strategy, the generals listened "shivering lest either of them should suddenly put their foot right into it and reopen some of the differences we had reconciled with such difficulty." Fortunately, Roosevelt and Churchill performed well, sticking no feet into anything inappropriate.

A tentative date for Roundup had been established: May 1, 1944. The operation had acquired a new, temporary name—Roundhammer—suggested by Admiral King and indicating its mixed parentage. Working under what Marshall called "terrific" pressure to reach an agreement with the British (the pressure presumably came from the commander in chief), the U.S. Joint Chiefs had agreed to support an operation larger than Sledgehammer but not as large as Roundup. This was Marshall's concession, but he coupled it with a refusal to send any further resources to the Mediterranean, and he insisted that some units be withdrawn from the theater after the conclusion of Operation Husky, the attack on Sicily, for the invasion buildup in England. "Roundhammer" was not destined to last long as a designation. Soon the proposed 1944 operation would have a new code name: "Overlord."

Both Roosevelt and Marshall had done their social best to make Trident a success. The president had taken Churchill, Lord Beaverbrook, and others off to Shangri-La, his simple camp in the Catoctin Mountains, during the first weekend of the conference. An amusing incident occurred as the presidential procession passed through the streets of Frederick, Maryland, home of the legendary or semilegendary Barbara Frietchie. "'Shoot, if you must, this old gray head,'" quoted Harry

Hopkins, and he was able to add the next line but no more: "'But spare your country's flag,' she said." Unable to endure the ensuing silence, Churchill, a great memorizer of verse in his youth, went back to the beginning of the poem and recited it all—a performance he followed by delivering to his captive audience a lengthy impromptu lecture on "the characters of Stonewall Jackson and Robert E. Lee, two of the noblest men ever born on the American continent." After a while, the prime minister recorded, "silence and slumber descended upon the company . . ." The kind of monologue that often exasperated Churchill's own associates when it came in the hours after midnight, the performance was much less familiar to the Americans, and perhaps they realized that the speaker himself had already taken on much greater legendary proportions than the intrepid Barbara Frietchie had ever possessed.

For his part, General Marshall outdid himself as a host, thanks to the work of Frank McCarthy, who had been assigned the duty of arranging a weekend of feasting and relaxation for the visiting British chiefs in Colonial Williamsburg. With the aid of John D. Rockefeller, Jr., who had presided over the restoration of the old Colonial capital, McCarthy produced repasts of peacetime magnificence, built on terrapin, crabmeat, and Virginia ham accompanied by a variety of cheeses and fruit; Rockefeller's butler personally brought from the family estate outside of New York a supply of fresh cream; Merrill Pasco, McCarthy's assistant, came from Washington with bourbon for the visitors' juleps, which were drunk from silver goblets.

Watching Brooke, a fervid bird-watcher, at his favorite pursuit, Marshall thought that his guest's "persistence and his pleasure in the task were very appealing." Air Chief Marshal Portal had a different kind of adventure; having borrowed swimming trunks that were somewhat on the large side, Portal emerged from the pool after a dive without even the protection a fig leaf would have given him. This was the only mishap recorded on what proved to be an eminently successful outing—but a weekend that, however delightful, represented only a truce in the Anglo-American argument. Yet, coincidentally or not, it was in the meeting of the U.S. chiefs back in Washington on the following Monday that Marshall, in a piece of statesmanship, suggested the compromise that led finally to Roundhammer.

* * *

The chief of staff's association with his British friends and fellow debaters did not end with the close of Trident on May 25. When Marshall appeared at the White House late that evening to bid farewell to the prime minister, he found Roosevelt and Churchill working together over a much-edited and retyped draft of the message they intended to send Stalin about the decisions that had just been reached. "We were puzzling what to put in and what to leave out," Churchill said, and finally he offered to take the pages with him, put them into shape on the plane, and send an edited statement back from Gander, the air base in Newfoundland that was to be his first stop. At this psychological moment Marshall arrived. Although he may have been informed earlier that the prime minister wished him to come to Algiers, where Churchill intended to grill Eisenhower about his plans, Marshall was surprised when the president, in response to a suggestion from his visitor, said, "Why don't you go with Winston? You can talk over the Russian communiqué together." This gave the chief of staff only six hours' notice, since he had not intended to travel with Churchill, but he assented—"agreeably," the prime minister said.

What had happened was that Churchill had become an even more zealous believer than Brooke in the idea of an Italian campaign after Operation Husky. Before the end of Trident, he had after all almost "put his foot right into it" by talking against the compromise that had been reached, which—remarkably—had left the great Italian question unsettled. In going to Algiers the prime minister intended by personal argument to win over Eisenhower and his advisers to the Mediterranean project. To demonstrate that everything was open and aboveboard, he wanted Marshall to be on hand. This was indeed a straightforward move on Churchill's part, since in the chief of staff he had chosen the strongest opponent he could have found. Curiously, Stimson feared that Churchill hoped to use the long hours of the trip to convert Marshall to the new Mediterranean view, but such a triumph was hardly possible even for a rhetorician of Churchill's power.

The trip had barely begun when Marshall found himself at work. After laboring vaguely and vainly over the sheaf of scrawled sheets he had brought with him from the president's study, Churchill handed the whole mess over to Marshall. The chief of staff's own associates were familiar with his prowess as a boiler-down, clarifier, and emender of documents but, seeing this side of Marshall for the first time, the prime minister was "immensely impressed" with the flawless draft Marshall gave him two hours later. Not altering a word, Churchill sent it back to Roosevelt, who dispatched it unchanged to Stalin. Essentially a concise summary of the agreements reached by the Combined Chiefs of Staff together with the supporting reasons, Marshall's draft was lucid rather than profound, but to Churchill, never short on hyperbole, it revealed the chief of staff not only as "a rugged soldier and a magnificent organiser and builder of armies—the American Carnot"—but, even more, as "a statesman with a penetrating and commanding view of the whole scene."

Later in the day Marshall demonstrated another kind of resourcefulness, but this time Churchill apparently did not realize what was happening. "I was trying to keep him from bringing up the subject of the Washington conference," Marshall said, knowing as well as anybody that Churchill would at least try to convert him to Mediterranean adventures of one kind or another—matters about which the chief of staff had no intention of debating until he had talked with Eisenhower. Having just read the famous essay on Warren Hastings in a volume of Macaulay he had borrowed from Lord Halifax, Marshall "hurriedly thought up something to talk about" and asked Churchill questions about the effect of Hastings's trial on later procedures in Parliament. This diversionary tactic worked magically; the prime minister went off into a twenty-minute disquisition that not only kept him busy but fascinated his listener. Then Marshall, fishing for a subject, asked Churchill about the circumstances of Rudolf Hess's sensational landing in Scotland in 1941. Again the prime minister "opened up in the most fascinating way," this time luring Brooke into listening. Hess proved to be good for about fifteen minutes' worth of Churchill's time, and at the end of the lecture, making "a desperate grab and in a most impolitic way," Marshall questioned the prime minister about his role in the abdication crisis of 1936, when Edward VIII renounced the throne to marry Wallis Simpson—"It was a marvelous lecture, just marvelous"—and then, to Marshall's great relief, the steward announced dinner, after which would come bedtime. The chief of staff was safe.

Since the Trident discussions had given Eisenhower, as the commander on the spot, an important vote in deciding what operations should follow Husky, the U.S. general found himself the object of concentrated attention when his high superiors arrived in Algiers. Talking day and night, Churchill pressed his case for Italy, holding out the glorious possibility of the capture of Rome. Marshall sang his usual song: After Sicily, operations in the Mediterranean ought to be restricted; Allied forces must be built up in England for the cross-Channel operation in 1944. Trying to talk with Churchill throughout the week the two spent in Algiers, Marshall was met only with monologue; he had "never heard anyone talk like this before." Churchill was a wonderful man, the chief of staff later remarked to Sir Charles Wilson, "but he won't look at things like a man who has been all his life a soldier. I must have facts." Although Churchill persuaded himself that he had converted Marshall to the idea of an Italian campaign, the Algiers discussions ended in an agreement that Eisenhower should make the decision on the basis, as Marshall desired, of the German reaction to the invasion of Sicily.

He "wished to emphasize," Marshall had carefully said, "that we must exercise great discretion in the selection of an operation to follow Husky, calculating closely what would be required and basing calculations upon an accurate knowledge of what was to be faced." When Anthony Eden observed that Turkey would probably come into the war on the Allied side "when our troops had reached the Balkan area," Churchill rushed in to say that he did not advocate "sending an army into the Balkans now or in the near future." Plans for Italy had presented problems enough without getting Marshall stirred up over vague talk of activity in the Balkans. "I like Eisenhower and Marshall," Eden noted in his diary, but the Americans certainly showed an "instinctive distrust" of any kind of operation that might divert the Allies from the cross-Channel invasion.

One day in Algiers sixty seasoned war correspondents, half of them American, half British, gathered in a large room in the Hotel St.-Georges for an off-the-record interview with General Marshall. Although his approach to press conferences differed utterly from the complex bantering, teasing, sometimes lecturing style perfected by Roosevelt, who if he wished could say almost nothing but enchant the reporters, the chief of staff had developed a distinctive method of his own. Most of the newsmen present were encountering it for the first time. A door opened, the reporters stopped their chatter, and the general walked in. "To save time," he said quietly, "I'm going to ask each of you what questions you have in mind." He turned to the first correspondent and then went systematically around the room, nodding politely, until all sixty had presented their queries—challenging questions, ranging from matters of strategy to technical details of the war in all theaters. Next the general gazed into space for half a minute or so. Then for forty minutes he delivered what one correspondent called "a smooth, connected, brilliantly clear narrative that encompassed the war"; good enough to constitute a chapter in a book, it included a full answer to every question the reporters had asked. As the crowning touch, when Marshall made any point that related to a reporter's question, he looked directly at the man who had asked it.

The reporters were bowled over, some enthusiastically saying they had just encountered the greatest military mind in history, others marveling at the mass of specific detail Marshall could recall, all exclaiming that it was the most brilliant interview they had ever attended. "You must understand," Marshall said later in response to such praise, "I was bound to know what these things were." Not only was he deeply involved in the subject, he had received excellent training from his many sessions before committees on Capitol Hill. "You see," he explained, "I'd been doing this with Congress all the time without any notes, because I found that the minute you began to read you lost your audience."

In spite of his disclaimers, Marshall in this press session had displayed a formidable grasp of facts and a striking ability to build them into a clear and convincing picture. "He is an expert at talking to the press," noted Eisenhower's friend and aide, Captain Harry C. Butcher. "His memory is uncanny." This triumph with the reporters contributed to a stream of admiration for Marshall, one that both in Washington and across the United States gave every sign of swelling into a tide. The general might still have to weigh in with his opinions on such questions as the draft of eighteen-year-olds, but more and more the feeling in Congress could be summed up, as one reporter put it with reference to the issue of manpower, "'If Marshall says he needs men, he does,' say Congressmen. 'You can trust him.'" Those working in the War Department did not disagree. "It is not enough to say that he meets his responsibilities," one officer declared of the chief of staff. "He rises with them. He seems to have no mental ceiling." Stimson thoroughly agreed: "You've no idea the admiration I've had during all these months in witnessing the constant mental growth of General Marshall."

On Capitol Hill the slogan suitable for any military problem was said to be "Trust to God and General Marshall." Revealing more than many persons realized, this maxim proclaimed that, in contrast to its behavior before Pearl Harbor, Congress had gone to the other extreme and decided to leave broad military questions to the presumed experts, personified by the chief of staff "who stands so completely above factions and feuds." Although he had been chosen by Roosevelt himself, Marshall could be openly admired by persons who hated FDR, war or no war; in fact, without in any way seeking such a position, the chief of staff faced the flattering but unnerving possibility of becoming a cult figure—a state of affairs that would soon pose a peculiar problem for the President.

During these months of 1943, Roosevelt faced and dealt with another problem, small but ominous. Grace Tully had noted signs of "cumulative weariness" in her boss—the dark circles that would not fade from under his eyes, the slump that came readily to his shoulders as he sat at his paper-strewn desk, the increasing tremor of his hand as he lit a cigarette. So bad had the shaking become that one day FDR asked Miss Tully to buy him a coffee mug twice as big as his usual one, so that he would not spill the contents.

In the early 1930s a trim and precise young woman named Mona Nason, "plucked from the Maine woods" just out of her teens, had come to Washington to work as a government stenographer at a salary of $1,400 a year. Having done extremely well in a high school office course, she soon revealed secretarial skills beyond those expected of stenographers and found herself assigned to the General Staff. One day in the autumn of 1942 her boss gave her the news that he had recommended her to succeed the retiring Maude Young as General Marshall's personal secretary. It seemed an overwhelming idea to this "prim New England girl with braids."

Although she had been a prizewinner in stenographic competitions in her home state, Miss Nason, on a friend's advice, enrolled in a night course in stenography, in addition to classes in English, French, letter writing, and filing. When the day came for the move into Marshall's office, the young woman was "as ready as I could possibly be." As she sat in front of the big, hand-carved walnut desk used by every commanding general or chief of staff since the 1880s, she quickly discovered that Marshall knew just what he wanted to say when he began dictating and could produce a two- or three-page memo almost without pausing and with no changes; one day with the aid of a stopwatch Miss Nason and a fellow worker calculated that the general dictated at the very fast pace of 160 words a minute. But Marshall proved to be an easy man to work for in one sense—everyone knew what he expected: perfection. "He was a perfectionist himself," Miss Nason said, "and he did the others the honor of expecting *them* to be perfect too." This, she felt, "was one of the secrets of his success." An unspoken feeling pervaded the office: "Times were hard and everybody wanted to do the very best he could."

The officers posted to the General Staff during the period just before Pearl Harbor and in the months afterward made up an outstanding group, many of them "Marshall men" from Fort Benning, including Omar Bradley, J. Lawton Collins, Robert L. Eichelberger, Harold "Pinky" Bull, Maxwell Taylor, and Robert N. Young. To Miss Nason, "the officers who came to that office were the crème de la crème." Frank McCarthy was the first of the reserve officers, and on the morning after Pearl Harbor he was joined by a fellow alumnus of the Virginia Military Institute, Merrill Pasco, a Richmond lawyer who came in the wake of Pearl Harbor to help keep the chief of staff's office manned around the clock. Marshall later professed ignorance of the background of these staff officers and other VMI alumni who rose to high positions; even so, he warned the school's alumni secretary "not to brag about it." In Miss Nason's view, the VMI connection called for no apologies from anybody. The tone of the office, calm and highly professional and even "elegant," seemed to her exactly right. Starting with the chief of staff himself, "they were Virginia gentlemen." From the top down, office relationships were "dignified, cool, and mutually respectful."

Miss Nason proved a capable and completely discreet personal secretary for Marshall. But the Fates had surely indulged a playful mood the day they presented George Marshall with a personal secretary named Mona Nason; a man who had trouble with names like "McCarthy" had little hope of getting those tricky *n*'s right. One day she took advantage of an opening to attempt a double mission. As she was leaving Marshall's office, he asked her to "send in that fellow—what's his name? Carty? Carter? McCarty?" Turning around, Miss Nason said in her precise way, "Sir, his name is McCarthy—M-c-C-a-r-t-h-y—and, sir, my name is Nason and not Mason."

Laughing heartily, the general said, "What have I been calling you?"

"Well," she said, "sometimes you call me Nason, and sometimes Mason, but it's *Na*son, sir."

When Miss Nason came out, she took a bit of pleasure in telling Colonel Robert Young, the secretary of the General Staff, that she had just enlightened General Marshall on two counts.

"Well, hell, Mona," Young snapped, "while you were at it why didn't you tell him that *my* name is Young and not Taylor?" (The "Taylor" whose name Marshall misused was another staff officer, Colonel Maxwell Taylor.)

On another occasion, General Wedemeyer, whose name is pronounced as if spelled with two *d*'s, arrived to see the chief of staff. Marshall called out "Come in, *Wee*demeyer" when he saw his subordinate at the door. (It was well known that the chief had a deep-seated, almost phobic aversion to seeing callers push open his door, stare at him, then withdraw and close the door behind them; in fact, the door bore a sign ordering anyone who opened it to WALK IN.) Hearing Marshall say "Weedemeyer," Miss Nason, who greatly admired the chief of staff but was not at all reduced to fear and trembling by him, said firmly: "General, his name is '*Wedd*emeyer'!"

Miss Nason not only admired General Marshall, she sensed a special quality in his outlook, which she saw as "a sense of mission—that he was the one to do this work." He seemed born to be chief of staff, and not simply because of his air of quiet command, which everyone felt ("In an ordinary business suit," one top official said later, "he could walk into a cocktail party full of high-level U.S. and foreign dignitaries dressed to the collars in gold braid, and the minute he entered, their chattering din would turn to whispers"). "General Marshall was the man for the hour," Miss Nason believed, "as Churchill was the man for the hour. He fitted the job like a walnut fits its shell."

The general not only fitted the job, he had the capacity to take a long and wide view of his responsibilities. Although in the aftermath of Pearl Harbor he had seemed rather detached about the evacuation of Japanese Americans from the western states, in early 1943 he moved to redress what he realized had been the grave constitutional wrong done these people. His concern led to programs written and put into effect by an already well-known war correspondent and military writer, a reserve lieutenant colonel named S.L.A. Marshall (no relation to the chief of staff), in which the army recruited the all–Japanese-American 442nd Regimental Combat Team, opened up jobs outside the relocation camps, and promised U.S. citizenship to those who had been born in Japan. The chief of staff invested the creation of the fighting units with special importance, because he felt that after the war the Japanese Americans would probably encounter great trouble from their fellow citizens.

In performing another assignment for the chief of staff's office, Colonel Marshall mentioned to the general that "not even the General Staff had dependable data on our fighting operations."

Looking surprised, the chief of staff asked, "Then what is the historical section of the General Staff doing?"

"Sir," the colonel replied, "it is still bogged down researching World War One."

Although perfectly courteous, General Marshall showed no particular reaction to the colonel's revelation that no historians were covering the present war. But one June morning not long afterward, the younger officer met in a cubicle on the top floor of the Pentagon with two other officers to begin planning the capture of the battle history of the U.S. Army in World War II. Responsive as usual to the needs presented to him, "the soldier I admired above all others," as Colonel Marshall called him, had taken appropriate action.

The great swell of feeling about General Marshall—a tide fed by persons like Mona Nason, by Washington officialdom, by the national press, by most of the public, and by the army itself—soon presented President Roosevelt with a strange kind of problem. In June a Pittsburgh judge serving on active duty as a colonel suggested in a letter to FDR that on July 4 Marshall should be made "General of the Armies," as Pershing had been. Marshall had earlier scotched such talk, but now, as the summer progressed, the president found himself in a position to bestow a plum that, for any soldier, would far outrank any promotion.

For a year now, Marshall and Brooke had waged their battle over the cross-Channel issue, but to most observers the matter seemed to be settled. Although the scope and timing of Operation Overlord might still be debated—Marshall and others might still fear that the British would try to keep their commitment as elastic as they could—few doubted that, if the Americans kept pushing, 1944 would see an Allied attack on the German Army in Western Europe. What shape would the structure of command take for this operation, which almost certainly would grow into the greatest Allied effort of the war? Would the commander come from Britain or from the United States?

Earlier in 1943 the command of Overlord had appeared to be Churchill's plum to award. Since an American held the supreme post in the Mediterranean, northwestern Europe seemed to represent Britain's turn at the top. Besides, the operation would be mounted in Britain. Not long after Casablanca the Allies had appointed a British officer, Lieutenant General F. E. Morgan, to the newly created position of chief of staff to the supreme commander (designate), but in mid-1943 Overlord suffered from the lack both of adequate funds and of a flesh-and-blood supreme commander. (One American newcomer to COSSAC—the acronym both for General Morgan and for his organization—suspected that Morgan's men also lacked drive because the British did not really believe in the invasion; he found himself in "a world of interminable politeness—and inaction.")

The Britons at the top, however, had no more doubt than the American leaders that the Allies would have to carry out a Roundup-Overlord operation to finish off the enemy. Just a few days after returning from Anfa, Churchill had told Brooke of his wish that the CIGS take command of operations across the Channel when the time came, and on July 7 the prime minister confirmed the offer. Though surprised at the rumor when it reached his ears—not from Brooke, who never spoke of the subject—Admiral Leahy later thought the CIGS "undoubtedly would have been a good commander." Brooke, eager, "too excited to sleep" after the talk with Churchill, turned the possibility over and over in his mind. Two days later the successful landings in Sicily brightened all the Allied prospects—the European Axis was finally undergoing attack at home.

From August 14 to August 24, as Husky—the Sicilian campaign—was drawing to a close, the American and British political leaders met in Canada, at the Chateau Frontenac in the old upper town of Quebec. Prior to the launching of Husky, Marshall had promised the British that if Sicily were taken quickly enough, he would approve an attack on the Italian mainland. Since the Sicilian campaign had required only thirty-eight days, the chief of staff not only agreed to a leap onto the Italian peninsula but proposed that it take the form of a daring amphibious landing at Salerno—because he felt that this move would offer the greatest possibility for bringing the Mediterranean campaign to a quick end.

By the time the Quebec conference opened, General Morgan and his staff had prepared a plan for the Overlord assault—a five-division seaborne landing supported by two airborne divisions. This was not yet the grand operation dreamed of by American strategists since they had first thought about intervention in Europe. The small scale came not from a controlling strategic concept but from the shortage of landing craft, particularly LSTs (for tanks); until more of these specialized vessels were in prospect, Overlord must remain only an "attendant lord." Unfortunately for Overlord's devotees, the Combined Chiefs at the Quebec conference (code-named "Quadrant") approved Admiral King's plan for a major amphibious drive through the Central Pacific toward the Japanese homeland—and once he was promised such priceless jewels as landing craft, the admiral would hardly release them except on the direct order of the president.

During the years since the "planes" conference of 1938, Roosevelt had amassed an impressive record of overruling his chiefs of staff when his strategic and political judgment required it. In just the past year he had come forth with three decisive interventions: the decision to stage Torch; his order, against the advice of the chiefs, to sustain British nonmilitary imports at the rate of twenty-seven million tons a year (thus using shipping for which the chiefs had other designs); and his move at Trident to reduce Roundup to Roundhammer. Earlier, he had repeatedly disagreed with his advisers on questions ranging from aid to Britain in 1940 and 1941, to basing the Pacific Fleet at Pearl Harbor, to establishing an air force in the Caucasus (Marshall proposed the plan, FDR turned it down). Now, at Quadrant, when the Joint Chiefs wished him to stand with them in coercing the British into signing on the dotted line with respect to Overlord—giving the operation virtually unrestricted top priority in the European theater—FDR called them off. His own policy forbade him to force the British into a corner, although in reality he felt ready to proceed with the operation. Events had long since destroyed his faith and hope that air power, which before the war had seemed economical and direct, might do the job. His eager generals had for a year and a half pulled and tugged at him to approve the delivery of the knockout blow; realistically, he had restrained them until he felt sure such a blow could be landed.

By the summer of 1943, thanks in good part to the ULTRA code-breaking operation, which had managed after long effort to crack the Germans' deadly Shark naval cipher (and thanks also to the British Admiralty's long-withheld acknowledgment that one of their own naval ciphers was not secure), the Battle of the Atlantic had turned decisively in the Anglo-Americans' favor; the lifeline from America to Britain had now become safe. The great American productive machine produced the other major development favoring Overlord. By the summer of 1943 the U.S. war economy was running in high gear, pouring out matériel and munitions in an unprecedented flood—just as the president had always anticipated. As in many other spheres of national life, FDR took a jaunty view of production problems. Planners are "always conservative," he told Marshall in a White House discussion on August 9; the economy or the armed forces could always do more than they thought, he liked to say, "if they really try." If they wanted ships, they could find or produce ships; if they needed landing craft, one way or the other they would get them. The United States was now reaching the position, dramatically different from that of a year and a half earlier, when she could pay a strategic Paul in full without robbing a strategic Peter. Roosevelt could preside over a strategy aimed at bringing the war home to both Germany and Japan.

His handling of the whole question of strategy had been utterly in character. He had approached the war after Pearl Harbor in exactly the way he had approached the national economy in 1933—the *what* took precedence over the *how*. American forces must become directly involved in the war against Germany—that was his prime objective. If his generals wished to try Roundup and even Sledgehammer and could carry the British with them, then he would approve such a move. But if the British dissented, then the U.S. forces must find other places in which to grapple with the Axis armies. No sulking or crying over spilt milk was allowed. When the situation had ripened, the Allies could make their climactic move. Though it was not quite ripe at Quebec, little more time would be required. (When accused by the British of rigidity in their strategic thinking, or of conservatism by the president, the U.S. chiefs could point in their own defense to the unprecedented complexity involved in properly arming and equipping forces that had to be carried thousands of miles to the theaters in which they would operate; improvisation, though perhaps an attractive approach, could not take the place of timetables.)

Even though General Morgan offered a limited plan, the statesmen and military staffs at Quadrant approved it as submitted. It would now move into the stage of concrete preparations—and the fact that the assault would not be as large as once contemplated did not mean that the ensuing operations would take place on a lesser scale; Overlord, after all, was to be the knockout blow delivered to the Wehrmacht, and its commander would become the supreme Allied field general of the war. In a conversation at Hyde Park prior to the opening of the Quadrant conference, Roosevelt and Churchill had taken up the question of command. According to the prevailing Anglo-American theory, the leadership of an operation should come from the country furnishing the majority of the forces. By the time of Quadrant it was obvious that Britain had reached her peak, her economy and manpower strained to the limit, whereas the American effort was still expanding; in many ways, the great American boiler was just beginning to bubble. In the assault phase of Overlord, the British Commonwealth and the United States would contribute more or less equal strength, but from that point on the operation would take an increasingly American tone (just before receiving Churchill, Roosevelt had even instructed Marshall "to have a preponderance of U.S. divisions available on the target date").

Which American should command Overlord? Neither Roosevelt nor Churchill seems to have entertained any doubts on this question. A year earlier, after the London meetings that buried Sledgehammer, the prime minister in a cable to the president had suggested that General Marshall be "designated for Supreme Command of Roundup." Now that the moment seemed to have arrived, Churchill made the same offer with respect to Overlord, and by the time Quadrant came to its end, everyone took it for granted that the post would go to the U.S. chief of staff. According to one of Brooke's recollections, Churchill told him on August 15 that Roosevelt had "pressed hard" for the appointment of an American, although the prime minister himself later stated that he had suggested the idea to the president. (It was a bitter dose for Brooke, a sensitive man behind his supercilious mask; looking down upon the Plains of Abraham from the Citadel of Quebec, he saw "all that scenery . . . swamped by a dark cloud of despair.")

The decision to appoint Marshall supreme commander of Overlord was not made public at the time, but the president nevertheless gave the press a piece of official news about the chief of staff. Marshall's four-year term came to an end on September 1, and Roosevelt announced that he would continue in office indefinitely; editors greeted this news with no surprise and a great deal of approval. "He is a great soldier," said one paper, "and we salute him for a grateful people." Meanwhile, in as quiet a way as she could, Mrs. Marshall was packing up and moving the family's furniture out of Quarters One at Fort Myer, sending it a few pieces at a time down to Leesburg in a little trailer covered by a sheet of green canvas to conceal its contents. (Highly eclectic in nature, this furniture consisted of her own antiques, various inexpensive pieces picked up at auctions, and items like vases and rugs bought by the general in China.) Soon, Mrs. Marshall believed, the old Revolutionary War house in the picturesque town would change from a weekend retreat to her full-time home while her husband served across the Atlantic as the supreme commander of Overlord. For his part, Secretary Stimson, who just before the opening of Quadrant had urged Roosevelt to insist on an American commander for Overlord, was more than delighted. "The shadows of Passchendaele and Dunkerque still hang too heavily over the imaginations of the British leaders," he wrote, whereas Roosevelt, "far more fortunate than was Mr. Lincoln or Mr. Wilson," had at hand a general who was not only perfectly fitted for the post but was known by everybody to be so. Stimson also told the president that Marshall's influence both at home and with the British would be enhanced if he were promoted to General of the Armies (a title that for American soldiery "carries a unique distinction far beyond Field Marshal, of whom they have seen many—some of little consequence").

Suddenly, however, a storm blew up. Anybody aware of Marshall's feelings knew that he, like Brooke—or any other general—would prize the invasion command above all other posts (although he always refused to suggest assignments for himself, one day, pressed by Stimson, Marshall finally conceded that "any soldier would prefer a field command"). But that point did not seem to be understood by the anti-New Deal publisher of the civilian but influential *Army and Navy Journal,* which in September declared editorially that "powerful influences" were working to get rid of General Marshall—in effect, to kick him not upstairs but thousands of miles overseas. A few days later a similar publication joined in the outcry. Scenting New Deal blood, antiadministration congressmen added their howls to what quickly became a bizarre chorus. A complex conspiracy theory rapidly evolved, in which the chief malefactors were Churchill, with his sinister British influence on Roosevelt, and Harry Hopkins. If Marshall were out of the way, the idea seemed to be, Churchill could control Allied strategy and Hopkins could install as chief of staff his friend General Somervell, who as an engineer officer had been associated with Hopkins in WPA projects.

Administration foes saw it all with paranoid clarity: Roosevelt intended to take advantage of the war not only to win the election in 1944 but to create a global New Deal; Marshall would simply be sacrificed to this doubly sinister cause. Shaping the whole affair, readers in one city were told by their local daily, was "Hopkins' slimy hand." Whoever cooked up the story, Robert E. Sherwood concluded, "wanted to create the maximum amount of public alarm and was smart enough to know that the best way to do that was to inject the fell name of Hopkins, the White House Rasputin." Some of the "plot" stories, said Joseph Harsch of the *Christian Science Monitor,* came from men in the War Department itself—officers who feared for their positions "when any major change is proposed in the war-making machinery in Washington" and consequently rationalized their objections to this change as resistance to improper outside—British—influence. The commotion reached across the Atlantic, prompting the Germans to declare over Paris radio that the Americans had made a sort of Hitlerian change at the top: "General George C. Marshall, the U.S. Chief of Staff, has been dismissed. President Roosevelt has taken over his command." Marshall sent the dispatch to his friend Hopkins with an amused query: "Dear Harry: Are you responsible for pulling this fast one on me?" When shown this note, Roosevelt seized his pencil and added a correction: "Dear George—Only true in part—I am now Chief of Staff *but* you are President. FDR."

One opponent of Marshall's move to Overlord even approached the eighty-three-year-old General Pershing. Although in the first war the general of all people had not looked on command of a great field force as a post inferior to the chief of staff's position, this was indeed a different war, and from Pershing's quarters at Walter Reed Hospital came a letter written, or at least signed, by the old general urging the president not to transfer Marshall to "a tactical command in England." Aside from this inadequate description of Overlord, however, the letter contained an observation about Marshall with which few could quarrel: "I know of no one at all comparable to replace him as Chief of Staff."

FDR answered Pershing in a small masterpiece, the kind of graceful cameo that showed his political craftsmanship at its best: "You are absolutely right about George Marshall—and yet, I think, you are wrong too! He is, as you say, far and away the most valuable man as Chief of Staff." But, FDR went on to point out, the new command would not be "a mere limited area proposition" but would, he thought, include "the whole European theater." As his main point, showing that he understood Marshall perfectly, the president declared that "I think it is only fair to give George a chance in the field—and because of the nature of the job we shall still have the benefit of his strategical ability. The best way I can express it is to tell you that I want George to be the Pershing of the second World War—and he cannot be that if we keep him here." FDR could hardly have made a more telling point: Pershing surely did not want his protégé Marshall to be the March of the Second World War.

But Pershing's argument was shared by much of Congress, the press, and the public, and by the other members of the Joint Chiefs as well, all of whom felt and said that Marshall was simply too valuable to lose from Washington. Leahy, King, and Arnold each had a private word with FDR, but, not content with that, King told newspapermen—one of them the well-known columnist Marquis Childs—to inform their readers how much Marshall was needed as chief of staff. Acknowledging that the question was "none of my business," Harold Smith, the able and conscientious director of the budget, told his "tolerant and considerate boss," the president, that "just the thought of moving General Marshall to some other post gives me a sinking feeling"; Smith hoped that there was "nothing to the rumors." And in a warning to FDR that the West Coast would be unhappy if Marshall became "submerged as a front line General," the the "safety chairman" of Pasadena, California, declared literarily: "We on the Pacific Coast realize this is a war for keeps and don't want the 'General to die at Dawn', so this is our 'Message To Garcia'." A woman in Mt. Carmel, Illinois, said she and her neighbors were "shocked and grieved and resentful" at the thought of losing General Marshall as chief of staff, partly because he was a strong man who would see to it that the wily British did not "shove our men out into the worst fighting and save their own men." "The more I think of the deal that General George C. Marshall is getting," wrote a man in Los Angeles, "the mader [*sic*] I get."

Looking for a way out, Roosevelt and Hopkins, with Marshall's faithful supporter Stimson, hoped to induce the British to agree to the expanded command Roosevelt referred to in his letter to Pershing, in which Marshall would function as an Anglo-American supercommander over both the Mediterranean and Overlord. Picking up such a rumor, the *New Republic* declared that it would be absurd to regard the change as "in any way a demotion"—precisely the reaction Roosevelt had hoped for. Determined "not to embarrass the President one way or the other" and believing that "he must be able to deal in this matter with a perfectly free hand," Marshall thanked Stimson but said that he did not think the British would agree to such a proposition. Indeed, however much Churchill might admire Marshall, he could hardly consent to placing an American general over all his own commanders, even if he liked the idea, any more than Roosevelt could have agreed to a British supercommander.

Marshall had been put in a strange position: The great national faith and trust in his wisdom and integrity stood in the way of the move both he and Roosevelt hoped to make—although FDR was acting more out of a sense of fair play than out of personal preference. All the evidence that congressmen trusted him far more than the president only increased Marshall's embarrassment. "I could get many things, if I asked for them, which he couldn't"; more than one Democratic or Republican leader "would ask if I wanted it or if I were speaking for the President." Not surprisingly, the president sometimes resented suggestions of his own advisers that Marshall do the talking on Capitol Hill. Even so, it appeared as the weeks passed that Marshall would shortly take command of Overlord activities, and on this assumption he began to choose various generals and colonels to accompany him.

In the midst of all the stir, Mona Nason carefully made up her own mind. It became clear to her that if Marshall received the great task of commanding Overlord, she should offer to serve with him. After much deep thought she approached him one day as he sat at his bare desk in front of the big portrait of General Pershing with his red sash. If the chief was appointed, she said, she wanted to accompany him to Europe.

Marshall was "visibly touched" by her offer, but he proceeded to point out problems the change would pose for her. "Of course you know it would mean a cut in your pay," he said. "You would have to get into uniform. It would be dangerous."

"I know that, sir." She assured him that she was not afraid and would still like to go. Then she said, "Sir, I suppose you've had offers from many of the others."

Quietly, almost sadly, he said, "No, you and Colonel Sexton are the only ones."

Knowing the distance Marshall's austere style of behavior could place between himself and an associate, Miss Nason said with her Down East candor, "It's difficult for people to offer because you're so reserved, sir."

Raising his voice slightly, giving it an edge, Marshall said, "I *have* to be, or they'd walk all over me."

As if the September-October hubbub had not made enough noise, on November 6 a Democratic senator from Colorado could not resist the temptation to attack Roosevelt through use of General Marshall's name. Declaring that "the New Deal is dead," Edwin C. Johnson called on his party to draft Marshall as its candidate for president in 1944. Listing the general's virtues, which ranged from being "a very great soldier" to being "a fine Christian gentleman," the senator called him "the man of this tragic hour." When told that rumor held Marshall to be a Republican, the senator could not believe it; reporters checking the general's biographical sketch in *Who's Who* found no party affiliation. But the congressional elections in 1942 had yielded substantial Republican gains, and the 1943 state and local elections just four days earlier had produced Republican victories, leading Johnson and other senators to look for a way around a fourth-term nomination for FDR. A Tennessee Democrat in the House of Representatives, the impressively named J. Percy

Priest, fired back at Johnson in an attack cleverly deploring attempts to drag both Marshall and MacArthur into "partisan squabbles." It was, he said, unfair to embarrass these "two great soldiers and generals" in this fashion. Evidence that MacArthur was embarrassed by efforts to involve him in presidential politics was indiscernible, but Marshall's reaction was clear beyond question. Horrified, he immediately drafted a statement for Stimson to make at a press conference; it declared unequivocally that the general would "never permit himself to be considered as a possible presidential candidate." When Stimson delivered these words to the reporters, the air rushed out of the trial balloon hovering above Capitol Hill.

The president still had not told Marshall that he was to command Overlord, nor had he gone all the way in supporting the operation as the supreme event its strongest proponents had always envisioned. FDR liked to defer hard-and-fast decisions as long as possible, to let causes ripen, and he would wait on one more great event. For a few further weeks he would hold on to his great plum—which, fortunately, was not perishable.

CHAPTER SIXTEEN

THE WHITE CLIFFS OF CAIRO

One autumn day in 1943 Captain McCrea, the White House naval aide, presented to the president his new assistant, a career navy man named Bill Rigdon whom he had known from prewar days on the battleship *Pennsylvania.* A native of Statesboro, Georgia, Rigdon was introduced by his full name: William McKinley Rigdon. FDR's eyes twinkled, and when Rigdon said that he had a brother named Lincoln, the president observed that their father "must have been a most courageous man."

Rigdon quickly learned that McCrea had brought him to the White House as part of a replacement team. The captain was soon to take command of the new battleship *Iowa,* and his assistant had asked to go along with him; the president's new naval aide would be Rear Admiral Wilson Brown, who had served Roosevelt in the same post in the 1930s and, much to FDR's envy, had departed to take command of the Atlantic Fleet. A small, sturdy man who held the rank of warrant officer, Rigdon was an experienced stenographer, a skill not only useful for the naval aide's assistant in the White House but essential for travel with the president; FDR did not take women on his long wartime trips, and Rigdon would serve as his personal secretary. One of his important duties would be the keeping of the log. Thus during the evening hours of Thursday, November 11, 1943, he began the record of a presidential mission whose hazards and logistical complexities would make the journey to Casablanca resemble a fishing trip.

Rigdon's first entry reported the fact that at 9:30 P.M., in "the utmost secrecy," Roosevelt and his party had left the White House for a drive to the marine base at Quantico, Virginia. At

10:38 P.M. they boarded the yacht *Potomac*. Admiral Brown did not conceal his fears for the president's safety. He fretted about "the submarine menace in the Atlantic and Mediterranean; the new destructive glider-bomb that was raising havoc against shipping in the Mediterranean; attack by air throughout the Mediterranean while traveling in helpless transports and the ordinary risks of air travel in proceeding anywhere beyond Cairo." Even with the most severe censorship, rumors of the president's whereabouts were almost certain to be picked up by Axis agents who lurked in every port of call. The best the admiral could do to comfort himself was to point to the great contribution the trip could make to "teamwork for the war and for the postwar period."

Roosevelt felt the same way. As the world's leading proponent of personal diplomacy, FDR had reached out to Churchill in 1939 and with him had built a personal alliance that had no modern precedent between the heads of great powers; but for two years now the president had hoped to turn the Big Two into the Big Three, to bring Joseph Stalin within range of his smile and his talk, yet he had always met Stalin's refusals: The Soviet premier must direct operations, the situation on the front was tense, his colleagues would not allow him to leave, he could not be absent "for even a single day." How true were these evasions? No one could really be sure, any more than anyone knew what happened to the tons upon tons of lend-lease supplies that were handed over at the gates of Russia as if the whole country were one vast private estate to which deliverymen were not admitted.

In any case, 1943 had not proved a good year for the cause of unity between the Anglo-Americans and the Russians. Roosevelt and Churchill had performed the unpalatable task of telling Stalin that Roundup would be delayed to the latter part of the year, and then, even less pleasant, they had been forced to tell the Soviet premier that the invasion would not take place in 1943 at all. Besides that, the Allies had had little choice but to suspend the hazardous convoys from Britain to North Russia; FDR had argued for them as strongly as he could, but the weather and German U-boats, surface raiders, and aircraft based in Norway simply took too great a toll. The Russians complained darkly and bitterly both about Western indecisiveness with respect to Roundup and the refusal, as they professed to regard it, of the British and the Americans to maintain the convoys. A diplomatic rift also opened over what seemed to be Soviet designs on Poland. But for the Red Army, 1943 had thus far proved a glorious year, with the final defeat of the German Sixth Army at Stalingrad, and in July and August the repulse of the major German armored offensive at Kursk.

Now that he held some aces of his own, Stalin showed more readiness to come to the table with the Western leaders. His messages began to indicate that a meeting of the Big Three might, after all, prove worthwhile. In May 1943 Roosevelt sent the Soviet premier a "personal note" suggesting a "meeting of the minds" between himself and Stalin only, "on your side or my side of the Bering Straits." A good idea, Stalin answered, but not just yet. Churchill thought this cozy tête-à-tête not a good idea at all, and protested; Roosevelt explained, not altogether convincingly, that he had envisioned this meeting as merely a preliminary to a full-dress conference of the Big Three.

Stalin now suggested that the Russian situation at the front was so acute that if a meeting was to take place, it would probably have to be at Astrakhan or Archangel. From this followed an extensive three-way correspondence about possible sites in which Stalin offered a series of *nyets* to Asmara, Bagdad, Cairo, Fairbanks, Scapa Flow. Only one place would do: Tehran, which Stalin insisted on because all three participating states had diplomatic representation in Iran. Roosevelt objected that Tehran would pose constitutional problems, because bad flying weather might make it impossible for him to sign and return legislation to Congress within the required ten-day period. The Soviet premier, who had his own view of constitutional matters, declared that on the insistence of his "colleagues" he must keep in continual contact with the Soviet Supreme Command, a need Tehran could meet "since there are wire telegraph and telephone communications with Moscow."

After Roosevelt stuck to his point in subsequent messages, Stalin told Cordell Hull, who had flown to Moscow for a conference of foreign ministers, that "he did not see why a delay of two days in the transmission of any state papers could be so vitally important, whereas a false step in military matters was not a grammatical error which could be subsequently corrected but might cost thousands of lives." Finally, after Stalin suggested that perhaps Molotov would have to take his place at any meeting, Roosevelt found a lawyerly solution to his constitutional dilemma and Tehran became the venue (FDR even wrote

Stalin that if he had to veto a bill he would fly to Tunis to meet the messenger from Washington and then return to Tehran). Stalin's quiet little threat had turned the trick, because both the president and the prime minister regarded the need for a Big Three meeting as urgent. Before the conference even began, the marshal, as Stalin had called himself since the victory at Stalingrad, had shown the Western leaders what sort of player they were up against.

The Western Big Two also agreed to meet at Cairo for joint planning and for sessions with Chiang Kai-shek. The road to this Cairo conference had also been rocky. Bubbling over with plans for activities in the Mediterranean—notably an assault on the German-held island of Rhodes—Churchill had pressed Roosevelt for a meeting of the Combined Chiefs of Staff at which such projects could be discussed. Marshall drafted a reply for the president, declaring him "not in sympathy with this procedure," which would only result in putting "the heaviest form of personal pressure on General Eisenhower," who had declared himself opposed to such ventures. On October 22 the prime minister telegraphed FDR: WHATEVER HAPPENS, WE HAVE GOT TO MEET SOON.

At the same time the U.S. chiefs were debating whether it would "be wise to ask the Ruskies Staff to meet with us," as Admiral Leahy put it; Marshall opposed the Russians' becoming formal members of the Combined Chiefs for an interesting reason—he "felt certain the Russians would feel that we were endeavoring to penetrate their strategical and operational plans"; besides, "it would be next to impossible to reach final decisions with such a variegated group." Instead, he suggested in a message drawn up for FDR and Churchill to send to Stalin that a Russian military representative sit in on Anglo-American staff meetings and take notes for home consumption. Churchill rejected this idea, declaring that such a representative "would simply bay for an earlier second front and block all other discussions" and that the Anglo-Americans surely had the right to control the destiny of their own forces.

Finally, after much discussion, one problem solved itself when the Russians bowed out of any participation in the conferences at Cairo on learning that Chiang Kai-shek would be present. "Due to some reasons, which are of a serious character," Stalin said euphemistically, "Mr. Molotov, unfortunately, cannot come to Cairo." The "serious character," of course, came from the fact that the Soviet Union was not at war with Japan and wanted no trouble from that quarter. The Cairo conference, code-named "Sextant," would begin on November 22.

The production of a mammoth enterprise such as the Tehran conference—code-named "Eureka"—called for the kinds of logistical labors used in creating military campaigns. After the leaders had managed to choose the site, advance parties had to fly there to supervise the work of making it suitable for the chiefs and their delegations. Since much of the travel would be by air, the Air Transport Command had to draw up arrangements for providing planes, scheduling, security, and routing, and for accommodating members of the delegation en route. The planning staffs produced guides containing detailed instructions for the travelers; the air force investigated flying conditions so that excessive altitude could be avoided; medical teams administered inoculations. Besides officers, all sorts of enlisted personnel—security men, clerks, typists, communications specialists, and messengers—were put on orders. Reams of classified records likewise had to make the journey and, because of the information they contained about future operations, had to be guarded beyond all possibility of compromise; if the papers could not be removed from the planes at stops, officers and enlisted men had to stand guard at all times. Having been told to bring every paper that might have any bearing on the proposed agenda, the secretary of the U.S. Joint Staff Planners decided to play it safe by packing up eight boxes, each as big as a foot locker; "the more I thought about it," he said, "the more convinced I was that almost any phase of the war might be brought up for discussion." Papers being worked on after the boxes were packed were carried in briefcases nicknamed "albatrosses" because their bearers could never let go of them until the destination was reached. The U.S. military group for Tehran numbered 107, with the president's party adding about twelve, depending on the phase of the trip (Lieutenant Franklin D. Roosevelt, Jr., for example, joined the travelers for a few days in North Africa, but, unhappy at being away from his ship, persuaded his father to relieve him of his duty as a temporary aide).

At 3:36 in the morning, Friday, November 12, the *Potomac* anchored off Cherry Point, Virginia, near the mouth of the river whose name she bore. Five miles away, out in the bay, members of the president's party could see the great dark shape of the

U.S.S. *Iowa,* one of the new class of superbattleships that were called 45,000 tonners but actually displaced 58,000 tons, which would carry them to Africa. The president's traveling companions included Harry Hopkins, Admiral Leahy, Admiral McIntire, Pa Watson, and Lieutenant Commander George Fox, his masseur. But the group lacked one person who had strongly wished to be included. When FDR had told his wife about the forthcoming meetings with Chiang Kai-shek and Stalin, she asked to take part in them. It was not that she was afflicted with wanderlust—she had recently come back from a long and complex trip across the Pacific to Australia and New Zealand, with stops at such outposts as Christmas Island, Bora-Bora, Tutuila, and Guadalcanal. In her old role as traveling eyes and ears for the president, revamped to fit wartime needs, she had acted as a goodwill ambassador in the British dominions and had visited U.S. bases, hospitals, and rest camps. It had been a grueling trip in military aircraft, trucks, and jeeps, with hops made at all hours; she had seen, she judged, 400,000 service men, and she had returned exhausted physically and mentally.

Her travels had "left a mark from which I think I shall never be free," she wrote. To all the young men who had been maimed or killed, society owed a full reward: "a peaceful world in which there exists freedom from fear both of aggression and want." Now that the emphasis in the Allied camp had turned from staving off defeat by the Axis to achieving victory efficiently, at Cairo and Tehran questions of policy would likely receive answers that could well determine whether the sacrifices by the young men had brought the better world for which they struggled, or whether, once again in the world's history, the suffering and dying had won immediate goals but had not received their full reward. If she were at her husband's side, she might make a difference.

Perhaps wishing to have no importuning voice in his ear or hand pulling at his sleeve, FDR turned down Eleanor's offer to accompany him to Cairo and Tehran. No women would be there, he told her. Far from deaf to the kinds of points she made with him, FDR, after teasing or argument and, frequently, delay, would often act in the manner she desired. But at Sextant and Eureka he wanted to be on his own.

The president was not the only high official to feel the force of Mrs. Roosevelt's ideals. In the 1930s her visits to CCC camps, coal mines, schools, folklife centers, and almost every other kind of institution had made her a sort of national ombudsman or court of last resort for people who felt oppressed; with the coming of the war she had evolved into a military inspector general without portfolio. As such, she did not believe in wasting time by raising issues with subordinate officers. From information and impressions picked up through her innumerable contacts and in her continual travels came a variegated stream of personal queries that she sent directly to the chief of staff, signed in her oddly tentative hand. As soon as one of her letters was clocked in, it was flagged with a special slip of paper; General Marshall required that the letter be acknowledged immediately and the matter investigated at once. Mrs. Roosevelt pulled no punches. Writing for instance about USO camp shows, she informed the general that they were "second rate" and left a bad taste in the mouths of the men. Her travels took her everywhere in the non-Axis world, as suggested by her concession to Marshall that "Bob Hope was highly spoken of, although the men on Galapagos were disappointed that he did not come there." Replying to this complaint, the chief of staff described new types of organization for traveling shows and offered Mrs. Roosevelt the information that "the authors of 'Oklahoma' are at this time rewriting the script of their show, simplifying the production for use overseas."

Although giving specific attention to problems encountered by any person in the service, Mrs. Roosevelt in an era of segregation put special emphasis on the troubles of black soldiers, such as complaints that the post theater at Carlsbad Army Air Field discriminated in its seating arrangements, and that the post exchange refused to allow black soldiers to eat inside the building. After a "telegraphic investigation" General Marshall reported that these complaints were not well founded—"the seats reserved for the colored soldiers" were actually quite desirable—but to make absolutely sure that the reports were false he was dispatching a War Department inspector to Carlsbad. (Before the United States entered the war, Marshall himself had once gone, incognito, to a southern army town to check on the recreational facilities for soldiers; finding none, he was led by the absolute bleakness of the scene to set up the organization that later became the USO. And often, when driving in civilian clothes, he would pick up hitchhikers or soldiers waiting for a bus and chat with them about anything that was on their minds.)

While Marshall was on the Sextant-Eureka trip, Mrs. Roosevelt wrote him to pass along a proposal by the noted black tenor Roland Hayes that a chorus of two hundred black GIs who had accompanied him in two concerts at the Royal Albert Hall be returned to the United States for a concert tour. Agreeing that here was a chance to give due recognition to black soldiers, the first lady told Marshall that the blacks "have something to gain in the war." Although acknowledging the merits of Hayes's proposal, General McNarney, acting in Marshall's absence, turned down the idea because he thought it unwise to return to the United States any group of men who had served overseas only briefly. But even though the ombudsman or inspector general could not always guarantee results, she was assured of a very careful hearing at the highest levels of the army. Marshall saw to that.

The president was the commander in chief, the chief strategist, and at Sextant and Eureka he would survey the scene from the mountaintop; the first lady, back home, would go on working her way through the valleys.

At nine o'clock Friday morning, November 12, the *Potomac* came alongside the *Iowa* to transfer the presidential party; FDR used his special gangway, which had been rigged from the after sun deck of the yacht to the battleship's main deck, to board the big ship in his wheelchair. He was greeted by the skipper of the *Iowa,* his friend Captain McCrea, while the *Potomac* sailed away to remain out of the world's sight for a week, as if Roosevelt were on a holiday cruise as in the long-gone days of peace.

Marshall, Arnold, and King, and an imposing array of accompanying officers, had boarded the *Iowa* the previous afternoon from King's flagship, the U.S.S. *Dauntless,* which had once been the yacht of the automobile-making Dodge family. Thus the entire American strategic directorate had now gathered in one vulnerable spot. The *Iowa* would be escorted by an antisubmarine screen of three destroyers, which would be relieved at two points along the way by other groups of three. The battleship herself was fast, her 212,000-horsepower engines enabling her to reach thirty-two knots; she cruised at twenty-five. Two escort carriers in the Atlantic provided air cover.

Captain McCrea and his staff had performed their own work thoroughly. Everybody from Hopkins to the president's valet, Arthur Prettyman, was met by an assigned escort from the ship's crew who showed him to his quarters. Each person received a form indicating his cabin and phone number, the mess to which he was assigned, his abandon-ship station, and his action station. Overall the battleship in her high-echelon areas had turned herself into a seagoing luxury hotel. The guests received lists of records in the ship's library—classical and romantic (heavy on the latter), popular and jazz—and of the new books available, including a large assortment of current fiction (Hervey Allen, James Hilton, Sinclair Lewis, Helen MacInnes) and nonfiction (politics, education, biography, and history). One of these had a title, at least, of high relevance: *We Cannot Escape History*. "My fellow citizens: We cannot escape history"—Abraham Lincoln had said it, and his successor on board the *Iowa* certainly knew it too. Indeed, he displayed no intention of escaping history and every intention of making it.

Because of the president's infirmity, the navy since the 1930s had installed a variety of special "cruise gear" on any ship he used, one set of it now being kept on the West Coast, the other at Norfolk, Virginia. On the *Iowa,* FDR took up residence in Captain McCrea's in-port quarters, the skipper moving up to his sea cabin for the duration of the voyage. A private elevator was put in so that the president could move easily in his wheelchair from one deck to another; ramps built over the coamings and deck obstructions likewise furthered his mobility. A bed a foot longer than the standard length was provided, and the bathroom was fitted with a tub with metal railings for him to grasp and with a toilet bowl raised to the level of his wheelchair. Since he disliked the standard-issue canvas shower curtains, his bathroom was brightened with a more colorful one. His staff even saw to it that a favorite old leather reclining chair was placed in his quarters. As for food, Bill Rigdon had quickly learned that the boss posed no problem at all: "Give him corned beef hash for breakfast, and coffee in his big cup, four and a half inches in diameter, and the day was well started." No problem with FDR's tastes, but that oversize coffee cup, as Tully had seen, represented trouble of another kind.

The members of the Joint Chiefs were assigned quarters more or less on the basis of seniority; Leahy berthed in the chief of staff cabin, Marshall in the flag (admiral's) cabin, and King in an ordinary officer's stateroom (the admiral declined McCrea's offer of one of his two sea cabins). As a member of FDR's entourage, Leahy dined with the president, Hopkins, and the aides in the flag mess; Marshall and the other generals and admirals messed separately, thus creating essentially civilian and military separate tables. Marshall, still wary of casual social contacts with the seductive FDR, no doubt found this arrangement most satisfactory.

With fueling completed at 10:20 in the evening of Friday, November 12, Captain McCrea prepared to depart Hampton Roads. But Roosevelt insisted on a short delay. As an avid sailor, he professed to share the old salt's aversion to inviting bad luck by beginning a voyage on a Friday; accordingly, the *Iowa* did not weigh anchor until six minutes after midnight. After dropping the pilot two hours later, she stood out to sea, rendezvoused with her three escorting destroyers (one of which, the *William D. Porter,* would on the following day create an incident unique in American presidential annals), and increased her speed to twenty-five knots.

Bearing her array of statesmen, strategists, commanders, and high-level planners, the *Iowa* plowed eastward through heavy seas. On Sunday, the second day out, the weather cleared, and after lunch the commander in chief was wheeled to the deck just outside his quarters to observe antiaircraft exercises. Supplied with cotton for their ears, FDR and his companions watched the gun batteries put up the kind of impressive curtain of fire that would greet any attacking enemy planes. Suddenly an alarm clanged, the *Iowa* changed course as abruptly as a battleship could, and over the loudspeakers a voice cried: "Torpedo defense! This is not a drill!" At the same time the shock wave from an underwater explosion hammered the ship's hull. From the bridge above the deck where Roosevelt sat, an officer shouted, "It's the real thing!"

Worried, Harry Hopkins yelled at FDR, asking whether he wished to go inside. Instead, the president called for his valet: "Arthur! Take me over to the starboard rail. I want to watch the torpedo!" This response was exactly what anybody who had known Roosevelt for a long time would have expected; he always showed extraordinary coolness in the face of physical danger. In February 1933, when Giuseppe Zangara killed Mayor Anton Cermak of Chicago with five shots meant for Roosevelt, FDR's nerve had held throughout the evening—not only while he was surrounded by crowds, "to whom nothing but courage can be shown," as one of his assistants said but later when he sat with his intimates; not even "the twitching of a muscle, the mopping of a brow, or even the hint of a false gaiety" suggested that

that this evening had anything extraordinary about it; FDR had simply been as his easy, confident, normal self. Ray Moley, the assistant, felt that he had never witnessed anything more magnificent. To a man who many years earlier had looked assassination in the face, a torpedo attack on a giant battleship no doubt seemed a diverting but relatively minor business. But always alive to such a possibility, the Secret Service agents guarding the president had made careful plans to lift him into a lifeboat; because he could not walk, agents were always close at hand.

Fortunately, the single torpedo, which exploded a thousand yards astern of the *Iowa* in the turbulence stirred up by the ship's abrupt evasive maneuver, did not signal the presence of a U-boat. Instead, the sneak attack had been launched by the *William D. Porter,* which had been using the battleship as an aiming point in a drill. (Originally blamed on a short circuit, the release of the torpedo was later determined to have resulted from a spectacular case of carelessness.) Enraged, Admiral King was not immediately concerned with the specific cause of the launching of a live torpedo. He and his navy had abased themselves not only in front of their commander in chief but in the presence of their ancient foes, the U.S. Army. If a yardarm had been handy, the luckless skipper of the *William D. Porter* might rapidly have found himself swinging from it—except that the president would have intervened. As it was, when he learned that King had already prepared a message informing the *Porter*'s captain that he was summarily relieved and that "he should get a boat and come over to the *Iowa,*" FDR told King to withdraw the order. The skipper had won a reprieve, but his chances of rising to flag rank under King's regime had surely become indiscernible. As the most practical result of the torpedo incident, the escorting destroyers quit using the *Iowa* as a practice target.

"I doubt," noted Hopkins, "that the Navy will ever hear the last of it."

On Saturday, November 20, at 8:09 in the morning, the *Iowa* dropped anchor at Mers el-Kébir, the "great harbor" of Oran in Algeria. In a new procedure for going ashore, the president was lifted into the *Iowa*'s motor whaleboat as it hung in the port davits; the boat was then lowered into the water and it proceeded to the pier. FDR was met by two of his sons, Colonel Elliott Roosevelt and Lieutenant Franklin D. Roosevelt, Jr., and by a delegation of Allied dignitaries led by General Eisenhower, the theater commander. Accompanied by Ike and by his sons, the president entered a waiting sedan for the fifty-mile drive to La Senia airport for the flight to Tunis, where the presidential party would spend the night. Like everybody else along the complex path from the White House to Cairo and Tehran, Eisenhower's people had made scrupulously careful arrangements for the entertainment and transshipment of the travelers, even to the point of producing a printed guide to the ruins at Carthage.

After a flight of three and a half hours, the three C-54s carrying the president, the Joint Chiefs, and their aides and supporting staffs arrived at El Auoïna airport, twelve miles northeast of Tunis. From there, FDR was driven to Eisenhower's local *pied-à-terre,* a villa previously used by the Germans and called, Roosevelt noted, "the Casa Blanca—most apt." Eisenhower, the complete host, also turned over a small cottage near Carthage to Marshall and King. "Outspokenly delighted" at the offer, the two men spent part of the afternoon walking over the barren plain where Carthage had sat two thousand years earlier. Then they had an evening in which to relax while the president played host at dinner to Eisenhower.

One of the attractions drawing Roosevelt to a stay in Tunis was the opportunity to take a long close-up look at the commanding general of the Allied forces. In his characteristic way, he would do this without appearing to make a point of it. If George Marshall did become commander of Overlord, then Ike appeared a likely successor in the chief of staff's chair; and if the pressures to keep Marshall in Washington proved too great to be resisted, FDR might well pass the coveted Overlord plum to Eisenhower, who had already displayed a remarkable flair for promoting an inter-Allied spirit and creating an inter-Allied team. Certainly the Overlord command, the greatest prize an officer might hope for, could not be awarded lightly.

Admiral King had the question much on his mind. When Ike dropped in at the cottage to freshen up before dining with the commander in chief, King in Marshall's presence brought up the matter by saying—certainly with no beating about the bush—that the president wished to give the supreme command to Marshall but that the other Joint Chiefs wanted him to stay in Washington. Listening to this surprising speech, Marshall "remained completely silent; he seemed embarrassed." As King recalled the evening, Marshall "said *nothing.*" As often as he had met with Marshall, the admiral nevertheless could still show surprise that the chief of staff did not enter a discussion concerning his professional future—the kind of talk Marshall actually would have only with his wife. Undeterred, King plowed on, declaring to Ike that he was "the proper man to become the supreme commander for the Allies in Europe." When Eisenhower arose to depart for the Tunisian "White House," King walked him to the front door of the cottage, saying, "I hate to lose General Marshall as chief of staff, but my loss is consoled by the knowledge that I will have you to work with in his job." Now it was Eisenhower's turn to suffer embarrassment, since Marshall had never said a word to him about his probable next assignment and even now made no comment.

Actually, Eisenhower had developed his own realistic hope. He did not want to become chief of staff and he did not expect to be given the supreme command of Overlord, but the position of ground commander for the invasion—the same role General Alexander had performed in the Mediterranean—seemed a reasonable expectation. (In a conversation with Hopkins, Ike's friend and confidant Captain Harry C. Butcher gave FDR's influential associate some substantial food for thought: Not only did the army need Marshall in Washington because of his "remarkable acumen and diplomacy" in dealing with Congress, but if he were to receive the command of Overlord it would take him at least six months to get the "feel" needed to administer the application of land, sea, and air power to the enemy, whereas Ike through direct experience had already developed this indispensible quality.)

The president had hoped to fly from Tunis early the next morning, but postponed his departure until evening when Eisenhower declared that a daytime flight might bring on an attack by German fighters. The sixteen-hour delay took on special significance, because it meant that Roosevelt would spend an entire day in close company with Ike. The general gave the president a tour of battlefields that perhaps had seen clashes between Romans and Carthaginians and more recently had provided the arena for heavy fighting between Allies and Germans, as he explained how Allied breakthroughs at Medjez el-Bab and Tebourba had produced an almost immediate collapse of the enemy.

When the party stopped for a roadside picnic lunch, FDR engaged in a bantering conversation with Ike's Anglo-Irish driver, Kay Summersby, whose romantic relationship with her boss was at least a half-open secret. Calling her "Child," a form of address he often used with young women, the president seemed charmed by her and by Telek, the Scottie dog whose ownership she shared with Ike and whose presence stimulated FDR to tell stories about Fala. (The president fared better with Telek than General Marshall had on a post-Casablanca visit to Eisenhower's headquarters in Algiers. On that occasion the poorly trained and willful dog leaped onto the chief of staff's bed, squirted a puddle on the maroon silk coverlet, and then, before Harry Butcher could grab him, bolted up to the head of the bed and lifted his leg on the pillow. Having subjected the most disciplined soldier of the age to these unwarranted acts not only of indiscipline but of outright lèse majesté, Ike could do little more than disloyally tell Butcher: "Get that goddamned dog out of here!" Miss Summersby seemed to feel that Marshall's appreciation of her role was not much higher than his opinion of Telek's performance.)

During the lunch interval, Admiral Brown, while walking across a plowed field, picked up a horseshoe and took it over to the car where Roosevelt sat with Ike and Miss Summersby.

"Mr. President, this ought to be good luck for somebody," the admiral said.

"Gosh!" exclaimed Ike, leaping from the car with what Brown saw as "instant appreciation of a tactical opportunity." Turning to the admiral, Ike said, "Let's you and me have our picture taken with it and the President." An accompanying army photographer duly complied with the general's wish.

At one point, FDR remarked to Eisenhower that he dreaded the thought of losing Marshall from Washington but went on to say, "Ike, you and I know who was the chief of staff during the last years of the Civil War, but practically no one else knows, although the names of the field generals—Grant, of course, and Lee, and Jackson, Sherman, Sheridan, and the others—every schoolboy knows them." Looking ahead, the president expressed his worry that "fifty years from now practically nobody will know who George Marshall was. That is one of the reasons why I want George to have the big command—he is entitled to establish his place in history as a great general." To this candid bit of thinking out loud, Eisenhower—though the possibility of his going back to Washington had him "sweating it out in big drops"—responded that he was a soldier and would do his best wherever the government might send him. But the president himself did not yet know where that would be. He would not have much more time to make up his mind.

On taking up his quarters in one of the comfortable villas surrounding the Mena House Hotel at the foot of the Pyramids, where the Cairo meetings were to be held, Colonel Charles Donnelly, secretary of the U.S. planners, found the arrangements not completely ideal. The food and service were excellent, but flies abounded; worse still was the stench of burning camel dung, which, since it was the cheapest and most accessible fuel, the servants used for cooking their own meals outdoors, just under the windows—"but it did help," Donnelly said charitably, "to take our minds away from the flies."

A forty-seven-year-old reserve officer who had graduated from Michigan State, Donnelly had served with the Joint Chiefs only since the end of June, when he had reported for duty in the drab old Public Health Building, where the JCS had taken up permanent residence after the Federal Reserve Board declined to give up its elegant marble palace next door. The building was a busy place, housing most of the committees and agencies that worked under the JCS—bodies dealing with strategic and logistic planning, intelligence, communications, munitions production and allocation, transportation, meteorology, new weapons, civil affairs, and postwar problems. The building continued to be the headquarters also of Sir John Dill and other members of the British mission, together with their secretariat and planning staffs.

Donnelly quickly realized that "high-level war planning is an awesome responsibility," because "the success or failure of the plans and decisions determines the future welfare of the nation and, more immediately, the lives of the participants in combat." He also learned that the whole business had to be conducted in an impersonal way: "The war had been going on long enough to determine with considerable accuracy what losses of men and matériel could be expected in a particular operation." What then followed was a purely mathematical calculation. In human and material terms, would the operation prove to be cost-effective? Would the projected gains "be sufficient to offset expected losses and leave enough margin to make it worth while"? The staffs had to make plans on the basis of numbers, not of individual human beings.

At Cairo, Donnelly would find himself sitting in on meetings of the Combined Chiefs of Staff at which such speculations would be carried on at the highest levels. In one of his first moves, he paid a call on his British opposite number, Colonel Arthur Thomas Cornwall-Jones, who in both looks and personal style strongly resembled the eminent actor Alec Guinness. When Donnelly told "CJ," as Cornwall-Jones was known, that he had been with the JCS only five months and had become secretary of the Joint Staff Planners less than seven weeks earlier, CJ offered his full help. Although observing that the British and American governments had different axes to grind and that each man owed his first loyalty to his own Chiefs of Staff, CJ explained that certain times arose when "to expedite matters, as secretaries we should be frank with each other, always with the understanding that any confidential matters would be kept strictly between ourselves." In CJ's view, the secretaries had considerably higher responsibilities than the recording of events. When they saw that their superiors had become bogged down in mutual misunderstanding, they could discuss the question frankly among themselves and devise some way of breaking the impasse. "Then we would approach our respective committeemen, suggest a certain course of action which would prejudice neither side, and indulge in private gratification as we watched negotiations end in agreement." Sometimes, as Donnelly soon found, the disputes arose from causes no deeper than the different shades of meaning given to some simple word. When, in seeking aircraft or other matériel, the British submitted their "demands" to the Americans, they were slow to grasp the fact that "requests" would earn them a much friendlier hearing.

Even now, after two years of full American participation in the war, Donnelly felt, like many a U.S. representative before him, that in the delicate art of negotiation the Americans still had much to learn from their allies. The thorough British preparation for meetings was demonstrated by the presentation of a "cockshy"—a target to be thrown at—a designation the British gave, with light irony, to the draft of a proposal behind which, in fact, they would all unflinchingly stand; the actual playing at cockshy would be done by the disunited Americans. Besides the maintenance of a solid front before foreigners, this British success drew on still other sources. An American novelist caught part of the essence: "When you get around a table with them, you shake hands with Sir Gordon Fewks, KCB. Then you shake hands with Field Marshal Sir Guy Douglas Jones-Smyth-Jones, KCB, CBS. Then before you know it, there they are, right in control, telling you what to do exactly. You must do this and you cawn't do that, really, old thing. You may have a few simple ideas of your own, but they always get lost somewhere, and you mustn't hurt the feelings of the British. Sometimes you wouldn't have known we had won the Revolution."

Donnelly ascribed much of the British superiority to one specific factor, their willingness to take the risk of including a broad group of names on their need-to-know list. "When they were trying to swing us to their point of view in some particular matter," they would bring up the question in a number of different Allied committees and discussion groups. Not having been briefed on the subject or included on the need-to-know list, U.S. representatives would sometimes express a view opposite to the official American position—"leading to our embarrassment when the British would say, 'Why, your Admiral X on the Combined Munitions Committee thought it was a splendid idea when it was discussed with him recently.'" Lacking any foreknowledge, poor Admiral X had no inkling that he had ventured onto thin ice. Even such a high-level personage as Hap Arnold found his footing giving way beneath him as he "got talked into a commitment to furnish the British with 300 C-47 transports for a Far East operation" before his logistics experts informed him that the arrangement was out of the question. "It took a couple of months to get him off this hook." Of course the British practice of spreading sensitive information among a wide group had its dangers, but at the time these did not make themselves felt.

Despite the decisions reached at Quebec, General Marshall and the other U.S. chiefs approached the Cairo meetings burdened with their familiar worries. A staff paper produced in early November declared that "the British, always extremely cool toward Overlord, have repeatedly stated the conditions which must exist before Overlord can be mounted. They feel that it is doubtful that all these conditions will be met." Some dedicated Anglophobes on Marshall's staff even believed that the British looked on the Bolero buildup in England as merely a gigantic deception, in which the Americans played the role of the deceived party. The British, they thought, would be willing to see the great buildup carried to its completion—at the expense of the American effort against Japan—even though the Bolero troops would never see battle.

As the Sextant conference opened, the head of the U.S. military mission in Russia dealt the old Roundup-first stalwarts a totally unexpected blow. Major General John R. Deane, who had gone from the General Staff to Moscow, reported that the Soviets seemed to have lost their obsessive concern with the second front in Western Europe. Their recent successes against the Germans, he felt, had convinced them that they could end the war quickly, and at Tehran they therefore might argue not for Overlord, planned for six months in the future, but for a stronger Allied push in Italy and "some venture in the Balkans." Although Deane qualified his report by calling it merely an impression, it horrified the War Department disciples of Grant and Pershing, including the chief of staff himself. If the Russians and the British teamed up to urge a new Mediterranean strategy, what chance would Overlord have? Even before receiving Deane's message, the Joint Chiefs had informed the president that they regarded a "Balkans-Eastern Mediterranean strategy" as unsuitable. At a meeting with the JCS aboard the *Iowa* en route to Africa, the president said amen to this argument and told the chiefs that during the first few days of Sextant the U.S. delegation should "definitely stand on it." In another session on the *Iowa* four days later, Roosevelt observed with regard to "U.S. policy on nonparticipation in operations of eastern Mediterranean-Balkan area" that the Soviet attitude would be important.

Marshall spoke up. "We must see the question of this Balkan matter settled," he said firmly. "We do not believe that the Balkans are necessary. To undertake operations in this region would result in prolonging the war and also lengthening the war in the Pacific." A million tons of supplies stockpiled in Britain would go to waste through "going into reverse"; logistical lifelines stretching as far west as the Rocky Mountains would suffer disruption. Reaching back for an old alternative, the general declared that if the British made any push to "ditch" Overlord, "we could say that if they propose to do that we will pull out and go into the Pacific with all our forces." The general produced this suggestion in reaction to a problem that had not yet arisen and might not arise. It represented no thought-out plan, it did not even address a more likely issue: How should the Americans respond if the British proposed not to abandon Overlord but to subject it to a short postponement?

While Roosevelt and Marshall fretted themselves over the

issue, the British, as their chief planner put it, had "crystallized" their ideas as to the strategy they would advocate at Cairo. They would argue for continuing the offensive in Italy, increasing the flow of supplies to partisan groups in the Balkans, trying to lead the Balkan countries into breaking away from Germany, inducing Turkey to enter the war . . . and "accepting" a postponement of Overlord. Brooke, as impatient and condescending as ever, prepared for "a pretty serious set-to with the Americans" because he was "tired of seeing our strategy warped by their short-sightedness."

Then, with everything seemingly set for battle, Roosevelt upset the expectations of all parties. Having taken up residence in the villa of the U.S. ambassador to Egypt, the president played host on the first evening to Churchill and Lord Mountbatten, and scarcely was dinner over when a preliminary meeting of statesmen and military staffs began, attended not only by American and British representatives but by Chiang Kai-shek, Madame Chiang, and three Chinese generals. FDR had confounded the British hope that at Sextant the generalissimo would arrive late and say little; Chiang's own stipulation had been that he see the president "at any time before his meeting with Stalin." The next morning, at a full-dress meeting of Roosevelt, Churchill, and the Combined Chiefs with Chiang, the generalissimo appeared with his wife at his side. Brooke saw her as clearly the dominant member of the pair, giving every indication of intending to extend her domination to a wider field. "Although not good-looking, she certainly had a good figure which she knew how to display at its best." The vehicle for this display was a clinging black satin dress slit to an interesting height; at one point a movement by Madame caused a rustle among the gentlemen, and from a group of the younger members Brooke thought he heard a "suppressed neigh."

To Churchill's disgust, Roosevelt had moved Chiang Kai-shek (or both Chiangs) to center stage at Cairo. Having come ready for tough bargaining over operations in Europe, so that the Western Allies could appear at Tehran with an agreed-upon strategy in hand, the British saw the president devoting what seemed endless hours to the Chinese, while Chiang's accompanying generals had little to say in talks with the Western military staffs. "All hope of persuading Chiang and his wife to go and see the Pyramids and enjoy themselves till we returned from

Teheran fell to the ground," Churchill said, "with the result that Chinese business occupied first instead of last place at Cairo."

Churchill felt that the Americans, and Roosevelt in particular, were catering to the Chinese because they believed, with little justification, that after the war Chiang and his country would become one of the dominant forces in the world. Sir Charles Wilson viewed the matter a little differently. Churchill looked at the Chinese through the eyes of a Victorian, seeing only members of an alien race, whereas "to the President, China means four hundred million people who are going to count in the world of tomorrow." More concretely, Roosevelt had in preparation an important role for these four hundred million. His plan for maintaining peace in the world after the war rested primarily not on a revamped and revised League of Nations but on the unity of the great Allied powers around the globe; a strong China must be ready to play her part as one of the "Four Policemen."

In an attempt to boost Chinese morale, FDR apparently promised Chiang that the Allies would support operations in Burma by launching an amphibious attack on the Andaman Islands (Operation Buccaneer). This news thrilled neither the British nor Roosevelt's own advisers. An amphibious assault would require landing craft, the precious vessels every theater cried for. If landings were to take place in the Bay of Bengal, then some proposed operation in Europe would suffer. Here FDR was foxier than anyone knew. During the first full day of Sextant he cabled Washington, asking James Byrnes, the director of war mobilization, whether with a top priority the factories could increase the production of landing craft during the first five months of 1944. On Thanksgiving Day, two days later, Byrnes replied that by April and afterward sizable increases would be possible, but not much could be done earlier. This meant, specifically, that if Overlord were postponed from May 1 to July 1, it could draw on twenty-two new LSTs, together with another ten that were allocated to the invasion but probably would not reach England in time to take part in a landing in May. Thus an attack in the Bay of Bengal might well take place without hampering activities in Europe. It would all depend on the possibility of postponing Overlord—not for long, merely for a few weeks. At this point, FDR was keeping his options open.

Although Roosevelt had not acted merely on impulse, he had failed to discuss his promise to Chiang with Marshall and the other Joint Chiefs. This put them in the embarrassing position of defending with the British an operation that seemed likely to delay the delivery of their own cherished baby, Overlord. Earlier Marshall had agreed that sixty-eight LSTs due to depart for England in December might be retained in the Mediterranean until January 15, with the understanding that this action would not delay the cross-Channel operation. But for some time Churchill had dreamed of a special use in the Mediterranean for assault craft and other matériel and forces. Though he had never succeeded in selling the idea, he continued to argue for an attack on the island of Rhodes in the Aegean, as a key element in his eastern Mediterranean strategy, which called for involving Turkey in the war. He had carried his assault to Marshall during the evening of the first full day of Sextant, while the other U.S. chiefs were dining with their British colleagues, and he threw the matter on the table at a session that included himself and the Combined Chiefs. Having resisted the prime minister's arguments until two o'clock in the morning, Marshall did not give the proposal a sympathetic hearing. "Churchill was red hot," Marshall said, and "all the British were against me"—although he thought, probably inaccurately, that the British officers were actually lukewarm on Rhodes but were simply supporting their leader, as the Americans had to do with Roosevelt on Operation Buccaneer. "It got hotter and hotter." Finally, Marshall recalled, Churchill stood before him, his hands clutching his lapels, and declared that "'His Majesty's Government can't have its troops staying idle. Muskets must flame'—and more English like that." Marshall fired back: "God forbid if I should try to dictate, but not one American soldier is going to die on that Goddamned beach!" The others reacted with horror, Marshall reported, although he felt that they were glad to hear him make the point. Churchill did not hold the outburst against him, he said, "but Ismay had to stay up with him all night." Although disagreeing with the prime minister about the merits of this particular scheme, Marshall thought he was right to challenge the staffs with new projects. Left to themselves, staffs tended to be "ultraconservative everywhere."

Dead set as they were against operations in the Aegean, Marshall and his U.S. colleagues found themselves standing on shaky legs when they appeared to favor Buccaneer. Brooke suggested that if Buccaneer were postponed, "the full weight of our resources could be brought to bear on Germany, thus bringing the war as a whole to an end at the earliest possible date." It was an unusually American-flavored argument to come from the mouth of the British chief, but it had the effect of infuriating the Americans, who felt that Brooke was brushing off their Asian concerns. The temperature in the meeting room soared so alarmingly that once again the chiefs ordered their subordinates to leave. In what Brooke called the "father and mother" of a row, Admiral King became so angry, noted one participant, that he "almost climbed over the table at Brooke. God, he was mad." But here, as was often the case, Brooke's abrupt and dogmatic manner of presenting his view was surely responsible in good part for the fiery American reaction, since the U.S. chiefs themselves held no special brief for Buccaneer. Marshall admitted to the British that "for political reasons it could not be interfered with," and Leahy declared that he and his American colleagues "were not in a position to agree to the abandonment" of the proposed operation.

Socially the president provided the high point of the Sextant conference by giving a Thanksgiving Day dinner. Certainly not only the Americans but all of the Allies had much to give thanks for on this holiday—the Red Army in its great resurgence had taken Kharkov and Kiev; Italy had surrendered to the Anglo-Americans, whose forces had held on at Salerno in a close-run battle; the U.S. offensive in the Central Pacific had opened with the capture of Tarawa, albeit in bloody fighting, just two days earlier and marines had landed on Bougainville; and at Cairo the battles, though heated, were hardly proving lethal. FDR had brought along his own turkeys, the gifts of Undersecretary of State Edward R. Stettinius, Jr., and Joe Carter of Burnt Corn, Alabama. Although the chief guest, Churchill, wore his standard blue zip-up coverall, FDR appeared in a dinner jacket and, as always, exercised his favorite hostly prerogative of carving (saying at one point, "Can you imagine how surprised Joe'll be, when he finds out how far his birds have flown before they were eaten?"). During dinner a GI orchestra played popular songs and old-time favorites, with Churchill asking for "Ol' Man River" and "Carry Me Back to Old Virginny" and Roosevelt returning the compliment with a request for "The White Cliffs of Dover." When the musicians played the "Marine Hymn," the prime minister leaped to his feet, flashing his famous V-for-Victory sign as the president sang along with the music. In a graceful toast to Churchill, FDR said that "with the United

Kingdom in our family we are a large family and more united than ever before." Churchill responded with a toast to Roosevelt that Bill Rigdon called "the greatest utterance I had ever heard, even from him."

The chief merriment of the evening was produced when, after Churchill's daughter Sarah, the only woman present, sought a brief rest from dancing with the men, the prime minister, as irrepressible socially as in every other way, insisted that Pa Watson waltz with him; as the two whirled about the room, Roosevelt's laughter, Rigdon said, "was enough to wake the Pharaohs." As was customary, the president's guest list included Hopkins, Admiral Leahy, and his aides; his son Elliott and son-in-law Major John Boettiger and Hopkins's son Robert joined the party, together with three ambassadors, including Averell Harriman from Moscow; except for his aide, Commander Thompson, Churchill's contingent was entirely civilian. The Combined Chiefs held their own separate dinner. Although they always seemed able to leave their disputes at the door of the meeting room, no one chronicled any singing and dancing.

All hands found the food plentiful at Cairo. Impressed at the contrast with life at home, now entering its fifth year of austerity, a British officer noted that during Sextant the delegates consumed, all told, 800 pounds of turkey, 22,000 pounds of meat, 78,000 eggs, 4,600 pounds of sugar, 5,000 tins of fruit, 500,000 cigarettes, and 1,500 cigars. Good hosts, the British had taken abundant care of the liquid side of matters, having ordered the cruiser *London* to pick up and deliver thirty dozen bottles of whisky and twelve dozen bottles of sherry. But the intellectual output produced by all these sources of energy proved disappointing to the military staffs and to Churchill, if not to FDR. The delegates departed for Tehran on Saturday morning, November 27, with little agreement among them. During one session at Sextant, Averell Harriman had warned the U.S. chiefs not to confront the Russians with the strategy of the war all settled. They would take offense, he said. Roosevelt had expressed the same kind of concern when he told Churchill that he did not wish to give Stalin the impression that the Western Allies were "ganging up on him."

As he flew toward Eureka, General Marshall still could not be sure: Was the president's heart in Overlord, or was it not?

The chief of staff had fought for the invasion, sometimes with the president, always with Alan Brooke, for almost two years now. Would he finally receive FDR's full support? With no agreed-upon plan in hand and with Stalin, an utterly new factor, joining the Allied deliberations, Marshall had to be prepared for one more great battle.

CHAPTER SEVENTEEN

EUREKA!

At 3:15 on Sunday afternoon, as President Roosevelt sat working on his mail with Bill Rigdon, a distinguished caller entered the room—a short man, perhaps five feet six, with white hair and pockmarked face, stockily built. Above the left breast pocket of his tunic hung a single decoration—the gold star signifying Hero of the Soviet Union. Marshal Stalin had come to welcome his guest to the Soviet compound in Tehran.

Where the president would live during the Eureka conference had been much discussed. Mike Reilly, head of the White House Secret Service detachment, reported from Tehran before FDR left Cairo that the U.S. legation would provide adequate quarters. But the Russians were pressing the Americans to lodge the president in a building inside the Soviet embassy compound; at the same time, the British invited FDR to become their house guest. Inspecting the Russian building on Roosevelt's behalf, Major General Patrick J. Hurley, a former Republican secretary of war whom FDR liked to use for special assignments, wired the boss that "from the standpoint of conference communications and security, these quarters are far more desirable than your own legation." The president would have a six-room suite, including a reception room and a large bedroom with adjoining bath. The building was not then used as a residence, but the Russians showed themselves ready to carry out a whirlwind conversion. Checking it on Saturday, November 27, Averell Harriman and a Russian-born American major found that the Soviets had installed plumbing, making possible the promised bathroom, and freshly painted the suite "with a paint that was not only dry but seemed quite odorless." In the reception hall the observers saw a great round meeting table put together during the night by Russian carpenters; oak shavings still littered the floor.

The president had arrived in Tehran that afternoon expecting to take up residence in the U.S. legation, but his stay there proved to be only a one-day affair. The Soviet and British embassy compounds stood side by side in the center of the city, thus enabling them to form one united enclave patrolled by British troops and Red Guards wielding machine guns, whereas the U.S. legation was situated a mile away through narrow, crowded streets. Late Friday evening Harriman had been summoned to the Soviet embassy, where Foreign Commissar Molotov spoke darkly of danger lurking for the Big Three in Tehran.

"Do you think this would be an attempt at assassination or a demonstration?" Harriman asked.

To this simple question Molotov returned a fuzzy answer, speaking of parachutists and saboteurs, assassination and enemy propaganda victories. The Russian-speaking U.S. major accompanying Harriman was amazed "to see how childish and at the same time evasive an experienced Soviet diplomat could be." Later the two Americans concluded that the person most likely to encounter danger was not the president but Stalin, who might become the target of one of the many displaced persons who had fled to Iran from persecution in the Soviet Union. Harriman further thought that the most probable plotters on hand were Russians wishing to see the American president installed inside Soviet walls, where he could be watched and listened to, but since protocol required that social functions rotate among the headquarters of the Big Three, coming and going through the streets of Tehran would unquestionably pose some danger for any of the leaders.

Roosevelt looked beyond considerations of convenience and safety. By accepting the Soviet invitation he could make a positive gesture toward the suspicious Stalin. FDR readily ruled out a move to the British embassy, where he and Churchill might appear to be solidifying an anti-Russian western front. In the president's mind Eureka must serve the primary purpose of enabling him to reach out to Stalin and to begin to build a genuine relationship based on mutual understanding of motives. What better way to start than by accepting Russian hospitality? The American party made its move to the Soviet compound after lunch on Sunday, November 28.

Outside the white-columned, yellow stone building, NKVD agents stood among the trees and flowers of the gardens, staring across sunlit lawns with their carpet of red and gold autumn leaves (which had been left unraked so that they would crackle under any intruding foot). Inside, Roosevelt set to work with Rigdon in his sitting room, a chamber that neatly reflected both sides of its Russian heritage with its decor of czarist gilt and Communist red stars.

When Stalin entered the room, the president looked up at his visitor and stretched out his arms, saying, "At last!" Then, pointing to a wall on which hung a picture of Stalin smoking his pipe, FDR declared that he wanted a photograph of the Three (he did not call them the "Big" Three) as smokers—Stalin with his pipe, Churchill with his cigar, and himself with a cigarette in its holder.

Stalin observed that he had wanted for a long time to meet the president. "It was not my fault," Roosevelt countered. "I did my best to meet sooner." The marshal accepted the blame for the delay; he had, he said, been immersed in military concerns. After a general discussion of a variety of questions, the two men broke off their conversation to prepare for the first general session of the Eureka conference, which was to begin at four o'clock in the adjacent reception room.

That morning, before moving from the U.S. legation, the president had met with the Joint Chiefs in a session devoted to reading Kremlin tea leaves. What should they expect from the Russians? Strongly influenced by the impressions reported from Moscow by General Deane, General Marshall believed that the Soviets were looking for "immediate help"—but just what did that mean? Facing up to the problems that such a desire might pose for his cherished cross-Channel attack, Marshall told Roosevelt that the Russians probably sought "a more immediate operation than Overlord." Both they and the British seemed, cold-bloodedly enough, to want Turkey in the war—a move calculated in Marshall's glum analysis to be a diversion from the operations in Italy, just as Italy was from Overlord. Humanely, FDR said that he "did not have the conscience to urge the Turks to go into the war." What would they have to gain?

For the four o'clock plenary meeting, the statesmen and their military advisers gathered around the specially built oak table, which offered room for four representatives from each country, with the other participants sitting in outer rings. FDR was flanked by Harriman and Charles E. "Chip" Bohlen, a diplomat stationed in Moscow who served as interpreter, and Hopkins sat at Bohlen's left. Although its makers had purposely created a table having no head or foot, the president as the only chief of state present occupied the seat of honor and, in accordance with a Big Three agreement, acted as chairman. Smiling, welcoming "the new members to the family circle," he seemed to one British participant "very much like the kind, rich uncle paying a visit to his poorer relations." But FDR had not come to Tehran to dispense Christmas baskets. To him, the table at which he sat represented not so much an arena for a meeting as a setting for a great poker game. He had in mind the sort of pot he wished to win, although the path taken by his thoughts was no more direct than it tended to be generally. His mind "didn't move through a series of logically related steps," his son James observed; rather, it "ran in many directions at once, leaping, skipping, pirouetting through, over and around possibilities. Always he knew the results he wanted, and the mind usually fashioned a journey toward that end which few others could have shaped or even fathomed." Bill Rigdon expressed a similar thought: Roosevelt could be hard to follow because he thought well into the future; Churchill's way of thinking was the same.

Sitting at the round table in this and succeeding meetings, FDR could not claim to control the cards as they came from the deck, but he knew how he intended to play whatever hands the dealer gave him. Gambling for stakes as great as any statesman had ever sought to win, he was determined to involve the Soviet Union as a willing partner in postwar settlements, basing his betting on the belief that Russia needed peace and in exchange for it would cooperate with the West. He would try to see Stalin's point of view on issues and at the same time display his own openness. He would strive to promote the process of bringing the aloof, suspicious Russians back into the family of nations they had left in 1917, working on the assumption that the interests of a victorious Soviet Union would not inevitably clash with those of the Western European countries and the United States. The face-to-face talks with Stalin would merely begin the process.

General Marshall and his planners had made an important contribution to this stream of thought. Several months earlier the War Department had produced "a very high level United States military strategic estimate" which acknowledged that, with Germany crushed, Russia would automatically take the dominant position in Europe. The document did not discuss any countervailing moves the Western Allies might make—such as the creation of a new balance-of-power situation through a restored France or a future democratic Germany—but declared instead that the conclusion was obvious: "Since Russia is the decisive factor in the war, she must be given every assistance and every effort must be made to obtain her friendship." This foray into political speculation, which appeared not to draw on the thoughts of any specialists in Soviet affairs, came as a perfectly logical corollary to the doctrine of unconditional surrender. Having acquiesced in the idea behind the doctrine—that Germany should not only be defeated but, as a power, should be demolished—the U.S. military appeared to see little choice but to woo Russia and hope for the best. The planners, however, had not drawn up the strategic estimate as an exercise in intellectual speculation. They wanted Roosevelt to be fully aware that "the most important factor the United States has to consider in relation to Russia is the prosecution of the war in the Pacific." Without Soviet help, Americans would find the cost and the casualties of efforts against Japan "immeasurably increased" and operations might even become "abortive." To save American lives the president must therefore work harmoniously with Stalin.

Like other Western observers, Roosevelt saw the "restless self-assertion" the Russians already displayed in respect to such potentially troublesome areas as Poland and Finland as the Red Army pushed the Wehrmacht westward, and he could hardly be blind to the risks involved in his approach to the great poker game. Somewhere in the meeting room, though in whose conscious mind no one can know, lurked the specter of the Lenin who had once observed after meeting a French diplomat: "We shook each other's hand . . . aware that each one of us would readily hang his partner. But our interests coincided." Whether or not FDR thought of Lenin's cynicism, the alternative to his own approach raised in his mind a horrifying picture—"a Russia excluded, aggrieved and driven in on itself to prepare for the inevitable war of continents." With the fall of Germany, as the War Department said, no military power at all would stand between the Soviet Union and the English Channel.

In their talk before the plenary meeting, Stalin, responding to FDR's description of his good-neighbor policy in the Americas, had volunteered the reassuring thought that he "had no desire to own Europe." The Russians, he said, would find "plenty to do at home, without undertaking great new territorial responsibilities." The president promptly expressed his belief in the marshal's good intentions. Seizing such opportunities to tell Stalin of his readiness to take his word formed part of FDR's overall strategy: Eureka ought to produce, in general, not a series of international compacts but a spirit of confidence and trust. The only one of his standard weapons FDR could not wield with Stalin was the use of first names; regretfully deciding that it was almost impossible to address somebody by his first name when talking through an interpreter, the president settled for "Marshal."

As had come to be customary, Roosevelt had brought with him to Eureka his professional military advisers but no equivalent professionals on the diplomatic side; Bohlen, though a career diplomat who had spent some six years in Russia and knew the language well, had come not as an adviser but simply as a translator; Harriman, the ambassador to the Soviet Union, had acquired considerable overseas experience since 1941 but was not a professional diplomat. In contrast, Churchill was accompanied by Anthony Eden, who, though not a professional in the career-officer sense, had specialized in foreign affairs since entering the House of Commons in 1925 and was on his second tour as foreign secretary. Stalin, on the other hand, had gone Roosevelt one better; he had brought neither diplomatic nor military staff assistance. His companions were two old Bolsheviks, the faithful Molotov, who in discussion seemed to have many thoughts that had already occurred to Stalin and none that had not, and Voroshilov, also called "Marshal" though early in the war his incompetence as a soldier had caused Stalin to take away his command; Westerners unflatteringly but accurately applied to him the term "stooge." Stalin had certainly ensured that he would meet no argument from his own people; he apparently also felt no need for any consultation. Although the rough exterior he displayed caused many who saw him in action to regard him as an uneducated peasant, he proved on acquaintance to be a man of considerable cultivation with great intelligence and a remarkable grasp of detail. "I found him better informed than Roosevelt, more realistic than Churchill," Harriman said. Nevertheless, at Tehran Stalin posed himself quite a challenge. As an autocrat, he enjoyed the advantage of having no Congress or

Parliament to second-guess his actions. Nor, perhaps, did he wish his own generals to hear what he said to Roosevelt and Churchill, nor anyone else to comment on his behavior in the company of such archcapitalists.

The marshal indicated right away the sort of approach he favored in conferences. Following brief opening remarks by the president and the prime minister, Stalin commented that "this fraternal meeting" offered the three leaders great opportunities and bluntly suggested: "Now let us get down to business."

After presenting a general survey, the president came to "the most important theater of the war—Europe." For more than a year and a half, he said, he and the prime minister had been most concerned with relieving German pressure on the Russian front, but because of the problems presented by "sea transport" had not been able to set a date for a cross-Channel operation till the conference at Quebec. If the participants in Eureka should decide that further operations in the Mediterranean would bring the greatest aid to the Soviet armies, then they would have to accept a possible delay of up to three months in Overlord; a large Mediterranean operation might even force the cancellation of the invasion. Aside from Italy, possible fields of activity included the Adriatic, the Aegean, and Turkey. Roosevelt then cast a firm vote for Overlord. In his own opinion, "the large cross-Channel operation should not be delayed by secondary operations." What did Marshal Stalin think?

Stalin produced a surprising response, although it confirmed some earlier reports from Moscow. With no equivocation, the marshal declared at the outset of his remarks that after the defeat of Germany, the Soviet Union would join the other Allies in the war against Japan. Many besides Marshall's staff had feared that the Russians would have to be negotiated, wheedled, or entreated into the Pacific war; they had not considered the strong possibility that Stalin would have reasons of his own for wishing to conquer Japan and take part in the peace settlement. To them, the marshal's declaration came as both unexpected and pleasing news. Then, after conducting his own brief survey of the war from the Soviet side, Stalin made it clear that General Deane's impression of his wishes in Europe, if it had ever been correct, was no longer so. Italy was not a suitable place from which to attack Germany, Stalin said, as the Russian field marshal Suvorov had discovered in 1799 when he had been routed while attempting to cross the Alps. The best method to get at the heart of Germany would be an attack through northern or northwestern France, perhaps even through southern France.

Here Stalin had delivered the statement for which George Marshall had hoped and waited; the Russians had not, after all, switched their affections away from a cross-Channel invasion: Overlord had just received a mighty vote of confidence. But, in a most atypical irony, Marshall was not present to register that vote. He, King, and Arnold were billeted at a U.S. Army base several miles outside Tehran, and after the Sunday morning conference had returned to the base for lunch. Then, having been told by Roosevelt that no other meetings would be held that day, Marshall and Arnold went for a drive in the country; King, who wanted to work on some papers, turned down their invitation to accompany them. In a short while, to the admiral's surprise, FDR changed his mind and summoned the Joint Chiefs to the four o'clock conference. Since Marshall and Arnold were off touring the mountains, Leahy and King had to represent the JCS. When King heard Stalin conferring his blessing on Marshall's cherished project, he had the pleasant thought that he would have the chance to describe the moment to the chief of staff.

He would have more than the bare facts to convey. When Churchill attempted to argue that new Mediterranean operations should probably be undertaken during the many months that remained before the mounting of Overlord, Stalin asked sharp questions about the effects such activities would have on the cross-Channel invasion. Roosevelt surprised his own advisers with a different sort of proposal, suggesting "a possible operation at the head of the Adriatic to make a junction with the Partisans under Tito and then to operate northeast into Rumania in conjunction with the Soviet advance from the region of Odessa." Marshall's heart would have sunk had he heard these words, and Hopkins wondered who was "promoting that Adriatic business that the President continually returns to?" The idea, King thought, was entirely Roosevelt's own. ("We were always scared to death of Mr. Roosevelt on the Balkans," Marshall later remarked.) But no one should have been worried; Stalin was buying none of these ideas. In a remarkable development, the Western Allies had come to Tehran to place the decision for their 1944 operations in Stalin's hands, and the marshal did not hesitate to oblige them. It was unwise "to scatter the British and American forces," he said; Overlord should become "the basis for all 1944 operations."

During the Big Three dinner that followed this lengthy session, Stalin gave his Western companions a little lesson in *Realpolitik*. When, in discussing what should be done with Germany, Roosevelt said that the very word *Reich* should be stricken from the German language, the marshal retorted that eliminating the word would hardly suffice; Germany must be rendered impotent, unable ever again to plunge the world into war. The various measures Roosevelt and Churchill had suggested did not seem harsh enough; he appeared to favor at least dismemberment of Germany. Nevertheless he questioned the advisability of the unconditional-surrender principle, which "merely served to unite the German people." If the Allies drew up specific terms, however harsh they were, German capitulation would probably come sooner than as matters now stood. But on this point Roosevelt did not change his mind. As far as the dismemberment of Germany was concerned, the Allies had already discussed the fixing of occupation zones, on the assumption, as Marshall said, "that we would be rather remote from Berlin at the time the Russians got there." So it seemed in 1943, when the only Allied soldiers on the Continent were embroiled with the Germans far away in southern Italy.

In objecting to unconditional surrender, Stalin was expressing not only what he truly believed but what his dinner companions could have known he believed. Despite the fact that press, public, and statesmen in Western countries liked to peer at the Kremlin through a cloud of mystery, one keen and knowledgeable observer declared that Soviet motives actually lay spread out in the open visible to anybody who wanted to take a good look. The phenomenon reminded him of the Paris police probing chair cushions and sofas for the famous purloined letter that sat unconcealed in front of them.

With respect to his views on Germany, Stalin had expressed himself with vigor and clarity in his talk in the Kremlin with Harry Hopkins in July 1941. The marshal spoke with the bitterness of a man who had been swindled by a company with which he had enjoyed doing business. The German invasion "aroused a hatred of Hitler that nothing but the death of the German Chancellor could lessen"; Stalin had loyally devoted himself to observing his treaties and commitments and his partner "had suddenly revealed himself as a rabid dog." But this hatred did not extend to the German people or to "the Reich as a body politic." *It did not even extend to the German General Staff!* Stalin said so openly. Indeed, until the coming of Hitler in 1933 the German and Russian staffs had worked closely together, and for Lenin, Germany had always held a high place as the most important foreign country, the arena in which socialism had been deemed most likely to develop, the power with which the Soviet Union should ally herself against the enmity of the West. To Stalin, the doctrine of unconditional surrender could represent nothing but tactical shortsightedness and intellectual gibberish.

By a remarkable coincidence, these points and other insights appeared in a book published during this very month in which Roosevelt and Marshall and the other Allied generals and politicians made their great trek to Tehran, although it perhaps came too late to have been bought by the White House, or circulated in the General Staff, or placed in the ship's library of the *Iowa* for leisurely reading on transoceanic trips. The author, David J. Dallin, a double émigré, had been exiled from imperial Russia as a young man of twenty-two in 1911, had returned in 1917, and then had sat in the Moscow soviet until departing again in 1921. During his first period of exile, Dallin had acquired a doctorate in political science at Heidelberg; he had spent the 1920s and 1930s in Germany, Poland, and France, and in 1940, like many another wandering European, he had fled France to take up residence across the Atlantic. His book gained its strength not only from the author's informed background but also from his ability to write about the Soviet government not as a disillusioned or resentful factionalist but as a genuine historian capable of the scholarly objectivity that one might bring to a study of the First Triumvirate or the Wars of the Roses. For those too pressed to read his relatively short book, he had even presented a summary of his conclusions about Russia's war aims in Europe in a magazine article that had appeared on newsstands in September.

Only those who chose to be blind, said Dallin, could fail to see the many areas of disagreement between the Soviet Union and the Western Allies. Unconditional surrender merely represented one example, though certainly an important one. In a variety of ways Moscow was already offering Germany "a tempting conditional peace" through the manifestos of the so-called Free Germany Committee and other devices (in spite of

Stalin's harsh words to Roosevelt and Churchill). Behind relations with Germany or any other country lay principles Lenin had enunciated in relation to German invasion of Russia in 1918: "Against the advance of the predatory Germans we utilized the equally predatory counterinterests of other imperialists. We resorted to maneuvering, dodging, falling back, which are obligatory in all wars, while waiting for the moment when the international revolution finally ripens." The true Soviet view seemed in essence to be what Molotov had said in October 1939: "A strong Germany is the necessary condition of a lasting peace in Europe," the assumption behind this idea being that such a Germany served as a counterweight to the Western imperialists.

Besides unconditional surrender, points of discord between west and east already included several major areas: 1) the United States granted full recognition to small nations (e.g., the Baltic states) that Russia considered integral parts of her own sovereign domain; 2) the Western powers favored postwar regional European federations, which the Soviet Union firmly opposed; 3) Soviet-sponsored refugee committees and underground forces run by Soviet intelligence services actively opposed governments-in-exile and other underground groups favored by Britain and the United States.

Soviet territorial ambitions matched those the Bolsheviks had discovered in 1917, carefully detailed in the czar's secret archives. The czar and his ministers had aimed at acquiring a "security sphere" made up of East Prussia and parts of Pomerania and Silesia from Germany; Galicia and northern Bukovina from Poland and Romania; Turkish territory around the Bosporus. Slavic areas—now Czechoslovakia, Yugoslavia, and Bulgaria—were to come within the Russian sphere of influence, which would also surround the nominally independent Hungary and Romania. Aside from the acquisition of the Turkish areas, said Dallin, the czarist plan still applied, with the added feature that in taking over territories, the Communists would completely disrupt the social systems of the people whom they subjected; the countries would be communized, and thus the East would experience political mobilization against the West.

Russia did not have to follow this course, Dallin declared. Instead, she could "seek her security in the demilitarization of Germany and in an alliance with the great nations of the west." It was almost as though the author had eavesdropped in advance on Roosevelt's talks with Stalin. He feared, however, that the Soviets would not make this great and promising departure from the dogma and tradition they had established since 1917. If they continued with their version of the plan they had inherited from Nicholas II, he observed, they would control all of Eastern and Central Europe east of a line from Stettin on the Baltic to Trieste on the Adriatic. The only blemish on this remarkable forecast was Dallin's failure to call this line the "iron curtain."

In a meeting of the Allied generals held the morning following Stalin's discussion of unconditional surrender, Voroshilov, stooge or not, showed himself a persistent military questioner. Pressing Marshall and Brooke on the details both of the projected landings in southern France and of Overlord itself, he made it plain that in Marshall he recognized a dedicated ally. It was clear, he said, that the United States considered Overlord "of the first importance." Bluntly he asked whether Brooke held the same view. Yes, answered the CIGS, but the Germans had created strong defenses in northern France; the invasion must be mounted at a time "when it would have the best chances of success." The talk repeatedly returned to the importance of landing craft, about which the Russian demonstrated his ignorance. During its recent advances, the Red Army, said Voroshilov, had been forced to cross several large rivers, but these crossings "were the results of the efforts of all their people. They had the will to do it."

Countering this ideological assertion, Brooke described crossing the English Channel as a "technical matter," and Marshall added a telling comment: "The difference between a river crossing, however wide, and a landing from the ocean is that the failure of a river crossing is a reverse while the failure of a landing operation from the sea is a catastrophe"; this was so because the repulse of a seaborne attack meant "the almost utter destruction of the landing craft and personnel involved." His military education had been based on roads, rivers, and railroads, Marshall said, but during the last two years he had been "acquiring an education based on oceans and he had to learn all over again." Before the present war, he had "never heard of any landing craft except a rubber boat. Now he thinks about little else."

Voroshilov responded to his ally's comment with a flattering observation: "If you think about it, you will do it."

So concerned was the president to avoid giving Stalin any reason to believe that the Western leaders were making a common front against him that he turned down Churchill's invitation to lunch, a rebuff that irritated the prime minister, who was experiencing hard going at the conference. That afternoon, in a private meeting with Stalin, Roosevelt moved toward the accomplishment of his main aim for Eureka. He told the marshal that he had in mind "a great many other matters relating to the future of the world which he would like to talk over informally." He was willing to discuss "any subject, military or political, which the marshal desired."

After receiving the bland reply that they could talk about anything they liked, FDR sketched his design for a postwar organization to keep the peace. Made up originally of the members of the wartime United Nations, it would consist of three principal bodies—an assembly to discuss world problems and make recommendations for action; an "executive committee" to deal with nonmilitary questions, such as agriculture, health, and economic matters; and the entity on which Roosevelt placed his real reliance, at least for the foreseeable future, the Four Policemen, who would "deal immediately with any threat to the peace and any sudden emergency which requires this action." Ever mindful of congressional opinion, however, FDR then undercut his own position. In case of trouble in Europe, he said, he envisioned sending only U.S. aircraft and ships, not troops; Britain and the Soviet Union would have to supply the land armies. What if the aggressor was one of the Four Policemen themselves? The question did not arise. But with his grand design, Roosevelt hoped and intended to make such a possibility unlikely.

At the conclusion of this talk, the two men moved from Roosevelt's sitting room into the great hall for the second plenary meeting of Eureka. This session opened with a moving event, the presentation by Churchill to Stalin of a gift from King George VI—a sword specially designed and wrought to commemorate the heroic Russian defense of Stalingrad. As Stalin bent and kissed the sword, Roosevelt thought he saw tears in his eyes. "This afternoon," said Sir Charles Wilson, "this hard-boiled Asiatic thawed and seemed to feel the emotions of ordinary people." After taking the sword, the marshal handed it to Voroshilov, who clumsily allowed the blade to slide from the scabbard, but caught it before it hit the floor. A Soviet honor guard then carried the sword away.

After listening to reports from Brooke and Marshall on the morning's meeting of the military staffs, Stalin wasted no time in coming out with the key question of the afternoon. The British and American chiefs of staff having spoken of the preparations for the cross-Channel invasion, Stalin asked: "Who will command Overlord?"

General Marshall? One can imagine the faces in the room turning to the U.S. chief of staff. Here was the president's opportunity to settle the question dramatically, once and for all, to reassure the Russians by appointing to the command of Overlord its longtime greatest advocate, to fix the British firmly to the plan (changes would scarcely be possible with Marshall at the helm). But FDR merely said that the command had not yet been decided.

Well, said Stalin with no embellishment, "nothing would come out of the operation" unless one man had the responsibility for planning it and carrying it out. In front of the marshal sat a pad on which he doodled wolf heads, while puffing on cigarettes that looked as if he had rolled them himself and stuffed them loose into his pocket. He appeared to be fully aware of the Anglo-American disarray and to have decided that aggressive conversational tactics were called for. The Western Allies had arrived at Tehran with their plans up in the air; the capitalists were not "ganging up" on him at all.

Leaning over to Admiral Leahy, FDR whispered, "That old Bolshevik is trying to force me to give him the name of our supreme commander. I just can't tell him yet because I have not made up my mind."

Given a vote, the "old Bolshevik" would unquestionably have cast it for Marshall. Although the chief of staff was meeting Stalin for the first time in this plenary session, the marshal and Voroshilov saw him as their great strategic friend. During informal conversations, Marshall said, Stalin "pressed for me all the time, and made it quite a point." Whether this was because of his ability or simply because Stalin thought the appointment would ensure the second front, Marshall modestly professed not to know. But the marshal was "very insistent." He would make "sort of semi-affectionate gestures," even when they were disagreeing, standing with a hand on Marshall's shoulder. This behavior came in pointed contrast to Stalin's treatment of Brooke, to whom the Russians showed antagonism; at one dinner Stalin assailed the CIGS with what Marshall called "some very acid but amusing remarks." (Had Stalin been able to see into Brooke's mind, his remarks might have been more than acid. Brooke said later he believed that, with Russia now seeming out of mortal danger, Stalin thought he needed no help from the Allies in the eastern Mediterranean, nor any Allied troops pouring in through the Dardanelles. Stalin's "political and military requirements could now be best met by the greatest squandering of British and American lives in the French theatre.")

Churchill had no intention of going down without a fight. The name of the commander of Overlord could be announced within a fortnight, he said, but the participants in the conference faced problems whose "number and complexity" concerned him; agreement must be reached on "big military, political and moral questions." After sitting through a lengthy verbal Churchillian guided tour from Overlord to Turkey, Stalin responded that the only really important operation was Overlord. "Nothing should be done to distract attention" from it. Mediating, the president observed that the discussion had been most interesting and that everybody agreed on the importance of Overlord ("There was no Goddamn alternative left," Hopkins commented). The only question concerned the timing of the operation. After further comments, Stalin said that he would like to see it undertaken in May; "he did not care whether it was the 1st, 15th or 20th," but a definite date was important.

At dinner that evening, ignoring the rule that the first duty of a host is not to make his guests uncomfortable, Stalin concentrated on Churchill, losing no opportunity, said Chip Bohlen, "to get in a dig." The marshal even suggested that the prime minister nourished a secret affection for Germany and wished to see a soft peace. The Russians might be a simple people, Stalin said, but "it was a mistake to believe that they were blind and could not see what was before their eyes." With this heavy-handed "teasing," Stalin gave a satiric twist to his Overlord theme. Then he declared that truly effective measures must be found to control Germany. For one thing, 50,000 German officers of the high command should be shot—perhaps even 100,000. As Churchill began to rumble in objection, Roosevelt said lightly that the punishment should apply to only 49,000 officers. Anthony Eden also signaled the prime minister to treat Stalin's remarks as a joke. But Churchill flamed with anger, declaring that he would choose to be shot himself rather than sully his and his country's honor. He arose from his chair and stalked into the next room, consenting to return only when Stalin and Molotov went after him—although he was not "fully convinced that all was chaff . . ." Roosevelt also teased Churchill, with the aim of showing Stalin that Eureka was a meeting of three equal allies, not of the two Western powers against the Soviet Union.

With respect to Stalin, Marshall was "surprised to find that seemingly none of our people had read his early history." They did not really understand the kind of force they were up against. He had "robbed banks and everything" in order to get money to support the Bolsheviks, but he nevertheless possessed social graces and a dry wit, and, as everybody saw, was an astute negotiator: "When he didn't intend to do business with you, you got absolutely nowhere." Since he was "a rough SOB who made his way by murder and everything else," he should have been dealt with accordingly, Marshall thought, not as "a product of the foreign services."

Although Marshall did not say so, Stalin's style in discussion drew part of its strength from his ability to tell enormous lies with an absolutely straight face; he would bluntly deny obvious fact, thus making genuine negotiation impossible. Roosevelt encountered this stone wall when a translator's error led Stalin to think that the president was raising a question about the absorption of the Baltic republics—which were virulently anti-Soviet—into the USSR. The people in these countries had voted to join the Soviet Union, Stalin asserted, and there was nothing more to be said about the matter. In a later conversation, Roosevelt brought up the same question deliberately, in the context of "internal American politics." He began by observing that 1944 would be an election year, and though he agreed with Stalin's wish to see Poland's boundaries shifted westward—the whole country being lifted up and then set down again like a piece of luggage—he could take no public part in making any such arrangement: There were "six to seven million Americans of Polish extraction, and as a practical man, he did not wish to lose their vote." Likewise, he said, Americans of Latvian, Lithuanian, and Estonian origin would look askance at the incorporation into the Soviet Union of the three small republics without "some expression of the will of the people." What Roosevelt was proposing, openly, was a bit of political window dressing, a plebiscite to show the world. Stalin, to whom appeals for votes no doubt appeared as a highly abstract and clumsy way to achieve a political aim, suggested that "some propaganda work should be done."

In seeking to further his relationship with Stalin by making this move, FDR was inevitably assuring the marshal that the United States would not stand in his way over the borders of Poland or the fate of the Baltic republics. Roosevelt believed, in any case, that the United States and Britain could do little to stop the Russians from working their will on their own frontiers. (A remark FDR made to General Giraud, who visited Washington in the summer of 1943, suggested that the president drew a clear distinction between events in Eastern and Western Europe. FDR spoke disapprovingly of General de Gaulle's *flirt* with the Russians, which he feared might lead to communism's making rapid progress in Western Europe "with the more or less sincere complicity if not of General de Gaulle, at least of his entourage.")

The Russian-born U.S. officer who had accompanied Averell Harriman on his inspection of the president's quarters participated in the conference as one of the assistants who "stood at the doors, answered telephones, and in general were at the conferees' beck and call." Since the plumbing permitted only one toilet besides the one in Roosevelt's suite, this facility was a busy place. It was to the right of the entrance, by the telephones and the duty officer's station. One day Churchill had no sooner gone in and closed the door than Stalin strode up. He rattled the knob so fiercely that Oleg Pantuhoff, the Russian-born U.S. officer, feared that it would come off in his hand. The American rushed over to tell "the Father of Mankind" that the prime minister was inside. *"Tchort vozmi!"* Stalin muttered. "The devil take it!" Pantuhoff, the son of White Russian émigrés and hardly an admirer of the marshal's, thought this conduct showed Stalin at his most jovial.

The greatest social occasion during the Eureka conference came on Churchill's sixty-ninth birthday—Tuesday, November 30. This dinner, held at the British legation and attended by the whole company, politicians and military advisers, crowned a day in which the Combined Chiefs of Staff agreed to launch Overlord in May 1944 and to support it with a landing in southern France "on as large a scale as possible, depending on the number of landing craft available for this operation." The military leaders had taken on a sizable order, since they already had a loaded agenda without the addition of any such item as an invasion of southern France. During the afternoon's plenary meeting, the Big Three had ratified the agreement, declaring the two operations the "supreme" undertakings for 1944. Surely, Churchill said, the United States and Britain, with all their great productive capacity, could find the needed landing craft.

The prime minister also discussed the necessity of "some form of cover plan" to deceive the Germans, because the vast preparations in England could not be concealed; "truth," he said, "deserves a bodyguard of lies." Although he did not wish to refer to it in Stalin's presence, a crucial element in this bodyguard, and indeed in the Allied calculations, was the existence of the high-level decrypting operation called ULTRA, headquartered at Bletchley Park, some fifty miles from London. The ULTRA code breakers could not themselves fight battles, but their detailed eavesdropping on the Germans could play an important part in winning them. Stalin had not officially been told of the ULTRA operation, although information it produced relevant to the eastern front had been funneled to him by a variety of means, but deception he understood. To conceal the location and the timing of Soviet offensives, he said, his forces made use of "dummy tanks, aircraft, fake landing fields and false information on the military radio."

As their next step, the president said, the Western Allies must appoint a commander for Overlord. This, he felt sure, would be done shortly after he and the prime minister had returned to Cairo. Then, indeed, Overlord would begin to take on a life of its own. But FDR did not say who the commander would be. Still the man who liked to wait for events to force his hand, he had come almost to the end of the string. Within a few days the matter would be settled—and, everyone still presumed, settled in General Marshall's favor.

Eureka had proved to be an utterly paradoxical undertaking. The greatest attention of the participants had been claimed by questions of Anglo-American strategy whose settlement did not require the politicians and the generals to journey deep into the Middle East. But Stalin had seen the decisions about Overlord made literally before his eyes—had even participated in making them—and the president had put out every effort to create a personal understanding with the marshal. What Stalin thought of these efforts could not be recorded, but Roosevelt had come prepared to gamble and he had played his game. (On returning to Moscow, Stalin told Marshal Zhukov that "Roosevelt has given his word that large-scale action will be mounted in France in 1944. I believe he will keep his word." Earlier Zhukov had noted that Stalin "trusted Roosevelt more, and Churchill less." But this trust did not necessarily exist on a lofty plane. Only a few months later Stalin privately compared the two Western leaders in folksy terms: "Churchill is the kind who, if you don't watch him, will slip a kopeck out of your pocket. By God, a kopeck out of your pocket! And Roosevelt? Roosevelt is not like that. He dips his hand in only for bigger coins." As a pick-pocket, FDR simply appeared the more elegant of the shifty Western pair.)

Now, tonight, a festive mood reigned in the British legation, with toasts and pledges of friendship exchanged among the Big Three. For good or ill, great military decisions had been taken. As the commander in chief of U.S. forces, the president had shepherded the Allied strategic debate to its conclusion. The motive for attacking Germany had never been in dispute; the means were now at hand, or were about to be; and the opportunity had been chosen. For Roosevelt, for Marshall, for the whole Allied directorate, motive, means, and opportunity had finally come together. The die was finally cast in Europe.

Near the end of the dinner, a gesture by Brooke marked the occasion with a unique example of high-level Anglo-American military cooperation. In keeping with the exotic decor of the legation dining room, which reminded the CIGS of a Persian temple as it would be built by His Majesty's engineers, the chef produced a masterpiece of a dessert, consisting of a small block of ice with a candle rising from its center and sitting above it, like a canopy, a large plate of ice cream supported by a perforated iron pillar. "The total effect," Brooke said, "was beyond description." Solemnly, waiters paraded two of these works of art around the table. As Stalin was speaking, with his interpreter, Pavlov, translating, Brooke kept his eye on an approaching waiter and saw that the heat from the candle had begun to melt the ice, eroding the foundation of the pillar so that it was tilting like the Tower of Pisa. The guests sat transfixed as the waiter went into a desperate waltz. Then, grabbing the neighbor on his right, General Somervell, Brooke cried, "Duck!" The two generals buried their faces in their plates as the whole "wonderful construction" slid over their heads and exploded on the table right in front of Pavlov, splashing him from head to foot with white ice cream, even depositing large lumps of it on his shoes. But, as a man who knew the importance of keeping first things first, Pavlov did not even pause in his translating: "Marshal Stalin, he say . . ."

"I suppose," Brooke observed, "it was as much as his life was worth to stop interpreting."

Before leaving the Soviet embassy, the president, as a good houseguest, told Bill Rigdon to obtain a list of the household servants so that they could be given presents. Pavlov, Rigdon's contact, stalled and temporized; no list appeared. After FDR's departure, many of these servants appeared in the uniforms of Soviet officers. The tall, white-jacketed waiter who stood behind Stalin's chair at meals proved to be a major in the NKVD. Stalin's safety had been constantly assured; likewise, FDR's every movement—and perhaps word—had been noted by a trained audience.

One afternoon during the conference, the Big Three had moved out to a portico of the building, at the top of a long flight of steps, to pose for photographers—Stalin in his remarkable iridescent, mustard-colored uniform with its starry shoulder boards, Churchill attired as an air commodore, Roosevelt, always the civilian, in a plain blue suit. The chairs in which the statesmen sat appeared to have been snatched up at random in a furniture warehouse; no two matched. When, not long after the conclusion of Eureka, the pictures appeared in the American press, they evoked an unusual and thoughtful reaction from one reader, a physician in Iowa City: "Witness Mr. Churchill slouched comfortably in a well-stuffed piece, apparently of period design, a piece that typifies a bygone era." But the prime minister did not really seem comfortable. His expression indicated "his realization that the elegance that was England is no more . . ." Next, Roosevelt, who sat in the middle, occupied "a partially upholstered chair of modern design," which to the doctor typified "the New World where the ideal of utilitarianism and comfort in a piece of furniture is but one manifestation of a nation full of ideals." The occupant of the chair reflected its attributes, with his "expression of the idealist, the poet of politics with head high." As for Stalin, who sat in a sturdy, unadorned swivel chair of the sort one might find in an insurance office, his expression reflected perfectly the pure utilitarianism of the chair: "It is that of the executive, the chief, the big shot." He seemed to sense "that he is in the driver's seat, that he is the

No. 1 man. Yet there is present that suggestion of coldness and suspicion, call it caution or wariness if you will. He knows what he wants and means to get it."

One more step remained to be taken. Back in Cairo, to which the Americans and the British returned on December 2, the military staffs resumed their detailed wrangling about operations and resources. It quickly became clear that, as they had on other occasions, the Anglo-Americans had taken too great a mouthful to be swallowed. Something would have to go, and that something, receiving Roosevelt's reluctant assent on December 5, was Buccaneer—the proposed landing in the Andaman Islands. Although the president feared that the canceling of the operation might lead Chiang to leave the war, he had little choice but to renege on his promise to the generalissimo—the operations planned for France must have first call on the landing craft.

But the big question remained: Who would command Overlord? On Saturday evening, December 4, FDR began to make his move, with an approach Rooseveltian in its most oblique form. The facts had not changed: the strong preference for Marshall on the part of both Hopkins and Stimson; the similar preference, freely expressed at Tehran, on Stalin's part; Churchill's blessing of Marshall, long since bestowed; the weight of authority Marshall would bring to the post; FDR's own wish to give the chief of staff "the historic opportunity which he so greatly desired and so amply deserved."

Another given, however, was the domestic furor about the appointment, with its implication that the president wished to get rid of Marshall, in some Machiavellian way, to demote him and ease him out of Washington. This argument could have been met had the British agreed to give Marshall command of all Anglo-American forces fighting Germany, but the allies, not surprisingly, had seen no reason to accept such a proposal. Thus this way out, never likely of access, had been closed to the president. If he appointed Marshall, he would have to face the dissonant music at home. Besides, he would lose the incomparable master of Congress, the man who had quietly made himself a politician without peer. And General MacArthur, Admiral King, Churchill, and Brooke—such ferocious figures might chew up any other man, including Ike, presuming to sit in the chief of staff's chair. Only Marshall could keep everything in balance.

That Saturday evening Roosevelt dispatched Hopkins to Marshall's quarters. The general did not seem to understand exactly what his friend had come to say—something to the effect that "the President was in some concern of mind over my appointment as Supreme Commander." Although Hopkins would hardly have been sent to give Marshall good news—FDR would have reserved this pleasure for himself—the chief of staff "could not tell from Hopkins' statement just what the President's point of view was." If Roosevelt had hoped that Hopkins's vague mission would solve his problem, he did not know his man as well as he should have known him; Marshall of all people would scarcely reject an offer that had not been made. He would not even say anything to Hopkins indicating that he had any idea what *might be* on the president's mind. He simply commented that he would "go along with whatever decision the President made. He need have no fears regarding my personal reaction." Marshall felt that he "should not embarrass the President one way or the other, that he must be able to deal in this matter with a perfectly free hand." He had believed, however, that the question of the command had been settled at Quebec. Otherwise, his wife would never have been encouraged to begin packing up at Fort Myer.

What message did Roosevelt really expect Hopkins to bring back to his villa? The president left no record on this point, but he cannot have been surprised that the question had not been settled between his emissary and the general; whatever his expectation, he had thought the hope was worth indulging. In any case, he would have to employ follow-up tactics. At midday the next day, in response to a summons, Marshall appeared at FDR's villa. The chief of staff bore in mind one guiding principle from his memories of World War I and his studies of military history: This time the good of the country, not the feelings of the individual, must be the predominant consideration. "I was utterly sincere," he said, "in the desire to avoid what happened so much in other wars." Marshall also felt a keen awareness of "all this business that had occurred in Washington"—the political attacks on FDR for proposing to appoint him to the command of Overlord.

Eyeing his visitor, Roosevelt talked about this and that, and "after a great deal of beating around the bush" asked the general what he wanted to do. For years Marshall had wished more than anything else to lead troops in the field, to command well-trained, well-armed formations driving toward a great objective. At VMI the fact of serving in a commanding role had brought out the soldier latent in the fun-loving young Flicker Marshall. Now, almost four decades later, one of the supreme command prizes in the history of warfare lay before him on the table, waiting to be picked up. Cleverly, FDR had placed it there and then stepped back; perhaps as a shrewd judge of men he knew that Marshall was not only selfless to a remarkable degree but proud. He wanted the prize above all others but did not want to reach for it. In no way would the general make the president's decision for him. Instead, "I just repeated again, in as convincing language as I could, that I wanted him to feel free to act in whatever way he felt was to the best interests of the country, and to his satisfaction, and not in any way to consider my feelings." The answer illustrates the essence of the character Marshall had created for himself through the years—an eighteenth-century sense of responsibility and duty, as he had perceived it especially in the writings of an author he greatly admired, Benjamin Franklin.

He would not attempt to estimate his own capabilities, Marshall told the president. He would "cheerfully go whichever way he wanted me to go."

Roosevelt's inescapable moment had come. Well, he said, "I feel I could not sleep at night with you out of the country."

That was that. Marshall's dream of command in the field had ended forever. He now must perform one specific chore as a consequence of Roosevelt's next decision. He drafted for the president a brief message to Stalin: "The appointment of General Eisenhower to command of Overlord operation has been decided upon." Checking the note, FDR picked up his pen and inserted one word: "immediate." With the thoughtfulness he constantly displayed, Marshall later recovered the note from the message center and sent it to Ike, adding his own words: "Dear Eisenhower: I thought you might like to have this as a memento. It was written very hurriedly by me as the final meeting broke up yesterday, the President signing it immediately. G.C.M."

When Admiral Leahy heard the decision, he felt that "the failure to name Marshall was taking a chance." But regardless of other considerations, the chief of staff was simply too important to be spared from Washington. In making his decision, the president had acted in accordance with plain fact and also with high principle. Strong and independent, Marshall had consistently demonstrated the shallowness of the commentators who had called him a yes-man. Unwaveringly, he had pushed for a large and balanced army and for one particular use of it—the invasion of northwestern Europe. In Eisenhower, whose appointment became inevitable after the president ruled out Marshall, Overlord would have as its commander Marshall's protégé, an officer groomed by him for high command, a man whom in all problems and difficulties he had supported and sheltered—almost, indeed, a son.

On December 22, after a trip across the Pacific, General Marshall arrived back in Washington. Although he was not to head Overlord, within a few days he had won another honor. During the last week of the year, *Time* magazine appeared with Marshall on its cover as Man of the Year. Below his portrait ran the line: "He armed the Republic." Although the American people normally do not like or trust the military, said the editors, "they like and trust George Marshall. This is no more paradoxical than the fact that George Marshall hates war. The secret is that American democracy is the stuff Marshall is made of."

Strange words to write about a general. "He has only one interest," one of his friends was quoted as saying—"to win this damned war as quick as he can, with the fewest lives lost and money expended, and get the hell down to Leesburg, Va., and enjoy life." The most trusted soldier since George Washington, Marshall was something more than a general, something remarkable and truly unmilitary. As even Congress could see, "this man is a trustee for the nation."

Those who mistrusted Roosevelt, those who hated him, could focus their need for a leader to respect and admire on the tall figure of the chief of staff. His own unique kind of politics had produced remarkable results.

CHAPTER EIGHTEEN

UNENDING MARTIAL STRAINS

Early in the morning of March 27, 1944, a navy doctor named Howard G. Bruenn received a surprising telephone call. A heart specialist, Dr. Bruenn had served in civilian life as chief of the cardiac clinic at Presbyterian Hospital in New York. Thirty-six years old at the time of Pearl Harbor, he had decided shortly afterward to offer his services to the navy. A trim man, standing perhaps two inches under six feet and weighing about 160 pounds, Bruenn passed easily through boot camp at Sampson, New York, and then became "just a ward physician" in the new hospital at the base. But near the end of 1942, higher responsibilities claimed him; he was summoned to Bethesda Naval Hospital outside Washington to become chief of the cardiac service.

The caller who threw Dr. Bruenn's department "into a tizzy" that March morning in 1944 was Vice Admiral Ross McIntire, President Roosevelt's personal physician and also, as surgeon general of the navy, Dr. Bruenn's toweringly superior officer. The admiral informed the naval reserve lieutenant commander that at eleven o'clock that same morning the president of the United States would arrive at Bethesda for a general checkup; Dr. Bruenn would be in charge. The president had not been feeling well, it seemed; he had been suffering from an upper respiratory infection "but had not made a very good recovery." Dr. Bruenn should see what he could find. Admiral McIntire gave one further order: Bruenn would tell neither the patient nor anybody else anything about his findings but would disclose them only to the admiral.

Although Bruenn was flattered by the confidence being

placed in his medical skill, the illustriousness of the patient coupled with the urgent orders for secrecy—with even the patient himself coming under the absolute proscription—combined to render the doctor a bit nervous. With a presidential election approaching, the news that FDR had been seen by a heart specialist would clearly be explosive. Bruenn's frame of mind was not improved by another phone call, this one placed by him to Dr. McIntire. Would the admiral send over the records of the patient's previous examinations? He would need them, the doctor explained, to help him assess his own findings. If he did send such records, McIntire replied, they must be returned to him immediately, along with Bruenn's report. But, incredibly, the president's personal physician then said that he might not be able to find FDR's chart; he was not sure just where it was. This remarkable admission did nothing to calm Dr. Bruenn's nerves.

It was an unusual morning for the president, with nothing on his calendar except the eleven o'clock appointment at Bethesda. Around 10:30, as he was getting ready to leave the White House, McIntire dutifully asked him how he felt. The admiral received a startling answer, one wholly out of the Roosevelt character as it had been built up and sustained through the years. The president said, "I feel like hell!"

When FDR returned to Washington from the Eureka conference, he had been welcomed at the south entrance of the White House by Cabinet officers, agency directors, and other well-wishers. One of the greeters, Judge Sam Rosenman, was struck by the president's facial expression. "I do not remember ever seeing the President look more satisfied and pleased than he did that morning," Rosenman noted. FDR seemed a little tired, perhaps, but perfectly healthy. "He was indeed the 'champ' who had come back with the prize." That prize had been summed up in the declaration issued at the end of the Eureka conference; its last paragraph, which breathed the Roosevelt spirit, declared: "We came here with hope and determination. We leave here, friends in fact, in spirit and in purpose."

During Roosevelt's presidency, Rosenman, who had been appointed to the Supreme Court of New York in 1932, had worked on presidential speeches informally but with increasing frequency until 1943, when he resigned his judgeship to become a full-time member of the White House staff. Through the unprecedented years in which Roosevelt had carried the burdens of

Depression and world war, Rosenman had seen the extraordinarily strong feelings FDR's associates could develop for the boss: Louis Howe, in a sense Roosevelt's discoverer, whose only ambition in life had been fulfilled when his beloved Franklin had won the presidency and from then on acted like "a one-man dog who felt that anybody who came close to the master came with the idea of hurting the master or hurting the dog"; Harry Hopkins, who likewise vigilantly guarded his place next to Roosevelt, but more on the level of ideas. "Harry felt that the President was a great hero," Rosenman said, "and that his objectives and his philosophy and what he had done to carry them out were an inestimable service to America and to civilization." Roosevelt was just as great a hero to Rosenman as he was to Hopkins: Both regarded the boss with a feeling of "worship."

Thus, on that December day at the south entrance of the White House, the judge was assessing the president with an eye both affectionate and knowing. He understood his man about as thoroughly as anyone could; Roosevelt, many times the "champ" with that same triumphant expression, was convinced that once again he had won the prize, and this one a big one.

The glow engendered by Eureka, which left the president saying of Stalin that "we are going to get along very well with him and the Russian people—very well indeed," found no match in the mood that met FDR on his return to Washington. General Marshall wrote him just a week later, in a Christmas Eve note: "I am distressed that you cannot enter the holidays free to enjoy the contemplation of the military and naval successes or victories of the past year. It seems too bad that your mind must be burdened with such serious difficulties on the home front." On October 29 the president had seized the coal mines, which had been shut down by a labor dispute. Now the war effort was dangerously threatened by a walkout of 170,000 steelworkers and a proclaimed strike of 1,450,000 railroad workers. Reluctantly, revealing to the delight of some conservatives that in relation to labor his velvet glove had room inside for an iron hand, the president stuck by the official anti-inflation principle called the Little Steel formula; the steelworkers yielded but the railroaders refused to withdraw the strike order, leading FDR on December 27 to grant the War Department absolute power over every one of the 233,670 miles of railroad track in the United States.

At his press conference the very next day, FDR in a related

move presided at the last rites of an illustrious medical man. To the eighty-odd reporters who crowded around his desk, Roosevelt described how the New Deal had come into existence because in 1932 "there was an awfully sick patient called the United States of America," suffering "from a grave internal disorder." Under the care of the kindly old family practitioner, Dr. New Deal, the patient during the past ten years had succeeded in getting well. "He's all right internally now—if they will just leave him alone." But "two years ago, after he had become pretty well, he had a very bad accident"—breaking a hip, breaking his leg in two or three places, breaking a wrist and an arm. Well, since old Dr. New Deal knew a great deal about internal medicine but nothing about these new problems, he called in his partner, an orthopedic surgeon named Dr. Win-the-War. "And the result is that the patient is back on his feet. He has given up his crutches. He isn't wholly well yet, and he won't be until he wins the war"—which was why, the president declared, the "principal emphasis, the overwhelming emphasis" must now go to winning the war. A week earlier FDR had confided to a reporter that he no longer saw the need for a New Deal and he hoped somebody would think up a catchy slogan about winning the war. Quickly becoming famous, his own pair of medical practitioners seemed likely to solve the problem.

Dr. Win-the-War soon found other vocal supporters besides the president. On December 31, while his solemn portrait with the clear blue eyes gazed from red-bordered *Time* covers on newsstands across the United States, General Marshall summoned Washington correspondents to an off-the-record meeting. What the startled reporters encountered at the conference was not *Time*'s nonpolitical, Olympian "trustee for the nation" in a mellow birthday mood but, instead, a reincarnation of the fiery-tempered young major who had attacked Black Jack Pershing more than a quarter of a century earlier. Unacquainted with the subterranean Marshall, the journalists were shocked. This time, departing from all his own precedents, Marshall took on not one man but the whole American labor movement. Ignoring still another of his personal precedents, he spoke without carefully weighing the evidence. His indignation at the strikes and threatened strikes had boiled over because he saw a sharp contrast between conditions at home and those on the Pacific islands from which he had just returned.

"Although not a blasphemous man, he swore bitterly," reporters noted with amazement as the person believed almost to be above such flaws banged a white-knuckled fist on the desk and declared that the strikes might literally cost hundreds of thousands of American lives. When one newspaper leaked the identity of the speaker, upset labor leaders counterattacked, and the chief of staff found himself in an extremely unfamiliar position, at the center of a hot public controversy. Marshall "is perhaps more universally admired in the United States than any other individual," the British embassy in Washington noted in a report to London, being "regarded as a figure of such unimpeachable impartiality, integrity, efficiency and ancient American virtue as to be almost beyond criticism." Had the general now descended from his mountaintop and revealed himself as crudely partisan?

If the denunciation of the strikers had come from anybody other than Marshall, it seemed clear, the indignant reactions would have made much more noise. Certainly labor had become unpopular in many quarters, but as one editorial cartoonist saw the issue, labor was only one member of a seedy barbershop quartet, along with the farm bloc, the oil bloc, and the anti-higher-tax bloc, all of whose voices were raised in a new anthem: "My country, 'tis of ME." Despite all the stir, reasonably dispassionate observers concluded that the chief of staff had not intended to make a political statement of any kind. Still, the British observer concluded, "respected and admired though Marshall will doubtless continue to be, his unique position, as a figure lifted above the political battle, has been, at any rate temporarily, shaken."

By abandoning his own concept of the off-the-record press conference, which called for it to serve as a high-level briefing session for commentators and other senior journalists, Marshall, at a moment when he was receiving great national adulation, had ironically managed to produce a personal failure in public relations. He rarely allowed his temper to run away with him during these years, but when it did explode, it showed itself as volcanic as ever. The whole affair constituted a curious beginning of 1944 for the Man of the Year of 1943. But, like Roosevelt, the general saw how the behavior of the special interests had increasingly created an urgent need for the ministrations of Dr. Win-the-War. To be sure, not all the reactions to Marshall's outburst were unfavorable. From his office in Rockefeller Center Captain Eddie Rickenbacker, the famous World War I flying ace who had become president of Eastern Air Lines, fired off a lengthy letter in which he managed both to praise the chief of staff and to attack the New Deal. "Stand by your guns," said Captain Eddie, "and you will have millions standing shoulder to shoulder with you including my humble self." Marshall drily replied in three short lines: "I have noted it with interest and appreciate your writing me so frankly." Among the roles the chief of staff emphatically did not envision for himself, leadership of a right-wing political movement took a leading place.

Several weeks later, still feeling that the public did not fully understand the "realities of war," Marshall returned to the fray. This time, instead of a press conference in which he would cloak himself in anonymity, he took as his forum a nationwide radio broadcast. To illustrate his point, he doggedly chose an unsavory example. "I speak with an emphasis that I believe is pardonable in one who has a terrible responsibility for the lives of many men," he said. Here at home the people had not yet faced "the savage, desperate conditions of the battlefronts." What disturbed him was the "vehement protests I am receiving against our use of flame throwers" in the Pacific island campaigns. The objectors simply demonstrated no "understanding of the meaning of our dead on the beaches of Tarawa." He hammered away at his point, his constant theme: "Our soldiers must be keenly conscious that the full strength of the nation is behind them. They must not go into battle puzzled or embittered over disputes at home which adversely affect the war effort." The time had come for a "stern resolution on the part of the whole people of the United States to make every sacrifice that will contribute to the victory." Politically, Marshall said later, "all our instincts pointed to the necessity of ending the war at the earliest possible moment." When General Brooke and other Britons proposed sideshows and end runs, speaking of such possibilities as invading Rhodes and the Balkans, they ran squarely not only into the traditions of the U.S. Army but into the emotions of the American public.

That same week Vice-President Henry Wallace, in response to a reporter's question, offered an interesting political prediction. Would President Roosevelt seek a fourth term in the White House? "There is no doubt in my mind," Wallace said, "that the President will run," although he conceded that FDR himself might have some questions about it. Anyone who saw the president close up would not have expressed surprise at any reluctance he might display. Certainly the White House offered increasing and convincing evidence that it was hazardous to the health of its occupant.

Despite the optimism with which the Americans had come away from Eureka, each of the Big Three, in fact, suffered physically in the aftermath. Churchill developed a serious case of pneumonia, and from the shadowy depths of the Kremlin came rumors that Stalin had suffered a heart attack that required several weeks of recuperation. Roosevelt, though he enjoyed a merry family Christmas at Hyde Park, returned to Washington with an explosive cough. Always prey to sinus and respiratory problems, he was now divined by Dr. McIntire to be suffering from flu, which "hung on and finally left behind a nagging inflammation of the bronchial tubes." Coughing spells racked him through the day and interrupted his sleep at night. After two weeks in Washington grappling with domestic problems that had awaited his return from Eureka, FDR felt the need of more rest and went back to Hyde Park. "I know he will return made over," Eleanor Roosevelt said—a holiday on the Hudson had always restored him—but soon she noted: "FDR says he feels much better but I don't think he longs to get back and fight."

For the man who had always been the true happy warrior of the political battlefield, this lack of combativeness represented a significant change. "More disturbing than anything else," Dr. McIntire later said, was "the definite loss of his usual ability to come back quickly." Besides the more or less continual respiratory infections, FDR experienced bouts of abdominal pains, with swelling and profuse perspiration, and he continued to speak of "unusual and undue fatigue." His zest and vitality, personal characteristics so pronounced as almost to seem identified with him, appeared to have drained away. His once-healthy complexion turned a sickly gray.

These symptoms contrasted oddly with the tone of a statement Dr. McIntire gave reporters on the eve of the president's sixty-second birthday—and contrasted also with what the admiral later declared his views to have been at the time. According to McIntire, Roosevelt in 1943 had enjoyed "one of the best years since he entered the White House," even though all the high-level conferences had made it one of the hardest. Actually, the doctor said, FDR was in better health than at any time since he entered the White House in 1933, thanks to his continuing "ability to bounce back" after fatigue or illness. This judgment was typical of the statements McIntire had made throughout Roosevelt's presidency. He spoke to the press of the stamina, "far above average," that enabled FDR to snap back from "extra-heavy strain or some little illness," and of the "much better than average health and energy" with which he had been endowed. These qualities, the admiral said, made him "just an average patient, with no operations and no interesting complaints."

As a reward for producing such insights, McIntire was nominated in February for promotion to the rank of vice admiral. No routine affair, this move, made at Roosevelt's specific behest, broke the precedent which decreed that bureau chiefs such as the surgeon general should hold no higher rank than rear admiral; for good measure the president included two other chiefs in his list of nominees and the Senate confirmed all three. A month later, on March 4—the president's eleventh anniversary in office—McIntire declared in a radio speech that Roosevelt was enjoying "the finest possible health"; he was, indeed, "in perfect shape."

Described in the press as a "comfortable, relaxed Westerner who never raises his voice or his blood pressure," McIntire with his calm approach and soaring pronouncements did not allay Grace Tully's fears. Earlier she had taken unhappy note of her boss's cumulative weariness as the weighty presidential years pressed down on him, the circles darkening under his eyes and the tremor of the hands increasing; she now became seriously alarmed. Sometimes FDR would nod over his mail or doze off during dictation with open mouth and unfinished sentence; upon waking, he would produce a mildly embarrassed grin and go on with his work—and his words seemed as clear and sparkling as ever. But these flights from wakefulness occurred more and more frequently. It became clear to Tully that the burden the president bore had finally become too heavy; ahead might lie collapse.

Greatly troubled, Tully sought out the person closest of all to FDR, his daughter Anna. Having come to the White House for a visit in November, Anna, whose husband, John Boettiger, was serving overseas, sensed "Father's need to have one of his children near him," as her brother James put it; she decided to give up her job on a Seattle newspaper and move into the White House. She saw a man at the summit of power and fame, the generally acknowledged leader of the United Nations, whose life was hollow at its center. Not only did her father appear to be succumbing to the weight of the burdens he had carried all those unprecedented years from the run on the banks in 1933 to the Eureka conference, he was a lonely man, his children like those of many another family scattered around the world, his wife often away on her extensive missions and often not precisely a comfort when she was in residence. In December Harry Hopkins, FDR's closest working confidant, had moved out of the White House to his own house at 3340 N Street in Georgetown, and was no longer on hand for those dinners on a tray and long evening talks in the president's study. At New Year's, Hopkins was sent to Bethesda with what Roosevelt thought was the flu; it was a widespread epidemic, the flu-ridden president cabled Churchill, "but while it is not serious it makes you feel the way an Italian soldier looks." Dr. McIntire assured Roosevelt that Hopkins, though suffering from digestive complications, would be back on the job in a month; but in fact, his stomach problem was far more serious, and his help and companionship were lost to the president. To Admiral Brown, FDR's naval aide, Hopkins "had no more sense than a child in caring for his own health or the health of Franklin Roosevelt." Having long lived on borrowed time, Hopkins seemed finally to have exhausted his credit.

Roosevelt had been a phenomenon, the first humorous president—not a maker of jokes or, like Lincoln, a master of the parable or telling anecdote, but a man who could fill his high office with appropriate dignity and still show the public that one could laugh at care, that even at a time of crisis life at the top did not have to be grim. But the companions, most of them, had gone and the fun had fled. Anna Roosevelt, who did not care whether she was "pouring tea for General de Gaulle or filling Father's empty cigarette case," took on the task of unofficial secretary, trying to help her father with his work and to "make his life as pleasant as possible when a few moments opened up for relaxation."

When Grace Tully came to talk with Anna, the president's daughter proved equally worried, and the two women independently carried their case to Dr. McIntire. As he had done for years, the doctor saw the president every day. Each morning about 8:30 he parked his Lincoln convertible in front of the White House annex and walked along the corridor into the mansion itself and up the stairs to FDR's room, where he joined in the bedside talk between the president and his aides, usually offering a story or two or some fresh news about FDR's beloved navy. With "a fine mind and a retentive memory," said Admiral Brown, Dr. McIntire could "discuss anything from the best batting average in either league for the past twenty years to the latest discoveries of science, members of Congress, the good points and bad of his own brother naval officers. Franklin Roosevelt was fond of him and valued his opinion on any subject." Including McIntire among the butts of his kidding, FDR once had a barber pole set up before the doctor's door, but the victim was not seen laughing.

Credited with "the best bedside manner any White House physician ever had," Dr. McIntire talked with Roosevelt as a friend, never breaking into a flow of conversation with specific medical questions; his successful bedside manner was thus the seeming absence of any such quality. A graduate of Willamette Medical School in Oregon, McIntire had come to FDR's attention as an ear-nose-and-throat specialist who could treat the chronic presidential sinus trouble. His prowess as a deep-sea fisherman had confirmed him as a member of Roosevelt's entourage; he also enjoyed singing. He was, a colleague said, "a very pleasant person." He had become eminent because he was the White House doctor, rather than the other way around.

So important was the president's well-being not only to the United States but to the admiral personally that even if he were capable of assessing his patient's condition, he perhaps could not allow himself to realize that FDR was far from well and that, despite his displaying occasional heartening flashes of his bouncy old self, the president was growing steadily worse. "The White House group," said the medical colleague, "just felt that the President was immortal"—as suggested in the doctor's case by the fact that almost three months had gone by since the onset of Roosevelt's post-Eureka problems, and only after the visits from Grace Tully and Anna Roosevelt did McIntire order a full-dress physical examination. And those mislaid medical records could prove embarrassing, whether or not they were found. If they remained missing, that in itself indicted McIntire as heedless—he had, after all, one supreme patient, the president of the United States. If the charts turned up, they might when examined by another doctor offer evidence that could make the admiral blush. The available records at Bethesda were scanty at best; no presidential blood pressure had been recorded there for three years, although the last known check had indicated a hypertensive 188 over 105.

Returning to Washington from a wide-ranging mission through Latin America, Eleanor Roosevelt saw a still-suffering husband. Wondering what might be wrong, she even considered the possibility that the president had acquired undulant fever from the cows at Hyde Park. "FDR is not well," she noted, "but more will be known by Monday & I think we can help keep him in good health but he'll have to be more careful. I think the constant tension must tell . . ." Actually, Mrs. Roosevelt took a Spartan view of her husband's life as well as of her own. Although she "hated the idea" of the fourth term, the two of them never talked about it. "Either he felt he ought to serve a fourth term and wanted it or he didn't. That was up to the man himself to decide and no one else." Indeed, "he never gave his health much thought and neither did any of us." But beyond that, as Eleanor observed some months later, she felt that Franklin accepted the fact that "if he had to go on in office to accomplish his work, it must shorten his life, and he made that choice. If he can accomplish what he set out to do, and then dies, it will have been worth it. I agree with him."

Wheeled by his valet, Arthur Prettyman, who had accompanied him to Tehran, the president passed through lines of applauding doctors, nurses, and patients and into the examining suite where Dr. Bruenn awaited him. Later, dressed in a flimsy hospital gown, FDR was lifted by attendants onto the examining table. Quickly studying the patient, the doctor observed the purplish lips and fingernails, the shallow breathing, the tremor of the hands. "He appeared to be very tired," Bruenn noted, "and his face was very gray." The doctor also observed that the patient was "in good humor." As was his custom in any company, FDR chatted amiably with the doctor, but, following another custom, he said nothing at all about his health. Anything Bruenn discovered would have to come from his own findings and from McIntire's records, which fortunately had been dug up and had arrived during the examination. Taking a quick look at the chart, Bruenn saw "a few notations of some increase in the blood pressure over the past year or so—two years, perhaps." These rising figures, however, had not moved Dr. McIntire to medical action.

The president himself displayed no interest in Bruenn's

work; as the examination progressed, he asked none of the usual little questions about the doctor's findings. Could his involvement in his own health really be so slight? Or, perhaps, were his energies devoted to denying that any significant problem existed? Bruenn could not be sure.

When all the procedures—direct examination, electrocardiogram, fluoroscopy, X rays—had been finished and the president was dressed, Bruenn to his relief was spared any questions. The president merely said, "Thanks, doc." The doctor spent the rest of the day analyzing and writing up his findings and outlining a series of recommendations. The next morning, in response to a summons from Dr. McIntire, he reported to the admiral in the clinic next to the map room on the ground floor of the White House. His findings, together with the chart supplied by McIntire, "made a fairly complete picture."

Dr. Bruenn's diagnosis was sweeping and appalling. The president of the United States suffered from hypertension, hypertensive heart disease, and congestive heart failure as well as from chronic bronchitis. Except for the lung problems, Bruenn noted later, the existence of these disorders had been *completely unsuspected up to this time.* This surprising oversight was due, Bruenn felt, to the fact that no one had paid "much attention to the President's so-called general health." Yet "the type of heart disease he had, and his blood pressure, made his life span questionable"; the president could die any day. On the other hand, he might survive for some time, but to try to ward off the "possibility of something happening," the doctors must see that certain definite steps were taken: immediate bed rest for one or two weeks; cutting down on appointments; administration of digitalis for the heart, codeine to control the cough, and sedation (phenobarbital) to ensure a good night's sleep; adoption of a light diet with restricted sodium and a plan for gradual reduction in weight. By no means radical at the time, this program would have been drawn up by Bruenn for any patient with FDR's problems; but, though reduction of stress constituted perhaps its main aim, McIntire rejected it "because of the exigencies and demands on the President." Instead, the admiral agreed, on FDR's behalf, to accept modified bed rest and cough syrup with codeine. He made another move as well. Picking up the telephone, he put in a call to Captain John Harper, the commanding officer at Bethesda, to inform him that Commander Bruenn was immediately being placed on detached service at the White

House, where he would function as an attending physician to the president—and where he would also serve directly under McIntire and act only on the admiral's orders. Secrecy would certainly be maintained.

But, not to Bruenn's surprise, limited gestures failed to halt the president's decline. Pushed by the younger doctor, McIntire called in the navy's two most eminent medical consultants—the president of the American Medical Association and Dr. Frank Lahey of the famous Lahey Clinic in Boston—who were bound to rigid confidentiality with respect not only to the public but to the president and his wife and children. None of the family would be told about FDR's true condition. For public consumption McIntire later declared that FDR's examination revealed "a moderate degree of arteriosclerosis, although no more than normal in a man of his age; some changes in the cardiographic tracing; cloudiness in his sinuses; and bronchial irritation." It seemed desirable, the admiral said, that the president quit smoking, in order to get rid of the sinus and throat trouble. McIntire ladled out similar soothing syrup to Mrs. Roosevelt and Anna. The doctors found FDR "well and active," Eleanor recorded, advising him only to rest every day to ease the strain on a heart weakened by the stress of war. If he should run again, McIntire assured her, he "could quite easily go on with the activities of the Presidency." James Roosevelt later suggested that the doctor was "indoctrinated, as one is in the White House," to "feel that he couldn't apply the same principles he would to somebody not having such responsibilities." Where normally McIntire might discourage a patient from performing some activity, James felt, with a president the doctor would allow it. Conceding that in some ways the doctor may have made the right decision, James nevertheless said, "I wish we had taken better care of my father."

Widespread rumors about the president's physical condition led White House correspondents to ask Steve Early, the press secretary, for a report. He was sure he could get word from Admiral McIntire, Early told the reporters, and during the secretary's regular morning press conference on April 3, the admiral appeared to make his statement in person and to answer questions. Calmly he told the correspondents that FDR's checkup, about which they had been informed, was a yearly event, like those given senior military officers. "It's quite comprehensive," he said. "You don't miss a thing." But when it came to substance, his verdict on the president's physical condition, though positive, emerged a bit less glowing than usual. It was, he said, "satisfactory," not, as customary, "better than ever," or, as it had been just a month earlier, "perfect." The problem had been created by "this acute flare-up of his sinuses and chest," for which the cure was simply some sunshine and more exercise. But in a summation of this unprecedented public report the doctor declared, "When we got through we decided that for a man of 62-plus we had very little to argue about." He was in fact speaking of a man who was far more likely than most men of sixty-two to die any day.

In scenes suggestive of toga-swathed surgeons debating the fate of a Roman emperor, Dr. Bruenn stood up to the eminent physicians McIntire had called to Bethesda. At first they "pooh-poohed" Bruenn's diagnosis. Then, after the two top consultants had gone to the White House and examined the president, "there was much discussion." One point of the game appeared to be not so much to decide what medications should be prescribed as to agree on how much medicine the president would take before asking questions. But Bruenn also felt that, since all the drugs in question could have side effects, the consultants wished to move with special care when prescribing anything for the president of the United States. At one point the lieutenant commander became "brassy" enough to tell McIntire that if his recommendations were not accepted, he would prefer to withdraw from the case. Finally, by doggedly sticking to his point, he won the right to administer digitalis to Roosevelt. He would also be allowed to put the president in a Gatch bed, whose raised head would ease his breathing by causing fluid to remain in the bottom of his lungs. "At no time," said Bruenn, who examined the patient several times a week, "did the President ever comment on the frequency of these visits or question the reason for the electrocardiograms and the other laboratory tests that were performed from time to time; nor did he ever have any questions as to the type and variety of medications that were used." Even for a Grotonian, this was unnatural reserve. The doctor held himself ready to speak to Roosevelt about what was wrong with him; he believed that if FDR understood his condition, he would be more likely to cooperate in his treatment than if he remained in the dark. But, said Bruenn, "the President never asked me a question about his condition, but accepted me literally as part of the environment." Given no opening, the doctor did not feel himself authorized to make one.

Dr. Bruenn took a strong liking to Roosevelt, finding him "an extraordinary person." The president returned this liking, and the resulting rapport was noted by Dr. McIntire, for whom it constituted a firm reason to keep Bruenn on the case. "But nobody," said Bruenn, "nobody asked me about the relationship between the President's physical condition and the question of a fourth term, and since nobody asked me, I wasn't volunteering anything—because of the implications involved."

Thanks chiefly to Dr. Bruenn's efforts, Roosevelt began to feel better. What he needed now, everyone agreed, was a vacation away from Washington, where he could truly rest and relax. Never averse to playing host to the president, Bernard Baruch offered his estate, called Hobcaw Barony, near Georgetown in South Carolina. There were "few better places to rest than Hobcaw," Baruch felt, with its complete lack of annoying distractions, even of a telephone. "The gardens would be in bloom when the President was there, and then it would be one of the loveliest places on earth." He thought of going to Guantanamo, Roosevelt told reporters off the record, but he and his advisers decided against it because "Cuba is absolutely lousy with anarchists, murderers, et cetera, and a lot of prevaricators."

On Easter Sunday FDR arrived at Hobcaw for what was supposed to be a two-week stay, but the visit stretched out to a whole month, spent chiefly in cruising and fishing, sitting in the sun, and sleeping ten to twelve hours a day. Admiral McIntire came along, as always, but this time Commander Bruenn joined the party. From now on, wherever Roosevelt went, there Bruenn would also go. Bill Rigdon served as the link with the outside world, carrying outgoing messages in his jeep to Georgetown, where signals personnel maintained a communications car on the presidential train parked on a siding. He reported to friends that he enjoyed the fishing.

"The whole period of time was very pleasant," said Dr. Bruenn, but on April 28 a fresh problem arose; late in the afternoon the president began to suffer abdominal pains. After examining him, Bruenn deduced a gall-bladder attack, a diagnosis later confirmed by X rays showing gallstones. To the restrictions already imposed on the president—cutting down on cigarettes, quiet dinners in quarters, limited activity generally—were now added the austerities of a bland, low-fat, 1,800-calorie diet, designed not only assuage the abdominal symptoms but to bring about some loss of weight. The diet, however, seemed to cause its own problems. Liking his looks as the pounds departed, FDR became so fond of the results that "it was with difficulty that we persuaded him to eat a little more to hold his weight." The persuasion did not always succeed, and FDR even turned somewhat anorectic. Since the most visible change came in his face, which began to seem not only lean but haggard, the press began to speculate about the cause. Nothing mysterious was involved—nothing, said Bruenn, "in the way of a disease." When tense or worried, said Mrs. Nesbitt, who managed the domestic side of the White House, FDR had always tended to turn testy about the food. Once several years earlier he had made headlines by rebelling against liver and green beans.

Flying in for a quick one-day visit, Eleanor Roosevelt noted that "F. looks well but said he still has no 'pep.'" Dr. McIntire assured her that with a "strict regimen" the president should soon recover. When the presidential party returned to Washington on May 7, McIntire told reporters that his charge was in "excellent shape"—indeed, "as good as a year ago." But even though FDR came back to the White House with an improved color and with some of the seams of weariness smoothed from his face, Baruch shrewdly advised a presidential associate to try to take up all the important business in the morning. The president was tiring, and he functioned best early in the day.

For Franklin D. Roosevelt, it had been almost twenty-three years since that summer day at Campobello when paralysis had struck. It had been an amazing era, with no parallel in history, for during it he had become the first paraplegic to have been chosen to lead a nation. Although far more handicapped than almost any member of the public knew, he radiated an aura of such potency that even his associates did not think of him as having any disability. He had become at home in the White House before he had been there a day, and he had loved the job of being president. To use the terms of one method of classifying presidential character, he showed himself "active-positive"—he did a great deal in office and he felt good about it. He had sought his high position not out of some sense of grim duty but because it would give him the work he liked best. Even earlier in his third term, after eight years of coping with unprecedented problems of both domestic and foreign policy, he could still boom to a visitor: "I can take anything these days!" He would beckon a caller into the office with his famous trademark gesture—right arm stretched out, head arched back, cigarette holder atilt. To one interviewer who saw him from time to time through those years, "he made almost everybody close to him feel bigger, heartier, more vigorous, by reason of his own luminous expansiveness."

And yet he could not walk. With the vitally important aid of his natural charm and ebullience, he had constructed a public personality that simply overwhelmed the fact of his paraplegia. As his cousin Joseph Alsop summed it up, Roosevelt's whole approach to his disability drew on "guts, optimism about finding a way out, and the kind of tough obstinacy that refuses to accept defeat"—qualities that also proved of first importance in the critical times in which FDR had served. His son Franklin, Jr., said that one of the chief lessons he learned from his father was "not worrying."

Roosevelt seemed specially designed to have been president. A scholarly member of the early Brain Trust said of him, "He came to the manipulation of powerful forces and vast interests as naturally as I had to studying them." He could deal with power in all its seriousness because he thoroughly understood—perhaps intuitively—that somewhere in its background, as John O'Hara once expressed it, stands "even the power of life and death, to stay an execution, or to break a man financially, or to have him machine-gunned in a South Side garage, or to ruin his reputation." Or to go to war.

He seemed a natural president, but in the 1920s he had been forced to develop entirely new perceptions—to learn to see what one polio survivor has called "the view from low down," at wheelchair level. Following the polio attack, from now on he would look at the world from an inferior position, as a child sees it. He would take account of this inescapable fact and build it into the personality he re-created (and it was this position of literal physical inferiority which, on one desperate day, General Marshall had sought to exploit).

Roosevelt had succeeded at everything he had tried to do, but with the turn of the year 1944, all seemed suddenly to have changed. He suffered from unaccustomed great fatigue, from aches and pains, from increasing tremors and muscle weakness.

For more than two decades he had physically been an overachiever like most polio survivors, except that his efforts produced spectacular results. But now he no longer even took his usual pleasure in performing little chores, in shaving and dressing himself and in driving. These new patterns of behavior represented something apart from the circulatory problems discovered by Dr. Bruenn.

At a January press conference a reporter who had been out of Washington for two years missed "that surpassing warmth, that almost electric personal magnetism that was such a tangible thing."

What had happened?

After coming home triumphant from Tehran, why had Roosevelt entered on a precipitous decline? It almost seemed that he had kept himself together until he had held his meeting with the Russians and until the strategy of the Allied coalition had been fixed beyond recall. Great fatigue, wandering pains, breathing problems, loss of stamina, weakness, tremors, and associated with these physical symptoms—as cause or result or both—classic signs of depression: This cluster of symptoms had no name and, in fact, did not find recognition as a cluster. But for twenty-two years Roosevelt had wrung extraordinary efforts from his body, making each muscle that functioned perform the work of two or three. Whether from this overwork or from decay of the controlling nerves, with surprising suddenness he experienced what polio survivors speak of as a "falling-apart" pattern. Such a condition, nameless in FDR's day, has lately been called postpolio syndrome, or postpolio sequelae. Even loss of weight is often part of it. Its special mark is the seeming suddenness with which it arrives, expressed especially in the overwhelming fatigue that can make last week's routine task seem a mountainous undertaking today. As polio survivors describe the onset, "it's like hitting a brick wall—a polio wall." After twenty or thirty years of living with his condition, adjusting to it and often mastering it, the polio survivor who has proved to the world that he can rise above his affliction finds himself attacked by an insidious new enemy. As in most disorders, stress plays an important part; the degree of stress experienced by a wartime president hardly calls for comment. From a fourth to a half of polio survivors, specialists estimate, experience this postpolio syndrome. FDR seems likely to have been one of them; certainly such a retrospective diagnosis explains the bleak picture of early 1944 that disheartened the president's associates and admirers.

The doctors, in their way, did not help. In some respects, they had little choice about what they did—the president's heart and lung problems meant that his activity had to be restricted. Some of the limitations, however, could hardly fail to lower his spirits. The White House pool offered help, but, Dr. Bruenn observed, "he wouldn't float but insisted on swimming, which produced more fatigue," and "we had to stop it"; actually, this was a bad move from a polio survivor's point of view not only because swimming is enjoyable but because through the freedom of movement it confers, it maintains or builds self-esteem. And FDR now had to eat his bland, low-fat, salt-free dinners off a tray in his room, removed from the possible stress—but also the enjoyable stimulus—of table companions. The president had come a long, lonely way from White House social evenings like those he had enjoyed during the Arcadia conference little more than two years earlier.

Nevertheless, in late May FDR seemed better, even if he was not as well as Dr. McIntire suggested to Eleanor. "The doctors are very pleased with Pa's comeback & say he is really fine again," she wrote to James, who was serving in the Pacific as a marine officer. She thought FDR was enjoying his new freedom from doing things that bored him; "but it isn't necessity," she said, "just preference." A person who could express the thought that "the constant tension must tell" as though it were a fresh insight may well not have been the most perceptive of observers; indeed, the concern that Mrs. Roosevelt confided to a friend involved the fear that her husband might be willfully succumbing to the attractions of invalidism.

Roosevelt was as great an actor in the White House as he was on the world stage. This was uniquely evident to persons whose comings and goings were not announced and who could thus catch him unawares. Even Mrs. Nesbitt, one of the less philosophical members of the staff, saw that the president was always cheerful with people around him. But "sometimes I'd come into a room where he was alone, when the jovial air had dropped off and he looked tense and tired. Withdrawn is the only word I know to describe him. Only then could you see what he was going through"—and these observations were made well before the onset of the 1944 troubles.

FDR now faced a new challenge. During the summer he would take a trip to Hawaii, to meet with the always arguing army and navy chiefs—General MacArthur and Admiral Nimitz—and try to settle on a Pacific strategy for the advance to Japan.

On February 9 General Marshall sent a proposal to Harry Hopkins at Bethesda Naval Hospital. He had unsuccessfully tried to reach Hopkins by telephone, the general said, but "should have gotten off a letter—several of them—because you have been daily on my mind." Hopkins and Sir John Dill were the two persons outside the family who evoked the strongest expressions of feeling from Marshall, Hopkins perhaps even more than Dill. Though both men had physical problems—Hopkins's very survival often seemed a genuine miracle—Marshall could talk to his fellow American in a worried-father style that he could hardly use with Dill. Encouraged by a note in which Hopkins said he expected to leave Bethesda in about a week, Marshall had developed a complete plan for follow-up care at White Sulphur Springs, West Virginia, where the army had transformed the famous resort hotel into a rest and recuperation center. His description of the establishment was embellished with travel-brochure superlatives, as though he were a tour director and Hopkins a finicky potential customer: The cottages were "luxuriously furnished" and the surroundings "delightful even in the winter season." Mrs. Hopkins would go along too, of course, and the couple could be flown in from Washington.

But "things have gone none too well for me," Hopkins wrote back; he had been ordered to Florida to soak up the sun in preparation for a new and serious operation to be performed at the Mayo Clinic. A few days later, while en route to Miami, Hopkins received a telegram from FDR containing the shattering news that his son Stephen, eighteen years old, had been killed in the fighting on Kwajalein, which had been invaded by army troops on February 1; Marshall comforted Hopkins in a "warm and sympathetic" letter. The chief of staff also suggested that Hopkins's son Robert, serving with the army in Italy, could be removed, at least temporarily, from the thick of the fighting. "I hope you will not send for him," Hopkins answered. "The last time I saw him in Tunis he told me he wanted to stay until we get to Berlin."

Hopkins underwent stomach surgery at the end of March, and in the middle of May he was ready to take up Marshall's invitation to White Sulphur Springs. A few days before Hopkins's operation, Marshall had flown with Dill for a brief holiday in Bermuda. Remembering their visit two years earlier, when Marshall had read the second lesson with its string of tongue-twisting Asia Minor churches, the chief of staff cabled Hopkins that this time he had read the first lesson and Dill the second: "I wished for you and my prayers of the day were for you." On the day of the operation Marshall cabled: MY PRAYERS ARE FOR YOUR EARLY AND COMPLETE RECOVERY. I KNOW YOU HAVE ONE GREAT RESERVE IN YOUR FAVOR AND THAT IS COLD NERVE AND GREAT COURAGE.

Delighted at the good reports that began to come in from White Sulphur Springs, Roosevelt wrote Hopkins not only to express his pleasure but to admonish him to lead a prudent life after he was discharged from the hospital. Hopkins's fondness for a bit of racy living despite his physical frailty evoked friendly censure from FDR. "I, too, over one hundred years older than you are," Roosevelt said, "have come to the same realization and I have cut my drinks down to one and a half cocktails per evening and nothing else—not one complimentary highball or night cap. Also, I have cut my cigarettes down from twenty or thirty a day to five or six a day. Luckily they still taste rotten but it can be done." The president urged Hopkins to stay away from Washington "until the middle of June at the earliest." As for himself, FDR said, he had enjoyed "a really grand time down at Bernie's—slept twelve hours out of the twenty-four, sat in the sun, never lost my temper, and decided to let the world go hang. The interesting thing is the world didn't hang."

Not everyone shared Marshall's and Roosevelt's great concern for Hopkins's health and well-being. On May 22 a Republican congressman from Ohio telephoned the army surgeon general's office to ask "by what authority the War Department permitted Mr. Harry Hopkins to be treated in an Army hospital." After checking with the judge advocate general, a staff officer informed the congressman that the secretary of war possessed the authority to extend army medical treatment to anyone he wished. On the bottom of the memo Marshall wrote a note to Stimson pointing out that the reply had been made before he had been informed of the query: "The responsibility for Hopkins's presence at White Sulphur is wholly mine." The staff officer had expressed concern that Stimson might incur congressional criticism for this act of medical largess, but if that happened, Marshall seemed to suggest, the heat ought to be deflected onto him. In a contest to determine whether such treatment was justified, the chief of staff was unlikely to be bested by such an antagonist as Congressman Ramey of Ohio. But the fact that the issue had been raised represented an example, war or no war, of the fury Hopkins's very existence continued to stir up in conservative congressional circles. All his traits of outlook and behavior combined to make Roosevelt's confidant and Marshall's best political friend a sort of Washington lightning rod.

During the following summer, Marshall, still worried about his friend, managed to turn birthday greetings to Hopkins into a letter nobody else could have written. "The conventional expression of the wish that you may have 'many more' does not meet the situation," said the general, seeming to base his view on the austere and impersonal needs of national policy. "Your good health is a matter of great and professional interest to me." But immediately he added "I missed you much and sadly during the recent period of your indisposition and I am worried now, particularly with the Washington sultry heat, that you may again be overdoing." Marshall then reverted to mention of his friend's "great service to the country," but in a final striking paragraph he burst out in unmistakable strong feeling: "I don't wish, I ask you to be more careful, to conserve your energies and not to overdo and I am also prepared to damn you for your cigarettes, your drinks, and your late hours. Confine your excesses to gin rummy." Although only ten years older than Hopkins, Marshall spoke as if he were trying to shake some sense into a teenager—a beloved teenager. Like Eisenhower in his military sphere, the civilian Hopkins evoked paternal language from Marshall. Anywhere the chief looked, it seemed, he could find a son.

Both Hopkins and Dill had a special tie to Marshall because they interpreted him to others and brought back to him the thoughts of those others. These two communicators served his purposes in a special way, as he returned value to them. But with each one, strikingly different as they were, he went beyond the professional tie to create a warmly personal friendship. Of all the great figures of the war, his communicators were closest to him.

CHAPTER NINETEEN

THE PHOENIX ONCE AGAIN

The illnesses of President Roosevelt and Harry Hopkins meant that two thirds of the informal American strategic directorate had gone on either full or partial sick leave—the chief strategist himself and his personal chief of staff. Fortunately for General Marshall, the American strategic situation had changed; it did not demand the constant discussion and debate—by personal visit, telephone call, and memo—that had been required before matters were settled at Tehran. With his own personal fate determined by Roosevelt's choice of Eisenhower for the command of Overlord, the chief of staff could now devote himself to administering the army in all its complexity and, in particular, to counseling and supporting Ike as the Overlord operation took shape across the Atlantic. It had been Marshall's dream, but his service was now to be given as an enabler, not as an executor.

As soon as Eisenhower, the supreme commander, and Montgomery, the ground commander for the assault, received their assignments, they began pressing for an operation larger in scope than General Morgan's planners had designed under their limited directives. A three-division assault, Ike declared, could not be expected to succeed in sticking in France; the plan was "impracticable," said Montgomery. Not only did the weight and width of the assault demand that the plan be rethought, but a host of other activities had to be fitted into it. Overlord would be the greatest amphibious operation ever undertaken, and it must succeed. Failure in other landings, in Italy or in the Pacific, might be accepted and overcome; the troops could be repulsed and return again; the overall Allied strategy would require no change. But in Overlord the Allies had something utterly different. If the assaulting troops were driven off the beaches of Normandy, the supreme Allied operation of the war against Germany would have failed, not to be mounted again for at least a year—and in a year's time who could know what might happen elsewhere? What would Stalin think? The possibilities envisioned ranged from Stalin's making a separate peace with Hitler to a sweep to the Rhine by the Red Army, leaving the United States and Britain powerless on the Continent. Still another Allied concern related to the possible introduction of German secret weapons, about which Hitler had first spoken in a speech in 1939. For one thing—and a major one—the British and the Americans were attempting to create nuclear weapons; they must assume that the enemy with all his renowned scientific prowess was engaged in the same pursuit. Overall, the price of a failure of Overlord would be incalculable. As Eisenhower wrote to a friend, "We are putting the whole works on one number." The gamble must succeed. So true was this that no alternative plan existed.

Aside from the traditional weapons of attack, Overlord—as it quickly became clear—would depend for success upon less tangible factors, upon strategic deception and signal intelligence. The Germans must be misled about the place and timing of the invasion landings. Intelligence and deception would live in intimate relationship, since the intelligence would provide revelations about the success (or lack of success) of Churchill's "bodyguard of lies." Radio messages intercepted and decrypted by the ULTRA operation at Bletchley Park would not only furnish the Allies with information about the German forces across the Channel, their strength and disposition, but would serve as a check on the workings of the deception plans, which were designed to make the enemy believe in the existence of nonexistent ("notional") Allied forces and unplanned Allied landings. On January 9 the code breakers produced evidence that the deception plans were beginning to work; the Germans were speaking to each other of a notional U.S. army group as though it were a real formation.

In still another realm of activity, Overlord drew on British and American ingenuity and engineering skill. The success of the invasion would turn partly on such new devices as artificial harbors, which would be towed across the Channel and sunk in place. A host of other devices—"invasion funnies," the British called them—would supplement the standard tools of war.

Could preparations in all of these areas, including landing craft, have been completed in time for a mounting of Roundup in 1943, as Marshall and his fellow American officers had urged? Aside from other factors essential for victory, the state of signal intelligence was questionable. The assault on the Normandy coast probably could not succeed without ULTRA, but in early 1943 the Americans had not yet been integrated into the operation. U.S. Army cryptanalysts, translators, and other intelligence officers only began arriving at Bletchley Park for permanent duty in August 1943. Had Americans not joined the operation, U.S. forces in northwestern Europe would have found themselves wholly dependent on the British for signal intelligence.

Thoroughly mindful of the Pearl Harbor fiasco, with its ineffective coordination and tangled lines of authority between army and navy, its bungling and amateurishness, General Marshall wanted no repetition in Europe. The Americans must have their own thoroughly indoctrinated and trained signal intelligence personnel, not only at Bletchley Park but in the field with the U.S. forces; American signal officers must brief American commanders. In a letter of March 15, 1944, to "Dear Eisenhower," the chief of staff explained emphatically the importance of ULTRA and its proper use in the field. The precious information would be entrusted to special security officers who would be attached to the headquarters of large American units, and it must be handled with the greatest care. "In order to safeguard the continued availability of this enormously important source of intelligence," said Marshall, "it is vital that these security regulations be meticulously observed." This statement was followed by a detailed list of procedures.

To one of the U.S. intelligence officers looking back on these events, a basic fact seemed clear: Without ULTRA, "the chances of any second front whatever would have been small." Together with all the other related facts, this view suggests that Roundup could have met catastrophe if the Allies had attempted to mount it in 1943. Yet all the great arguments pro and con between Marshall and Brooke and their respective supporters seemed to turn on other considerations, factors certainly of great importance but far more traditional. Brooke thought that the Americans could not produce the divisions that would be needed to assault the coast of France; Marshall believed otherwise, but it was on such bases that the Allies transmuted Roundup into Overlord and 1943 became 1944.

"In Washington," a British staff officer remarked in late 1943, "ideas are too theoretical, and there is a lack of operational experience and a sense of reality." Nevertheless, "in the end, I suppose we shall probably go into France, with little opposition, and then the historians will say that we missed glorious opportunities a year earlier." But he did not really believe it. As for Marshall, once Overlord was unalterably set on its course, he was too busy with the present to worry about the past. His philosophy on such points was elementally simple: "When something is done, it's done." Or, as a colleague expressed it, "he has analyzed worry and has it licked." Whether, as ULTRA took on increasing importance, the general reconsidered his view on the timing of the invasion cannot be known.

Of all the U.S. command questions, East or West, probably the most vexed arose in China, where the astringent and sarcastic "Vinegar Joe" Stilwell served as commander of U.S. forces and also as chief of staff to Chiang Kai-shek in the generalissimo's role of Allied theater commander. Pitting himself against Stilwell in this looming tragedy was Major General Clare Chennault, founder of the famous Flying Tigers and commander of the Fourteenth Air Force. Marshall saw Vinegar Joe as "a splendid fighting man," a bold and brave leader of an army; but in a diplomatic situation he was overmatched by Chennault, "a superb performer at the game." In February, Marshall grudgingly acceded to Roosevelt's directive that the War Department issue a commission as first lieutenant in the air force to the president's distant cousin Joseph Alsop, a well-known newspaper columnist who had become the charismatic Chennault's public relations adviser. Resenting Chennault's attempts to overthrow Stilwell and take the top job for himself, Marshall considered Alsop a troublesome amateur who unfortunately had the president's ear. Besides, Alsop criticized Stilwell behind his back to the Chinese and the British, and nothing but trouble could come from accepting "subordinates who are determinedly critical and disloyal to the commander" in the theater. Alsop, Marshall sarcastically told FDR, was either a great strategist or "a seriously destructive force." But the appointment stood, and to crown the affair, the president did not even keep Marshall's dissent on file but returned it to the War Department. "He did that time and again. He wouldn't take the unfavorable thing and file it. He'd send it back to you so it would be on your side of the fence." Even after years of close association with the president, Marshall could find such undisciplined behavior baffling. The army certainly did not work that way.

At a January meeting of an Allied group called the Pacific War Council, which brought together representatives of China and other powers around the rim of the ocean, the president passed on some details of special interest from Eureka. Approvingly, he told the representatives that with reference to the Far East the Western Allies and the Russians had reached agreement on three points: a) the Soviet Union should have an ice-free port in the region—Stalin favored Dairen; b) the Manchurian railroad should become the property of China; c) the Soviet Union should receive from Japan the Kurile Islands and the southern half of Sakhalin Island. He, Stalin, and Chiang Kai-shek concurred, said Roosevelt, on all the principal questions concerning the Pacific.

Although the doctors ordered as much of a reduction in the president's activities as they dared, FDR, despite his illness, could not simply "let the world go hang." He and Marshall had to deal together with such matters as the tangled situation in China, as well as many other issues, with the chief of staff and his aides producing drafts of messages to Churchill and furnishing answers to assorted queries. With Hopkins absent, Admiral Leahy had to play an enhanced role, and with it came "a new appreciation of the tremendous selfless contribution Hopkins had been making to his country."

Ultimately the relationship between Stilwell and Chiang Kai-shek turned so sour that the generalissimo refused to have Vinegar Joe in any capacity, and the president ordered him recalled. Although disappointed, Marshall acknowledged Stilwell's complicity in his own fate; he "always got in his own way and just was duck soup for Chennault's gambling," even though he was "being undercut by his commander in chief, the President." At Cairo the chief of staff had taken Stilwell to task for his truly remarkable and chronic social indiscretion. If he wanted to stay in China, Marshall said, he must stop his "outrageous talking," most notably his habit of referring to Chiang as "the Peanut." Stilwell's place was taken by General Wedemeyer.

Previously Marshall had described an operational triumph to

the president. "In France in 1918," he said, "a Division attack order was sometimes fifteen or twenty pages long," and "even as late as 1927 when I took over the Infantry School I found a battalion order three and four pages in length." He had never forgotten that officer years ago on the riverbank in China, struggling to compose his detailed prose, and now he could demonstrate how completely he had won his campaign for clarity and brevity. "All our field orders," he told FDR, "have five paragraphs, each one dedicated to a certain purpose: the first, to information regarding the enemy and our friendly troops; the second, to the general plan; the third, to the details for the operation; the fourth, to supply matters; and the fifth, to the location of command posts (CP's)."

On January 27, in a note of birthday felicitations to the president, Marshall observed that "last year at this time we were treasuring our great hopes as a result of the recent Casablanca conference. It seems to me much more was realized than we anticipated then, and I have the feeling that the Lord will bless our efforts in the coming months, again beyond our expectations." Further, he said, "I wish to thank you for the strong support you have given me personally" as well as to the entire army. That was "a mighty nice note," FDR replied, and, switching to a tone a little more characteristic of such semiformal correspondence, he told Marshall: "One thing that I am devoutly thankful for in these days—and that is the very splendid help I have had from you in all of our common tasks. It has meant a teamwork which has succeeded and will succeed. Take care of yourself."

"I thought you might be interested in a comparison that was brought to my attention yesterday by General McNair," Marshall wrote FDR on February 6. In discussing means for finding urgently needed infantry replacements, McNair had reported that "while only *11%* of the army—air and ground—is composed of infantry soldiers, they are bearing *60%* of the present losses in Italy." Several days later the president asked for an accounting of the number of army divisions that would be serving in the continental United States on the date of the launching of Overlord. Although the figure would be forty-one, Marshall replied, on June 1 the United States would have in the United Kingdom 1,514,700 soldiers, together with 2,804 four-engine bombers, 711 medium bombers, and 4,346 fighter-bombers or fighters.

During February Marshall also moved to bring the president more completely into the intelligence picture. For some time G-2, at the chief of staff's instruction, had worked at developing a convenient presentation of the information on Japanese plans gained from the Magic code-breaking operation. As Marshall described it, the intelligence staff was "separating the wheat from the chaff and correlating the items with past information in order that I may be able quickly and intelligently to evaluate the importance of the product." Frequently two or three of these "black books" were produced in a single day, but Marshall had not realized that the president seldom saw this material. Apparently the one copy of each book that went to the White House had been kept by Admiral Leahy for his own use. From now on Roosevelt would receive his own set of black books.

In response to fresh evidence that strategic plans could never be considered cast in concrete, Marshall in late February had to engage in a fresh battle for Anvil, the planned landing in southern France. In a White House meeting he told the president that the British wished to cancel the operation because the Allied armies were "having hard going in Italy" and had no troops to spare. But, said Marshall succinctly, "we say Anvil should not be canceled."

Well, the president asked, had the British made any mention of the Allied agreement with Russia? It had taken "three days at Tehran to get the British to agree to Anvil, and the Russians were tickled to death in that their suggestion had been accepted." They would not be happy now "even if we told them the abandonment of Anvil would mean two or more divisions for Overlord." General Eisenhower, who no doubt experienced heavy pressure from the British staff in London, should be informed that "we are committed to a third power" and the president had no intention of trying to go back on that commitment: "He felt that we have given up promises in the past and had better not do it again."

During this period many messages of a political-military and sometimes almost purely military nature came not through the elaborate Anglo-American machinery but directly from Churchill to Roosevelt. As the president's agent, Admiral Leahy often turned to Marshall for a reply, a good example being a mid-February exchange of messages concerned with the development of China as a great Pacific base and the consequent need for the Allies to keep her supplied and for the British to "back to the maximum a vigorous and immediate campaign in Upper Burma." Marshall and Leahy thus became a two-man message-producing team, a trend accentuated by Hopkins's absence from the White House—an absence that meant the loss not only of Hopkins's individual outlook and experience but of a purely civilian contribution. The State Department played little part in this message stream.

Even though he was running in slow motion, the president still liked to poke his finger into various pies, particularly when they were tempting navy pies. Throughout the war, just as he had in World War I as assistant secretary of the navy, he had kept an eye on ship construction, even to the point of asking Knox and King to discuss "the relative advantages of 13,600 ton heavy cruisers vs. the 11,000 ton heavy cruisers." Showing how closely he followed the navy's use of task forces, at one point he had suggested that five of the new two thousand-ton destroyers, which could be complete in a year, might take the place of one heavy cruiser or one light cruiser, which took two years to build; but, he asked, "what is the relative anti-aircraft total fire of five of the new D.Ds., with full anti-aircraft batteries, as against the total anti-aircraft fire by one of the largest type C.A.s or C.L.s?"

One of Roosevelt's interventions had proved decisive. A convinced believer in the potential value of small aircraft carriers, he had ordered Admiral King to build a number of them and to award the contract to an aggressive industrialist named Henry J. Kaiser, who had previously been rejected by the U.S. Bureau of Ships; King had no choice but to comply. FDR turned out to be right, both about the great usefulness of the baby flattops and about the effectiveness of Kaiser as a shipbuilder. Now, in February 1944, Roosevelt suggested to King that small boats be sent to Britain for use during Overlord as rescue craft. For a number of specific reasons, King turned down the idea. "I rather suspected that Admiral King would answer as he did," FDR noted to Leahy, though he thought that the small craft "ought to be far better than the British small craft which operated at Dunkirk in 1940." He offered his underlying thought: "I should hate to be accused of not doing all we can in case a lot of drowning people are floating around in the Channel." Like the unemployed in the 1930s, the victims of combat lived in Roosevelt's mind as individual persons.

* * *

Having stayed in bed an extra hour or two because summer vacation had just begun, a schoolboy in middle America came downstairs on the morning of June 6, 1944, to be told the news: "The invasion has begun." Nobody needed to say where in the world the operation was taking place or how important it was. So completely did all Americans, military and civilian, expect the great event that nothing was required anywhere beyond the single word: *invasion.* It was something even schoolchildren had waited for. But nobody not involved in Overlord could know the incredible complexity of the operation on which depended Allied hopes for ending the war, and few could appreciate the fact that by landing on the coast of France the Allied armies had begun to fulfill the dream that George Marshall shared with Grant and Pershing. The world would now see American strategic doctrine at work.

Before his press conference began that afternoon, FDR asked his staff why they all wore such smiles. "You don't look like you're so solemn yourself, Mr. President," one of them replied. Even Fala, frolicking about the executive office, seemed to have caught the mood. Showing that despite his physical condition he could still rise to an occasion, FDR looked well to a staff member, as he sat behind his desk in a white shirt, with a dark blue polka-dotted bow tie. Eager for news, one of the largest groups of reporters for any of FDR's press conferences crowded into the office. "I think this is a very happy conference today," the president told his audience; indeed, he had heard that "the whole country is tremendously thrilled." But he also wanted to make a serious point. Quoting one of the mythical friends he liked to use as the subjects of his little parables, he said that this man, a welder, had already left the war plant where he worked because the war was effectively over and he wanted to get a permanent job as soon as he could.

But "the war isn't over by any means," the president declared. "This operation isn't over. You don't just land on a beach and walk through—if you land successfully without breaking your leg—walk through to Berlin. And the quicker this country understands it the better."

General Marshall and the other Joint Chiefs flew to Europe on June 8 to see Overlord for themselves. On the evening before their departure they attended a White House dinner for the head of the Polish government-in-exile, Stanislaw Mikolajczyk, a man whose position seemed progressively shakier the farther west the Russians advanced. On this occasion Marshall evoked a remarkable silent tribute from Bill Hassett, one of Roosevelt's secretaries. After chatting with the general as the two stood in line, Hassett told himself: "Wherever this man goes he inspires reverence—may God spare him."

While overseas, Marshall not only witnessed the fighting in Normandy, where he was favorably impressed by the quality of the Allied effort, but also engaged in a fresh argument about Operation Anvil. (Soon a new problem would arise in Normandy, where the hedgerows—dense barriers formed by bushes and trees growing in mounds of earth—caused unexpected problems for Lieutenant General Omar Bradley's troops. Strangely, the great 16,000-person Overlord bureaucracy seemed not to have anticipated the problem. "We didn't know we were going to hit such rough country," Marshall said. "G-2 let me down every time in everything." But the culprits would not be found only in G-2 in Washington; the intelligence officers at Eisenhower's SHAEF headquarters also bore culpability. The specialists in the Inter-Service Topographical Department, the Allied Central Interpretation Unit, the Military Intelligence Research Section, the Joint Photo-Reconnaissance Committee—all had missed the troublesome hedgerows.) Though Churchill hated Anvil, the British themselves did not present a united front against it, but the operation nevertheless would not stay in place. It resembled a heavy picture, which, once hung, kept pulling out the nail that supported it. Anvil, renamed Dragoon, began on August 15; its successful launching did not end the debate.

Marshall also performed a special personal mission. Just eight days before D Day in Normandy, Lieutenant Allen Brown, Marshall's "friend in need" during his courtship of Katherine Brown, had been killed by sniper fire as his tank unit advanced toward Rome. In Italy, Marshall not only visited his stepson's grave at Anzio but did his best to reconstruct the action in which he had died, studying the terrain and interviewing the members of Allen's crew. The next day he began his journey home.

On returning to the United States, the Joint Chiefs gave the president a report that read like essence of Marshall. Proclaiming the line FDR had followed at his June 6 press conference, the members of the U.S. high command spoke of "a state of mind in this country against which we believe the public should be warned"—as, duly, the public was by the release of this report on June 29. The U.S. armed forces were progressing on all fronts, the chiefs said, showing "not only the courage that was expected of them but a toughness and a technical skill that has made them more than a match for the veterans whom they opposed." (Did this particular sentence ever chance to come before the long-skeptical eye of Field Marshal Sir Alan Brooke?) But, sounding exactly like the president, the chiefs declared that "some people" were wrong in believing that "the war is as good as won, and that accordingly they can throw up their war jobs and go back to civilian life." A tough fight still awaited the Allied forces, and "desertions on the home front" would protract the war just as would desertions on the fighting fronts.

The invasion had survived all the hazards that had troubled its commanders and planners; the troops had arrived in France to stay. Now the army created under the command of General Marshall and under the specific supervision of General McNair would face its great test. McNair had designed a force not only lean but mobile—its trucks, cars, and other vehicles making it by far the most mobile army in the world and contrasting strikingly with the Germans' anachronistic dependence on horse-drawn transport. GIs had grown up as tinkerers and backyard mechanics; a mechanized army thus seemed the logical American fighting force. But this lean army came to France with the traditional American mission: It must crush the enemy by the application of superior power. How well was it suited for this role?

Some auguries were favorable. Before American involvement in the war and during the year following Pearl Harbor, "a bunch of unregimented and inquiring minds" in the artillery had devoted themselves to improving the gunnery techniques acquired in World War I from the French textbook on the subject, with its instructions for box barrages, rolling barrages, and "how many rounds would you have to fire to destroy a pillbox that was six yards wide, four yards deep, and three yards high at a range of so and so, using so many guns." In the first war results had been achieved by massing the batteries, but twenty-five years later the experiment-minded gunners learned with the aid of radio to mass the fires without having to mass the guns, and thus developed "the ability to move and mass fires to support a moving, fighting army instead of a relatively static army." In the field, U.S. artillery proved itself deadly.

Yet American tanks still seemed to reflect the spirit of Jeb Stuart rather than the method of U. S. Grant. If an institution can be seen as the lengthened shadow of a single person, then the absence of that person can account, at least partly, for the existence of a truncated shadow. In August 1941 General Chaffee, the leading American advocate of the armored division, died after suffering a physical breakdown brought on by his day-and-night labors to build up the armored force. (In a highly typical example of his thoughtfulness, George Marshall had rushed honors for the general through the bureaucracy—an Oak Leaf Cluster for the Distinguished Service Medal Chaffee had won in World War I, nomination for a permanent major general's rank, and promotion to temporary lieutenant general, though Chaffee was too sick even to be told of the latter gestures.) Lacking Chaffee's dedicated leadership, the advocates of armor as concentrated power also saw armored divisions losing their glamour as Russia reeled but failed to crumple under the attacks of the German panzers. Just a month after Chaffee's death, General McNair and his associates settled on the thirty-three-ton medium tank later designated the M4 and widely known as the Sherman. The choice of the Sherman as the standard U.S. tank followed perfectly from McNair's fondness for mobility over power; tanks existed primarily not for punch but for pursuit.

General Marshall believed early on that he had the problem of tank design well in hand. "As to mobility, speed, handling, and matters of that sort the American tank was incomparable," he said, but he acknowledged that in "fighting characteristics" the British tanks were far ahead. "My effort," the general said, "was to bring about the settlement of the thing on the basis of what the Americans did best and what the British did best." Actually, early in the war American M3 tanks—General Grants—proved far superior to existing British tanks when put to work in the desert fighting against Rommel. But later, in Tunisia, the Germans outgunned the Shermans with the sixty-three-ton Tiger, which then appeared in France alongside the forty-seven-ton Panther, whose frontal armor simply brushed aside the fire from the Sherman's 75. Mechanical problems frequently immobilized the Tigers, but with its potent 88mm gun this tank made a formidable foe, and the hard-shelled Panther always posed a serious problem for the crews of the American Shermans. "Only by swarming around the panzers to hit them on the flank," said General Bradley, "could our Shermans knock the enemy out." And the cost, in tanks and crews, often proved high. On learning of the problem, General Eisenhower expressed surprise, but at this point in the war, though the armament might be improved, a new tank could hardly appear in time to change the situation. Yet the Sherman still had mobility and mechanical reliability, as its great advocate, the pursuit-minded George Patton, pointed out. If his Third Army had been equipped with Tigers, he said, "the road losses would have been 100%"; the Tiger was useful only on defense, as a sort of stationary gun, and could never have been employed by an advancing army. The Sherman would appear in numbers beyond compare: American factories would turn out almost fifty thousand of them. "Our tank superiority," said Bradley, "devolved primarily from a superiority in the number rather than the quality of tanks we sent into battle." In spite of Marshall's earlier intervention, it seemed, American strategists still suffered from cognitive dissonance: The dashing Jeb Stuart's free-flowing red beard made a strange ornament for U. S. Grant's somber features.

In pursuit of his aim of having trained regular officers serve in the field overseas instead of on staff duty at home, Marshall had "a reserve officer of thirty-one years as the secretary of the General Staff, operating in the broadest way possible: being sent for by the president at midnight to sit with Churchill and himself in some of their discussions; going with me to the various theaters of operations" and often acting as secretary of Allied meetings. Reflecting on the responsibilities assumed by this reserve officer, Marshall as an old regular found himself amused.

Frank McCarthy took over as secretary of the General Staff at the beginning of 1944, when Bill Sexton left for service with the field artillery. Not all of McCarthy's duties proved as lofty as midnight missions to Roosevelt and Churchill. As a general, Marshall had long been accustomed to the automatic availability of certain kinds of services; McCarthy looked after the repair of the general's house, the painting of his office, and the shoeing of his horse. As secretary of the General Staff, McCarthy found that the chief continued "to assign me some of the little personal tasks that I have been doing for him for a long time—such as meeting certain very special people at the front door and taking short trips with him." Like Mona Nason and others who worked for the chief of staff, McCarthy knew that Marshall required nothing except perfection. Within two weeks of his appointment as secretary of the General Staff, he learned to be "psychic," because "that is what a successful Secretary has to be." McCarthy was supposed to know what was happening, or not happening, in the chief of staff's office; *how* McCarthy was supposed to know it did not concern the chief; that was McCarthy's problem—one the secretary solved by developing his own special means.

Since Marshall's office could be reached directly from the corridor, McCarthy had no way of knowing whether anyone had come to see the general without passing through the anteroom to be noted by a secretary. After Marshall had expressed his displeasure when McCarthy interrupted a meeting with such an unheralded visitor, McCarthy resolved not to be caught that way again, and at night, while the chief of staff was home at Fort Myer, a new feature was added to his office. McCarthy had a weight-activated buzzer installed under the visitor's chair facing the desk; now a secretary would always know whether the general had unexpected company.

McCarthy revered Marshall, but the chief of staff's eminence and austerity did not cause the secretary to act in an inhibited way. When Bedell Smith sent a case of champagne and a case of cognac from France, as gifts for Marshall, McCarthy told the chief that, acting on Smith's advice "to deduct the middle-man's profit, I have relieved you of one bottle of the cognac." Very properly, he enclosed with this note the draft of a letter of thanks to Smith.

Though an all-around convivial fellow, McCarthy represented something more and different to the chief of staff—he seemed a perfect example of the ideal Marshall for twenty-five years had held, the citizen soldier, and he no doubt earned the distinction of being called "Frank" not merely from the chief's inability to keep his last name straight but from his winning personal qualities and devotion to duty. Marshall once dispatched him on a mission with full authority to "issue instructions in my name," these orders to take precedence over any previously issued orders, and in a Christmas note the chief told McCarthy: "You have my complete confidence"—a statement Marshall did not make lightly. At Casablanca earlier in the war, as the two walked side by side on the beach, chatting, they had been amused to see Admiral King strolling with his aide, who carefully kept several paces behind his master.

McCarthy's "southern charm" also led to a friendship with Joan Bright, who appeared at the Allied conferences as a leading figure in the British secretariat. Gifted with "an innate understanding of English humour," Marshall's aide found many friends among the British representatives; Miss Bright thought him "sensitively quick in his reactions, thorough in his work, an ace organiser," and readily saw why General Marshall "treated him on terms of affectionate familiarity and equality." The chief of staff, she thought, "must have thanked Providence" for his aide. At the conclusion of the Tehran conference the British Chiefs of Staff had played host to the Americans on a visit to Jerusalem en route back to Cairo. During the evening the chiefs attended their own formal dinner while the lesser lights danced in the room next door. After a handsome feeding, the generals and admirals moved into the room where the staffs were at play and watched their juniors "bouncing rather self-consciously around the floor." First to break ranks, Marshall cut in on McCarthy, who was dancing with Miss Bright. Speaking of his aide, Marshall said to her, "He is a very nice person." "And so are you," thought the young woman.

One Monday morning back in Washington, another young woman had the same thought and expressed it aloud. The general had given up his chauffeured limousine in favor of driving himself to the Pentagon in his little black sedan. That morning at a bus stop he beckoned three secretaries into the car.

"It's nice of you to stop on such a rainy morning," said one.

Marshall assured her that the rain had been the factor causing him to give them a ride, because "usually I think you girls ought to walk."

One of the passengers thought of giving this austere sentiment the kind of answer it clearly deserved—something like "with these long hours we work, I ride when I can to conserve energy." But then she saw four stars on a folded coat: General Marshall! When they drove into the general's parking spot, he invited them upstairs for a look around, and then they went off to their offices.

"He is a very tall man with a kind voice," observed the woman who told the story, "and I've never seen such shiny shoes."

Despite what Marshall chose to tell his passengers, he frequently gave rides to war workers he saw on the way to the office. He practiced the same hospitality when on an airplane trip. Once, returning to Washington from North Africa, he ordered the takeoff delayed until a member of his staff found two wounded privates to occupy the spare seats. But he took special pleasure in picking up hitchhikers while driving in civilian clothes from Washington to Leesburg. Since to many of his passengers he seemed only a friendly but anonymous Good Samaritan, he heard opinions and reactions he could have picked up nowhere else. Any ruler probably has a bit of the Haroun al-Rashid in his makeup, a desire to roam his domain incognito. In giving rides to GIs, Marshall found a way to satisfy this wish and perform a service as well. He had, said one observer, "a profound apprehension of the dignity of the individual soldier in a democratic army." As he had told Frank Hayne twenty years earlier in China, every soldier was an American citizen.

What was the matter with the president? For months rumors had circulated about the state of his health, and a photograph taken three weeks earlier at San Diego, before he left on his Pacific voyage, had shown him slack-jawed, looking gaunt and old. But now, as he delivered a report to the nation on his trip to Hawaii for talks on strategy with General MacArthur and Admiral Nimitz, listeners could hardly credit the sounds emerging from their radio speakers. The once clear, lustrous, perfectly controlled voice had turned mushy and muffled. The delivery was uncertain and halting, as if Roosevelt had not quite decided how to phrase his remarks. The speech itself rambled, seeming to have little point or direction. Even a listening youngster felt it: Something *must* be wrong with the president. Sitting by his radio in Washington, Sam Rosenman "had a sinking sensation." Had the old master lost his touch—and, possibly, more than his touch? Having been nominated in July for a fourth term in the White House, was FDR going to be able to beat back the challenge mounted by the Republican nominee, Thomas E. Dewey, a vigorous and articulate ex-prosecuting attorney only forty-two years old?

The President spoke in the late afternoon of August 12, 1944, from the deck of the destroyer *Cummings,* moored inside a flooded drydock at the Puget Sound Navy Yard in Bremerton, Washington. Because he would be appearing before a throng of ten thousand shipyard workers, he had chosen to stand as he delivered the speech, which meant that he had to put on his heavy leg braces, not often used during the war; since he had last worn them, he had lost weight and they no longer fitted his legs. Uncertain supports at best, the braces proved even less effective on this day because the deck on which the president stood was curved. A crisp wind rocked the ship, causing him to pull against the lectern for support. Where she lay in drydock, the destroyer was surrounded by high buildings, from which the president's words coming through loudspeakers echoed and re-echoed. To compound his problems, FDR had not given great thought to the "informal summary of the trip I have just taken," and he frequently interpolated ad-libs that only enhanced its vagueness.

In many ways the speech resembled the kind of discursive monologue FDR liked to throw off as he sat with friends. He spoke of the afternoon he "played hookey for three hours" and "caught one halibut and one flounder"; he discussed at length the geography of the Pacific region, which had greater distances "than anywhere else on earth"; with some insight he spoke of the great future Alaska could enjoy as an American equivalent of Norway and Sweden. He did not fail to point out the benefits derived from his talks in Hawaii with "my old friend General Douglas MacArthur." He did not, of course, reveal to his audience that he had expressed support for MacArthur's wish to retake the Philippines, as part of the Allied advance toward Japan, rather than bypassing the islands and striking first at Formosa, as the navy desired; in the popular saying of the day, that was a military secret. Nor did the president comment on the fact that he had conducted these meetings on strategy without the help of his highest-ranking advisers, the army chief of staff and the chief of naval operations. (Not pleased at being excluded from the discussions, General Marshall dispatched his own emissary to MacArthur's headquarters in Brisbane to reach an understanding with the suzerain of the Southwest Pacific.)

Radio listeners might sense the fact that in its ideas, construction, and phrasing the Bremerton speech represented an inferior Roosevelt production, but they could hardly be aware of the technical problems facing the president. Nor could they know that as he delivered the first half of the speech—during a period of perhaps some fifteen minutes—FDR experienced what Dr. Bruenn described as "substernal oppression with radiation to both shoulders." A heart attack, angina, or muscle spasms resulting from the president's struggle to keep himself upright? Listeners would have been horrified had they realized that during much of the speech terrible pains threatened to choke FDR into sudden silence.

Back in the captain's cabin after he had finished speaking, the president got rid of the hated, painful braces and underwent an EKG and a blood count. In a telling phrase, Dr. Bruenn noted "no unusual abnormalities."

A curious by-product of the president's long journey, which on the way home had included stops in Alaska, came from his visit to the naval air station on Adak Island in the Aleutians. Somehow a rumor arose that after the presidential cruiser had gone a considerable way from Adak toward her next stop, FDR discovered that Fala, his Scottie, was missing, presumably left ashore on the island. The commander in chief thereupon was said to have ordered a destroyer to speed back to Adak and pick up the dog and hurry him back to the cruiser. By acting in this imperial fashion, FDR had revealed a double callousness—he had pulled a valuable warship from her proper duty of fighting Japs and he had wasted thousands of dollars of the taxpayers' money. As the story spread among Roosevelt haters, it acquired such persuasive detail that precise—though varying—dollar amounts appeared.

Following the disastrous speech at Bremerton, public-opinion polls showed Roosevelt's support slipping; his opponent, the immaculate but aggressive young racket-busting lawyer, enjoyed a corresponding rise in the standings, with his repeated declaration that it was "time for a change." In the midst of a great war, FDR had chosen in 1944, as in 1940, to appear presidential rather than gladiatorial, to cruise above the battle. In view of all the rumors about his uncertain health, his supporters fretted that this battle might go by default. But one day, while attending a second Anglo-American conference in Quebec, FDR summoned Grace Tully and, deriving great amusement from the chore, dictated a paragraph for use in a forthcoming address. Later he showed it to Robert Sherwood, saying, "I'm going to give a speech to Dan Tobin's boys next Saturday night and I expect to have a lot of fun with that one." This speech, in effect the opening of his real campaign, would have special importance because the Democrats more than the Republicans depended on large turnouts of voters. If he wanted to win, Roosevelt must fire his supporters with enough excitement to drive them to the polls.

FDR's renomination had come as an inexorable event. It took no account of his physical problems, of his exhaustion, of the fact that as a handicapped person he had produced twelve years of extraordinary effort in the White House, presiding over not only economic recovery and war but over a fractious, quarreling, contentious country, government, and political party. The president had approached 1944 like a man in free fall; nothing could stop him, whatever he or anyone else might desire. On the Saturday evening of the speech—September 23—Anna Roosevelt expressed the fears that assailed her. Since Bremerton she had wondered whether her father still had any fight in him. As her father's helper she had read and commented on successive drafts of this major new speech; she knew that its effectiveness would depend on the way her father delivered it, and she was worried. She asked Rosenman: "Do you think Pa will put it over?" Full of his own doubts, Rosenman did his best to give Anna a cheerful answer.

"Dan Tobin's boys" were the Teamsters' union, and at the head table in the banquet hall of the new Statler Hotel in Washington, FDR was flanked by Tobin, president of the union, and William Green, president of the American Federation of Labor. Nearby sat FDR's favorite shipbuilder, Henry J. Kaiser. Just before the dinner the Teamsters had unanimously endorsed Roosevelt for a fourth term; he could not have appeared before a more enthusiastic audience, as was shown by the four-minute ovation that greeted him. This time, unlike the scene at Bremerton, he spoke indoors, with admiring listeners close at hand to respond to his words, and he was sitting comfortably; he also had a carefully prepared text on which he had enjoyed the help of Rosenman and Sherwood.

To the delight of his audience, the president at the beginning of his speech demonstrated good voice and prime fighting fettle; perhaps the Teamsters—and the Democrats generally—would, after all, hear the kind of political rallying call they hoped for. Conceding that he was four years older than he had been during the last campaign, FDR observed that "there are millions of Americans who are more than eleven years older than when we started in to clear up the mess that was dumped in our laps in 1933." He asserted that the Republican Old Guard could not succeed in passing itself off as the New Deal. Accusing the opposition of using Hitler's technique of the "big lie," he told the approving Teamsters and his radio audience how he had rubbed his eyes when he read Republican charges that the Great Depression had been "not a Republican depression but a Democratic depression." He suggested that in making such a charge, the Republicans were committing a tactical error: "Now there is an old and somewhat lugubrious adage which says, 'Never speak of a rope in the house of a man who's been hanged.'" If "I were a Republican leader speaking to a mixed audience, the last word in the whole dictionary that I think I would use is that word 'depression.' Not even Goebbels would have tried that one." The Teamsters loved it.

But in a few moments they would be moved to much greater merriment. FDR came to the passage he had dictated to Tully and shown to Sherwood. Here, amazingly, the president's tone and delivery achieved absolute harmony with his material; he displayed timing that was perfection itself, with intonations and pauses that could not have been bettered by Bob Hope or Jack Benny or any other contemporary master of comic delivery. He had never been better. Keeping his expression serious, giving his voice a tone of regretful indignation as mockery played about his words, he said: "These Republican leaders have not been content with attacks on me, or on my wife, or on my sons—no, not content with that, they now include my little dog, Fala. Well, of course, I don't resent attacks, and my family don't resent attacks, but Fala does resent them. You know, Fala's Scotch and, being a Scottie, as soon as he learned that the Republican fiction writers in Congress and out had concocted a story that I had left him behind on an Aleutian island and had sent a destroyer back to find him—at a cost to the taxpayers of two or three or eight or twenty million dollars—his Scotch soul was furious. He has not been the same dog since.

"I am accustomed to hearing malicious falsehoods about myself—such as that old, worm-eaten chestnut that I have represented myself as indispensable. But I think I have a right to resent, to object to libelous statements about my dog."

The laughter that exploded in the Statler banquet hall swept across the country. With those words the president had taken charge of the campaign. Foolishly trying to respond to the speech, Dewey sputtered but could find no effective answer.

From then on, said Paul Porter of the Democratic National Committee, the race was "between Roosevelt's dog and Dewey's goat." The Scottie could scarcely lose.

Once again, President Roosevelt had done it; despite all the grim evidence to the contrary, he had shown that he could still bounce back. He still had unsuspected reserves on which he could draw. Rosenman thought it "the finest speech he ever made." Before the very eyes of his admirers, Roosevelt had once again proved himself a political phoenix rising from what seemed the ashes of a crumbled body.

CHAPTER TWENTY

THE ARGONAUTS GO FORTH

When a young navy lieutenant named Robert Myers came to work in the White House map room, he discovered that his job brought with it one unforeseeable challenge. Occasionally he had to push the president around the room in his wheelchair, a trickier assignment than it looked; one day the lieutenant managed to maneuver FDR into a corner, and, said Myers, "there were words." One evening he learned something else. Not sure he was doing the right thing, he took some dispatches upstairs at midnight and was relieved to find the president not asleep but working on his stamp collection. He seemed in a friendly mood.

"I never know whether to bring these to you at night, sir," Myers said. "Do you have any instructions?"

"Well," said FDR, "if you bring them and they're not important you're in trouble, and if you don't bring them and they *are* important you're in trouble."

Myers got no further guidance. In private, the president spoke more quietly than Myers had expected, but his voice carried its Rooseveltian resonance; no New Dealer, the lieutenant nevertheless noted with approval that FDR's manner had nothing pompous about it.

Many mornings the president would appear at the map room in the company of Admiral Leahy, who was well liked by the watch officers; as one of them said, "by reputation he was crusty, but he never gave map room personnel any trouble." Myers regarded the admiral as an "incredible" worker "absolutely committed to the President." Leahy would actually have much of his homework done before the president arose. His staff had set up a system of classifying dispatches and reports by color—pink for incoming messages from field commanders, green for papers of the Joint Chiefs, white for papers of the Combined Chiefs—and quickly realizing that many of these colorful matters ought to be brought to the president's attention every day, the admiral had developed the habit of making a selection from the overnight dispatches and other material, placing the papers in a folder, and meeting the president as he was wheeled from the elevator on the way to his office. FDR would greet him with a cheery "Good morning, Bill." Since, as Leahy said, "war is no respecter of schedules," Roosevelt, still abed, would frequently look up from his newspaper to find the admiral at the bedroom door, bringing news requiring decisions that could not be put off even for an hour. Sometimes Leahy would launch into a discussion while FDR was shaving with his old-fashioned straight razor. "The President," the admiral later observed, "kept himself informed minutely on the progress of the war."

Admiral Brown, Roosevelt's naval aide, viewed the president's morning journey to his office as "an amusing parade." Husky Secret Service agents would lead the march, one of them laden with baskets of papers that had constituted the presidential evening reading; "the President's wheel chair was pushed out smartly by his valet." To Brown, FDR's "Good morning" was an intentional indicator of his state of mind. "By his expression and tone we had come to know whether it indicated satisfaction with the day's news, annoyance at persistent difficulties, or grim determination to tackle and overcome them." With his navy cape thrown about his shoulders, the president seemed "more like the winner of a Roman chariot race than a confirmed cripple. Admiral Leahy had to hustle to keep abreast of the chair on one side, and I was equally hard pressed on the other." Watching the lively parade, Sherwood felt that "nobody who worked for him had a right to feel tired." But as the war ground on, FDR, for all his great zest and courage, had proved mortal; his body had given ominous evidence that it could not continue to support the demands of his schedule or his will. Yet in the "Fala speech," as the Teamsters address quickly became known, he had astonished those closest to him, and he had gone on to win the election; his dog had indeed driven Tom Dewey's goat from the field.

The October campaigning weeks had proved to be a remarkable interlude. Under the stimulus of the kind of fight he loved best, with his carefully calibrated daily routine thrown out the window, FDR displayed a renewed interest in food, his blood pressure levels declined, and despite such political follies as a full day's exposure to a driving cold rain in New York City, he contracted no respiratory infections. But by mid-November he had again lost his appetite and the flesh began to fall away from his body. One day at Warm Springs, after swimming, his blood pressure read 260 over 150. The doctors forbade further exercise in the pool.

On January 20, 1945, Roosevelt for the fourth time took the oath as president of the United States. Speaking from a White House portico to an outdoor crowd on a cold, windy Washington day, he was racked again by the spasms that had struck him as he had stood on the deck of the *Cummings,* and as soon as he had finished his address and gone inside he downed half a glass of whiskey to kill the pain. After the day's ceremonies he would have little time to rest; he must now gather together all the personal forces he could find to meet a new physical and diplomatic challenge.

Robert Bogue, a Washington attorney in his twenties, had gone into naval intelligence because Admiral King believed that young lawyers made the best watch officers in the operation to track down German U-boats. But by the autumn of 1943 the Allies, guided by radio intelligence, had won the Battle of the Atlantic, and as a result of the slackened demand for personnel in the antisubmarine F-35 operation, Bogue became available for transfer to the White House map room. Here he, like Myers, developed an admiration for Admiral Leahy and a particular liking for Harry Hopkins, a "bright, engaging fellow who would put his feet on the table and talk to twenty-five-year-olds as if they were peers." Bob Myers liked Hopkins too, although disapproving of him politically; Hopkins had "a great sense of humor," but he posed a unique problem in the map room through his habit of tossing lighted cigarettes into wastebaskets.

As FDR traveled the world, map room personnel always went along as communications officers. Lieutenant Bogue had taken his cipher apparatus in a railroad car to Bernard Baruch's Hobcaw Barony and to the Anglo-American conference in Quebec in September 1944. Now Bogue and his map room partner, Major Hal Putnam, were about to have an opportunity to learn that they did not care for salami, rice, and tea for breakfast, and they would find that when they complained about this fare it would be replaced by tangerines and toast. Lunch and dinner would present a somewhat different scene, with the table graced by a pot of beluga caviar. Putnam would consider this arrangement highly satisfactory, but unfortunately Bogue did not care for caviar.

It would be another great production on the model of the Sextant-Eureka conferences at Cairo and Tehran, and because this time the American and British participants would journey to the shores of the Black Sea to meet Stalin, the operation received the code name "Argonaut," in commemoration of Jason's storied quest for the Golden Fleece. Although the conference would take place at Yalta in the Crimea, observers having classical inclinations might have recalled that the original Argonauts pursued their quest to Colchis in the Caucasus, where the prize they sought hung in a grove protected by dragons breathing fire, and they might also have noted that Marshal Stalin was himself a native of this same region. (Less evocatively, the two stages of the operation, at Malta and at Yalta, bore the respective designations Cricket and Magneto.)

Sailing on the cruiser *Quincy,* the president and his party departed from Newport News at 8:31 in the morning, January 23, only three days after the inauguration. At this point in the war the Germans, after throwing considerable fright into General Eisenhower's Allied forces, were retreating from the "bulge" they had created with a surprise thrust through the Ardennes. On the eastern front the Russians had opened a powerful winter offensive on January 12; alarmed at the pressure exerted by the Germans in the Ardennes, Eisenhower and Churchill had tried to hasten the launching of the great attack by the Red Army, Eisenhower by dispatching his deputy, Air Chief Marshal Sir Arthur Tedder, on a mission to Moscow, Churchill through a direct message to Stalin. He would hurry matters along, Stalin replied, in order that the Russians might "do all in our power to support the valiant forces of our allies." (Tedder left London for Moscow on January 1, the Allies began their counterattacks on the Bulge on January 3, Churchill cabled Stalin on January 6 and received the marshal's reply within two days, and after a series of delays and disasters Tedder reached Moscow only on January 15. He therefore had no effect on the timing of the Russian offensive; whether or not Churchill's request exerted any influence was another question.) At Yalta,

Stalin might well claim credit for having voluntarily helped the Western Allies.

Interviewed on his eightieth birthday, the long-forgotten General Peyton C. March had some sharp words about the failure of Allied intelligence with respect to the Ardennes front. Unlike General Pershing, the old World War I chief of staff had no relationship with Roosevelt or Marshall, but he had always thought that the war would be long and hard, and in 1943 he had not shared in any Allied optimism about achieving victory in 1944. Now he said that when he heard Allied excuses about bad weather and difficult terrain, "I just fall on my knees and weep." Allied intelligence officers, he acidly observed, had allowed the enemy to assemble a force of 200,000 men right under their noses. "Imagine the population of Richmond, Virginia, being assembled across the Potomac and we not knowing about it!" Not being privy to the secret of ULTRA, March could not know that in addition to other oversights, Eisenhower's team had failed to take note of several clues to German intentions offered by signal intelligence. Aside from the specific failures of Allied G-2, the Anglo-American leaders and staffs had—not for the first time in the war—been overconfident and underestimated German skill and resiliency. The Allies fell again into the false logic that caused Pearl Harbor: A major German attack would constitute an illogical use of the enemy's remaining resources; therefore such an attack would not take place. General Marshall kept hands off the Ardennes. Referring to impressions gained on a tour of the front in October, he said, "I was worried about this thing," but primarily because he thought German strength opposite U.S. forces would upset Allied plans to attack; he said later that he did not believe General Bradley took even a calculated risk by manning the Ardennes thinly; he simply "got soaked" by the German offensive.

In traveling all the way to Yalta, the president was once again putting himself under a great strain in order to accede to Joseph Stalin's desires. Harry Hopkins, back from the hospital, believed that the Big Three urgently needed to meet; since "there was not a chance of getting Stalin out of Russia at this time in the light of the military situation," the Allies might as well agree at the outset to meet somewhere in the Soviet Union and spare themselves "a lot of long-winded, irritating cables back and forth . . ." To his brand-new secretary of state, Edward R. Stettinius, Jr., who had succeeded the physically failing

Cordell Hull, FDR observed that he did not expect "U," as he called Stalin (for Uncle Joe), to be willing to fly; he had offered to meet with the marshal in Armenia or Sicily, the President said, but the leaders would probably end up in what Stettinius called "someplace where all the old Russian palaces used to be." Showing his suppleness, Stalin in insisting on staying close to home this time adduced as his reason not military considerations but his doctors' advice "against long journeys."

Hopkins flew to London for preliminary talks with Churchill, who told him that in view of what he had heard about conditions at Yalta, "we could not have found a worse place for a meeting if we had spent ten years on research." Hopkins at this point needed to call on all his talents as an inter-Allied soother, since Churchill and the Americans had stumbled their way into a public controversy over what the State Department, and much of the press and public, regarded as the prime minister's promonarchical actions in Greece and Italy; in Greece, particularly, Churchill had upset American liberals by intervening with British troops against Communist-led insurgent forces. (Honoring a previous agreement with Churchill whereby Greece was to fall into the British sphere of influence, Stalin dutifully looked the other way.) During December Hopkins had advised Churchill to refrain from issuing statements and ride out the storm, advice that had proved sound. But differing viewpoints continued to divide the British and the Americans, as Churchill was to see at Malta.

This war-battered island came into the story because Roosevelt needed a junction at which to switch from ship to airplane. One of the many problems Yalta posed as a meeting place was the fact that the Aegean, the Bosporus, and the Black Sea had not yet been cleared of German mines, and no one wanted to be responsible for causing a warship with the president of the United States aboard to meet an explosive end en route to the conference. From Malta the Allied delegations would fly in a great stream of planes to the Crimea, where the Americans would be awaited by the U.S.S. *Catoctin,* which would provide communications facilities and could also serve as a hotel if, as seemed likely, "the old Russian palaces" proved uninhabitable.

The responsibility for ensuring the safe delivery of the president through waters in which he would be exposed to possible U-boat and air attack fell on the shoulders of Admiral Brown, who felt that Hopkins had committed a piece of utter frivolity by arguing for Yalta, remote and long occupied by the Germans, as the meeting place. Never convinced that the adventurous Hopkins showed proper concern for Roosevelt's health and safety, the admiral felt further distress when, halfway across the Atlantic, the *Quincy* received a message from Churchill declaring that a veteran British pilot had found the motor trip from the Crimean landing field over the mountains to Yalta "a most dangerous and frightening experience" and reported Yalta itself to be "rife with typhus and lice." FDR, however, "treated it all as a joke." But the U.S. admiral commanding in the Mediterranean had dispatched what Brown called a highly modern delousing unit to Yalta.

En route to Malta the president celebrated his birthday at a party graced by no fewer than five birthday cakes, and he could take great pleasure from the company of "Sis," his beloved daughter Anna. At Gibraltar the *Quincy,* heavily protected by destroyers and air cover, sped at thirty knots through a reputed concentration of U-boats, and at midday on February 2, under sunny skies, she steamed into the Grand Harbor of Valletta, where on the stony quay an array of Anglo-American generals and admirals awaited the presidential party. Churchill waved greetings to FDR from the deck of a British ship. Having as always enjoyed his sea voyage, the president appeared to Admiral Brown to be ready for the busy official day arranged for him at Malta, but when Admiral King came aboard, he was alarmed at Roosevelt's appearance. Far from looking fit, King thought, the president had deteriorated just in the two weeks' time since the inauguration.

Flying in a four-engine C-54, General Marshall and his party had left Washington on a bitter-cold January 25. After conferring at Marseille with Eisenhower, the chief of staff arrived at Malta on January 29 to take part in much-needed talks with the British chiefs before the entire high-level Allied group departed for the Crimea. Marshall, along with Leahy and King, came to these discussions bearing a fresh distinction. On December 11, after what Leahy called a "tortuous legislative journey," the Senate had approved a House bill authorizing the creation of four new five-star ranks for each service, to give the top American officers supposedly equal status with British field marshals and admirals of the fleet. King had long believed the move necessary and had suggested "arch-admiral" and "arch-general" as names for the ranks.

Marshall had objected to the idea, whatever the ranks might be called, since he did not wish to appear avid to share Pershing's lofty status. Later he offered another reason, wholly typical of him, that probably carried more weight and explained why he told a congressman that he would refuse to testify in favor of the bill. A good part of Marshall's influence with Congress had come from the clear fact that he never sought to use any legislator for his own personal purposes; he did not now wish to be "beholden to Congress for any rank or anything of that kind. I wanted to be able to go in there with my skirts clean and with no personal ambitions concerned in any way . . ." As for dealing with the British, Marshall believed that "the important thing at a military conference is not your relative rank. The important thing is to know your story, and have lots of money and lots of men." If he knew his position, he said, and had the power to back it up, he could "sit at the foot of the table as a brigadier and have as much influence as anybody there." Nevertheless, on December 15 he became the senior holder of a new rank, General of the Army. Although some observers thought that this title was adopted because of the obvious absurdity of "Field Marshal Marshall," the chief of staff said that he had never raised this objection—yet, seeing the possibility, Churchill had "twitted" him about it. In any case, the title of "field marshal," with its un-American echoes, was not likely to receive congressional approval. "Fleet admiral" for the navy posed no problems.

The discussions at Malta thrashed out Anglo-American differences about Eisenhower's plans and about Allied command arrangements in Europe. "The session," said Marshall, was "a very hot one." Dissatisfied with Eisenhower's handling of the fighting in his theater, Churchill had proposed that Field Marshal Alexander replace Tedder as deputy supreme commander and in effect take charge of the land battle; ever since North Africa, the prime minister and his advisers had sought to interpose one or another British general between Ike and the actual conduct of operations. Marshall had already made unmistakably clear his objection to the appointment of a British ground commander in whatever guise, but at Malta disagreements flared over the strategy whereby Ike intended to fix final defeat on the Germans.

One highly useful participant could not be present at this "hot" session; this time Marshall's traveling company did not include Sir John Dill. During the past year Marshall had made a series of extremely unusual moves concerning Dill. Fearing that Churchill was considering the recall of Dill because in some British eyes the field marshal had become too sympathetic to American ideas (or "gone native"), Marshall had set to work to endow the Briton with so much prestige that the prime minister would not dare remove him. Invading the Ivy League, the chief of staff managed in February to obtain for the field marshal the Howland Memorial Prize (described in the press as "the highest special award within the gift of Yale University"), which had been established to honor persons promoting international understanding. Marshall took a high-level group with him to New Haven and encouraged full publicity in the newspapers. On April 3 the College of William and Mary conferred an honorary degree on the chief of staff's great friend, and on May 20 Dill received an honorary degree of doctor of laws in a special convocation at Princeton. (The world had rarely found itself in such a fluid state, the field marshal told his distinguished audience. "Old patterns have broken down, old beliefs have been challenged, many of the old ways of life have ceased to operate." What people must understand was that "none of God's creatures can live safely" while "others in this shrunken world are, through no fault of their own, existing in want with no hope for themselves or for their children.") In obtaining these honors for Dill, Marshall worked persistently through associates who had connections with the various schools, and, he said, he "sent Churchill stories about him," dramatizing the impact Dill had made in America.

But the chief of staff could do nothing about the state of Dill's health. Subject to a variety of physical problems during the preceding years, the field marshal developed pernicious anemia, and though he struggled mightily to keep up his work, he fought a hopeless battle; he died in Washington on November 4. He received an outpouring of tributes, public and private, marked by their unusual intensity. At Marshall's request, for the first time flags in Washington flew at half-staff to honor a foreign officer. At the funeral Marshall, now a veteran at this procedure, read the lesson—"with such real feeling," Lady Dill wrote him—and as Marshall had arranged, Dill was buried in Arlington National Cemetery, the first foreigner to be so honored. "Marshall's face was truly stricken," said one of those present at the graveside service. The general made a practical move by sending Mrs. Chamberlin from his office as "domestic help" for Lady Dill. "Officially the United States has suffered a heavy loss," Marshall wrote the field marshal's widow, "and I personally have lost a dear friend, unique in my lifetime, and never to be out of my mind." Strong words for strong feelings on the part of this reserved man, and truly unique words to utter about the military representative of another country, but Marshall had not only lost a close friend who was a great gentleman, he had experienced the end of a relationship with a professional peer, the only equal in the world with whom he had enjoyed the opportunity to be on close terms. General Hull in his thinking linked Marshall with George Washington as a military leader; of Dill, Hull said, "He had many of the qualities of Robert E. Lee." The two men had thus made a formidable force for Allied discussion, compromise, and unity; as Hull put it, "I do not know of another case in history where the friendship between two such outstanding allied military leaders had as much influence in welding together the military efforts of their respective countries."

Fortunately for this unity, Allied disagreements, even in the hot session at Malta, could no longer arise over such fundamental issues as Europe versus the Pacific but concerned such questions as the proper meaning of the concept "closing the Rhine" (to Marshall, some of the argument represented nothing more than an unnecessary semantic scramble). In any case, the power in what, for all the disagreements, constituted a remarkably—even unprecedentedly—intimate and successful alliance now rested heavily on the American side. But the Combined Chiefs succeeded in producing a report that took account of British fears about Eisenhower's broad-front strategy, and at six o'clock on February 2, on board the *Quincy,* they were able to tell their political masters that "complete agreement" had been reached. Brooke had insisted on spelling out his desire for Eisenhower to concentrate his strength in the north, and Marshall, concerned primarily with preserving Ike's independence of action, had assented. At this point, barring some German scientific miracle, the war in Europe presented no real question except how best to end it.

During the evening of February 2, after playing host at a small dinner at which both he and Churchill had a daughter present, the president boarded his new C-54 transport, which reporters soon nicknamed the *Sacred Cow.* At Dr. McIntire's insistence, this plane had been equipped with an elevator so that the president would not have to come aboard by means of a ramp; but FDR, who liked to make very little fuss over his infirmity, looked on this innovation as something of a frill. Since he was, most cooperatively, subjecting himself to being lifted and hauled in and out, and since he had to cover great distances by ship and plane in order to seek a meeting of the minds with Joseph Stalin, an elevator seemed a not unreasonable expense.

At the unlikely hour of 3:30 A.M., having waited through the noisy night while other planes in the great Allied fleet departed Malta at ten-minute intervals, the *Sacred Cow* lifted off for Saki in the Crimea, 1,375 miles away. Already weary, the president stood only at the beginning of his difficult quest for the golden fleece of understanding between Russia and the West.

For all their extraordinary personal characteristics and achievements, Roosevelt and Churchill came to the Crimea as figures in a long-running political mainstream. Though from time to time they might harbor suspicions about each other's wisdom, about attempts to gain commercial predominance in an area or to extend imperial control, they had grown up in the same world of discourse, and they could share an outlook their common background made possible. But in facing Stalin they confronted an unusual problem, different enough in degree from ordinary problems to be different from them in kind—or, perhaps, simply intrinsically different. Since Tehran, developments in the war had sharpened the difference. It had been the Western leaders who had pressed for this new meeting, and in coming to Yalta they brought with them questions relating to the future of Germany, to the fate of Poland (and other eastern and southeastern European states through which the Red Army had moved or was moving), and to the establishment of a new world order based on international organization. To these essentially political or diplomatic questions was joined a great military question, one of particular concern to General Marshall: What form would Soviet intervention against Japan assume and what schedule would it follow?

In taking on their formidable task, the Western delegations came to the Crimea with an invisible theme. Others besides Roosevelt were among those with physical impairments, though his were certainly the most severe; on seeing him, Sir Charles Wilson (who had now become Lord Moran) noted bluntly that "to a doctor's eye, the President appears a very sick man. He has all the symptoms of hardening of the arteries of the brain in an advanced stage, so that I give him only a few months to live." (Dr. Bruenn disagreed; the president's circulatory problems, he said, were not of a kind to affect his thinking.) Hopkins, after his preliminary trip to England and other points, arrived in Malta diarrhetic and debilitated, his yellow skin stretched tight over prominent bones; only his internal fire had enabled him to take part in the Allied talks.

Churchill, who had suffered numerous bouts of pneumonia during the war, arrived at Malta running a temperature—"a good beginning," Lord Moran observed drily, "to a winter journey of three thousand miles." One of Churchill's secretaries said of the prime minister that his work had "deteriorated a lot in the past few months," and that he had become "very wordy, irritating his colleagues in the Cabinet . . ." On this trip Churchill was also taking a gastrointestinal medication that tended to produce nausea and vomiting and also may have caused or contributed to his fever. But, as a British medical observer later remarked, great men are not easy patients: "Owing to their exceptional personalities, fortitude and avidity for power, they are liable to cause special difficulties to the attendant physician," particularly since "they are skilled in concealing their real feelings and thoughts."

Churchill was not the only British representative in subpar condition. Anthony Eden, the prime minister's right hand, felt the strain of five wartime years of unremitting work in high office. "He is tired, tired, tired," said his friend Harold Nicolson. Not only was Eden tired, he suffered from internal pains not yet diagnosed. The foreign secretary did not see this kind of tiredness as confined to the top men; Britain herself, he noted in his diary, was now conspicuously war-weary. Looking toward Yalta, Eden had glumly noted that he was "much worried that the whole business will be chaotic and nothing worth while settled, Stalin being the only one of the three who has a clear view of what he wants and is a tough negotiator. P.M. is all emotion in these matters, F.D.R. vague and jealous of others." Weariness seemed the theme of the American and British representatives, men sick and prematurely aged; Eden was only forty-seven, Hopkins fifty-five, Roosevelt sixty-three, Churchill, at seventy, the senior. (Molotov, the Soviet foreign minister, apparently sensed this weariness; he is said to have spoken of Roosevelt and Churchill as "two tired old men" who "have no choice but to give us what we want.")

What sort of partner or opponent would the stress-worn Western leaders encounter at this stage of the war in Joseph Stalin? How true was Eden's perception?

Milovan Djilas, a loyal Yugoslav Communist meeting the marshal for the first time, had taken note of his sparse hair and his strange coloring, white except for ruddy cheeks; later Djilas heard this coloration described as "Kremlin complexion," characteristic of those who, like Stalin, spend their lives indoors. The combination of "strawberries and cream" complexion and thinned hair suggested to one physician-author the possibility that Stalin suffered from a severe thyroid deficiency called myxedema, which not only has physical effects but in some cases can produce mental changes that may bring hallucinations or psychotic delusions of persecution.

Whatever the state of his glands, Stalin appeared to Djilas as an extraordinarily complex man—a "cold calculator" with a "passionate and many-sided nature." On a visit to Moscow in the winter of 1944–1945 Djilas found himself subjected to an outburst of anger from Stalin. He later decided that he could not tell how much of this behavior was theatrics and how much was real; with Stalin, it seemed impossible to separate one realm from the other. "With him, pretense was so spontaneous that it seemed he himself became convinced of the truth and sincerity of what he was saying."

Stalin came to the meetings with the Western leaders not only as a complex individual person but as master in his own house and as the ideological chief of a world political movement. This ideology, like many others, made some use of the term "democracy," but Lenin, the guiding theoretical spirit of the movement and first head of the Soviet state, had long ago made it clear that the "dictatorship of the proletariat" he preached represented what a scholar writing in the 1940s called "a flat negation of bourgeois-democratic principles"; "a parliamentary republic," Lenin said, "would be a step backwards." The dictatorship of the proletariat, he declared repeatedly, is "won and maintained by the use of violence and unrestricted by any laws" (Lenin, unlike many other ideologues in power, seemed to show little fondness for violence but to view it as a sort of unfortunate necessity; the victims of the violence perhaps regarded his feelings as irrelevant). For the past century, democracy, basing itself on the idea of individual rights, had fought for such principles as universal suffrage; the Soviet system rejected these ideas. Lenin not only disliked but despised democracy and openly held dictatorship to be a superior form of government, although he would sometimes borrow the language of the other world and declare that the Soviet Union was "a million times more democratic than any bourgeois democracy."

In 1937, with the adoption on New Year's Day of "Stalin's constitution" by the Soviet Union, the successor dictator became the pope of communism at home and internationally. While changing some governmental structures, the new constitution confirmed the country as a dictatorship of the proletariat guided by "the most active and politically conscious citizens"—a one-party state. Such one-party rule, observed the 1940s scholar, "can scarcely be described as government 'by' the people, at least without doing violence to the common sense meaning of words." Indeed, one day Roosevelt had spontaneously remarked to Hopkins that the Russians didn't seem to use words the way Americans used them. Hence, in entering this politically charged meeting (contrasting with the military orientation at Tehran), Roosevelt and Churchill could expect not only political disagreement but complete ideological opposition and, very likely, semantic incomprehension—all of it made more complex by the individual drives and variegated personality of Joseph Stalin.

Formally, Roosevelt came much better prepared to this conference than to Tehran. For one thing, he brought with him a secretary of state—a notable first. On December 22, speaking of Yalta, the president had told Stettinius, "I want you to go"—words he could never have said to Cordell Hull. Only forty-four, Stettinius cut a striking figure with his silver hair and bushy black eyebrows; a businessman unusually sympathetic to the New Deal, he had no background in diplomacy, although he had served as lend-lease administrator, but he was a capable executive and popular with Congress and as secretary of state would not set up as a rival to FDR in the management of foreign affairs. In discussing possible postwar problems with the new secretary, FDR played one of his favorite tunes. If he and Churchill could "sit around a conference table again with Marshal Stalin," matters could be settled. Stettinius brought a new harmony to the scene, though his contribution to American policy did not seem likely to be large; but he had with him from the

State Department the experienced Soviet hand Chip Bohlen, who had developed a close relationship with Harry Hopkins and in December had officially been named to a useful and long-needed position—State Department liaison with the White House.

At Yalta, Bohlen would play a much larger role than at Tehran, since he would serve not only as interpreter but as expert on Soviet affairs. To this experienced diplomat, the Soviet Union resembled "the act of love. You can read and memorize every page of all the literature about it. But you can't possibly tell what it's really like, until you've experienced it yourself." Though a product of the Ivy League, Bohlen himself was an unusual member of the Foreign Service, unpressed, never seen in striped pants, never observed striding along the pavement walking stick in hand. Justly enough, he regarded himself as essentially a realist with respect to the Soviet Union and its aims, and *vis-à-vis* the White House he saw himself as a professional dealing with amateurs. At the beginning of his job as liaison, he recalled, "I went to the White House with some trepidation, thinking I was going into hostile territory." But he received a welcome even from Admiral Leahy, who had previously won no renown through any fondness for diplomats or State Department officials.

Bohlen also found his own views changing. Earlier he had approached foreign affairs with the outlook of a technician; now, in almost daily contact with Hopkins and in frequent touch with Roosevelt, he began to see that "foreign policy in a democracy must take into account the emotions, beliefs, and goals of the people." He grew to understand that the government could not act, or fail to act, in disregard of the public, just as Marshall had learned in 1942 that strategy could not be formulated without taking popular opinion into account: The public must be "entertained." Bohlen therefore saw what Roosevelt had on his mind as he set off for Yalta: "The American people, who had fought a long, hard war, deserved at least an attempt to work out a better world. If the attempt failed, the United States could not be blamed for not trying."

Much earlier, the chiefs of staff had told the president of the importance they gave to Soviet support in the climactic phases of the war against Japan. The American public likewise counted on Soviet participation. Hence Roosevelt gave high priority to securing the necessary commitments from Stalin. The president also felt that he must make the best use of this opportunity to keep the United States firmly on the internationalist path—well away from the shadows of isolationism—by obtaining full agreement on the United Nations. To win what he wanted, perhaps he would have to compromise on other questions that came before the leaders.

Along with Hopkins and the Joint Chiefs, FDR would have with him at the coming conference the secretary of state, the White House liaison, and some ten State Department officers. He would also have the thorough but nonhuman aid of a series of specially prepared black books analyzing every problem likely to arise during the Argonaut meeting. He had taken these briefing books with him on the U.S.S. *Quincy;* no one, however, had noticed him spending much time with them.

CHAPTER TWENTY-ONE

THE FLEECE AND THE DRAGONS

"It was thrilling to watch this operation," Colonel Charles Donnelly recalled of the airlift from Malta to the Crimea. As soon as one four-engine plane took off, the next one taxied to the end of the runway, warmed up its engines, and with throttles wide open departed literally at the scheduled second. The flights were scheduled at night to cut down the chances of German interference. "I had a feeling that history was in the making and was proud to be a part of it," said Donnelly, who had already witnessed a fair amount of history at Sextant and Eureka. "Russia was a land of mystery to most Americans, even to those who had been there; now we were about to descend on a historic outpost of this ancient land, two hundred and fifty strong, like beings from another planet . . ."

The Allied planes flew eastward from Malta, over the Ionian Sea, past Mount Olympus, and over the Chalcidice Peninsula with its three great prongs extending into the Aegean (one of the prongs suggestively bearing, in this association-rich corner of the world, the name Kassandra), then over European Turkey and the Black Sea, the flights finally ending on a landing strip that seemed to have been dug out of a mud flat on "a grim and treeless plain." The *Sacred Cow* made the trip from Malta in six hours and forty minutes, arriving at 12:10 local time. The president remained aboard until Churchill's plane arrived twenty minutes later. When the prime minister disembarked and came over to the *Sacred Cow,* FDR, wearing his navy cape, rode the elevator down to the ground; he was then lifted by his bodyguard, Mike Reilly, into a jeep driven by a Russian in a visored cloth cap, and the two leaders moved closer to the guard of honor, which was splendidly attired in new dark green uniforms with gold shoulder boards and gold buttons; its officers carried sabers. The band played the American and British national anthems and the "Internationale" and the president and the prime minister reviewed the guard; as he watched, Churchill puffed on one of his trademark eight-inch cigars.

The open attitude with which many of the Americans approached the Yalta Conference showed itself in a strange example of dereliction of duty. As the welcoming ceremonies progressed, Bill Rigdon happened to notice that the U.S. cipher machine that had been unloaded lacked an escort; the officers responsible for guarding it had failed to resist the lure of the Russian refreshment tent, which offered smoked fish and a variety of liquors, including a slightly sweet and very smooth version of vodka. (Such a lack of wariness might have been expected of officers serving a military that in 1943, when planning the postwar defense establishment, had been unable to identify a possible adversary for the United States. The Germans and the Japanese would have been beaten, and who else was there?)

At a few minutes after one, the procession departed for Yalta, eighty miles away over mostly unpaved roads. The drive took the visitors through rolling, snow-covered country without trees, past gutted buildings, burned-out tanks, demolished railroad cars, a military cemetery with red stars over the graves. After passing through Simferopol, the caravan began to climb, taking the "Route Romanoff" over high mountains and along the east coast of the Crimea. The American passengers found the ride exciting. "The curves were short and sharp without retaining walls," said Admiral Brown, and they "were on the very edge of a continuous precipice. The driver's tenacity in holding his place in line despite hell and high water was a fine example of discipline through fear. Passengers were thrown about in the constant change of direction; one escape from the edge was quickly followed by another hairbreadth escape." Brown compared the whole experience to being driven for six hours in a jeep at breakneck speed over rough fields. For FDR, whose railroad train always moved at a measured pace so that he could readily keep his balance, the jolting ride in his car with his daughter Anna and secretary Stettinius represented a rude introduction to Russia. All along the way, closely spaced, stood Red Army sentries, a number of them what Stettinius termed "sturdily built" women.

The ride posed special problems for Colonel Donnelly. Like other American officers he had enjoyed the treats offered by the Russians in their tent, and without realizing what he was doing had consumed an unwise amount of the subtly flavored, highly deceptive vodka. Moving with some difficulty, he had then joined other officers aboard a rickety bus bound for Yalta. The driver performed his task with determination as relentless as that shown by the president's chauffeur. Donnelly soon realized that he had made a horrendous mistake by not visiting a latrine before leaving the landing strip, since his head and stomach problems were compounded by great pressure from his bladder—a state of affairs shared by several of his companions. "But the driver refused to stop. Threats to urinate in the bus had no effect; the driver had his orders and was following them literally with no consideration for the comfort of his passengers." So desperate did Donnelly and some of his fellow Americans become that after debate they resolved to overpower the driver and force him to stop. As they were about to launch their operation, the bus itself came to the rescue; its worn old engine overheated, removing any power of choice from the driver. Within seconds, the passengers were out of the bus and lined up in an open field, facing downwind. Even if Soviet discipline through fear would not acknowledge human need, it had to yield to mechanical failure.

After passing through Yalta, a small resort city with a prewar population of about thirty thousand, the president's motorcade drove around a curve and up a hill and into the grounds of Livadia Palace, about two miles from the city. In the Yalta region, on the south side of the mountains around and through which they had passed, the visitors experienced a more benign climate than the raw atmosphere of the landing strip at Saki. Nostrils chilled by wintry travel now sniffed the fragrance of laurel. Finished in 1911, the palace itself had been intended as a summer residence for Czar Nicholas II, although he and his family used it only four times before revolution swept them away. The long stone building, more or less Italianate, had some fifty rooms and stood on high ground overlooking the town and the sea, with a panorama of mountains to the east and north. The Russians had performed prodigies of rehabilitation to undo the damage inflicted by the occupying Germans; they had apparently stripped Moscow hotels of everything—beds and chairs, kitchen equipment, rugs and pictures—to make Livadia and the other villas inhabitable. But they could not replace or expand the bathing and toilet facilities, which were archaic and limited (the entire U.S. delegation had to make do with one bathroom for the men and one for the women, with only the president having private accommodations; except for the war, said one U.S. officer, "the bathrooms were the most generally discussed subject at the Crimean conference"). And as the Americans discovered during their first night, some of Churchill's pessimism rested on solid ground—the Russians had not been able to rid the place of bedbugs, nor had American exterminators won the same battle.

While the Americans were doing their best to settle in at Livadia, the British were undergoing the same process at the Vorontsov villa, about twelve miles south of Livadia; members of the British party had been enjoined to bring "plenty of flea powder and toilet paper." Headquarters for Stalin and his party would be the Koreis villa, once the estate of Prince Yusupov, who won a place in history as the leader of the assassination conspiracy against the czarina's favorite, the *starets* Rasputin.

The president was quartered in the first-floor bedroom originally used by the czar; the imperial billiard room served as FDR's private dining room. Stettinius and other American civilians likewise enjoyed ample accommodations, but fortune did not treat the military staffs so generously. So many American officers had come to Yalta that five to seven generals had to share one room and ten colonels another. In the days of empire, the second floor had been the domain of the czarina and her four daughters; now the imperial bedroom housed the chief of staff of the U.S. Army, and the empress's adjacent boudoir was occupied by Admiral King. Thoroughly familiar with the running hostilities between the U.S. armed services, a British observer was shocked to see on the door of the suite a card reading: GENERAL MARSHALL AND ADMIRAL KING. It could not be, she thought; it seemed "an impossible equation." With detachment made possible by his own comfortable accommodations, Stettinius reported that in general "the overcrowded conditions for the military contingent were a source of much amusement." No one, however, would go hungry. Food appeared in unlimited quantities, and dinner began with the best brown-grained caviar.

At nine o'clock on the first evening, the final member of the American party, Lieutenant Robert Bogue, arrived at Livadia.

He had stayed behind at Malta to handle last-minute U.S. communications and had caught one of the last planes out. But he did not discriminate among kinds of caviar; he did not care for any of it.

The president slept well that first night, and at eleven o'clock the next morning, Sunday, February 4, began the round of conferences that would consume the ensuing week. As a general pattern, what were termed "formal meetings"—involving the Big Three and their advisers—took place at Livadia Palace in the late afternoon and early evening; at other times throughout the day the statesmen conferred with their political, diplomatic, and military advisers. In one notable difference between this and previous conferences, the ailing Hopkins spent almost all of the time in bed, making appearances only for the plenary sessions—and, in fact, he missed the first of those. Moving further into the civilian realm, Admiral Leahy to some extent took Hopkins's place. "Bill," Roosevelt had said to him, "I wish you would attend all these political meetings in order that we may have someone in whom I have full confidence who will remember everything that we have done."

Not only did a secretary of state take part for the first time, but FDR had introduced other novel features into the American delegation. Sitting in the Grand Ballroom close to the big round table along with diplomats and military types was James F. Byrnes, former senator and Supreme Court justice who directed the Office of War Mobilization and Reconversion; as czar of the home front, Byrnes had acquired the popular title "assistant president." He had no background in foreign affairs and had expressed astonishment at being invited to go to Yalta. But Roosevelt had his reasons. He also seemed to have his reasons for including in his party a person whose foreign experience was even more modest than that of Byrnes—his old friend and political counselor Ed Flynn, for many years Democratic boss of the Bronx. The president, however, had not brought these two men to the Crimea because he wished to draw on their wisdom in council. They would take on their value back home, as interpreters of the Argonaut proceedings to two important groups—Byrnes to the Senate and Flynn to American Catholics—and so as promoters of the president's strongest wish, popular and Senate approval of American membership in the proposed new United Nations organization.

Byrnes and Flynn did not owe their presence at the conference exclusively to Roosevelt's fear of repeating Woodrow Wilson's fiasco over the old League of Nations. The fact was that the administration found itself in trouble. At the end of December, Stettinius had told the president that public faith in U.S. foreign policy had declined in the past six months. And in January opinion polls revealed "increased public skepticism" concerning the intention of the great powers to uphold the ideals proclaimed in the Atlantic Charter and the subsequent declaration of the United Nations. If idealism seemed to have vanished from the great Allied coalition, FDR feared, then the American public might turn again, as it had turned twenty-five years earlier, to isolationism. The doubts came in reaction to certain recent and current events, including British actions in Greece, in which a grim pattern seemed to be showing itself; these doubts crystallized on the issue of Poland. At Yalta other questions, such as the voting principles to be followed in the new international organization, might after discussion find seemingly acceptable answers. But the Polish question pitted worried West against adamant East.

At Tehran, practicing statecraft by wink, Roosevelt had given his assent to Stalin's territorial desires with respect to Poland. Although room remained for argument over details, the country's eastern boundary essentially would follow the line Ribbentrop and Molotov had drawn in 1939, with compensation for the area lost to Russia coming from German territory on the west; almost literally, the great powers would pick Poland up, walk it westward, and set it down again. To be sure, such action would have abundant precedents: For centuries, countries in Eastern Europe had known boundary shifts and territorial compensations and even periods of extinction.

What about the nature of the postwar Polish government? The Americans and the British continued to recognize the Polish government-in-exile set up in London early in the war. The leaders of this government had repeatedly entreated the Western Allies to insist that the Russians not prevent the establishment of a free and independent Poland in postwar Europe. But since July 1944 the Soviet government had promoted the claims of the Communist-dominated Polish Committee of National Liberation, the group commonly called the "Lublin Poles," and on December 27 Stalin informed Roosevelt that "in the event of the Polish Committee of National Liberation becoming a Provisional Polish Government," the Soviet government would proceed to grant it recognition. The marshal stated this position coolly, as though the Lublin Poles were merely a group of splendid unattached patriots whom the Red Army had happened to encounter as it moved into their country. Roosevelt immediately replied that he was "disturbed and deeply disappointed" at Stalin's plan, but, he said, "I am more than ever convinced that when the three of us meet, we can reach a solution of the Polish problem . . ." Would Stalin therefore delay his recognition of the Lublin committee? No, Stalin would not. He promptly presented Roosevelt and Churchill with a *fait accompli;* the decision, he said, had already been made by the Presidium of the Supreme Soviet and communicated to the Lublin Poles. (In discussions with the Western leaders, Stalin often spoke of his "colleagues" and their wishes, as though the Soviet Union were governed by a sort of oligarchy of which he was only one member; the Anglo-Americans could never decide exactly how much weight to give these assertions.)

Earlier, in August 1944, other Soviet behavior in Poland had disturbed the American and British governments and people. On the first day of the month, underground forces in Warsaw rose against the occupying Germans and within three days had gained control of large parts of the city. But then Nazi SS detachments arrived on the scene and, to the accompaniment of the kinds of infamous atrocities for which they had won their evil renown, shattered the Polish "Home Army," ferociously pursuing its members even through the sewers beneath the city streets. As all these violent and pathetic events took place, a Soviet army limited itself to watching with interest from the other side of the Vistula. In defense of this inaction, Stalin told the protesting Western leaders that "sooner or later the truth about the group of criminals who have embarked on the Warsaw adventure in order to seize power will become known to everybody." These "criminals" were affiliated with the London Polish group, which like any other Polish government over the centuries viewed the Russians with deep distaste but nevertheless had cooperated with the Red Army as it moved into Poland, even helping liberate Lublin, the seat of the Russian-inspired countergroup. Whether or not the Russians could have helped the Home Army in its deadly struggle, however, what aroused Western concern was Soviet refusal to allow British and American aircraft bringing supplies to Warsaw to land on Russian airfields. Even so, Western leaders and the press did not exhibit the anger that might have been expected. With the war going well, nobody wanted to rock the boat of the great coalition. For Stalin the slaughter in Warsaw had served a highly useful political purpose, the extermination of the only organized body of Polish patriots who could oppose him and the Lublin committee.

In September, watching Soviet behavior in Poland and similar moves to dominate countries in the Balkans, a worried Averell Harriman wrote from Moscow that "when a country begins to extend its influence by strong arm methods under the guise of security, it is difficult to see how a line can be drawn. If the policy is accepted that the Soviet Union has a right to penetrate her immediate neighbors for security, penetration of the next immediate neighbors becomes at a certain time equally logical."

The president had come to Yalta to win certain goals and to make it evident to the American people that he had won them. He wished to help the London Poles, and he believed that he still must concern himself with those millions of U.S. Polish voters about whom he had spoken with Stalin: They must feel satisfied that he had looked after the interests of the land from which they or their forebears had come. In relation to Poland the Americans and the British aimed at the establishment of a government that would be free and independent and also would be friendly to the Soviet Union. They would soon find out the nature of the task they had taken on themselves.

Except for the first session, all the meetings at Yalta followed a principle of strict segregation between political and military representatives; only Admiral Leahy crossed the line to sit with the civilians. At the plenary sessions of the Big Three and their advisers, the president was flanked at the big table by the admiral and Stettinius on his right and by Bohlen and Harriman on his left. But for all the organizational effort that had gone into the creation of this remarkable event, Yalta, like Tehran, lacked one contemporary feature found everywhere in the business world: No stenotypist recorded every word; in fact, there was no official record of the meetings; each delegation kept its own minutes. In the American delegation, Bohlen resembled the legendary pruritic paperhanger, since in addition to interpreting and acting as an adviser he also had to keep the American record.

The subject of Poland did not arise until the third plenary

session, on February 6. During the opening session on Sunday, which had been devoted to the general military situation, Stalin collected a bit of psychological credit for the Soviet winter offensive by observing that the Russians had advanced its date not because of any contractual obligation but because "they felt it to be their duty to their allies to do so." No one could blame Stalin for seeking credit, but in fact the offensive had long been scheduled for a date between January 15 and January 20, depending on the weather; the two army groups involved launched their operations on the twelfth and the fourteenth, respectively, when the arrival of a cold front had hardened the ground; hence the change in timing could hardly be considered significant. Since the Germans tended to run a kind of east–west shuttle operation with troops, tanks, and artillery, Eisenhower clearly had reasonable grounds for dispatching Tedder to Moscow to learn Soviet plans. But because the issue of the Battle of the Bulge had in fact been settled well before January 12, Churchill's telegram to Stalin, which could only be viewed as an appeal for help, was ill-judged.

At the second plenary meeting the Big Three discussed the treatment they wished to administer to Germany after her surrender, focusing on possible reparations and the participation of France—urged by Churchill—in the occupation of the defeated Reich. Stalin expressed eagerness to have "dismemberment" included in the unconditional-surrender terms. Earlier, at the second Anglo-American conference in Quebec, in September 1944, Roosevelt and Churchill had shown an equally vindictive spirit by approving Henry Morgenthau's proposal to convert Germany into an "agricultural and pastoral" country, a land of shepherds and farmers—"as if," said Anthony Eden, "one were to take the Black Country and turn it into Devonshire." Churchill apparently gave his support with the idea of thereby earning American economic aid, but after colliding head on with Eden's disapproval and with that of Stimson, Hull, and the British Treasury, the two leaders backed away from the impracticable plan. Later, telling Stimson that he had no idea how he could have initialed such a proposal, Roosevelt lightly described the whole affair in his own style: "Henry Morgenthau pulled a boner."

The statesmen opened the third session at Yalta with a discussion of the voting procedures to be used in the Security Council of the postwar United Nations organization. To answer previous Russian insistence on a strong great-power veto, the Americans put forward a plan whereby any of the great powers could veto any motion unless it was a party to the dispute in question; if the motion involved sanctions, that power would simply abstain from voting, and since the rules declared that the great powers had to be unanimous, the motion would automatically fail. Thus the American plan allowed for talk about any issue but not for action contrary to the will of one of the great powers. These were important matters, said Stalin; his "colleagues in Moscow" could not forget that during the 1939–1940 Finnish war Britain and France had caused the Soviet Union to be expelled from the League of Nations. He did not wish to see that kind of thing happen again.

Then, after a brief intermission, President Roosevelt, who as the only chief of state had the chair here as at Tehran, opened the discussion of the Polish question. The subject went on to consume more time than anything else that came up at Argonaut. Over and over, day after day, the Western Allies pressed for a Polish government that would be independent, democratic, and friendly to Russia, with free elections and the other appurtenances of democracy as generally understood in the world. Stalin could even speak some of the same language, assuring his partners that in due course such elections would take place. But with his ideological and nationalistic background and his personal psychology, what could words like "independent," "democratic," "friendly to Russia" mean to him? How could those words help creating in his brain such images as "subservient," "Communist," "controlled," and would not "influence" mean "domination"? The Western leaders seemed to believe that Stalin, if he tried, could see the issue through their eyes. But he gave only the most superficial evidence of even wishing to do so. No doubt, he was literally incapable of it.

"It must never be forgotten," said Churchill during the February 6 opening discussion, "that Great Britain had gone to war to protect Poland against German aggression at a time when that decision was most risky, and it had almost cost them their life in the world." Britain (and France) had not managed to do anything to help Poland, but the point had meaning nevertheless; and two days later, as the leaders still hammered away at the subject, Churchill had one of his finer hours. Since the Russians insisted on the Lublin committee as the basis of the postwar Polish government—with perhaps a garnish of a Pole or two from London—the prime minister declared with accuracy and concision that "we take different views of the same basic facts." As the president had earlier told Hopkins, the language spoken was different. The Lublin government did not "commend itself to the overwhelming masses of the Polish people," Churchill said, and it had no acceptance abroad. He held no special fondness for the London Polish group, he conceded, but if he broke altogether with this lawful government, he would be "subject to the most severe criticism in England." If a new start were made on both sides, any new government must be pledged to "an election on the basis of universal suffrage by secret ballot with the participation of all democratic parties and the right to put up their candidates."

Yes, they were "all agreed on the necessity of free elections," said the president, who held inter-Allied harmony as his chief goal. The only problem was "how Poland was to be governed in the interval." After this lengthy and demanding and inconclusive discussion on February 8 came a tripartite dinner meeting, as such functions were termed. Forty-five toasts were drunk; none involved the participation of General Marshall or Admiral King, both of whom through some piece of incompetence had been left off the guest list, though the British and Soviet chiefs attended. At the end of this arduous day Dr. Bruenn found FDR "obviously greatly fatigued," his face gray, his pulse alternately strong and weak. He must cut down on his activities, the doctor said, with no visitors until noon and an hour's rest in the afternoon, before the plenary meetings. For the first few nights of the conference a "paroxysmal cough" had disturbed the president's sleep; it "disappeared with the use of terpin hydrate and codeine." Joining the presidential party one evening, General Hull, who had not seen the president close up for several weeks, reacted with shock to Roosevelt's appearance; he "looked dreadful, with sagging jaw, dull eyes, drooping shoulders." Even so, Bill Rigdon noticed no decline in the quality of FDR's work.

The talk and the wrangling went on through the next day and the next. But the Russians enjoyed the incalculable advantage of having a large army already occupying Poland. The final statement of the Big Three declared that Molotov and the British and American ambassadors in Moscow would help the "present government"—the Lublin government—reorganize itself through "other Polish democratic leaders from within Poland

and from abroad." The agreement also used the battered phrases about universal suffrage and the secret ballot.

"Mr. President," said Admiral Leahy, "this is so elastic that the Russians can stretch it all the way from Yalta to Washington without ever technically breaking it."

"I know, Bill—I know it," said FDR. "But it's the best I can do for Poland at this time."

The parties to the disagreement had sat around a table, as FDR wished, but they had not solved the problems that faced them. Disappointingly, the method that had value in American domestic politics did not travel well.

A photograph taken during the conference unintentionally captured the spirit of the debate over Poland, the essence of the conflict: Averell Harriman and Joseph Stalin shake hands as though encountering in a hallway—two men headed in opposite directions. American and Russian, they stare off in the distance, past each other. The handshake has no more life than a prayer produced by the turning of a wheel.

With reference to the war against Japan, the Joint Chiefs of Staff in mid-January had declared to the president: "Russia's entry at as early a date as possible consistent with her ability to engage in offensive operations is necessary to provide maximum assistance to our Pacific operations." The planners had proposed and the chiefs had agreed on several general tasks for the Soviet forces in the Far East. They were to take on the Japanese Army in Manchuria, bomb Japan from bases in eastern Siberia (in partnership with U.S. air units), and attack Japanese shipping between the home islands and the Asian mainland.

The reference in the chiefs' report to an early date was not incidental. Some weeks previously the planners had told the chiefs that Russia would unquestionably enter the Pacific war, because of her "interests in the Far East and in post-war world politics . . ." The task thus became not to induce the Russians to take part in the war against Japan, but to bring about this desirable intervention as soon as possible after the defeat of Germany—the chiefs concerned themselves not with *whether* but with *when*. At Tehran Stalin had offered his promise to intervene, and in subsequent meetings with Allied representatives, Soviet spokesmen had repeated the pledge. Since it could be presumed that Stalin saw Soviet selfish interest as clearly as American planners in Washington could discern it, no one at

Yalta had reason to question Soviet intentions with respect to the Japanese war on the basis either of pledged word or of self-interest. The issue at Yalta turned on timing.

To Marshall and his army planners, Soviet participation held crucial importance. The Joint Chiefs of Staff had declared that the "over-all objective" in the war against Japan was to force unconditional surrender by "lowering Japanese ability and will to resist by establishing sea and air blockades, conducting intensive air bombardment, and destroying Japanese air and naval strength" and by "invading and seizing objectives in the industrial heart of Japan." A full-scale invasion, carrying the land war to Tokyo—that was the picture playing before Marshall's eyes. The U.S. chiefs contemplated landings in Kyushu and Honshu in the winter of 1945–1946, but the war in Europe might progress more slowly than anticipated, with the result that the invasion of Japan might not take place "until well into 1946." And the war would not end with those landings; after the invasion would come fighting of a ferocity perhaps not yet seen in the entire war.

Thus far the Americans had treated the Japanese Navy cruelly, reducing it to little more than a ghost of the imposing fleet of December 1941; in the air the enemy had turned in desperation to the kamikaze weapon (which, though created for use by the weak against the strong, could pose a serious hazard to an Allied invasion fleet off the Japanese coast). On the ground the war told a different story. The Japanese still possessed powerful land forces ready for combat—perhaps two million in the home islands and two million more in Manchuria, Korea, and China, with another million scattered across Southeast Asia and on Pacific islands and fighting General MacArthur's forces in the Philippines. If the Japanese should decide to struggle to the end, as Marshall expected, the Allies would have a mighty task on their hands. The fighting could well consume the bulk of 1946, perhaps even continuing into 1947—two years in the future. No one could know how high the figures on casualties might go. From somewhere came an estimate of one million Americans killed, wounded, missing. But Marshall believed that a drive straight to Japan, coordinated with Russian operations, would produce fewer casualties than a proposed plan unfolding by stages, with a landing in Korea. MacArthur agreed and likewise emphasized the importance of Soviet participation.

Everyone did not share the view of the chief of staff and the

Pacific theater commander. Some naval and air officers felt or at least hoped that blockade and air bombardment might force the Japanese to surrender before any land invasion took place. At the time of the Yalta Conference, the U.S. B-29 attacks on Japan had not yet produced impressive results, but air force officers regarded such results as entirely predictable. An air force general representing Hap Arnold, who had suffered his fourth heart attack in less than two years, attempted to report to the president on B-29 operations; Marshall, he said, belittled his efforts, remarking that his account was so imprecise that "it sounded like the State Department." But if the B-29s should produce the kinds of results their advocates anticipated, then U.S. strategy might indeed require revision. On the other hand, in the European theater bombing had never lived up to the hopes and claims of Arnold and Eaker and its other prophets. Certainly, in February 1945, Marshall appeared to hold an unwavering belief that victory in Japan, as in Europe, meant victory through defeating the enemy on land. In the enduring tradition of the U.S. Army, the Americans must not only strangle but smash the Japanese.

For the time being, no divergence of views would have any practical effect, because blockade and bombing would play important roles in softening up Japan before any landings were attempted; if these approaches brought about a capitulation, no one would complain. But if Roosevelt accepted Marshall's view that a Japanese counterpart of Overlord must be staged, then the cooperation of the Russians loomed as a matter of the first importance. "My job was military planning," Marshall said. In pressing for the Russians to join in the Pacific war, his "motivation was to save the lives of Americans."

One other factor existed as a possible influence on American commanders and planners. Just before New Year's, Marshall had received a brief Top Secret report from Leslie R. Groves, the large-girthed but energetic engineer officer who had supervised the building of the Pentagon. Now a major general, Groves since September 1942 had directed a project that in both size and importance dwarfed the great army headquarters. In his message he told the chief of staff that the first "atomic fission" bomb "should be ready about 1 August 1945. The second one should be ready by the end of the year . . ." The general appeared to regard his tidings about the "gun type bomb" as good news, but he also had bad news to report. "Scientific difficulties" had dashed previous hopes that another type of bomb—an "implosion (compression) type"—might be ready by late spring; it now seemed that the project would probably not produce the first bomb of this type until the latter part of July. Its makers believed that it would produce a blast equal to that of five hundred tons of TNT—certainly a mighty explosion but nothing like the expected yield of the gun-type bomb, which Groves thought might amount to the equivalent of a "ten thousand ton TNT explosion." Thus it appeared that by August the United States might have one bomb of extraordinary and unprecedented power and another bomb, certainly powerful enough, but only about one twentieth as potent as the gun-type model. Groves also observed that once production of the implosion bomb began, its effectiveness "should increase towards 1000 each" and perhaps even more.

Marshall stood in an official relationship to the atomic bomb project not only because he was Groves's boss but because in the autumn of 1941, when British and American scientists and officials were discussing the possibility of trying to make such a bomb, President Roosevelt had appointed him to the "Top Policy Group" along with Vice-President Wallace, Stimson, and two scientists, Vannevar Bush and James B. Conant. In practice, however, the birth and growth of this great new enterprise had enabled the secretary of war to establish his own special box on the War Department organizational chart. In May 1943 Stimson had assumed official responsibility for the administration of the Manhattan Engineer District (originally the code name for the operation to construct facilities, the term became synonymous with the overall project; "we might have called it Hoboken," Marshall said, "but we called it Manhattan") and also served as FDR's senior adviser on the military uses of atomic energy. As Stimson and the committee saw it, the government's policy was "to spare no effort in securing the earliest possible successful development of an atomic weapon." The group regarded this weapon as "a new and tremendously powerful explosive, as legitimate as any other of the deadly explosive weapons of modern war. The entire purpose was the production of a military weapon; on no other ground could the wartime expenditure of so much time and money have been justified."

Marshall saw his role as that of provider, furnishing the men and the money to accomplish the enormous task. He had a fatherly but nontechnical interest in what seemed a great but necessary scientific gamble. As the Allies conferred at Yalta, the gamble looked increasingly promising. But the new bomb did not yet exist. Even several months later one of the physicists would write: "All the problems are believed to have been solved at least well enough to make a bomb practicable," but he did not know how effective the first explosion would be. "Even if the first attempt is relatively ineffective, there is little doubt that later efforts will be highly effective; the devastation from a single bomb is expected to be comparable to that of a major air raid by usual methods." That, of course, was the kind of language generals and fliers immediately understood. One bomb equaling the fury of a major air raid would surely be remarkable, but such a raid or even many of them had not ended the war in Europe and they did not seem likely to do so in the Pacific. A bomb with the explosive force of ten thousand tons of TNT would equal the effect of five thousand of the air force's largest general-purpose bombs; it would be comparable to the tonnage (much of it incendiary) dropped by the British and the Americans on Hamburg in the deadly week at the end of July and the beginning of August 1943. Hamburg had been devastated—but the Germans had carried on. Besides, it seemed that the Manhattan Project would provide at most two of these bombs by the end of 1945. Even if they worked, and worked with the expected power, they did not constitute a supply on which military planners could base their strategy. A new and untested weapon had to be viewed as such. Who could envision a "transformation in the whole character of war itself"? Scientists, perhaps; it was not so easy for the generals.

Although an early friend of air power and a supporter of General Chaffee's work with armor, Marshall made no claim to any technical expert knowledge. He liked tactical innovations and often tried to push Eisenhower—sometimes rashly—to make more use of SHAEF's airborne divisions, but such thinking lay a whole dimension away from the atomic realm. Early in the war a writer who was neither soldier nor scientist observed that military officers "have always regarded fire power as the number of hands on javelins, the number of fingers on triggers, the number of grenade pins in sets of human teeth, while time without number a handful of men have turned the tide of battle with a new tool." In "some not distant future," this writer declared, "a hundred men with a hundred new bombs might, quite literally, fight the whole of a war against a great nation in half an hour. It is that weapon we should anticipate—that style of mind we need even now for victory." Still, Marshall could say with cold accuracy that at the time of Yalta "we had no idea of the destructive power of the atomic bomb. We could only guess at what it really was . . ."

The smaller bombs described by Groves represented something different for Marshall. He expected the Japanese to be "determined and fanatical like the Moros," and believed "we would have to exterminate them almost man by man. So we thought the bomb would be a wonderful weapon as a protection and preparation for landings." Such a tactical use of the implosion bomb had also been foreseen by Conant. The idea seemed reasonable to Marshall because "the casualties from the actual fighting would be very much greater than might occur from the after-effects of the bomb action." Radioactivity would present problems, but they would not be as great as those caused by the fire of the enemy.

Roosevelt apparently held great hopes for the big bomb. His son James, home from the Pacific for the inauguration in January, remarked in one conversation that he would not see his father again for a long time because his outfit's next mission would probably be the invasion of Japan. His father, James recalled, "paused and looked out the window, and then swung back to me and said, 'You know, you may never have to make that landing in Japan.'" That was as close as FDR could let himself come to revealing the secret; perhaps he wanted James to infer that "we had a weapon."

Since from the outset the bomb had been treated as primarily an army matter, decisions concerning it rested primarily on the army—on the secretary of war and the chief of staff. This suited Admiral Leahy, who had little faith in the bomb, once describing it as "a professor's dream." So far as Marshall was concerned, "I was for Russia entering the Pacific war. We needed everything we could get to save American casualties." With the bomb still only a theory, he so advised the president, and on the evening of their arrival at Livadia the Joint Chiefs presented the Soviet staff with a request to discuss "details of possible participation in the war against Japan." During the next week such discussions took place, although an American participant noted that the Russian officers did not feel free to make commitments. That power was reserved for Stalin.

Engaged in his military talks while Roosevelt dealt with all the political issues, Marshall looked with detachment on FDR's possible problems. Having told the president that the Joint Chiefs desired "Russia's entry at as early a date as possible," the chief of staff "did not ask the terms or point out what political concessions the U.S. and Britain should be willing to make. My job was military planning." Stalin presented the president with a familiar argument: To justify Russia's entering the war against Japan, he must have something to take home to show his colleagues. After several discussions, the two leaders agreed that Russia would conclude an alliance with China and would retain control of Outer Mongolia, receive the southern half of the island of Sakhalin (taken from Russia by Japan after the Russo-Japanese war forty years earlier) and the Kurile Islands, receive Port Arthur as a naval base, and establish with China a joint company to operate the Chinese Eastern and South Manchurian railroads. Since many of these arrangements concerned Chinese territory and interests, they would naturally be of the deepest concern to Chiang Kai-shek. Some of the way had already been prepared a year previously, as Roosevelt had told the Pacific War Council after Tehran. But for the present the agreement would not be made public or communicated to the Chinese. Understandably eager to avoid a kamikaze version of Pearl Harbor at Vladivostok, the Russians wished to keep the document sealed until they were ready for action.

At four o'clock Sunday afternoon, February 11, after a final luncheon of the Big Three and their leading civilian advisers, Marshal Stalin took leave of the president and drove away from Livadia Palace. The Americans left shortly afterward. Each of the Big Three carried something of value away from Yalta. Churchill had won the fight to have France recognized as an Allied power that would participate in the occupation of Germany and in the Allied Control Council, Stalin had the agreement on the Asian territories to show his "colleagues," and Roosevelt—in an interesting reversal of his 1942 discussions with Molotov—had received specific Soviet promises to open a second front against Japan and had also achieved agreement on a voting formula for the United Nations organization. Thus FDR had won both his main points. Hopkins, usually the specialist in realism, later told Sherwood that he saw Argonaut as "the dawn of the new day we had all been praying for and talking about for so many years." Harriman, the hardheaded capitalist-diplomat, praised Stettinius for discussions that had "resulted in a tremendous stride in the direction of greater mutual confidence which will stand us in good stead in future negotiations." Leahy had been impressed by the way the Big Three worked together "on the action that should be taken to destroy Germany as a military power," and the president, the admiral noted, was "tired but happy."

Roosevelt had arrived at Yalta weary and he departed weary (though Admiral Brown, who sat in the final plenary meeting, described FDR as dominating it—he was "alert, tactful and resourceful"). The arrangements with respect to Japan and to the United Nations pleased the president, but his euphoria did not match that of Hopkins. In private, FDR adhered to the theme he had used with Leahy: "It was the best I could do." He believed in personal diplomacy, but he also recognized the new realities of power.

The departing Americans carried away from Livadia Palace not only protocols and agreements but tangible rewards—gift packages presented by their hosts, containing vodka, several kinds of wine, champagne, caviar, butter, oranges, and tangerines. Bill Rigdon offered Robert Bogue a quart of caviar, but his offer was turned down. When Bogue, newly married, returned to Washington and, in describing the Yalta trip to his mother-in-law, happened to mention his rejection of Rigdon's offer—a whole quart of the best Black Sea caviar—the lady was upset: "She nearly threw me out of the house!"

CHAPTER TWENTY-TWO

PARTINGS

The guest of honor was late for the party.

For most of the past four days, the hostess had devoted herself to making all the preparations. Though the fact that she had just bought "a goddamned pig that weighed three hundred pounds" had provided the incentive for the party, she had never presided over a barbecue, and for this special occasion she was particularly anxious to do everything right. She had made Brunswick stew before, but never in the quantities now called for—more than sixty people were expected. She had known the guest of honor for years in a casual, small-town way, without ever having felt responsible for his enjoying himself, and that made all the difference. "Awfully restless" one night as she lay in bed, she had even thought of calling the whole thing off. But as the time came closer she had bustled about, preparing hogs and lamb, hens and stew meat, and the guest of honor's favorite black nut cake with raisins, to go with the stew he preferred to barbecued pork and lamb.

Spring had come to Georgia. The day was fine, the lawn bright with flowering quince and dogwood. Most of the guests came at four that Thursday afternoon, but the president of the United States was late.

He had arrived in Warm Springs on March 30, being driven in his own blue Ford convertible from the railroad station up the hill to the modest white cottage called the Little White House, where the doctors had ordered him for "a period of total rest." His companions included two favorite cousins, Laura Delano and Margaret Suckley (whom he always called Daisy), and two men friends. They all, said Daisy, "had only one thought—to make everything peaceful and happy and restful for him." Except for the encouragement they might draw from unpredictable flashes of the old buoyancy, usually in the morning, FDR's weariness had become the theme dominating the concerns of those around him—his companions, his political associates, the staff, and Dr. Bruenn. Even Admiral McIntire could discern problems, although he had assured FDR that medical tests proved him "organically sound"; nevertheless, said the admiral, the president must realize that he could no longer behave like a young man who could take chances with his health. Even later, McIntire stuck to his view that FDR's blood pressure "was not alarming at any time." The doctor had seen no reason to accompany his patient to Warm Springs.

Tired as he was on leaving Yalta, Roosevelt had nevertheless flown to Egypt and there boarded the *Quincy,* which lay at anchor in the Great Bitter Lake. For the next three days he took part in an exotic pageant, entertaining successively King Farouk of Egypt, Emperor Haile Selassie of Ethiopia, and King Ibn Saud of Saudi Arabia—the last-named having been ferried to the meeting by the U.S. destroyer *Murphy* with an entourage including the royal astrologer, the royal food taster, and a flock of royal sheep. After enjoying all this entertainment, FDR moved on to Alexandria for a short stop, during which Churchill came on board the *Quincy* for lunch and talk.

Since leaving the Crimea, Pa Watson had stayed in his cabin as the result of a heart attack he had suffered at Sevastopol. On February 20, following a stroke, Pa died at sea. "Outwardly the President took the death of General Watson calmly," said Dr. Bruenn, but FDR felt the loss of his close friend as a cruel blow. "I shall miss him almost more than I can express," he said in a statement bearing an intimate tone. "There was never a cloud between us in all these years."

Desperately sick, Hopkins left the *Quincy* at Algiers to rest for a few days and then fly home (FDR could not understand how Hopkins could find dry land more soothing than a warship rolling in the high seas), and Rosenman came aboard to help the president prepare the speech he would make to Congress and the country about the results of the Yalta Conference. Like everyone else seeing FDR again after a separation of even a few weeks, the judge felt disheartened; the president seemed "all burnt out." FDR did not even show any interest in conversation: "I had never seen him look so tired." Nor could Rosenman induce the boss to take much interest in the forthcoming speech. Yet, in talking with the wire-service reporters aboard the *Quincy,* FDR offered some lively comments. During one press conference he described Yalta as "Hollywood and our South all rolled into one," and he remarked confidentially that he would "give anything to write a funny story" about Farouk and Haile Selassie but "I don't dare do it." The coffee Ibn Saud's royal coffee server presented was pronounced "godawful" (FDR had drunk two very small cups). In another talk with the press the president seemed to enjoy chatting about such subjects as the reforestation and irrigation of the Middle East, and the fact that "dear old Winston," would never learn that the world of the old empires had gone.

Radio brought the presidential party aboard the *Quincy* good news about the reception the American press and public figures had given the official communiqué issued at the close of Argonaut. The agreements "justify and surpass most of the hopes placed on this fateful meeting," declared the *New York Times.* The conference gave "another great proof of Allied unity," said the *New York Herald Tribune.* In a message from the White House, a staff member told the boss that "newspapermen feel unquestionable best report any Big Three conference so far"—and even Herbert Hoover had expressed approval.

Thus FDR approached his speech to Congress along a well-prepared path, although his own optimism remained tempered by inferences he drew about the scope of Stalin's power. He could not feel sure that those often-invoked colleagues back in the Kremlin would support the actions Stalin had taken at Yalta; perhaps, "when the chips were down," Stalin would not be able to "carry out and deliver what he had agreed to." But if Stalin managed to stay on top, then the future looked promising.

Shortly after noon on March 1, just thirty-six hours after getting home, the president, along with his wife and their daughter and son-in-law, entered a limousine for the drive to the Capitol. Always haunted by his memory of Woodrow Wilson's mistakes in dealing with Congress, FDR wanted to lose no time in relaying to the legislators—particularly the all-powerful senators—his view of the achievements of Yalta and their meaning for the postwar world. For this speech he adopted a modified tone and style, sitting at a small table in the well of the House instead of standing at a lectern. At the outset he ad-libbed an explanation for this "unusual posture," breaking a personal precedent by referring to the difficulty of carrying "about ten pounds of steel around on the bottom of my legs." But the posture, together with the simple and direct style in which Roosevelt spoke, led a reporter to view the president's performance less as a "speech" than as a talk in which the president appealed for the full partnership of Congress. Members later expressed special pleasure at this approach and at the fact that the president had not only chosen to use Congress as the forum for his report but had moved so quickly. One staunch critic of FDR's course in foreign affairs conceded that he liked the "great earnestness" of the speech, its "friendly and almost intimate tone."

But Bill Hassett of the White House staff thought it a speech of "prodigious length" with far too many ad-libs. So chatty did FDR appear that in lifting his head to look at his audience he frequently seemed to lose his place in the text and would improvise a line until he reoriented himself. Careful listeners noted that his voice, for all the intimate quality the legislators admired, sounded mushy and some words were slurred. Those in the chamber could see his hand tremble when he took a sip of water. Rosenman, who had gone over the speech time and again between Algiers and Washington, felt dismay as he sat in the audience, a reaction in striking contrast with the feelings of persons who looked at the president from a different point of view. To one journalist, Roosevelt appeared on top of things, "tanned and glowing."

Since the Big Three had produced a lengthy communiqué at the conclusion of Argonaut, the speech, aside from personal touches, contained little information new to its audience. The president made his purpose plain at the beginning. If Congress did not concur in the "general conclusions" reached at Yalta, then his 14,000-mile travels would have been pointless. "This time," he said, "we are not making the mistake of waiting until the end of the war to set up the machinery of peace." The conference in the Crimea constituted a turning point "in the history of the world" and would shortly lead to the presentation to the Senate and the American people of a "great decision." The three leading nations had found the "common ground of peace."

Soon after the speech, however, this common ground began to quake beneath the president's feet, and in a related affair, demonstrating a lack of his usual dexterity, he managed to create a needless controversy. The latter dispute grew out of a concession the president had made to Stalin at Yalta. The people of White Russia and the Ukraine had suffered such devastation at the hands of the Germans, the marshal argued, that they deserved the encouragement of receiving a vote for each of their republics in the General Assembly of the United Nations; Molotov suggested a parallel with the British dominions, which had gradually achieved their own positions of international importance. Roosevelt and Churchill agreed to support the admission of the two units of the Soviet Union when the founding UN meeting at San Francisco took up such questions, and the president won the acquiescence of the others to a matching (if illogical) three votes for the United States if he should decide such a move necessary. Though Chip Bohlen for one thought the concession to Russia unwise, the United States, if she chose, could thereby maintain voting parity in the General Assembly with the Soviet Union. In any case, the Security Council, not the General Assembly, had been conceived as the center of power.

But FDR made a grave oversight. This little agreement received no mention in the Big Three communiqué or in the president's report to Congress and the country. Perhaps he wished to discuss the arrangement privately with the senators before making it public, but for an old Washington hand he seemed amazingly shortsighted in not anticipating a possible leak to the press. Having made sure that Congress would be well represented in the U.S. delegation to San Francisco, the president met on March 23 with the five members who had been chosen; in his talk with the group he spoke of the Russian request for the extra votes and of his and Churchill's promise of support for the idea. Within a few days the Washington leaker had done his work, and on March 29 the first news of the concession to the Soviets appeared in the *New York Herald Tribune*. The revelation quickly took on much greater weight than its intrinsic substance warranted. If Roosevelt had kept a fact like this to himself, might not other secret deals lie locked in his bosom, waiting to be uncovered? The storm broke, said Leahy, "in full force."

Although a genuine problem, the question of these votes could be classified as no worse than awkward. But a number of graver issues loomed with the Soviet Union. One of these concerned American prisoners of war in camps overrun by the Red Army. At Yalta the powers had agreed that each country would allow the others to send officers behind its lines with "immediate access" to their own freed prisoners, but now it became clear that the Russians would permit no American mission to work in Poland on behalf of U.S. soldiers reported to be experiencing rough treatment at Soviet hands. No American relief planes would be allowed to land in the area. As always a master at what would later be called stonewalling, Stalin even turned the argument around by accusing the Americans of beating Soviet ex-prisoners of war in U.S. camps.

The problem of the prisoners had arisen by the end of February. In Romania another Allied agreement proved as short-lived as the one on prisoners. In the "Declaration on Liberated Europe" adopted at Yalta, the Big Three, using all the standard phrases, had agreed that they would jointly help the people of a liberated or a former Axis state set up interim governments "broadly representative of all democratic elements in the population . . ." But on February 27, Andrei Vyshinsky, who had served Stalin with grisly effectiveness as prosecutor in the purge trials of the 1930s, arrived in Bucharest and, banging his fist on the desk, forced King Michael to appoint a Communist government. The Soviets brusquely rejected U.S. protests.

Increasingly the Russians painted for more and more eyes to see a picture of the security zone they intended to create and maintain, with the features that had been precisely drawn in advance by David Dallin. Early in March the loosely worded Yalta agreement on Poland began to unravel. Refusing to invite more than one of the London Poles to have a hand in creating the new government, Molotov acted as though the whole affair should involve nothing more than a trifling enlargement of the Lublin group—a view the Yalta agreement specifically rejected in favor of "reorganization." As Harriman reported from Moscow on March 7, "the Lublin Government every day is becoming more and more the Warsaw Government and the ruler of Poland." After the U.S. and British ambassadors had made no progress by protesting to Molotov, Roosevelt and Leahy met with a State Department group (a striking example of the changes taking place since Hull's departure) to discuss and draft a long message to Stalin. If the Polish question is not settled, said the president in the final version of the message (sent on April 1), "all of the difficulties and dangers to Allied unity which we had so much in mind in reaching our decisions at the Crimea will face us in an even more acute form." But the Western Allies were learning the folly of anything less than a painfully meticulous agreement with the Soviet Union (like a paranoid person, a paranoid government could expand a real or imagined loophole into an escape hatch). Stalin brushed off the president with a bland answer indicating that the U.S. and British ambassadors had chosen to misunderstand the Yalta decision by seeking to do away with the Lublin government.

The controversy over Poland, illustrating the Soviet drive for security and control in what the Kremlin deemed its sphere, flared up simultaneously with another important fight, this one dramatizing Russian fears that even at this late date the Western Allies might in one way or another sell them out to the Germans. In this controversy the president and Admiral Leahy turned to General Marshall. The dispute arose from the attempts of a German SS general in Italy to discuss a surrender. Although both the general's authority and his real purposes were unclear, the Anglo-Americans felt they must pursue any possibility that offered the chance to save the lives of Allied soldiers. When told that such talks might occur, the Russians raised no objections—but, said Molotov, he wanted three Soviet officers to take part in them. Even though unconditional surrender remained the only formula under which the Allies would deal with the Germans, Roosevelt feared that the presence of the Soviet officers might frighten the skittish Germans away and thus destroy a chance to shorten the war in Italy (perhaps Molotov was aware of the same point). Besides, said Harriman, the Soviets would regard Allied acceptance of Molotov's proposal as a "sign of weakness," which they would view with contempt; they certainly allowed no U.S. officers on their front. The argument led to a dialogue between East and West in which the voices turned harsh and bitter. Roosevelt messages on Italy went to Stalin on March 24, March 31, and April 5.

Though bearing the president's signature, the cables to Stalin were not his handiwork. Drafted by Leahy, the first message politely assured the marshal that he apparently had been misinformed; these preliminary talks would concern nothing more than the possibility of a military surrender of the sort German commanders might make to Soviet forces "at Königsberg or Danzig" and would have "no political implications whatever." In his reply Stalin rejected the Königsberg-Danzig analogy and accused the Allies of a serious offense—allowing the Germans to switch divisions from Italy to the eastern front.

This time, with Roosevelt's assent, Leahy made an interesting move, turning to Marshall for an answer to this blunt Soviet accusation of bad faith. Certainly the storm blowing up had military origins, but it involved considerations far greater than the surrender in the field of German divisions. It reached to the highest levels of the American and Soviet governments, and as a diplomatic—and psychological—dispute of the first importance, it called for civilian attention. But the State Department's new relative prominence did not extend to participation in the Italian affair. As Secretary Stettinius busied himself with preparations for the United Nations conference in San Francisco, the White House, as it had throughout the war, turned to the military for an answer. The letter produced in the chief of staff's office deplored the new "atmosphere of regrettable apprehension and mistrust" and explained again that no actual negotiations had taken place in Italy; if such negotiations should occur, Stalin's representatives would be present. Further, Stalin was misinformed in supposing that the proposed talks had led to any transfer of German divisions from Italy to the east. Perhaps, said the letter, the German officer had raised the possibility only to "create suspicion and distrust between the Allies. There is no reason why we should permit him to succeed in this aim."

The correspondence between Washington and Moscow on Poland and on the surrender in Italy moved back and forth like a tennis game played with two balls. On March 29, during the busy exchange, the president left the White House for a proposed stay of perhaps two weeks in Warm Springs. The next evening, after FDR was installed in the cottage, Bill Hassett had a somber talk with Dr. Bruenn. "He is slipping away from us," Hassett said, "and no earthly power can keep him here." He understood the doctor's reluctance to admit defeat in dealing with the president's condition, but in his own view "the Boss was beyond all human resources." During these days the failing president contributed little besides his approval to the White House telegrams. He had lost twenty-five pounds now, he told Hassett; he simply had no appetite.

After dispatching on April 2 the long message concerning Poland, the White House two days later received Stalin's answer to the March 31 Leahy-Marshall letter about the possible Italian surrender. As the Americans might have expected, Stalin's paranoiac fears or his wish to put the Western Allies on the defensive broke through the usual crust of diplomatic restraint. His "military colleagues" told him, he said, not only that negotiations had already taken place but that the Allies had gone much further, by promising to give the Germans easy armistice terms in exchange for allowing Anglo-American troops to "move east." These colleagues, he said, "are not very far from the truth." To gain a momentary advantage, the Allies had taken a "hazardous step," literally allowing the enemy to cease the war against Britain and America. They were destroying the "trust between Allies."

At the White House this blast was "received with astonishment," as the reply drafted by Marshall and his staff declared. This reaction conveyed no more than the truth, because the Americans had consistently refused to consider moving into Central Europe with German connivance or without it. The advances of General Eisenhower's forces were military successes, said the U.S. reply, made possible to a great extent by Allied air power. The Germans had not been consulted; in addition, the Allied armies could move fast now because Eisenhower had been able to "cripple the bulk of the German forces . . . while they were still west of the Rhine." No help from the Germans had been involved. "I wrote the message and repeated it to Mr. Roosevelt at Warm Springs," Marshall said; "more and more Mr. Roosevelt utilized my services in connection with matters of this kind." The message closed with two paragraphs having a strikingly personal tone—but these words, sounding as though they might have come from Roosevelt's hand, had been drafted in the chief of staff's office:

"Finally I would say this, it would be one of the great tragedies of history if at the very moment of the victory, now within our grasp, such distrust, such lack of faith should prejudice the entire undertaking after the colossal losses of life, material and treasure involved.

"Frankly I cannot avoid a feeling of bitter resentment toward your informers, whoever they are, for such vile misrepresentations of my actions or those of my trusted subordinates."

On April 7 Stalin assured the president that he had never doubted "your integrity or trustworthiness." But after this semblance of an apology, he went on to declare that his informants—"honest and unassuming people"—must be correct because the Germans were readily surrendering important cities to the Western Allies while at the same time fighting desperately for obscure towns in Czechoslovakia "which they need just as much as a dead man needs a poultice." He also accused General

Marshall of having furnished the Russian staff with false information about planned German counterattacks in the east. The marshal chose to overlook the fact that without any Anglo-American connivance whatever, the Germans, driven by their dread and fear of the Russians, were far more likely to surrender armies and cities to the Western Allies than to the Red Army. Stalin also ignored Marshall's later advisories to the Soviet staff.

Roosevelt and Leahy produced a mild reply, telling Stalin that the Italian affair had "faded into the past . . ." It had been a "minor" misunderstanding. Harriman wanted to delete "minor" before passing the message on to the marshal, but the president and Leahy said no. In a message Roosevelt did write himself, dispatched on April 12, he told Churchill that they should minimize the "general Soviet problem" because most of the difficulties that arose tended to straighten themselves out. "We must be firm, however," he told Churchill in his last line, "and our course thus far is correct." Which course—firmness or conciliation? Presumably, the president meant as the correct formula a careful mixture of the two: a tricky course, he might concede, but the correct one. The man who had refused to give in to polio in an era when surrendering would have been easy and acceptable had no thought of yielding to any other challenge.

After a few days in Warm Springs, Dr. Bruenn, whom Bill Hassett considered "a man of superior intellect and integrity," began to feel encouraged about his eminent patient. In the balmy spring weather FDR began "to eat with appetite, rested beautifully, and was in excellent spirits." He took short drives through the hills in the afternoon, and one day he amused Hassett by deciding not to buy a set of scarce books he saw listed in a catalogue because he could not afford the required $17.50. "The Boss feeling the pinch of poverty this morning," Hassett noted in his diary. One set of findings puzzled Dr. Bruenn—the president's widely varying blood-pressure levels, ranging from 170/88 to 240/130; "there was no apparent cause and effect." On Tuesday, April 10, FDR cheerily accepted the invitation to a Georgia barbecue to be given on Thursday by Mayor Frank Allcorn of Warm Springs and Ruth Stevens, the manager of the Warm Springs Hotel. But he didn't like barbecued pork, he said; he would rather have Brunswick stew.

The hostess, he was told, was already well aware of the fact. As preparations proceeded, FDR suggested additions to the guest list—Elizabeth Shoumatoff, an artist, and another guest who had come to Warm Springs, Lucy Mercer Rutherfurd. The President had seen her at various times during the later part of the war, but never before had Lucy's name received public mention in connection with his.

At midday on Thursday he devoted himself to reading and signing the papers that had come in the morning's pouch from Washington, at the same time posing for the portrait on which Madame Shoumatoff was working. With her constant requests for the president to move and turn this way and that, the artist upset Hassett. He left the cottage, intending to ask Dr. Bruenn to forbid this "unnecessary hounding of a sick man." Lucy Rutherfurd sat quietly watching as the artist worked.

About one o'clock the president put his left hand up to his head and in a low voice said to his cousin Daisy Suckley, "I have a terrific pain in the back of my head."

Late in the afternoon of April 12 a message passing through the Pentagon for transmission to four young men in uniform brought Colonel Frank McCarthy news that was just beginning to spread through the highest circles of the United States government. He must tell General Marshall at once. By this time of day, the general had gone home to Fort Myer. At no point during the war had he felt that he must symbolize his devotion to duty by putting in a twelve-hour day at his desk and then lugging home a swollen briefcase. To him, that did not represent sound administration. His dictum that nobody ever has a good idea after three o'clock in the afternoon (his stepdaughter Molly remembered his allowing one more hour but some associates claimed that the general even said two o'clock) had become famous all over Washington. Asked by an admirer how one might achieve such executive efficiency, Marshall said drily, "Get yourself a McCarthy." But it was not only McCarthy, it had been Sexton and Ward and all the others.

McCarthy got into his car and drove the short distance, not much more than a mile, from the Pentagon to Quarters One at Fort Myer. He found the chief of staff sitting comfortably on his front porch. On the war fronts that day, in Europe units of the 2nd Armored Division had established a bridgehead across the Elbe River, on Okinawa the Tenth Army was locked in deadly battle with ferocious Japanese defenders, in Manila General MacArthur had just established the headquarters of the Southwest Pacific Area. And in Georgia, McCarthy reported, the armed services had suffered a notable casualty: The commander in chief was dead. What Mrs. Roosevelt had said in her message to their sons, the source of McCarthy's information, was that their father had "slept away."

In January 1944, replying to birthday greetings from General Marshall, President Roosevelt had praised their partnership because it produced "teamwork which has succeeded and will succeed." The team had survived all the stresses of peace, twilit neutrality, limited intervention, and total war. Of all the leaders of the Western Alliance, Roosevelt and Marshall had been the only ones to serve at their respective posts from the first day of the war. They had built a partnership on a remarkable paradox—Marshall, the representative of the military, had become the country's most effective politician, and Roosevelt, the civilian, had presided over the military as chief strategist until the design for victory was set. Though roles had not precisely been reversed, leadership at the highest level had known a historic exchange. And now, after all its strains and triumphs, the team was disbanded.

Marshall and his wife rushed to the White House to offer Mrs. Roosevelt sympathy and help. On her last day as first lady, the widow charged the general with making all the arrangements for FDR's last journey, from Warm Springs to Washington for the funeral service, and to Hyde Park for burial. At the White House, the new president, Harry Truman, spoke to Marshall, but as the general told his wife, "I have the arrangements for the funeral to consider so thought it best not to stay any longer." As ever, he wasted no time in debating his priorities.

At twenty minutes to five Georgia time (an hour earlier than Eastern War Time), as the guests at the barbecue listened to folk tunes played by an old mountain fiddler whom FDR enjoyed, a major in the White House signal detachment asked Ruth Stevens to stop the music. Then he told the mayor why the guest of honor was late, saying, "The Boss is dead." The news, said Mrs. Stevens, was "more than we could take." She became almost hysterical, and with his arms around her, the major "sobbed like a child." The old fiddler pulled off his hat as tears rolled down his cheeks, and he said over and over, "What a good man to leave us!"

Knowing the crowds and confusion that would descend on Warm Springs, the town FDR had almost literally created, Mrs. Stevens gathered the party food together to take it to the hotel so that people could eat when they had to. The country had lost a president, but Warm Springs had lost its greatest friend. Soon it became amazingly clear that Americans across the country shared the feelings of FDR's friends in the little Georgia town. Six hours later Bob Trout, one of the greatest of the radio reporters, declared on CBS: "There has not been time to think. The news is known but the brain does not quite grasp it." Working on an editorial for the army magazine *Yank,* a young soldier wrote: "He was the Commander in Chief, not only of the armed forces but of our generation."

Eleanor Roosevelt came from Washington to Warm Springs to accompany the president's body back to the capital. That night, looking out from her berth on the Washington-bound funeral train at the people lining the tracks, she was surprised: "I never realized the full scope of the devotion to him until after he died." Although her husband had certainly made unrelenting enemies, she was looking out on a nation in mourning, and next day, on the streets of Washington, those who did not weep seemed dazed. The death of a man they had never met had moved them like a personal loss. The crowd felt what the cab driver had once said to the reporter: "That guy has a slant in my direction." He was a wartime president, but people everywhere seemed to mourn the creator of the New Deal, the man who, they believed, had cared for them as individual persons, the first real friend they had ever had in Washington. High school seniors had known no other president since they had entered the first grade; to a whole generation, the words "president" and "Roosevelt" seemed to have been coined in the same moment.

More than time was involved. FDR had filled every nook and cranny of the presidential office, in a way not known before. Although bound to a chair, he ranked among the most action-oriented of presidents, turning his energies outward rather than employing them in deep reflection. "When stimulated by concern for his place in history," one writer observed, "he responded not by writing an *apologia* but by building a library." Yet even in this area he could enjoy playing a little game with reporters. Once, when probed by a young journalist seeking to learn his ideological principles, FDR finally produced the famous reply "I am a Christian and a Democrat. That's all." He was indeed both of those things, and sincerely so, but was that really all? James Roosevelt saw the response as "half-facetious, a moment of levity." Sometimes reporters did not quite know how to take this man; most persons hearing FDR's remark put it down as a piece of exhaustive presidential self-examination.

"*He's* dead, *he's* dead," said a tall man standing in a corridor of the Capitol. "He was like a daddy to me." The bereft politician was a congressman from Texas, Lyndon B. Johnson.

Struggling from his hospital bed in Minnesota to come to Washington for the funeral, Harry Hopkins, "the skin of his face a dreadful cold white with apparently no flesh left under it," told Bob Sherwood: "Goddamn it, now we've got to get to work on our own. This is where we've really got to begin."

Seven months later a different parting took place. All members of the General Staff were on hand that November day in the office of the secretary of war, from Somervell down to a younger officer George Marshall had long respected, Brigadier General Buck Lanham, and their attention was focused on the chief of staff.

In the months since April 12 great individual events had taken place, and the overall context of all events had changed; a world had died and another had been born. The unconditional surrender of Germany had become official on May 8, V-E Day; the bloody battle for Okinawa, the most costly U.S. campaign against Japan, had ended in a flag-raising ceremony on June 22; in July at Potsdam, Germany, a new Big Three—the veteran Joseph Stalin and newcomers Harry Truman and Clement Attlee—had met to discuss the Japanese surrender and other issues; on July 16 the hopes and questions about the atomic bomb appeared to find answers in a successful test of one of the three existing bombs in the New Mexico desert; on August 6, a B-29 flying from Tinian dropped a "gun-type" atomic bomb on Hiroshima; just two days later (but also exactly on the schedule as promised by Stalin at Yalta), the Soviet Union declared war on Japan; and the day after that, the only American implosion bomb was dropped on Nagasaki; on August 14, after some discussion, Japan surrendered, and the Second World War was over. The nuclear age had begun. In his final report Marshall wrote: "Certainly the implications of atomic explosion will spur men of judgment as they have never before been pressed to seek a method whereby the people of the earth can live in peace and justice." These hopes were not certainties, he cautioned: "If man does find the solution for world peace it will be the most revolutionary reversal of his record we have ever known." Therefore, "our diplomacy must be wise and it must be strong."

At noon on V-E Day, at a little celebration in his office, Secretary Stimson had spoken some words directly to Marshall. As everyone knew, the secretary both admired the general and depended on him, and was never happy when the chief of staff was not close at hand. With interesting insight, he considered Marshall "a great and good citizen." And on V-E Day, having seated Marshall in the center of a semicircle of fourteen generals and high civilian officials, the secretary said directly to the general: "I have seen a great many soldiers in my lifetime and you, sir, are the finest soldier I have ever known." And for all his worries about Roosevelt's methods of administration, Stimson had praised the president's refusal to intervene with "personal or political desires" in the appointments of commanders; he thought him "a superb war President—far more so than any other President of our history."

Now, in November, Stimson had retired; his place as secretary of war had been taken by his old friend Undersecretary Robert Patterson. As is traditional, the ceremony honoring the departing chief of staff had an informal tone but nevertheless was expected to follow a certain ritual. Patterson spoke words of praise for Marshall and then turned to the general. After clearing his throat several times, fighting to control his feelings, swallowing, Marshall uttered but few words—of his fondness for his old friends, his pride in their work, his gratitude for their help. Then, instead of following the ritual by waiting for the line of generals to move past him in the order of rank and seniority, he turned and walked quickly to the door. Holding out his hand to the brigadier at the end of the line, the most junior officer in the room, Marshall smiled and said, "Come on, Lanham!"

A military career that had begun early in 1902 under President Theodore Roosevelt and Secretary of War Elihu Root had come to an end, having given what Stimson called "a new gauge of what such service should be." In spite of all the tributes that came to him as the war ended, tributes of a kind rarely heard by a living subject, Marshall managed to retain a notable degree of humility. One day, driving to Leesburg with his wife, he stopped for gasoline. As usual on these trips, he wore civilian clothes (and he was potentially a deadly driver, since he liked to speed down the highway with the hood ornament of his Plymouth lined up with the center stripe). The Marshalls were just about to leave the service station when a car with two army privates and two girls drove up and parked squarely in front of them. In no hurry, the young men joked with the girls, making no progress toward the selection of the soft drinks they appeared to have promised their passengers. After about five minutes, Marshall politely asked one of the soldiers to move so that he could go on his way. Ignoring the older man in his civilian clothes, the soldiers continued their chatter a bit longer, finally deciding how many Cokes and how many 7-Ups to buy, and then one of them, passing the Marshalls' car on his way into the station to pick up the drinks, leaned in the window and said, "Keep your shirt on, buddy, just keep your shirt on."

When the Marshalls got home, Mrs. Marshall told the story to Molly, who said, "What did Colonel do?"

Mrs. Marshall gave her a simple answer: "He kept his shirt on."

Marshall's retirement from public affairs lasted barely a month. On the day he and his wife left Fort Myer for good, the new president summoned the general within minutes of his arrival at Leesburg; the telephone was actually ringing while Marshall was carrying bags into the house. Seeking reliable help in a complex diplomatic situation, Harry Truman said: "General, I want you to go to China for me." Marshall had no conceivable desire for further assignment, office, or distinction, but without hesitation he said, "Yes, Mr. President." Thus began the series of high governmental tasks Marshall took on at the request of President Truman, who seemed to admire him above all other men. Moving completely into the civilian realm, Marshall in 1947 began his distinguished service as secretary of state. This was a period during which in some quarters—notably, with the Marshall Plan for European recovery—he achieved greater renown than he had ever won as a soldier. And in 1950, during the Korean War, he again came from retirement to fill the civilian post of secretary of defense.

Marshall sought none of these positions but accepted them because he had grown up to put duty ahead of desire. In this he acted as a true soldier. But all his political flair, all his strikingly successful experience with Congress, all the thinking beyond the purely military he had been required to engage in during the war—everything prepared him to take on these later tasks and to perform them, perhaps using military techniques here and there, with a purely civilian outlook. One day, while still in uniform, he observed that the creation of the United Nations made it "especially important historically" to understand points of view besides one's own. "I seem during the past three years to have spent most of my time disagreeing," he said, "but I have made a very conscious effort to understand the background of the other fellow's situation before voicing my disagreements."

"To all of us he was always 'General Marshall,'" remarked another secretary of state, Dean Acheson. "The title fitted him as though he had been baptized with it"; but "there was no military glamour about him and nothing of the martinet." In one sentence an editor meeting Marshall late in the war captured something close to his essence: "I noticed the lightness of his handclasp and thought, 'Here is a man who is not intent on appearing powerful.'" He was a man who, perhaps, was half civilian and all soldier, and the most important body over which he exercised command was his own.

In Marshall's postwar political career his patriotism came under attack in the Senate from various right-wing opportunistic figures, mostly forgotten now except for Joseph McCarthy, whose contempt for evidence caused his surname to take a permanent place in the language of allegation. When an aide assembled some material intended to help the general refute the charges, Marshall thanked the man but declined his help, saying, "If I have to explain at this point that I am not a traitor to the United States, I hardly think it's worth it."

General Marshall died in October 1959 after suffering two strokes earlier in the year. In February his goddaughter, Rose Page Wilson, had come to see him in the hospital at Fort Bragg, near the Marshalls' winter home at Pinehurst, North Carolina. She found the general in good spirits and the two chatted gaily, but after a while Colonel Marshall, as she always called him, told her he wanted to ask a very confidential question; she must swear not to repeat it to anybody. After she promised, he said: "Will you please tell me? Where am I?" The thought that the Colonel's "prodigious mind" might be deteriorating struck Rose as worse than the prospect of his death. Certainly it was the strangest question George Marshall had ever asked anybody.

As the general had requested, the funeral services in the little brown brick chapel at Fort Myer were simple—among the simplest ever held for a person of his eminence. They lasted only twenty minutes, with no eulogy. The honorary pallbearers included General Omar Bradley, former Secretary of Defense Robert A. Lovett, and other notables, and two army sergeants, James W. Powder, Marshall's former driver, and William Heffner, the general's orderly.

EPILOGUE: A NATURAL STATE?

The old chuck-wagon army that George Marshall sometimes pined for when finding himself facing political and technical challenges had been long gone in 1939 when the general took note of his nostalgia. But to later generations, Marshall's tiny, insular, unpopular prewar army has seemed equally simple and remote.

Much of the postwar big change grew out of the new strategic and economic roles brought to the armed forces by the Cold War. Earlier, however, Franklin Roosevelt had demonstrated his view of the services as a pool of talent to be drawn upon for civilian purposes. Showing a particular liking for former professional heads of his beloved navy, FDR appointed Admiral Leahy ambassador to Vichy France and Admiral William H. Standley ambassador to the Soviet Union. In choosing these two men the president displayed two personal predilections—not only his liking for military or naval officers in civilian posts but his fondness for bypassing the State Department, a fondness that showed up even more clearly in his frequent use of surrogate diplomats not to fill official foreign posts but to act as special envoys supplementing and outflanking the duly appointed ambassadors. Since he could not himself go to London or Moscow to sit talking around a table, his "personal representatives" would carry out his wishes and perhaps impress foreign leaders as emissaries coming directly from the White House.

So thoroughly did FDR control the foreign affairs of interest to him that months after the Tehran Conference poor Cordell Hull complained that he had never even been allowed to read the minutes of the meetings; and the exclusion of Hull automatically meant exclusion of State Department foreign-service officers and area experts. But none of Roosevelt's appointments and assignments occurred in secret; he moved openly, making full use of his legal authority to conduct foreign relations, often with the advantages of publicity in mind. Yet in using his own methods to affirm presidential supremacy in foreign affairs and to blaze a bypass around one of the great executive departments, he unavoidably established a precedent that could be emulated, or corrupted, or parodied, as the case might be, by any successor.

In seeking counsel as he formulated his plans and in choosing agents to carry them out, Roosevelt naturally turned during the war to the Joint Chiefs of Staff, the only organized body of advisers whose existence he encouraged—or even tolerated. One of the reasons he preferred military over State Department associates, besides his fixed view of diplomatic professionals as reactionaries, was surely that generals and admirals are trained to present themselves as brisk pragmatists who receive an assignment and then go back to their offices and devise ways of carrying it out—unlike civilian professionals who tend to wrinkle their brows, pull out their pipes, and begin presenting objections to a proposed line of action. Many General Staff memos of Marshall's day contain as their underlying principle the thought that it is the staff's purpose to discover the president's wishes not in order to frame a dissent but to proceed to carry them out promptly. Roosevelt was viewed as the commander in chief and therefore the unquestioned superior officer.

All of these reasons combined to dictate a close relationship between Roosevelt and the Joint Chiefs of Staff. And, though FDR always nurtured a special fondness for the navy, his partnership with Marshall counted most heavily. As the uproar over his possible appointment to Overlord demonstrated, the general ranked in everyone's eyes as *primus inter pares*. On another occasion the House Republican leader, Joseph W. Martin, made the point succinctly: "Everybody knows who runs the Joint Chiefs of Staff."

Marshall, though a professional soldier with no aspirations to become anything else, had to assume the mantle of statesman, a garment Leahy could sometimes wear but one that King would never even have lifted from the rack. Thus it came about that Marshall and his aides drafted the important telegrams of the exchange with Stalin in early 1945, and the chief of staff threw himself into the part so thoroughly, speaking in the April 5 message of "bitter resentment" and "vile misrepresentations," that so shrewd an observer as Churchill concluded that these words came from the hand of the president himself.

In many ways this change for Marshall could hardly be considered a profitable transaction for the United States, not only because it demanded new kinds of thought and effort on the part of a general who already had his hands full, but because it diluted his freedom to offer the president detached, professional military advice that could then take its place in the creation of overall national policy. By dispatching Marshall to China and then appointing him secretary of state, President Truman completed the general's evolution from professional soldier to political official that had begun in the days before Pearl Harbor with his remarkable successes on Capitol Hill.

Several years after Marshall came to the State Department, one of his most eminent army disciples resigned from a military position of high importance to run for president. By winning the election of 1952, General Dwight D. Eisenhower became the only professional soldier besides U. S. Grant to be chosen president of the United States (other presidents who had held military rank either flourished in the preprofessional era or were men whose service had been limited to wartime).

In the years following the moves first of Marshall, then of Eisenhower, into the civilian realm, a type of U.S. officer little known in the past began to appear—a type long known in Europe, the political general. Alexander Haig, a notable example, shuttled back and forth between the military and the civilian worlds, coming from active military duty to the National Security Council (NSC), returning to regular service to become vice chief of staff, thence becoming head of the White House staff, then going to Europe as U.S. commander and moving up to become supreme Allied commander, finally taking office as secretary of state and seeking the Republican presidential nomination. Was he a political general or a military politician? Brent Scowcroft, an air force lieutenant general, served as Henry Kissinger's deputy at the NSC, then moved into the top job (and in 1989 returned to this post under President Bush). A general took office as U.S. ambassador to the United Nations.

Some of these developments no doubt grew out of the fact that, beginning in the 1950s, the Department of Defense took on a variety of overseas responsibilities, the distinction between peace and war became blurred, and the armed forces no longer lived behind the wall that had kept them apart from civilian society (or at least the wall acquired a number of doors and windows, encouraging access from the military to universities, corporations, and other branches of the government itself).

The post of presidential national security adviser seems to exert a special attraction for serving officers. (When an officer takes this or any lesser assignment with the National Security Council, he is placed on "administrative release"—which means that his military career continues but that, in this civilian appointment, he is temporarily removed from the chain of command. Otherwise, an NSC staff member pointed out, a lower-ranking officer might find himself issuing orders to the chairman of the Joint Chiefs. Or an officer may, if he chooses, retire from service upon taking the top job at NSC; General Scowcroft did so at the time of his first tour at the top in 1975.) We now have in the United States a generation of political generals, many of whom have retained higher ambitions in the military or in the civilian realm or in both. This is something new in American life.

Even if every national security adviser and his deputy were to take retirement on moving into the presidential circle, a problem would remain, for the obvious reason that anticipation of wielding power in the civilian world could distort an officer's professionalism. The trouble here resides not merely in the difference between the "military mind" and some other sort of mind. Though soldiers have often tended to display a simplistic view of the untidy civilian realm, it is also true—as Eisenhower in particular demonstrated throughout his presidency—that generals often do not compare as fire-eaters with some of their most scholarly civilian advisers. The greater and continuing problem seems to lie in another area altogether: By the nature of his job the military officer controls the nation's organized force, which must hold itself constantly ready to serve the civilian authority, whatever policies that authority may follow.

Under the Defense Department reorganization of 1986, to take the most important example, the chairman of the Joint Chiefs moved up to a special position, replacing the collective JCS as the president's principal source of military advice and assuming powers of decision over all the services. Congress passed the legislation, with which former Senator Barry Goldwater and Senator Sam Nunn were heavily identified, in an effort to overcome the parochialism that often resulted in the chiefs' offering their civilian superiors the lowest (but not the cheapest) common military-naval-air denominator, which a former defense secretary called "generally irrelevant, normally unread and almost always disregarded." By being raised above his colleagues on the JCS, the chairman now holds unprecedented power. The 1986 law also gave him a seat on the National Security Council, thereby creating a legal break in the fragile wall of separation between the civil and the military. Can a president afford to worry about the political reliability of this officer?

In a speech delivered shortly before leaving office, Lieutenant General Colin Powell, President Ronald Reagan's last national security adviser, discussed diplomatic situations in the world, east and west, north and south, just as any civilian, political member of the White House staff might do. Crediting Reagan's policies with a large part in bringing about a "democratic" resurgence in the world, for instance, he observed that America must not be "weak," as he implied had been the case before Reagan took office. The point here is not the accuracy of any of the general's comments but the fact that he made them. During the question period, one member of the audience asked whether the general had thought of becoming chairman of the Joint Chiefs. More immediately, however, General Powell would move back into normal duty status and go off to a new assignment. In any case, in view of the tenor of his remarks it is hard to imagine any future Democratic president (if there ever is one) appointing the general to high office, not because of any professional deficiencies but because he has been politicized.

Of course, no one would realistically argue that the political, civilian world can be totally separated from the military world. But the tragic results that can come from blurring the two clearly stand out in the adventures of one of President Reagan's national security advisers, Vice Admiral John Poindexter, a brilliant man who was first in his class at Annapolis and who earned a Ph.D. in nuclear physics. After being blown from office when the Iran-Contra affair exploded in the White House basement, Poindexter delivered testimony to a congressional committee that Admiral William Crowe, the chairman of the Joint Chiefs, found disturbing. He was "shocked" at Poindexter's doings, Crowe told an interviewer, "not just as a military officer but as an American."

The interviewer then posed a broad question: Should a military officer ever serve as the president's national security adviser? The chairman of the Joint Chiefs uttered an emphatic no: Such an officer, he said, has his natural loyalties to the military, and when he is thrown "into the political caldron" he is "forced, rightfully so, to put the President's interests right there first."

President Roosevelt and the whole U.S. civilian government were well served by the officers of World War II, many of whom in their private thinking deplored the New Deal but served their commander in chief in a highly professional manner, faithfully adhering to the distinction between the military and the civilian realms—except when called on to do otherwise—and, in fact, giving no evidence that any other thought ever occurred to them. Even the famous proconsul in the Pacific represented only a fleeting exception with his political ambitions.

In the United States, civilian supremacy is customarily taken for granted, but the world is always teaching nations new lessons. It has been well observed that "civilian control of the military is not a natural state for a polity and may even be unnatural, considering the experiences of others." In becoming the "trustee for the nation" and filling his expanded role with the president, General Marshall gave no evidence that he saw himself and Roosevelt taking the first steps in any new political-military direction. He was simply doing what the president asked of him and what the situation, as he saw it, demanded of him day by day. Working together throughout the greatest of all wars, Roosevelt and Marshall made up the most triumphantly effective political-military team in American history—a team whose achievements rested on candor and hard-won mutual respect.

"Don't you think so, George?" At the outset of the relationship, FDR had asked what seemed to be a simple, routine question.

"I don't agree with that at all": Marshall's swift reply had staked for him an immediate claim to independence, and in accepting the answer not as an affront but merely as a statement of honest opinion, FDR had demonstrated his own strength.

How many future soldier-politicians are likely to have Marshall's eighteenth-century ideals? What future Roosevelt will be strong enough to want a new Marshall, or fortunate enough to find one?

ACKNOWLEDGMENTS

A book of this kind cannot come into being without the active participation of a great many persons. As I have had occasion to say before, the most pleasant discovery a writer makes in pursuit of information is the remarkable readiness with which his requests for help are met. So many have offered so much that as I sit down to express my thanks, I do so with some trepidation: How unfair it would be to overlook anyone who made a contribution. Let me say, therefore, that nobody is intentionally left out; I am deeply grateful to all who helped.

I must first record my thanks to two persons closest to the principals of my story—to James Roosevelt, son of the late president, and to Molly Brown Winn, General Marshall's stepdaughter. Mr. Roosevelt not only answered questions and offered opinions but graciously agreed to read parts of the manuscript, especially those dealing with his father's physical condition. (He, of course, bears no responsibility for any of the statements I make.) Mrs. Winn was a gracious hostess and told many insightful and delightful anecdotes about General Marshall and his family life.

Other persons supplying first-hand information in interviews and correspondence included Colonel John L. Bates (who is referred to in the chapters on Tehran and Yalta as Oleg Pantuhoff, the name by which he was known in his younger days), Robert W. Bogue, Howard G. Bruenn, M.D., Colonel Donald S. Bussey, Major General Marshall S. Carter, the late Brigadier General Carter W. Clarke, the late Colonel C. J. George, Sergeant William J. Heffner, the late Frank McCarthy, Colonel W. A. Muir, Robert H. Myers, Mona Nason, H. Merrill Pasco, Forrest C. Pogue, William M. Rigdon, and General Albert C. Wedemeyer. I am especially grateful for the spoken insights and written material given me by JoAnn Berryman, Flora Morgan, and Rita D. Whitt, all of them members of the Polio Survivors Organization; they helped me acquire a perspective I found invaluable. In their fight to live full lives despite their handicap, these survivors are inspiring inheritors of the FDR tradition. (I must point out again that any conclusions I reach are mine, not theirs.) I am also indebted to Kevin Nelson, M.D., for discussing with me his work with polio survivors, and I absolve him from any responsibility for my observations about postpolio sequelae. I further thank Colonel Bates for supplying a chapter of his draft memoirs and photographs taken by him at Yalta, Mr. Bogue for making available to me detailed information about U.S. communications at Yalta, Dr. and Mrs. Bruenn for lending me a photograph of the doctor as a young practitioner, and Miss Nason for lending me a photograph and for taking time to read and suggest corrections in passages of the book dealing with her experiences as General Marshall's personal secretary.

Other persons who helped with spoken or written information were Robert Adams; T. S. Boggess, Jr.; Brigadier General William Buster; Captain Mark Clodfelter of the U.S. Air Force Academy; Laura Crawford; Dr. Gary Goldberg; Jim Kitchens; and Robert M. Johnson II of the Historical Research Section at Maxwell Air Force Base; Linda McClain; my longtime if intermittent colleague, Bernard C. Nalty; Sally L. Parker; and officers of the National Security Office at the White House.

For helpful suggestions offered at the outset of the project, I am indebted to a friend and associate of many years' standing, the late Mel Bookstein. I also thank my friend and fellow author Charles Bracelen Flood for his continuing advice and encouragement, and I owe a special debt of gratitude to Professor George Herring of the University of Kentucky for reading the entire manuscript and offering constructive comments. And, in a mixed-media age, it is surely appropriate for me to thank David Haller, an accomplished actor, for tape-recording a reading of the Prologue as it existed in an early version.

Intellectual as well as personal acknowledgment is important, I think. As anyone familiar with the writings of Professor Samuel P. Huntington of Harvard University will see, I have drawn on a number of his ideas concerning civil-military relationships; I acknowledge a similar indebtedness to the work of Professor Russell F. Weigley of Temple University with respect to questions of army organization and doctrine. It is a pleasure also to make mention of another important thinker in the overall civil-military area, Dean Louis Smith. And my work has been made vastly easier by the great contribution of Larry I. Bland and his colleagues at the Marshall Library in producing the first two volumes of the Marshall papers and in making available, early in my research, the transcripts and notes of the twenty-three interviews conducted with General Marshall by Forrest C. Pogue. These extensive interviews, undertaken by Dr. Pogue as the general's official biographer, were important sources of the immediacy I sought in telling this story. I wish to thank Dr. Pogue, the unrivaled authority of authorities on General Marshall, for our many pleasant and enlightening conversations about the general and other subjects; I am happy to have his friendship. I also thank Professor Huntington for taking time to discuss civil-military relations with me.

Much of this book is based on information from archival sources. I am grateful to Dr. William Emerson, director of the Franklin D. Roosevelt Library at Hyde Park, N.Y., for his cordial reception and helpful suggestions; it is perhaps unfair to single out members of the staff of this outstanding library, but I must thank Susan Elter for the efficiency with which she furnished requested photographs. At the U.S. Army Military History Institute, Carlisle Barracks, Pa., a very efficient organization presided over by Dr. Richard J. Sommers, I benefited in particular from the thoughtful help of David Keough. And it is a pleasure once again to thank my good friends at the George C. Marshall Library, Lexington, Va., Royster C. Lyle, Jr., and John Jacob, who as always did everything possible to further my work. I also extend thanks to Rodney Dennis, director of the Houghton Library at Harvard University, for his helpfulness. At Georgia Southern College, where I consulted the papers of William Rigdon, I met with a wonderful reception from the staff of Julius Ariail, the director; for all their help I thank Edna Earle Brown, the associate director, and Bunny Akins, the records coordinator. And no list of such acknowledgments would be complete without a nod to John E. Taylor, the wonderfully unbureaucratic wizard of the Modern Military Branch, National Archives, in Washington.

I express special thanks to my neighbors, the tireless staff members of the Hutchins Library at Berea College—to Thomas Kirk, the director; to Phyllis Hughes, head reference librarian, and her associates Edith Hansen and Molly Pitts, and to Eileen Hart. I am also grateful to Paul Willis, director of libraries at the University of Kentucky, for the many courtesies extended to me by him and his staff, in particular William J. Marshall and William Cooper. I have also made considerable use of the library of Eastern Kentucky University, where I am indebted to Dean Ernest Weyhrauch for extensive loan privileges.

Since writers do not exist by information alone, I wish to thank the following persons whose hospitality constituted an important element in my research: Ann Allen and Robert Schwoebel of Swarthmore, Pa.; the late Lassor Blumenthal and his wife, Dr. Susan Blumenthal, whose Dutchess County retreat was conveniently close to the Roosevelt Library; Fritz and Joann Heimann of Westport, Conn.; my fellow author Charles B. MacDonald of Arlington, Va., who not only put me up but is always cheerfully willing to answer questions; and Samuel and Ellen Stevens of Belmont, Mass.

Once again I thank Ann Pollard, who has typed manuscripts for me for quite some time now, but whose work is inadequately suggested by such a mundane description. I also thank Sara Hext for her work with the bibliography and Lillian McGuire and Arlene Nance for transcribing tapes. A special word of thanks for her cooperativeness must go to Susan Wallen, assistant to James Roosevelt.

I am especially grateful for the interest and support of my editor at William Morrow, the renowned Bruce Lee, whose recent retirement means that this book was among the last he edited for Morrow; I am pleased at this distinction but very sorry that he has left his editorial desk. I thank, too, Bruce's assistant, John Harrison, for his help.

Perhaps only a writer can know how valuable an agent can be, but let me say that Stuart Krichevsky of Sterling Lord Literistic, Inc., who represents me, is devoted, imaginative, efficient and cheerful—an ideal agent; I would not like to have to get along without him. His constant interest and encouragement have been important factors in the creation of this book.

Finally, I acknowledge with special pleasure the help of my dear friend Nancy Coleman Wolsk, who once again offered not only continuing encouragement but sound advice, who took an active part in research, and—most important—who provided unfailing love and support.

SOURCES

Aside from the archival and the other unpublished sources on which I have drawn, the following listing does not attempt to include all the materials that make up the written and spoken background of this book. Such a bibliography would constitute a book in itself—an enormous one—since the literature of the World War II era is not only vast but continues to grow (a state of affairs about which, of course, I can hardly complain). I have listed here every work of any kind cited in the Notes and others that either had overall importance or were of direct use in the writing of the book. I have tried to keep in mind the idea that the bibliography should serve both as a listing of sources and as a convenience for anyone wishing to do further reading in the subject.

The book is based on interviews and correspondence, on manuscripts and other archival materials, on other unpublished works such as lectures and dissertations, and on published articles and books, some of these last-named being first-hand accounts, others serving as secondary but valuable sources. A basic source is the series of interviews with General Marshall conducted during 1956–1957 by Forrest C. Pogue, the general's official biographer; in the Notes these are cited as Interviews, followed by a column (not page) number, the reference being to the arrangement of the interviews as recently made available by the George C. Marshall Library and Research Center, Lexington, Va. Other interviews, whether conducted by the present author or by someone else, appear individually as citations in the Notes.

ARCHIVAL MATERIALS

It ought to be pointed out here that nowadays, thanks to photocopying, a given document may well be found in any of several repositories. A citation in the Notes therefore indicates the file and the collection in which I encountered the particular document; accordingly, persons wishing to consult a document may find another of its archival homes more convenient for their purposes. (In any case, it must be said that a copy can never provide the excitement that comes from handling the original piece of paper.) The principal manuscript sources consulted for this book were the Franklin D. Roosevelt Library, Hyde Park, N.Y. (FDRL); the Marshall Library (GCML); the collections of the U.S. Army Military History Institute, Carlisle Barracks, Pa. (MHI); and the William Rigdon Papers in the Zach S. Henderson Library, Georgia Southern College, Statesboro, Ga. (RP).

The papers consulted at Hyde Park include the President's Personal File (PPF), the President's Secretary's File (PSF), the Official File (OF), the Map Room File (MR), and the president's appointments diary, and the papers of Francis Biddle, Wilson Brown, Anna Roosevelt Halsted, William D. Hassett, Harry L. Hopkins (including material collected by Robert E. Sherwood), John L. McCrea, Lowell Mellett, William Rigdon, Anna Eleanor Roosevelt, Samuel I. Rosenman, Harold Smith, Rexford G. Tugwell, Henry Wallace (vice-presidential papers), and Claude Wickard. Other sources at Hyde Park were the diaries of Henry Morgenthau, Jr., the oral histories, and the file of reminiscences of FDR by his contemporaries.

At the Marshall Library, the principal manuscript sources consulted, in addition to the George C. Marshall Collection and the George C. Marshall Papers, were the Marshall Andrews Papers, the Harvey A. DeWeerd Papers, the C. J. George Collection, the Thomas T. Handy Papers, the Frank B. Hayne Papers, the George F. Howe Collection, the Frank McCarthy Papers, the Reginald N. MacDonald-Buchanan Papers, the Marshall Foundation National Archives Project, the Reminiscences About George C. Marshall File, the Paul M. Robinett Collection, the William T. Sexton Papers, the Mark Skinner Watson Notes, and the Reginald Winn Collection.

At Carlisle Barracks, the most useful sources were the papers of John L. Bates (Oleg Pantuhoff), Richard Collins, Charles Donnelly, and John E. Hull; oral history interviews; and reports.

I also consulted the James Parton Papers and other documents at the Houghton Library of Harvard University.

OTHER UNPUBLISHED MATERIALS

BUSTER, WILLIAM. "The Constitution and the Military." Lecture, September 20, 1987.

FERDON, NONA S. "Franklin D. Roosevelt: A Psychological Interpretation of His Childhood and Youth." Ph.D. diss., University of Hawaii, 1971.

HARRELSON, ELMER HARVEY. "Roosevelt and the United States Army, 1937–1940: A Study in Challenge-Response." Ph.D. diss., University of New Mexico, 1971.

HARRIS, DENNIS EARL. "The Diplomacy of the Second Front: America, Britain, Russia, and the Normandy Invasion." Ph.D. diss., University of California, 1969.

HIGGINBOTHAM, DON. "George Washington and George Marshall: Some Reflections on the American Military Tradition." The Harmon Memorial Lectures on Military History, U.S. Air Force Academy, 1984.

JOHNSON, WILLIAM THOMAS. "Forging the Foundations of the Grand Alliance." Ph.D. diss., Duke University, 1986.

KUTER, LAURENCE S. "Malta-Yalta Army Air Force Observations." Microfilm. Maxwell Air Force Base, n.d.

LAZALIER, JAMES H. "Surrogate Diplomacy: Franklin D. Roosevelt's Personal Envoys, 1941–1945." Ph.D. diss., University of Oklahoma, 1973.

McCLAIN, LINDA. "The Role of Admiral W. D. Leahy in U.S. Foreign Policy." Ph.D. diss., University of Virginia, 1984.

MARSHALL, GEORGE C. Interviews and Reminiscences for Forrest C. Pogue, 1956–1957.

PARKER, SALLY L. "Attendant Lords: A Study of the British Joint Staff Mission in Washington, 1941–1945." Ph.D. diss., University of Maryland, 1984.

POGUE, FORREST C. "George C. Marshall: Global Commander." The Harmon Memorial Lectures on Military History. U.S. Air Force Academy, 1968.

———. "The Wartime Chiefs of Staff and the President." U.S. Air Force Academy Symposium, 1973.

STRANGE, JOSEPH L. "Cross-Channel Attack, 1942: The British Rejection of Operation Sledgehammer and the Cherbourg Alternative." Ph.D. diss., University of Maryland, 1984.

ARTICLES

"A Dutchess County Boy." *New Republic,* April 15, 1946. Special FDR edition.

ALEXANDER, JACK. "The Stormy New Boss of the Pentagon." *Saturday Evening Post,* July 30, 1949.

ALLEN, FREDERICK LEWIS. "Marshall, Arnold, King: Three Snapshots." *Harper's,* February 1945.

AUCHINCLOSS, LOUIS. "The Inner F.D.R." *New York Review of Books,* November 21, 1985.

BARNETT, LINCOLN. "General Marshall." *Life,* January 3, 1944.

BERGER, MEYER. "They Speak As If He Still Lives On." *New York Times Magazine,* April 14, 1947.

BRUENN, HOWARD G., M.D. "Clinical Notes on the Illness and Death of President Franklin D. Roosevelt." *Annals of Internal Medicine,* April 1970.

BUSCH, NOEL F. "General Drum." *Life,* June 16, 1941.

BUTOW, R.J.C. "The F.D.R. Tapes." *American Heritage,* February–March 1982.

CARTER, MARSHALL S. "Unforgettable George C. Marshall." *Reader's Digest,* July 1972.

CBS NEWS. "The Chairman," segment of *Sixty Minutes,* March 20, 1988.

CRAWFORD, BRUCE. "Long Life for the Proverbial Soap Dish." *Military History,* December 1987.

DALLIN, DAVID J. "Russia's Aims in Europe." *American Mercury,* October 1943.

DAVIS, FORREST. "What Really Happened at Teheran." *Saturday Evening Post,* May 13 and May 20, 1944.

DAVIS, KENNETH S. "FDR as a Biographer's Problem." *The American Scholar,* Winter 1984.

DE WEERD, H. A. "Marshall: Organizer of Victory." Part I. *Infantry Journal,* December 1946.

———. "Marshall: Organizer of Victory." Part II. *Infantry Journal,* January 1947.

EISENHOWER, DAVID. "Franklin Delano Roosevelt: Commander in War." Review of *Commander in Chief,* by Eric Larrabee. *Book World, Washington Post,* June 8, 1987.

EMERSON, WILLIAM. "Franklin Roosevelt as Commander-in-Chief in World War II." *Military Affairs,* Winter 1958–1959.

FALLS, CYRIL. "A Window on the World: General George Marshall." *Illustrated London News,* January 22, 1949.

GROW, ROBERT W. "The Ten Lean Years: 1930–1940." *Armor,* November 1987.

HAGOOD, JOHNSON. "Soldier." *Saturday Evening Post,* July 15, 1939.

HAIGHT, JOHN McVICKAR, JR. "Roosevelt as Friend of France." *Foreign Affairs,* April 1966.

HARBUT, FRASER. "Churchill, Hopkins, and the 'Other' Americans." *International History Review,* May 1986.

HOPKINS, HARRY L. "The Inside Story of My Meeting with Stalin." *American,* December 1941.

IGNATIUS, DAVID. "They Don't Make Them Like George Marshall Anymore." *Washington Post,* June 8, 1987.

JOHNSON, T. M. "America's No. 1 Soldier." *Reader's Digest,* February 1944.

JOHNSON, WALTER. "Roosevelt in the War Years." Review of *The Public Papers and Addresses of Franklin D. Roosevelt, 1941–1945,* edited by Samuel I. Rosenman. *Yale Review,* Summer 1950.

KENNEDY, PAUL. "At His Best, Even When He Failed." Review of *George C. Marshall: Statesman 1945–1959,* by Forrest C. Pogue. *New York Times Book Review,* June 28, 1987.

KRAUSKOPF, ROBERT W. "The Army and the Strategic Bomber: 1938–1939." *Military Affairs,* Winter 1958–1959.

LIEBLING, A. J. "Chief of Staff." *New Yorker,* October 26, 1940.

MARSHALL, GEORGE C. "Some Lessons of History." *Maryland Historical Magazine,* September 1945.

"Mrs. Marshall's Story." Unsigned review of *Together,* by Katherine Tupper Marshall. *Infantry Journal,* January 1947.

PAINTON, F. C., AND JOHNSON, T. M. "Vignettes of America's No. 1 Soldier." *Reader's Digest,* January 1944.

PERKINS, JEANNE. "The President's Doctor." *Life,* July 31, 1944.

POGUE, FORREST C. "The Military in a Democracy." *International Security,* Spring 1979.

POTTER, DAVID. "Sketches for the Roosevelt Portrait." *Yale Review,* September 1949.

"The President and War Aims," "Democracy and Filibuster." *New Republic,* March 10, 1941.

REYNOLDS, DAVID. "Roosevelt, the British Left, and the Appointment of John G. Winant as United States Ambassador to Britain in 1941." *International History Review,* August 1982.

SHALETT, SIDNEY. "Mammoth Cave, Washington, D.C." *New York Times Magazine,* June 27, 1943.

———. "Marshall, Soldier Without Frills." *New York Times Magazine,* October 3, 1943.

STOLER, MARK A. "The 'Pacific-First' Alternative in American World War II Strategy." *International History Review,* July 1980.

STRANGE, JOSEPH L. "The British Rejection of Operation Sledgehammer: An Alternative Motive." *Military Affairs,* February 1982.

SUTHERLAND, JOHN P. "The Story Gen. Marshall Told Me." *U.S. News and World Report,* November 2, 1959.

"A Three-Sided Controversy on Aid to Britain." *School and Society,* February 1, 1941.

U.S. DEPARTMENT OF STATE. "George C. Marshall, Soldier-Statesman." *Bulletin,* June 1982.

VISHNIAK, MARK. "Lenin's Democracy, and Stalin's." *Foreign Affairs,* July 1946.

Extensive use has been made of *Collier's,* the *George C. Marshall Library Newsletter, Life,* the *New Republic,* the *New Yorker,* the *New York Times,* the *Polio Survivors Organization Quarterly Newsletter,* the *Reader's Digest,* the *Saturday Evening Post, Time, U.S. News and World Report,* and the newspaper wire services.

BOOKS

ADAMIC, LOUIS. *Dinner at the White House.* New York: Harper, 1946.

ADAMS, HENRY H. *Harry Hopkins.* New York: Putnam, 1977.

———. *Witness to Power: The Life of Fleet Admiral William D. Leahy.* Annapolis: Naval Institute Press, 1985.

AGLION, RAOUL. *Roosevelt and de Gaulle: Allies in Conflict.* New York: Free Press, 1988.

ALSOP, JOSEPH. *Franklin D. Roosevelt: 1882–1945: A Centenary Remembrance.* New York: Viking, 1982.

ALSOP, JOSEPH, AND KINTNER, ROBERT. *American White Paper: The Story of American Diplomacy and the Second World War.* New York: Simon & Schuster, 1940.

———. *Men Around the President.* New York: Doubleday, 1939.

AMBROSE, STEPHEN E. *Eisenhower.* Vol. 1: *Soldier, General of the Army, President-Elect.* New York: Simon & Schuster, 1983.

———. *The Supreme Commander.* Garden City, N.Y.: Doubleday, 1970.

AMBROSE, STEPHEN E., AND BARBER, JAMES A., JR., EDS. *The Military and American Society: Essays and Readings.* New York: Free Press, 1972.

ARNOLD, H. H. *Global Mission.* New York: Harper, 1949.

ASBELL, BERNARD. *When F.D.R. Died.* New York: Holt, Rinehart & Winston, 1961.

ASTLEY, JOAN BRIGHT. *The Inner Circle.* Boston: Atlantic-Little, Brown, 1971.

AVON, LORD. *The Eden Memoirs.* Vol. 3: *The Reckoning.* London: Cassell, 1965.

BALDWIN, HANSON W. *The Crucial Years: 1939–1941.* New York: Harper & Row, 1976.

BARBER, JAMES DAVID. *Political Leadership in American Government.* Boston: Little, Brown, 1964.

———. *Power in Committees: An Experiment in the Governmental Process.* Chicago: Rand McNally, 1966.

———. *The Presidential Character: Predicting Performance in the White House.* Englewood Cliffs, N.J.: Prentice-Hall, 1972.

BARNETT, LINCOLN. *Writing on Life: Sixteen Close-Ups.* New York: William Sloane, 1951.

BARUCH, BERNARD M. *Baruch: The Public Years.* Vol. 2 of *My Own Story.* New York: Holt, Rinehart & Winston, 1960.

BEAL, JOHN ROBINSON. *Marshall in China.* Garden City, N.Y.: Doubleday, 1970.

BEITZELL, ROBERT, ED. *Tehran, Yalta, Potsdam: The Soviet Protocols.* Hattiesburg, Miss.: Academic International, 1970.

BELL, CORAL. *The Debatable Alliance.* New York: Oxford University Press, 1964.

BERLIN, ISAIAH. *Personal Impressions.* Edited by Henry Hardy. New York: Viking, 1981; Penguin edition, 1982.

BESCHLOSS, MICHAEL R. *Kennedy and Roosevelt.* New York: Norton, 1980; Harper Perennial edition, 1987.

BINION, RUDOLPH. *Hitler Among the Germans.* New York:

Elsevier, 1976; Northern Illinois University Press edition, 1984.

BLAND, LARRY I., ED., AND RITENOUR, SHARON R., ASSISTANT ED. *The Papers of George Catlett Marshall.* Vol. 1: *The Soldierly Spirit: December 1880–June 1939.* Baltimore: Johns Hopkins University Press, 1981.

BLAND, LARRY I., ED., RITENOUR, SHARON R., AND WUNDERLIN, CLARENCE E., ASSISTANT EDS. *The Papers of George Catlett Marshall.* Vol. 2: *We Cannot Delay: July 1, 1939–December 6, 1941.* Baltimore: Johns Hopkins University Press, 1986.

BLUM, JOHN MORTON. *From the Morgenthau Diaries.* Vol. 2: *Years of Urgency 1939–1941.* Boston: Houghton Mifflin, 1965.

———. *From the Morgenthau Diaries.* Vol. 3: *Years of War, 1941–1945.* Boston: Houghton Mifflin, 1967.

———. *Roosevelt and Morgenthau: A Revision and Condensation of From the Morgenthau Diaries.* Boston: Houghton Mifflin, 1970.

BOHLEN, CHARLES E. *Witness to History, 1929–1969.* New York: Norton, 1973.

BORKLUND, CARL W. *Men of the Pentagon: From Forrestal to McNamara.* New York: Praeger, 1966.

BRADLEY, OMAR N. *A Soldier's Story.* New York: Holt, Rinehart & Winston, 1951.

BRENDON, PIERS. *Ike: His Life and Times.* New York: Harper, 1986.

BRYANT, SIR ARTHUR. *Triumph in the West. A History of the War Years Based on the Diaries of Field Marshal Lord Alanbrooke, Chief of the Imperial General Staff.* Garden City, N.Y.: Doubleday, 1959.

———. *The Turn of the Tide: A History of the War Years Based on the Diaries of Field Marshal Lord Alanbrooke, Chief of the Imperial General Staff.* Garden City, N.Y.: Doubleday, 1957.

BROWNLOW, LOUIS. *A Passion for Anonymity: The Autobiography of Louis Brownlow.* Vol. 2. Chicago: University of Chicago Press, 1958.

BUELL, THOMAS B. *Master of Sea Power: A Biography of Fleet Admiral Ernest J. King.* Boston: Little, Brown, 1980.

BULLITT, WILLIAM C. *For the President: Personal and Secret.*

Edited by Orville H. Bullitt. Boston: Houghton Mifflin, 1972.

BURNS, JAMES MacGREGOR. *Leadership*. New York: Harper & Row, 1978.

———. *Presidential Government: The Crucible of Leadership*. Boston: Houghton Mifflin, 1965.

———. *Roosevelt: The Lion and the Fox*. New York: Harcourt, Brace, 1956.

———. *Roosevelt: The Soldier of Freedom*. New York: Harcourt Brace Jovanovich, 1970.

BURNS, RICHARD DEAN, AND BENNETT, EDWARD M., EDS. *Diplomats in Crisis: United States-Chinese-Japanese Relations, 1919–1941*. Santa Barbara, Calif.: Clio Press, 1974.

BUSH, VANNEVAR. *Modern Arms and Free Men: A Discussion of the Role of Science in Preserving Democracy*. New York: Simon & Schuster, 1949.

BUTCHER, HARRY C. *My Three Years with Eisenhower*. New York: Simon & Schuster, 1946.

BUTOW, R.J.C. *The John Doe Associates: Backdoor Diplomacy for Peace, 1941*. Stanford, Calif.: Stanford University Press, 1974.

CANTOR, MILTON, ED. *Great Lives Observed: Hamilton*. Englewood Cliffs, N.J.: Prentice-Hall, 1971.

CHURCHILL, WINSTON S. *The Second World War*. Vol. 1: *The Gathering Storm*. Vol. 2: *Their Finest Hour*. Vol. 3: *The Grand Alliance*. Vol. 4: *The Hinge of Fate*. Vol. 5: *Closing the Ring*. Vol. 6: *Triumph and Tragedy*. Boston: Houghton Mifflin, 1948–1953.

CLAUSEWITZ, KARL VON. *On War*. Edited by Anatol Rapoport. Penguin edition, 1968.

CLINE, RAY S. *Washington Command Post: The Operations Division*. Washington, D.C.: Office of the Chief of Military History, Department of the Army, 1951.

COAKLEY, ROBERT W., AND LEIGHTON, RICHARD M. *Global Logistics and Strategy, 1943–1945*. Washington, D.C.: Office of the Chief of Military History, Department of the Army, 1968.

COFFEY, THOMAS M. *Hap: The Story of the U.S. Air Force and the Man Who Built It, General Henry H. "Hap" Arnold*. New York: Viking, 1982.

COFFMAN, EDWARD M. *The Hilt of the Sword: The Career of*

Peyton C. March. Madison: University of Wisconsin Press, 1966.

COLE, WAYNE S. *Roosevelt and the Isolationists, 1932–1945.* Lincoln: University of Nebraska Press, 1983.

CONN, STETSON, AND FAIRCHILD, BYRON. *The Framework of Hemisphere Defense.* Washington, D.C.: Office of the Chief of Military History, Department of the Army, 1960.

CRABB, CECIL V., JR., AND MULCAHY, KEVIN V. *Presidents and Foreign Policy Making: From Franklin D. Roosevelt to Reagan.* Baton Rouge: Louisiana State University Press, 1986.

DALLEK, ROBERT. *Franklin D. Roosevelt and American Foreign Policy, 1932–1945.* New York: Oxford University Press, 1979.

DANCHEV, ALEX. *Very Special Relationship: Field Marshal Sir John Dill and the Anglo-American Alliance, 1941–1944.* London: Brassey's Defence Publishers, 1986.

DANIELS, JONATHAN. *White House Witness, 1942–1945.* Garden City, N.Y.: Doubleday, 1975.

DARLAN, ALAIN. *L'Amiral Darlan parle.* Paris: Amiot-Dumont, 1953.

DAVIS, ANDREW. *Where Did the Forties Go? A Popular History.* London and Sydney: Pluto Press, 1984.

DAVIS, KENNETH S. *F.D.R.: The New York Years, 1928–1933.* New York: Random House, 1985.

DEBOE, DAVID C., SMITH, VAN MITCHELL, WEST, ELLIOTT, AND GRAEBNER, NORMAN A. *Essays on American Foreign Policy.* Austin: University of Texas Press, 1974.

DHERS, PIERRE. *Regards nouveaux sur les années quarante.* Paris: Flammarion, 1958.

DIVINE, ROBERT A. *Roosevelt and World War II.* Baltimore: Johns Hopkins University Press, 1969; Penguin edition, 1970.

DIZIKES, JOHN. *Britain, Roosevelt and the New Deal.* New York: Garland, 1979.

DJILAS, MILOVAN. *Conversations with Stalin.* Translated by Michael B. Petrovich. New York: Harcourt, Brace & World, 1962.

DORN, FRANK. *Walkout: With Stilwell in Burma.* New York: Crowell, 1971.

EDWARDS, KENNETH. *Men of Action.* London: Collins, 1943.

EHRMAN, JOHN. *Grand Strategy.* Vol. 5: *August 1943–September 1944.* London: Her Majesty's Stationery Office, 1956.

EISENHOWER, DAVID. *Eisenhower at War, 1943–1945.* New York: Random House, 1986.

EISENHOWER, DWIGHT D. *At Ease.* Garden City, N.Y.: Doubleday, 1967; Avon edition, 1968.

———. *Crusade in Europe.* Garden City, N.Y.: Doubleday, 1948.

———. *Dear General.* Edited by Joseph P. Hobbs. Baltimore: Johns Hopkins University Press, 1971.

———. *The Eisenhower Diaries.* Edited by Robert H. Ferrell. New York: Norton, 1981.

EISENHOWER, JOHN S.D. *Allies: Pearl Harbor to D-Day.* Garden City, N.Y.: Doubleday, 1982.

EUBANK, KEITH. *Summit at Teheran.* New York: Morrow, 1985.

FABER, HAROLD. *Soldier and Statesman: General George C. Marshall.* New York: Ariel Books, 1964.

FEIS, HERBERT. *The Atomic Bomb and the End of World War II.* Princeton, N.J.: Princeton University Press, 1966.

———. *The Road to Pearl Harbor: The Coming of the War Between the United States and Japan.* Princeton, N.J.: Princeton University Press, 1950.

FENNO, RICHARD F., JR., ED. *The President's Cabinet: An Analysis in the Period from Wilson to Eisenhower.* Cambridge, Mass.: Harvard University Press, 1959.

———. *The Yalta Conference.* Second Edition. Lexington, Mass.: D. C. Heath, 1972.

FERRELL, ROBERT H. *General George C. Marshall.* New York: Cooper Square, 1966.

FINER, S. E. *The Man on Horseback.* New York: Praeger, 1962.

FRASER, DAVID. *Alanbrooke.* New York: Atheneum, 1982.

FREIDEL, FRANK. *Franklin D. Roosevelt: The Ordeal.* Boston: Little, Brown, 1954.

FRYE, WILLIAM. *Marshall: Citizen Soldier.* Indianapolis: Bobbs-Merrill, 1947.

FUNK, ARTHUR LAYTON. *The Politics of Torch.* Lawrence: University Press of Kansas, 1974.

GADDIS, JOHN LEWIS. *The United States and the Origins of the Cold War, 1941–1947.* New York: Columbia University Press, 1972.

GALLAGHER, HUGH GREGORY. *F.D.R.'s Splendid Deception.* New York: Dodd, Mead, 1985.

GEDDES, DONALD PORTER, ED. *Franklin Delano Roosevelt: A Memorial.* New York: Dial Press, 1945.

GILBERT, MARTIN. *Winston S. Churchill*. Vol. 5: *1922–1939: The Prophet of Truth*. Boston: Houghton Mifflin, 1976.

GIRAUD, HENRI HONORÉ. *Un seul but, la victoire*. Paris: René Julliard, 1949.

GOLDBERG, RICHARD THAYER. *The Making of Franklin D. Roosevelt: Triumph Over Disability*. Cambridge, Mass.: Abt Books, 1981.

GOODPASTER, ANDREW J., AND HUNTINGTON, SAMUEL P. *Civil-Military Relations*. Washington, D.C.: American Enterprise Institute for Public Policy Research, 1977.

GRAFF, ROBERT, AND GINNA, ROBERT. *F.D.R.* New York: Harper, 1963.

GRAHAM, OTIS L., JR. *An Encore for Reform: The Old Progressives and the New Deal*. New York: Oxford University Press, 1967.

GREENFIELD, KENT ROBERTS. *American Strategy in World War II: A Reconsideration*. Baltimore: Johns Hopkins University Press, 1963.

———. *Command Decisions*. Washington, D.C.: Office of the Chief of Military History, Department of the Army, 1960.

GREENFIELD, KENT ROBERTS, PALMER, ROBERT R., AND WILEY, BELL I. *The Army Ground Forces: The Organization of Ground Combat Troops*. Washington, D.C.: Historical Division, Department of the Army, 1947.

GRIGG, JOHN. *1943: The Victory That Never Was*. New York: Hill & Wang, 1980.

GUNTHER, JOHN. *Roosevelt in Retrospect: A Profile in History*. New York: Harper, 1950.

HARGROVE, ERWIN C. *Presidential Leadership: Personality and Political Style*. New York: Macmillan, 1966.

HARRIMAN, W. AVERELL, AND ABEL, ELIE. *Special Envoy to Churchill and Stalin, 1941–1946*. New York: Random House, 1975.

HARRISON, GORDON A. *Cross-Channel Attack*. Washington, D.C.: Office of the Chief of Military History, Department of the Army, 1951.

HARRITY, RICHARD, AND MARTIN, RALPH G. *The Human Side of F.D.R.* New York: Duell, Sloane & Pearce, 1960.

HASSETT, WILLIAM D. *Off the Record with F.D.R., 1942–1945*. New Brunswick, N.J.: Rutgers University Press, 1958.

HATHAWAY, ROBERT. *Ambiguous Partnership, 1944–1947*. New York: Columbia University Press, 1981.

HAYES, GRACE PERSON. *The History of the Joint Chiefs of Staff in World War II: The War Against Japan.* Annapolis: Naval Institute Press, 1982.

HEARDON, PATRICK J. *Roosevelt Confronts Hitler: America's Entry into World War II.* De Kalb: Northern Illinois University Press, 1987.

HOWARD, MICHAEL. *The Mediterranean Strategy in the Second World War.* New York: Praeger, 1968.

———. *Soldiers and Governments.* London: Eyre & Spottiswoode, 1957.

———. *War and the Liberal Conscience.* New Brunswick, N.J.: Rutgers University Press, 1978.

———, ED. *The Theory and Practice of War.* New York: Praeger, 1966; Indiana University Press edition, 1975.

HOWE, GEORGE F. *Northwest Africa: Seizing the Initiative in the West.* Washington, D.C.: Office of the Chief of Military History, Department of the Army, 1957.

HULL, CORDELL. *The Memoirs of Cordell Hull.* 2 vols. New York: Macmillan, 1948.

HUNTINGTON, SAMUEL P. *The Soldier and the State: The Theory and Politics of Civil-Military Relations.* Cambridge, Mass.: Belknap Press, Harvard University, 1957.

ICKES, HAROLD L. *The Autobiography of a Curmudgeon.* New York: Reynal & Hitchcock, 1943.

———. *The Secret Diary of Harold L. Ickes.* Vol. 2: *The Inside Struggle: 1936–1939.* New York: Simon & Schuster, 1954.

———. *The Secret Diary of Harold L. Ickes.* Vol. 3: *The Lowering Clouds: 1939–1941.* New York: Simon & Schuster, 1954.

INGERSOLL, RALPH. *Top Secret.* New York: Harcourt, Brace, 1946.

ISMAY, GENERAL LORD. *The Memoirs of General Lord Ismay.* New York: Viking, 1960.

ISRAEL, FRED L. *Nevada's Key Pittman.* Lincoln: University of Nebraska Press, 1963.

JACOBSEN, HANS-ADOLF, AND SMITH, ARTHUR L., JR., EDS. *World War II Policy and Strategy: Selected Documents with Commentary.* Santa Barbara, Calif.: ABC-Clio, 1979.

JAMES, D. CLAYTON. *The Years of MacArthur.* Vol. 1: *1880–1941.* Boston: Houghton Mifflin, 1970.

JAMES, ROBERT RHODES. *Anthony Eden.* New York: McGraw-Hill, 1986.

JANEWAY, ELIOT. *The Struggle for Survival: A Chronicle of Economic Mobilization in World War II.* New Haven: Yale University Press, 1951.

JESSUP, PHILIP C. *Elihu Root.* Vol. 1: *1845–1909.* New York: Dodd, Mead, 1938.

JOHNSON, GERALD W. *Roosevelt: Dictator or Democrat?* New York: Harper, 1941.

KAHAN, STUART. *The Wolf of the Kremlin.* New York: Morrow, 1987.

KAMMERER, ALBERT. *Du débarquement africain au meurtre de Darlan.* Paris: Flammarion, 1949.

KECSKEMETI, PAUL. *Strategic Surrender: The Politics of Victory and Defeat.* Stanford, Calif.: Stanford University Press, 1958.

KENNAN, GEORGE F. *American Diplomacy, 1900–1950.* Chicago: University of Chicago Press, 1951; Mentor edition, n.d.

KENNEDY, SIR JOHN. *The Business of War.* Edited by Bernard Fergusson. New York: Morrow, 1958.

KERSAUDY, FRANÇOIS. *Churchill and de Gaulle.* New York: Atheneum, 1981.

KERWIN, JEROME G., ED. *Civil-Military Relationships in American Life.* Chicago: University of Chicago Press, 1948.

KIMBALL, WARREN F. *The Most Unsordid Act: Lend-Lease, 1939–1941.* Baltimore: Johns Hopkins University Press, 1969.

KUTER, LAURENCE S. *Airman at Yalta.* New York: Duell, Sloane & Pearce, 1955.

LANGER, WILLIAM L., AND GLEASON, S. EVERETT. *The Challenge to Isolation, 1937–1940.* New York: Harper, 1952.

LANGHORNE, RICHARD, ED. *Diplomacy and Intelligence During the Second World War.* Cambridge England: Cambridge University Press, 1985.

LARRABEE, ERIC. *Commander in Chief. Franklin Delano Roosevelt, His Lieutenants, and Their War.* New York: Harper & Row, 1987.

LASH, JOSEPH P. *Eleanor and Franklin: The Story of Their Relationship, Based on Eleanor Roosevelt's Private Papers.* New York: Norton, 1971.

———. *Roosevelt and Churchill: 1939–1941.* New York: Norton, 1976.

LEAHY, WILLIAM D. *I Was There.* New York: Whittlesey House, 1950.

LEASOR, JAMES. *War at the Top.* London: Michael Joseph, 1959.

L'ETANG, HUGH. *The Pathology of Leadership.* New York: Hawthorn Books, 1970.

LEUCHTENBURG, WILLIAM E. *In the Shadow of F.D.R.: From Harry Truman to Ronald Reagan.* Ithaca, N.Y.: Cornell University Press, 1983.

LEWIN, RONALD. *The American Magic: Codes, Ciphers and the Defeat of Japan.* New York: Farrar, Straus & Giroux, 1982.

———. *Churchill as Warlord.* New York: Stein & Day, 1973.

LIPPMANN, THEO, JR. *The Squire of Warm Springs.* Chicago: Playboy Press, 1977.

LIPPMANN, WALTER. *U.S. Foreign Policy: Shield of the Republic.* Boston: Little, Brown, 1943.

LOEWENHEIM, FRANCIS L., LANGLEY, HAROLD D., AND JONAS, MANFRED, EDS. *Roosevelt and Churchill: Their Secret Wartime Correspondence.* New York: Dutton, 1975.

LURTON, DOUGLAS, ED. *Roosevelt's Foreign Policy, 1933–1941.* New York: W. Funk, Inc., 1942.

MacARTHUR, DOUGLAS. *Reminiscences.* New York: McGraw-Hill, 1964; Crest edition, 1965.

McFARLAND, KEITH D. *Harry H. Woodring: A Political Biography of F.D.R.'s Controversial Secretary of War.* Lawrence: University Press of Kansas, 1975.

McINTIRE, ROSS E., AND CREEL, GEORGE. *White House Physician.* New York: Putnam, 1946.

MacISAAC, DAVID, ED. *The Military and Society.* Proceedings of the Fifth Military History Symposium, United States Air Force Academy, October 5–6, 1972. Washington, D.C.: Office of Air Force History and United States Air Force Academy.

MCJIMSEY, GEORGE. *Harry Hopkins.* Cambridge, Mass.: Harvard University Press, 1987.

MANCHESTER, WILLIAM. *American Caesar.* Boston: Little, Brown, 1978; Dell edition, 1979.

MARQUAND, JOHN P. *Melville Goodwin, USA.* Boston: Little, Brown, 1951.

MARSHALL, GEORGE C. *Memoirs of My Services in the World War: 1917–1918.* Boston: Houghton Mifflin, 1976.

MARSHALL, GEORGE C., ARNOLD, H. H., AND KING, ERNEST J. *The War Reports*. Philadelphia: Lippincott, 1947.

MARSHALL, KATHERINE TUPPER. *Together: Annals of an Army Wife*. New York: Tupper & Love, 1947.

MARSHALL, S.L.A. *Bringing Up the Rear*. San Rafael, Calif.: Presidio Press, 1979.

MASTNY, VOJTECH *Russia's Road to the Cold War*. New York: Columbia University Press, 1979.

MATLOFF, MAURICE, ED. *American Military History*. Washington, D.C.: Office of the Chief of Military History, Department of the Army, 1969.

MATLOFF, MAURICE, AND SNELL, EDWIN M. *Strategic Planning for Coalition Warfare: 1941–1942*. Washington, D.C.: Office of the Chief of Military History, Department of the Army, 1953.

MAY, ERNEST R. *The Ultimate Decision: The President as Commander in Chief*. New York: Braziller, 1960.

———, ED. *Knowing One's Enemies: Intelligence Assessment Before the Two World Wars*. Princeton, N.J.: Princeton University Press, 1984.

MICHEL, HENRI. *Pétain, Laval, Darlan: trois politiques?* Paris: Flammarion, 1972.

MILLER, NATHAN. *F.D.R.: An Intimate History*. Garden City, N.Y.: Doubleday, 1983; Meridian edition, 1984.

MILLER, SALLY R., AND WINSTEAD-FRY, PATRICIA. *Family Systems Theory in Nursing Practice*. Reston, Va.: Reston, 1982.

MILLIS, WALTER. *Arms and the State*. New York: Twentieth Century Fund, 1958.

———. *The Martial Spirit*. New York: Literary Guild, 1931.

MILLIS, WALTER, WITH HARVEY C. MANSFIELD AND HAROLD STEIN. *Arms and the State: Civil-Military Elements in National Policy*. New York: Twentieth Century Fund, 1958.

MOCH, JULES. *Rencontres avec Darlan et Eisenhower*. Paris: Plon, 1968.

MOLELLA, ARTHUR P., AND BRUTON, ELSA M., EDS. *FDR: The Intimate Presidency: Franklin Delano Roosevelt, Communication, and the Mass Media in the 1930's*. Washington, D.C.: National Museum of American History, Smithsonian Institution, n.d.

MOLEY, RAYMOND. *After Seven Years*. New York: Harper, 1939.

MORAN, LORD. *Churchill: Taken from the Diaries of Lord Moran.* Boston: Houghton Mifflin, 1966.

MORGAN, KAY SUMMERSBY. *Past Forgetting: My Love Affair with Dwight D. Eisenhower.* New York: Simon & Schuster, 1976.

MORGAN, TED. *FDR: A Biography.* New York: Simon & Schuster, 1985.

MORGENTHAU. *See* Blum.

MORISON, SAMUEL ELIOT. *The Two-Ocean War.* Boston: Little, Brown, 1963.

MORTON, H. V. *Atlantic Meeting: An Account of Mr. Churchill's Voyage in H.M.S. "Prince of Wales" in August, 1941, and the Conference with President Roosevelt Which Resulted in the Atlantic Charter.* New York: Dodd, Mead, 1943.

MURPHY, ROBERT. *Diplomat Among Warriors.* Garden City, N.Y.: Doubleday, 1964; Pyramid edition, n.d.

MURRAY, WILLIAMSON. *The Change in the European Balance of Power, 1938–1939.* Princeton, N.J.: Princeton University Press, 1984.

NELSON, OTTO L., JR. *National Security and the General Staff.* Washington, D.C.: Infantry Journal Press, 1946.

NESBITT, HENRIETTA. *White House Diary.* Garden City, N.Y.: Doubleday, 1948.

NICHOLAS, H. G., ED. *Washington Despatches, 1941–1945: Weekly Political Reports from the British Embassy.* Chicago: University of Chicago Press, 1981.

NICOLSON, HAROLD. *The War Years.* Vol. 2 of *Diaries and Letters.* Edited by Nigel Nicolson. New York: Atheneum, 1967.

O'HARA, JOHN. *My Turn.* New York: New American Library, 1966.

ORDIONI, PIERRE. *Tout commence à Alger, 40–44.* Paris: Stock, 1972.

PALMER, JOHN MCAULEY. *Washington, Lincoln, Wilson: Three War Statesmen.* Garden City, N.Y.: Doubleday, Doran, 1930.

PARRISH, NOEL FRANCIS. *Behind the Sheltering Bomb.* New York: Arno Press, 1979.

PARRISH, THOMAS. *The Ultra Americans.* New York: Stein & Day, 1986.

———, ED. *The Simon and Schuster Encyclopedia of World War II*. New York: Simon & Schuster, 1978.

PARTON, JAMES. *"Air Force Spoken Here."* Bethesda, Md.: Adler & Adler, 1986.

PERKINS, FRANCES. *The Roosevelt I Knew*. New York: Viking, 1946; Harper Colophon edition, 1964.

PERSHING, JOHN J. *My Experiences in the World War*. 2 vols. New York: Stokes, 1931.

POGUE, FORREST C. *George C. Marshall: Education of a General, 1880–1939*. New York: Viking, 1963.

———. *George C. Marshall: Ordeal and Hope, 1939–1942*. New York: Viking, 1966.

———. *George C. Marshall: Organizer of Victory, 1943–1945*. New York: Viking, 1973.

———. *George C. Marshall: Statesman 1945–1959*. New York: Viking, 1987.

———. *The Supreme Command*. Washington, D.C.: Office of the Chief of Military History, Department of the Army, 1954.

PRANGE, GORDON W., GOLDSTEIN, DONALD M., AND DILLON, KATHERINE V. *Pearl Harbor: The Verdict of History*. New York: McGraw-Hill, 1986.

PRESCOTT, FREDERICK C., ED. *Alexander Hamilton and Thomas Jefferson*. New York: American Book, 1934.

PURYEAR, EDGAR F., JR. *Nineteen Stars: A Study in Military Character and Leadership*. Orange, Va.: Green, 1971; Presidio edition, 1981.

RAUCH, BASIL. *Roosevelt from Munich to Pearl Harbor: A Study in the Creation of a Foreign Policy*. New York: Creative Age, 1950.

———, ED. *The Roosevelt Reader: Selected Speeches, Messages, Press Conferences, and Letters of Franklin D. Roosevelt*. New York: Holt, Rinehart & Winston, 1957.

REYNOLDS, DAVID. *The Creation of the Anglo-American Alliance, 1937–1941*. Chapel Hill: University of North Carolina Press, 1982.

RHODES, RICHARD. *The Making of the Atomic Bomb*. New York: Simon & Schuster, 1986.

RIGDON, WILLIAM M., WITH JAMES DERIEUX. *White House Sailor*. Garden City, N.Y.: Doubleday, 1962.

RIENOW, ROBERT, AND RIENOW, LEONA TRAIN. *The Lonely*

Quest: The Evolution of Presidential Leadership. Chicago: Follett, 1966.

ROBERTSON, ESMONDE M., ED. *The Origins of the Second World War*. New York: St. Martin's, 1971.

RODINE, FLOYD H. *Yalta—Responsibility and Response*. Lawrence, Kans.: Coronado Press, 1974.

ROLLINS, ALFRED B., JR. *Roosevelt and Howe*. New York: Knopf, 1920.

ROMASCO, ALBERT J. *The Politics of Recovery*. New York: Oxford University Press, 1983.

ROOSEVELT, ELEANOR. *This I Remember*. New York: Harper, 1949.

ROOSEVELT, ELLIOTT. *As He Saw It*. New York: Duell, Sloan & Pearce, 1946.

ROOSEVELT, FRANKLIN DELANO. *F.D.R.: His Personal Letters, 1928–1945*. 2 vols. Edited by Elliott Roosevelt. New York: Duell, Sloan & Pearce, 1950.

ROOSEVELT, JAMES, AND LIBBY, BILL. *My Parents: A Differing View*. Chicago: Playboy Press, 1976.

ROOSEVELT, JAMES, AND SHALETT, SIDNEY. *Affectionately, F.D.R.* New York: Harcourt, Brace, 1959.

ROOSEVELT, JAMES, WITH SAM TOPEROFF. *A Family Matter*. New York: Simon & Schuster, 1980.

ROOSEVELT, SARA DELANO. *My Boy Franklin*. New York: Crown, 1933

ROSE, LISLE A. *The Long Shadow*. Westport, Conn.: Greenwood Press, 1978.

ROSENMAN, SAMUEL I. *Working with Roosevelt*. New York: Harper, 1952.

ROSENMAN, SAMUEL AND DOROTHY. *Presidential Style: Some Giants and a Pygmy in the White House*. New York: Harper & Row, 1976.

ROSKILL, STEPHEN. *Churchill and the Admirals*. New York: Morrow, 1977.

RUDDY, T. MICHAEL. *The Cautious Diplomat*. Kent, Ohio: Kent State University Press, 1986.

RUSTOW, DANKWART A., ED. *Philosophers and Kings: Studies in Leadership*. New York: Braziller, 1970.

SAINSBURY, KEITH. *The North African Landings, 1942*. Newark: University of Delaware Press, 1979.

SCHACHT, JOHN N., ED. *Three Faces of Midwestern Isolationism*.

Iowa City: Center for the Study of Recent American History, 1981.

The Secret History of World War II. New York: Richardson & Steirman, 1986.

SHERWOOD, ROBERT E. *Roosevelt and Hopkins: An Intimate History.* Rev. ed. New York: Harper, 1950; Grosset & Dunlap edition, n.d.

SMITH, GADDIS. *American Diplomacy During the Second World War, 1941–1945.* New York: Wiley & Sons, 1965.

SMITH, LOUIS. *American Democracy and Military Power: A Study of Civil Control of the Military Power in the United States.* Chicago: University of Chicago Press, 1951.

SMYTH, HENRY DE WOLF. *Atomic Energy for Military Purposes: The Official Report on the Development of the Atomic Bomb Under the Auspices of the United States Government, 1940–1945.* Princeton, N.J.: Princeton University Press, 1945.

SNOW, C. P. *Variety of Men.* New York: Scribner, 1966.

SPECTOR, RONALD H. *Eagle Against the Sun: The American War with Japan.* New York: Free Press, 1985.

STEEHOLM, CLARA AND HARDY. *The House at Hyde Park.* New York: Viking, 1950.

STEEL, RONALD. *Walter Lippman and the American Century.* Boston: Little, Brown, 1980.

STEELE, RICHARD W. *The First Offensive.* Bloomington: Indiana University Press, 1973.

STEIN, HAROLD, ED. *American Civil-Military Decisions.* Tuscaloosa: University of Alabama Press, 1963.

STETTINIUS, EDWARD R., JR. *The Diaries of Edward R. Stettinius, Jr., 1943–1946.* Edited by Thomas M. Campbell and George C. Herring. New York: New Viewpoints-Watts, 1975.

———. *Roosevelt and the Russians.* Garden City, N.Y.: Doubleday, 1949.

STERN, FRITZ, ED. *The Varieties of History: From Voltaire to the Present.* New York: Random House, 1956; Vintage edition, 1972.

STEVENS, RUTH. *"Hi-Ya Neighbor."* New York: Tupper & Love, 1947.

STIMSON, HENRY L., AND BUNDY, McGEORGE. *On Active Service in Peace and War.* New York: Harper, 1948.

STOLER, MARK A. *The Politics of the Second Front: American*

Military Planning and Diplomacy in Coalition Warfare, 1941–1943. Westport, Conn.: Greenwood, 1977.

SULZBERGER, C. L. *A Long Row of Candles*. New York: Macmillan, 1969.

———. *Such a Peace: The Roots and Ashes of Yalta*. New York: Continuum, 1982.

TERHORST, J. F., AND ALBERTAZZIE, RALPH. *The Flying White House: The Story of Air Force One*. New York: Bantam, 1980.

THOMPSON, KENNETH W., ED. *The Roosevelt Presidency*. Washington, D.C.: University Press of America, 1982.

THOMPSON, LAURENCE. *The Greatest Treason: The Untold Story of Munich*. New York: Morrow, 1968.

THORNE, CHRISTOPHER. *Allies of a Kind: The United States, Britain, and the War Against Japan, 1941–1945*. New York: Oxford University Press, 1978.

TOMAN, WALTER. *Family Constellation*. New York: Springer, 1961.

TRUMAN, MARGARET. *Harry S. Truman*. New York: Morrow, 1972.

TUGWELL, REXFORD G. *In Search of Roosevelt*. Cambridge, Mass.: Harvard University Press, 1972.

TULLY, GRACE. *F.D.R., My Boss*. New York: Scribner, 1949.

U.S. STATE DEPARTMENT. *Foreign Relations of the United States. The Conferences at Washington, 1941–1942, and Casablanca, 1943*. Washington, D.C.: U.S. Government Printing Office, 1968.

———. *The Conferences at Washington and Quebec, 1943*. Washington, D.C.: U.S. Government Printing Office, 1970.

———. *The Conferences at Cairo and Teheran, 1943*. Washington, D.C.: U.S. Government Printing Office, 1966.

———. *The Conference at Quebec, 1944*. Washington, D.C.: U.S. Government Printing Office, 1972.

———. *The Conferences at Malta and Yalta, 1945*. Washington, D.C.: U.S. Government Printing Office, 1955.

UNOFFICIAL OBSERVER. *The New Dealers*. New York: Literary Guild, 1934.

VANDENBERG, ARTHUR H., JR., ED. *The Private Papers of Senator Vandenberg*. Boston: Houghton Mifflin, 1952.

WALLER, WILLARD. *War in the Twentieth Century*. New York: Dryden, 1940.

WARD, GEOFFREY C. *Before the Trumpet.* New York: Harper, 1985.

Washington Merry-Go-Round. New York: Horace Liveright, 1931.

WATSON, MARK SKINNER. *Chief of Staff: Prewar Plans and Preparations.* Washington, D.C.: Historical Division, Department of the Army, 1950.

WATT, DONALD CAMERON. *Too Serious a Business: European Armed Forces and the Approach to the Second World War.* Berkeley: University of California Press, 1975.

WEDEMEYER, ALBERT C. *Wedemeyer Reports!* New York: Holt, 1958.

WEIGLEY, RUSSELL F. *The American Way of War: A History of United States Military Strategy and Policy.* Bloomington: Indiana University Press, 1973.

———. *Eisenhower's Lieutenants: The Campaign of France and Germany, 1944–1945.* 2 vols. Bloomington: Indiana University Press, 1984.

———. *History of the United States Army.* Bloomington: Indiana University Press, 1984.

WELLES, SUMNER. *The Time for Decision.* New York: Harper, 1944.

WEYGAND, JACQUES. *Weygand, mon père.* Paris: Flammarion, 1970.

WHITE, GRAHAM J. *FDR and the Press.* Chicago: University of Chicago Press, 1979.

WHITE, WILLIAM S. *Majesty and Mischief: A Mixed Tribute to F.D.R.* New York: McGraw-Hill, 1961; Macfadden edition, 1963.

WILSON, ROSE PAGE. *General Marshall Remembered.* Englewood Cliffs, N.J.: Prentice-Hall, 1968.

WILSON, THEODORE A. *The First Summit.* Boston: Houghton Mifflin, 1969.

WINANT, JOHN G. *A Letter From Grosvenor Square.* London: Hodder & Stoughton, 1947.

WRIGHT, MONTE D., AND PASZEK, LAURENCE J., EDS. *Soldiers and Statesmen.* Proceedings of the Fourth Military History Symposium. Washington, D.C.: Office of Air Force History and United States Air Force Academy, 1973.

WYLIE, PHILIP. *Generation of Vipers.* New York: Rinehart, 1942.

ZHUKOV, G. K, *The Memoirs of Marshal Zhukov.* New York: Delacorte, 1971.

NOTES

In addition to the abbreviations given in the introduction to the Sources section (page 508), various short forms are used in the following notes. *F.D.R.: His Personal Letters* is cited as *Personal Letters;* the Forrest C. Pogue Interviews with GCM are cited as Interviews; the *Papers of George Catlett Marshall* are cited as *Papers;* the U.S. Department of State series *Foreign Relations of the United States* is cited as *FRUS,* followed by the short title of the specific volume to which reference is made. Translations from French sources are by the present author.

PREFACE

12 Importance, immediacy, suspense: Robert K. Massie presented these ideas in the 1987 Prichard memorial lecture at the University of Kentucky Library Associates, March 24, 1987. I have made a slight adaptation by substituting "importance" for Massie's word "relevance."

PROLOGUE

15 "Buried my youthful": Interviews, 22.
16 Bullitt and FDR: Watson, 131–132.
"Possesses antennae": Berlin, 27.
17 "From the North to the South Pole": Watson, 137.
"He could not influence": Frye, 254.
"Were, in his mind": Watson, 138.
18 "Way off to the side" and following quotations: Interviews, 87.

CHAPTER ONE
THEMES

19 The hosing episode: Interviews, 49.
The bee episode: Interviews, 38–39.

20 "Sometimes she may have been": Interviews, 19.
"A very painful time": Interviews, 20.
"Star": Interviews, 20.
21 "A very famous record": Interviews, 40.
The incident with Stuart: Interviews, 21, 58.
"It was about time": Interviews, 68.
Handsome houses: These not only still stand in the two towns but retain their elegance.
"Accustomed to a very bountiful living" and "there were always people": Interviews, 36.
"Pleasant little life": Interviews, 21.
22 "Finally get ahead": Interviews, 21.
"Splendid large boy": James Roosevelt's entry in his wife's diary, quoted by Goldberg, 4.
23 "The well-born must never compromise": Leuchtenburg, 235.
Bird anecdote: Sara Roosevelt, 15–16.
"A world whose boundaries": Quoted by Morgan, 54.
24 "Dictatorial, Spartan, and immaculate": Gunther, 171.
"A little inexpensive dredging": Gunther, 174.
FDR's management style: Barber, *Presidential Character,* 220.
25 Roosevelt's plan: The fellow law clerk was Grenville Clark.
26 "First on the bandwagon": *The New Dealers,* 245.
27 "I get my fingers": Burns, I, 50.
"Just another rich man's son": Miller, 146.
"Long whining whistle": Quoted, Miller, 150.
"Twentieth century Apollo": Quoted, Morgan, 222.
"As handsome a figure": Quoted, Goldberg, 18.
28 "The best time to lay plans": Burns, I, 76.
Navy scandal: *New York Times,* July 20, 1921.
"Caught every bug that came along": Quoted, Morgan, 169. The plight of polio victims in the period discussed here is well described in Gallagher, 30–31.
29 "What had constituted": Marshall, *xv*.
30 "Crocodile" episode from Interviews, 119–120.
"An exceptionally capable man": *Papers,* I, 47.
Hagood's tribute: Quoted in Frye, 119–120.
31 "He just gave everybody hell" and two following quotations: Interviews, 175.

"His eyes flashed": *Papers,* I, 122.
"You must appreciate" and "We have them every day": Interviews, 176.
"All I can see": Interviews, 176.
32 "Off away from the others": Interviews, 176.
"Who could listen to severe criticism": Interviews, 89.
"General Pershing as a leader": Interviews, 218.
"'Vitriolic' and 'bitter' and 'het up'": Interviews, 189.
32–33 "Which was being prepared" and "had to take troops": Interviews, 132.
"A terrific problem": Interviews, 198.
"It seldom happens": Pershing, II, 285.
34 "What a magnificent body": G. C. Marshall, *Memoirs,* 217.
"The Duchess of Sutherland": *Memoirs,* 218.
"The usual crowd": *Memoirs,* 219.
"Je suis très beau": Memoirs, 12.
Citizen-army discussion: Interviews, 406.
35 Pershing as possible candidate: Interviews, 228–229.
"Almost boyish": Interviews, 228.
"Had no hesitation": Interviews, 177.
36 Scene concerning General March: Interviews, 90.
Thoughts on Pershing: Interviews, 90–91.
"I know nobody": John McA. Palmer, quoted in *Papers,* I, 210.
37 Letter to General Mallory: GCM, *Memoirs,* xv.

CHAPTER TWO
ON THE HORIZON

40 "A wife and five children": Alsop, 70.
41 "Beloved and Revered": Rollins, 53.
42 "Did not think": Quoted, Morgan, 273.
43 "A double back flip": Quoted, Miller, 222.
"The demand for Mr. Roosevelt": *New York World,* quoted, Lash, 317.
"Too bad about this unfortunate sick man": Burns, *The Lion and the Fox*, 103.
44 "A little on the dull side" and following quotations: Rosenman, 19.
"It went over fine": Rosenman, 20.

"He always went through" and following quotations: Rosenman, 22.
"A history and a sermon": Rosenman, 23.
45 "Aloof, reserved" and quotations in following sentence: Rosenman, 24.
"An unspoken dignity": Rosenman, 16.
46 "I pledge you": August 2, 1932. Rauch, *Roosevelt Reader,* 74.
"The forgotten man": FDR speech, April 8, 1932. Rauch, *Roosevelt Reader,* 66.
47 "Silly attitude": Quoted, Morgan, 361.
48 "You remember": Barber, *Presidential Character,* 234.
"A most efficient officer": Pogue, I, 417, note 46.
48–49 GCM in Tientsin: Frank B. Hayne to Edgar F. Puryear, Jr., March 7, 1963. Reminiscences File, GCML.
"One of the best . . . one of the most capable": Pogue, I, 419, note 24.
"A very lovely-looking": Interviews, 74.
50 "Very much in love": Interviews, 71.
"To an extraordinary degree": Frye, 201.
GCM with Hayne: Frank B. Hayne to Edgar F. Puryear, Jr., March 7, 1963. Reminiscences File, GCML.
"Twenty-six years": *Papers,* I, 315.
51 Comments by the secretary of the Infantry School: Frank H. Partridge to Edgar F. Puryear, Jr., September 10, 1962. Reminiscences File, GCML.
52 General Collins quoted in Frye, 204.
"The even tenor": Quoted, Pogue, I, 267.
"A noticeable change" and following quotation: Thomas F. Taylor, n.d. Reminiscences File, GCML.
53 "Think on their feet": This paragraph based on *Papers,* I, 336–338.
54 The sketchy map: Pogue, I, 268.
"The most brilliant": Quoted, Pogue, I, 281.
"During the two years": Bradley, 33.
55 "Way of looking": Quoted, Pogue, I, 281.
"This certainly was": K. T. Marshall, 2.
"Interested in her own date": Molly Winn interview, April 24, 1987.
Conversation between GCM and Mrs. Brown: K. T. Marshall, 3.

56 Fort Benning reception: K. T. Marshall, 6–7.
"Lieutenants do not dance": K. T. Marshall, 9.
57 "He loved trees": Perkins, 177.
"Moral and spiritual" and "a vast army": Quoted, Freidel, 260.
"'You couldn't just open the forest'" and next quotation: Perkins, 178.
58 "'Relief through the creation'": Quoted, Freidel, 261.
FDR quoted in Freidel, 261.
59–60 "Fascinated by the opportunity" and following quotations: K. T. Marshall, 13.
"Ate, breathed and digested": Reuben E. Jenkins, quoted in *Papers,* I, 393.
"After six weeks": K. T. Marshall, 13.
"Without moonshine": K. T. Marshall, 13.
"Colonel Marshall had his regiment": K. T. Marshall, 17.
61 "Outstanding and suitable": *Papers,* I, 409.
"Of threatened civic disorders" and following quotation: *Papers,* I, 406.
62 "What? He can't do that." Quoted, Frye, 226.
"He had a grey, drawn look": K. T. Marshall, 18.
"As enthusiastic and energetic": K. T. Marshall, 20.

CHAPTER THREE
RUMORS AND WARS

63 "Had he been in the treadmill": Brown MS, Wilson Brown Papers, FDRL.
64 "Like a club": Quoted, Israel, 27.
"He was drunk all the time": Quoted, Freidel, 491.
65 "An isolationist": Hull, I, 398.
"It was evident": Hull, I, 400.
"Suggesting wild-eyed measures": FDR to Edward M. House, September 17, 1935. *Personal Letters,* I, 506.
"I have seen war": Quoted, Divine, 11.
66 Conversation with Captain Brown: Brown MS, 136, FDRL.
"I must get started": *Papers,* I, 446–447.
"General Pershing asks": *Personal Letters,* I, 479.

67 Craig "is strong for you": *Papers,* I, 480.
"I have possessed myself": *Papers,* I, 482–483.
68 "Rather glowered": Tully, 230.
69 "When an epidemic": Rauch, *Roosevelt Reader,* 191.
"War is a contagion": Rauch, *Roosevelt Reader,* 192.
Newspaper comments: *New York Times,* October 6, 1937.
CHICAGO TRIBUNE UNDOMINATED: *Time,* October 18, 1937.
"There are a lot of methods": Quoted, Burns, *Lion,* 319.
70 "As far as I could": James Roosevelt, *My Parents,* 117.
"Impetus to the efforts": Welles, 66
71 "We in the United States": *Personal Letters,* II, 776.
"I just called to congratulate": K. T. Marshall, 21.
"I am sure": *Papers,* I, 492.
72 "Such a welcome": K. T. Marshall, 24.
"Two of the happiest years": K. T. Marshall, 25.
"One of our most delightful periods": *Papers,* I, 513.
Pershing and GCM's goiter: *Papers,* I, 520.
"All the common diseases": Interviews, 88.
73 "Strange to say": *Papers,* I, 538.
"Usually patients for thyroid operations": *Papers,* I, 521.
"You know as soon": *Papers,* I, 575.
"I went to the hospital" and "two big maneuvers": *Papers,* I, 574.
74 The partially color-blind officer: *Papers,* I, 575.
"Three polar bears": K. T. Marshall, 25.
75 "The Christmas baskets": Pogue, I, 321.
76 "The political football": GCM to Pershing, September 19, 1937. *Papers,* I, 559.
"Saw him off here in Vancouver" and following quotations: GCM to Charles G. Dawes, October 8, 1937. *Papers,* I, 561.
"Was much amused" and "the tumultuous welcome": GCM to Pershing, November 17, 1937. *Papers,* I, 561.
77 "A country boy who rides": GCM to Frank R. McCoy, March 9, 1938. *Papers,* I, 583.
"I am fond of Craig": GCM to Pershing, May 27, 1938. *Papers,* I, 598.

CHAPTER FOUR
"ALL I HAVE DREAMED OF"

78 The call on the Craigs: K. T. Marshall, 41.

78–79 The discussion of Root and the General Staff owes much to Jessup, to Nelson, and to Huntington; the thinking of the last-named was particularly influential in this chapter and in Chapter Six.

"Coordinate" and "vertical" systems: See Huntington, 186–189.

80 "Under this system": Huntington, 253.

For Root's thinking see, e.g., Nelson, 48–65. The idea of the General Staff as the "brain of the Army" came from a British writer, Spenser Wilkinson, who influenced the reorganization of the British Army after its less-than-stellar performance in the Boer War.

"Supervision" and "command": See Nelson, 59.

"Directing brain": Root, December 1, 1902. Quoted, Nelson, 55.

"A master administrator": Interviews, 246.

"A very arbitrary, tactless man": Interviews, 226.

"Rank and precedence": Quoted, Nelson, 231.

81 "He would be better": Quoted, McFarland, 108.

82 PWA: Public Works Administration; WPA: Works Progress Administration.

"He loved peace and harmony": Sherwood, 9.

"A man of bewildering complexity": Quoted, Sherwood, 9.

"The most complicated": Perkins, 3; "not clear, not simple": Perkins, 4.

83 "Would enjoy the prestige": Sherwood, 71.

"General Craig was sitting": K. T. Marshall, 72.

84 "Rumor is destroying me": *Papers,* I, 636–637.

85 West Virginia speech: September 4, 1938. *Papers,* I, 620–625.

86 Johnson-Craig exchange: Frye, 248.

87 "This is no time": Watson, 140.

"Features of the defense mechanism": *Papers,* I, 655.

"Made the familiar remark": Interviews, 440–441.

88 FDR with advisers described in Watson, 142–143, and McFarland, 169.

The existing strength: McFarland, 171.
"Had a tremendous effect" and "rather intricate": Interviews, 441.
89 "After nearly six years" and following quotations: Anne O'Hare McCormick, *New York Times Magazine,* October 16, 1938.
FDR assured Monnet: see Haight, "Roosevelt as Friend of France."
90 "To make the Frenchman": Haight.
"The peace and safety": Quoted, Alsop and Kintner, 30–31.
"Self-protection is part" and "I hope to God": Transcript of conference, January 31, 1939, quoted in McFarland, 189.
"To regard France": *New York Times,* February 1, 1939.
91 "Deliberate lie": Quoted, McFarland, 190.
Secret recordings: Butow.
"Drum, Drum!": Quoted, Busch, "General Drum."
92 "The biggest stuffed shirt": Dorn, 25.
Hopkins and Wilson: Sherwood, 100–101.
93 "The entry to the President": Sherwood, 100.
94 "We consider [it] very fine": Watson, 151.
95 "In connection with the final vote" and following quotations: *Papers,* I, 704–705.
"I have for years": Cole to GCM, February 20, 1939. *Papers,* I, 705.
"Johnson wanted me": Quoted, Pogue, I, 343.
"Reference any publicity" and following quotations: *Papers,* I, 641–642.
96 "Resumed": Quotations in this paragraph from *Papers,* I, 682.
97 FDR in Georgia: *Personal Letters,* II, 875–877.
"It was an interesting interview": Quoted, Pogue, 347. See also *Papers,* I, 713.
98 "I want to say in compliment": Interviews, 87.
"On the recommendations": Interviews, 181.
"Tremendous pressure was exerted": Quoted, *Papers,* I, 713.
"It would be unkind": Quoted, Pogue, I, 348.
99 "Vigorous, keen": *Time,* May 8, 1939.

"Brilliant, taciturn": *Time,* August 22, 1938.
"George's appointment has met": Quoted, Pogue, I, 348.
Mrs. Marshall to FDR: May 10, 1939. *Papers,* I, 714.

CHAPTER FIVE
"TRAGIC MESSAGES IN THE NIGHT"

101 "In the event of any action": Jacobsen and Smith, 16–17.
"Certain types of propaganda": Hoover, *Reader's Digest,* September 1939.
102 "The last effort to enforce civilization": *Reader's Digest,* March 1939, 128.
"We are already engaged": Thompson, *Reader's Digest,* June 1939.
"We can remain untouched": Broun, *Reader's Digest,* June 1939.
GCM and the young matron: Wilson, 218.
103 "In order to suppress": Interviews, 248.
"Latin America is a vitally strategic area": Wilson, 219.
104 GCM's meeting Rose Page (Wilson): Wilson, 1–3.
Humorous verse: *Papers,* I, 208.
General MacArthur's "sweetheart": Wilson, 11.
Rose and the senator: Wilson, 10.
105 Activities in Brazil: *Papers,* I, 717–718.
"A regular Lindbergh reception": Interviews, 249.
"General Marshall received all honors" and "had never seen its equal": K. T. Marshall, 46.
106 Craig's letter: June 30, 1939. *Papers,* I, 721.
FDR to the attorney general (Frank Murphy): July 1, 1939. *Personal Letters,* II, 899–900.
107 "Two weeks more": Alsop and Kintner, 40.
"One of the Congressional": Alsop and Kintner, 43.
108 The best account of this important meeting is found in Alsop and Kintner, 44–46. The quotations on p. 108 come from this source, as does the final quotation on p. 109.
109 "Painfully aware": Peter Drucker, *Wall Street Journal,* January 6, 1988.

"Must never cease" and following quotations: Hargrove, 3.
"Possessed of high competence": Brownlow, 357.
112 "During the long years of the World War": *Personal Letters,* II, 916.
"And thus neglect the task": Quoted, Alsop and Kintner, 6.
"For all the great": Interviews, 9.
113 "She sort of shrank": Interviews, 10.
"Memorable and touching": K. T. Marshall, 55.
"Our special welcome is for 'Flicker'": Quoted, K. T. Marshall, 56.
"I will not trouble you": *Papers,* II, 55.
"For almost 40 years": Quoted, K. T. Marshall, 56.

CHAPTER SIX
SOLDIERS AND CIVILIANS

114 Figures of army strength: Marshall in Marshall, Arnold, King, 16.
"Ineffective": Marshall, Arnold, King, 16.
"We had no field army": Marshall, Arnold, King, 16.
The situation and the tradition of the army are well discussed in Weigley, *Eisenhower's Lieutenants,* Chapter 1.
115 "Relentless, continuous pressure": John Simon, talk to the Madison County (Ky.) Civil War Round Table, April 10, 1987.
116 Short and decisive wars: For discussion, see, e.g., Maurice Matloff in Howard, *Theory and Practice of War,* 215–241.
"Spirit and aggressiveness": Pershing, I, 181.
"The mission of the infantry": See Matloff, in Howard, 215–241.
117 "Extreme firmness": Quoted, Ambrose, *Supreme Commander,* 312.
Patton a great favorite, and following description: Molly Winn interview, April 24, 1987.
"He would say outrageous things": Interviews, 546.
117–118 "Satisfied a whole area of need" and "always very good with young people": Winn interview.

GCM and Allen: K. T. Marshall, 3.
Call GCM "Colonel": Winn interview.

119 "He controlled the conversation" and following quotations: Winn interview.
GCM and the prisoners: William C. Moore, November 28, 1962. Reminiscences File, GCML.
"He listened" and following quotation: B. B. Talley, September 9, 1962. Reminiscences File, GCML.

120 Return of Major Black: *New York Times,* November 30, 1939."An exceptional opportunity": Chaffee to GCM, December 11, 1939. Marshall Papers, GCML.

121 "It is not advisable": GCM to Chaffee, December 20, 1939. Marshall Papers, GCML.

122 GCM and Johnson: Quoted, Pogue, I, 21–22, from GCM interviews, November 14 (?), 1956.

123 Constitutional discussion owes much to Huntington, Chapter VII.

124 "To create a 'standing army'": Brig. Gen. William Buster, "The Constitution and the Military," lecture, September 20, 1987.
GCM and the congressman: Interviews, 39.

125 "The spectacle of General Craig": Janeway, 39.
GCM made a striking point: This discussion comes from Interviews, 271–273.

126 The staff officer: Reminiscences File, Marshall Papers, GCML.
No one press Roosevelt: GCM to Brig. Gen. Asa L. Singleton, November 22, 1939. *Papers,* II, 108.

127 "People would think": Alsop and Kintner, 75.
"We have definitely taken sides": Vandenberg, 3.

128 "I am almost literally walking": FDR to Lord Tweedsmuir (governor-general of Canada), October 5, 1939. *Personal Letters,* II, 934.
"Pathetically incomplete square divisions" and following quotations: Marshall in Marshall, King, Arnold, 18.
"It will react to our advantage": Quoted, Watson, 164.

129 Marshall speeches—to AHA, December 28, 1939, and to ROTC (radio address), February 16, 1940: Cited, Pogue, II, 17 and 458, notes 23 and 24.

"So mellifluous that it would put up" and following quotation: Liebling, "Chief of Staff."

130 "A sudden expansion" and following quotations: Marshall in Marshall, King, Arnold, 20.

"Involved in infinite possibilities": GCM to Mrs. Reynolds Brown, April 8, 1940. Marshall Papers, GCML.

131 "German victory": Alsop and Kintner, 82a.

CHAPTER SEVEN
"FORCES OF DESTRUCTION"

132 The examples here are from *Time,* June 3, 1940.

"All you have to do": Watson, 166.

133–134 The scene in FDR's office: Interviews, 301–302, from which the quotations come. The meeting is also described in Blum, II, 140.

"Stood right up to the President": Blum, II, 141.

Speech to Congress and fireside chat: Lurton, 240–242.

"Threatened by forces of destruction": Quoted, Lurton, 247.

135 Chat with Grace Tully: Tully, 78–79.

136 "I just sent a message" and following discussion: Interviews, 303.

137 Lunch at Fort Myer: James T. Williams, Jr. Reminiscences File, GCML.

Management specialist: Peter Drucker, "Leadership: More Doing Than Dash." *Wall Street Journal,* January 6, 1988.

138 Lieutenant (Alexander L.) Jones: *Papers,* II, 394–395.

Bedell Smith and the jeep: Interviews, 244–245. See also K. T. Marshall, 59–60, and Smith to GCM, July 29, 1943—Marshall Papers (Smith File), GCML.

139 "Would not speak of the Navy": Interviews, 575.

"He is used to winning acclaim": Toman, 115.

"If I didn't give the orders": One of the best-known Roosevelt anecdotes, this story comes from Sara Delano Roosevelt, 15–16.

Best predictor of "achievement behavior": Ferdon, 73–74.

140 "Sent for Baruch": Interviews, 574.

"If the opportunity": GCM to Baruch, April 3, 1940. Marshall Papers, GCML.

"Let me take over": Baruch, 278.

Dialogue with the senator: Interviews, 574.

"I presume everything is all set": Baruch to GCM, April 22, 1940. Marshall Papers, GCML.

141 "He wanted to get in with me": Interviews, 574.

"For your eyes alone": GCM to Baruch, May 14, 1940. Marshall Papers, GCML.

Baruch's suggestions: Baruch to GCM, June 25, 1940. Marshall Papers, GCML.

"Had them studied: GCM to Baruch, June 29, 1940. Marshall Papers, GCML.

142 "Rectitude, wisdom": Stimson and Bundy, xviii.

"The voice and force": Churchill, *Their Finest Hour,* 24.

143 "Emblazoned on the sides of the Flatiron Building": *Time,* June 3, 1940.

"Recognition of the early defeat": Quoted in Watson, 109.

144 "The public indifference": *Papers,* II, 225.

"By tradition and training": Watt, 57.

On the question of legality, see Blum, II, 150.

"One of the smartest men": Ambrose, *Eisenhower,* 75.

145 "Knows more about the techniques": Ambrose, *Eisenhower,* 76.

"Overcome nationalistic considerations": Eisenhower, *Crusade,* 18.

"It is a military consideration": Blum, II, 150.

Manure for language instruction: Blum, II, 152–153.

146 "It would be seriously prejudicial": *Papers,* II, 247.

"Lay off on the four-engine bombers": Quoted, Blum, II, 163.

"They were in danger": Churchill, *Their Finest Hour,* 401.

"Intended to be a complete prohibition": *Personal Letters,* II, 1048–1049.

147 "The pacifists and the anti-third-termers": Ickes, III, 215.

“A tip on Mr. Stimson”: *Papers,* II, 252.
GCM’s visit: *Papers,* II, 252.

148 “Began to know and appreciate” and following quotations: Stimson and Bundy, 331.
“Is a splendid fellow”: *Papers,* II, 141.

149 GCM and Stark with FDR: Watson, 112–113.
“Not abstract ideals”: Huntington, 272.

150 “A very difficult period” and following quotations: Interviews, 279.

151 “I understood what we needed”: Interviews, 276.
The “imminently probable” eventualities: *Papers,* II, 218.

152 “My relief of mind”: *Papers,* II, 264.
“More occurs here” and “read or slept”: GCM to Roy D. Keehn, July 15, 1940. *Papers,* II, 267.
Marshall and the youngster: GCM to Arthur J. Hayes, July 17, 1940. *Papers,* II, 268–269.
GCM chastised the senators: Watson, 196.
“For the first time”: *Papers,* II, 311–312.

153 FDR quotations: Lurton, 301.
“It was agreed”: *Personal Letters,* 1050–1051.

154 “A decidedly unneutral act”: *Their Finest Hour,* 404.
“I tried not to crowd” and “a certain amount”: Interviews, 241–242.
“Experimental”: Interviews, 264.
“Prevent the complete collapse”: Interviews, 290.

155 “Why should we go on”: Sherwood, 175.
“Almost tearful”: Ickes, II, 283.

156 “Holding conversations”: Churchill, *Their Finest Hour,* 407.
“It just keeps rolling”: *Their Finest Hour,* 409.
The calculating machine: Morison, 29.

157 “Congress is going to raise hell” and following quotations: Tully, 244–245.

CHAPTER EIGHT
“THE BEST IMMEDIATE DEFENSE”

158 Letters to FDR: PSF (Personal File), FDRL.
The “phony islands”: Quoted, Adams, 195.

160 Lothian's condition: L'Etang, 83.
British Empire was not poor: See Kimball, 32.
"That was loanable": Ickes, II, 367.
"Useful to us": Quoted, Blum, II, 203.

161 "I feel that you will expect": The letter is quoted from Loewenstein, 122–123.
"A full statement": Churchill, *Their Finest Hour,* 558.
"The bustle of Washington": Quoted, Kimball, 111.

162 "With a desire": Sherwood, 224.
Hopkins later told Churchill: Churchill, *Their Finest Hour,* 567.
The Morgenthau working group: Blum, II, 207. See also Kimball, 115.
"I didn't know": Sherwood, 224.
The press conference: Rauch, *Speeches,* 268–271.

163 The polls: See, e.g., Kimball, 57–58.

164 "There were probably very few": Sherwood, 225.
FDR speech: Rauch, *Speeches,* 312–315.

165 Hopkins told associates: Sherwood, 278.

166 FDR talk with Morgenthau: Blum, II, 210–211.
"Pompous, arrogant": Kimball, 160.
"The President's dictator bill": Kimball, 163.

167 "Events developed too rapidly": *Papers,* II, 398.

168 Quotations from Marshall's speech and Roller's reaction: *Papers,* II, 387–388.
Marshall's reply to Roller: January 15, 1941. *Papers,* II, 388.

169 Robinett material from MS diary, and from biographical article written by Col. Howard V. Conan for use in Robinett's 1974 senatorial campaign in Missouri (GCML). The quotations are all by Robinett.

170 "Frankly, while you have your difficulties": *Papers,* II, 533.

172 "Take the guts": Blum, II, 226.
The technical compromise: See *Newsweek,* February 24, 1941, p. 72.
"Gave a ripping good speech" and "made a great impression": Quoted, *Papers,* II, 437.

173 Senator's letter: *Newsweek,* March 17, 1941, p. 18.
"Intimate relationship": Interviews, 290.

174 Letter from mother and GCM's reply: *Papers,* II, 553.

175 "Afraid of fear": Sherwood, 367.
"Whenever the Congress": Stimson and Bundy, 377.
176 Quotations from GCM's report: Marshall in Marshall, Arnold, King, 22.
"He let me do all the talking": Interviews, 558.
Discussion of task force: *New York Times,* July 16, 1941.
177 "There is evidently": GCM memo to FDR, July 6, 1941. *Papers,* II, 567.
"Urgently requested": *New York Times,* August 1, 1941.
177–178 GCM to congressmen: Quoted, Watson, 229–230.
178–179 GCM at the Army and Navy Club: Interviews, 276–277.
180 "If you don't watch your step": *New York Times,* August 13, 1941.
The scene in the House is described in various newspaper and newsmagazine articles.
"Positive tones" is from the *New York Times,* August 13, 1941.
180–181 Fish and Wheeler comments: *New York Times,* August 14, 1941.
181 "Is a fighting man": Leland M. Ford, quoted, *Papers,* II, 613, note 2.

CHAPTER NINE
LORD BEAVERBROOK'S CRYSTAL BALL

182 "All members of party": *New York Times,* August 8, 1941.
Details of the presidential trip come from "The Log of the President's Cruise on board the *U.S.S. Potomac* and *U.S.S. Augusta,* Newfoundland Conference," 3–16 August 1941. RP.
"A case of sheer exasperation": Sherwood, 293.
183 McIntire's comments: McIntire, 130.
FDR's deception of Starling: James Roosevelt, *Affectionately, FDR,* 337.
184 *Herald Tribune* reporter: K. T. Marshall, 95.

"You and I occupied": Churchill, *Gathering Storm,* 440.
FDR-Hopkins conversation: Sherwood, 230.
185 Press conference: Sherwood, 231.
"A lot of people": Quoted, Adams, 199.
Churchill's "Who?": Sherwood, 234.
"*Churchill* is the gov't": Sherwood, 243.
186 "Still has the country": Ickes, II, 513.
"As a complete surprise" and following quotations: Interviews, 261.
187 "A large and ugly fish": "Log," 5.
"We were in a very desperate plight": Interviews, 262.
Arnold—quotation and principles: Theodore Wilson, 6.
189 "One look": McIntire, 131.
"Dying on his feet": Quoted, Adams, 231.
190 "Harry returned dead-beat": Churchill, *Grand Alliance,* 428.
"Unbelievable courage": Quoted, Adams, 241.
"Would have liked to go ahead": Interviews, 262.
191 "I have an idea": Quoted, Morton, 150.
"Had no mind": McIntire, 133–134.
"A general agreement" and "aims and desires": Welles, 175.
192 Quotations from Atlantic Charter from Thomas Parrish, *Encyclopedia,* 35.
FDR's notes: James Roosevelt, *Affectionately, FDR,* 338.
193 "Adlai" a strange name: As a Democrat and a political scholar, FDR would of course have been familiar with the career of Stevenson's grandfather, the first Adlai, who was vice-president during Grover Cleveland's second term.
The member of Churchill's party: Morton, 99.
194 "Crammed with almost eatable": Morton, 105–106.
The mission to London: Watson, 113–114.
"In an operation dubbed 'Magic'": Thomas Parrish, *Ultra Americans,* 59–66.
195 "We are not now prepared": Quoted, Watson, 116.
"As unfavorable a moment": Quoted, Watson, 117.
"Presented for the purpose": Quoted, Watson, 118.
196 "It would be": Quoted, Watson, 121.

"That do not have": Quoted, Watson, 122.
"Not be through my doings": Quoted, Watson, 122.
"Begin shooting": Quoted, *Papers,* II, 362, note 2.
"Not willingly to engage" and following quotations: Quoted, Watson, 122–123.

197 "We would stand": *Papers,* II, 392.
"Hitler's principal objective": Quoted, Watson, 125.
"Secret staff talks": Watson, 119.
"Know a great deal more" and "realistic ideas": *Papers,* II, 362–363, note 2.
"Would consist of a small party": Quoted, Watson, 84.

198 "Rather disturbed" and following quotations: Interviews, 259–260.
The British position: Matloff and Snell, 34.
"Compelled to resort to war": Quoted, Watson, 373.
"Contribute most directly": Watson, 373.

199 "And it was up to the British": Matloff and Snell, 37.

200 "I don't know what will happen": Sherwood, 373.
"All the British people": Sherwood, 373–374.

201 GCM's description of Kimmel and following discussion: *Papers,* II, 411–413.

202 "The average young American": Morison, 39.
"Involved an element of danger": Prange et al., 108.
"Without a naval superiority": Quoted, Watson, 466.
"Fantastic" and "no move against Pearl Harbor": Quoted, Watson, 469.

203 FDR conversation: Butow, "The F.D.R. Tapes."
GCM letter to Molly Winn: *Papers,* II, 627.

204 "I didn't understand": Interviews, 259.
Widespread opinion: Shared by various interests—the British, the U.S. Navy, air advocates—and promoted, notably, by the columnist Walter Lippmann.

205 "An intelligence officer": Pogue, II, 199.
"We were likely to be attacked": Stimson diary, quoted, Pogue, II, 199.
"Hostile action possible": Cited in the congressional hearings—*Pearl Harbor Attack,* Part 14, 1329. See Prange et al., Appendix 3.

206 "Jap situation": Biddle diary, FDRL.
The prophylactic station: GCM to Rep. Andrew J. May, December 3, 1941. *Papers,* II, 691.

"At a trot": Quoted, Pogue, II, 227.
207 "If possible to the Secretary of State" and following discussion: Thomas Parrish, *Ultra Americans,* 74–75.
208 Scene in FDR's study: Sherwood, 430.
"I never thought": Prange et al., 460. Or, as Kimmel phrased it another day, "I very much doubted their ability to plan and execute an attack such as they made." His colleagues all doubted it too. See Prange et al., Chapter 25 and Chapter 31.
"American habits and customs": Robinett diary, GCML.

CHAPTER TEN
TWENTY-FOUR DAYS IN ARCADIA

209 Robinett's speculations from diary, GCML.
210 "Allies are the most aggravating": Diary of Sir William Slim, quoted, Danchev, 36.
211 Foreign Office clerk: Sir William Hayter, *A Double Life,* quoted in Thorne, 76.
"We shall declare war": Winant, 277.
212 "Hoped to reach agreement": Message of December 18, 1941, in Hopkins-Sherwood Papers, FDRL.
"Germany is still the prime enemy": Quoted, Sherwood, 445.
"Immediate military measures" and following quotations: December 18, 1941. Hopkins-Sherwood Papers, FDRL.
213 "A different man": Moran, 9.
214 "Our people were always ready": Interviews, 563.
"They strike me as very crude": Thorne, 97.
"The Americans, more than any other people": Thorne, 106.
"The reason they dislike us": Quoted, Thorne, 105.
"Cherokee": Thorne, 105.
215 "To be on a very warm": Interviews, 551.
"Panting to meet the President": Moran, 7.
"The house . . . large enough": Winant to secretary of state, December 21, 1941. Hopkins-Sherwood Papers, FDRL.

"We live here as a big family": Churchill, *Grand Alliance,* 686.
The president looked "extraordinarily fit": Adamic, 15.
"One of my Scots ancestors": Adamic, 18.
216 "A couple of emperors": Adamic, 61.
"Apparently he had not even found out": Robinett diary, GCML.
217 Brooke's opinion of Dill: Bryant, 204.
"A good deal of discussion": Bryant, 227.
The British strategy: See, e.g., Matloff and Snell, 99.
218 "Must come to grips" and "feasible from a logistics viewpoint": WPD study, quoted in Matloff and Snell, 101.
"Very doubtful": Matloff and Snell, 102.
"Closing and tightening the ring": Matloff and Snell, 103.
Embick's views: Matloff and Snell, 104.
219 White House session: From GCM's notes, quoted in Matloff and Snell, 105.
220 "The British had heard": Robinett diary, GCML.
United Nations Declaration: Thomas Parrish, *Encyclopedia,* 324.
221 Christmas dinner: K. T. Marshall, 100–102.
221–222 "He took the view" and following quotations: Robinett diary, GCML.
222 "With differences between groups" and following quotations: Sherwood (from the official minutes), 455–457.
"A broader solution" and he "was afraid": Robinett diary, GCML.
"Solve nine-tenths of our troubles": Sherwood, 455.
222–223 "In a most persuasive manner" and following quotations: Robinett diary, GCML.
223 "We had to do something": Interviews, 559.
"When he said this": Robinett diary, GCML.
223–224 Eisenhower "moved quietly" and following quotations: Robinett diary, GCML.
224 Admiral Pound: Interviews, 327.
"Acted explosively": Interviews, 559.
"Work on Churchill": Sherwood, 456.
GCM and Churchill: Interviews, 559.

225 "To meet the urgent wishes": Churchill, *Grand Alliance,* 675.
"If success should come" and following quotations: Robinett diary, GCML.
Fox Conner quotation: Ambrose, *Eisenhower,* 76.
Marshall was "the key": Moran, 22.
227 FDR's editing: Sherwood, 468.
Wilson's reflections: Moran, 21.
228 "Post-Arcadia Collaboration": Historical Section, JCS. Donnelly Papers, MHI.
229 "I tried to give Arnold": Interviews, 400.
Origin of the JCS from Historical Section document, Donnelly Papers, MHI.
King and Arnold: Coffey, 254.
"His prestige and influence": Churchill, *Grand Alliance,* 688.
230 "Our best general": *Newsweek,* September 27, 1943.
Churchill cable: January 20, 1942. Hopkins Papers, FDRL.
231 "I think this suggestion": FDR to Hopkins, January 21, 1942. Hopkins Papers, FDRL.
Marshall on Dill: Interviews, 379.
"I hope that you and the President": Dill to Hopkins, January 16, 1942. Hopkins Papers, FDRL.
232 FDR's message to "Former Naval Person": Hopkins Papers, FDRL.
Dill on trips: Interviews, 545.
232–235 McCrea material from his draft memoirs, FDRL.
235 "At present this country": Dill, January 3, 1942. Bryant, *Turn of the Tide,* 234.
"It is good for Winston": Moran, 14.
Churchill "just flits": Moran, 828.
236 "It is fun": Churchill, *Hinge of Fate,* 71.
236–237 Development of the map room from McCrea draft memoirs, FDRL.
237 "Send us a dumb one": Nesbitt, 274.
Map room routine: Robert H. Myers interview, June 30, 1986.
238 "His asides": McCrea draft memoirs, FDRL.
Montgomery's special pins: Rigdon, 7–8.
"We were always pleased" and following quotations: McCrea draft memoirs, FDRL.

239 "An amateur strategist": Emerson, "Franklin Roosevelt as Commander-in-Chief."
"'President' ought to do": Joseph Lash diary, quoted, Burns, *Soldier of Freedom,* 185.
"He relished the title" and "please try to address me": Hull, 1111.

CHAPTER ELEVEN
"WE'VE GOT TO GO TO EUROPE"

240 The maneuvers: See, e.g., Watson, 237–238.
"My God, Senator": Interviews, 424.
241 Driving GCM to Lake Charles: Col. J. E. Raymond to Forrest C. Pogue, April 14, 1961. Reminiscences File, GCML.
GCM and Eisenhower: Eisenhower, *Crusade,* 18–22.
241–242 "Awfully cold" and Marshall's challenge: Ambrose, *Eisenhower,* 134.
242 "As big a baby" and "still likes his boot lickers": Eisenhower, *Diaries,* 44.
"He's a hero": Eisenhower, *Diaries,* 54.
Eisenhower on GCM: *At Ease,* 241, and, with reference to anger, *Diaries,* 52.
243 GCM and Mrs. Marshall: K. T. Marshall, 110.
243–244 GCM's principles of selection: Eisenhower, *Crusade,* 34–35.
244–245 Hull on GCM's office procedure: Hull MS, MHI.
"Would seem to have all the time": James T. Williams, Jr., Reminiscences File, GCML.
246 General Staff rumbles: Nelson, 327–329.
"A true hatchetman": Interviews, 591.
247 "To fight the current war": Quoted, Nelson, 349. The plan was explained in War Department Circular 59, March 2, 1942. See Nelson, 371–389.
Operations Division: See Cline, 122.
"Built itself a hero": Eisenhower, *Diaries,* 51.
249 GCM scene with King: Interviews, 399–400.
250 GCM with FDR: Interviews, 396 and 588.
251 "Integrity of purpose": GCM to Leahy, December 23, 1940. Quoted, McClain, 37.
"I was willing to trust": Interviews, 395.

Announcement of Leahy appointment: *New York Times,* July 22, 1942.
GCM with Leahy: Interviews, 588.
253 "Becoming more and more interested": Matloff and Snell, 166.
These FDR-GCM messages are in PSF, FDRL.
254 The signal company: Col. W. A. Muir to the author, July 10, 1987.
"He wasn't always clear-cut": Quoted, Pogue, II, 23.
The notebooks: Interviews, 587.
255 "We've got to go to Europe": *Diaries,* 44.
"Staggered" and following quotations: Stimson and Bundy, 416–417.
256 "It is the only place" and following quotations: Undated memorandum for the president, Hopkins-Sherwood Papers, FDRL.
258 Hopkins to Churchill: Sherwood, 521.

CHAPTER TWELVE
THE DOORS OF PERCEPTION

259–260 Wedemeyer in Germany and with GCM: Interview, June 28, 1986; also *Wedemeyer Reports!*
260 The memo: Interview and Wedemeyer, 62.
261 Marshall orders estimate: *Papers,* II, 517–518.
"Although the procedure": Wedemeyer, 17.
"Over-all production requirements": Watson, 538.
262 "Beyond his imagination": Wedemeyer, 67.
The scene on December 5: Interview and Wedemeyer, 15–16.
"Wedemeyer, there's blood": Interview.
263 FBI visit: Interview.
"Wedemeyer thinks and says": Wedemeyer, 24.
German reaction: *New York Times,* December 6, 1941.
"How did he get into my safe" and "General Marshall never doubted me": Interview.
265 "Apparently everyone on the island": Wedemeyer, 99.
"All of you be prepared": Wedemeyer, 100.
"Execrable coffee": Wedemeyer, 104.

266 "It was perfectly clear": Sherwood, 523.
"Displaying his talents" and following quotations: Hopkins memo, April 8, 1942. Hopkins-Sherwood Papers, FDRL.
267 Meeting with the British chiefs: Minutes, C.O.S. Committee, April 9, 1942. Marshall Papers, GCML.
British planners had foreseen a return: Strange, "Cross-Channel Attack," 162–163.
268 "A long talk": Bryant, I, 285.
269–270 British statement: C.O.S. (42) 97 (0), April 13, 1942, "Comments on General Marshall's Memorandum." Marshall Papers, GCML.
270 He was "anxious" and following discussion: Minutes, C.O.S. Committee, April 14, 1942. Marshall Papers, GCML.
Defence Committee meeting from Ismay's minutes in Churchill, *Hinge of Fate,* 317–320.
271 Mountbatten quotations: Harrison, 18.
"Would march ahead": Churchill, *Hinge of Fate,* 319.
Hopkins observed to the group: Sherwood, 538.
"We wholeheartedly agree": Churchill, *Hinge of Fate,* 320.
272 "Simple, straightforward soldier": Bryant, I, 284.
"To hustling and getting things done": Bryant, I, 284.
Brooke thoughts on GCM: Bryant, I, 288–290.
"With their ingrained habit": Wedemeyer, 132.
273 English poet: William Blake, "The Marriage of Heaven and Hell."
Ismay later remarked: Ismay, 249.
"The classic waffling manner": Alison Lurie, *Foreign Affairs* (New York: Random House, 1984), 192.
GCM to McNarney: Matlock and Snell, 189.
274 "Workmanlike divisions": Interviews, 551.
"While I had been chief": Interviews, 555.
"Simply to restrain": Wedemeyer, 135.
275 "A horror of bodies": Interviews, 552.
"For the time being": Quoted, Strange, "The British Rejection of Operation Sledgehammer."
276 The White House valet: Eleanor Roosevelt, 251.
"Were fraught with serious consequence": Churchill, *Hinge of Fate,* 332.
277 FDR-GCM-Molotov: Sherwood, 563.

"In the course of the conversations": *Britannica Book of the Year,* 1943, 451.

279 Tobruk "should be held at all costs": Churchill, *Hinge of Fate,* 370.

CHAPTER THIRTEEN

"TAKING UP YOUR DISHES"

280 "Thoughtful moments": Churchill, *Hinge of Fate,* 377.

281 Sledgehammer discussion: Matloff and Snell, 234.

"Poor quality": Interviews, 544.

"To follow up a crack" and "he did not wish to send": Sherwood, 583.

"We must never let": Churchill, *Hinge of Fate,* 340.

282 "Trying to prevent stupid things": Danchev, 33.

282–283 GCM quotations about FDR and Dill: Interviews, 379–380.

283 To "bring additional pressure": Stimson and Bundy, 419.

"King wobbled around": Stimson diary, quoted, Buell, 206.

284 "Additional expeditionary proposal" and "an essentially American project": Stimson to FDR, June 19, 1942. Stimson and Bundy, 423.

"Greatly impressed": Ismay, 251.

"What P.M. and President": Bryant, 325.

285 "Prior to September 15, 1942": June 20, 1942. Sherwood, 581.

286 McCrea with FDR and Churchill: McCrea draft memoirs, FDRL.

287 "Impressed by the tact": Bryant, I, 329.

"What can we do?": Churchill, *Hinge of Fate,* 383.

"Everyone's thoughts": Ismay, 256.

Marshall horrified: Strange, "Cross-Channel Attack," 354–355, based on Stimson diary.

Marshall memo: June 23, 1942. Marshall Papers, GCML.

288 "I had never seen": Churchill, *Hinge of Fate,* 386.

288–289 GCM's note: July 3, 1942. Marshall Collection, GCML.

289 "Hopkins had ten blood transfusions": Interviews, 546.
"Even though that house": Eleanor Roosevelt, 257.
"A rather staggering crisis": Stimson and Bundy, 424.
290 "Tend to concentrate": Quoted, Matloff and Snell, 268.
King quotation: Matloff and Snell, 268.
Subordinate committee of the Joint Chiefs: Stoler, "The Pacific-First Alternative."
290–291 "Pacific Ocean alternative" and "detailed, comprehensive outline": Matloff and Snell, 270.
291 Dill alerting his colleagues: See Parker, 224.
"He and I would make up the reply": Interviews, 380.
"Not approved": July 15, 1942. PSF (Safe File), FDRL.
292 Draft of FDR substitute memo, "Instructions for London Conference": July 15, 1942. PSF (Safe File), FDRL.
"All ready to do any sideshow": Interviews, 554.
"Defeat of Germany": FDR substitute memo, July 15, 1942. PSF (Safe File), FDRL.
"Taking up your dishes": Stimson and Bundy, 425.
293 Code names from Sherwood, 606.
293–294 "British authorities are most fearful": Eisenhower's comments from GCM memo to Dill, July 14, 1942. Marshall Papers, GCML.
294 Important help from British planners: See Truscott to Eisenhower, July 20, 1942. Truscott Papers, GCML. See also Strange, "Cross-Channel Attack," 429. For further discussion of the Sledgehammer controversy, see GCM interview by Col. L. M. Guyer and Col. C. H. Donnelly, February 11, 1949. National Archives Project, GCML.
"Long arguments": Bryant, I, 342.
Tongue "shooting out and round his lips": Bryant, I, 451.
"He talked so damned fast": Buell, 275.
Cockney: H. Merrill Pasco interview, June 24, 1986.
Barber, *Power in Committees,* 47.
"A matter of invention":
295 Hopkins's notes: Reproduced in Sherwood, 608, 609.
"The blackest day in history": Butcher, 29.

Keeping Allied options open: See Harrison, 30, and Matloff and Snell, 280.

296 "What I fear most": July 25, 1942. Hopkins-Sherwood Papers, FDRL. This wording represents the version of the message published by Sherwood in 1948. What Hopkins actually said was that "the thing I fear" was "delay and procrastination": Such variations result from security requirements, under which messages sent in cipher were paraphrased before being published.

"Full speed ahead": Sherwood, 612.

297 "I did not realize": Interviews. GCM made this observation several times.

"Please make it before election day": Interviews, 563.

Time quotation: January 3, 1944.

CHAPTER FOURTEEN
DECISION AT ANFA CAMP

315 FDR's note: K. T. Marshall, 127.

316 "I have set it up": December 30, 1942. PPF, FDRL.

"Became stronger": Interviews, 585.

"Harry Hopkins used to rib us": Tully, 262.

Bessie Boggess's background from T. S. Boggess, Jr., interview, March 11, 1988.

316–317 Miss Boggess and the stenographer: Shalett, "Mammoth Cave, Washington, D.C."

317–318 Background and details of the Pentagon from Defense Department publications and various 1943 articles.

318 "All personnel being moved": *Reader's Digest,* January 1943.

319 The *Dixie Clipper* and Howard M. Cone: TerHorst, 98–100.

Trip details here and on following pages from "Log of the President's Trip to the Casablanca Conference, 9–31, January 1943" (RP), and Harry Hopkins's handwritten notes, n.d. (Hopkins Papers, FDRL).

"He was tired of having other people": Hopkins notes.

321 Soviet premier rejected two invitations: Churchill, *Hinge of Fate,* 666.

The "next-best thing": Hopkins notes.
"There's only one son of a bitch": McCrea to Sherwood, Sherwood, 968.
"In view of Stalin's absence": Loewenheim, 295.
322 "Scarcely any large-scale": Hull, II, 1110.
323 To "clear the ground": Churchill, *Hinge of Fate,* 568–569.
Molly Winn's view: Interview.
Review of *Brother Rat: New York Times,* November 5, 1938.
GCM and McCarthy's name: Winn interview.
"He was one jump behind": Pasco interview.
324 "Get me that fellow": McCarthy to William Sexton, January 31, 1944. McCarthy Papers, GCML.
"One of the best laughs": McCarthy quoted, Pogue, III, 613, note 27.
325 "A car had scarcely been ordered": Giraud, 87–88.
British chiefs slept in bomb bays: Astley, 87.
"Every quantitative calculation": Bryant, I, 443.
"They had left most of their clubs": Sir Ian Jacob in diary, quoted, Bryant, I, 443.
"The British would be ready": Interviews, 572.
326 The British "will have a plan": Matloff and Snell, 379.
"Shooting off the hip": Interviews, 572; "shooting off the cuff," Interviews, 577.
"A slow and tiring business": Bryant, I, 448.
Field Marshal Dill's aide: Reginald Winn MS in Reginald Winn Collection, GCML.
326–327 Wedemeyer on Brooke: Interview.
327 "One of the finest gentlemen": Hull MS, MHI.
"Like most truly great people": Donnelly MS, MHI.
"You know as well as I do": Bryant, I, 450.
328 "It would keep me from flying missions": Thomas Parrish, *Ultra Americans,* 237.
"If these people are going to be that stupid": Interview by Lt. Col. Joe Green, Eaker Papers, Oral History, MHI. See also James Parton Papers, Houghton Library, Harvard University.
British opinion of Marshall: Kennedy, 283.
329 "Fascist around the edges": Michel, 118.
"Obedience and legality": Kammerer, 11.
"Legalism and hierarchy": Kammerer, 12.

“Does not extend” and “blind obedience”: Kammerer, 16.
330 “The assembled specialists”: Darlan, 184.
331 “Little by little”: Darlan, 14.
“Farouche”: Darlan, 177.
Darlan “would head up”: Quoted, Funk, 247.
“It is impossible to say”: Moch, 161.
332 “The actual state”: Ambrose, *Eisenhower,* 208.
“All of these Frogs” and “I find myself getting absolutely furious”: Ambrose, *Eisenhower,* 204.
“The first quisling” and “a rat”: Quoted, Kammerer, 542.
“Idealistic as hell”: Ambrose, *Eisenhower,* 206.
“I brought down a group”: Interviews, 452.
333 “Incredibly stupid”: Ambrose, *Eisenhower,* 208.
FDR’s message to Eisenhower: Map Room File, FDRL.
FDR’s statement: Sherwood, 653–654.
“I am only a lemon”: November 21, 1942. Moch, 187 (“un citron que les Américains vont rejeter après en avoir exprimé tout le jus”).
334–335 Giraud on GCM and FDR: Giraud, 88–89.
“The President’s knowledge”: Aglion, 151.
335 “Did not need these gentlemen”: Giraud, 103.
Hopkins on the Secret Service detail: Sherwood, 685.
“American publicity”: Giraud, 109.
336 Press conference: No. 875, transcript in FDRL.
“We had so much trouble”: Sherwood, 696.
337 FDR with his advisers: Minutes of meetings of the president with the Joint Chiefs (January 7, 1943). Map Room File, FDRL.
Veblen’s insight: See Howard, *War and the Liberal Conscience,* 83.
337–338 Churchill-War Cabinet messages: Churchill, *Hinge of Fate,* 684, 686.
338 Stalin’s and Maisky’s comments: *FRUS, Washington and Casablanca,* 493.
339 The five national goals summarized in Watson, 354.
340 The “total defeat” of Germany: Watson, 356.
“A secular church”: Howard, *War and the Liberal Conscience,* 91.

340–341 "The confident will of whole peoples" and "the idea and hope of Europe": Quoted, Davis, 65.
341 "Came to our minds": Interviews, 382.
Chiefs "talked politics": Interviews, 581.
Wedemeyer's reflections: Wedemeyer, 192.
"They swarmed upon me": Interview.
342 White quotation from Walter Johnson, "Roosevelt in the War Years."

CHAPTER FIFTEEN
THE PRESIDENT'S PLUM

343 He "stepped out of it": K. T. Marshall, 140.
He "was not a quarrelsome man" and following quotations: Interviews, 346.
344 "To deny this request" and following quotations: Pasco interview.
345 "Stiff reprimand": Interviews, 569.
"When we lose the next war": Quoted, Morgan, 778–779.
Huey Long dangerous: Tugwell, 116.
"'Mac' is certainly not 'running away'": Vandenberg, 77.
345–346 Incident with Coast Guardsmen: K. T. Marshall, 140–141.
346–347 British and American chiefs' meeting: *FRUS, Washington and Quebec,* 44–45.
348 "The man from London": *FRUS, Washington and Quebec,* 19.
"Spinach": Notation on JCS memo to president of May 8, 1943. Map Room File, FDRL.
"Sledgehammer or Roundup": *FRUS, Washington and Quebec,* 30.
"More valuable than building up": *FRUS, Washington and Quebec,* 46.
"Fiddle fuddle" and "limp along": Quoted, Coakley and Leighton, 65.
348–349 Where Marshall and Brooke really differed: See Fraser, 342.

349 "There would be a most unfortunate": Pogue, II, 194.
350 "Easily excited": Wedemeyer interview.
"It was the most difficult day": Bryant, I, 509.
"Shivering lest either one of them": Bryant, I, 510–511.
"Terrific" pressure: Coakley and Leighton, 71.
351 Churchill and "Barbara Frietchie": Churchill, *Hinge of Fate,* 795–797.
"Persistence and his pleasure": Quoted, Bryant, I, 506–507, note 35.
352 "We were puzzling": Churchill, *Hinge of Fate,* 811.
The edited document: Loewenheim et al., 336.
353 "A rugged soldier" and "a statesman": Churchill, *Hinge of Fate,* 813.
Marshall quotations from Interviews, 516–518.
354 He had "never heard anyone": Moran, 110.
He "wished to emphasize": Minutes of the Algiers Conference, June 7, 1943. JCS document, Map Room File, FDRL.
Eden and Churchill: Avon, 388–389.
354–355 Algiers press conference: Painton and Johnson, "Vignettes of America's No. 1 Soldier." GCM duplicated this performance on other occasions.
355 "You must understand" and following quotation: Interviews, 325.
"He is an expert": Butcher, 324.
"If Marshall says he needs men": T. M. Johnson, "America's No. 1 Soldier."
355–356 "It is not enough to say" and "You've no idea": Barnett, "General Marshall."
356 "Who stands so completely": T. M. Johnson.
"Cumulative weariness": Tully, 273.
The coffee mug: Bishop, 5.
356–357 Details of Mona Nason's background and work with GCM from interview, June 26, 1986. Miss Nason very kindly read and supplemented a draft of my account.
357 "Not to brag about it": Interviews, 591.
358 "Send in the fellow" and "General, his name is '*Wed*demeyer'!" Nason interview. General Wedemeyer also recalled the latter story, with great amusement.
"In an ordinary business suit": Quoted, Borklund, 89.

359 GCM and the Japanese Americans: S.L.A. Marshall, 54.
GCM and battle history: S.L.A. Marshall, 55–57.
360 "A world of interminable politeness": Ingersoll, 8.
"Undoubtedly would have been a good commander": Leahy, 178.
"Too excited to sleep": Bryant, 542.
361 FDR overruling chiefs of staff: For discussion, see Greenfield, *American Strategy,* 56.
362 Events had destroyed his faith in airpower: See Noel Parrish, 18.
FDR on production: Greenfield, *American Strategy,* 130, note 53.
363 "To have a preponderance": GCM memo to FDR, July 8, 1943. Map Room File, FDRL.
Marshall "designated for Supreme Command": Sherwood, 615.
363–364 Roosevelt had "pressed hard" and "all that scenery": Bryant, I, 578.
364 "He is a great soldier": K. T. Marshall, 155.
"The shadows of Passchendaele": Stimson to FDR, August 10, 1943. Map Room File, FDRL.
365 "Any soldier would prefer": Stimson and Bundy, 440–441.
"Powerful influences": Quoted, Sherwood, 760.
"Hopkins' slimy hand": Quoted, Sherwood, 760.
"Wanted to create the maximum amount": Sherwood, 761.
"When any major change": *Christian Science Monitor,* September 23, 1943. Official File, FDRL.
Rumor of GCM's dismissal: The broadcast and the note are reproduced in Sherwood, 763.
366 Transfer GCM to "a tactical command": September 16, 1943. PSF, FDRL.
FDR's reply to Pershing: September 20, 1943. PSF, FDRL.
366–367 Letters about GCM from Official File, FDRL.
367 *New Republic* quotation: October 11, 1943.
Determined "not to embarrass the President": Interviews, 315.
"I could get many things": Interviews, 547.

368 GCM-Mona Nason from Nason interview and subsequent correspondence.
Senator Johnson: *New York Times,* November 7, 1943.
369 Representative Priest: *New York Times,* November 10, 1943.
Would "never permit himself": Pogue, III, 278.

CHAPTER SIXTEEN
THE WHITE CLIFFS OF CAIRO

370 Rigdon's background from interview and from Rigdon, *White House Sailor.*
"Most courageous": Rigdon, 5.
Trip details from "Log of the President's Trip to Africa and the Middle East." RP.
371 Brown quotations from "Log," Foreword. RP.
"For even a single day": Dallek, 368.
372 Roosevelt quotation from *FRUS, Cairo and Teheran,* 4.
"Since there are wire" and following quotation: *FRUS, Cairo and Teheran,* 33.
373 "Not in sympathy": GCM memo to Leahy, October 8, 1943. Marshall Papers, GCML.
"Whatever happens": *FRUS, Cairo and Teheran,* 37.
"Be wise to ask the Ruskies": Leahy memo to Marshall, King, Arnold, October 20, 1943. Marshall Papers, GCML.
"Felt certain" and "it would be next": GCM memo to Leahy, October 25, 1943. Marshall Papers, GCML.
"Due to some reasons": *FRUS, Cairo and Teheran,* 83.
374 Conference-planning details from Richard Collins Papers, MHI.
"The more I thought": Donnelly MS, MHI.
375 "Left a mark" and following quotation: Eleanor Roosevelt, 313.
376 "Second rate" and "Bob Hope": Eleanor Roosevelt to GCM, April 3, 1944. Marshall Papers, GCML.
"The authors of 'Oklahoma'": GCM to Eleanor Roosevelt, April 17, 1944. Marshall Papers, GCML.

"The seats reserved": GCM to Eleanor Roosevelt, March 22, 1943. Marshall Papers, GCML.

377 Eleanor Roosevelt letter to GCM about Hayes proposal, November 23, 1943. Marshall Papers, GCML.

377–378 Details of passenger arrangements from various items in Hopkins Papers, FDRL.

378 "Give him corned beef hash": Rigdon, 61.

379 "It's the real thing": Sherwood, 768.

Moley on FDR's nerve: Moley, 139.

380 "He should get a boat": Rigdon interview.

"I doubt": Sherwood, 768.

381 "The Casa Blanca": Eubank, 156.

"Outspokenly delighted": Eisenhower, *Crusade,* 196.

"Remained completely silent": Eisenhower, *Crusade,* 196.

"Said *nothing*": Buell, 414.

382 "The proper man": Buell, 416.

"I hate to lose": Butcher, 446.

"Remarkable acumen": Butcher, 449.

382–383 FDR with Kay Summersby: Summersby, 151.

383 Telek's behavior with GCM: Summersby, 105, and Brandon, 104.

Horseshoe incident from Brown MS, FDRL.

"Ike, you and I know": Sherwood, 770.

"Sweating it out": Butcher diary, quoted in Ambrose, *Eisenhower,* 268.

384 Cairo background and quotations from Donnelly MS, MHI.

385–386 "When you get around a table": Marquand, 373.

386 Donnelly material from Donnelly MS, MHI.

"The British": Coakley and Leighton, 274.

387 Deane message quoted in Coakley and Leighton, 275.

"Definitely stand on it": JCS minutes, November 15, 1943. Map Room File, FDRL.

"U.S. policy on nonparticipation" and following quotations from JCS minutes, November 19, 1943. FDRL.

388 "Crystallized" and "accepting": Kennedy, 312.

"A pretty serious set-to": Bryant, II, 67.

"At any time before": AFHA message, October 10, 1943. Hopkins Papers, FDRL.

"Suppressed neigh": Bryant, II, 78.

388–389 Churchill on Chiang: *Closing the Ring,* 328.
"To the President": Moran, 140.
390 "Churchill was red hot" and following quotations: Interviews, 586–587.
"The full weight of our resources": *FRUS, Cairo and Teheran,* 364.
391 "Father and mother" of a row: Bryant, II, 84.
"Almost climbed over the table": Buell, 428.
"For political reasons": *FRUS, Cairo and Teheran,* 364.
"Were not in a position": *FRUS, Cairo and Teheran,* 365.
"Can you imagine": Elliott Roosevelt, 159.
392 The toasts: Rigdon, 74–75.
"Was enough to wake": Rigdon, 75.
Supplies at Cairo from Hollis, 258. Liquor from Astley, 118.
"Ganging up on him": FDR to Churchill, November 11, 1943. Loewenheim, 393.

CHAPTER SEVENTEEN
EUREKA!

394 "From the standpoint": November 26, 1943. MR, FDRL.
"With a paint": Bates (Pantuhoff) MS, MHI. Many background details in this chapter, including the following Harriman-Molotov conversation, come from this source.
396 "At last!": Bates MS, MHI.
"It was not": Bates 547, MHI.
"Immediate help": *FRUS, Cairo and Teheran,* 481.
"A more immediate": *FRUS, Cairo and Teheran,* 479.
"Did not have": *FRUS, Cairo and Teheran,* 479.
397 "The new members": *FRUS, Cairo and Teheran,* 481.
"Very much like": A. H. Birse in Eubank, 256.
"Didn't move through a series": James Roosevelt, *A Family Matter,* 40.
398 The high-level strategic estimate: Sherwood, 748.
"Restless self-assertion": Forrest Davis, May 13, 1944.

"We shook each other's hand": Quoted in Dallin, *Russia and Postwar Europe,* 66.
"A Russia excluded": Forrest Davis, May 13, 1944.

399 "Had no desire" and "plenty to do": Forrest Davis, May 13, 1944.
"I found him better informed": Harriman and Abel, 536.

400 "This fraternal meeting": *FRUS, Cairo and Teheran,* 487.
"Now let us": *FRUS, Cairo and Teheran,* 497.
"The most important theater" and following quotations: *FRUS, Cairo and Teheran,* 488.

401 "A possible operation": *FRUS, Cairo and Teheran,* 493.
Who was "promoting": Sherwood, 780.
"We were always scared": Interviews, 311.

401–402 "To scatter the British": *FRUS, Cairo and Teheran,* 505.

402 "The basis for all": *FRUS, Cairo and Teheran,* 494.
"Merely served to unite": *FRUS, Cairo and Teheran,* 513.
"That we would be rather remote": Interviews, 295.
"Aroused a hatred of Hitler" and following quotations: Hopkins, *American Magazine,* December 1941.

403 "A tempting conditional peace": Dallin, *American Mercury,* October 1943.

404 "Against the advance": V. I. Lenin, *Works,* XXIII, 182; quoted in Dallin, *Russia and Postwar Europe,* 66.
"A strong Germany": Dallin, *Russia and Postwar Europe,* 114.
"Security sphere": Dallin, *Russia and Postwar Europe,* 177.
"Seek her security": Dallin, *Russia and Postwar Europe,* 221.

405 "Of the first importance": *FRUS, Cairo and Teheran,* 521.
"When it would have the best chances": *FRUS, Cairo and Teheran,* 523.
"Were the results": *FRUS, Cairo and Teheran,* 526.
"A technical matter": *FRUS, Cairo and Teheran,* 526.
"The difference between": *FRUS, Cairo and Teheran,* 527–528.

"He had been acquiring": *FRUS, Cairo and Teheran,* 528.
"If you think about it": *FRUS, Cairo and Teheran,* 528.
406 "A great many other matters": *FRUS, Cairo and Teheran,* 530.
The role of the Four Policemen: *FRUS, Cairo and Teheran,* 530.
"This afternoon": Moran, 146.
407 "Who will command": *FRUS, Cairo and Teheran,* 535.
"Nothing would come": *FRUS, Cairo and Teheran,* 535.
"The old Bolshevik": Leahy, 208.
"Pressed for me" and following GCM quotations: Interviews, 313.
408 "Political and military requirements": Bryant, II, 91.
"Number and complexity" and next quotation: *FRUS, Cairo and Teheran,* 535.
"Nothing should be done": *FRUS, Cairo and Teheran,* 537.
"There was no Goddamn alternative": Moran, 147.
"He did not care": *FRUS, Cairo and Teheran,* 538.
"To get in a dig": Bohlen, *FRUS, Cairo and Teheran,* 553. See also Bohlen, 146.
"It was a mistake": *FRUS, Cairo and Teheran,* 553.
409 "Fully convinced": Churchill, *Closing the Ring,* 374.
"Surprised to find" and following quotations: Interviews, 314.
"A rough SOB": Pogue, III, 313.
FDR-Stalin discussion: *FRUS, Cairo and Teheran,* 594–595.
410 "With the more or less sincere complicity": Giraud, 199.
"Stood at the doors" and following discussion: Bates MS, MHI.
"On as large a scale": *FRUS, Cairo and Teheran,* 576.
411 "Truth deserves a bodyguard": *FRUS, Cairo and Teheran,* 578.
"Dummy tanks, aircraft": *FRUS, Cairo and Teheran,* 578.
412 "Roosevelt has given his word": Zhukov, 493.

"Trusted Roosevelt more": Zhukov, 364.
"Churchill is the kind": Djilas, 73.
"The total effect": Bryant, II, 100–101.

413–414 "Witness Mr. Churchill" and following quotations: *Time,* January 3, 1944.

415 "The President was in some concern" and "could not tell from Hopkins' statement": Sherwood, 803.
"Go along with whatever decision" and following quotations: Interviews, 315.
"I was utterly sincere" and "all this business": Interviews, 316.
"After a great deal": Interviews, 315.

416 "I just repeated again": Interviews, 315.
"Cheerfully go whichever way": Interviews, 315.
"I feel I could not sleep at night": Sherwood, 803. Marshall also recalled the line as having been "sleep at ease," but, either way, the meaning is unmistakably clear. Message with covering note to Eisenhower: December 7, 1943. Marshall Papers, GCML.
"The failure to name": Leahy, 215.

417 Man of the Year quotations: *Time,* January 3, 1944.

CHAPTER EIGHTEEN
UNENDING MARTIAL STRAINS

418 Background material on Dr. Bruenn, and his quoted remarks, come from the author's interview with him. Some details of the examination are drawn from Bishop, 5–7.

419 For a thought on Dr. McIntire's motivation, see Leahy, 220.
"I feel like hell": Bishop, 4.
"I do not remember": Rosenman, 411.
"We came here with hope": "Log of the President's Trip to Africa and the Middle East." RP.

420 Rosenman on Howe and Hopkins: Interviews, Oral History File, FDRL.
"We are going to get along": Rosenman, 413.
"I am distressed": GCM to FDR, December 24, 1943. PPF, FDRL.

420–421 Press conference reported in Rosenman, 415, and *Time,* January 10, 1944.

421 "Although not a blasphemous": *Time,* January 10, 1944.

422 "Is perhaps more universally": Nicholas, 301.
Cartoon: Fitzpatrick, *Time,* January 10, 1944.
"Respected and admired": Nicholas, 301–302.

423 "Stand by your guns": Rickenbacker to GCM, January 6, 1944. Marshall Papers, GCML.
"I have noted it": GCM to Rickenbacker, January 6, 1944. Marshall Papers, GCML.
GCM broadcast quoted from *Time,* February 14, 1944.
"All our instincts": Interviews, 589.
"There is no doubt": *Time,* February 14, 1944.

424 "Hung on and finally left behind": McIntire, 182.
"I know he will return": Lash, *Eleanor and Franklin,* 694.
"More disturbing than anything": McIntire, 182.
FDR's symptoms from Bruenn, "Clinical Notes."
"One of the best years" and "ability to bounce back": *New York Times,* January 29, 1944.

425 "Far above average" and following quotations: *New York Times,* January 29, 1944.
"The finest possible health": *New York Times,* March 6, 1944.
"Comfortable, relaxed Westerner": *Life,* July 31, 1944.
"Father's need to have": James Roosevelt, *Affectionately, FDR,* 348.

426 "But while it is not serious": Adams, 352.
"Had no more sense": Brown MS, FDRL.
"Pouring tea for General de Gaulle": James Roosevelt, *Affectionately, FDR,* 348–349.

427 "A fine mind": Brown MS, FDRL.
The barber pole: Nesbitt, 247.
"The best bedside manner": *Life,* July 31, 1944.
"A very pleasant person": Bruenn interview.
"The White House group": Bruenn interview.

428 Blood pressure: Goldberg, 182.
Undulant fever: Eleanor Roosevelt, *This I Remember,* 327.

"FDR is not well": Lash, *Eleanor and Franklin,* 697.
"Hated the idea" and following quotations: *New York Times,* August 9, 1956.
"If he had to go on": Lash, *Eleanor and Franklin,* 695.
"He appeared to be" and "in good humor": Bruenn, "Clinical Notes."
"A few notations": Bruenn interview.

429 "Made a fairly complete picture": Bruenn interview.
"Much attention to the President's" and following quotations: Bruenn interview.
"Because of the exigencies": Bruenn, "Clinical Notes."

430 "A moderate degree": McIntire, 184.
"Well and active": *New York Times,* August 9, 1956.
"Indoctrinated, as one is in the White House" and following quotation: James Roosevelt interview.

430–431 "It's quite comprehensive" and following quotations: *New York Times,* April 5, 1944. It should be mentioned that the records of FDR's examinations have never been found.

431 Bruenn and the consultants: Bruenn interview.
"There was much discussion": Bruenn, "Clinical Notes."
"At no time": Bruenn, "Clinical Notes."

431–432 "The President never asked me" and following quotations: Bruenn interview.

432 Description of Hobcaw: Baruch, 335–336.
"Cuba is absolutely lousy": Press conference No. 948, May 6, 1944. RP.
"The whole period of time": Bruenn, "Clinical Notes."

433 "It was with difficulty": Bruenn interview.
"In the way of a disease": Bruenn interview.
"F. looks well": Lash, *Eleanor and Franklin,* 698.
"Excellent shape": *New York Times,* May 8, 1944.
The first paraplegic: This point is made by Gallagher, xiii.
"Active-positive": The classification comes from Barber, *Presidential Character,* 12.

434 "I can take anything" and "he made almost everybody": Gunther, 314.

"Guts, optimism": Alsop, 96.
"He came to the manipulation": Tugwell, 301.
"Even the power": O'Hara, 114.
"The view from low down": Rita Whitt interview.

435 "That surpassing warmth": *Time,* January 31, 1944.
"Falling-apart pattern" and "polio wall" are phrases used by Rita Whitt and JoAnn Berryman in interviews. The description here of the postpolio syndrome is drawn mainly from talks with these members of the Polio Survivors Organization.

436 "He wouldn't float": Bruenn interview.
A bad move: Berryman makes this point in interview.
"The doctors are very pleased": James Roosevelt, *Affectionately, FDR,* 350.
Mrs. Roosevelt's fear: Gallagher, 191.
"Sometimes I'd come": Nesbitt, 279.

437 "Should have gotten off a letter": GCM to Hopkins, Marshall Papers, GCML.
"Things have gone": Hopkins to GCM, February 10, 1944. Marshall Papers, GCML.
"Warm and sympathetic" and "I hope you will not": Hopkins to GCM, February 16, 1944. Marshall Papers, GCML.

438 "I wished for you": GCM cable to War Department for Hopkins, March 26, 1944. Marshall Papers, GCML.
"I, too, over one hundred years" and following quotations: Sherwood, 6.
"By what authority": Memo, Persons to Chief of Staff, May 22, 1944. Marshall Papers, GCML.

439 "The conventional expression": GCM to Hopkins, August 18, 1944. Marshall Papers, GCML.

CHAPTER NINETEEN
THE PHOENIX ONCE AGAIN

440 "Impracticable": Churchill, *Closing the Ring,* 444.

441 "We are putting the whole works": Thomas Parrish, *Ultra Americans, 172.*

442 Marshall letter to Eisenhower: SRH-026, Record Group 457, National Archives.

"The chances of any second front": William P. Bundy, quoted in Thomas Parrish, *Ultra Americans,* 285.

443 "In Washington": Kennedy, 310.

"When something is done": Lincoln Barnett, *Life,* January 3, 1944.

"He has analyzed worry": T. M. Johnson, *Reader's Digest,* February 1944.

"A splendid fighting man" and "a superb performer": Interviews, 343.

"A seriously destructive force": GCM to President, February 15, 1944. Marshall Papers, GCML.

443–444 "He did that": Interviews, 343.

444 "A new appreciation": Leahy, 220.

"He always got in his own way": Interviews, 531.

"Being undercut": Interviews, 569.

445 Discussion of field order: GCM to President, March 27, 1943. Marshall Papers, GCML.

Marshall birthday note: PSF, FDRL.

FDR reply: January 31, 1944. PSF, FDRL.

February 6 memo: Leahy File, GCML.

446 "Was separating the wheat": GCM to President, February 12, 1944. Leahy File, GCML.

White House meeting: President and JCS, February 21, 1944. Map Room File, FDRL.

446–447 "Back to the maximum": GCM to Leahy, February 24, 1944. Marshall Papers, GCML.

447 "The relative advantages": FDR to Frank Knox, quoted in Buell, 309.

"What is the relative anti-aircraft total": FDR to Knox, August 12, 1942 (A 16-3). FDRL.

"I rather suspected": FDR to Leahy, February 26, 1944. Map Room File, FDRL.

448 Press conference scene: Rauch, *Selected Speeches,* 357, and Daniels, 225–226.

449 "Wherever this man goes": Hassett, 249.

"We didn't know we were going": Interviews, 553.

Marshall in Italy: Pogue, III, 404–405.

449–450 JCS report: no date, Map Room File, FDRL.

The U.S. Army in France: see, particularly, Weigley, *Eisenhower's Lieutenants,* Chapter 2, 17–41 (book-club edition).

450–451 "A bunch of unregimented and inquiring minds" and following discussion: Richard Collins interview, Collins Papers, MHI.

451 "As to mobility, speed, handling": Interviews, 241.
"My effort": Interviews, 412.

452 "Only by swarming around": Bradley, *A Soldier's Story,* 322.
"The road losses": Patton to Maj. Gen. Thomas T. Handy, March 19, 1945. Handy Papers, GCML.
"Our tank superiority": Bradley, *A Soldier's Story,* 322.
"A reserve officer of thirty-one years": Interviews, 469.

452–453 "To assign me" and following quotations: McCarthy to Sexton, January 31, 1944. McCarthy Papers, GCML.

453 McCarthy and the buzzer: Donald Bussey interview, April 5, 1988.
"To deduct the middle-man's profit": McCarthy to GCM, November 29, 1944. McCarthy Papers, GCML.
"Issue instructions in my name": GCM "to whom it may concern," May 26, 1943. McCarthy Papers, GCML.

454 McCarthy and Joan Bright: Astley, 127.
Marshall and the secretaries: Faber, 57.

455 "A profound apprehension": *Life,* January 3, 1944.
"Had a sinking sensation": Rosenman, 462.

456 "Informal summary": Transcript of speech, August 12, 1944. RP.
Quotations from speech: Transcript, RP.

456–457 "Substernal oppression" and "no unusual abnormalities": Bruenn, "Clinical Notes."

457 "I'm going to give a speech": Sherwood, 821.

458 "Do you think Pa": Rosenman, 478.

458–459 Quotations from Teamsters speech: *New York Times,* September 24, 1944.

460 "Between Roosevelt's dog": Rosenman, 479.
"The finest speech he ever made": Quoted, Bishop, 203.

CHAPTER TWENTY

THE ARGONAUTS GO FORTH

461 Myers and FDR: Myers interview, June 30, 1986.
"By reputation": Robert Bogue interview, July 1, 1986.
Myers quotation: Interview.
461–462 Leahy's procedures: Leahy, 98–99.
462 FDR's morning journey: Brown MS, FDRL.
"Nobody who worked for him": Sherwood, 216.
463 Blood pressure from Bruenn, "Clinical Notes."
Bogue background and quotation from interview.
"A great sense of humor": Myers interview.
464 "Do all in our power": *Secret History,* 239.
March comments: *New York Times,* December 28, 1944.
465 "I was worried about this thing": Interviews, 317.
"There was not a chance": Quoted, Sherwood, 844.
466 "Someplace where all the old Russian palaces": Stettinius, *Diaries,* 202.
"Against long journeys": October 29, 1944. *Secret History,* 209.
"We could not have found a worse place": Quoted, Sherwood, 847.
467 Reported conditions at Yalta: Brown MS, FDRL.
"Tortuous legislative journey": Leahy, 282.
King thought: Sherwood, 849.
468 "Beholden to Congress" and following quotation: Interviews, 419–420.
"Sit at the foot of the table": Quoted, Frye, 370.
"The session was a very hot one": Interviews, 367.
469 "The highest special award": *New York Times,* February 17, 1944.
"Old patterns have broken down": *New York Times,* May 21, 1944.
"Sent Churchill stories": Interviews, 588.
"With such real feeling": Nancy Dill to GCM, November 9, 1944. Marshall Papers, GCML.
"Marshall's face": Quoted, Danchev, 1.
470 "Domestic help": Nancy Dill, November 9, 1944.
"Officially the United States": Quoted, Danchev, 3.
Hull quotation: Hull MS, MHI.

“Complete agreement”: *FRUS, Malta and Yalta,* 541.
471 Departure scene at Malta: Donnelly MS, MHI.
472 “To a doctor’s eye”: Moran, 242.
Dr. Bruenn’s disagreement: Bruenn interview.
“A good beginning” and following quotation: Moran, 232.
“Owing to their exceptional personalities”: L’Etang, 212.
“He is tired, tired, tired”: Nicolson, 421.
“Much worried that the whole business”: Avon, 504.
473 Description of Stalin: Djilas, 61.
Thyroid deficiency: L’Etang, 202.
“Cold calculator”: Djilas, 69.
“With him, pretense”: Djilas, 97.
“A flat negation” and following discussion: Vishniak, “Lenin’s Democracy, and Stalin’s.”
474 “I want you to go”: Stettinius, *Diaries,* 202.
“Sit around a conference table”: Stettinius, *Roosevelt and the Russians,* 13.
475 “The act of love”: Quoted, Ruddy, 1.
“I went to the White House”: Bohlen, 166.
“Foreign policy in a democracy” and “the American people”: Bohlen, 177.

CHAPTER TWENTY-ONE
THE FLEECE AND THE DRAGONS

477 “It was thrilling” and following quotes in this paragraph: Donnelly MS, MHI.
477–478 “A grim and treeless plain”: Avon, 512.
The scene at the landing field is described in the Bates (Pantuhoff) MS, MHI, and by Rigdon, *White House Sailor,* 144.
478 Unable to identify a possible adversary: See Noel Parrish, 53.
The automobile ride is chiefly from the Brown MS, FDRL.
“Sturdily built”: Stettinius, *Roosevelt and the Russians,* 81.
479 “But the driver”: Donnelly MS, MHI.
480 “The bathrooms were the most”: Kuter, 122.

"Plenty of flea powder": Astley, 175.
"An impossible equation": Astley, 186.
"The overcrowded conditions": Stettinius, *Roosevelt and the Russians,* 92.
481 "Bill, I wish you would": Leahy, 207.
482 "Increased public skepticism": Quoted, Gaddis, 157.
"In the event of the Polish Committee": *Secret History,* 223.
483 "Disturbed and deeply disappointed": *Secret History,* 226.
"Sooner or later": Quoted, Thomas Parrish, *Encyclopedia,* 668.
484 "When a country": Harriman to secretary of state, September 20, 1944. Quoted, Mastny, 213.
485 "They felt it to be their duty": *FRUS, Malta and Yalta,* 588.
"Agricultural and pastoral": Blum, III, 372.
"As if one were to take": Avon, 476.
"Henry Morgenthau pulled a boner": Stimson and Bundy, 581.
486 Stalin's comment: *FRUS, Malta and Yalta,* 666.
"It must never be forgotten": *FRUS, Malta and Yalta,* 668.
487 "We take different views" and following discussion: *FRUS, Malta and Yalta,* 778–779.
Dr. Bruenn and FDR: Bruenn, "Clinical Notes."
"Looked dreadful": John L. Hull MS, MHI.
Rigdon noted no decline: Rigdon interview.
488 FDR-Leahy exchange: Leahy, 315–316.
Joint Chiefs' report to FDR: January 23, 1945. *FRUS, Malta and Yalta,* 396.
"Interests in the Far East": Quoted, Pogue, III, 529.
489 "Lowering Japanese ability" and following quotations: *FRUS, Malta and Yalta,* 395–396.
490 "It sounded like the State Department": Laurence Kuter, quoted in Noel Parrish, 58.
"My job was military planning": Sutherland interview with GCM, *U.S. News and World Report,* November 2, 1959.
490–491 Groves letter to GCM: *FRUS, Malta and Yalta,* 383–384.
491 "We might have called it Hoboken": Interviews, 388.

"To spare no effort" and following quotation: Stimson and Bundy, 613.

492 "All the problems" and following quotation: Smyth, 223.

"Transformation in the whole character": Noel Parrish, xiii.

"Have always regarded fire power": Wylie, 262.

493 "We had no idea": Sutherland interview with GCM, *U.S. News and World Report,* November 2, 1959.

"Determined and fanatical" and "we would have to exterminate them": Quoted, Feis, 11.

"The casualties from the actual fighting": Interviews, 390.

FDR and James: Interview with James Roosevelt, May 9, 1988.

"A professor's dream": Leahy, 431.

"I was for Russia": Sutherland interview with GCM, *U.S. News and World Report,* November 2, 1959.

"Details of possible participation": JCS to General Antonov, February 3, 1945. *FRUS, Malta and Yalta,* 564.

494 "Russia's entry at as early a date": JCS to president, January 23, 1945. *FRUS, Malta and Yalta,* 396.

"Did not ask the terms": Sutherland interview with GCM, *U.S. News and World Report,* November 2, 1959.

Reversal of 1942 discussions: This point is neatly made by McClain, 238.

"The dawn of the new day": Sherwood, 870.

495 Harriman's comment: Stettinius, *Diaries,* 257.

Leahy's comments: Leahy, 322.

"Alert, tactful, resourceful": Brown MS, FDRL.

"It was the best": Quoted, Dallek, 521.

"She nearly threw me out of the house": Bogue interview, July 1, 1986.

CHAPTER TWENTY-TWO
PARTINGS

496 The description of preparations for the party comes primarily from Stevens, 84–91.

"Bought a goddamned pig": Hassett, 332.
"Awfully restless": Stevens, 85.
"A period of total rest": Bruenn, "Clinical Notes."

496–497 "Had only one thought": Oral History Interview by Rexford Tugwell, August 1957, FDRL.

497 "Organically sound": McIntire, 238; "was not alarming": McIntire, 239.
"Outwardly the President": Bruenn, "Clinical Notes."
"I shall miss him": "Log of the President's Trip to the Crimea," RP.
"All burnt out" and "I had never seen him": Rosenman, 522.

498 "Hollywood and our South" and next four quotes: Press conference from "Log," February 19, 1945. RP.
"Dear old Winston": Press conference from "Log," February 23, 1945. RP.
Press-reception quotes from "Log," RP.
"When the chips were down": Quoted by Rosenman, 526.

499 "Unusual posture": Quotations from speech from transcript, *New York Times,* March 2, 1945.
"Speech": *New York Times,* March 2, 1945.
"Great earnestness" and following quote: *New York Times,* March 2, 1945.
"Prodigious length": Hassett, 318.
"Tanned and glowing": *New York Times,* March 2, 1945.

500 "In full force": Leahy, 342.

500–501 "Immediate access": *FRUS, Malta and Yalta,* 985.

501 "Broadly representative": *FRUS, Malta and Yalta,* 977.
"Reorganization": *FRUS, Malta and Yalta,* 973.
"The Lublin Government": Harriman and Abel, 427.
"All of the difficulties": *Secret History,* 262.

502 "Sign of weakness": Harriman and Abel, 433.
"Königsberg or Danzig" and following quote: *Secret History,* 253.

503 "Atmosphere of regrettable misapprehension" and following quotation: *Secret History,* 258.
"He is slipping away": Hassett, 327–328.
He had lost twenty-five pounds: Hassett, 329.

504 "Move east" and following quotations: *Secret History,* 263–264.

"Received with astonishment" and following quotations from Roosevelt message to Stalin, April 5, 1945, from Rigdon White House files (RP). This message was identical with the draft reply forwarded by Leahy to the president on April 4, except that in the penultimate paragraph the draft read "materiel" instead of "material" (see Leahy File, GCML).

"I wrote the message": Interviews, 383.

"Honest and unassuming" and following quotation: *Secret History,* 267.

505 "Faded into the past" and "minor": quoted, Harriman and Abel, 439.

April 12 message: Churchill, *Triumph and Tragedy,* 454.

"A man of superior intellect": Hassett, 328.

"To eat with appetite": Bruenn, "Clinical Notes."

"The Boss feeling": Hassett, 329.

"There was no apparent cause": Bruenn, "Clinical Notes."

506 "Unnecessary hounding": Hassett, 334.

"I have a terrific pain": Oral History Interview by Rexford Tugwell, August 1957, FDRL.

"Get yourself a McCarthy": Don Bussey interview, April 5, 1988.

507 Mrs. Roosevelt's message has appeared in varying versions, e.g., "Father slept away" (Bishop, 805), "Daddy slept away (Pogue, III, 557).

"Teamwork which has succeeded": FDR to GCM, January 31, 1944. PPF, FDRL.

"I have the arrangements": K. T. Marshall, 243.

The scene at the barbecue: Stevens, 92.

508 "There has not been time": Asbell, 116; "He was the Commander in Chief": Asbell, 120.

"I never realized": Asbell, 161.

"When stimulated by concern": Potter, "Sketches for the Roosevelt Portrait."

"I am a Christian": Potter, "Sketches for the Roosevelt Portrait."

509 "Half-facetious": James Roosevelt interview, May 9, 1988.

"He's dead": White, 10.
"God damn it": Sherwood, 881.

509–510 "Certainly the implications": *War Reports,* 152.

510 "A great and good citizen": Stimson and Bundy, 664; "I have seen": Stimson and Bundy, 664.
"Personal or political desires" and following quotation: Stimson and Bundy, 666.
"Come on, Lanham": Frye, 371.
"A new gauge": Stimson and Bundy, 664.

510–511 Description of Marshall's driving from C. J. George interview, June 23, 1986.

511 Service-station scene from K. T. Marshall, 281.
"General, I want you": Truman, 301.

512 "I seem during the past three years": Marshall, "Some Lessons of History."
"To all of us": Acheson, 123.
"I noticed the lightness": Allen, "Marshall, Arnold, King."
"If I have to explain": Ignatius, *Washington Post,* May 31, 1987.
"Will you please tell me": Wilson, 394.

EPILOGUE
A NATURAL STATE?

514 The implications of FDR's use of surrogates are well discussed by Lazalier; see, especially, 248–249.

516–517 The discussion of the changing civil-military relations owes much to Huntington in Goodpaster and Huntington, e.g., 10.

518 "Generally irrelevant": James Schlesinger, quoted, *New York Times,* May 25, 1986.
Colin Powell speech: National Press Club, October 27, 1988.

518–519 Quotations from Admiral Crowe: Mike Wallace interview, *Sixty Minutes.*

519 "Civilian control": Orville D. Menard in Goodpaster and Huntington, 82. This point forms a main theme in Finer.

INDEX